October 3–5, 2012
Seattle, Washington, USA

I0028939

**Association for
Computing Machinery**

Advancing Computing as a Science & Profession

SIGDOC '12

Proceedings of the 30th ACM International Conference on
Design of Communication

Sponsored by:
ACM SIGDOC

Supported by:
HCDE and University of Washington

Association for
Computing Machinery

Advancing Computing as a Science & Profession

The Association for Computing Machinery
2 Penn Plaza, Suite 701
New York, New York 10121-0701

Notice to Past Authors of ACM-Published Articles
ACM intends to create a complete electronic archive of all articles and/or other material previously published by ACM. If you have written a work that has been previously published by ACM in any journal or conference proceedings prior to 1978, or any SIG Newsletter at any time, and you do NOT want this work to appear in the ACM Digital Library, please inform permissions@acm.org, stating the title of the work, the author(s), and where and when published.

ISBN: 978-1-4503-1499-2 (Digital)

ISBN: 978-1-4503-1497-8 (Print)

Additional copies may be ordered prepaid from:

ACM Order Department
PO Box 30777
New York, NY 10087-0777, USA

Phone: 1-800-342-6626 (USA and Canada)
+1-212-626-0500 (Global)
Fax: +1-212-944-1318
E-mail: acmhelp@acm.org
Hours of Operation: 8:30 am – 4:30 pm ET

Printed in the USA

From the Conference Chair

Welcome to the 2012 ACM Conference on the Design of Communication!

Our conference this year provides a premiere opportunity to hear researchers and practitioners share the latest investigations and experiences in the design of communication. Over the three days of the conference, you will interact with an exciting, international group of academic and industry researchers as well as practitioners.

The conference program embraces a variety of perspectives, reflecting how the design of communication intersects with the related areas of user experience design, information architecture, interaction design, and documentation. From the many submissions made to the conference this year, we have put together a strong program, with exceptionally high quality work. The varied methods used in the studies discussed this year are intriguing, ranging from large-scale surveys to ethnographies, from deployment studies to discourse analyses. The diversity of perspectives is also mirrored by geographic diversity among contributors. Following the international meetings of the conference in the last two years, SIGDOC 2012 has continued to attract the attention and participation of researchers from outside North America.

Our program includes many different opportunities to engage with fellow design of communication thinkers, including workshops, papers, panels, experience reports, and posters. The program also offers an opportunity to reflect on the past in a special session dedicated to the work of SIGDOC, which celebrates its 30th anniversary at this year's conference.

SIGDOC requires a significant amount of work on several fronts. A team of dedicated individuals have made the conference possible this year. Our success with SIGDOC 2012 is due to the tireless efforts of the chairs, paper reviewers, and student volunteers. Profound thanks to all those who have made this event possible. We also appreciate the financial support received from our generous sponsors.

Please enjoy SIGDOC 2012 and all the excitement that our host city has to offer.

Mark Zachry
SIGDOC 2012 Conference Chair

Program Chair's Welcome

Welcome to the *2012 ACM Conference on Design of Communication – SIGDOC'12.* Over the last 30 years, SIGDOC has evolved considerably. At first, SIGDOC focused on documentation for hardware and software. But in 2003 SIGDOC refocused on the design of communication, emphasizing the potentials, the practices, and the problems of multiple kinds of communication technologies, such as Web applications, user interfaces, and on-line and print documentation.

Today, SIGDOC focuses on the design of communication as it is taught, practiced, researched, and theorized in various fields. Here, people of different fields and disciplines study how people communicate in classroom and workplace activities, in using websites and web applications, in managing information, and in writing and documentation. This year's program features speakers from academics and industry and from fields as diverse as computer science, information science, information architecture, usability, communications, rhetoric, and technical communication, all gathered in Seattle to share their insights about the design of communication. These speakers address *settings* from enterprises to retirement centers; *media* from help systems to instant messaging to art installations; and *concerns* from documentation frameworks to processes to research methodologies. We accepted 44 papers this year, including 32 research papers and 12 experience reports, representing various fields and viewpoints on the design of communication.

Thanks to everyone involved in making SIGDOC'12 possible. Our executive committee provided guidance and vision. Mark Zachry, our conference chair, has worked hard to pull the conference together, helped ably by Doug Divine and Toni Ferro on the Local Arrangements Committee; Behzod Sirjani, the Publication Designer; and Jonathan T. Morgan, the Master of Websites. Liza Potts served as Publicity Chair, while Aristidis Protopsaltis served as European Liaison. Stewart Whittemore and Huatong Sun served as Poster Chair and Experience Reports Chair.

Thanks also to the conference volunteers, and special thanks to our outstanding program committee, who worked hard this year to review papers and provide solid comments for authors.

The Rigo Award is given biannually to an individual or individuals who have made an outstanding lifetime contribution to the field of documentation design. This year's winner is Gerhard Fischer, whose work on computer-supported collaboration and cultures of participation, users as co-designers, contextually-aware systems, and social creativity has contributed greatly to the design of communication. His work as Director of University of Colorado's leading-edge Center for Lifelong Learning and Design has inspired generations of students and researchers. Prof. Fischer also delivers our keynote, "Meta-Design and Cultures of Participation: Transformative Frameworks for the Design of Communication."

Finally, and especially, we thank two SIGDOC leaders. Our immediate past president, Brad Mehlenbacher, has decided to step down after tirelessly and expertly guiding this organization for many years. Our interim president, Rob Pierce, has stepped up to the plate and drawn on his considerable experience to guide us through the transition.

On to the conference!

Clay Spinuzzi
SIGDOC'12 Program Chair
University of Texas at Austin

Tablet of Contents

Session 5: Processes for Improving Communication

Session Chair: Carlos Evia *(Virginia Tech)*

Session 6: Social Media in Education

Session Chair: William Hart-Davidson *(Michigan State University)*

Keynote Address

Session Chair: Mark Zachry *(University of Washington - Seattle)*

Session 7: SIGDOC Past, Present, and Future

Session Chair: Scott Tilley *(Florida Institute of Technology)*

Session 8: Social Tools for Supporting Work - II

Session Chair: Brian McNely *(University of Kentucky)*

Session 9: Reading and Navigating

Session Chair: Laura Palmer *(Southern Polytechnic State University)*

Session 10: Design Methodologies
Session Chair: Kathy Haramundanis *(HP)*

Session 11: Domains of Care - II
Session Chair: Manuela Aparicio *(ISCTE)*

Session 12: Interactivity and Multimedia
Session Chair: Huatong Sun *(University of Washington - Tacoma)*

Session 13: Interaction Histories and Knowledge Systems
Session Chair: David Farkas *(University of Washington - Seattle)*

Session 14: Frameworks and Models

Session Chair: Michael J. Albers *(East Carolina University)*

Session 15: Interfaces

Session Chair: Carlos Costa *(ISCTE)*

Session 16: Design of Communication: The Big Picture

Session Chair: Liza Potts *(Michigan State University)*

Poster Abstracts

SIGDOC 2012 Conference Organization

General Chair: Mark Zachry *(University of Washington, USA)*

Program Chair: Clay Spinuzzi *(University of Texas, USA)*

Experience Reports Chair: Huatong Sun *(University of Washington - Tacoma, USA)*

Posters Chair: Stewart Whittemore *(Auburn University, USA)*

Local Arrangements Chair: Doug Divine *(University of Washington, USA)*

Student Volunteers Chair Toni Ferro *(University of Washington, USA)*

Publicity Chair: Liza Potts *(Michigan State University, USA)*

Workshops Chair and Webmaster: Jonathan Morgan *(University of Washington, USA)*

Publications Designer: Behzod Sirjani *(Northwestern University, USA)*

European Liaison: Aristidis Protopsaltis *(Coventry University, United Kingdom)*

Program Committee: Aristidis Protopsaltis *(Serious Games Institute, Coventry University, United Kingdom)*
Brad Mehlenbacher *(North Carolina State University, USA)*
Brenton Faber *(Worchester Polytechnic Institute, USA)*
Brian Butler *(University of Maryland, USA)*
Brian McNely *(University of Kentucky, USA)*
Carlos J. Costa *(ISCTE, IUL, Portugal)*
Christa Teston *(University of Idaho, USA)*
Dave Clark *(University of Wisconsin-Milwaukee, USA)*
David Farkas *(University of Washington, USA)*
David Novick *(University of Texas-EP, USA)*
Douglas Eyman *(George Mason University, USA)*
Huatong Sun *(University of Washington – Tacoma, USA)*
Jason Swarts *(North Carolina State University, USA)*
John Stamey *(Coastal Carolina University, USA)*
Johndan Johnson-Eilola *(Clarkson University, USA)*
Junia Anacleto *(UFSCar, Brazil)*
Kathy Haramundanis *(HP, USA)*
Liza Potts *(Michigan State University, USA)*
Manuela Aparicio *(ISCTE, Portugal)*
Marco Winckler *(Université Paul Sabatier, Brazil)*
Mark Perry *(Brunel University, United Kingdom)*
Maurice Hendrix *(Serious Games Institute, United Kingdom)*
Michael J. Albers *(East Carolina University, USA)*
Quan Zhou *(Metropolitan State University, USA)*
Rebecca Walton *(Utah State University, USA)*

Program Committee (continued)

Renata Fortes *(ICMC, USP, Brazil)*
Robert Pierce *(IBM, USA)*
Rudy McDaniel *(University of Central Florida School of Visual Arts and Design, USA)*
Ryan Moeller *(Utah State University, USA)*
Simone Barbosa *(PUC-Rio, Brazil)*
Steve Murphy *(IBM Canada Ltd, Canada)*
Stewart Whittemore *(Auburn University, USA)*
Stuart Selber *(Penn State University, USA)*
Sarah Read *(DePaul University, USA)*
Sean Zdenek *(Texas Tech University, USA)*
Shihong Huang *(Florida Atlantic University, USA)*
William Hart-Davidson *(Michigan State University, USA)*

Additional reviewers:

Godwin Agboka
Pam Brewer
Kellie Carter
Michael Gurstein
Kyle Mattson
Sushil Oswal
Lee Tesdell
Christopher Toth

SIGDOC 2012 Sponsor & Supporters

Sponsor:

Supporters:

HCDE Human Centered Design & Engineering
University of Washington

W UNIVERSITY *of* WASHINGTON
OFFICE OF PLANNING & BUDGETING

Dynamic Adaptive Search Based Software Engineering*

Mark Harman[1], Edmund Burke[2], John A. Clark[3] and Xin Yao[4]
[1]CREST Centre, University College London, Gower Street, London, WC1E 6BT, UK
[2]University of Stirling, Stirling, FK9 4LA Scotland, UK
[3]Department of Computer Science, University of York, Deramore Lane, York, YO10 5GH, UK
[4]School of Computer Science, The University of Birmingham, Edgbaston, Birmingham B15 2TT, UK

ABSTRACT

Search Based Software Engineering (SBSE) has proved to be a very effective way of optimising software engineering problems. Nevertheless, its full potential as a means of dynamic adaptivity remains under explored. This paper sets out the agenda for Dynamic Adaptive SBSE, in which the optimisation is embedded into deployed software to create self-optimising adaptive systems. Dynamic Adaptive SBSE will move the research agenda forward to encompass both software development processes and the software products they produce, addressing the long-standing, and as yet largely unsolved, grand challenge of self-adaptive systems.

Categories and Subject Descriptors

D.2 [Software Engineering]

General Terms

Search Based Software Engineering (SBSE), Evolution, Automatic Programming, Measurement, Testing

Keywords

SBSE, Search Based Optimization, Self-Adaptive Systems, Autonomic Computing

1. INTRODUCTION

Current software development practices achieve adaptivity at only a glacial pace, largely through enormous human engineering skill and effort. We force highly experienced engineers to waste their time and expertise adapting many

---

*This position paper is written to accompany Mark Harman's keynote talk at the 6th International Symposium on Empirical Software Engineering and Measurement (ESEM 12) in Lund, Sweden. It is joint work with Edmund Burke, John Clark and Xin Yao, funded by the EPSRC programme grant DAASE (EP/J017515/).

tedious implementation details. Often, the resulting software is equally inflexible: users often find themselves relying on their innate human adaptivity to compensate with 'workarounds'. This has to change.

To address the twin goals of adaptivity and automation, we advocate a development of the Search Based Software Engineering (SBSE) agenda that we call 'Dynamic Adaptive Search Based Software Engineering'. We seek greater software engineering automation through the development of hyper heuristics for SBSE. At the same time we seek greater adaptivity through the use of dynamic optimisation; optimisation embedded into the deployed software to re-tune its performance parameters and even to replace large portions of code with automatically re-evolved code.

2. SBSE

Search Based Software Engineering (SBSE) is the name given to a field of research and practice in which computational search (as well as optimisation techniques more usually associated with Operations Research) are used to address problems in Software Engineering [39]. The SBSE approach seeks to optimise software engineering processes and products using generic, robust, flexible, scalable and insight-rich computational search. SBSE provides a mechanism for managed automation of software engineering activities.

SBSE has proved to be a widely applicable and successful approach, with many applications right across the full spectrum of activities in software engineering, from initial requirements, project planning, and cost estimation to regression testing and onward evolution. Few aspects of development and deployment of software systems have remained untouched by the SBSE research agenda.

There is also an increasing interest in search based optimization from the industrial sector, as illustrated by work on testing involving Berner and Mattner and Daimler [49, 64], Ericsson [3], Google [69] and Microsoft [14, 50], and work on requirements analysis and optimisation involving Ericsson [70], Motorola [9] and NASA [20].

The increasing maturity of the field has led to a number of tools for SBSE applications, including AUSTIN (for C language test data generation, [49]), Bunch (for modularisation, [55]), Code-Imp (for automated refactoring, [56]), eTOC (for Java class testing, [63]), EvoSUITE (for Java test data generation, [26]), GenPrg (for automated bug patching, [52]), MiLu (for higher order mutation testing, [46]), ReleasePlanner (for Requirements Optimisation, [58]), and SWAT (for PHP server-side test data generation [5]).

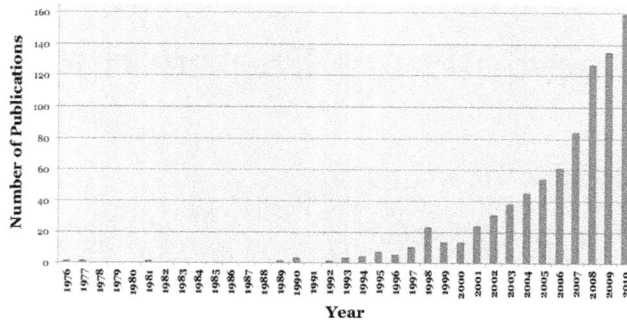

Figure 1: Yearly SBSE publication rates 1976-2010. Source: SBSE Repository [72].

Interest and research activity concerning SBSE has grown rapidly in the past ten years (see Figure 1) and there are now many excellent surveys and reviews on SBSE from which more information can be obtained. Rather than repeating this information, here are some pointers to specific SBSE surveys and reviews on:

- Requirements [71];
- Predictive Modelling [1, 34];
- Non-Functional Properties [2];
- Program Comprehension [32];
- Design [61] and
- Testing [2, 4, 33, 54].

In addition to this topic-specific SBSE literature, there are several more general SBSE surveys [18, 27, 31, 37, 40] and a review covering the relationship between other Artificial Intelligence techniques and SBSE [38]. There is also an SBSE tutorial aimed at those with no prior knowledge of SBSE who seek to adopt and apply search based optimization to software engineering problems of their own [42].

3. HYPER HEURISTIC SBSE

Current work on SBSE has produced significant advances in automated software engineering, particularly in the realms of testing, bug fixing and decision support. SBSE also shows great promise as a technique for handling non-functional properties and noisy, incomplete, and conflicting information concerning fitness.

Current SBSE automates specific problems in isolation, rather than the entire software engineering process. A dramatic increase in the breadth of automation lies within the grasp of the SBSE research and practitioner community. Such a 'holistic' optimisation-centric approach would ensure that SBSE achieves its full potential as a means to embed automated processes throughout the full range of software development and deployment activities.

To illustrate this vision for a more holistic SBSE, suppose we automate large parts of the development process using computational search: requirements engineering, project planning and testing could then become unified into a single automated activity.

To achieve a generic and holistic optimisation that connects diverse engineering activities, we turn to hyper-heuristic search [13] as a methodology for selecting or generating heuristics. That is, while most heuristic methods in the literature operate on a search space of potential solutions to a particular problem, a hyper-heuristic operates on a search space of heuristics. A Hyper Heuristic Search Based Software Engineering would address two important open questions in SBSE:

1. **To reach deeper, we need a holistic SBSE:** Why do we currently need to design special search based algorithms for each problem instance? This is unrealistic: every software engineer cannot be expected to be a computation search algorithm designer too.

2. **To reach wider, we need a generic SBSE:** Why do we currently optimise silos of software engineering activity? This is unrealistic: engineering decision making needs to take account of requirements, designs, test cases and implementation details *simultaneously*.

The Hyper Heuristic SBSE research agenda will raise fundamental questions. For example: how best do we draw the dividing line between adaptive automation for small changes and human intervention to invoke more fundamental adaption and to provide oversight and decision making? While automation is important, it is essential to understand the points at which human oversight, intervention, resumption-of-control and decision making should impinge on automation [35].

In the context of SBSE, this dividing line is the fine line between automated decision taking and automated decision support. Previous work on SBSE has tended to focus on automated decision making for those aspects of the development thought to occur later in the cycle, such as testing. The community has tended to reserve decision support for the early development cycle activities such as requirements analysis, and estimation. However, in a more holistic SBSE, there will be a far more intimate relationship between decision making and decision support, posing new methodological, engineering and pragmatic constraints and concerns.

Our vision of this new Hyper Heuristic Search Based Software Engineering is that it will provide the intellectual and technical tools to address the challenge of deeper, more holistic SBSE that cuts across the traditional software engineering boundaries such as requirements, design, modelling and testing. This vision is unashamedly experimental [67] and empirical [12]. It also aligns well with more agile and adaptive development practices, in which different software engineering activities such as design, re-factoring, testing and requirement elicitation are seen as iterative, integrated and inter-related activities, rather than as separate phases of development.

We also believe that the same Hyper Heuristic Search Based Software Engineering agenda will allow SBSE to reach a wider practitioner audience, by moving us from the bespoke to the generic. Instead of designing bespoke optimisation algorithms for specific instances, we advocate the design of 'reasonably good' hyper heuristic optimisers that have the generality to be applied more readily 'out of the box'. The results obtainable from a carefully crafted, specific, bespoke algorithm will surely out-perform those of a generic hyper heuristic SBSE algorithm.

We do not dispute this. Rather, we seek to surrender a little result quality for a lot of generality, believing that this balance of the meta objectives of quality and applicability will better address the factors that will influence uptake of SBSE. Our motivation is that ease of applicability will often trump quality of results, at least for the initial adopters, without whom there will be no take up. Has it not ever been thus in all technological development?

The hyper heuristic approach will require little tuning and will reduce the need for specific details, thereby significantly reducing the time to deployment and use. The key question will be whether sufficient optimisation power can be maintained so that the increased usability of the approach outweighs the reduction in result quality. This, in itself, is of course a twin-objective, cost-benefit optimisation trade off.

4. DYNAMIC ADAPTIVE SBSE

Self-adaptivity has been a goal of software and systems engineering research for some time, with work on architectures to support adaptive middleware [11, 59], Artificial Immune Systems (AIS) [45] for intrusion detection [47] and fault tolerance [68] and the vision of autonomic systems [29].

This research agenda is far from fully achieved: many authors still seek to address the outstanding grand challenge of self-adaptive systems, with large integrated projects such as the Self Managing Situated Computing project [25] and conferences and workshops, such as the Dagstuhl Seminar on Software Engineering for Self-Adaptive Systems [16].

SBSE has a potential to make a significant contribution to the realisation of this grand challenge. Unlike all other engineering optimization problems it is for *software* that optimisation has the most potential, because of the virtual nature of this extraordinary engineering material [36]. While computational search has been successfully applied to the design of engineering artefacts in civil, mechanical and electronic engineering, the search process cannot directly optimise these materials; the search ranges over a design space, guided by a simulation of a model of reality.

The search space and guidance are very different when we apply computation search to software. We find a new and potent possibility for search based optimisation: we can *directly* optimise the engineering material: the programs themselves. This opens up the possibility for in-situ, on the fly, optimisation to re-balance, re-configure, and even to *redevelop* the deployed software as it operates. This is the goal of Dynamic Adaptive Search Based Software Engineering.

The SBSE community has already developed techniques for tuning the performance of systems by identifying performance affecting parameters and treating them as configuration search spaces [19, 48]. There have also been exciting recent breakthroughs in the use of genetic programming to re-design aspects of systems to fix bugs [8, 65], to migrate to new platforms and languages [51] and to optimise non-functional properties [66].

These results can be thought of as early indications of the potential for Dynamic Adaptive SBSE. The work on parameter tuning shows that we can identify and tune performance parameters. If we can do this off-line, why not perform the tuning *on-line*. That is, compile into the deployed software an optimization algorithm that can identify and tune parameters that affect non-functional requirements. In this way, we would have self-monitoring, self-optimising systems.

By focusing on non-functional requirements we may partly escape the intricacies of requirements capture, with their inherent uncertainties. Functional requirements analysis is known to be plagued by difficulties of knowing exactly what the customer wants [15], something the customer may not even know themselves. Fortunately, the fitness function is often clear and unequivocal when it comes to non-functional requirements. The customer merely needs to state the non-functional requirements that matter (perhaps with acceptable tolerances, thresholds or ranges) and we can seek to optimise for these requirements.

By focusing on non-functional properties, we shall not be in a niche ghetto of 'optimisable software space'. The technological and business winds of change are clearly prevailing in a very non-functional direction. The advent of smart devices as an important computational platform, raises issues of power consumption, memory use and code size. The use of internet-enabled computing, in context aware mobile systems demands attention to bandwidth and response time. Cloud migration brings with it demands on throughput, heat dissipation and other service level properties.

Notice how this migration, from what might be termed the 'discrete' world of functional properties to the more 'continuous' world of non-functional properties, clearly illuminates the age-old debate about the difference between those two recalcitrant siamese twins: computer science and software engineering.

A focus on non-functional requirements such as power consumption, heat dissipation, throughput, response time, memory profile, bandwidth and information leakage will render a kind of Software Engineering more akin to traditional engineering disciplines. The inherent engineering character of software development and deployment will become more compelling than would have ever been thought by those who even ventured to doubt that there was such a thing as software *engineering* or that it could ever share the qualities of traditional engineering disciplines [22, 44, 43]. The rising importance of non-functional properties will also mean that software engineering will become ever more amenable to SBSE-style approaches.

Identification and optimisation of performance sensitive parameters will be one way to achieve Dynamic Adaptive SBSE. However, this will still leave the code largely unchanged. We will be extracting parameters, exposing them at the 'top level' and then searching for sensible settings, as the software executes. While this is likely to have many practical benefits, it merely scratches at the surface of the software.

Perhaps an even more exciting (yet demanding) challenge would be to seek a re-development of part of the software as deployed, while it executes, in situ, to replace the code with a better alternative. This dynamic adaptive SBSE would allow software to be more fundamentally adaptive. With this form of search-based adaptivity, we could hope that software systems would re-develop themselves, over time, to handle changing environments, platforms and contexts, while still seeking to meet the same overall functionality.

To some, such a vision of truly self-modifying code, might seem more of a nightmare than a dream: surely such code would be impossible to understand and to control? How would we ever apply source code analysis to such dynamically adapting code? Would the code not become unreadable?

However, with hindsight it may seem like merely another step on the pathway from assembler code to higher levels of abstraction. We already cede to the compiler a great deal of sovereignty over the code that it produces, seldom interfering with (or even enquiring about) the optimisation choices the compiler makes in producing object code.

With the advent of Dynamic Adaptive SBSE, we will make a further step towards the goal of greater abstraction. What we think of as source code today, may become the object code of tomorrow. In a world where non-functional, performance related requirements are 'optimised in' as the code executes, the programmer can move to a higher plain of abstraction. She will surely want to focus purely on the functional requirements of the system and will be happy to leave the optimisation of non-functional aspects to the SBSE compiler (and the 'on board re-evolver').

We hope to reach the point at which we are able to use Dynamic Adaptive SBSE to simultaneously meet the goals cherished by early pioneers of declarative languages [21] as well as the initial advocates of self-adaptive and autonomic computing [29, 59]: The program would be written in a purely declarative style. Why would anyone wish to code for performance-related details when these can be 'optimised in'? Initial results from new forms of SBSE-inspired genetic programming have indicated that this goal may be within our reach:

Bug fixing: With automated bug fixing, it is already possible to find and fix non trivial bugs [30]. The changes made by an automated patching system, are relatively small changes compared to the overall size of the program. One might think that they would simply be just that: a patch, deployed as a temporary measure to buy time for the more trusted code changers (the humans) to take over. However, there is recent evidence that there may be a longer-term future for such machine-generated patches [28].

Migration: Recent work on code migration using evolutionary improvement [51] showed that it was possible to automatically port the core computation of the unix utility `gzip` from a desk top platform supporting C code to a GPGPU platform supporting CUDA code. The automated re-evolution of the core computation of this utility demonstrates that it is not just patches that can be evolved, but larger pieces of code. It also indicates that it is possible to evolve new code for completely different architectures and languages than those for which the original code was designed. A key insight in this work is that the original program can act as an oracle for the functional requirements of the system to be re-evolved in this way [7].

Trading Functional and non-functional requirements: Previous work on searching for alternative balances between functional and non-functional requirements has also been promising. White et al. [66] showed how different versions of a pseudo random number generator could be evolved with a range of power-consumption characteristics. Crucially, in this work, functionality was sacrificed for non-functional properties. This may seem a curious approach to adopt after several decades of emphasis on correctness of functional requirements. However, for battery-powered platforms, power consumption is king:

$$correctness + flat\_battery = useless$$

A user might sacrifice the 'sacred cow' of complete functional correctness (did we ever attain that anyway?) should it come into stark conflict with longer battery life.

Indeed, do we not already do so when we switch off features of our smart phones to enable longer lifetime to the next re-charge?

The road to achieve our vision is not without challenges. There are fundamental obstacles to be overcome in computational search itself. It is still unclear whether it is even theoretically possible to evolve and adapt software from just a declarative description of functional requirements. There is a need to understand what is and is not possible using the SBSE approach and how efficient and effective such an approach is in evolving software dynamically.

5. EXPERIMENTAL VS. EMPIRICAL

The essence of science and engineering and their considerable achievements rest upon the careful construction of experiments, from which (often painstaking) observations are made. Experimentation is the foundation stone on which rests much of science, widely believed to be the principle driver behind the growth of scientific knowledge. Experimentation is the scientific credo enshrined in the Popperian view of science [60].

There has been much debate about the role of experimentation in computer science and software engineering too, with many arguing the case for experimental approaches [10, 57, 62]. However, there is a subtle distinction between purely experimental and empirical research in software engineering. This distiction is less important (and thus under-emphasied) in other science and engineering disciplines.

A scientific experiment is normally taken to mean the careful observation of one or more dependent attributes, under carefully controlled circumstances. The control of circumstances is crucial; one often uses the phrase 'under laboratory conditions' for such experiments.

By contrast, the term 'empirical' is typically used to define *any* statement about the world that is related to observation or experience. It is helpful to distinguish pure experimentation from the more general class of empirical investigation. Of course, a scientific experiment is an act of observation and experience; the experience of the scientist making those 'careful observations'. Therefore, any experimental approach is inherently empirical. Nevertheless, the controlled scientific experiment enjoys a special place in the scientific discovery process, because it is a way to determine and *measure* the effect of one quantity on another.

There is a long history of empirical observation dating back to the Babylonian astronomers, who provided data charting the movements of the heavenly bodies, from which present day astronomy continues to profit. As such, the concept of empirical observation considerably predates the scientific method of experimentation. Indeed, these ancient empirical stargazers were not only forerunners of present day astronomy, they were also astrologers, concerned as much with magic and mysticism as there were with reason and scientific experimentation [24].

Arbitrary empirical observations on their own, can provide no more than case studies in the observation of real world phenomena. While real world empirical observations have an important place in the testing of engineering artefacts in situ and in their final operation context, the first duty of scientist and engineer lies within the realm of pure experimentation, under laboratory conditions, where laboratory control serves as a mechanism for removing selection bias, confounding effect and miss observation.

6. SYNTHETIC DATA IN SOFTWARE EN-GINEERING

In software engineering, pure experimentation often makes use of synthetically generated problem instances. For example, to understand the effect of a requirements analysis problem by generating instances of hypothetical requirements or the effects of a data mining approach by construction of a large number of different kinds of data set.

Curiously, in stark contrast to similar experimental work in longer-established scientific and engineering disciplines, pure experimentation is often frowned upon by computer scientists and software engineers. However, under properly controlled laboratory conditions it remains the primary way in which scientists can investigate the effects of the independent variables on the dependent variables — a principle widely accepted in all fields of science and engineering.

Therefore, it is important not to overlook the value of purely experimental studies. While laboratory conditions are not the same as real world conditions, they can be controlled. In empirical software engineering we need both laboratory controlled data and data based on real world empirical experimentation, not one or the other.

However, caution is needed. The empirical software engineering researcher might fall into the trap of using synthetic data as a *surrogate* for real data rather than as an *augmentation*; seeking to answer research questions that really should be answered using real data. When using purely experimental research for appropriate questions the experiment must be carefully designed.

Nevertheless, this does not mean that synthetic data has no role to play in empirical software engineering. For example, a data mining researcher might use synthetic data to investigate whether their algorithm could reveal interesting surprises about system behaviour. This is a question clearly best answered by real data: a 'surprise' found in synthetic data cannot really be a genuine surprise (by definition). However, synthetic data could be used to test the scalability of the data mining algorithm.

Naturally, similar issues arise as with pure experimentation in other sciences and engineering; field trials are always required to augment laboratory testing. Fortunately, a 'best of both worlds' is also sometimes possible. Repositories may be large enough that one can find sufficiently many examples to cover a wide range of possibilities in the fine granularity required for experimental research questions. However, there are questions that can only be answered with experiments on synthetic data. For example, when exploring behaviour with corrupted, noisy and atypical cases, it may be not only necessary, but desirable to use synthetic examples.

6.1 The Role of Synthetic data in SBSE

Synthetic data can be useful as a means of experimenting with algorithms based on computational search. Such experiments cannot fully answer whether some SBSE approach will be useful in practice; evidence for this must ultimately accrue from empirical investigations using real world systems. The generation of synthetic data sets also requires care. For instance, the data must be reasonable and represent characteristics that may be found in the real world data sets that the techniques may encounter. Nevertheless, there are a number of experimental SBSE research questions that can be addressed using purely experimental analysis on synthetically generated data sets:

Scalability: How well does the algorithm scale with characteristics of the data? Scalability concerns resource consumption (typically space and time) of the search based algorithm as the characteristics of the input data vary. Scalability is a paramount concern in almost all software engineering applications. The input data variation is not necessarily merely a matter of the sheer size of the data set (though this is often important). The performance of some optimisation algorithms may also depend on other characteristics, such as density of dependence relations, correlations between elements and other non-size-based data characteristics. A purely experimental approach allows precise, fine-grained variation of data characteristics to explore the relationship between empirical algorithmic scalability and theoretical complexity bounds.

While general empirical and theoretical algorithm performance may be known for arbitrary problems, the specific software engineering problem in hand may exhibit peculiar scalability trends. Scalability is influenced by choices of representation and fitness function as well as the choice of search algorithm. An empirical scalability study can also determine the size and data characteristics at which an 'intelligent' search outperforms a purely random search, as has been done for requirements engineering problems [73].

Robustness: How resilient are the results on the presence of bias, noise, incompleteness and incorrectness in the inputs? Software engineering problems are often characterised by noisy, incomplete and even inconsistent data. SBSE has been argued to be well-suited to this paradigm [31]; search algorithms are naturally robust in the presence of incomplete and noisy data, and cope well with competing and conflicting objectives. However, the degree to which the choice of algorithms, fitness and representation cope with forms of bias, noise and incompleteness is often best assessed in laboratory conditions, where precise control can be exerted over the degree of challenge with which the algorithm is presented.

Algorithmic Performance Comparison: How do a set of search based algorithms compare for a problem over a wide range of data sets. There has been much recent progress in theoretical analysis of SBSE problems [6, 17, 41, 53]. Nevertheless, there remain many SBSE problems for which the only way to determine the best choice of search algorithm remains entirely empirical. In these situations one would certainly like to know how each algorithm performs on real world problems. These real world results can often be complemented by a more thorough purely experimental study, in which the factors that affect the choice can be explored in more detail. A study that exploits the full control afford by an experimental design unfettered by the availability of suitable real world data sets. Such a purely experimental approach necessitates the separate research problem of instance generation, a problem that has been considered in comparative studies of SBSE algorithms for requirements engineering [23].

Non-Functional Properties: How does the approach behave with respect to non-functional properties? Such properties of the search algorithm, such as its power consumption, response to change and communication bandwidth have not traditionally been the subject of intense investigation. However, in order to realise the Dynamic Adaptive SBSE agenda outlined in this paper, it will be necessary to compile (or otherwise embed) the search based computation into the deployed software to achieve search based adaptivity.

In this new paradigm of Dynamic Adaptive SBSE, non-functional characteristics of the search algorithms will be inherited by the software it is used to create. The complex interplay between several non-functional properties and the many problem characteristics that potentially influence them will mean that a full and thorough empirical evaluation will require a large and diverse body of data sets. Once again, the best way to ensure controllability of experimental method may be to create synthetic problem instances.

Adaptability: How well does a proposed SBSE approach cope with changes in the context or environment? The Dynamic Adaptive SBSE agenda will require algorithms and approaches that retain strong performance and result quality in the presence of changes in context and operating environment. Controlling for the operating environment of an approach is something that, almost inherently, calls for some form of laboratory experimentation, rather than a 'real world' evaluation; achieving laboratory control of experimental variables in a production deployed environment is unlikely to be realistic. Of course, results from such laboratory experiments should be augmented with field trials, but a field trial may not enable the researcher to report results for a wide variety of challenging contexts, which a purely experimental study can.

In many of the situations above, a purely experimental study alone will be insufficient and should be augmented with real world studies. Where real world data is abundant (for example when studying open source code as the subject of the empirical study), it may even be possible to find scale and variety in the available real world data sets sufficient to support a detailed experimental evaluation. However, in many situations, it is the very nature of the research questions asked that prohibits the use of real world data. For example, when attempting to assess scalability or robustness beyond what could reasonably be *currently* expected, the researcher must, to some extent, generate the experimental data set in order for it to be demanding.

7. THE DAASE PROJECT

The research agenda briefly outlined in this paper forms the focus of the DAASE project (DAASE: Dynamic Adaptive Automated Software Engineering).

DAASE is a major research initiative running from June 2012 to May 2018, funded by £6.8m from the Engineering and Physical Sciences Research Council (the EPSRC). DAASE also has matching support from University College London and the Universities of Birmingham, Stirling and York, which will complement the 22 EPSRC-funded post doctoral researchers recruited to DAASE with 26 fully funded PhD studentships and 6 permanent faculty positions (assistant and associate professors).

The DAASE project is keen to collaborate with leading researchers and research groups. We are also interested in collaboration with industrial parters and other organisations interested in joining the existing DAASE industrial partners which include Berner & Mattner, British Telecom, Ericsson, GCHQ, Honda, IBM and Microsoft. We have a programme for short and longer term visiting scholars (at all levels from PhD student to full professor) and arrangements for staff exchanges and internships with other organisations.

For more information, contact Lena Hierl, the DAASE Administrative Manager (crest-admin@ucl.ac.uk) or Mark Harman, the DAASE project director.

8. CONCLUSION

Dynamic adaptive search based software engineering is a development of the SBSE research agenda in which we seek to embed into the deployed code the optimisation techniques developed over the past decade of SBSE research. In so doing we seek to address the goals espoused by advocates of self-adaptive and autonomic computing, not merely to fix faults and cope with anomalies, but as a routine and natural means of on-line adaptivity to meet new challenges, environments and platforms. The approach may be particularly effective in the emerging world of more continuous non-functional properties.

We also look towards a Hyper-Heuristic future for SBSE, in which hyper heuristic search is used to improve the applicability and generality of SBSE techniques at the expense of some loss in quality of results. We argue that this may prove to be an important step in the wider practitioner uptake.

Both real world empirical studies and purely experimental studies (using laboratory-controlled synthetic examples) will be required to evaluate the practical aspects of Dynamic Adaptive SBSE. Theoretical analysis of problem characteristics, algorithm choices and solution space properties will also be needed to provide a sound scientific underpinning for this optimisation-based approach to dynamic adaptivity.

Acknowledgements: We would like to thank those whose ideas influenced this work (with apologies to those whom we may have failed to list here specifically): Enrique Alba, Nadia Alshahwan, Andrea Arcuri, Peter Bentley, Lionel Briand, Javier Dolado, Robert Feldt, Stephanie Forrest, Carlo Ghezzi, Rob Hierons, Mike Holcombe, Yue Jia, Bryan Jones, Kiran Lakhotia, Bill Langdon, Claire Le Goues, Spiros Mancoridis, Phil McMinn, Tim Menzies, Riccardo Poli, Marc Roper, Martin Shepperd, Paolo Tonella, Shin Yoo, Wes Weimer, Joachim Wegener, David White, Andreas Zeller & Yuanyuan Zhang. Thanks also to Lena Hierl for proof reading.

9. REFERENCES

[1] W. Afzal and R. Torkar. On the application of genetic programming for software engineering predictive modeling: A systematic review. *Expert Systems Applications*, 38(9):11984–11997, 2011.

[2] W. Afzal, R. Torkar, and R. Feldt. A systematic review of search-based testing for non-functional system properties. *Information and Software Technology*, 51(6):957–976, 2009.

[3] W. Afzal, R. Torkar, R. Feldt, and G. Wikstrand. Search-based prediction of fault-slip-through in large software projects. In *Second International Symposium on Search Based Software Engineering (SSBSE 2010)*, pages 79–88, Benevento, Italy, 7-9 Sept. 2010.

[4] S. Ali, L. C. Briand, H. Hemmati, and R. K. Panesar-Walawege. A systematic review of the application and empirical investigation of search-based test-case generation. *IEEE Transactions on Software Engineering*, pages 742–762, 2010.

[5] N. Alshahwan and M. Harman. Automated web application testing using search based software engineering. In 26th *IEEE/ACM International Conference on Automated Software Engineering (ASE 2011)*, pages 3 – 12, Lawrence, Kansas, USA, 6th - 10th November 2011.

[6] A. Arcuri. It does matter how you normalise the branch distance in search based software testing. In *International Conference on Software testing (ICST 2010)*, pages 205–214, Paris, France, 2010. IEEE Computer Society.

[7] A. Arcuri, D. R. White, J. A. Clark, and X. Yao. Multi-objective improvement of software using co-evolution and smart seeding. In 7th *International Conference on*

Simulated Evolution and Learning (SEAL 2008), pages 61–70, Melbourne, Australia, December 2008. Springer.

[8] A. Arcuri and X. Yao. A Novel Co-evolutionary Approach to Automatic Software Bug Fixing. In *Proceedings of the IEEE Congress on Evolutionary Computation (CEC '08)*, pages 162–168, Hongkong, China, 1-6 June 2008. IEEE Computer Society.

[9] P. Baker, M. Harman, K. Steinhöfel, and A. Skaliotis Search based approaches to component selection and prioritization for the next release problem. In *22nd International Conference on Software Maintenance (ICSM 06)*, pages 176–185, Philadelphia, Pennsylvania, USA, Sept. 2006.

[10] V. R. Basili, R. W. Selby, and D. H. Hutchens. Experimentation in software engineering. *IEEE Transactions on Software Engineering*, 12(7):733–743, July 1986.

[11] J. S. Bradbury, J. R. Cordy, J. Dingel, and M. Wermelinger. A survey of self-management in dynamic software architecture specifications. In D. Garlan, J. Kramer, and A. L. Wolf, editors, *Proceedings of the 1st ACM SIGSOFT Workshop on Self-Managed Systems (WOSS 2004)*, pages 28–33, California, USA, October 31 - November 1 2004. ACM.

[12] L. Briand. Embracing the engineering side of software engineering. *IEEE Software*, 2012. To appear.

[13] E. K. Burke, B. McCollum, A. Meisels, S. Petrovic, and R. Qu. A Graph-Based Hyper-Heuristic for Timetabling Problems. *European Journal of Operational Research*, 176(1):177–192, 2007.

[14] C. Cadar, P. Godefroid, S. Khurshid, C. S. Păsăreanu, K. Sen, N. Tillmann, and W. Visser. Symbolic execution for software testing in practice: preliminary assessment. In *33rd International Conference on Software Engineering (ICSE'11)*, pages 1066–1071, New York, NY, USA, 2011. ACM.

[15] B. Cheng and J. Atlee. From state of the art to the future of requirements engineering. In L. Briand and A. Wolf, editors, *Future of Software Engineering 2007*, Los Alamitos, California, USA, 2007. IEEE Computer Society Press. This volume.

[16] B. H. C. Cheng, R. de Lemos, H. Giese, P. Inverardi, and J. Magee, editors. *Software Engineering for Self-Adaptive Systems (Dagstuhl Seminar)*, volume 08031 of *Dagstuhl Seminar Proceedings*. Internationales Begegnungs und Forschungszentrum für Informatik (IBFI), Schloss Dagstuhl, Germany, 2008.

[17] J. F. Chicano, J. Ferrer, and E. Alba. Elementary landscape decomposition of the test suite minimization problem. In M. B. Cohen and M. Ó. Cinnéide, editors, *3rd International Symposium on Search Based Software Engineering (SSBSE 2011)*, volume 6956 of *Lecture Notes in Computer Science*, pages 48–63, Szeged, Hungary, 2011. Springer.

[18] J. Clark, J. J. Dolado, M. Harman, R. M. Hierons, B. Jones, M. Lumkin, B. Mitchell, S. Mancoridis, K. Rees, M. Roper, and M. Shepperd. Reformulating software engineering as a search problem. *IEE Proceedings — Software*, 150(3):161–175, 2003.

[19] A. Corazza, S. D. Martino, F. Ferrucci, C. Gravino, F. Sarro, and E. Mendes. How effective is tabu search to configure support vector regression for effort estimation? In *6th International Conference on Predictive Models in Software Engineering (PROMISE '10)*, Timisoara, Romania, 12-13 September 2010. IEEE.

[20] S. L. Cornford, M. S. Feather, J. R. Dunphy, J. Salcedo, and T. Menzies. Optimizing Spacecraft Design - Optimization Engine Development: Progress and Plans. In *Proceedings of the IEEE Aerospace Conference*, pages 3681–3690, Big Sky, Montana, March 2003.

[21] J. Darlington and R. M. Burstall. A system which automatically improves programs. *Acta Informatica*, 6:41–60, 1976.

[22] E. W. Dijkstra. On a political pamphlet from the middle ages (A response to the paper 'social processes and proofs of theorems and programs' by DeMillo, Lipton, and Perlis). *ACM SIGSOFT, Software Engineering Notes*, 3(2):14–17, 1978.

[23] J. J. Durillo, Y. Zhang, E. Alba, M. Harman, and A. J. Nebro. A study of the bi-objective next release problem. *Empirical Software Engineering*, 16(1):29–60, 2011.

[24] P. Fara. *Science: A 4000-year history*. Oxford University Press, 2009.

[25] A. Filieri, C. Ghezzi, A. Leva, and M. Maggio. Self-adaptive software meets control theory: A preliminary approach supporting reliability requirements. In P. Alexander, C. S. Pasareanu, and J. G. Hosking, editors, *26th IEEE/ACM International Conference on Automated Software Engineering (ASE 2011)*, pages 283–292, Lawrence, KS, USA, November 2011. IEEE.

[26] G. Fraser and A. Arcuri. Evosuite: automatic test suite generation for object-oriented software. In *8th European Software Engineering Conference and the ACM SIGSOFT Symposium on the Foundations of Software Engineering (ESEC/FSE '11)*, pages 416–419. ACM, September 5th - 9th 2011.

[27] F. G. Freitas and J. T. Souza. Ten years of search based software engineering: A bibliometric analysis. In *3rd International Symposium on Search based Software Engineering (SSBSE 2011)*, pages 18–32, 10th - 12th September 2011.

[28] Z. P. Fry, B. Landau, and W. Weimer. A human study of patch maintainability. In *International Symposium on Software Testing and Analysis (ISSTA'12)*, Minneapolis, Minnesota, USA, July 2012. To appear.

[29] A. G. Ganek. Autonomic computing: Implementing the vision. In *Active Middleware Services*, pages 2–3. IEEE Computer Society, 2003.

[30] C. L. Goues, M. Dewey-Vogt, S. Forrest, and W. Weimer. A systematic study of automated program repair: Fixing 55 out of 105 bugs for $8 each. In *International Conference on Software Engineering (ICSE 2012)*, Zurich, Switzerland, 2012.

[31] M. Harman. The current state and future of search based software engineering. In L. Briand and A. Wolf, editors, *Future of Software Engineering 2007*, pages 342–357, Los Alamitos, California, USA, 2007. IEEE Computer Society Press.

[32] M. Harman. Search based software engineering for program comprehension. In *15th International Conference on Program Comprehension (ICPC 07)*, pages 3–13, Banff, Canada, 2007. IEEE Computer Society Press.

[33] M. Harman. Open problems in testability transformation. In *1st International Workshop on Search Based Testing (SBT 2008)*, Lillehammer, Norway, 2008.

[34] M. Harman. The relationship between search based software engineering and predictive modeling In *6th International Conference on Predictive Models in Software Engineering (PROMISE 2010)*, Timisoara, Romania, 2010.

[35] M. Harman. Why source code analysis and manipulation will always be important. In *10th IEEE International Working Conference on Source Code Analysis and Manipulation*, pages 7–19, Timisoara, Romania, 2010.

[36] M. Harman. Why the virtual nature of software makes it ideal for search based optimization. In *13th International Conference on Fundamental Approaches to Software Engineering (FASE 2010)*, pages 1–12, Paphos, Cyprus, March 2010.

[37] M. Harman. Software engineering meets evolutionary computation. *IEEE Computer*, 44(10):31–39, Oct. 2011.

[38] M. Harman. The role of artificial intelligence in software engineering. In *1st International Workshop on Realizing Artificial Intelligence Synergies in Software Engineering (RAISE 2012)*, Zurich, Switzerland, 2012.

[39] M. Harman and B. F. Jones. Search based software

engineering. *Information and Software Technology*, 43(14):833–839, Dec. 2001.

[40] M. Harman, A. Mansouri, and Y. Zhang. Search based software engineering: Trends, techniques and applications. *ACM Computing Surveys*, 2012. To appear.

[41] M. Harman and P. McMinn. A theoretical and empirical study of search based testing: Local, global and hybrid search. *IEEE Transactions on Software Engineering*, 36(2):226–247, 2010.

[42] M. Harman, P. McMinn, J. Souzà, and S. Yoo. Search based software engineering: Techniques, taxonomy, tutorial. In B. Meyer and M. Nordio, editors, *Empirical software engineering and verification: LASER 2009-2010*, pages 1–59. Springer, 2012. LNCS 7007.

[43] C. A. R. Hoare. The engineering of software: A startling contradiction. In D. Gries, editor, *Programming Methodology, A Collection of Articles by Members of IFIP WG2.3*. Springer-Verlag, New York, NY, 1978.

[44] C. A. R. Hoare. How did software get so reliable without proof? In *FME '96: Industrial Benefit and Advances in Formal Methods: Third International Symposium of Formal Methods Europe*, number 1051 in LNCS, pages 1–17. Springer-Verlag, Mar. 1996.

[45] S. A. Hofmeyr and S. Forrest. Immunity by design: An artificial immune system. *Proceedings of the Genetic and Evolutionary Computation Conference (GECCO '99)*, 2:1289–1296, 1999.

[46] Y. Jia and M. Harman. Milu: A customizable, runtime-optimized higher order mutation testing tool for the full C language. In 3rd *Testing Academia and Industry Conference - Practice and Research Techniques (TAIC PART'08)*, pages 94–98, Windsor, UK, August 2008.

[47] J. Kim, P. J. Bentley, U. Aickelin, J. Greensmith, G. Tedesco, and J. Twycross. Immune system approaches to intrusion detection - A review. *Natural Computing: An international journal*, 6, Dec. 2007.

[48] K. Krogmann, M. Kuperberg, and R. Reussner. Using genetic search for reverse engineering of parametric behaviour models for performance prediction. *IEEE Transactions on Software Engineering*, 36(6):865–877, November-December 2010.

[49] K. Lakhotia, M. Harman, and H. Gross. AUSTIN: A tool for search based software testing for the C language and its evaluation on deployed automotive systems. In 2nd *International Symposium on Search Based Software Engineering (SSBSE 2010)*, pages 101 – 110, Benevento, Italy, September 2010.

[50] K. Lakhotia, N. Tillmann, M. Harman, and J. de Halleux. FloPSy — Search-based floating point constraint solving for symbolic execution. In 22nd *IFIP International Conference on Testing Software and Systems (ICTSS 2010)*, pages 142–157, Natal, Brazil, November 2010. LNCS Volume 6435.

[51] W. B. Langdon and M. Harman. Evolving a CUDA kernel from an nVidia template. In *IEEE Congress on Evolutionary Computation*, pages 1–8. IEEE, 2010.

[52] C. Le Goues, T. Nguyen, S. Forrest, and W. Weimer. GenProg: A generic method for automatic software repair. *IEEE Transactions on Software Engineering*, 38(1):54–72, 2012.

[53] P. K. Lehre and X. Yao. Runtime analysis of search heuristics on software engineering problems. *Frontiers of Computer Science in China*, 3(1):64–72, 2009.

[54] P. McMinn. Search-based software test data generation: A survey. *Software Testing, Verification and Reliability*, 14(2):105–156, June 2004.

[55] B. S. Mitchell and S. Mancoridis. On the automatic modularization of software systems using the bunch tool. *IEEE Transactions on Software Engineering*, 32(3):193–208, 2006.

[56] I. H. Moghadam and Mel Ó Cinnéide. Code-Imp: A tool for automated search-based refactoring. In *Proceeding of the 4th workshop on Refactoring Tools (WRT '11)*, pages 41–44, Honolulu, HI, USA, 2011.

[57] A. Newell and H. A. Simon. Computer science as empirical inquiry: symbols and search. *Communications of the ACM*, 19:113–126, 1976.

[58] A. Ngo-The and G. Ruhe. A systematic approach for solving the wicked problem of software release planning. *Soft Computing - A Fusion of Foundations, Methodologies and Applications*, 12(1):95–108, August 2008.

[59] P. Oreizy, M. M. Gorlick, R. N. Taylor, D. Heimbigner, G. Johnson, N. Medvidovic, A. Quilici, D. S. Rosenblum, and A. L. Wolf. An architecture-based approach to self-adaptive software. *IEEE Intelligent Systems*, 14:54–62, May 1999.

[60] K. R. Popper. *Conjectures and Refutations: The Growth of Scientific Knowledge*. Routledge, 2003.

[61] O. Räihä. A survey on search–based software design. *Computer Science Review*, 4(4):203–249, 2010.

[62] W. F. Tichy. Should computer scientists experiment more? *IEEE Computer*, 31(5):32–40, May 1998.

[63] P. Tonella. Evolutionary testing of classes. In *Proceedings of the 2004 ACM SIGSOFT International Symposium on Software Testing and Analysis (ISSTA '04)*, pages 119–128, Boston, Massachusetts, USA, 11-14 July 2004. ACM.

[64] J. Wegener and O. Bühler. Evaluation of different fitness functions for the evolutionary testing of an autonomous parking system. In *Genetic and Evolutionary Computation Conference (GECCO 2004)*, pages 1400–1412, Seattle, Washington, USA, June 2004. LNCS 3103.

[65] W. Weimer, T. V. Nguyen, C. L. Goues, and S. Forrest. Automatically finding patches using genetic programming. In *International Conference on Software Engineering (ICSE 2009)*, pages 364–374, Vancouver, Canada, 2009.

[66] D. R. White, J. Clark, J. Jacob, and S. Poulding. Searching for resource-efficient programs: Low-power pseudorandom number generators. In *2008 Genetic and Evolutionary Computation Conference (GECCO 2008)*, pages 1775–1782, Atlanta, USA, July 2008. ACM Press.

[67] C. Wohlin, P. Runeson, M. Höst, M. C. Ohlsson, B. Regnell, and A. Wesslén. *Experimentation in Software Engineering*. Kluwer Academic Publishers, 2000.

[68] S. Xanthakis, C. Karapoulios, R. Pajot, and A. Rozz. Immune system and fault-tolerant computing. *Artificial Evolution (Lecture Notes in Computer Science)*, 1063:181–197, 1996.

[69] S. Yoo, R. Nilsson, and M. Harman. Faster fault finding at Google using multi objective regression test optimisation. In 8th *European Software Engineering Conference and the ACM SIGSOFT Symposium on the Foundations of Software Engineering (ESEC/FSE '11)*, Szeged, Hungary, September 5th - 9th 2011. Industry Track.

[70] Y. Zhang, E. Alba, J. J. Durillo, S. Eldh, and M. Harman. Today/future importance analysis. In *ACM Genetic and Evolutionary Computation COnference (GECCO 2010)*, pages 1357–1364, Portland Oregon, USA, 7th–11th July 2010.

[71] Y. Zhang, A. Finkelstein, and M. Harman. Search based requirements optimisation: Existing work and challenges. In *International Working Conference on Requirements Engineering: Foundation for Software Quality (REFSQ'08)*, volume 5025, pages 88–94, Montpellier, France, 2008. Springer LNCS.

[72] Y. Zhang, M. Harman, and A. Mansouri. The SBSE repository: A repository and analysis of authors and research articles on search based software engineering. crestweb.cs.ucl.ac.uk/resources/sbse_repository/.

[73] Y. Zhang, M. Harman, and A. Mansouri. The multi-objective next release problem. In *GECCO 2007: Proceedings of the 9th annual conference on Genetic and evolutionary computation*, pages 1129 – 1137, London, UK, July 2007. ACM Press.

User Assistance for Complex Systems

Robert Pierce

Watson core technology

IBM Corporation

robertp@us.ibm.com

ABSTRACT

There is much opportunity for innovation in the areas of design, development, and delivery of technical communication for "systems of systems."

Systems can be extremely complex, and contain many subsystems and components. The presentation of technical communication for a system of systems adds layers of complexity both to explaining the basic concepts of the system and all the details required for each area of the system that may be applicable to each type of user or role, function, and operation. It becomes more critical and yet more difficult to provide clear and comprehensive overviews and details of a system and its subsystems and components, as the complexity increases.

Categories and Subject Descriptors

D.2.7 [**Software Engineering**]: Complex systems, Information design, Best practices, User assistance, Documentation, Personas, Topic types – *documentation.*

General Terms

Documentation, Design, Systems, Standardization, Theory

Keywords

Software documentation, User assistance, User technologies, Computer documentation, Information development, Best practices, Development process, Software development, Usability, Information architecture, Task-based design, Task modeling, Personas.

1. INTRODUCTION

Managing the complexities of large bodies of information for any one role or audience is an ongoing and increasing challenge. However, it is also an opportunity for innovation in the design of communication.

The challenges to designing, developing, and delivering user assistance for complex systems are many and this paper addresses the issues and provides specific solutions to those systems. It includes examples and best practices for working with several

different audience types both in terms of user role, context, and delivery level of content to make complex systems understandable and more useable.

The benefits of following information and software development best practices for complex systems are a focus and include methods for identifying, developing, and managing both the content and the relationships as an information consumer and supplier.

Unlike an individual tool, a process or an integrated system with a clear collection of user roles and tasks, a complex system has too many components, capabilities, tools, contexts, and user roles to be made available to any one audience. There may be concepts that provide for a basic understanding of the system but there is also much detailed information for specific user roles.

Defining a set of personas that represents the user roles or work contexts for the system is one way to manage system complexity and make appropriate subsets of information available to different audiences.

Each persona may encompass a set of use case scenarios that spans multiple tools and tasks. Each user role needs to understand what tools, processes, and capabilities apply to them and how to perform each task to do their job. And since their role is not performed in isolation but rather interacts with the tasks performed by other user roles, users as collaborators and contributors, need to understand how their work is integrated and interacts in the complete system.

1.1 What is a complex system?

The IBM Watson computer system that won the game show Jeopardy is a good example of a complex system that is made up of many subsystems and components. There are subsystems for natural language processing, deep question and answering technology, and machine learning to name just some of the broad areas it covers. Each of these subsystems has many components. [2]

The following image provides an example of a complex system. Each box represents a subsystem that is comprised of many different components. In this example, end users can ask questions through devices to a backend system that analyzes the question, generates possible answers, searches for supporting evidence for all possible, or specified number of, answers, weighs or scores the evidence and ranks the answers and then returns the top answer or requested number of possible answers. "Answers" in this example is only one possible type of question analysis response. For example, instead of answers, a system may return diagnoses, treatments, or problem resolutions, or monetary transactions.

Each subsystem and component that must be installed and configured or can be customized or monitored must be documented.

There may be several different role types for the users who interact with the system.

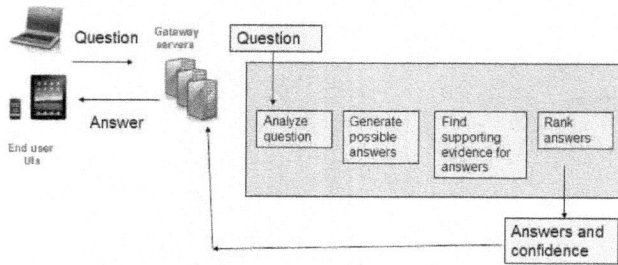

In IBM Watson, there is a vast amount of data in a knowledge base for question answering. There are many different algorithms and analysis components that operate on the data. There are several kinds of tests to run for training the system and for testing it. Many capabilities can be customized for industry-specific solutions. [1]

2. DESIGNING COMMUNICATION FOR SERVICE SYSTEMS

Dr. Claudio Pinhanez, IBM Research – Brazil, in a keynote talk at the SIGDOC 2010 conference, titled, "Designing the Interaction and the Communication with Service Systems," discussed complex systems and he also discussed the design of communication for such systems. He described many aspects of design of communication in complex systems where a solution is actually a system of systems, such as in IBM Watson.

He talked about a design focus moving from human-computer interaction (HCI) to systems human interfaces (SHI). IBM Watson is an example of a SHI since it provides interfaces to talk to or enter text to ask questions and receive answers with additional information to show the confidence of an answer and the sources that support the answer. [7]

IBM Watson provides a good example of these key attributes inherent in user interfaces:

- Inseparability: Services are produced and consumed at the same time. IBM Watson supplies answers but also uses the questions to get smarter for future answering of questions.

- Heterogeneity: Service processes are highly tailored and quite unique to each customer. IBM Watson Solutions are domain, industry, or enterprise specific. The sources of data and the types of specific questions would be tailored for each customer.

- Intangibility: Most services create outputs that have highly intangible aspects. For example, answers might be recommendations such as treatments for various diagnoses.

- Perishability: The capacity to produce a service is lost when there is no request for it. The system is available and does not advance if it is not trained and used.

- Coproduction: The customer performs part of the production process. Asking or supplying questions as well as indentifying information resources for the knowledge base are parts of the process for making IBM Watson better.

- Customer as Input: The customer is a significant part of the input. Since IBM Watson is going to be tailored for specific

customer solutions, the customer must be involved in determining the goals of the solution.

The design of communication for these types of interfaces and interactions in general and IBM Watson in particular reveals several subsystems and capabilities that map to different user roles or personas. Thus, not all information needs to be available at all times to all users and in all contexts. Providing a subset of the user assistance based on user context makes improves the usability of the product or offering. [7, 18, 19, 21]

Service systems and systems of systems represent an area for design of communication that requires detailed thought and planning for audience type, purpose definition, and context of use.

Careful thought in the design of communication around your audience in many different contexts yields a much more usable system, in part through better communication or user assistance. [19, 20]

In addition to the work in designing interfaces for online services is the design of the technical content and how to make it available. For example, different content can be made available to developers, administrators, and solutions consultants or even third parties for industry or customer specific solutions as well as to managers, team leads, and various other administrators, analysts, and other users of a solution. [8, 9, 11, 20]

Thus, a key aspect to all design is in determining and defining what interfaces are to be visible and what is to remain transparent in a system of systems and services. From this perspective, the design of user assistance can then support optimal usability of the system with a solution design that provides the appropriate information and exposes different systems, components, services or functions in different scenarios, that is, to different user types, roles or contexts. [12, 17, 22]

For example, users may only see a service or system capability if they need to perform some specific action. One implementation could be to provide subsets of technical content based on logged in user role. [10, 13, 22]

Information developers must identify the subsystems and components and determine that ones that need to be documented. How the information is presented may not be the same for all audience types. For example, explaining the overall system architecture may only be needed by a fraction of the potential audience. The available services may only need to be visible to users who are able to access them or customize them.

If consumers of the system will only see a few of the services through a user interface such as a web browser or remote device, then they may only need user assistance on how to perform the tasks available through those UIs. But the developers, administrators, implementers and deployers of those services may need to see the much more complex picture or all the services that drive or have an effect on the services made visible to end users.

There are also considerations for whether it always is most helpful to have the user assistance directly in the user interfaces versus in a standalone help system. A combination is usually the optimal delivery mechanism, for example where specific task-type content is available in the UIs but more extensive content including the task as well as more conceptual content and additional reference materials and examples are available in the more complete help system. [14, 24]

2.1 Information types

The types of information to document for a complex system are similar to other projects, systems, and solutions. However, the added complexity provides additional information architecture design challenges as well as opportunity. [4, 12]

For example, in a complex system, not only may there be too many details to describe to any one audience, it would not even be useful for all audiences to see "everything," both in product functionality and in the associated user assistance. [10, 19]

There are several different options for presentation of technical content as well. Technical communication types may include online documentation but also recording, training materials and labs, tutorials, and videos. One of the currently most consumable and effective technical communication formats is videos made available on YouTube. For an example, see, http://www.youtube.com/watch?v=okpbxc5OYoG [1]

If your system requires or at least makes use of several different capabilities from different components or product offerings, how do you connect the user information for them all?

2.1.1 Concepts and overviews

Concepts may include product or system overviews, summaries and images that show the subsystems, what the system is designed for and ways to use it, and examples of it being used or how it could be used.

Introductory information should also provide a list and description of user roles so it becomes clear to your audience which portions of the product and user assistance are relevant to their role. [7]

There may be portions of the system that everyone needs to know about. And there may need to be general overviews of the system for an overall understanding of what the system is comprised of. Providing images that show models of the overall system architecture can be useful to many of the types of people working on and with a complex system. [4, 12]

For an overall conceptual coverage, you may first describe what the overall system does and how it works. Then, you could present a view into the subsystems – or at least the concepts around some of what those subsystems do.

Some areas of information may only be needed by specific roles only, for example by the developer who will be customizing a component in a specific subsystem.

2.1.2 Tasks and use cases

Part of the introductory information for a complex system may be to provide a list and description of use case scenarios or super-tasks. From this list of scenarios, you can provide the individual task topics to perform specific use cases. For example, if running system testing is only to be done by a tester, then the specific task topics to perform testing can all be made available from a parent topic for testers. [14]

2.1.3 Reference information

Reference content may include several different forms of technical content. APIs, error messages, logging and tracing information, data files and formats information such as the locations of required files that may be hard to find, are all examples of reference content. In addition, it can be useful to provide listings of and pointers to additional information resources for related tools, services, and technologies for understanding and performing specific tasks and completing scenarios.

2.1.4 Context sensitive help

For a system of systems, context-based user assistance can be an important feature to make tasks easier to perform. Because an information designer cannot know in advance who does what, and what tasks and contexts apply to which types of users in all scenarios, perhaps user assistance that applies to specific contexts must be tied to the actual product interfaces so that help is there when the user is using the product and performing whatever tasks they must perform. [6, 7, 20]

3. IDENTIFYING INFORMATION COLLABORATORS

It is always critical to correctly identify the target audience for a personal, or industry, or customer specific service or solution and to incorporate their ongoing feedback. Additionally, it is important to structure the user assistance accordingly for an opportunity to enhance a product offering and help support users of all types and contexts. [6, 15, 23]

An information collaborator is a resource who may be both a consumer and a supplier to the user assistance.

Consumers are looking for information to understand product or solution functionality and system capabilities and are also looking for information to perform specific tasks and accomplish real work goals.

- Consumers: Are looking for user assistance to complete the tasks to do their job.

- Suppliers: May be using the system already and can provide additional information to enhance the content quality and completeness based on their experience with products, systems, or solutions.

Actively working with information resources as collaborators can enhance the quality and completeness of user assistance and also enhance customer relations. [15, 23]

As the following image shows, collaborators are consumers of the user assistance (in an information center in the image) and may also be suppliers by providing feedback. They may use the information and provide feedback to it.

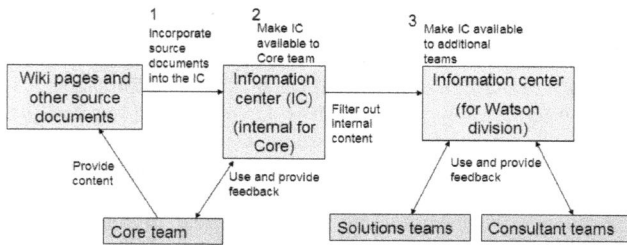

An internal core development team may create documents that form the initial technical information for a system, its components, subsystems, or specific functionality and use cases. Information developers may use these documents to create the first iterations of new content that may then become visible in a documentation deliverable such as an online help system or information center.

The developers of the core team may review that content and some new members of the core team can use it to learn about the technology.

At a more externalized but still internal level, consultants within an organization may be working with customers on industry or corporate specific solutions. They may need the user assistance to help them create the actual customer solutions. They may want to provide feedback and make requests for changes and additions to the content available at any given time or release. The content they see may be filtered so content for new work underway by the development team is now visible to the consultants until a newer code base or version of a solution is released to them.

In the same way, if the user assistance is made available to actual customers, it may undergo additional filtering so content that may be useful and appropriate for internal consultants is not visible to the customers.

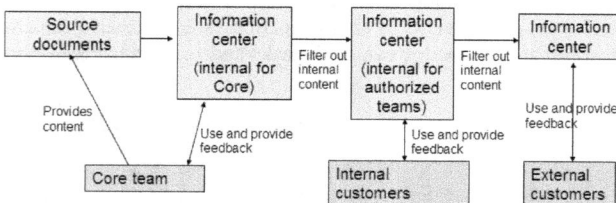

External customers, like internal audiences, may want to provide feedback on the content they have available to them or would like to see made available. One solution is to provide a reviewer commenting capability directly within the help system. [15]

Managing who can see what, and how each type of consumer can provide feedback provides opportunities for different review, collaboration, and change management tools, processes and best practices. [6, 23]

3.1 Personas and use cases

Personas represent the user roles that information developers and designers help define for system user interface (UI) and user assistance design. [6]

Personas can help provide a structure and strategy to drive the design of communication around your audience in many different contexts. Using personas as part of complex system design can also

help identify different layers of collaborators as well as clarify the complexity of the system itself. A complex system typically has many different user roles and thus information developers and designers may be able to organize the design of technical information around personas. [14]

The users in a system of systems may first include developers and administrators and testers of a system. Testers may be the first reviewers and consumers of user assistance who are trying to follow the tasks with the same goals in mind as customers or consumers of the system after it is deployed and made available.

The following image shows these three personas and some of their associated categories of user assistance.

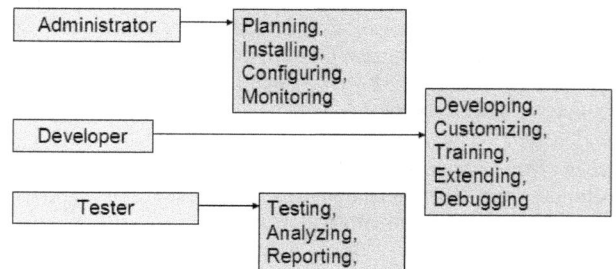

3.1.1 Developers, administrators, and testers of a system

Structuring documentation based on roles, such as Administrator, Developer, and Tester may benefit by customer input both before the new information architecture is designed and implemented and after it has been tested, delivered and used by customers for future enhancements. [15]

- Administrators install, configure, deploy, monitor, and manage systems that may include complex integrations for a solution.

- Developers may have a number of available services or capabilities to use to perform development tasks such as creating, testing, and debugging a feature in a product, new service, API class, or Java package.

- Testers may include testing the documentation by trying to follow it to perform actual tasks. By working with them, designers of communication can gain an awareness of how best to design and deliver the content in addition to developing the actual content. For example, in some cases, it may be good for context sensitive help to be available and in others, inline text may be better.

  Testers can also serve as both developers and administrators in validating content and contexts.

User assistance that applies to specific contexts may or may not be included to actual product interfaces – it may be part of an installation experience or it may be made available in a common framework such as from the web. [10, 11]

Other critical users will be the people who need to figure out how to install, configure, deploy, monitor, and administer both individual systems and services, and the integration of all of them into the complete "solution" or collection of solutions.

Thus, in a system of systems, there may be an audience for installing and configuring an array of hardware and software. System testing will be important before developers and testers begin using it and working on new and existing services in the system.

Some of the other common topic areas in a system of systems documentation project may include:

- Security - Authentication and authorization
- Extensibility and services (API or web services)
- Performance monitoring and tuning guidelines
- Configuration

If the system can be customized, then the user assistance can list the possible types of customization and in what context (that is, using what tools, services, subsystems) each type can be designed, implemented, tested, and deployed.

In a complex system, types of customization might include the following types of information:

- How data resources form a knowledge base.
- How to make a knowledge base available for queries.
- Understand the search algorithms and learn how to customize them.
- How to customize search mechanisms for improved results depending upon the data sources.
- How to use APIs to automate system monitoring and tuning for better performance.
- How to troubleshoot common runtime errors when they occur.

Some of the most difficult tasks for system developers and administrators may focus on installing, configuring, deploying, and using integrations, that is, solutions that comprise more than one software product.

More errors arise from installing and configuring integrations than any other area based on several customer support and problem resolution reports. Providing better error messages and resolution text for these types of errors can be beneficial. But even more important than providing troubleshooting text is providing the user assistance that helps prevent the errors in the first place. These areas are consistently identified as high value and high priority for making improvements including providing better documentation. [15]

3.2 Roles in a real complex system

A doctor or nurse who wants to use an IBM Watson for Healthcare Advisor application will only want to know how to use the system and what he or she can do with the available services. But, the healthcare organization making the system available to doctors will need to have the broader collection of technical content.

These topics, and how best to make them available, are all critical aspects of user assistance development.

In IBM Watson, the amount of data stored and the amount of analytics performed on the data, the algorithms used to search, retrieve, measure, and deliver a "best response" requires a massive amount of processing and data storage much of which may need to be described for administrators who may need to monitor and tune for performance.

If this system is made available for different applications of the technology, such as for health care decision support or financial planning, which services would the consumer of the information need to know about and configure?

If medical records are not written clearly, then they may be difficult to use for future reference. Developers might be able to create new innovations. For example, perhaps a search capability or machine learning solution could generate a health record based on the inputs (such as voice input requests for diagnoses and treatments for a patient) and responses (the answers the system returned). [16]

3.2.1 Personas example in a complex system

For the core technology that enabled IBM Watson to compete in a game show, and rapidly and effectively answer questions with a high level of accuracy, there's a front end, a back end and a pipeline between them that manages the complexity and performs most of the processing between questions and answers as requests and responses.

In this simplified perspective, what portions of the system need to be explained? The ones that some kind of user can do something with – configure it, tune it, and test it.

Some of the topics to document might include:

- Getting a system installed and configured – that is, ready for it to have data imported into it.
- Getting the data into the system.
- Training the system – machine learning and testing – algorithms for the question and answering processing technology – through testing and tuning the results for better results.
- Monitoring the system – to manage and improve the performance and resolve any issues.
- Designing how to surface the system into an offering.
- Deploying the system and making it available.

But the final design, development, and delivery will evolve based on the ongoing work.

4. IDENTIFYING THE ROLES OF COLLABORATORS

A person working for a company may have a job that aligns with more than one defined role in a given Help system. For example, a consultant who helps implement customer solutions may take on both the Administrator and Developer roles to complete a solution. Because roles do not necessarily translate to different people and because a product may be highly customizable and thus open-ended for information to provide, it is not always clear what would be the most beneficial list of user tasks to document. Getting input from real customers helps validate a design strategy and identify the primary user tasks.

When working with information consumers and suppliers, it is important to identify the primary user roles or audience types and then find collaborators who fit those roles. This direct type of collaboration can help validate or correct the accuracy of your perceptions and definitions of your audience. [15, 23]

Also, by targeting portions of content for each role or audience type rather than providing everyone all the content, an information design may enable a more effective collaboration network and receive better and more actual feedback. For example, in the following image, if there are several solutions team members and consultants, there may be smaller groups in these organizations who perform the actual Developer role tasks versus the tasks for Administrators or Testers.

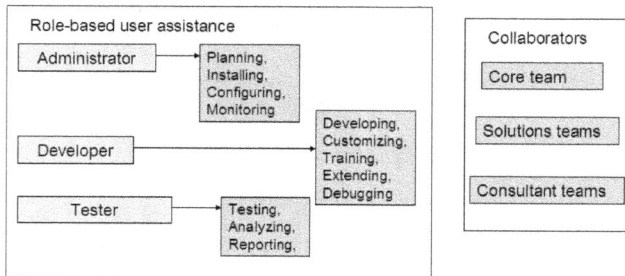

While the roles may span different tools and platforms for performing a number of tasks, the more common situation is where different platforms and different roles map more consistently. For example, in several products, there may be an Eclipse-based set of services or tools for developers and web interfaces for administrators or testers. [8, 9]

4.1 Integrations

Design of communication for a complex system shares some of the same challenges as designing user assistance for product integrations. In both situations, there may be multiple products, or components to install, configure, tune, monitor, customize, and use. [13]

For a two-product integration, there are two sides to the integration. Does the order of installing the two products matter? And is this clearly documented in the user assistance of each product? Is there content redundancy and possible inconsistencies in the two product documentation sets on the integration, or is there consistent content reuse? Is there cross product team collaboration to ensure content consistency, and if so, how is that collaboration managed and tracked? If something critical changes from one product version to another how are the user assistance teams of each product notified and how do they coordinate the updates needed in both documentation sets? [3, 5]

Multiple product solutions are another complex kind of system that requires information design, development, and delivery challenges and opportunity. For example, if five different software products are integrated into one solution for an enterprise, and all five products have their own user assistance, how are the five sets of content going to be integrated? What is the user experience for finding information that is relevant to the integration? What information for one product that may not be relevant for the integration can be made not visible? There are information architecture, filtering and metadata implementations available to address aspects of these challenges, but no actual working examples that demonstrate true success. [11]

In addition to installing and configuring the integrations, there are the use cases for using the integration. Do one product's capabilities simply appear in the user interfaces (UI) of the other product? Or,

does one product launch the other product UI? Or, is there a common UI where capabilities of different products appear?

A good example of a common platform is Eclipse, where capabilities from products can be installed as Eclipse plugins to the based Eclipse integrated development environment (IDE). The Help plugins for multiple Eclipse products can also be installed and they will all appear in one Eclipse Help system.

But even in this one Help system are the Help systems truly integrated? No, they are aggregated. User can search and find integration topics but might not find what they actually need for the integration they are using.

What user assistance is needed for the subsystems for natural language processing, big data, content analytics, and machine learning? And how best to coordinate with other user assistance (UA) collaborators if some of the components or capabilities have existing UA?

5. MANAGING DIFFERENT LEVELS OF REVIEWER FEEDBACK

If there are multiple types or levels of collaborators, then a well-defined design and effectively managed process for seeking and responding to reviewer or consumer feedback is important.

There are several considerations for and ways to manage an ongoing review process, communication and the content changes.

The following image shows one possible solution for managing two audience levels that each may include a number of the user roles for the system.

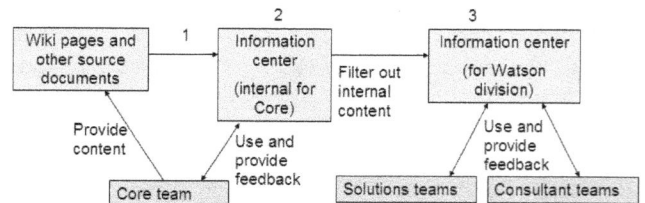

Filtering mechanisms can be used to manage the visibility of what content can be seen by which users. As the picture shows, each type of review has access to view just the relevant version of the content for their use and reviewer feedback. The information developers manage all feedback from all audience types and manage the content updates and the communication with the reviewer to ensure that updates to the content resolve the reviewer requests for content updates.

There are several communication and visibility options for working with all types of collaborators including internal audience such as a team of consultants and for working with external customers. [3, 11]

6. MANAGING CONTENT DEVELOPMENT AND CHANGE

Agile development and software development processes are commonly applied to information development projects. In Agile development, iterative development cycles of 3-6 week sprints are frequently used in software development projects. [5]

Technical communicators can manage information development in an agile development environment by using similar tools and processes. However, careful planning is required for managing the development and visibility of technical content through each iteration or sprint. [5, 8]

Content changes can be managed through a change management system so requests become visible and can be tracked by interested stakeholders. [3, 5]

As in other information development projects, managing multiple versions of the content for different audiences or different release versions including the review of the content can be managed through a content management system and metadata. [3]

7. SUMMARY

The design of communication for complex systems can enhance the consumability of the system by delivering user assistance solutions that provide the appropriate subsets of information in different scenarios or contexts for different user roles and objectives. [11]

Creating images and multimedia to illustrate complex integrations, and developing effective inline text and context-sensitive help are also options for improving product consumability. [4, 12]

There may be a kind of matrix for defining all the technical content that needs to be developed that includes user roles, product capabilities, and tasks. Personas can help map tools, tasks, and goals.

Designers of communication can use personas to help define the different kinds of use cases in the system. They can also use personas to map user roles to specific tools, services, capabilities, and products that support the tasks that users must perform to accomplish their objectives.

Some tasks are accomplished in one tool or system and some are accomplished through an integration of tools or multiple systems or components.

Collaborating with people working on and with complex system solutions can help validate the set of tasks and contexts that apply to each type of user role.

Collaborators may feel that accurate and relevant use cases are more important than defined personas or role-based technical content since each person often fills different roles. In addition, not all use cases may fit strictly into one defined role.

However, promoting a culture of collaboration with consumers of content makes them active participants in creating more accurate and complete content and is also a key to validating content development designs and delivery.

REFERENCES

[1] *This is Watson*, IBM Journal of Research and Development, Volume 56 Issue 3.4, 2012, http://ieeexplore.ieee.org/xpl/tocresult.jsp?reload=true&isnumber=6177717.

[2] Ferruci, D., Brown, E., Chu-Carroll, J., Fan, J., Gondek, D., Kalyanpur, A. Lally, A., Murdock, J.,Nyberg, E., Prager, J., Schlaefer, N., Welty, C., *Building Watson: An Overview of the DeepQA Project*, AI Magazine. (Fall 2010), 59-79.

[3] Agerfalk, P.J., Fitzgerald, B., *Flexible and Distributed Software Processes*, Communications of the ACM, Vol. 49 No. 10, (Oct. 2006), pages 27-34.

[4] Clements, P., Bachmann F., et al. Documenting Software Architectures: Views and Beyond. Addison-Wesley Professional. September 26, 2002.

[5] Cockburn, A., Agile Software Development, Addison-Wesley, 2002.

[6] Heximer, Erin E., Markova, Wu, and Yoon, *A Multidisciplinary Approach to Improving the User Experience - Information Development, Test, and User Experience Design Teams Working Together*, SIGDOC '02, Toronto, Ontario, Canada, ACM, 2002.

[7] C. Pinhanez. *A Service Science Perspective on Human-Computer Interface Issues of Online, Service Applications*, International Journal of Information Systems in the Service Sector, 1(2): 17-35, 2009.

[8] Sulaiman, S., Idris, N. B., Sahibuddin, S., *Production and Maintenance of System Documentation: What, Why, When and How Tools Should Support the Practice*, APSEC '02 Proceedings of the Ninth Asia-Pacific Software Engineering Conference, page 558, IEEE Computer Society Washington, DC, USA, 2002.

[9] Stefanovic, M., Matijević, M., Erić, M., Simic, V., *Method of design and specification of web services based on quality system documentation*, Information Systems Frontiers, Volume 11 Issue 1, March 2009, pages 75-86, Kluwer Academic Publishers, Hingham, MA, USA.

[10] Karatkevich, S. G., Litvintseva, L. V., Ul'Yanov, S. V., *Intelligent control systems. II. Design of self-organized robust knowledge bases in contingency control situations*, Journal of Computer and Systems Sciences International, Volume 50 Issue 2, April 2011, pages 250-292, Springer-Verlag, New York, Secaucus, NJ, USA.

[11] Casanovas, P., Pagallo, U., Sartor, G., Ajani, G , *Introduction: complex systems and six challenges for the development of law and the semantic web*, AICOL-I/IVR-XXIV'09 Proceedings of the 2009 international conference on AI approaches to the complexity of legal systems: complex systems, the semantic web, ontologies, argumentation, and dialogue, pages 1-11, Springer-Verlag, Berlin, Heidelberg, 2010.

[12] Pratten, G. D., *POSD-a notation for presenting complex systems of processes*, ICECCS '95 Proceedings of the 1st International Conference on Engineering of Complex Computer Systems, page 125, IEEE Computer Society Washington, DC, USA, 1995.

[13] Luqi, Zhang, L., Berzins, V., Qiao, Y., *Documentation Driven Development for Complex Real-Time Systems*, IEEE Transactions on Software Engineering, Volume 30 Issue 12, December 2004, pages 936 - 952, IEEE Press Piscataway, NJ, USA.

[14] Williams, A., *User-centered design, activity-centered design, and goal-directed design: a review of three methods for designing web applications*, SIGDOC '09 Proceedings of the 27th ACM International Conference on Design of Communication, pages 1-8, ACM New York, NY, USA, 2009.

[15] Pierce, R., *Using customer input to drive change in user assistance*, SIGDOC '08 Proceedings of the 26th annual ACM International Conference on Design of Communication, pages 23-30, ACM New York, NY, USA, 2008.

[16] Chu-Carrol, J., Fan, J., Schlaefer, N., Zadrozny, W. *Textual Resource Acquisition and Engineering*, IBM Journal of Research and Development, Vol. 56, No. 3, 4. May/July 2012.

[17] Thomas, B., Tilley, S., *Documentation for software engineers: what is needed to aid system understanding?* SIGDOC '01 Proceedings of the 19th annual international conference on Computer documentation, pages 235 – 236, ACM New York, NY, USA, 2001.

[18] Albers, M., *Multidimensional analysis for custom content for multiple audiences*, SIGDOC '03 Proceedings of the 21st annual international conference on Documentation, pages 1 – 5, ACM New York, NY, USA, 2003.

[19] Albers, M., *Human-information interaction*, SIGDOC '08 Proceedings of the 26th annual ACM international conference on Design of communication, pages 117-124, ACM New York, NY, USA, 2008.

[20] Albers, M., *Design of complex information*, SIGDOC '02 Proceedings of the 20th annual international conference on Computer documentation, pages 1 – 9, ACM New York, NY, USA, 2002.

[21] Murray, Schell, and Willis (1997). *User centered design in action: Developing an intelligent agent application*, SIGDOC 1997, 181-188.

[22] Priestly, M., *A wizard for wizards: Decision support for the new or despairing user*, SIGDOC 1998, 98-102.

[23] Rivera, Tate and Will, *Actively involving our information development teams with clients*, SIGDOC '03 Proceedings of the 21st annual ACM international conference on Design of communication, 167-170.

[24] Seifert and Crawford, *Managing innovation — 15 minutes of fame*, SIGDOC '03 Proceedings of the 21st annual ACM international conference on Design of communication, pages 210-13.

Design Templates in Instructional Design

Josephine Walwema
Oakland University
2200 N. Squirrel Road, Rochester,
Michigan
C1-248-370-4136
walwema@oakland.edu

ABSTRACT

Instructional design lies at the interface of systems theory, theories of teaching and learning, technology, and design. These fields together pose epistemological challenges to instructional designers. In this report I examine one element widely used by instructional designers, specifically the template designed and widely distributed by the Commonwealth of Learning (COL). In analyzing how the template serves intended users (who are instructional designers), I find that efficiency and effectiveness rooted in scientific models of objectivity to effectively corral massive information into manageable yet accessible knowledge for specific needs while expedient can have its drawbacks. I argue that a key emphasis on thinking as an active transaction between an individual and the data to which that individual is exposed permeates not just information, but also Instructional Design. Formalized within that role is a system of reasoning used to generate solutions to problems and in fostering skills in acquiring concepts. And it is missing in a template application such as COL's.

Categories and Subject Descriptors

Design, Theory

General Terms

Design, Instruction, Theory

Keywords

Instructional design, Template, Information design, Distance Learning, episteme, techne

1. INTRODUCTION

Instructional Design has emerged as a factor in the context of educational technology and its effectiveness in providing solutions in distance education. It brings together education and technology to serve one purpose: foster learning. What is problematic however, is the possibility of tipping the scales to education, or to technology, without necessarily striking a balance between the two. And yet practitioners see their role cut out for them as "how to carry out the reflective and analytic thought that leads to more learning" [1]. Pairing the two—education and technology—becomes a pitch between craft technology on the one hand and techne, on the other to meet educational needs.

2. About Instructional Design

Instructional Design is widely understood as the practice of translating "principles of learning and instruction" [2] (into material means for instruction.

Such materials are infused with activities, evaluative exercises, and feedback. As such, it is seen by many as a problem solving discipline based on systematic and careful application of design solutions [3].

As a discipline, Instructional Design is informed by an amalgamation of theories ranging from systems theory and human factors [4], cognition and learning [5] to design [6], making for a rather broad and diverse discipline. There is a history to this diversity.

At a time when knowledge was equated with objective/rational thinking, when education was systems based, John Amos Comenius bucked that paradigm to introduce visuals in teaching [8]. Comenius' vilification of the educational practices of his day in favor of the position that acquiring new material began through the senses was encapsulated in the word pansopy—a concept of expanding universal education. That view, of course, drew criticism from René Descartes, who sought to free science (reason) from theology (senses/emotions) in a quest to gain knowledge objectively. In time, Comenius's desire to make learning enjoyable and more meaningful through the use of dramatic productions and other innovative methods waned in favor of Descartes' rational objectivity. And yet his visual foundation is what John Dewey later built upon to create a link between educational psychology, and later evaluation and assessment [8]. Today, Instructional Design capitalizes on visual forms of communicating knowledge (icons, levels of heading) to appeal to learners' proclivity to process visual information. Instructional Design perceives visual forms as points of emphasis for main ideas, even as those forms draw attention away from less relevant details precisely because it recognizes that design *choices* affect the perception and even cognition of would-be learners. This material aspect of design is not merely an analogy.

Instructional designers associate design with efficiency in teaching and learning as dependent on carefully designed instruction. That process, according to Robert Mager, includes several goals of instruction.

These include strategy and the medium through which to attain that goal, and evaluation [9] – all working together. And from them, the generic ADDIE model (an inclusive term coopted to visualize a systematic approach to instructional design), whose five phases—Analysis, Design, Development, Implementation, and Evaluation— have emerged. The ADDIE model aims to offer dynamic yet flexible guidelines and illustrates the process of materials development in a systematic manner. ADDIE shows the level of instructional planning and precision that goes into the development of designing instruction. A simplified and generic systems design model, ADDIE operates in a series of stages that are formatively evaluated at each juncture through built in tests, and assessment. Notice the linearity that produces the formalized type of design suggesting that design solutions are decided upon beforehand.

One of the goals of Instructional Design is to improve quality and timeliness in the design and delivery of instructional material. This goal is often attained at the conceptual level through Instructional Design elements that include course structure, learning objectives, and content. The challenge for designers involves selecting the most effective instructional strategies to facilitate learning, a matter of creative and sound judgment.

For a long time, design strategies were dominated by traditional forms of Instructional Design characterized by an instrumentalist approach whose primary goal was optimal delivery of content. That's partly due to the dominant media format of the time (text, audio, video, and later, online delivery) that lent itself more toward quantity with emphasis on learning new material, and with it, the "duration of learning tasks" [10]. The media and the message being so intertwined, so the lack of interaction therein is cause for concern. And without such built-in mechanisms for engagement, students might as well access content on their own in from the many repositories.

Given the dominant ADDIE model and others modeled after it, Instructional Design has developed a built-in linearity that offers a step-by-step process toward attaining effective instructional material [11]. Unfortunately, this prescriptive model is what has resulted in established ways of *knowing* embedded in the template. That model, in many ways, cedes the agency of designing to the template. Abbie Brown and Timothy Green have attributed this disparity to the separation of the design process from the developmental process with the result that the processes do not inform each other [12]. For example, the developmental process focuses on effectiveness without knowing how efficient those strategies will be, while the design process simply implements the decisions made by the developmental process. This disparity, they say, can be traced back to the scientific and objective paradigm that Instructional Design draws from [13]. It is certainly consistent with the weaknesses we know from the body of work on designing instruction that learners and their needs are often ill-defined [14]. Hence the notion of replicating existing models [15] is fraught with uncertainty, making the case for design being amenable to shifting needs of learners, their diversity, and their contexts. Long dependent on a systems approach to Instructional Design, the discipline is beginning to recognize the need for active agents in designing and controlling instructional content.

As noted earlier, Instructional Design exists to tailor instructional materials to particular learners for prescribed objectives. But while historical accounts hold that Instructional Design emanates from research in the psychology of learning and system theory [15] from which the learning models are

constructed, Instructional Design also relies on "information and communication technologies" [16]. Even more importantly, designing instruction is didactic. It strives to make content transparent, through structuring, ordering, and presenting it in ways that learners find cognitively accessible [17]. Thus Instructional Design is a theoretically grounded, detail-oriented, practice and yet production based in its bid to foster instruction. This dynamic presents an epistemological challenge to practitioners.

As some models of Information Design have shown, our faith in technology, particularly in its electronic forms [18] has given us the Instructional Design template as a solution to materials development in educational contexts. These templates, often more experienced-based and effective for what they were specifically designed are often transferred as universal solutions without due regard to their reliability or effectiveness in other learning contexts. A major contributor to this eagerness to transfer template technology is what I call the *ethos of expertise* that the template takes on owing to, among other things, strong association with its designer, and testament of its initial success. As a result, the concern for those on the receiving end is the ease of template technology adaptation for pragmatic reasons.

I wish to draw attention to some shortcomings of the universal approach to Instructional Design inherent in the resources from the Commonwealth of Learning (COL). Before I discuss these concerns, I need to offer a brief overview of COL, an organization whose vision for designing quality educational materials is enshrined in the Learning Instructional Design template.

2.1 Commonwealth of Learning (COL)

In 1931, an organization calling itself The Commonwealth of Nations was established to bring together, on a voluntary basis, an association of independent sovereign states historically under British rule. Among its goals were to foster an educated citizenry, and "to encourage the development and sharing of open learning and distance education knowledge, resources and technologies" (www.col.org).

In pursuance of this mission, COL devised a number of resources to promote open and distance learning (ODL) throughout its member states. Among these resources is COL's *Learning Instructional Design Template*, meant to "aid the sustainable adoption of ODL methodologies" to help promote what COL considered quality education. The template is accessible at http://www.col.org/resources/ and is licensed under a Creative Commons Attribution-ShareAlike 2.5 License. It is accompanied by a comprehensive 70 page user guide.

Practical Challenges

Against this background are unique challenges emanating from member states. For each member state, quality learning materials are crucial to enhancing learning programs to produce students with adequate knowledge of various disciplines. Institutions of learning in developing and developed countries alike devote vast amounts of energy and funds to develop instructional materials. Developing countries, in particular, have enormous difficulty dealing both with the marginal suitability of materials developed from their scarce and often stretched resources in meeting their learners' goals. This limitation in resources further constrains those countries' ability to pay highly trained design personnel or to purchase costly learning materials, further perpetuating a paucity of high quality instructional materials. Compounding this situation is the desire to improve the capacity for delivery of higher education in countries where the demand is high, but access is limited, hence the turn to distance education. For their part, providers of distance education wish to assure one major theme. The warrant that there is no distance in education and that standards are not being compromised because of this model.

To remedy the problem of both quality personnel and learning materials, COL's freely downloadable template distributed in a Word format whose aim is meant to ease the burdens, costs, and obstacles associated with instructional materials development.. It satisfies your standard user manual-genre.

3. METHOD

To better investigate the merits of the COL template, I will base my analysis on what I categorize as techne and its related episteme. By techne, I mean a productive form of knowledge capable of creating and constituting novelties; the kind that demonstrates situated understanding (also "adaptive expertise" see Hatano and Inagaka), in tactually constructing material interfaces through technological dexterity and sophistry. A techne both artistic and epistemic promotes discovery, inquiry, and insight in an organic fashion [17].

I will limit my critique to the design process, the goal of my report.

3.1 COL Template

Unveiling the COL template was undergirded with the understanding that the conceptual structures underlying good education, teaching, and instruction are universal and that their language is shared worldwide. However, with Commonwealth member countries located in the Americas, Europe, Africa, Asia, and the Pacific and individual countries ranging from New Zealand to Namibia to Belize, the inherent diversity presented a tall order to COL's claim to offer high quality pedagogical content for such a diverse group of learners. One country that has adapted the COL template for its use is Namibia, whose Polytechnic of Namibia (PoN) offers courses in distance education. Georgina L Fröhlich of PoN [23] has documented the experiences of working with the COL template. I draw closely from that report in the course of this critique based on the template sections: Course Overview, Course Objectives, Unit Summary, Assignment, and Assessment—that offer content space meant for study material, assignments, assessment, feedback, and the unit summary.

There are several interpretations to be made from this frame. First, is the technological determinism inherent in the design-directive "add topic text here." Additionally, the template is replete with imperative expectations built into the words: 'add,' and 'complete' which demands specific mechanical action of the instructional designer. We see little regard to conceptual understanding and decision-making attributes that define designing instruction, to say nothing about the tactile dimension of techne as a material epistemic.

The template imperative stance reduces the instructional designers' task to cosmetic maneuvers. Fröhlich documents, for example, that "fonts were changed to more appealing ones, the color to black," and so on. These changes, as Fröhlich attests, amount to "fixing the technical style and formatting." It is, however, curious that the overseers reduced the work of the materials developer to simply entering content tailored to fit the COL template. In this act, the essential value of techne—of creating knowledge has been lost.

This brings us to an important consideration. What if we saw ADDIE and related models, not as templates, but rather as starting places for composing instructional texts? We might be able to see the numerous manifestations possible within the digital participatory space effectively and responsively. That way we

might take our eyes away from the product and focus on the design process. We might see then see the work of instructional design as the nexus of instantiating knowledge that's adaptive to situated design processes uniquely matched to the needs of learners in defined contexts.

Consigning design to the template invalidates intent in design. Without intent, we lose purpose, planning, and the creative act of actualizing practicable design. To design instructional materials as a techne requires a re-envisioned design frame that makes for mustering components that constitute a whole art. This model can help make learning more experiential and tangible for distance learners, who thrive in engaging spaces. It can certainly renders the act of designing as the conscious work of the instructional designers.

What unfolds in the template imperative affirms the results of a study by Ray Perez and Cathy Emery in which they monitor the design practices of those considered experts at design and those who are merely following instructions. That study finds that experts perform conceptually and practically, while novices pay more attention to the outward form of design, namely fonts, format and organization [20]. Further, those who had expertise were more reflective about their design strategies. Such conclusions are comparable to the findings by V. Goel and Peter Pirolli of architects and mechanical engineers. These findings suggest "strategies of incremental refinement" [21] as the designer progresses. And that sense of refinement is actualized through an epistemic process of inquiry. Thus we should not consign the term design to the outcome of a template designed learning material.

The perception of the COL template is that when beautifully executed (specter of Tufte) it yields quality instructional content that's purely objective and free from human error. The template aims to improve the current state of materials design pedagogy by assuring a standardized format of delivering instruction. Specifically, the COL template is touted as having built-in tenets and applications of accepted methods of ODL designed to teach learners to function across a variety of disciplines.

Unfortunately, the sentiment associated with Instructional Design as replicating existing designs has been understood the way it was intended as evidenced in the COL template's instantiation of mechanistic design. Consider the empirical evidence emanating from Namibia's adoption of COL templates in which it sees the immediate benefits of COL templates for their clarity, utility, and the supposed intelligence that is fixed in those formalized structures. For example, Fröhlich touts one benefit of the COL template for Namibia as precluding writers from having to "think for themselves" [22]. Thus for Namibia's Instructional Designers, templates are a no-brainer. Literally. Unfortunately, this perspective omits the thought, skill, and knowledge before action.

The Namibian experience touts COL templates for offering a tidy model for mechanical (re)production. As Fröhlich's account shows, the templates are themselves good for assuring standardized material. And because "writers do not have to think for themselves" (2), the template becomes a mechanism of standardization by substituting human thinking for thinking through technology. The Namibian experience shows a lack of depth, of elaboration in executing the design, and even less tactual handling of the process as an epistemic. The emphasis here is on the product. It may explain why the COL template lends itself to being focused on meeting formal structures rather than interrogating the process. Attending to Instructional Design as process is important because, as Patricia Hardrè, Xun Ge, and Michael Thomas observe, it helps designers emphasize "the systematic, circular, iterative, and holistic nature" [24] that characterizes Instructional Design.

4. Discursive Analysis of the Template

When we write about technological determinism (see Ellul Technological Society xvii), we often focus on technology as tool, and or as a means to an end, even an end in itself. However, there are several assumptions inherent in the notion of reliance on technology. These include social interactions that govern the "specific technological and managerial procedures" [25] necessary for the smooth running of a materials production team. What we see in COL is a design process that is determined by the technology of the template. We are perturbed that a complex design process is reduced to the effects of one part (mechanistic act) for the whole (design conceptual process).

The primacy of technology in the template is driving the design and shaping the interaction between designer, artifact, and eventually learner (cf. Winner, Agamben). The philosophical stance underlying this operation is steeped in the scientific model of cause and effect as demonstrated by the dominance of data graphics whose visual presentation is the product of a content-based approach to color and form [26]. In this paradigm, goals and objectives once predetermined are made to operate seamlessly without human intervention. The question, as Donna Harraway has noted, is "What kind of relationality is going on here and for whom? What sort of humanity is being made here in this relationship with artifacts, with each other…with institutions?" [27]. As we now know, the central tenet in Instructional Design comprises material relationships among the designer, technology, the conceptual framework, and learner needs. It takes into account the learning goals and how to achieve them artistically. That relationship is now compromised in the template.

Adapting form to content strives toward techne. Instructional designers leaning heavily on COL templates might want to question the power structures (Foucault) inherent in pre-established forms and the messaging of universalization. Further, standardization has its limits, and instructional designers especially need to recognize these limitations if they are to pay attention to the tactile predilection of this discipline. Taking this approach is participatory in that it musters the skills and knowledge of more than one designer. It is emblematic of a desire to create knowledge that's befitting of the time, the audience, and the purpose. It is techne.

One of the motivating factors for relying on templates is the supposed formal logic inherent in the reasoning embedded in them. Templates purport a logical structure, calling to mind what the Sophists were criticized for as lacking in method. However, the Sophists wanted to reach beyond the confines of human logic in order to apprehend knowledge in all its dimensions [28] and so went beyond method. Frank Walters is both supportive of this view and offers a counterstatement to the preeminence of logic. Singling out the "Antilogic" that Plato takes Gorgias to task about (with regard to method), Walters offers that it is better than dialectic (dialectic posits that once knowledge has been found, the case is closed) because antilogic, "is a continuous and recursive process. Though dialectic yields knowledge, the knowledge gained is yet a new logos for the continuation of the antilogic process" [29]. This antilogical process is thus a system of knowing and making known and is consistent with our understanding of techne specific to a design model [30]. That model offers a workable method comprising analytical skills that engage situations, confront problems, and offer workable epistemic solutions.

An Instructional Designer like a tactile artist must have a reasoned sense of ownership to execute her task. That is because information and instructional design are similar to the artistic tradition whose content in practical ways is inseparable from how the tactile activity expresses the specific form and content pertinent to the situation.

For perspective, consider that The US Geological Survey lists an Instructional Design team (IDT) as comprising five–to–ten people, whose roles range from instructors, subject matter experts (SME), illustrators, testers (students, design team SME), editors, and quality control personnel [31]. The wide-ranging skills of individual teams members on the team involve making decisions both initially and during crucial moments of the design process. The Instructional Designer operates in a hands-on manner to independently interpret subject matter in its functional role and to transform it into an artistic yet epistemic instructive tool.

A work of art is always a condensation of the complex reality of subject matter and art is the means through which one learns to perceive an intricate solution through simplified images (cf. Jacobson). Being invited to simply customize solidifies this low investment expectation resulting in a simplistic interface that conforms to the standards of mass production. And so the template as a technology for producing instructional discourse can be deemed overly simplified. It calls to mind Donald Norman's description of easy technologies and how they undermine users' sense of accomplishment, and ownership (see Emotional Design on the Betty Crocker simple, easy-to-use recipes). Similarly, technologies of meaning making that simply require users to add, mix, and publish undermine human agency, discount the material element, and to an extent, intentionality, in ways that render humans' cognitive and tactile affordances redundant. This redundancy is in part because the technology occludes the need to engage with the materialist and anatomical in working with the technology. In light of N. Katherine Hayles' Posthuman in which the body is what is lost in cybernetics, in which humans become information patterns, data that can be analyzed and incorporated into the apparatus.

Instructional designers can think in artistic, perhaps subjective-based ways, to address the subject matter and its delivery. They consider learner needs in the triumvirate of designer, materials, and learner. They need not limit themselves to rational means alone. As Alan Hill has shown in "Meaning of Education," rationalists can draw from Comenius' vision of a world of instruction, whose situated understanding of the learners and their conditions, recognized on the basis of experience and the subject matter is not subsumed by universal learning instructional maxims [31]. Similarly, Hurbert Dreyfus in "How Far is Distance Learning From Education?" makes the case for embodied learning, the kind that produces experts out of novices, but is somewhat diminished by disembodied ways of delivering instruction. Accordingly, Dreyfus calls for the kind of learning environment that is informed by a designer's "immediate intuitive situational response" [32]. That immediacy and situatedness is no doubt lost in ceding deliberative design choices to a preconceived template such as COL's. Moreover, Dreyfus' analysis distinguishes the defining role of Instructional Design as not simply making information available to learners, whose role it is to learn it. That belief is what fosters the notion of universal, replicable designs that are system-centered.

Granted, COL's overarching goal was to improve the educational content of the study materials and the educational quality as a whole. The vision for achieving this goal rested in standardized material designed through "relative ease of use" as Fröhlich attests in her piece. The unforeseen consequence of this quest for normalization is that it reveals the limits of standardization. The apparent simplicity of the ease in design that comes with templates makes them very attractive. However, a number of problems are associated with such simplicity and ease. For perspective, Information design in general, and Instructional Design in particular, demand a wider understanding of detailed information pertaining to the subject at hand. All possible information cannot be represented through simple forms. Thus the constraints imposed by the template and the user interface mean that the quantity of content in a controlled form of delivery must be limited.

It is borne out in practice that standardized ways of doing things tend to be tuned to attaining singular objectives avoiding human error, amounting to, in this case, a technologicalization of instruction. But how can we expect a single controlled technology to capture the processes of Instructional Design and delivery for subjects ranging from history to mathematics, to art, and business? Notice that specific mention of the template's shortcomings at PoN had to do with the shortcomings that showed up in "working with specific mathematical programmes that insert special characters as it threw out the formatting of the document" (Fröhlich 3). Once more, emphasis on the template dictating its form, without due regard to the genesis of knowledge gives the appearance of a "black box" effect in that the designer has little or no knowledge of the rules that govern the operation [32].

A techne offers ways in which craft activity amalgamates the instrumental, the artistic, technology, ethics, expertise, techniques, and material into a tactile interface [33]. This techne affirms "the profoundest rationality" as Hegel would say [34]. Therefore techne/craft as we learn from the corpus of the sophists, "cannot simply re-present given content, but must transfigure whatever it presents so that the form of its appearance is uniquely tied to its content" [34]. This articulation fulfills the theory of form as epistemic, of art as techne.

And it is certainly a departure from viewing knowledge principally through the prism of reason based on Cartesian and mechanistic forms aided by an external norming body (in this case COL) as opposed to the situated context of particular learners.

5. CONCLUSION

We know from research in Information Design that the media and its role in delivery is of great importance. We also know that the goal of Instructional Design, despite the ease of mass-production, is to design for learners placed in their immediate environment. Individual designers need to become active participants in the design process as they search for locally significant ways of meaning making and connection for those learners. For, to design means to think out a plan that oversees the production of artifacts, and is epistemic. We cannot conceive Instructional Design independently of the society the materials are meant to serve (cf. Margolin), making a single model of design for all, all but a farce [35, 36].

The technology of the template should be perceived as a material element, a choice format for presenting learning content rather than as the one in all determinant COL has (inadvertently) made it out to be. For it can be argued that the value-added formulas that drive the template are only as accurate as its inputs. Tenets of visual organization satisfy in the minds of instructional designers, scientific support of tried and true principles of composition and page layout. It may be true that COL's broader vision of a commonwealth of nations, bound by a shared colonial history, is altruistic enough to suggest its intentions for unity and a shared sense of belonging. And yet COL's mission promotes individual literacy while universalizing it.

It is clear that new emerging social and technological conditions that define the working space for Information designers call for an engaged material and tactile response that entails a techne.

In order to have a techne of Instructional design, designers should account for the material conditions, the conceptual, and the tactual elements— elements that influence the genesis of discourse and knowledge rather than seek to conform to the right method with no epistemic grounding.

I acknowledge that for a teaching module to be deemed successful, the instructional designer has to demonstrate technical correctness, derived from theories of learning and instruction. Indeed, Instructional Design demands that the designer find a rapprochement between two general principles, namely: learning and instruction, to develop "specific tasks or domains" [37] that are instructional. But that's not all. There has to be a manifested artistry in a dynamic interplay between techne and the systematic method in the process of making instructional knowledge. Perez and Emery attribute this burden to the fact that "Instructional Design theories are prescriptive in nature" [37] and therefore do not address what "designers actually think and do" [37]. Thus Instructional Design is not simply a technical, mechanical matter as COL's approach seems to reinforce. It has a tactile dimension, whose tactility is lost in universalizing the design of knowledge, and, along with it, materials that are immediate, engaging, and focused.

There is no question that instructional materials must have local appeal to the immediate learners. To do so, they must be engaging. The conflict inherent in the contrast between these realities can be resolved, and it should be, by recognizing the simple facts of the knowledge construction characteristics of design—their tactile epistemicity. It is not enough to impose the fixed conventions of a template on a given set of learners. However, grounding those epistemic qualities in techne and how it discovers and communicates knowledge accommodates the interplay among the instructional designer, content, and learner demands, in a non-mechanical approach.

Unfortunately, evidence from Namibia's PoN indicates that the appropriation of the COL template shows Instructional Design as a mechanical skill. In that respect, all instructional designers need is to acquire the skill long enough to get them through each materials development process. A new remediated techne would efface these tendencies.

Adhering to COL templates has a corresponding value of loss. This loss of vivacity renders moot the ability for instructional designers to generate a narrative that engages learners. Instructional designers who might have applied their material and situated knowledge, their epistemic techne, to the instructional design process are deprived of the process of invention and discovery.

By emphasizing the content format and discounting the narrative and poetic aspects of learning materials, COL templates have altered the content of the material itself. The templates present some truths as being self-evident and accessible to all learners if designed the COL way. As a result, the new formulation becomes decidedly illustrative rather than knowledge constructing. And it is non-epistemic.

Research in Information Design and media shows that advances in technology propel designers of information and instruction to experiment with newer technologies in attempt to determine the medium that can positively help with cognitive and problem solving skills. This knowledge presents takeaways, limitations, and challenges with implications for the field and future research on the merits of techne as a factor in instructional design.

6. REFERENCES

[1] R. Gagne. *The Conditions of Learning and the Theory of Instruction.* 4th ed. New York: CBS College Publishing, 1985.

[2] P.L. Smith. and T. J. Ragan. *Instructional Design.* New York: Wiley, 1999.

[3] W. Dick. and L. Cary. *The Systematic Design of Instruction.* Third Edition, Harper Collins, 1990.

[4] R.A. Reiser. Instructional technology: A history. In R.M. Gagné. *Instructional Technology: Foundations.* Hillsdale, NJ: Erlbaum, 1987.

[5] S. Dijkstra. Instructional design: international perspective. *Theory, Research, and Models.* Mahwah, NJ: Lawrence Erlbaum Associates, 1997.

[6] G. Rowland. What do instructional designers actually do? an initial investigation of expert practice. *Performance Improvement Quarterly.* 5, 2 65-86, 1992.

[7] Molenda, M. In search of the elusive ADDIE model. *Performance Improvement.* 42,5 June 2003.

[8] B. Persky and L.H. Golubchick. Early childhood education. *Doctorate Association of New York Educators.* American Federation of Teachers. Lanham, MD, University Press of America, 1991.

[9] R. F. Mager. *Preparing Instructional Objectives.* California, David S. Lake Publishers, 1984.

[10] V. Elliot. Developing Prescriptive Taxonomies for Distance Learning Instructional Design. *Instructional Design: Concepts, Methodologies, tools and Applications.* IGI Global. 270-287, 2011.

[11] J.E. Kemp. *Instructional Design: A Plan for Unit and Course Development.* Belmont, CA, Fearon, 1971.

[12] J.E. Kemp. *Instructional Design: A Plan for Unit and Course Development.* Belmont, CA, Fearon, 1971.

[13] A. Brown and T.D. Green. *The Essentials of Instructional Design: Connecting Fundamental Principles with Process and Practice.* Pearson, Merrill/Prentice Hall, 2006.

[14] A. Brown and T.D. Green. *The Essentials of Instructional Design: Connecting Fundamental Principles with Process and Practice.* Pearson, Merrill/Prentice Hall, 2006.

[15] PL. Smith and T.J. Ragan. *Instructional Design.* New York: Wiley, 1999.

[16] S. Thiagarajan. Rapid instructional design. http://www.thiagi.com/article-rid.htm, 2012.

[17] N. M. Seel and S. Dijkstra. *Curriculum, Plans, and Processes in Instructional Design: International Perspectives.* Mahwah, N.J. L. Erlbaum Associates, 2004.

[18] N. M. Seel and S. Dijkstra. *Curriculum, Plans, and Processes in Instructional Design: International Perspectives.* Mahwah, N.J. L. Erlbaum Associates, 2004.

[19] R. Gagne, J. Leslie, L. Briggs, and W. W. Wager *Principles of Instructional Design.* Fort Worth, TX, HBJ College Publishers, 1992.

[20] R.E. Clark. Media will never influence learning. *Educational Technology Research and Development.* 42, 2 21–29, 1994.

[21] R. S. Perez and C. D. Emery. Designer thinking: how novices and experts think about instructional design. *Performance Improvement Quarterly.* 8, 3 80-94, 1995.

[22] V. Goel and P. Pirolli. The structure of design problem space. *Cognitive Science.* 16, 395-429, 1992.

[23] D. S. Kaufer, and B.S. Butler. *Rhetoric and the Arts of Design.* Mahwah, NJ: Erlbaum, 1996.

[24] G. L. Fröhlich. Experiences of working with the COL electronic Template: paper presented at the 5th Pan-Commonwealth conference on Open Learning. London: Commonwealth of Learning. 13-17 July, 2008.

[25] P. L., Hardre X. Ge, and Thomas, M. K. 2006. An investigation of development toward instructional design expertise. *Performance Improvement Quarterly.* 19, 4 63–90.

[26] S. Katz and V. Rhodes. Beyond ethical frames of technical relations: digital being in the workplace. In *Digital Literacy for Technical Communication: 21st Century Theory and Practice*, Rachel Spilka. London: Routledge, 230-256, 2010.

[27] E. Tufte. *Envisioning Information.* Cheshire, Conn.: Graphics Press, 1990.

[28] L. Nakamura. Prospects for a materialist informatics: an interview with Donna Haraway. *Electronic Book Review*, 2003.

[29] S. P. Consigny. *Gorgias, Sophist and Artist.* Columbia, S.C: University of South Carolina Press, 2001.

[30] F. D. Walters. Gorgias as philosopher of being: epistemic foundationalism in sophistic thought. *Philosophy and Rhetoric.* 27.2, 143-55, 1994.

[31] US Geological Survey. Instructional systems design process usgs.gov/humancapital/ecd/ecd_telisd.html

[32] A. G. Hill. Wordsworth, Comenius, and the Meaning of Education. *The Review of English Studies.* New Series. 26, 103 301-312, 1975.

[33] H. Dreyfus. How far is distance learning from education? *Bulletin of Science, Technology & Society.* 21, 3 165-174, 2001.

[34] B. Latour. *Science in Action: How to Follow Scientists and Engineers Through Society.* Cambridge, MA: Harvard University Press, 1987.

[35] G.W.F. Hegel. Hegel's aesthetics lectures on fine art. Trans. T.M. Knox. I. Oxford, Clarendon Press,1988.

[36] R. D. Winfield.The challenge of architecture to Hegel's aesthetics. Ed. William Maker. *Hegel and Aesthetics.* Oxford: Oxford University Press, 2000.

[37] D. Buchanan. Design research and the new learning. In *Researching Design: Designing Research.* Ed. Jonathan M. Woodham. London: London Design Council, 2000.

[38] R.Gagne, J. Leslie, L. Briggs, and W.W. Wager. *Principles of Instructional Design* (4th Ed.). Fort Worth, TX: HBJ College Publishers, 1992.

[39] R. S. Perez and C. D Emery. Designer thinking: how novices and experts think about instructional design. *Performance Improvement Quarterly.* 8, 3 80-95, 1995.

[40] H.W. Levie and K. Dickie. The analysis and application of media. *Second Handbook of Research on Teaching.* Ed. R. M. W. Travers. Chicago: Rand McNally, 1973.

The Case of the Three Usability Tests – An Experience Report

Katherine Haramundanis
Hewlett-Packard Co.
PO Box 1365
Westford, MA 01886
1-978-692-2390
kathy.haramundanis@hp.com

ABSTRACT
In this paper, we describe three tests used to establish the effectiveness and accuracy of three documents, two for hardware products (affixing labels by customers or customer support to show hardware upgrade status), and one for installation of a software product, usually performed by customers.

Categories and Subject Descriptors
H.5.2 Training, Help, and Documentation – Subjects: User-Centered Design and Testing.

General Terms
Documentation, Human Factors, Standardization, Verification

Keywords
Hardware, software, installation, effectiveness, usability

1. INTRODUCTION
As part of a combined hardware and software release, we had the opportunity to examine three separate documents for their usability. Our intent was to determine if significant changes were needed to these documents to help make them more usable for customers and service engineers. The documents were:

- A hardware component upgrade
- A hardware upgrade for all components of a product
- A software upgrade installation

Only the hardware upgrade test was a full usability test run by an experienced usability test manager; the others were quick, heuristic tests, where several individuals used existing draft documents to perform the upgrade or installation, making notes of issues that were found.

In homage to Arthur C. Clarke and Claude Shannon we determined that: "Data is not information, information is not knowledge, knowledge is not wisdom, and wisdom is not foresight."

Permission to make digital or hard copies of all or part of this work for personal or classroom use is granted without fee provided that copies are not made or distributed for profit or commercial advantage and that copies bear this notice and the full citation on the first page. To copy otherwise, or republish, to post on servers or to redistribute to lists, requires prior specific permission and/or a fee.
SIGDOC'12, October 3–5, 2012, Seattle, Washington, USA.
Copyright 2012 ACM 978-1-4503-1497-8/12/10...$15.00.

We started with data (the full and quick-tests for usability), and concluded with information (how to implement the results); (no obvious increase in knowledge or wisdom).

Briefly, the usability process as it applies to technical documentation starts with:

- Task description/documentation
- Person to perform the task
- Equipment required to perform the task
- Observers
- Reporter/team lead

In a small-scale test, only the first three may be available. The person performing the task may record their thoughts (think-aloud protocol) for later review. Think-aloud protocols, however, may not capture all issues with a task description. The person performing the task may also mark up the task description where issues with it appear.

The result of the usability test is an improved task description more useful to the intended audience and more effective in completing the task.

Typically, there is an expectation of how long the task will take, but in a usability test, time to complete is not a constraint but a result.

2. HARDWARE COMPONENT UPGRADE
The hardware component upgrade was a 4-page document showing where to affix labels to specific components that were upgraded. The components that required labels were two batteries, a management module for disk arrays, and the rack where the management module was installed. The labels were for use by customers or field support to verify component upgrade level.

2.1 New scenario and upgrade process
During review of the first draft of the component upgrade document, the reviewing engineer questioned the figure showing the battery, and made a trip to a near-by manufacturing site to see the actual battery used in the hardware component. The original drawing of the battery (Figure 1) shows the callouts where a previous identification label was located (2) and where the upgrade label should be placed (1).

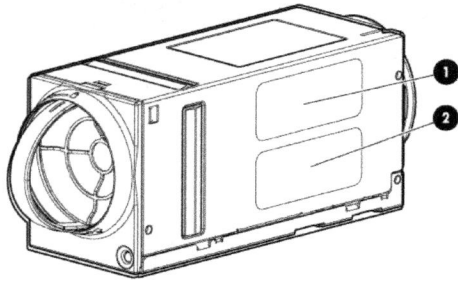

Figure 1. Original drawing of battery for affixing labels.

A subject-matter expert (SME) reviewer noticed that Figure 1 was a drawing of a fan battery, not the required module battery. The drawing was thereby changed (Figure 2), using an existing drawing of a module battery, with a single label and a single callout. An upgrade label was planned to be added to the drawing with an accompanying callout and description. The SME also planned to visit a nearby manufacturing site to obtain a photo of the new battery to verify label location.

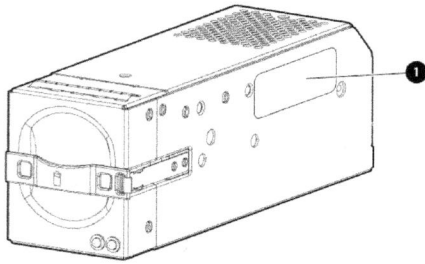

Figure 2. Second drawing of battery for affixing labels.

At the manufacturing site, the engineer obtained a photograph of the battery (Figure 3), which showed that the label had been moved to the bottom of the battery, that the original label was much larger than before, and that therefore placement of the upgrade label diagram and procedure would need to be changed.

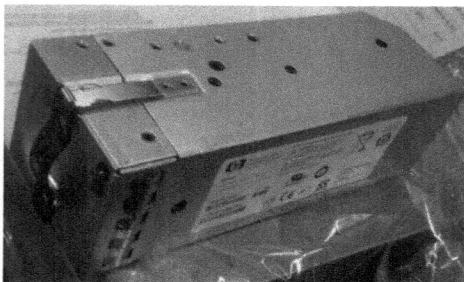

Figure 3. Photograph of battery with existing label.

3. HARDWARE UPGRADE
3.1 New scenario and upgrade process
As part of the hardware upgrade release, a full usability test was planned and executed. The separate Hardware Component Upgrade document described in Section 2 for affixing the labels showing information about the upgraded components was provided to the usability team. The goal was to ensure that a person doing the upgrade would be able to add the labels *before* putting in the components; otherwise, the installer would have to disassemble the upgraded components to install the labels.

3.2 Usability test
A full usability test of the full hardware upgrade process was done at about the same time as the work on the upgrade labels. The full hardware upgrade process included tasks to upgrade several components: the management module, the disk arrays, the module battery, the module fan, the fan battery, the rack in which all components were installed. During this full usability test, the participants determined that there was no way the person doing the hardware upgrade could install labels after completing the full upgrade process. Therefore, the label installation instructions were incorporated directly into the hardware upgrade instructions, eliminating an unnecessary document and reducing complexity for the customer.

4. SOFTWARE INSTALLATION
4.1 New scenario and upgrade process
A major reorganization of the installation guide for a popular software product had created a draft installation guide that was used by four participants to test its usability. A major difference in the reorganization from the previous version was to remove most screen captures of various stages of the process and rely on smooth operation of the software from each screen to the next. Elimination of unnecessary screen captures is increasingly common in software documentation [1].

Where appropriate, minimalist guidance on each task as seen in installation screens was provided in the reorganized document. The next sections show how the organization of the customer document evolved, from content before the test and after, with a final organization after resolving issues with the initial reorganization.

4.2 Initial content organization of content
The initial organization of the document contained the following major chapters in 64 pages:

1. Preparation
2. HP P6000 Command View software suite
3. HP Storage System Scripting Utility
4. HP SMI-S EVA
5. Browser configuration
6. Array configuration setup
7. Troubleshooting
8. Support and other resources
9. Glossary
10. Index

4.3 Proposed re-organization of content
The first draft re-organization of this content contained the following chapters and appendices in 59 pages:

1. Preparation
2. Installing server-based software
3. Installing (upgrading) array-based software
4. Logging in to HP P6000 browser-based applications
5. Installing HP EVAInfo software
6. Installing HP SSSU software
7. Installing HP SMI-S EVA software
8. Installation troubleshooting
9. Support and other resources
10. Appendices:
    a. General server-based software
    b. Server-based HP P6000 Command View
    c. Array-based HP P6000 Command View
    d. HP P6000 Performance Advisor
    e. HP P6000 Performance Data Collector
    f. Browsers
    g. HP P6000 software TCP ports
    h. Completing storage system installations
    i. HP SMI-S User Guide
11. Glossary
12. Index

Appendices were added to ensure that key information needed by the installer would be readily available so that the installer would not need to search elsewhere for essential information.

4.4 Usability test

Each member of the usability testing team had

- A copy of the reorganized install guide
- A copy of the software on a CD

Each member decided on a time to perform the test independently (within an agreed-upon window) and provided their results to the project lead for the product.

After the results were collected, the team met to discuss and take action on what was learned during the test.

The main conclusions were:

- Certain steps (when and if to configure the firewall during the installation) caused missteps to all participants. The project lead planned to work with the software project lead to obtain clear instructions as to how to clarify this task.

- Certain tasks needed pre-work before starting the installation (for example, checking what TCP ports were in use, which could be used, and what browser settings were in use and might need to be changed)

- Installers needed to verify what system the product was being installed on (for example, Windows 32-bit or 64-bit, UNIX, and so on).

- The number of screen captures could be reduced as the user had little interaction with them due to relatively smooth operation of most of the installation steps.

- Screen displays where crucial decisions by the installer were made should be clearly identified in the tasks described.

After considering and taking into account all these areas, a revision of the reorganized guide was prepared and reviewed by the key participants. Major changes were recommended to additionally simplify the overall organization of the document to make it more usable, and ensuring that all content, including supplementary content in appendices, was available to the customer using the document.

4.5 Final organization of content

The final re-organization of content, with some additions to the original content, contained the following chapters and appendices in 77 pages:

1. Preparation
2. Installing server-based software
3. Upgrading array-based software
4. Logging in to HP P6000 browser-based applications
5. Installing HP EVAInfo software
6. Installing HP SSSU software
7. Installation troubleshooting
8. Completing storage systems installations
9. Support and other resources
10. Appendices:
    a. HP P6000 Command View Software Suite components
    b. Characters illegal in names and comments
    c. Server-based software users
    d. Server-based HP P6000 Command View
    e. HP SMI-S EVA configuration
    f. Array-based HP P6000 Command View
    g. HP P6000 Performance tools
    h. HP P6000 software TCP ports
    i. Browser configuration
11. Glossary
12. Index

5. CONCLUSION

Usability tests, even the most minimal[2], are invaluable in finding and correcting errors in product documentation for both hardware and software. Evaluation of tasks is crucial to understanding issues for users and correcting them [3]. The challenge is to determine when in the product lifecycle to use them. Too early, and later changes may obviate the earlier results; too late, and the required changes may not be made.

6. ACKNOWLEDGMENTS

Our thanks to Hewlett-Packard Company for the opportunity to present this material and to reviewers and colleagues – Susan Benson, Joseph Calkins, Maureen Germano, Uma Kasinadhuni, Deborah Lienhart – who participated in the tests and provided valuable comments.

7. REFERENCES

[1] Haramundanis, Katherine, "Why use screen captures? – An Experience Report.," *Proceedings of the 29th ACM International Conference on Design of Communication, SIGDOC 2011*, pp. 219-221.

[2] Nielsen, Jakob, and Molich, Rolf. 1990. Heuristic Evaluation of User Interfaces. In *Proceedings of the SIGCHI Conference 1990*). CHI '1990. ACM, New York, NY, 249-256.

[3] Lindegaard, Gitte. and Chattratichart, Jarinee. 2007. *Usability Testing; What Have We Overlooked?*. CHI 2007 Proceedings, pp. 1415-1420.

Making Usable Documentation: Iterative Instructions and Media Richness

Jeremy Huston
Grinbath
2321 50th St Suite F
Lubbock, TX 79412
jeremyhuston@grinbath.com

ABSTRACT
Providing usable instructional documentation to users requires understanding their needs and best ways to meet those needs. This article reviews the types of instructional documentation for users of the Grinbath EyeGuide eye tracking system and discusses the lessons learned from each iteration of instruction. Media richness played a major role in the effectiveness of the documentation, with richer media providing better instruction for the user.

Categories and Subject Descriptors
H.5.2 [**Information Interfaces and Presentation**]: User interfaces – *Theory and methods, training, help and documentation, user-centered design*

General Terms
Documentation, Human Factors

Keywords
Documentation design, instructional design, iteration, usability, media richness

1. INTRODUCTION
Grinbath [1] makes eye tracking technology at a fraction of the cost of other systems on the market. The company sprang from the desire to use eye tracking at the Usability Research Lab (URL) at Texas Tech University. Clients would come to Dr. Still, the director of the URL, asking for usability testing done with eye tracking. Dr. Still would have to decline clients because the URL didn't have access to eye tracking, exacerbating funding issues. Dr. Still and his graduate students created a low-fidelity eye tracker for lab use to accommodate client demand. Shortly thereafter, they decided to make their eye tracker available to other researchers at a low cost and created Grinbath.

EyeGuide's low cost has opened up the viability and realistic attainment of eye tracking for researchers and UX experts worldwide. It also presents unique challenges to us on the Grinbath team as we have tried to craft effective, usable and interactive instructional documentation.

To identify how to design the instructional documentation for

EyeGuide, we ran some preliminary usability tests. We discovered that our eye tracker was hard to get used to and operate. We found that other eye tracking systems also suffer from similar usability problems. With our background in usability, we set out to improve EyeGuide's usability with instructional documentation.

2. USER PROFILES
Before determining how to focus our initial round of documentation, we identified potential user groups. We narrowed our profiles to three primary user groups who would be interested in our technology and developed instructional documentation with those groups in mind.

Users of the EyeGuide system, based on marketing data, were most likely to be researchers in academic institutions and UX and HCI professionals, which early sales bore out. We reasoned that if academic customers were in similar positions to the URL, many of our potential sales would be to people who knew about eye tracking but could not afford it. A huge part of our customer base might have no idea how to use eye tracking technology and might have no methodological background for incorporating eye tracking into their research. It was also possible that we could run into customers with more eye tracking experience than us. We formed user profiles that addressed these all of these issues.

2.1 Profiles
2.1.1 User 1
This user has never used eye tracking before for a number of reasons and is likely unfamiliar with using the technology *and* the methodology. They have unrealistic expectations of the technology and needs it to be as usable as possible. Instructions for them need to be simple and direct. They could also use a vocabulary and methodology primer as well as general support for every day issues (e.g. adjusting the hardware, turning on the hardware, modifying preferences, etc). They may not be able to articulate what they want to do with eye tracking and may not know how to get started.

2.1.2 User 2
This user has used eye tracking before but does not work with it now for functionality, usability, and/or cost reasons. This user has a reasonable expectation of what eye tracking can do and only needs two kinds of support: getting EyeGuide to work and adapting EyeGuide to their test plan. This user needs reference, not direct assistance. They need a place to go to in order to retrieve information about our system and its operations quickly. This user likely already has a head full of ideas and is ready to implement them. They just need to know how to use the technology to fit their plans in a detailed way.

2.1.3 User 3

This user has used eye tracking before and currently uses it in their research but is interested in what we offer in terms of functionality and price. This is a user that wants portability, flexibility, and cross-platform support and is willing to try us given the price point. User 3 clearly understands the capabilities and shortfalls of eye tracking; this user has something to teach *us*. They are comfortable with and versed in eye tracking vocabulary and methodology. We need to stay in contact with them in a way that is personal, sensitive, and immediate.

3. DOCUMENTATION TYPES USED TO INSTRUCT USERS

After identifying these groups, we determined that the best way to address these needs were through simple HTML instructions, an online support forum, support email, videos and live discussion through VOIP and webinars. After a few months of using these methods, though, we discovered that what our communications lacked was media richness. Our instructional communication had too much variance of interpretation or equivocality [2] and too little information to perform needed tasks, or too much uncertainty [3]. To combat the lack of media richness, we instituted supplemental methods of instruction; namely, hands-on training and an interactive tutorial.

3.1 HTML documentation

The HTML documentation (Figure 1) was built with User 1 chiefly in mind and their need for simple, task-based instruction. We tried to design it to meet the needs of all user profiles as well, so the HTML documentation also provides links to more detailed information in the support forum.

The HTML documentation is a website of simple, task-based instructions accessible from within the software that loads in the user's default browser. The documentation looks like any other webpage and adheres to basic web design conventions for ease of use [4]. The HTML documentation includes a step-by-step progression of how to operate the EyeGuide system. We implemented a task-based instructional approach in the documentation to avoid overwhelming or alienating users new to eye tracking [5]. The information was basic, intentionally leaving out detailed and arcane operation information or vocabulary. The tone was also more personable and less academic in order not to alienate potential audiences outside of academia. After a few rounds of review and usability testing, the instructions were finalized and embedded in the EyeGuide software.

3.1.1 Problems with documentation

The chief problem with our documentation is the chief problem of all documentation: no one reads instructions. One user in our usability tests clicked through pages and didn't read anything. Testing also revealed that users had trouble understanding how to use the hardware and software until they had a hands-on demonstration. Users had trouble interpreting the instructions until they saw them performed. Early customer service emails routinely directed users to the documentation for clarity and instruction.

Furthermore, the HTML documentation introduces some uncertainty due to the lack of information it presented. Users did not have the information they needed to make decisions. Succeeding iterations of the HTML documentation are clearer and

more inclusive, but that can't solve usability problems if no one reads the instructions in the first place.

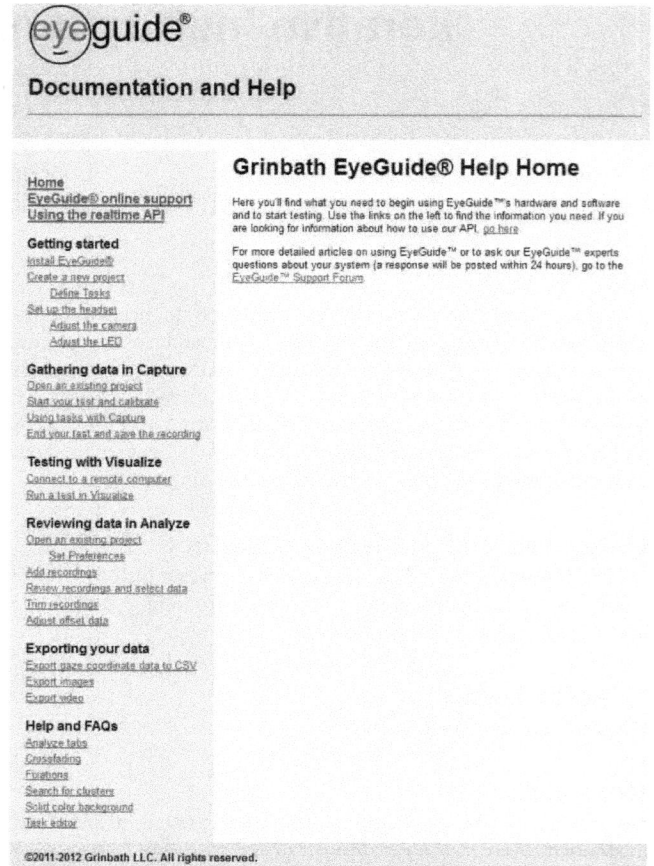

Figure 1: HTML documentation home page

3.2 Support forum

The support forum (Figure 2) was designed for Users 2 and 3 in particular. Those users needed access to quick and detailed information and we decided the forum was the best place to situate that information.

We initially hoped that users of the site would keep the community vibrant, creating a grassroots community around their use of EyeGuide. Another benefit we anticipated in the support forum was being able to sticky frequent questions or issues that cropped up. This would allow the instructional documentation to remain straightforward and clear, restricting more in depth discussion to the forum. We wanted this information to be separate from the documentation but still accessible to Users 2 and 3 from within the documentation, so we added a link to the support forum to the home page.

The support forum allows users to comment, offer feedback, ask questions, and get expert opinions from other EyeGuide users. Higher-end users are able to answer forum threads and head discussions as trustworthy, expert voices outside of the company in volumes that we simply cannot sustain as a small start-up.

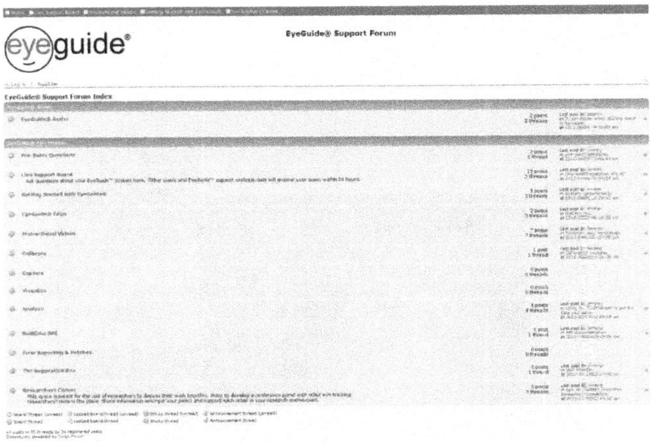

Figure 2: Forum home page

3.2.1 Problems with the forum

The sales numbers we have had with EyeGuide simply do not add up to the population needed to make for a robust online community. More often than not, questions posted in the forum had to be answered by staff at Grinbath after some research of our own. Also, most questions asked were sent via email. After some compiling, the most frequent issues addressed in email and VIOP communication became thread postings for users to see. Instead of being a site of user-generated content and support, the support forum is a repository of answers for the most common problems and their resolutions.

3.3 Email

Providing support through email is a basic affordance for our time. Users of all stripes have to interact with our website to get information and order EyeGuide. We took it as given that users would have email accounts with which to contact us.

We use email to address support concerns as they crop up and as a way to point new customers to old content that addresses the most common issues with the system; namely, lighting and calibration. Email is also used to provide proactive support, beginning with a follow-up email two weeks after they receive shipment. Customers also receive email notifications about new system updates and training opportunities, such as webinars and instructional videos.

3.3.1 Problems with email

At first, we used email to direct users to different documentation already in place. Simply redirecting customers was frustrating for users and time consuming for us, so we allowed users to create forum topics for forum users to answer. Permitting users to create forum topics was ineffective as well, as discussed in Section 3.2.

Also, as we found out with our usability testing of the documentation, users have better results using EyeGuide when they can see what to do and how to do it. Instructional emails contain too much equivocality for use as an effective instructional medium for all user profiles, even when we include pictures and screen grabs. Support emails are usually long chains of replies trying to describe actions and vocabulary to users that don't have an adequate frame of reference. Problems get addressed and resolved quickly (usually within 12-24 hours), but not without a lot of back-and-forth. Worse, emails with updates, follow-ups, and more instructional material are often ignored, which has compounded some support issues instead of relieving them.

3.4 Videos

Soon after user testing the HTML documentation, we created instructional videos as a richer media solution. We needed a way to show users from all three profiles how to use the unit and the software as well as illustrate what users could potentially do with EyeGuide. Instructional videos were employed as a stopgap solution to that quandary.

Our instructional videos (Figure 3) cover a number of instructional applications. Some are simple videos covering how to put on the headset, how set up a test with the software, or an explanation of the data output. Some videos are more specific and show direct application of certain features of the system in different types of eye tracking tests, such as video tracking, static image tracking, and video game tracking, complete with gaze plots, cluster analysis, and heatmaps.

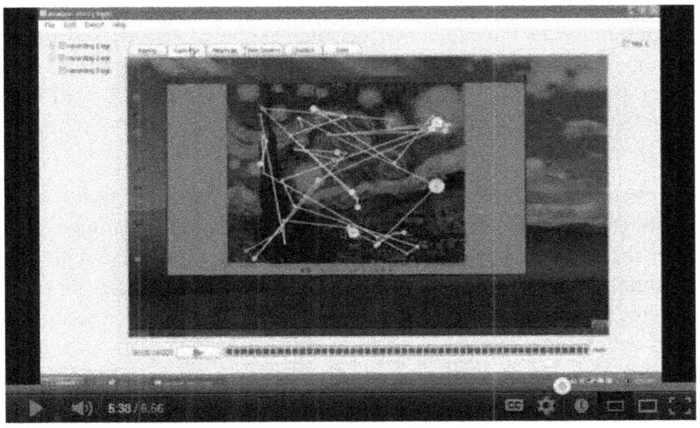

Figure 3: Still from and instructional video

3.4.1 Problems with video

Savvy internet users are naturally cynical of anything they see online. As such, users tend to videos to dismiss the instructional videos them as hokum or promotional fluff.

We lacked video creation and editing skills as a company early on. Our early videos do not instruct well, introducing equivocality exactly where we want to reduce it. As we have become more experienced with video, we have included shots of users setting up the hardware and software and shots that include the computer screen so users can see system at work.

Our videos are also short so it is easy to take time to watch them. However, eliding information causes uncertainty in the shorter videos because the instruction is less clear and less useful.

It is hard to get users to use the instructional videos. We link to the videos in email and on the forum, but we can't make users watch what they don't want to. Some customers saw the videos as promotional instead of instructional and simply ignored them.

3.5 VOIP and webinars

After seeing how users from profiles 1 and 2 were responding to instructive materials, we implemented more direct instruction: Skype and webinars. Real-time interaction with users often gave users the confidence and experience they needed to operate EyeGuide.

One-on-one sessions with users address questions and concerns that the users pose during the conversation. Even better, users do not need further assistance. The personal and immediate aspect of the instruction through VOIP and webinars gives users what they need, clearly and immediately.

3.5.1 Problems with VOIP and webinars

Sessions take a lot of time to set up and execute. It is not practical to offer this to all customers all the time and most non-essential issues (i.e., is the power on, are the batteries charged, etc.) can be resolved through email. Calls can also take longer than expected due to latency issues. Time zone differences add a wrinkle to the time issue since we have EyeGuide customers in places like Singapore and New Zealand.

Another problem can be how difficult it is for users to simultaneously see our screen and how we manipulate the headset, an essential aspect to getting lighting and positioning right. Switching between desktop sharing and a webcam can be tedious in Skype and outright impossible in webinars due to software conflicts.

3.6 Training

After deploying the other instructional methods, we decided that nothing could beat the effectiveness of hands-on instruction. We developed a two-day instructional course structured off of Dr. Brian Still's Certified User Experience Professional Workshop at TTU.

Users can purchase a unit and get hands-on, two-day training in Lubbock or a field representative can be go to the customer and train them on-site. Users receive the training they need with the personal attention they need respective to which user profile they fit into. For instance, one user fit the profile for User 3; she didn't need much help integrating eye tracking into her work. She just needed to know but how to get EyeGuide running. However, a different group trained later not only lacked eye tracking methodology training, but human subjects research training as well. Their training was more comprehensive but the nature of the training enabled the instruction to meet their individualized needs.

As a result of the training, none of the individuals who were trained have needed any more help getting the system to work or running their tests and have gone on to train other users. Customers who had the training were able to perform independently and successfully. Issues regarding equivocality and uncertainty were eliminated.

3.6.1 Problems with Training

The expense for the training puts some customers off despite the benefits. Only about 10% of all our customers have opted for this training. Further, Grinbath is a small start-up. It is difficult to send a trainer off for four days at a time when that person represents 1/8 of the workforce and fills so many different roles.

Luckily, we haven't had to deal with issues of international travel or language barriers yet, but instruction in other countries in other languages is a known problem, given that the staff at Grinbath knows only five languages collectively.

3.7 Tutorial

After realizing the success of the training, we decided to implement a slideshow tutorial (Figure 4) that would walk users through the most difficult parts of getting started at their own pace. We created the tutorial with Adobe Captivate so the tutorial played in the user's native browser after installing the software.

The tutorial shows users how to set up and interact with the system while they progress through a sample test. Users have the option to rewind a video or go back a slide to progress at their own pace.

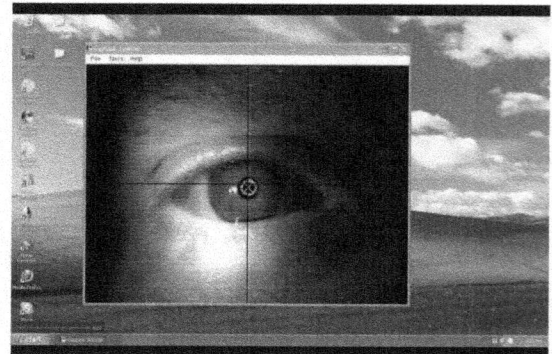

Figure 4: Tutorial sample slide

3.7.1 Problems with the tutorial

After some usability testing, we discovered that our familiarity with eye tracking had rendered us somewhat incapable to address users' needs latently; we were not our users anymore. The tutorial does alleviate some difficulty and makes EyeGuide easier to use; however, the tutorial cannot address equivocality or uncertainty as well as hands-on training. We are improving the tutorial's instruction and with user testing and feedback.

4. CONCLUSION

Relying on media poor instructional documentation alone (such as HTML documentation, support forums, and email) is inadequate for instructing users how to use EyeGuide; simply adding richer media options was also insufficient. Using the gamut of instruction we now provide allows users to more effectively learn how to use EyeGuide and makes it easier for us to support them. Media-rich instruction results in more effective learning and use. This is widely evident in the type of support emails we now receive. Instead of emails instructing users how to get started, emails can now focus on troubleshooting and compatibility issues.

5. REFERENCES

[1] Grinbath 2012. Grinbath, maker of EyeGuide Assist & Tracker. Retrieved July 11, 2012 from www.grinbath.com.

[2] Daft, R. & Lengel, R. 1986. Organizational information requirements, media richness and structural design. *Management Science*, 32. 554-571.

[3] Daft, R., Lengel, R. & Trevino, L. 1987. Message equivocality, media selection, and manager performance: Implications for information support systems. *MIS Quarterly*, 11. 355-366.

[4] Baehr, C. (2007). *Web Development: A Visual-Spatial Approach.* Pearson, Upper Saddle River, NJ.

[5] Barker, T. 2003. *Writing Documentation: A Task-Oriented Approach.* 2nd edition. Longman, New York, NY.

Think Aloud: Effects and Validity

Amy M. Gill
School of Computer Science
University of Guelph
gilla@alumni.uoguelph.ca

Blair Nonnecke
School of Computer Science
University of Guelph
nonnecke@uoguelph.ca

ABSTRACT

Think aloud is a commonly used usability method with roots in psychology. Although current think aloud practice was adapted from a standard method defined by Ericsson and Simon, there is no evidence of the use of a standard method by usability practitioners. We present the results of a study exploring usability practitioners' awareness of the effects of think aloud and whether validity as defined by Ericsson and Simon is relevant to usability practice. Results indicate that practitioners are aware of some of the effects of think aloud. However, it is not clear whether practitioners are aware of or concerned with the reactive effects of think aloud.

Categories and Subject Descriptors

H.1.2 [**Information Systems**]: User/Machine Systems – *human factors.*

General Terms

Design, Human Factors

Keywords

Usability, Think Aloud, Validity, Methodology

1. INTRODUCTION

Think aloud is a method commonly used during usability testing to gather insights about the design being tested. It is considered both cheap to implement and valuable for the insights it provides. Nielsen states that "think aloud may be the single most valuable usability engineering method" [10]. Think aloud guidelines describe it as a method which can be useful even with a few participants, requires little training, does not require expensive equipment, does not require extensive analysis and can be used at any stage of the design process [5, 6, 8-10, 13].

To use think aloud during a usability test, participants are asked to say their thoughts aloud while completing a set of specific tasks on a user interface. This allows usability practitioners to discover usability problems while they occur, determine why a problem occurs, learn about how users feel about the design and learn how users approach tasks [6, 10].

Although think aloud is commonly used and considered valuable, practices vary and there is no evidence of a standard think aloud method in usability practice [1].

According to Ericsson and Simon (who defined a standard think aloud method in psychology), think aloud may affect a participant's thought processes and performance if strict guidelines are not followed [3, 4]. For example, using think aloud may lead to reactivity, which is when a participant's thought processes and performance are altered. Thus when thinking aloud, a participant may perform tasks differently as compared to how the tasks would be performed if the participant was not thinking aloud. Furthermore, if think aloud guidelines are not followed participants may provide inaccurate information when thinking aloud [2]. Even when guidelines are followed, think aloud slows task completion and participants may have difficulty thinking aloud while performing complex tasks [3, 4].

Ericsson and Simon's method ensures validity by focusing on retrieving information from the short term memory (STM), which is where current or recently acquired information is stored [3, 4]. This is done by asking a participant to focus on a task while thinking aloud. The information that is in the STM is directly related to what the participant is doing (the task at hand). When using Ericsson and Simon's method, a moderator does not interact with a participant during a think aloud session except to remind the participant to "keep talking" [3, 4].

If Ericsson and Simon's guidelines are not followed, the resulting verbalizations may not be valid. Their model describes three levels of verbalization: levels 1 (L1), 2 (L2) and 3 (L3). L1 verbalizations occur when the information being verbalized is already stored in verbal form. L2 verbalization occurs when information needs to be encoded into verbal form before it is verbalized. L2 verbalization may be less complete than L1 verbalization and may also slow down task performance. The first two levels are accepted as valid verbalizations however L3 verbalization alters thought processes. Additional processing of information occurs before L3 verbalization is produced, for example:

- **Scanning or filtering processes:** When a participant is asked to talk about specific content. For example, if a moderator asks a participant to focus on specific areas of a website.
- **Inference or generative processes:** When a participant is asked to provide information that he or she would not normally verbalize. For example: why the participant behaved a certain way or a description of where the participant's eyes are focusing. Ericsson and Simon agree with Nisbett and Wilson's view that explanations may not be stored in the STM and participants may never have access to this information; thus a participant may not accurately describe why they behaved in a certain manner [13]. The participant's explanation may be based on a priori causal theories and may not be valid. In regard to descriptions of behavior, this type of

request requires a participant to concentrate on their behavior and internal processes.

Overall, processes which lead to L3 verbalization result in changes in thought processes and task performance.

In summary, Ericsson and Simon's think aloud method is used to study a participant's thought processes [3, 4]. The reliability and validity of information collected during think aloud is of paramount importance. Although usability practitioners may be interested in a participant's thought processes, the primary goal of using think aloud is to improve product design.

To explore the awareness of the effects of think aloud and the relevance of validity in usability practice, the following research questions are addressed in this paper:

- Are usability practitioners aware of the effects of think aloud on task performance and a participant's thought processes?

- Are the validity issues (as described by Ericsson and Simon) related to using think aloud relevant in usability practice?

2. METHOD

Usability practitioners were interviewed to learn about their use of think aloud protocols. A description of interviewees, their associated companies, interview questions, and interview analysis methodology are provided.

2.1 Interview Participants

To study how usability practitioners use think aloud, 20 usability practitioners were interviewed. These practitioners had varying degrees of experience (1 year to over 20 years) and varying educational backgrounds that include computer science, mathematics, English, psychology, interactive design, business administration, engineering, fine arts and communication.

At the time of the interviews, the interviewees worked for the following types of companies: telecommunications, usability consulting, technology and marketing and advertising companies which provide internal or external usability consulting services or both. Twelve of the interviewees worked for the same telecommunications company and were all members of a team conducting user research. Two interviewees were from a marketing and advertising company. The remaining interviewees all worked for different companies.

2.2 Data Capture and Analysis

During interviews which lasted from 30 to 60 minutes, notes were taken to capture interviewee responses to each question. Once all of the interviews were completed, the interview notes were compiled and organized by question. The notes were then coded and assigned keywords to discover themes and patterns and count their frequency. Once all of the notes were coded, they were organized into diagrams for each question to better understand and visualize responses.

2.3 Interview Questions

The following interview questions were asked to learn about interviewees' awareness of the effects of think aloud and to study whether validity as defined by Ericsson and Simon is relevant in usability practice.

1. Are there any situations in which you do not ask participants to think aloud?

2. Think back to any study in which you asked participants to think aloud. How would the study change if you did not instruct participants to think aloud?

3. How do you know if a participant's think aloud accurately represents his or her thoughts Do you use information that feels inaccurate?

4. Have you participated in think aloud studies in which task/test completion was timed?

3. RESULTS

The results in this section describe interviewees' awareness of the effects of think aloud on task performance and a participant's thought processes.

3.1 Timed Tasks and Task Complexity

Table 1 lists situations in which interviewees do not ask participants to think aloud. Ten interviewees (50%) do not ask participants to think aloud when the task is timed. For example one interviewee said: "If the goal is to get the task done and time it, think aloud would skew that". Also, 3 interviewees (15%) mentioned that a usability test would end much quicker without think aloud (see Table 2 for other impacts of the think aloud method). However, it is not clear if the remaining 10 interviewees are aware (or concerned with) the effect of think aloud on task performance.

Three of the 20 interviewees do not ask participants to think aloud when the task is challenging or the participant is having a difficult time. One interviewee indicated she does not ask a participant to think aloud "if they are having a hard time" and another had a similar response: when a participant is doing "something that is genuinely frustrating". Underlying this is the belief by the interviewees that asking or prompting participants to think aloud while completing a complex or difficult task will affect a participant's performance and attitude.

Table 1. Situations in which interviewees do not ask participants to think aloud

Situation	Number of Interviewees (n=20)
Timed Task	10
Benchmarking	3
Challenging Task or Difficult Time	3
Group Setting	2
Time Limited	1
Natural Usage: task completion without interruptions from the moderator	1

Table 2. Interviewees' perceptions of how a study would change if think aloud was not used

The impact of not using think aloud	Number of Interviewees (n=20)
Difficult to provide recommendations without underlying reasons for issues	4
Less problem information	4
Impacts results	3
Retrospective think aloud may be incorrect or incomplete	3
Quicker	3
Miss intentions	2
Miss out on a lot of things	2
Miss expectations	2
Data less rich	2
Results more subjective	2
Miss behavioral descriptions	2
More rigid testing required	1
Need to pay more attention to behavior	1
Miss thinking / thought processes	1
No mental model insights	1
More one-sided	1
Not as comfortable	1
Miss out on want	1
Miss out on need	1
No audio recordings for clients	1
More surprises (usually have focal points)	1
Difficult with paper prototypes	1
User would think everything was ok (even when there is a problem)	1

3.2 Inconsistent Information

Inconsistent information refers to when participants provide information which is inconsistent with their task performance and experience. For example, participants may feel embarrassed due to their lack of knowledge or may want to please or avoid offending the moderator. Interviewees acknowledged their awareness that participants may provide inaccurate information while thinking aloud. For example one interviewee said: "If they're trying to look good or to please us, we probe a little more deeply in a conversational way" and another interviewee said: "If they're doing something other than what they're saying, we will compare their behavior to what they have said".

More than half of the interviewees (55%) try to prevent inaccurate information using the methods listed in Table 3. In general, these methods were used to make participants comfortable. For example while providing instructions prior to a usability test, interviewees describe assuring participants that the test moderator did not design the product being testing. One interviewee said: "I tell participants that I am not part of the development team. I don't want the participant to hold anything back". Similarly, interviewees tell participants to share if something is wrong and

the software is being tested not the participant. For example, one interviewee said when a participant is having problems with the task and is not verbalizing it or not admitting that there is a problem the interviewee tells participants that it is "okay to tell us if something is wrong. Other people also had problems with this". This conversational probe is an attempt to encourage participants to open up and point out any problems encountered.

Table 3. Methods used by interviewees to prevent inaccurate information

Methods	Number of Interviewees (n=20)
Tell user you do not have an investment in the product	4
Make them comfortable (enough to tell the truth)	2
Tell the user that it is okay to tell the moderator if something is wrong	2
Tell the user that he or she is not being tested, the software is	1
Build in redundant tasks	1

Table 4. How interviewees treat inaccurate information

Treatment of inaccurate information	Number of Interviewees (n=20)
Probe for consistency	7
It is difficult to prove that information is false	4
Discount false information	2
Look at actions	1
Rare not to use information	1

Interviewees used different methods for treating inaccurate information (as outlined in Table 4). For example, 7 out of 20 interviewees probed for consistency. One interviewee said "If the participant hesitates during a task but rates it as easy, we try to talk to the participant and pull out more information". By approaching the subject from a different direction through prompting, practitioners may get an unguarded response and learn what the participant really thinks. Although practitioners developed ways to handle inaccurate information, 4 of 20 interviewees stated that it may be difficult to prove when information is inaccurate. For example, one interviewee said: "It is hard to tell. There are always people that try to please you". When trying to determine if information is inaccurate, interviewees study a participant's behavior, performance, and facial expressions (see Table 5). To evaluate think aloud information, interviewees compare participant's behavior to the information provided through think aloud. If their behavior corroborates the think aloud information, the participant is likely reflecting accurate information in the think aloud. However, if the behavior and think aloud are starkly contrasting in nature, the think aloud information is most likely inaccurate, e.g., the participant made up the content of their think aloud to please the moderator. For example, interviewees said: "Some people perform poorly but say it is working fine because they don't want to hurt your feelings" and "If they're saying something that doesn't match what they're doing on the screen or they tend to hesitate but then say the task was easy, I try to talk to them to pull out more information. Sometimes they don't want to admit that they did something wrong or that there's something they don't understand".

3.3 Reactivity

Only two of our interviewees showed their awareness of the reactive effects of think aloud. One interviewee does not use think aloud when interested in the natural use of a product (see Table 1). The interviewee said: "I don't use think aloud when I want to gauge more observational things. Like if I want to see how a user reactively does something. The reaction is more important than an explanation in this case".

This interviewee believed that think aloud alters how a participant behaves and performs during a usability study. Another interviewee said that there would be more surprises without think aloud (see Table 2). This interviewee said: "We would get more surprises that way. When we plan out questions, we have a goal in mind. Not using think aloud can lead to unexpected feedback".

This indicated that the interviewee may use think aloud to control a usability session through methods like prompting. For example, if a usability practitioner wants to test specific areas of the user interface, think aloud can be used to guide a participant to areas of interest. In this case, using think aloud alters how a participant completes a task and explores an interface.

Table 5. Methods used by interviewees to determine if think aloud information is inaccurate

Method	Number of Interviewees (n=20)
Compare behavior to think aloud	7
Compare ratings of task and test to user's performance	3
Judge user's facial expressions	1

It is not clear if the remaining interviewees are aware of the reactive effects of think aloud. What is clear is that interviewees use methods with reactive effects. For example, our study results showed that almost all of the interviewees (95%) prompt for reasons other than reminding participants to think aloud (see Table 6). Some reasons interviewees prompt test participants are: to learn about explanations of the participant's behavior, to give hints when participants are stuck, to ask planned questions, to draw attention to areas of the interface a participant did not focus on and to learn about a participant's expectations of the task or interface. According to Ericsson and Simon, prompting with anything other than 'keep talking' will lead to a change in thought processes [3,4]. However, none of our interviewees were familiar with Ericsson and Simon's think aloud method and its underlying principles. This may partially explain why interviewees were not aware of the reactive effects of think aloud.

4. DISCUSSION

This study illustrates that usability practitioners are aware that think aloud affects task completion time and can affect performance if participants are performing a complex task. Usability practitioners avoid using think aloud in certain situations. For example, think aloud is not used when determining the time it takes to complete a complex task. Another effect that practitioners are aware of is the possibility of think aloud resulting in inconsistent information. However, interviewees value and

perhaps depend on think aloud despite their awareness that information gathered through think aloud may be inconsistent. Interviewee responses indicate usability study results would not be as useful if participants were not asked to think aloud. For example, 4 of the 20 interviewees said it would be difficult to provide design recommendations without the underlying reasons discovered through think aloud (see Table 2 for other examples of how a study would change if participants were not asked to think aloud). One interviewee said: "We would miss the boat on a lot of things. We can't tease out the underlying reasons for issues, so that we can actually change the issue".

Table 6. Reasons for prompting (other than reminding participants to keep talking)

Reasons for Prompting	Interviewee
4.1.1.1 Direct the Session	
• Focus on a specific area of the interface	1,4,5,9,18
• Ask planned questions	16
• Give hints	17, 20
4.1.1.2 Support Participant	
• Have a conversation to make them comfortable	2,10
4.1.1.3 Understand Participant	
• Prompt when participant not understood	10
• Prompt to understand goal(s)	1,3
• Prompt for clarification	3,17
• Ask for an explanation	1,11,13,19
• Ask questions based on behavior	10,11,13,14,15
• Find out about expectations	3, 6, 8
• Prompt when struggling	7,8,9,17,20

Interviewees used methods with reactive effects. It is possible that interviewees were not aware of the reactive effects of think aloud. However, 3 out of 20 interviewees recognized that think aloud affects task performance in certain situations. For example, if the task is challenging or the participant is having a difficult time. It may be argued that performing any task, while thinking aloud and answering a moderator's prompts may be challenging and lead to changes in performance. For example, the results of a study which compared the use of think aloud with retrospective think aloud indicate that thinking aloud while performing given tasks has a negative effect on task performance [12]. Although comments from two interviewees indicate their awareness of the reactive effects of think aloud (see section 3.3), it is not clear if the remaining interviewees recognize the reactive effects of think aloud.

It is possible that preventing reactive effects as described by Ericsson and Simon is not as important in usability practice as the usability practitioner's goals are different. Ericsson and Simon's definition of validity was directly related to the goal of their think aloud method: capturing unaltered thought processes. Although thought processes may be unaffected using Ericsson and Simon's think aloud method, it may not provide design insights required by usability practitioners. Also Ericsson and Simon's method does not account for situations specific to usability. These include handling a participant when they are stuck or off track; how to handle bugs or system crashes; how to use think aloud while testing an incomplete prototype; and how to answer a participant's questions [1]. Consequently, using Ericsson and Simon's method may result in a useless usability session, if the goal of an effective usability session is to collect data that augments design-based decision making.

The goal of using think aloud in usability is to improve product design whereas the goal of Ericsson and Simon's method is to study thought processes and human problem solving. Usability practitioners use think aloud to improve product design by collecting information about problems encountered during a usability test. Some examples of this information are: a participant's description of their own behavior; a participant's explanation of their thinking or behavior and a participant's expectations of the interface. This information helps usability practitioners determine why participants encounter problems during a usability test. An understanding of design problems will lead to recommendations for design improvements [7].

In contrast, Ericsson and Simon are only interested in a participant's thought processes. The method defined by Ericsson and Simon ensures that their goal is met. Similarly in usability, think aloud is practiced using techniques to help improve product design. As mentioned above, Ericsson and Simon's definition of valid think aloud was directly related to their goal. Accordingly, the definition of valid think aloud in usability should correspond with the goal of improving product design.

5. ACKNOWLEDGMENTS
The authors would like to thank the University of Guelph for its support of this research, and the interviewees who made their time freely available.

6. REFERENCES
[1] Boren, M. T., and Ramey, J. 2000. Thinking Aloud: Reconciling Theory and Practice. *IEEE T. Prof. Commun.*43, 3 (Sept. 2000), 261 - 278. DOI = 10.1109/47.867942.

[2] Ericsson, K. A. 2003. Valid and Non-Reactive Verbalization of Thoughts During Performance of Tasks. *Journal of Consciousness Studies.*10, 9 – 10 (Sept. – Oct. 2003) 1 - 18.

[3] Ericsson, K. A., and Simon, H. A. 1993. *Protocol Analysis: Verbal Reports as Data* (Rev Ed.). The MIT Press, Cambridge, MA.

[4] Ericsson, K. A., and Simon, H. A. 1980. Verbal Reports as Data. *Psychol. Rev.*87, 3 (May 1980) 215 - 251. DOI =10.1037/0033-295X.87.3.215.

[5] Hertzum, M., Hansen, K. D. and Anderson, H. H. K. 2009. Scrutinising usability evaluation: does thinking aloud affect behaviour and mental workload?*Behaviour and Information Technology*. 28, 2 (Feb. 2009), 165 – 181. DOI=10.1080/01449290701773842.

[6] Lewis, C. 1982. *Using the "Thinking-aloud" method in Cognitive Interface Design. Research No. 40713.* IBM, Yorkton Heights, NY.

[7] Mehlenbacher, B. (1993). Software usability: Choosing appropriate methods for evaluating online systems and documentation. *SIGDOC'93: The 11th Annual International Conference Proceedings*. NY, NY: ACM, 209-222.

[8] Nielsen, J. 1993. Evaluating the thinking-aloud technique for use by computer scientists. In *Advances in Human-Computer Interaction*, vol. 3, Hartson, H. R. and Hix, D., Eds. Ablex Publishing Corp., Norwood, NJ, 69 - 81.

[9] Nielsen, J. 1994. Guerrilla HCI: Using Discount Usability Engineering to Penetrate the Intimidation Barrier. http://www.useit.com/papers/guerrilla_hci.html.

[10] Nielsen, J. 1993. *Usability Engineering* (1st ed.). Morgan Kaufmann,San Francisco, CA.

[11] Nisbett, R. E. and Wilson, T. D. 1977. Telling More Than We Can Know: Verbal Reports on Mental Processes. *Psychological Review*, 84, 3 (Mar 1977) 231 - 259. DOI= 10.1037/0033-295X.84.3.231

[12] Van den Haak, M. J., De Jong, M. D. T. and Schellens, P. J. 2003. Retrospective vs. concurrent think-aloud protocols: testing the usability of an online library catalogue. *Behavior and Information Technology*. 22, 5. (Sept. – Oct. 2003). 339 – 351. DOI = 10.1080/0044929031000.

[13] Wright, P. C. and Monk, A. F. 1991.The use of Think Aloud Evaluation methods in Design. *SIGCHI Bulletin*. 23, 1(Jan 1991), 55-57. DOI = 10.1145/122672.122685.

Babel or Great Wall: Social Media Use Among Chinese Students in the United States

Shaoke Zhang
Department of Psychology
Tsinghua University
Beijing, 100084, P.R.C.
shaoke.zhang@gmail.com

Hao Jiang
College of Information Sciences
and Technology
Pennsylvania State University
University Park, PA 16802
haojiang@psu.edu

John M. Carroll
College of Information Sciences
and Technology
Pennsylvania State University
University Park, PA 16802
jcarroll@ist.psu.edu

ABSTRACT

We investigated how social media support the acculturation process for an expatriate group: Chinese students in the United States. We interviewed 20 participants and found that 1) students extensively used Chinese social media to maintain their original self, especially through social bonding and information surveillance activities, while facing culture shock; 2) social media were also critical in helping students assimilate into their new (American) culture, through affordances for scaffolding, bridging, and surveillance; 3) the use of social media across the acculturation process is evolving in the context of the changing ecology of social media. This study expands existing HCI work on inter-cultural communication and collaboration activities toward consideration of acculturation strategies, online support for identity, and designing for individual development.

Categories and Subject Descriptors

H5.m. [**Information interfaces and presentation (e.g., HCI)**]: Miscellaneous.

J.4 [**Computer Applications**]: social and behavioral sciences - *Economics, Psychology, Sociology.*

General Terms

Design, Human Factors, Theory

Keywords

Social Identity, Social Media, Acculturation, Culture Shock, Uses and Gratifications, Online Community

INTRODUCTION

The era of globalization is marked by communications penetrating national or cultural boundaries in all sorts of areas. Unprecedented levels of mobilization or migration, and the boom of information communication technologies (ICTs) such as social media, which free people from the limitations of space and time, have been two highly salient features that are rapidly and irrevocably changing the world. In this paper, we explore how social media use is influencing the *acculturation* process (i.e. learning about, experiencing, and participating in a new culture) in an expatriate context: Chinese students living in the United States.

ACCULTURATION PROBLEMS

Increasing migration or expatriation has transformed cultural phenomena in recent decades. It has brought many new opportunities for learning and exchange, but also social problems and challenges. According to a report by the Department of Homeland Security [38] in August 2011, there were 46,471,516 nonimmigrant admissions to the US in the single year of 2010; 1,595,078 of these were students, greatly increasing the ethnic diversity of American universities.

These expatriates, confronting a new culture, may suffer from myriad difficulties in coping with acculturation, referred to sometimes as "culture shock" [25, 33] or "cultural fatigue" [19]. Some experience cognitive dissonance [32] or feelings of loneliness and alienation [31]. The challenges of acculturation can also undermine wellbeing, mental and physical health, psychological satisfaction, self-esteem, work performance, and grades in school [22].

Taft [33] identified six distinct sources of culture shock, confirmed by subsequent researchers (e.g. [24]): 1) strain due to the effort required to make necessary psychological adaptations; 2) a sense of loss and feelings of deprivation in regard to friends, status, profession and possessions; 3) being rejected by or rejecting members of the new culture; 4) confusion in role, role expectations, values, feelings and self-identity; 5) surprise, anxiety, even disgust and indignation after becoming aware of cultural differences; and 6) feelings of impotence due to not being able to cope with the new environment.

We are interested in the strategies adopted by expatriate students to cope with the challenges of culture shock. A priori there are a range of possibilities. At one extreme, expatriates might assimilate into the new mainstream (e.g. [25]). This is the *Babel strategy*, referring to the story of Genesis in which, after the Great Flood, all of humanity spoke a single language and shared a common culture. Babel is a traditional view of the cultural trajectory of minorities.

At the other extreme, expatriates might isolate themselves from the new mainstream cultural that confronts them. That is the *Great Wall strategy*, referring to the attempt of the early Chinese empire to prevent incursions from the north. For example, Duster [13] described the tendency of students (at Berkeley) to group themselves racially. Duster emphasizes positive consequences of such grouping, including the development of in-group affinities, cultural pride, ethnic identity, and social support. Other researchers (e.g. [10]) have argued that such self-segregation can also lead to increased ethnocentrism and racial intolerance.

This phenomenon not only denies the antiquated idea of mere assimilation, but also shatters the overmuch idyllic conception that diversity by itself benefits, which guided us to take a more rational and pragmatic perspective to explore how we could help. Researchers claimed that increasing interracial interactions were beneficial, because they enhanced cultural awareness and commitment to ethnic understanding [30], as well as college satisfaction and student retention [7]. We plan to investigate how these strategies are employed with the facilitation of social media.

IN LIGHT OF IDENTITY THEORIES

Many studies have discussed social identities including national and ethnic identities (e.g. [2, 5, 35, 36]), with a consensus that social changes such as expatriating or migration would trigger deep intra-individual changes in social identities over time [2]. Social identity being defined as "part of individuals' self-concept which derives from his or her knowledge of membership to a social group (or groups) together with the value and the emotional significance attached to it" [34], implies its multiplicity because the same individual could belong to a variety of groups. Chinese students, for example, when exposed to American culture, will experience fluctuations of and conflicts between Chinese identification (mainly based on ethnicity) and American identification (mainly based on living environment) in the context of social interactions.

Considering acculturation in light of social identities gives us an opportunity to examine identification processes separately, as well as how different identities become integrated [2, 28]. According to Turner et al. [37], social identification is a process of depersonalization "whereby people come to perceive themselves more as the interchangeable exemplars of social category than as unique personalities". In such identification processes, individuals identify strongly with their group, developing a prototype that embodies the beliefs, attitudes, feelings and behaviors associated with group membership. However, beliefs, attitudes, feelings and behaviors could be incompatible in different identification processes. For persons managing a multiplicity of social identities, these incompatibilities can create cognitive dissonance [32] and emotional exhaustion through the pursuit of self consistency [17].

Acculturation Strategies and Identity Structure

In response to these incompatibility and dissonance problems, people develop a variety of coping strategies that eventuate in different patterns of identity structures. Berry [5], for example, proposed a framework of four acculturation strategies depending on whether people value their native ethnic identity more or less than their new cultural identity. When individuals do not wish to maintain their native identity and seek adaptation into new culture, the *Assimilation* strategy is defined; when individuals place a value on holding a native identity while avoid engaging in new culture, the *Separation* strategy is defined; when individuals seek to maintain native identity while also adapting to the new culture, the *Integration* strategy is applied; and *Marginalization*, when individuals abandon the effort of reconciling identities, and display an interest in neither of them.

Roccas and Brewer [28] further developed a Social Identity Complexity, describing four kinds of identity structures according

to the subjective representations of multiple identities. Individuals may categorize themselves in an intersectional group (e.g. Chinese American) while maintaining both identities (i.e. *intersection*); they may also adopt one primary group identity to which all other group identities are subordinated (e.g. just a Chinese though temporarily living in U.S.), which is *dominance*; they may also maintain both identities, whether they are integrated (i.e. *merger*) or not (i.e. *compartmentalization*).

Berry's [5] analysis seems to oversimplify the situation individuals holding both identities and ignores possibility of compartmentalizing and situationalizing identities. It was unclear how well the identities were integrated in Roccas and Brewer's [28] intersection group. According to self-development view, people's identities could be constructed and re-constructed, which suggests that such categorizations may risk stereotyping. They regarded acculturation as a state instead of a process.

Furthermore, these categorizations are confounding different processes. For example, the assimilation strategy comprises both adaptation to new culture and resistance to original culture. A closer scrutiny of these acculturation strategies as in a quadrant (figure 1) reveals two basic underlying mechanisms, identification with the new culture (e.g. American identification as in this paper) and identification with the original culture (e.g. Chinese identification), that drive acculturation processes and lead to above states (i.e. categorizations).

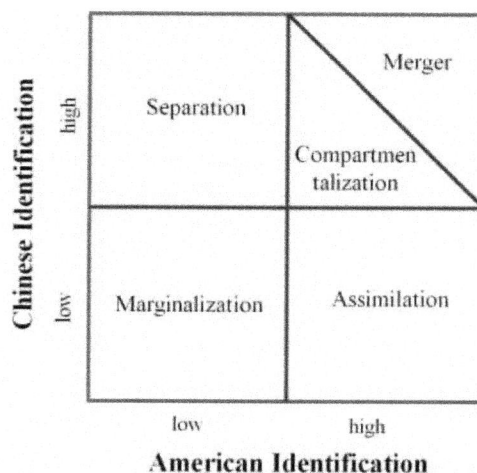

Figure 1. American Identification and Chinese Identification Underlying Acculturation Processes

SOCIAL MEDIA INFLUENCING ACCULTURATION

Most of studies on acculturation and identity structures were conducted offline, ignoring the fact that social media are radically changing the world. Social media, in terms of social network sites, weblogs, microbloggings, wikis, Internet forums, social news, social bookmarking, and multimedia sharing, etc., introduce "substantial and pervasive changes to communication between organizations, communities, and individuals" [20] with tremendous use all over the world. For example, Facebook [15] reported that it had more than 750 million active users in global, with half of them logging in at any given day. Twitter, as another example, has around 200 million users as of 2011, generating over

200 million tweets and handling over 1.6 billion search queries per day [42].

Functions of Social Media

Social media help people to present the self [18], and thereby support identity construction and maintenance. Several studies [6, 11, 16, 46] have discussed identity embodied in social media. Closer scrutiny of these studies, however, reveals that most of them presented a static conception of identity, grounded only in user profiles and other characteristics. Goffman [18] asserted, people try to control their self-presentations to other people through any type of social interactions, we view identity as a more dynamic conception of constructing self-presentations and studied identification through social interactions in social media [44, 45]. In this study, we further focus on exploring maintenance, change and integration of identities of Chinese students in U.S. in the context of acculturation.

Social media help maintain social ties. Young people are motivated to join social network sites to keep strong ties with friends, to maintain ties with new acquaintances, and to meet new people online [1]. Social networking systems (SNSs) have a strong association to maintaining or solidifying existing offline relationships [14]. They enable users to create and maintain a network of heterogeneous and weak ties due to the low maintenance cost [6, 12]. For Chinese expatriates in U.S., maintain "old" ties in China is an important commitment to Chinese identity; having opportunities to create "new" ties may largely facilitate American identification process.

Social media disseminate information rapidly and have a low threshold for participation. Barkhuus and Tashiro [3] reported that social media facilitate social events, and provide increased opportunities for engagement. For example, telephoning friends requires an explicit social approach and action commitment. However, interacting through Facebook is more of an incidental social interaction. For Chinese expatriates in U.S., social media provide their opportunity to easily engage in both Chinese and American groups, these engagements will definitely influence their identification processes.

Landscape of Chinese Social Media

There were 221 million bloggers, 176 million SNS users, 117 million bulletin board system users in China as of early 2010, which were huge amounts [8]. But the social media used in China are totally different from that in U.S. While most of social media hosted in U.S. are lack of access in China, the landscape of social media there is dominated by local players. As a result, we can find the counterparts of almost all kinds of social media in China (table 1): Renren, for example, as a counterpart of Facebook, and Weibo as a counterpart of Twitter. In contrast to the wave of "globalization" of social media, this phenomenon of "relocalization" [39] introduces interesting communication issues. There are already some studies specifically investigating these Chinese social media in CHI community (e.g. [27, 43]).

Chinese students in the United States as a result find themselves facing all these options, and often use different kinds of social media with both American and Chinese counterparts for their social life. This situation provide us a great scenario to explore *1) how they choose and use different kinds of social media;* and *2) how their use of social media influence their acculturation processes*, which serve as the research questions of this paper.

	American social media (US-based)	Chinese social media (CN-based)
Social network sites	Facebook, Myspace	Renren, Kaixin001
Microblogs	Twitter	Weibo
Online news Portals	New York Times	Sina News, Sohu
Wikis	Wikipedia	Baidu Baike
Online forums	Craigslist	MITBBS, Huaren
Instant messaging	MSN, Gtalk	QQ

Table 1. Examples of American and Chinese social media counterparts.

METHOD

We interviewed Chinese students who have stayed in the United States for more than two years, with behavioral interview techniques [23], accompanied with questionnaires. Each study took about 60 to 90 minutes.

Procedures and Questions

In the study, we first asked participants to introduce themselves with background questions and the Twenty Statements Test (TST, [21]), which had been widely used to explore self concepts in cross-cultural situations [40]. Participants were asked to give twenty brief descriptions of themselves, which helped us to understand their cultural identities (e.g. living in Pennsylvania, graduated from Beijing University, etc) and to relate them with social media use (e.g. connecting a college friend through SNS).

Then they were asked to report their general social media use with a comprehensive social media list adapted from Wikipedia [41] (by adding Chinese counterparts of these media) with about 40 application examples. With this list as a cue, participants reported which social media they use. They were asked to rate use frequency for each discussed social media application, with a 6-point Likert scale from 0 (never) to 5 (very frequently).

For each social media application that was used at least monthly, participants were asked to describe how they used it. With questions such as why and when they adopted it, what they usually did with it, who they usually interacted with, we leveraged behavioral interview technique, which were usually used in human competency assessment studies (e.g. [23]), asking participants to describe typical events in their past experience on how the applications influenced expatriate life, in a storytelling way while interviewers helped them clarify the story.

The interviews were followed by questionnaires about acculturation to understand the participants. We adapted the Multigroup Ethnic Identity Measure (MEIM, [26]) to measure both Chinese and American identification, with 10 items about cultural information searching, behavioral involvement, and emotional attachment. Based on bicultural identity integration [4], acculturation strategy [5], and social identity complexity model [28], we adapted the Bicultural Identity Integration questionnaire consisting of 5 items measuring integration level of Chinese and American identities (e.g. "these two cultures are just compatible", and "I usually feel conflicts between these two cultures"). We also leveraged the Culture shock Questionnaire [24], which consisted 7 items such as feeling of strains, homesickness, and feeling of acceptance by new environment. All questionnaires were in 7-point Likert scale.

Two of us took notes and discussed the data after each interview. The interviews were conducted in both Chinese and English, depending on participants' preferences. It was impossible to count the numbers because many conversations were conducted in a mix of both languages. In data analysis process we translated some of participants' reports from Chinese to English, with the agreement of translation between two interviewers.

Participants

We recruited participants by sending out a recruitment message twice in one month through a mailing list of Chinese students in a large eastern university in the United States. In the recruitment message, we asked for participants who had stayed in US for at least two years. In this way we recruited 20 participants, with 8 males and 12 females. Their ages ranged from 20 to 33, with average of 25.40 (std=3.38). Their years in the United States ranged from 2 to 6, with average of 3.47 (std=1.54). 15 participants were graduate students, and 5 undergraduates. Their average time staying on social media per day was 2.60 hours (std=1.38), ranging from half an hour to 4 hours. Participants were given $10 each to compensate for their time.

Demographic information	Overall
Number of participants	20
Chinese Identity	5.51 (0.64)
American Identity	3.77 (1.01)
Bicultural Identity Integration	3.74 (0.97)
Years in U.S.	3.47 (1.54)
Culture shock	3.21 (0.73)
Social media use (hrs)	2.60 (1.38)

Table 2. Demographic information of participants. (figures in parenthesis are standard deviations)

Table 2 presents the descriptive statistics of participants. According to paired-sample t test, Chinese identifications of all participants (mean=5.51, std=0.64) were significantly higher than their American identifications (mean=3.77, std=1.01), t(19)=6.95, p<0.001. Their Chinese identifications were all higher than four, which was reasonable because Chinese identities were their inborn ethnic identity.

USE OF SOCIAL MEDIA

Participants' usage of Chinese (CN-based) social media was reported higher than usage of American (US-based) social media. The existence of American and Chinese counterparts of different kinds of media (e.g. Renren vs. Facebook for SNS, Weibo vs. Twitter for microblogging) gave us opportunities to compare. Table 3 presents the average usage of some most popular media by different groups.

From table 3, we found that participants used almost every kind of social media in the acculturation context. The least used social media was US-based microblogs such as Twitter.

	Media	Overall usage
SNS	US-based (e.g. Facebook)	2.90
	CN-based (e.g. Renren)	3.85
Microblogs	US-based (e.g. Twitter)	0.30
	CN-based (e.g. Weibo)	3.25
News portal	US-based news portal	1.80
	CN-based news portal	2.50
Wikis	US-based (e.g. Wikipedia)	2.65
	CN-based (e.g. Baidu Baike)	1.80
Online Forum	American Forum (e.g. Craiglist)	1.50
	Chinese Forum (e.g. MITBBS)	3.40

Table 3. Usage of different social media (in use frequency).

The "Babel" and "Great Wall" Strategies

From the interview, all participants reported that they leveraged social media both to maintain their Chinese identity (as the "Great Wall") and to get assimilated to American identity (as the "Babel"). All participants used both US-based and China-based social media (table 3) and kept certain levels of American identity and Chinese identity (table 2). In below section we will analyze how their use of social media fulfilled both needs.

	Media	Total # of activities	# of activities for American Identification	# of activities for Chinese Identification
SNS	US-based (e.g. Facebook)	40	31	9
	CN-based (e.g. Renren)	45	0	45
Microblogs	US-based (e.g. Twitter)	5	4	1
	CN-based (e.g. Weibo)	42	0	41
News portal	US-based news portal	7	6	1
	CN-based news portal	13	0	13
Wikis	US-based (e.g. Wikipedia)	16	5	1
	CN-based (e.g. Baidu Baike)	3	0	1
IM	Instant messaging	51	7	35
Online Forum	American Forum (e.g. Craigslist)	4	4	0
	Chinese Forum (e.g. MITBBS)	31	14	17

Table 4. Number of social media use activities for American and Chinese Identification.

From the 20 participants, we collected 329 social media use activities. For each reported social media use activity, based on participants description of this activity, we further asked them to explicitly identify whether it was primarily about getting adapted to American culture (i.e. American identification), or maintaining their Chinese identities, ties, or events (i.e. Chinese identification), or not related to neither. Based on participants' reports, we get the statistics on social media use for different acculturation strategies as in table 4.

From table 4, we identified 71 social media use activities for American identification, and 164 social media use activities for Chinese identification, which suggested that 1) participants were using social media (especially US-based SNS such as Facebook) to cultivate their American identification; 2) participants were much more intensively using these social media (especially CN-based SNS such as Renren, CN-based microblogs such as Weibo, and instant messaging) to maintain their Chinese identification.

The other 94 social media use activities were not included in the table because they were reported as either not relating to cultural identification (e.g. using Facebook group for course project), or being hard to tell (e.g. discussing visa issue in MITBBS)

SNS: Maintaining Social Ties of American and Chinese

We collected 40 activities in US-based SNS (e.g. Facebook), and 45 activities in CN-based SNS (e.g. Renren). I found that CN-based SNS was exclusively for Chinese identification, while US-based SNS was mostly for American identification.

US-based SNS: cultivating American identity, in "understanding" level

The US-based SNS that participants reported were almost exclusive Facebook, which was originated in the United States and had gained popularity in many countries. Facebook users post messages not only for communication purpose but also for self-presentation [18] by publishing their personal information. It became a rich channel for participants to get to know everyday lives of American friends. Facebook was considered to provide critical information to maintain American ties and to cultivate American identification.

Facebook provides a window to closely observe American lives (i.e. information surveillance), as one participant informed us: "In Facebook I can learn how American friends' life is, what they usually do, what they usually think"; another participant reported "I don't have much to talk with them outside class, mainly due to our different cultural background. Facebook gives me some sense about their daily life". Facebook is critical for American identification as a scarce online communication channel with American friends. At least 5 participants had statements such as "besides email, Facebook is almost the only way to connect with American friends online".

The inter-cultural communication, however, often stayed at an "understanding" level with low level of interaction. While Facebook provided easy accessibility to American friends with information surveillance and simple actions such as "like", "birthday greetings", participants reported that they seldom interact deeply with American friends on Facebook. 12 participants described their passive use of Facebook as merely viewing others' posts to keep a peripheral awareness. A typical response was "I just check it every couple of days to know what's happening around, I don't write updates, neither do I share, though occasionally I give comments and add friends". Some participants explained it with cultural incompetency such as "I want to get involved but I don't know what to say", but some others claimed "It doesn't matter. I live well with so many friends online [in Chinese social media] and offline [with other Chinese students].Why force myself to adapt to American culture?".

Even when engaging in Facebook activities, a large part of these activities (9 of 40 as in table 3) could be interacting with other Chinese students: "more than half of my Facebook friends are Chinese; usually they were my target audience when I was writing status updates; sometimes I just type in Chinese". The awareness of the existence of American friends may even inhibit their active posting: "there are so many alien people [i.e. weak ties] in Facebook; to share something I would choose places like Renren", which demonstrated that their use of social media are largely influenced by their cultural identity and culture-based social ties.

CN-based SNS: maintaining Chinese identity, intensively

Accordingly table 2, table 3 and participants' report, CN-based SNS such as Renren and Kaixin001 were intensively used for Chinese identification. Participants used CN-based SNS actively and interactively, by updating status, uploading photos, playing social games, sharing articles and videos, commenting, and chatting. As one participant reported, "it is convenient because almost all my friends use it, whether they are currently in China or US, which makes my abroad life not that boring". They reported that Facebook and Renren corresponded to two different groups of people (although overlapping): in Facebook there are "alien people" or "professional" friends; but in Renren, there are "high school friends", "college friends", and "Chinese peers in US", which were all Chinese social ties.

Accordingly, the use (and perception of use) of these two media differed: "Facebook is for professional use, and is more formal; Renren is much more casual and informal. I will share my daily things in Renren, but I won't share them in Facebook because they look too trivial", which greatly supported their cultural inertia in the acculturation process

Microblogging: Surveillance on Chinese Ties and News

We collected only 5 activities on US-based microblogs (e.g. Twitter). Although 12 participants had registered in Twitter, most of they seldom used it, because "the [American related] contents are not relevant", and "my friends are not there". Only 2 participants used Twitter at least weekly. They followed celebrities such as famous movie critics, graphic designers, and industrial leaders to keep updated with the movies and industries. They have few friends to follow. In contrast with low use of Twitter, we collected 42 activities on CN-based microblogs (e.g. Weibo). 15 participants used Weibo, at least daily.

The use of microblogging tools is different from that of SNS. "Weibo is so lightweight" that they shared contents "more frequently and more casually" with Chinese friends than in any other social media including Renren. Updates in Weibo can be more "ad hoc", as a participant reported, "I will create an album in Renren for the photos of my trip to Las Vegas; but if I randomly take a picture of a lovely squirrel on the road, I will definitely share it in Weibo". According to participants, micro-blogs provide a more friendly way for instant sharing of trivial things that matters in daily bonding and acculturation. With these instant and rich updates, Weibo provided users quick and wide access to their friend's information, which provides participants the surveillance with regard to their Chinese friends, and thus maintaining the Chinese identity.

Besides keeping touch with Chinese ties, participants used Weibo as news portal to keep abreast of current affairs in China. One participant reported that "*every morning I open Weibo, I won't miss any piece of hot news*". Any valuable information (e.g. news, opinion) would be shared and repost (like "retweet" in Twitter) quickly and extensively in Weibo. In such way, the hot news and topics transmit much faster than traditional news portals. Nine participants mentioned that they used Weibo to get informed of Chinese news, especially in big events such as the Yunnan earthquake and bullet train crash in China. "*Although I am currently in US, I am really concerned about these things [that] happened in China*", as many participants reported.

As Weibo is so lightweight, every user could add opinion when resharing information about hot topics. Valuable and diverse opinions popularize through mass sharing, so that users could "*learn opinions from different perspectives*" that added value to the news. "*There are so many opinions, rumors, and debates. Weibo makes you open-minded and rational to these events*", especially when "*China is developing so fast with so many controversial events happening everyday*". They also re-share messages for emotional supports. For example, a participant re-reposted a message calling for people around in Beijing to buy vegetables from an old poor lady; another participant re-shared a very popular message of blessing a child victim in the bullet train accident: "*At that moment, I feel my heart is with people in China*".

Participants also sought for worldwide news and opinions (e.g. tsunami in Japan, uprising in Egypt) in Weibo. In such circumstances, the Chinese identity became salient due to the social categorization in the national level [2, 37]. With so many channels to understand the world, some of them chose Weibo to learn and share opinions with other Chinese people, which helped maintaining the Chinese identity.

News Portals and Wikis: to Understand the Cultures

We collected 7 activities on US-based online news portals, mostly for American identification, and 13 activities on CN-based news portal exclusively for Chinese identification. Participants reported that they read American news "*so that I know what's happening around, and I can have some topics to talk with American friends*", which implied an effort for American identification. More participants expressed that they were less interested in things happened in US. "*I am more concerned with a similar event happened in China than that in US*", as one participant reported.

We also collected 16 activities using US-based wikis (e.g. Wikipedia) and 3 activities using CN-based wikis (e.g. Baidu Baike). While many activities were to understand professional terms in their academic work, participants also used wikis to understand American cultural, historical events, and celebrities, as one participant reported: "*when I am communicating with American friends, I usually hear names or events that I have no idea. For example, one friend mentioned "the Ellen DeGeneres Show", but I never heard of it. When I come back I searched for it in Wikipedia. Actually later I even listened to some of her talk shows.*"

Online Forums: Scaffolding, and Bridging

Participants sometimes used US-based online forum such as Craigslist, but they used Chinese online forums a lot, including both Chinese forums located in US (e.g. MITBBS) and CN-based online forums. In the Chinese online forums in US (e.g. MITBBS, huaren.com) were specific online community of Chinese students in the US, which are divided into hundreds of subgroups of interests and topics, which were related to "*almost every aspect of our lives in US, from flea market, to travelling to certain place, to repairing a car, to any discipline we study, and to fans of certain soccer team*". These bulletin boards serve as a scaffold role for their lives in the US. "*Any time I have a question about, say, what are best Chinese restaurants in Boston when I travel there, I just enter certain subgroup to browse or to ask*", as one participant reported.

Such scaffolding role helps bridge Chinese identities with American identities. By interacting with Chinese peers in the US, they learned hand-down experiences on how to deal with their living and acculturation problems in US (e.g. the visa problem, how to cook, travel guidance, etc.). These interactions help them build up cultural competency, and thus better engage in American life.

Participants may also use American counterparts such as Craigslist. Although their usage of Craigslist was limited in things like purchasing "second-hand products" or house renting, it supported the American identification process in help solving living problems in the new environment.

Instant Messaging: for Social Bonding

Participants reported 51 instant messaging activities, with 7 for American identification and 35 for Chinese identification. They used instant messaging a lot to communicate with their Chinese strong ties. Fifteen participants reported that they had weekly video call with their parents in IM's such as Skype and Tencent QQ. One participant reported that "*I usually use QQ to chat with my college friends in China. We talk about everything. Especially when someone has some problems and needs to pour out their worries, I would become a very patient listener and tries to give some emotional support.*"

THE TEMPORARITY OF SOCIAL MEDIA USE

We found that participants' adoption and use of social media were influenced by two other processes: the changing landscape of social media, and individual acculturation phases.

Social Media Migration: Changing landscape

As the time in the U.S. of our participants varied from 2 years to 6 years, we had an opportunity to observe a phenomenon of "social media migration" according to their reports. As different social media emerged in different time, a rough migration path was from instant messages to blogs, to social networks, and then to micro-blogs. While they may use all of these social media, the usages seemed to have peaks of waves across the time. As one participant reported, "*when Xiaonei (the predecessor of Renren) became popular about five years ago, I began use it with my friends. It is much better than blogs because we can build tangible connection there. We do not need to bookmark each friend's blog anymore, and I got connected to friends who hadn't written blogs before*". Several others reported "*The use of Renren of my friends is not as high as a couple of years ago, mainly because we are using Weibo more frequently".*

Adoption and Decay of Media Use along Acculturation

Participants' use of social media also changed depending on their acculturation stages in the U.S. Most of participants reported a leap in use of social media at the time when they entered the U.S. One typical example was: "*I used Renren much more frequently when I came here three years ago, although I had its account earlier. When in China we could see friends around [so we didn't use it much], but right before I came abroad, I thought I should have something to stay connection with them".*

The social media migration phenomenon becomes much more complex when accompanied with participants' length of stay in the U.S. For example, the adoption (or leap in use) of certain social media largely depend on their time of entry. Both of the two participants who entered the U.S. in 2005 used blogs frequently to share their American lives; and most participants who came to the U.S. two year later chose to use social network sites.

12 participants mentioned the decay of use of at least one kind of social media. Facebook was a frequent example. One participant observed that the decay of Facebook use was common in his Chinese friends, "*now just a few of my friends are still actively using it [Facebook], so I don't use it either".* Although this decay could be partly attributed to the emergence of its Chinese counterparts (e.g. Renren) and new kind of social media (i.e. microblogging), participants indeed reported the influence of the acculturation phases. An interesting example is: "*when I came here [four year ago], I created a Facebook account to add friends. We used it a lot with silly features such as pokes and biting zombies. But a couple of years later my social network became pretty large, with many acquaintances, like some foreigner, or professional friends met once in conferences. I don't like having too much revealed to so many people with whom I am not familiar [weak ties]",* so now she just checked Facebook every couple of days but seldom posted anything.

A more salient example is the Bulletin Boards Systems. Most of participants reported that they used bulletin boards intensively in their first year in U.S., because they had "*so many things to ask for help".* But several years later, as they got more adapted in new cultural environment, their usage decreased, just as one participant reported that now she "*only check it weekly to keep updated, or to look for some deals when needed".*

DISCUSSION

The Acculturation Process

This study expands existing HCI work on inter-cultural communication and collaboration activities toward research on acculturation strategies, the online support of cultural identity, and designing for individual development. Living abroad can be exciting and enjoyable, but it can also be challenging and even difficult. People reconstruct and maintain identities throughout life, but for young people identity development is an important social project. Young adults living abroad face a particularly challenging identity construction project, due to cognitive dissonance and emotional exhaustion caused by the incompatibilities of values, feelings and behavioral patterns implied in different cultural identity [17, 32]. This challenge is even greater when the two cultural identities being managed are relatively more distinct, as

they are in case of Chinese and American culture. Studying Chinese students living in the United States is particularly important because the two cultures they are dealing with are quite different, because more and more Chinese students are pursuing education in the U.S., and because the two cultures are quite important ones geo-politically and are broadly engaging at a scale and rate that is unprecedented.

All participants in our study showed strong identification with their original culture and strong needs for maintaining original cultural identity. All participants maintained a higher Chinese identification than American identification. This cultural inertia can be seen as a result of living in a culturally different environment, because according to social identity theory, group identity becomes more salient with presence of contrasting groups [2, 37]. Living abroad is an extreme case of this kind, in which one has to interact with people from a different culture throughout everyday life. In this analysis, social media can be a tool to re-access and re-energize one's original culture, and thereby a tool for maintaining it within a contrasting cultural context.

In reacting to stimuli from wide social context, some participants showed certain level of neglect or resistance. This is a stage of cultural identity "separation" [5]. Our participants reported high use of social media to maintain Chinese ties (as the "Great Wall") providing emotional supports, which alleviate the culture shock [24, 33]. They also expressed high use of bulletin broad systems that are based in America but provide Chinese content as a Chinese online community, which is more of an indication of identity level maintenance.

Participants also exhibited efforts to get assimilated to American culture. For example, participants were using US-based SNS to connect with American friends and have an information surveillance of them; they used Wikipedia to understand culture and history of the United States; some participants even regularly use US-based news portals.

Use Social Media to Support Identity Development and Acculturation

The extensive use of Chinese social media can be a result of driving demands of maintaining one's original identity. Social network sites (SNS) and instant messages (IM) contribute to this a lot. Although both SNS and IM do not necessarily work on the social identity level, they do provide a strong mechanism for Chinese students living abroad to maintain *social* ties, and thus cultural identities reinforced or cultivated. From our participants' disclosure, these two types of social media kept the emotional connections between them and their Chinese friends (i.e. *bonding*). Facebook was not the most used social media for this purpose, although it is the most popular social network website. Instead, Chinese social network websites such as Renren served this purpose.

Another kind of social media that can help satisfy the need of maintaining and reinforcing Chinese cultural identity is Chinese news portal and a twitter-like system called Weibo. From these channels, Chinese students in the U.S can subscribe or read news related to China in a very timely fashion (i.e. *surveillance*). What we could see from our participants was that they cared about the happenings in their home country, showing high connection with original cultural identity.

Besides using social media as the "Great Wall" to maintaining their Chinese identity, participants also use social medial to cultivate American identity. Facebook serves as a place where Chinese students can observe American life and as a channel for Chinese students to have personal contacts with American people (i.e. *bridging*).

Social media run by Chinese expatriates in the U.S. provide content in Chinese and they cover almost every aspect of living in the US: traveling, finance, legal issues, health, and many others (i.e. *scaffolding*). Social media of this type plays a very important role in living abroad at least for the early years. These media provide information of very useful instrumental value at first, to help someone get one's life going. It also provides a forum where the new expatriates can raise questions and seek for help in Chinese when their secondary language is not proficient. This is very important in that being able to find help in an unfamiliar culture can alleviate culture shocks [24, 33]. A social learning of those seemingly trivial and concrete experiences of others can help foreign students adapt their lives into a new environment and lead to further identity integration.

Some Underlying Mechanisms

Looking at the use of social media in our participants, we see a pattern of temporality of social media use. In the first couple of years, social media that provide China-related information and interpersonal interaction are intensively used and appreciated by Chinese students. They used these channels to consolidate their connections with remote family members and friends, which is more emotionally bonded and less informational in nature. At the same time, U.S-based Chinese social media that provide content relevant to living in the U.S also was used intensively.

Use of these media becomes less after a period of time; but the use of social media such as Facebook that presents more American life continues, although with a relatively low interaction level with American ties. In later years, Chinese students also showed their interests in absorbing American news portals.

In terms of total social media use, we noticed the trend that the amount of time spent on social media decreased over time, accompanied with decreasing culture shock in our participants. One interpretation of this is that students with well-integrated cultural identity has less trouble in handling and reacting to social stimuli and they can spend more time on their offline life. It is not surprising, since as years spend in a new environment increases, familiarity and skills of coping in the environment will develop. However, this points to us that some social media are more of value to expatriates only for a period of time and the marginal value and actual use of these social media decrease over time.

We believe that it is a process of social construction. Both human agents and social media play interactively to achieve this cultural identity integration and successfully cultural coping. In the developing process, it is the agents actively choosing different social media to react to stimuli from the social world, and social media provide the possibility for human agents to do so. So in our case of Chinese students living in the U.S, it becomes a spiral circle: students living abroad experience difficulties to process culturally different events, certain social media can help; when students develop their understandings and skills of coping American culture in real life, not necessarily from those social media, old social media can lose their marginal value to the students and they may find new media and ways of life.

CONCLUSION AND FUTURE DIRECTION

In this paper we investigated how Chinese students in the United States used social media in acculturation process. Diverse social media were leveraged for accommodating American identity as well as maintaining Chinese identity. They provide value to participants such as bridging, social bonding, information surveillance, and scaffolding. This exploratory work expands existing HCI work on inter-cultural communication and collaboration activities toward research on acculturation strategies, and designing to support self development.

What we learned is that no single tool can serve well in cultural identity integration. Participants adopted different kinds of social media for different uses in the acculturation process. While Babel strategy represents an effort seeking for total assimilation into the host culture, the Great Wall strategy represents a resistance to adapt. Neither is enough as shown in the study. With supports of social media, we actually have better choice, to embrace cultural diversity and move towards a new self, by cultivating new identities and maintaining existing identities at the same time.

It should be noted that as we recruited participants through a mailing list of Chinese student in one university, the results could be biased due to the sampling issue. Most of the participants were graduate students, which further limited the generalizability of this study. While this is mainly a qualitative interview study, we presented some quantitative data, which suggested some trends without further statistical examination due to limited sample size. We plan to conduct a survey study with large sample of Chinese students in the United States based on this study.

REFERENCES

1. Acquisti, A. and R. Gross (2006). Imagined communities: Awareness, information sharing, and privacy on the Facebook. In *Proc. of the 6th Workshop on Privacy Enhancing Technologies*.

2. Amiot, C.E., de la Sablonniere, D., Terry, D. J., and Smith, J.R. (2007). Integration of social identities in the self: Toward a cognitive-developmental model. *Personality and Social Psychology Review*, 11 (4), 364-388.

3. Barkhuus, L. and Tashiro, J. Student socialization in the age of facebook. In *Proc. CHI 2010*. 133-142.

4. Benet-Martínez, V., Leu, J., Lee, F., and Morris, M. (2002). Negotiating biculturalism: Cultural frame-switching in biculturals with "oppositional" vs. "compatible" cultural identities. *Journal of Cross-Cultural Psychology*, 33, 492-516.

5. Berry, J.W. (1997). Immigration, Acculturation, and Adaptation. *Applied Psychology: An International Review*, 46 (1), 5-34.

6. boyd, D.M. and Ellison, N.B. (2007). Social Network Sites: Definition, History, and Scholarship. *Journal of Computer-Mediated Communication*, 210-230.

7. Chang, M.J. (1996). *Racial diversity in higher education: Does a racially mixed student population affect educational outcomes?* Unpublished doctoral dissertation, University of California, Los Angeles.

8. Colaizzi, M. (2010). Social media and China: What you need to know. Retrieved from http://smartblogs.com/socialmedia/2010/03/31/social-media-and-china-what-you-need-to-know/

9. Corbin, J. and Strauss, A. (2008). *Basics of Qualitative Research: Techniques and Procedures for Developing Grounded Theory.* Sage Publications, CA.

10. D'Souza, D. (1991). *Illiberal education: The politics of race and sex on campus.* New York: Free Press.

11. DiMicco, J.M. And Millen, D. (2007) Identity management: multiple presentations of self in facebook. In *Proc. GROUP 2007,* ACM Press, 383-386.

12. Donath, J. and Boyd, D. (2004). Public displays of connection. *BT Technology Journal.* 22(4), 71-82.

13. Duster, T. (1991). *The diversity project: Final report.* Berkeley: Institute for the Study of Social Change.

14. Ellison, N.B., Steinfield, C. and Lampe, C. The Benefits of Facebook "Friends:" Social Capital and College Students' Use of Online Social Network Sites. *Journal of CMC.* 12(4). (2007). 1143-1168.

15. Facebook. (2011). http://www.facebook.com/press/info.php?statistics. Retrieved on September 21, 2011.

16. Farnham, S.D., and Churchill, E.F. (2011). Faceted Identity, Faceted Lives: Social and Technical Issues with Being Yourself Online. In *Proc. of CSCW 2011.* 359-368.

17. Grice, T.A., Jones, L. and Paulsen, N. (2002) Multiple targets of organizational identification: The role of identification congruency. *Journal of Articles in Support of the Null Hypothesis,* 1 (2), 1-12

18. Goffman, E. (1956). *The Presentation of Self in Everyday Life.* NY: Anchor Doubleday.

19. Guthrie, G.M. (1975). A behavioral analysis of culture learning. In: Brislin RW, Bochner S, Lonner WJ (eds) *Cross-cultural perspectives on learning.* Wiley, New York, 95-115.

20. Kietzmann, J.H., Hermkens, K., McCarthy, I.P., and Silvestre, B.S. (2011). Social media? Get serious! Understanding the functional building blocks of social media. *Business Horizons,* 54 (3), 241–251.

21. Kuhn, M.H. and McPartland, T.S. (1954). An empirical investigation of self-attitudes. *American Sociological Review,* 19, 68-76

22. Liebkind, K. (2001). Acculturation. In R. Brown & S. Gaertner (Eds.), *Blackwell handbook of social psychology: Intergroup processes.* Oxford: Blackwell. 386–406.

23. McClelland, D.C. (1998). Identifying competencies with behavioral-event interviews. *Psychological Science,* 9(5), 331-339.

24. Mumford, D.B. (1998). The measurement of culture shock. *Social psychiatry and psychiatric epidemiology,* 33 (4), 149-154.

25. Oberg, K. (1960). Cultural shock: adjustment to new cultural environments. *Pract. Anthropol.* 7: 177-182.

26. Phinney, J. (1992). The Multigroup Ethnic Identity Measure: A new scale for use with adolescents and young adults from diverse groups. *Journal of Adolescent Research,* 7, 156-176.

27. Qu, Y., Huang, C., Zhang, P., and Zhang, J. (2011). Microblogging after a major disaster in China: a case study of the 2010 Yushu earthquake. In *Proc. of CSCW 2011,* 25-34.

28. Roccas, S. and Brewer, M.B. (2002). Social Identity Complexity. *Personality and Social Psychology Review,* 6 (2), 88-106.

29. Rudenstine, N. (1996). Why a diverse student body is so important. *Chronicle of Higher Education,* 42(32), B1-B2.

30. Smith, D.G., Gerbick, G.L., Figueroa, M.A., Watikins, G.H., Levitan, T., Moore, L.C., Merchant, P.A., Beliak, H.D., and Figueroa, B. (1997). *Diversity works: The emerging picture of how students benefit.* Washington DC: Association of American Colleges and Universities.

31. Suarez, S.A., Fowers, B.J., Garwood, C.S., and Szapocznik, J. (1997). Biculturalism, Differentness, Loneliness, and Alienation in Hispanic College Students. *Hispanic Journal of Behavioral Sciences,* 19 (4), 489-505.

32. Tadmor, C.T. and Tetlock, P.E. (2006). Biculturalism: A Model of the Effects of Second-Culture Exposure on Acculturation and Integrative Complexity. *Journal of Cross-cultural Psychology,* 37 (2), 173-190.

33. Taft, R. (1977). Coping with unfamiliar cultures *Studies in cross-cultural psychology,* 1, 121-153.

34. Tajfel, H. (1978). *Differentiation between social groups: Studies in the social psychology of intergroup relations.* London: Academic Press.

35. Ting-Toomey, S. (1981). Ethnic identity and close friendship in Chinese-American college students. *International Journal of Intercultural Relations,* 5(4), 383-406.

36. Ting-Toomey, S., Yee-Jung, K.K., Shapiro, R., Garcia, W., Wright, T.J., and Oetzel, J.G. (2000). Ethnic/ Cultural Identity Salience and Conflict Styles in Four US Ethnic Groups. *International Journal of Intercultural Relation.* 24, 47-81.

37. Turner, J.C., Hogg, M.A., Oakes, P.J., Reicher, S.D., and Wetherell, M.S. (1987). *Rediscovering the social group: A self-categorization theory.* Oxford, England: Basil Blackwell.

38. U.S. Department of Homeland Security. (2011). http://www.dhs.gov/files/statistics/publications/YrBk10NI.shtm

39. Warschauer, M. (2000). Language, Identity, and the Internet. In B. Kolko, L. Nakamura & G. Rodman (Eds.) *Race in Cyberspace.* New York: Routledge, 151-170.

40. Watkins, D. (1997). The Twenty Statements Test: Some Measurement Issues. *Journal of Cross-Cultural Psychology,* 28 (5), 626-633.

41. Wikipedia, http://en.wikipedia.org/wiki/Social_media.

42. Wikipedia, http://en.wikipedia.org/wiki/Twitter.

43. Yang, J., Ackerman, M.S. and Adamic, L.A. (2011). Virtual gifts and guanxi: supporting social exchange in a chinese online community. In *Proc. of CSCW 2011,* 45-54.

44. Zhang, S., Jiang, H., and Carroll, J.M. (2010) Social Identity in Facebook Community Life. *International Journal of Virtual Communities and Social Networking.* 2 (4), 66-78.

45. Zhang, S., Jiang, H., and Carroll, J.M. (2011) Integrating Online and Offline Community through Facebook. In *Proc. of International Conference on Collaboration Technologies and Systems (CTS 2011),* IEEE Press, 569 - 578.

46. Zhao, S., Grasmuch, S., and Martin, J. Identity Construction on Facebook: Digital empowerment in Anchored relationships. *Computers in Human Behavior,* 24 (5), 2008, 1816-1836.

Knowledge Workers and Their Use of Publicly Available Online Services for Day-to-day Work

Toni Ferro
University of Washington
428 Sieg Hall
Seattle, WA 98195
503-360-7226
tdferro@uw.edu

Doug Divine
University of Washington
428 Sieg Hall
Seattle, WA 98195
206-369-7317
rddivine@uw.edu

Mark Zachry
University of Washington
428 Sieg Hall
Seattle, WA 98195
206-616-7936
zachry@uw.edu

ABSTRACT

Researchers and organizations have been endeavoring to determine if and how social media can be leveraged to support the day-to-day work of knowledge workers. This study discusses a survey of the use of publicly available online services by knowledge workers that highlights new ways of examining the social media in relation to day-to-day work. Specifically, we examine the use of social media by workers in a variety of contexts as well as analyzing social media at the component level, the level of services, instead of simply at the site level.

Categories and Subject Descriptors

H.4.3 [Information Systems]: — Information Systems Applications – Communications Applications

Keywords

Social media, knowledge work, social networking site, SNS, publicly available online service, PAOS.

1. INTRODUCTION

Many knowledge workers are adopting social media technologies in the workplace to support communication and collaboration. Relatively little research investigates the use of social media services to support the day-to-day work of knowledge workers. The value of social media services to support work remains unclear and has resulted in workplace restrictions on the use of publicly available social media such as social networking sites [11] even as knowledge work becomes increasingly distributed and reliant on such systems [17]. In addition, most of the research that has been conducted to date has taken place within companies (for example, Microsoft and IBM), and therefore does not account for the variety of knowledge workers or their varied wants and needs. The lack of research regarding the potential value of social media to knowledge workers makes it difficult to proactively envision how these services can be designed to better support their day-to-day work.

Researchers have argued that social media sites will become as valuable to knowledge workers as email and IM have become, while at the same time acknowledge that it is difficult to

systematically study the value of systems focused on incidental communicative interactions [1, 16]. In addition, recent studies indicate that social media sites that are being deployed within companies are still not yet broadly adopted or used [1, 14].

Contributing to the challenge of understanding the value of social media to knowledge workers is the fact that many social media sites encompass a variety of services. Without an understanding of the services that make up the site it is difficult to pinpoint the features and functionality of the site that are providing value to users. To clarify the difference between a site and a service, we define sites as in Divine et al. [5] as "a set of related and connected web pages that are available on the Internet and typically identified through a common domain name, for example Amazon.com or twitter.com." Services are defined as a specific offering available through the site. For example, shopping sites typically offer the service of product search, product information, and a shopping cart among others [9].

Previous research identifies nine genres of Web 2.0 services that are offered through social media sites [9]. These services (listed in Table 1) include blog, microblog, and wiki. In this study, we take another step toward understanding the value of social media sites to knowledge workers by analyzing the services offered through the sites knowledge workers report as valuable to their work.

We have conducted a survey of knowledge workers and asked them about the publicly available social media they use for work. We have analyzed the usefulness of the sites to knowledge workers in different types of organizations as well as the services offered through the frequently reported sites.

Specifically, we asked participants about the social media sites they use that are publicly available as opposed to sites that are available only within their companies. Many Web 2.0 sites have been developed and deployed within enterprises for internal use only. These systems often offer similar services to those available publicly, for example, wikis and blogs. However, we focus on publicly available online services (PAOSs), which are created and maintained by a separate party and are available to the general public.

An examination of PAOSs is important, because they provide knowledge workers with capabilities that are not available through enterprise-proprietary online systems. For example, because PAOSs are public, they make it possible for knowledge workers to leverage information from a variety of sources outside their own company.

Our examination of a) the contexts of use of PAOSs and b) the services that are offered through the sites frequently reported as important to knowledge workers, is intended as an early step

Table 1 Web 2.0 service genres and their definitions from [9].

Genre	Description based on common user objective
network creator	an application through which individuals identify other online individuals with whom they have a relationship
blog	a journal through which a designated individual or group of individuals can publish ideas
microblog	an application through which users can enter free form text of constrained length, broadcasting it via the Internet
wiki	a webspace that publishes pages that can be read by individuals and edited/supplemented collaboratively by contributors
media sharing tool	a service through which people can submit primarily visual/audio material to be shared with others
social marking tool	an online tool that allows individuals to tag, classify, index, or otherwise mark information in a form that can be aggregated and shared with others
synchronous interaction tool	an online tool through which people engage in real-time exchanges via text, audio, and/or video
asynchronous forum	an online space to which contributors can add individual postings
knowledge transactor	a service through which people can submit information—alphanumeric, graphical, or otherwise symbolic--and have it transformed to be shared with others in a way not accounted for by any of the other service genres above

toward understanding the value of social media to knowledge workers. We also demonstrate the value of examining the context of the worker and analyzing sites at a service level when discussing the value of social media to knowledge workers.

2. RELATED WORK

As a background framework for our study, we begin with an overview of research regarding social media in work contexts and then discuss the phenomenon of knowledge workers using publicly available online services. Our research differs from previous studies by focusing on knowledge workers in a variety of contexts, knowledge workers use of publicly available sites, and the services offered through sites.

2.1 Social Media in Work Contexts

Studies of professional uses of social media typically focus on specific sites that have been implemented within a company for internal use (enterprise-proprietary sites). These studies provide insight into the factors that motivate employees to use social media.

For example, in studies of blog and forum use by company employees, researchers found that internal bloggers are motivated by the perception that others are reading their posts and that this may garner them increased support from their managers [18]. In a similar study of social media use at Hewlett-Packard (including, blogs, forums, and wikis), researchers found that the encouragement of management motivated employees to post for the first time in social media venues and that "comments and a diverse readership" motivated users to continue contributing [4]. A complementary study of blogging at Microsoft (on blogs hosted internally and externally) revealed that bloggers write to "share a passion for their work," "to document and organize their ideas and work practices," and "to find and engage others inside and outside of the organization" [8].

In a study of what motivated IBM knowledge workers to use Beehive (an enterprise-proprietary social networking site) researchers found that employees wanted to achieve "career advancement goals" or "champion a project idea" in a widely visible manner [7]. Another study of enterprise-proprietary social networking sites examined three different sites within three different companies: IBM's Bluepages, Accenture Ltd.'s People Pages, and SAP's Harmony. Participants reported using the sites for "identifying experts," "building personal context," and "fostering existing relationships" [14].

In a study of Yammer, an enterprise-proprietary microblogging service, researchers found that employees were motivated to use this online service to "publish news about their groups or business units," to stay aware of what others were working on, and to make new connections [19].

Other studies note reluctance among employees to use enterprise-sponsored social media, where workers may not perceive value in such activity [10] or where such activity was perceived to be in conflict with accomplishing more important work objectives [12]. However, when knowledge workers perceive that the properties of an online service complement the characteristics of a given work group, there is greater likelihood of adoption [3].

In these studies of online site use by knowledge workers, researchers have focused on what motivates knowledge workers to use a particular type of enterprise-proprietary site and/or what they value about a specific site. Our study is designed to complement and extend this line of inquiry by studying participants from a variety of different contexts (participants from different companies and working in different settings) and examining the sites and services they report as being the most valuable for their work.

In addition, some researchers [4, 7] have argued that employees using social media inside an enterprise are motivated differently than users of the same or similar sites hosted outside the enterprise, presumably even when they are using those sites for work purposes. Therefore, specific studies of how knowledge workers are using social media outside the enterprise (PAOSs) are needed to complement our existing understanding of knowledge work with enterprise-proprietary services.

2.2 Knowledge workers and publicly available online services

There are a few studies that have examined how knowledge workers at a single company use publicly available social media. For example, DiMicco and Millen studied knowledge workers motivations for using Facebook and found that they used Facebook to improve friendships with new co-workers, to keep in touch with current friends, and to maintain relationships with friends they were close to, but that did not live nearby [6]. Similarly, in a longitudinal study, Skeels and Grudin examined the use of social networking systems such as Facebook and LinkedIn at Microsoft and found that strengthening weak ties was the most important work-related benefit of social networking sites [16]. And in an update on that same study, Archaumbault and Grudin reported that the use of Facebook, LinkedIn and Twitter at Microsoft had increased over the four years of their study [1].

Zhao and Rosson found that knowledge workers at a large corporation that used Twitter valued it because it enabled them to "keep a pulse on people they do not encounter in their daily life activities" and to get trustworthy information about different topics from people they know personally [20].

In addition, some studies have discussed the task activities that knowledge workers accomplish using PAOSs, though these studies are not focused specifically on work tasks. For example Morris, Teevan, and Panovich studied information seeking via PAOSs at Microsoft [13] and DiMicco and Millen discussed managing identity on Facebook [6]. In addition, Sellen, Murphy, and Shaw conducted a study of knowledge workers to determine the general activities they performed through the web [15].

Our research contributes to the existing body of research by taking a high-level look at the use of PAOSs for work by knowledge workers in a variety of contexts. We examine the sites that are valuable to knowledge workers at the service level as well as the site level. Instead of examining a specific company and a specific site, we study participants from a variety of companies. .We study the use of sites that are publicly available (not specific to a certain company or enterprise), and the range of component-level services offered through social media sites..

By approaching the study of PAOSs at this level we can address questions such as, which PAOSs are knowledge workers finding valuable for their work? Does the context of the knowledge worker have an impact on the PAOSs they find valuable? Which services offered through publicly available social media sites do knowledge workers find valuable? What do the answers to these previous questions tell us about the way communication is changing for knowledge workers and what impact does this have on the design of workplace communication systems?

3. METHODS

Our research group conducted an online survey of knowledge workers each year from 2008 through 2011. Each year, participants were asked demographic and employment questions, and questions about their Internet use. Here we report primarily the 2011 data, the most recent data gathered through the survey.

Participants were recruited from technology-focused online groups such as those on meetup.com (an online site that facilitates the organization of location-specific interest groups). Technology-focused groups, such as the New York New Technology group (meetup.com) and the Akron Linux Users Group (Google Groups), were invited to take the survey, because the participants of these groups are the most likely to use PAOSs for work.

Therefore, the results do not generalize to the general population or to all knowledge workers, but instead represent the highest level of PAOS use among knowledge workers in the US. The survey was available to each invited group for two weeks during the spring of 2011.

This study is limited to US knowledge workers who use the Internet for work, therefore we eliminated participants who indicated they were not employed, not living in the United States, or not using the Internet for work at least 10% of their workday. A total of 154 participants met these criteria in 2011.

Our 2011 participants had an average age of 38 years (SD = 11.8), included managers (27.9%) and non-managers (64.3%), included mostly participants with computer-related jobs (82.5%), included mostly full-time employees (82.4%), included employees that work primarily from home (21.4%), and others that work primarily from a company office (69.5%). Our participants also included employees from companies smaller than 1000 people (65.6%) and from companies larger than 1000 people (34.4%).

3.1 Genres of services

This research is a longitudinal study of knowledge workers that started in 2008. Genres of services were identified previously as part of this study in [9]. In that report, we identified services that were offered through the sites frequently reported by participants between the years of 2008-2010 (shown in Table 1). Those services were than validated by a coding study in [5].

Eight of the services shown in Table 1 are specific services offered through websites. However, the ninth service genre, knowledge transactor, makes it possible to identify social elements of sites that are not in common use or contain primary elements of frequently reported PAOSs. In this way, knowledge transactor is not a commonly understood genre of service as the others, but instead provides an analytical method of accounting for uncommon social services offered through PAOSs. As is discussed in a later section, analyzing knowledge transactors can help identify services that are emerging as their own specific genres through PAOSs.

4. RESULTS

In this section we first discuss the overall use of PAOSs for work and the sites participants reported as important for work. Second, we identify the service genres present in the sites most frequently reported as important for work, the frequency of the presence of the services genres, and the relationships the service genres have to each other.

4.1 Results related to sites

Participants were asked to report how frequently they used PAOSs, the specific PAOSs valuable to their work, and information about their work context.

On average, participants reported using PAOSs for work 22.7% (SD=25.4) of their workweek. A majority of participants (66.4%), however, reported using PAOSs less than 20% of their workweek and 12.1% of participants (n=18) reported not using PAOSs for their work at all. Amongst the 18 participants who reported not using PAOSs at all, 17 worked primarily from company offices. 15 of the participants who reported not using PAOSs for work purposes were employed in companies of larger than 100 employees. Therefore, almost all of the participants that worked from home and almost all of the participants working for companies of less than 100 employees, reported using PAOSs for their work at least part of their workday. Figure 1 shows the percentage of time all participants reported using PAOSs for work.

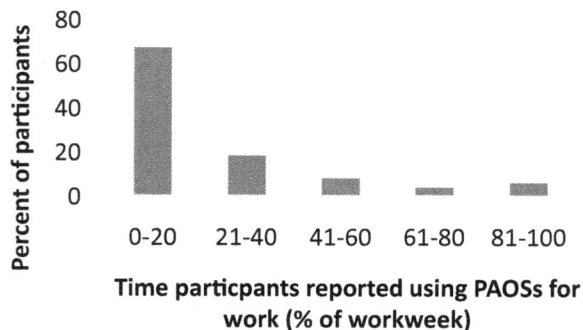

Figure 1. Participants use of PAOSs for work purposes

Participants were also asked to list the PAOSs that were most important to their work. Participants were instructed not to include email, general search engines, or instant messaging (IM) systems. In total, the participants reported 298 different sites with 231 (78%) of those sites being reported by only one person. Five sites were reported by at least 15% of participants and twelve sites were reported by more than 6% of participants. Table 2 shows the sites that were reported by 6% of participants or more along with the percentage of participants that reported them as important for work.

Table 2. Sites reported by 6% or more of participants as important to their work

Site	Participants (%)
Google Calendar	26%
LinkedIn	22%
Google Docs	21%
Twitter	19%
Facebook	18%
Google Reader	8%
Wikipedia	8%
Basecamp	6%
Dropbox	6%
Skype	6%
Flickr	6%
WordPress	6%

The context in which participants conducted their work was related to how frequently some websites were reported as used. For example, Table 3 shows that Skype was reported by 18% of the participants working primarily from home offices and by only 3% of the participants working primarily from company offices. Facebook was reported as being important for work by 23% of participants working for companies with 1,000 employees or less and only 8% of employees from companies with more than 1,000

employees. Other sites, such as Google Calendar were reported as being valuable for work by almost the same percentage of participants at each work location.

Table 3. Percent of participants reporting specific sites as valuable for work by primary work location

	Participant primary work location	
	Home office	Company office
Google Calendar	27%	25%
Twitter	12%	**21%**
Facebook	6%	**18%**
Linked In	**30%**	21%
Google Docs	**27%**	20%
Skype	**18%**	3%

Similarly, participants working for companies with 1,000 employees or less reported Google Calendar and Basecamp significantly more frequently than employees working at companies of more than 1,000 employees. Google Calendar was reported by 31% of participants from companies of 1,000 employees or less and by 10% of participants from companies of over 1,000 employees. In addition, 15% of participants from companies with less than 1,000 employees and 0% from companies with more than 1,000 employees reported Basecamp as important to work.

These results demonstrate that the value of PAOSs is not the same for all knowledge workers and therefore a more nuanced study of the use of social media sites is needed. Our study shows that some social media sites hold greater value for employees that work from home as well as employees working at companies smaller than 1,000 employees when compared to employees who work primarily from company offices and employees that work at very large companies. However, to date, the vast majority of the research into the value of social media for knowledge workers has been done at companies of well over 1,000 employees.

4.2 Frequently reported sites and their service genres

The genres of services offered through PAOSs were identified in [9] and validated in [5]. This report continues this prior research by examining the genres of services offered through the sites that participants frequently reported as valuable to their work. Table 4 shows that many of the sites reported by more than 6% of participants offer multiple service genres. Facebook and Flickr offer the most service genres with 6. And 6 of the 12 sites reported by more than 6% of participants offer 2 or fewer of the service genres identified in [9].

Google Calendar and Google Docs offer only knowledge transactors, offering no other service genres defined in [9]. However, these sites were reported by over 20% of participants as being valuable for use. This points to the potential for adding more service genres in the future.

Table 4. Sites reported by more than 6% of participants and the genres of services they offer

Site	# of services	Services
Facebook	6	knowledge transactor media sharing tool microblog network creator social marking tool synchronous interaction tool
Flickr	6	asynchronous forum blog knowledge transactor media sharing tool network creator social marking tool
Twitter	4	media sharing tool microblog network creator social marking tool
Linked In	3	microblog network creator social marking tool
Basecamp	3	asynchronous forum knowledge transactor media sharing tool
Wordpress	3	blog knowledge transactor social marking tool
Wikipedia	2	knowledge transactor wiki
Google Reader	2	knowledge transactor social marking tool
Dropbox	1	media sharing tool
Skype	1	synchronous interaction tool
Google Calendar	1	knowledge transactor
Google Docs	1	knowledge transactor

In addition, some genres of services were offered by many of the frequently reported sites while other genres of services were offered through only 1 of the frequently reported sites. Table 5 shows the list of service genres and the number of frequently reported sites through which they were offered. As is expected, knowledge transactors (described earlier as a social component of a site that is not described in another existing genre category) were offered through the most sites, with 8 out of 12 sites offering social aspects of their site that have not yet been defined through another genre. Examples of the knowledge transactors that were found during our analysis include Flickr's app garden that allows users to create apps and share them with other users as well as Flickr's mapping feature, which allows users to share information

about where their pictures were taken. An event coordination capability was included in Basecamp, Facebook, and Google Calendar and was the only type of knowledge transactor that occurred in more than two of the frequently reported sites.

Social marking tools were offered second most frequently with 6 of the 12 frequently reported sites including social marking. Media sharing tools were offered third most often, with 5 of the 12 frequently reported sites including media sharing. Wiki services were offered the least frequently with a wiki being offered through only one of the most frequently reported sites.

Some services were typically offered through the most frequently reported sites in pairs. For example, in every instance of a site offering a microblog, the site also offered a network creator. These sites are Twitter, Facebook, and LinkedIn. This illustrates that microblogs are typically used to share information with a network that has been created by the user. Flickr is the one site that offered a network creator, but not a microblog. This potentially demonstrates that creating a network has value outside of sharing small messages through a microblog.

Table 5. Service genres and the number of top-reported sites they are offered through

Service genre	Number of sites
Knowledge transactor	8
Social marking tool	6
Media sharing	5
Network creator	4
Microblog	3
Asynchronous forum	2
Blog	2
Synchronous interaction tool	2
Wiki	1

In addition, among the most frequently reported sites, network creators, are always paired with at least one form of social marking tool. This may indicate that the value of network creators is related to their ability to see how the members of their network have rated or tagged the information made available through the site. However, among the most frequently reported sites, network creators are not always paired with media sharing tools. In the case of LinkedIn, users can create networks, post status updates through a microblogging tool, and then "like" the status through a social marking tool; however, media sharing is not available.

Both of the sites that offer blogs (Flickr and Wordpress) also offer social marking tools. And media sharing tools and social marking tools are frequently paired with services; for example, network creators in Facebook and Twitter. Figure 2 shows a diagram of network creators and the three other services that they are paired with regularly in the most frequently reported sites.

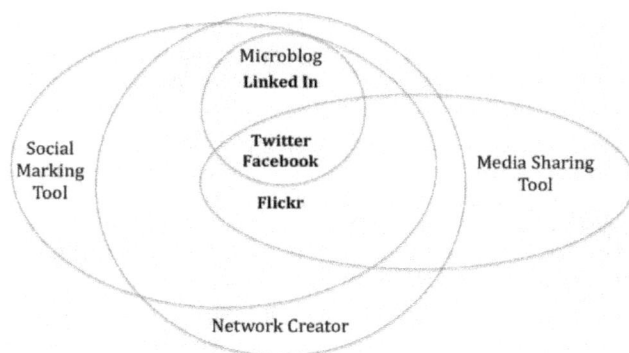

Figure 2. The sites that offer network creators and their relationships to three other service genres

5. DISCUSSION

Our discussion addresses both our findings related to the types of sites that were frequently reported by survey participants and the services available on those sites.

5.1 Sites

Researchers and organizations alike are working to figure out ways to leverage social media to support the day-to-day work of knowledge workers. As the work of knowledge workers becomes increasingly distributed, the need to collaboratively develop and exchange information grows.

As our survey indicates, many knowledge workers are using PAOSs for work purposes in some fashion. However, over 65% of the knowledge workers we surveyed (participants from technology-oriented online groups) use PAOSs for 20% or less of their workweek.

Knowledge workers in different contexts reported some sites as valuable at different levels. Specifically, the primary location of the work, whether at a home office or at a company office made a difference as to whether or not the participant used sites such as Skype. And the size of the participant's company also had an impact on the use of sites such as Basecamp.

The value of PAOSs resides in the ability of knowledge workers to leverage a wide variety of resources including experts outside of their own companies. Therefore, studying the value of PAOSs to workers in different contexts (beyond large companies such as IBM and Microsoft) is central to understanding the ability of PAOSs to support the day-to-day work of knowledge workers.

5.2 Services

Analyzing the genres of services offered through the sites that knowledge workers are finding valuable makes it possible to understand the value of social media to knowledge workers at a more detailed level. Recently Archambault and Grudin have reported that Microsoft employees are finding it difficult to post information on Facebook, because the user base of the system is so broad almost nothing is appropriate to post. It may be likely that users already appear to be using different social networking services to fulfill different needs [1]. An analysis of the genres of services available through these different sites suggests that it is possible to examine what knowledge workers are finding valuable in a new way. For example, LinkedIn, which has been reported as valuable for work in our survey every year offers a network creator (ability to connect to others), a microblog (ability to post a status), a social marking tool (ability to "like" information), and an

asynchronous forum (ability to join groups and post topics). However, LinkedIn does not offer media sharing or a synchronous interaction tool such as a chat service. Perhaps the absence of these services contributes to the professional perception and value of LinkedIn. Understanding the value of sites to knowledge workers at the service level may improve the design of PAOSs in the future.

In addition, a service-level analysis allows us to examine the value of services in relation to each other. Some services are frequently offered together, which may mean that their value is incumbent on the pairing. These pairings may prove to be important for knowledge workers. For example, in the sites frequently reported in our study, microblogging is never offered without a social marking feature to accompany it.

Analyzing sites at the component level also helps foreground key differences among sites that are considered to be similar and similarities among sites that are considered to be very different. For example, Boyd and Ellison define social networking sites (SNS) as allowing individuals to 1) create a profile, 2) create and share a list of other users they are connected to and 3) visit the profiles of their connections [2]. However, there are many sites that meet this definition that are not commonly thought of as SNSs in the same way that Facebook and LinkedIn are. For example, Flickr and YouTube have the three capabilities identified by boyd and Ellison and yet are thought of as photo sharing and video sharing sites instead of social networking sites. As shown in Figure 2, a comparison of Flickr's services and the services of the other network creators identified in our study, show that Flickr is the only network creator without a microblog. This analysis suggests that an updated definition of SNSs possibly should include a fourth feature, that of microblog.

Similarly, a service-level analysis foregrounds that there are key differences in Facebook and LinkedIn beyond the notion that one is thought of as a socially-oriented SNS and the other a professionally-oriented SNS. A look at the genres of services offered through both sites shows that LinkedIn does not include media sharing, a synchronous interaction tool (chat), or knowledge transactors like event planning or a question-posing tool.

A service-genre level analysis also makes it possible to identify emerging genres of PAOSs as they become increasingly valuable to knowledge workers. For example, in the 2011 survey, Google Calendar and Google Docs were reported by more than 20% of participants as important for work, however, the specific genres of services identified in [9] and validated in [5] do not include a specific service for either of these beyond the relatively generic service, knowledge transactor. Therefore, this analysis suggests that in further validation studies of service genres important for work, specific genres that represent the social services offered through Google Calendar and Google Reader should be identified and validated. This is especially relevant in the case of event planning services, as those were offered in three of the twelve sites reported frequently by participants in this study.

It is important to note that although some service genres appeared infrequently in the list of most reported sites, these service genres may be prevalent in the full list of over 200 unique sites reported by participants as important for work. For example only two sites offering blogs and only one site offering a wiki were reported by more than 6% of our participants. This infrequent inclusion of blogs and wikis is possibly due to the fact that blogs and wikis tend to be specific to industries and disciplines. It is not surprising that industry-specific blogs or wikis are not reported by more than

6% of participants. The blogs and wikis that were frequently reported, for example, Wordpress (one of the sites offering a blog) and Wikipedia (the only site offering a wiki) are broad-based sites that encompass a variety of industries and disciplines.

Another potentially important element of future service-level site analysis is that large companies such as Google are creating loosely affiliated suites of sites instead of integrating multiple services into a single site. For example, Google Calendar integrates with Google Plus such that it allows you to post your status (microblog) directly from Google Calendar, even though you cannot view your postings or the postings of others in your circles through Google Calendar. Therefore, for our analysis we did not indicate that Google Calendar included a microblog and instead suggest that the microblog is an element of Google+. However, in the future these distinctions could become increasingly more difficult to make, especially if other companies follow Google's lead.

6. CONCLUSION

Archambault and Grudin noted that the value of email and IM were not determined through research prior to their becoming pervasive in the workplace [1]. However, because of the complex nature of social media systems and PAOSs, further research can provide insights into the elements that are providing value to knowledge workers in all contexts.

Part of the difficulty in identifying the value of PAOSs for work is that these systems are not primarily task-based (for example, creating a work order or submitting an expense report). Instead, PAOSs are focused on the interactions that take place around these specific tasks. The social media sites that were reported most frequently support connecting and communicating with others in a variety of ways instead of straightforward task-based transactions. In addition, many communication-oriented sites include various combinations of Web 2.0 services that make it difficult to ascertain what specifically is valuable about the system for a knowledge worker.

This study is intended to illustrate that there are important areas of study that are being overlooked by many researchers and organizations. Knowledge workers in different contexts find different types of communication tools valuable. To understand more fully the value of social media to knowledge workers, it is important to understand what elements of social media sites workers value. Future research will include more detailed examinations of how knowledge workers are using the various services offered through social media sites.

7. REFERENCES

[1] Archambault, A., and Grudin, J. "A longitudinal study of Facebook, Linkedin, & Twitter use." *CHI*, 2012, 2741-2750.

[2] boyd, d. m., and Ellison, N.B. "Social Network Sites: Definition, History, and Scholarship." *Journal of Computer-Mediated Communication* 13.1, 2007, 210-230.

[3] Bradner, E., Kellogg, W.A., Erickson, T. "The Adoption and Use of 'Babble': A Field Study of Chat in the Workplace." *ECSCW*, 2002, 139-158.

[4] Brzozowski, M. J., Sandholm, T., and Hogg, T. "Effects of Feedback and Peer Pressure on Contributions to Enterprise Social Media Categories and Subject Descriptors." *GROUP*. 2009. 61-70. Print.

[5] Divine, D., Ferro, T., and Zachry, M. "Work through the Web: A Typology of Web 2.0 Services." *SIGDOC*. 2011. 121-127.

[6] DiMicco, J. M. and Millen, D.R. "Identity management: multiple presentations of self in Facebook." *Group*, 2007, 383-386.

[7] DiMicco, J. M., et al. "Motivations for social networking at work." *CSCW*. 2008. 711-720.

[8] Efimova, L. and Grudin, J. "Crossing boundaries: A case study of employee blogging." *HICSS*. 2007. 1-10.

[9] Ferro, T., and M. Zachry. "Networked knowledge workers on the web: An examination of trends 2008 - 2010." *Handbook of Research on Business Social Networking: Organizational, Managerial, and Technological Dimensions*. Ed. M. M. Cruz-cunha. Business Science Reference, 2011.

[10] Grudin, J. and Poole, E. S. "Wikis at work: success factors and challenges for sustainability of enterprise Wikis." *Proc. WikiSym*, 2010, 1-8.

[11] Half, R. "Whistle-but don't tweet- while you work." *Robert Half Technology*. 2009.

[12] Holtzblatt, L. J., Damianos, L.E., and Weiss, D. "Factors impeding Wiki use in the enterprise: a case study." *Extended Abstracts CHI*, 2010, 4661-4676.

[13] Morris, M. R., Teevan, J., and Panovich, K. "What do people ask their social networks, and why? A survey study of status message Q&A behavior." *CHI*, 2010, 1739-1748.

[14] Richter, A., and Riemer, K. "Corporate Social Networking Sites – Modes of Use and Appropriation through Co-Evolution." *ACIS*. 2009. 1-10.

[15] Sellen, A. J., Murphy, R., and Shaw, K.L. "How knowledge workers use the web." *CHI*, 2002, 227-234.

[16] Skeels, M. M. and Grudin, J. "When social networks cross boundaries: a case study of workplace use of Facebook and Linkedin." *Proc. Group 2009*, ACM Press (2009), 95-104.

[17] Spinuzzi, C. "Guest Editor's Introduction: Technical Communication in the Age of Distributed Work." *Technical Communication Quarterly*, 16.3 (2007): 265-277. Print.

[18] Yardi, Sarita et al. "Blogging at Work and the Corporate Attention Economy." *CHI*. 2009. 2071-2080. Print.

[19] Zhang, J., Qu, Y., Cody, J., Yuling, W. "A case study of micro-blogging in the enterprise: use, value, and related issues." *CHI*, 2010, 123-132.

[20] Zhao, D. and Rosson, M.B. "How and why people Twitter: the role that micro-blogging plays in informal communication at work." *GROUP*, 2004, 243-252.

Designing an Enterprise Social Tool for Cross-Boundary Communication, Coordination, and Information Sharing

Cleidson R. B. de Souza[1], Claudio S. Pinhanez, Victor F. Cavalcante, Fernando Aluani,
Vinicius Daros, Danilo Ferreira, Rogério de Paula

IBM Research Brazil
Rua Tutóia, 1157
São Paulo, SP, Brazil, 04007-005

cleidson.desouza@acm.org, {csantosp, victorfc, fealuani, vdaros, daniloff, ropaula}@br.ibm.com

ABSTRACT

This paper discusses the design of a social tool for cross-boundary communication, coordination, and information sharing in a large organization. Based on insights and requirements gathered in qualitative and quantitative studies conducted within the organization, the Live Corkboard, a virtual message board system enhanced with community features and text/history search is proposed as a tool to enhance communication, group awareness, and information sharing and reuse. We describe the requirements for our tool as well as how they influenced our design. The research was conducted in a large IT services delivery company which has recently changed its organizational structure from a customer-centered to a competency-centered model. Focus group evaluation results suggest that the tool will be useful to the employees in the organization.

Categories and Subject Descriptors

H.5.3 Group and Organization Interfaces.

Keywords

IT service delivery; cross-boundary communication; cross-boundary coordination; message boards; knowledge sharing; collaboration.

1. INTRODUCTION

In spite of many attempts to rethink the organizational structure of firms, most large-scale organizations are still structured in a hierarchical fashion. However, organizations today also need to be highly adaptable, innovative, integrated, and often, global [1]. Information and knowledge have to migrate to and from different organizational "silos". According to Scott [3] *"In situations of heavy information flow, the development of more direct lateral connections across work groups and departments is an obvious response. That is, lateral connections allow information to flow more directly among participants in interdependent departments or work groups, rather than up and over through hierarchical channels."*

Effectively supporting that information flow has been the subject of many studies [2, 3, 4, 5]. In fact, different approaches have been proposed ranging from task forces, project teams, and matrix

structures [3] to, more recently, social media [6] and social networks [8].

However, most studies [35] focus on examining how users adopt *existing* social tools (e.g., Twitter, blogs, etc) or how such tools can be enhanced with new techniques [36]. To the best of our knowledge, only a few papers describe the design of new social tools [37]. Even fewer papers can be found describing new social tools to address real-problems in the organizations. Accordingly, our paper tries to bridge this gap by reporting the motivation, design, prototype, and evaluation of the *Live Corkboard*, a social tool to facilitate cross-boundary communication, coordination, and information sharing among employees of a large IT service organization. We place particular emphasis on the motivation and how it influenced our design decisions. Note that the boundaries in this case are both organizational (employees from one department need to interact and share information with members of other departments), and geographical (employees are spread in different sites).

One of the key aspects of this work is the focus on an information technology (IT) *service factory*, that is, a large-scale IT service operation where hundreds or even thousands of support personnel take care of a network of thousands of servers, routers, and other IT equipment, often from multiple customers at the same time. We use the term factory purposely to reflect the fact that those organizations borrow a great deal of structural resemblance to traditional manufacturing factories. Employees from IT service factories have specialized skills and their jobs often focused on specific tasks that are repeated exactly many times a day. In particular, we look at a group of professionals referred to as system administrators, a.k.a. *sysadmins* or SAs, who are responsible for maintaining the customers' IT infrastructures running well and efficiently. Despite the specialization, the work of sysadmins is highly dynamic, collaborative, and interdependent [7]. Improving cross-boundary communication, coordination, and information sharing among them is the main objective of the efforts described herein.

The paper thus starts off describing the large IT service factory for which we designed our social tool, Live Corkboard. It focuses on sharing information about customers that came out from our research as one of the greatest challenges of the organization. It follows by describing qualitative and quantitative studies, which unearthed critical insights, use case scenarios, and the

---

---

[1] Cleidson de Souza is currently at the Federal University of Pará and the Vale Institute of Technology – Sustainable Development.

requirements needed for the design of the tool. We then discuss how these affected the design of the tool's prototype, influencing us to use the message board metaphor. This prototype was then evaluated by sysadmins in a process that in turn deepened our understanding of the coordination issues in the IT service factory. We conclude by discussing the findings in light of organizational and collaborative systems theory.

2. THE BIG SERVICE FACTORY (BSF)

For confidentiality reasons, we call the service factory we studied *Big Service Factory* (BSF). The BSF offers first-class service quality level, which places it among the top IT service providers in the world. In fact, it provides IT services for a wide range of organizations by means of outsourcing contracts in the U.S., Europe, and Latin America. In this paper, we call these organizations simply as customers of the BSF. The size of service coverage ranges from dozens to thousands of IT components.

2.1 The BSF's Organizational Structure

Traditionally, BSF's departments were structured according to customer, i.e., a given sysadmin would work only for a particular customer. The advantage of this approach is that employees more easily understand the important IT components and the IT architecture of the customer to which they deliver services. The disadvantages of this approach were, on the other hand, the inability to achieve economies of scale by means of sharing resources among customers, and the fact that technical knowledge was often not shared across those departments.

Because of the highly competitive market and aiming at economies of scale, about seven years ago, the BSF organizational structure was changed to departments organized according to technical competencies. That is, the organization moved from a product to a process organization [3]. Each department is now based on common skills, competencies, and activities performed. Two examples of departments are: *UNIX*, responsible for dealing with issues on UNIX-based server systems; and *security*, responsible for accountability, security updates, and similar issues in different types of operating systems. In the BSF, there are about 40 different technical departments.

The BSF implements almost all the principles proposed by the *Information Technology Infrastructure Library* (ITIL) [9] framework for IT organizations, the most important standard for the industry. The departments aforementioned (UNIX, security, etc) are those responsible for handling incidents, where an incident is defined as "*any event which is not part of the standard operation of a service and which causes, or may cause, an interruption to or a reduction in the quality of that service*" [9]. Each incident is managed via an IT object often referred to as a ticket, which aggregates all the key information about the incident. There are also departments responsible for process support: *Change Management, Process Management*, and more. For more details, see the ITIL framework [9]. In addition, traditional sales and marketing department in charge of bringing in new customers or selling additional services to current customers also exist at BSF. Within this department, a group of employees, dubbed *customer team*, is responsible for managing the overall relationship with the customer. They interact with BSF employees and customers, negotiating prices, contracts, and monitoring the quality of the services delivered.

Finally, it is important to mention that most BSF employees are spread in two different sites about 100 kilometers apart from each

other. Members of the technical and support departments are located in one large site, while some members of the customer teams work in a smaller site, closer to the sales and marketing organization. Also, some members of the customer team work geographically collocated with their customers. In other words, BSF employees are spread across many different sites, making face-to-face communication often quite difficult.

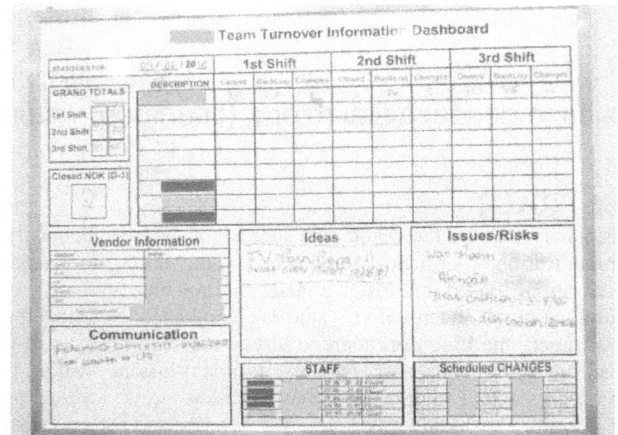

Figure 1 - Example of a Visual Board.

2.2 The Lean Service Delivery (LESD) Model

The BSF organization moved from a product to a process organization [3] when it adopted a new service delivery model referred to in this paper as the Lean Service Delivery (LESD) model. This model is a set of delivery practices based on Lean principles [10], which aim to enable a consistent delivery of high-quality services at even more competitive prices. One of the main aspects of this model is the standardization of delivery processes. This is done by means of pooling, i.e., the usage of shared resources "*to enable better utilization of skills and overall resources while simultaneously reducing average service times and response times*" [Fieldnotes from March, 2011]. In the LESD model, delivery centers are organized in "pools" of customers, meaning that an employee delivers services for a group of as many as 30 different customers. This should be contrasted with the previous organizational structure in which a sysadmin worked only for a single customer.

To centralize the knowledge specific to particular customers, the LESD model proposes the role of *customer experts* (CEs), responsible for understanding in greater detail the IT environment and the organizational structure of these particular customers. Given the large number of customers, some BSF employees are CEs for up to 5 different customers.

Another aspect of the standardization is the creation of roles. Within each department, BSF sysadmins are classified in three levels according to their expertise. But the key role created by the LESD is of the *dispatcher*, who is the person within a pool whose primary job is to monitor all tickets coming in and manage their assignment, progress, and completion. To do so, she has to segment these tickets into distinct groups according to their type and complexity. She then assigns these tickets to the sysadmins who meet technical expertise requirements.

LESD model also suggests *collocation*, i.e., all team members of the same department are encouraged to be located in the same geographical location to improve knowledge sharing and real-time problem solving, as well as to foster an apprenticeship approach for training and skill building. Following the Lean traditions, the LESD model suggests the usage of visual management systems [Fieldnotes from September, 2011]. At BSF, visual management systems are implemented as *visual boards*, consisting of whiteboards with key metrics posted visibly to all members of the pool and including information such as backlogs (i.e. tickets to be resolved), some exceptional events, team status, and the like. According to LESD internal guidelines:

> *"An effective visual board contains a useful mix of quantitative and qualitative information to help manage the pool. It stresses things that are important to customers, pool staff, and BSF. The team should be involved in the items displayed as well as in the analysis and discussion of the information."*

An example of a visual board is presented on Figure 1.

3. COMMUNICATION, COORDINATION AND CUSTOMER KNOWLEDGE PROBLEMS AT BSF

The problem of cross-boundaries communication and coordination came out of a qualitative study on service quality we conducted with the sysadmins from the BSF organization. The results of the qualitative study suggested the need of a quantitative study to better understand some key issues. The main activities of these two studies are described next.

3.1 Identifying the Problem

The qualitative approach used in this study consisted of an initial set of 12 unstructured and semi-structured interviews [11] and about 6 hours of non-participant observation [12] conducted over a period of one and half months in 2010. In this period, employees of different departments of the BSF and from different organizational positions were interviewed. The observations were conducted on sysadmins. Our interviews were open-ended and asked participants to describe some of the problems they see in their work. Observations focused on the collaborative work of sysadmins, the context of work during the daily delivery of services, and the usage of tools.

Based on the analysis of the data we collected, we identified a number of different issues. Among them, one of the problems reported by different informants was the difficulty of coordinating cross-department work, i.e., how the LESD model did not predict mechanisms to facilitate the communications and coordination across the different departments; and how the growth of the BSF organization increased this problem. There were also reports that the organization was "losing" critical specific knowledge about the customers' IT infrastructure and organization.

3.2 Validating the Problem

To validate the aforementioned problems, we conducted a series of eight semi-structured interviews [11] with senior personnel, including deployment leaders for the LESD model, managers, and mid-level executives in the organization. The problems of cross-boundary communication and coordination and the "loss" of customer-knowledge were regarded as highly relevant for the organization.

While carrying out the qualitative study, we became aware of an effort from senior management proposing solutions to the "loss"

of customer knowledge. We then acted as participant observers [12] in the meetings related to this effort, which did not produce effective results. Later on, we learned about another study conducted by a different group of researchers focused on four other IT service facilities of the BSF across different parts of the globe. One of the results of this study was also that customer knowledge and cross-department communication and coordination were major problems that were aggravated by the adoption of the LESD model.

3.3 Understanding the Coordination Problem

Having confidence that the problems we were tackling were highly relevant to the organization, we conducted 12 additional unstructured interviews [11] and more than 24 hours of non-participating observation [12] in the following months. Our goal was to deepen our understanding on how sysadmins communicate and coordinate their work. The data collection is next presented as vignettes[2].

Vignette 1:

> *"Frank is a sysadmin that works in the Intel department. A ticket from a particular customer has just been assigned to him by the dispatcher. This customer is problematic [...]. The description of the ticket mentions that a particular server is not very responsive. He runs some scripts and thinks that the problem is in the connection link to that server. This means that this ticket should not be handled by his department, but by another department. So, he "sends" the ticket to this other department only to later take notice of a similar ticket (unresponsiveness on a different server) for this same customer. The first ticket is sent back to him because the other department did not find any problem with the connection link. He discusses with his colleagues and finds out that, apparently, there has been a recent change in this customer's network configuration. No one is sure about it, but they all agree that this might be the cause of the problem in these two servers. He tries to talk to the CE of this customer from his department, but the person is not available. He calls the customer who reported the problem, who tells him that other locations are also reporting similar problems on their servers. After interacting with several other people, he is finally informed that indeed another sysadmin had made changes in the customer network environment and that this change was the root-cause of the problems he is observing now. So, he adds an observation to the tickets describing the change that happened. Basically, he needs to wait for the other sysadmin to finish making changes in the network environment before doing any additional work on this ticket. Therefore, Frank decides to work on another ticket."* [Fieldnotes from Apr 4, 2011].

There are two interesting aspects worth mentioning in Vignette 1. First, it illustrates the complexity of the work of the sysadmins: Frank needed to interact with five other sysadmins and tried to interact with another two in order to find out relevant pieces of information that could have helped him to figure out the problem.

---

[2] Our field notes were *much more* detailed than what we present here. We summarized them due to space constraints.

While some of these people are geographically collocated (because they work for his department), others are located miles away and working for different departments. Second, it suggests that while the work of sysadmins is segmented by departments, it is highly interconnected: events that take place in a particular department (in this case changes in the network configuration) might impact the work being conducted in a different one (the lack of responsiveness of servers observed in the UNIX department). More importantly, the work practices, work structures, and personnel of each department are *mostly* invisible to the others. Vignette 2 illustrates this problem and its affects.

Vignette 2:

> *"Jake is a sysadmin who works in the UNIX department. He tells that in some cases, the diagnostic of the problem described in the ticket is very hard. For instance, some tickets are initially assigned to a department, but then they are re-assigned to another department because the first sysadmin who worked with the ticket assessed that the ticket problem was associated to that other department. The second sysadmin, after some investigation, realizes that the problem is in fact of responsibility of the first department, so she sends the ticket back to it. The problem in this case is that the "clock is ticking", i.e., now Jake has considerably less time to work on the ticket. He tells me that he suggested to the leader of the Dispatchers to create everyday a collaborative chat with all the dispatchers from the different departments, so that they could avoid this type of problem."* [Fieldnotes from Sep 16, 2010]

Vignette 2 illustrates another key aspect of the cross-department work: the bouncing of tickets, i.e., the fact that tickets might move back and forth between departments until a sysadmin figures out the real root-cause of the problem. This vignette also illustrates how the sysadmins themselves recognized the difficulty of handling cross-department work and even suggested approaches (a collaborative chat among dispatchers) to trying to minimize this problem.

3.4 Validating the Problem in Large-Scale

While conducting the qualitative study, we decided to conduct a quantitative study to gather more information about the issues we identified and to understand to which extent our qualitative results were true across the BSF. In this case, we conducted a survey that is detailed in [13]. For the purposes of this paper, we should mention that we restricted the survey to sysadmins who worked handling tickets. Participants were selected based on a stratified random sampling [14] approach based on the following *stratum*: department, expertise level, and gender.

The survey had 45 questions and was designed to cover two main aspects of the employees' work: their overall daily work and their work handling complex tickets that demand additional effort. We described effort as the amount of mental and physical energy spent while working on the ticket. The survey had more than two hundred participants, which is sufficient to validate our results in large scale. Data from the survey was imported into a standard tool for statistical analysis.

Results from our survey, detailed in [13], suggest that the existent tools to store information about the customers are barely used. Since the tools are problematic, sysadmins have to gather

information about the customer from other BSF employees who have knowledge about the customers, namely the CEs and the customer team. Our results also indicate that *some* sysadmins are potentially overwhelmed with requests for information about the customers, while others do not face this challenge. Finally, we found out that 67,34% of the complex tickets involved more than one department. In addition, 76,42% of the complex tickets involved more than two BSF employees, with up to eight different people involved.

In general, the results confirmed our qualitative results: sysadmins' work is highly complex, collaborative, and requires information from different sources. Some sysadmins are overloaded with requests for information. Furthermore, although there are many different tools to document information about a customer, but the most important information "resource" used by sysadmins are other employees.

It should be noted that the BSF is aware of the cross-department communications and coordination problem and has adopted different approaches to minimize it. For instance, a formal approach adopted was simply to co-locate sysadmins in a single large open space during weekends when the number of sysadmins actively working is smaller than usual. Another approach attempted by the BSF was to strengthen the cross-departmental role of the dispatchers. Because of the routing work they perform, a dispatcher is the only person who has knowledge about which sysadmin is working on which ticket. This means that sysadmins from one department often contact the dispatcher of another to find out who is working on a particular ticket. To facilitate the interaction among the dispatchers, "fake" user ids were created on the instant message tool for each dispatcher of each department as a way to facilitate the access to them. An informal approach was the creation of the collaborative chat among dispatchers as discussed in Vignette 2.

4. THE LIVE CORKBOARD

The results of our study have shown both qualitatively and quantitatively that, given the highly interdependent and complex work performed by the sysadmins, the BSF's current organizational structure, work processes, and tools are insufficient (and often inadequate) to meet the knowledge, communication and coordination needs of the people involved in IT service delivery.

To meet those needs, we are developing and testing a web-based tool to gather, display, and manage information about people and knowledge related to a particular customer. By focusing on a single customer, we aim to virtually "reconstruct" the communication links that were removed when the organization adopted the LESD model. The main goal of this tool is to provide a framework where people from different departments can find each other, share information about on-going activities, and store pieces of knowledge as a result of the interaction among them. In other words, we aim to create a tool not only to facilitate cross-department coordination but also to store and manage knowledge about a particular customer.

4.1 Exploring Options

In the initial design sessions we explored a large range of community-based knowledge management platforms on the Internet, such as *Moodle.com, StackOverflow.com,* and *Answers.com*. However, most of those solutions lacked a good way to providing real-time information about a customer, what we knew from our qualitative and quantitative results was a key issue for better cross-organizational work in the BSF (see Vignette 1).

The most appealing solution coming out from the initial design sessions turned out to be some sort of virtual message board. The most important feature of a message board, in our context, is its ability to communicate with a group of people at the same time and, therefore, to foster *group awareness* [15] and facilitate the collaboration and coordination. The second key feature is *transiency*, the ability to effectively represent an instant of time: message boards can forget things. Previous research [16, 17] has studied many situations where message boards are a key element to promote group awareness.

As mentioned before, the BSF departments already employ physical whiteboards to share information and coordinate their daily activities. Those whiteboards have, however, some important shortcomings which result from the fact that they are physical objects [21, 22]: (i) they require all workers to be geographically collocated; (ii) they do not provide mechanisms for permanent storage of information, or a consistent historical perspective on how the information has changed over time; and (iii) it is hard to perform text or similar searches on the annotations.

In particular, physical whiteboards are not adequate as a mechanism to gather or consolidate information among departments that are not collocated. It is almost straightforward that this particular need suggests a design solution based on an Internet-based platform. We initially looked into solutions based on *wikis*, *blogs*, or *tweets*, which, to some extent, already were employed in primitive forms by the employees of the BSF. The main problem identified with wikis was the easiness in which the information uploaded becomes outdated: it is easy to add new information but there seems to take a lot of good will to remove old information and even more — somewhat surprisingly — to reorganize the content. Indeed, we have found many instances of quite stale content and knowledge about the customers and the service delivery process stored on the wiki-like framework provided by the BSF.

Given the collocation restrictions imposed by physical message boards, we searched and explored platforms for electronic message boards on the web, such as *Spaaze.com*, *Corkboard.me*, and *Posti.ca*. However, in all of the examples we examined, we saw very little support for a key issue detected in our studies: the

need for finding and connecting people. Some of the "augmented" message boards explored by the CHI community [18-22] were also considered but abandoned because of their complexity.

4.2 Design Requirements for the Prototype

Based on the results of this exploration and our study findings, we headed to the prototype design process with the aim of developing a (i) virtual (ii) transient (iii) message board where (iv) people and the (v) main IT components are first class objects with support for (vi) questions and answers, facilitated (vii) communication among people; and (viii) text search and history management capabilities.

The *virtual* requirement addresses the need of sharing information among non-collocated workers. The *transient* requirement relates to the need of representing the situation of the customer in a particular moment (needed in situations, such as, the ones described in Vignette 1) and to the speed in which information gets outdated in this context. As discussed before, the *message board* metaphor explores both as well as the familiarity the workers already have with visual boards in the context of the LESD model.

The importance of finding other people who have information and expertise about a customer was a key issue detected in our field studies, and having *people as first class objects* focused the design process on the issue. Similarly, as we noted before, some of the main IT components, notably servers, not only are the central figures in the incident management process, but often an important source of tickets. Sysadmins talk not only about customers, but also about specific servers and other IT components. Therefore, making certain *IT components as first class objects* was also elected as an important requirement of the design.

The three key functionalities (vi), (vii), and (viii) also came out from needs identified in the studies. As unearthed by the survey, customer experts spend considerable amount of time answering questions from colleagues, so support for both *questions and answers* dialogue and its persistence are desirable functionalities. The survey also pointed out that people spend considerable amount of time trying to find and establish communications, so it is important to have built-in facilities for *communications among people*. Finally, the need for better customer knowledge management, also resulted from our studies, can be partially addressed by adequate *text search and history management capabilities*.

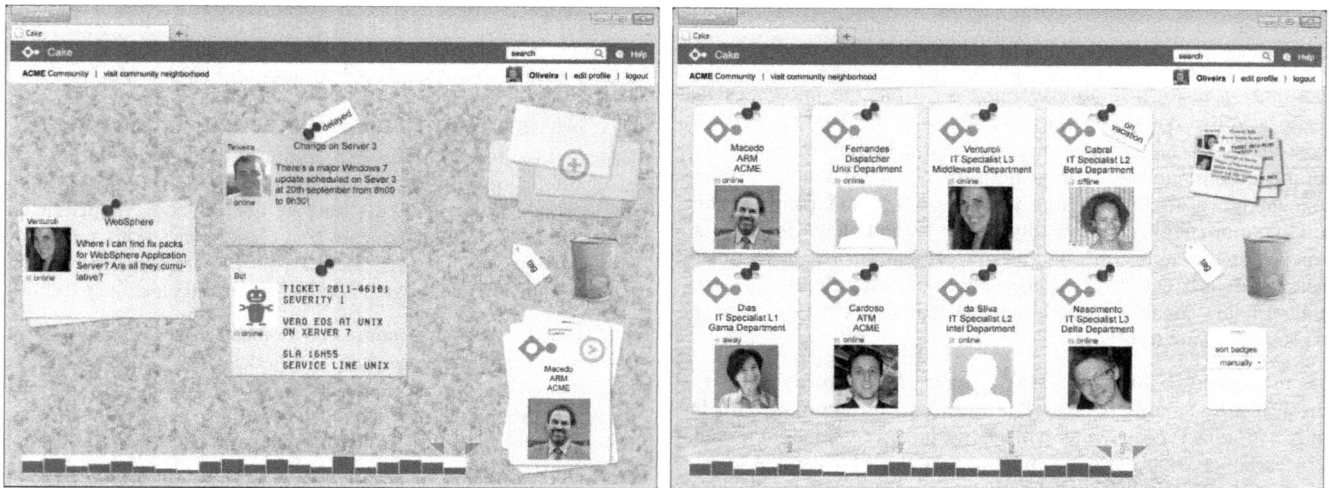

Figure 2. The *Live Corkboard* prototype: a) message posting area; b) community area.

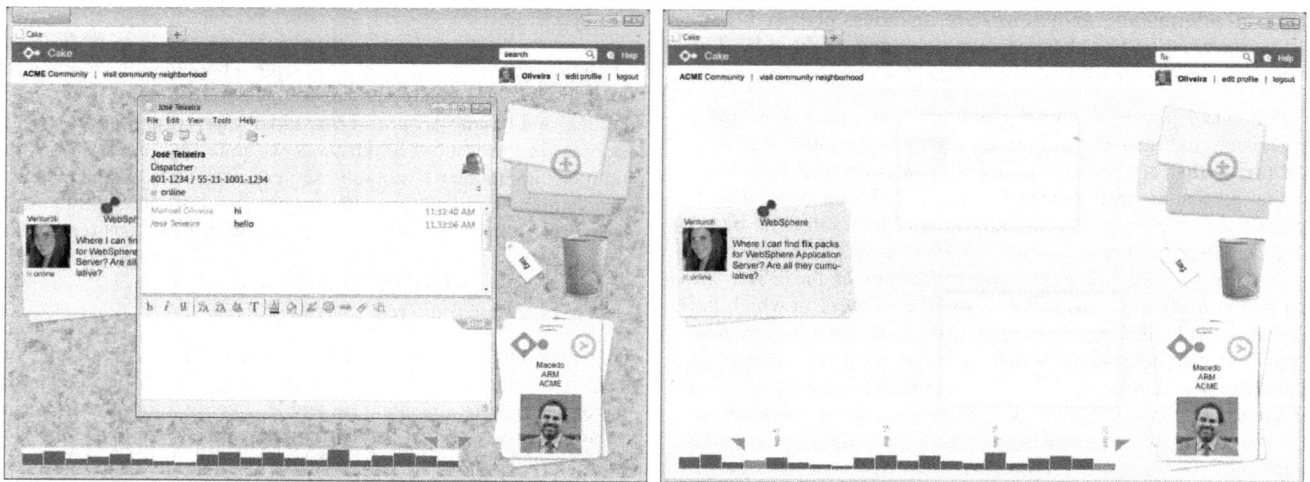

Figure 3. Usage of *Live Corkboard* prototype: a) opening a chat with the author of a post; b) results of a textual search in an interval of time using the temporal slider.

4.3 The Live Corkboard Prototype

There are two basic varieties of message boards, one based on *free writing boards* such as in chalkboards and whiteboards; and *message posting boards*, such as bulletin boards and corkboards. For implementation reasons we decided to design our prototype as message posting board. We had basically an aesthetic reason to choose a corkboard paradigm. As to be described next, since our message board explicitly represents people and authorship, we use the term *Live Corkboard* to refer to it.

Figure 2 shows representative images of the *Live Corkboard* prototype. The prototype consists of two main areas, the *message posting* area (Figure 2.a) and the *community* area (Figure 2.b). The main components of the posting area are *messages*, paper-like notes of multiple colors that contain text and eventually other media, such as, photos, drawings, and video. They are created by dragging them from the pile of blank notes on the top-right corner of the board, followed by typing a message or question. A message has some properties which address some of the needs identified before. It explicitly shows the author of the message through photo and name and can have an expiration date. As in a corkboard, a message can be pinned to different places on the

message posting area, and stacked below or on top of others. This allows the users to easily manage the visual impact of the messages on *Live Corkboard*. IT components such as servers can also "post" messages, which are visually distinguished from human users by a robot-like icon (see Figure 2.a).

To move from the message posting area to the community area, the user has to click on the pile of badges on the bottom-right corner of the message board (see Figure 2.a). The community area (Figure 2.b) uses the visual metaphor of a key hanger where *badges* representing people related to the customer are displayed. A badge includes the name of the person, her role, organization and department she belongs to, and other information. Badges can also be rearranged spatially. To move from the community area back to the message posting area, the user simply clicks on the pile of messages on the top-right corner of the community area.

Both messages and badges can be modified by *tags*, short comments attached to the pins holding them. For instance, a tag can be pinned to a badge with the words "on vacation", as shown in Figure 2.b.

The prototype of the *Live Corkboard* used in the evaluation described in the next section was developed by three people in a month of work using the Action Script 3 programming language. The prototype development was based on Agile methodologies [23]. Throughout the development, weekly meetings were held to determine which features should be implemented on the prototype. In order to guide that choice, three use case scenarios were created (based on the field notes of the qualitative study) defining typical work-flows that users would follow when interacting with the system.

4.4 Use Cases

Use Case 1: As described in Vignette 1, the everyday work of sysadmins often demands them to find experts from other departments and customer team members. The *Live Corkboard* addresses this need by allowing easy visual inspection of the community area and if necessary, textual and/or temporal search, as described later.

Use Case 2: Question and answer is supported by a mechanism that automatically stacks answers underneath the message with the question and allows easy browsing of the answers. Figures 2.a and 3.a show some of those stacks. This feature addresses the issue detected in the survey relative to people who spend considerable time providing information for colleagues. It allows easy recording of Q&A interactions in a non-transient artifact that can be recovered through search. However, since the need of fast and direct communication with co-workers has been repeatedly detected in our studies, we introduced specific functionality to allow the opening of chatting windows directly from the *Live Corkboard*. As shown in Figure 3.a, a simple click on the photo on a badge or message opens a chat window. The availability for status is also displayed close to the photo.

Use Case 3: Text and temporal search is provided by a combination of different mechanisms. Text search is available from a small text input area on the top-right corner of both the message posting and the community areas. After the search is performed, all the messages or badges, which do not match the query, are partially removed from the view. As in Figure 3.b, the messages not matching a query are faded. Temporal search is performed by using the temporal slide on the bottom of both areas. Search can be tuned to specific time intervals, and the results are shown in the same manner as in the textual search. Figure 3.b shows an example where temporal and textual search are combined, resulting in the highlight of only the messages that contain the text and were posted in a specific time interval. Other advanced search features are also being considered, such as, search by role, organization, and the like.

5. THE EVALUATION OF THE LIVE CORKBOARD

To evaluate the prototype we conducted four 1-hour focus groups [24] with a total of six sysadmins of different expertise levels and two dispatchers. The sysadmins belonged to different departments. In addition, four of them worked as CEs for particular customers.

5.1 Material and Methods

Each focus group session lasted for about 1 hour with two or three sysadmins at a time. We initially introduced the prototype with its metaphor and overall ideas. Then, we presented the three use cases described in the previous section. Afterward, we asked the

participants to provide feedback on the prototype. Our goal was to understand to which extent our approach would be useful in facilitating cross-boundary communication and coordination. This was done by exploring how the employees currently deal with the situations that are illustrated by our scenarios. Finally, we asked for other aspects on which we should focus on.

Presentation and feedback were video- and audio-recorded and later analyzed. We analyzed the feedback provided by the informants using grounded theory methods [25] to identify themes raised during the focus groups. These themes are described in the next section.

5.2 Results

When we presented to the participants Use Case 1 (the community area), they positively evaluated this aspect. Indeed, as our qualitative and quantitative analysis suggested, "finding" people is a significant problem in the BSF organization. Given the large number of different customers (close to 100), the study participants reported that even they get confused finding out who the CE is for a particular customer *in their own department* and significantly in other departments. To handle this situation, a database containing the names and contact information from all personnel working in service delivery has been created. Unfortunately, this database is not updated regularly and is not standardized: each department inputs its information in its own way. Therefore, using the database is not as easy as expected. Because of that, sysadmins often directly contact the dispatcher from the department from which they want information.

In addition, focus group participants liked the idea of employees from different departments to share information about customers. For instance, after we described the *Live Corkboard*, one study participant mentioned that information about servers that are undergoing scheduled work or upgrades (they call this "in project") would be very useful for him. For he often receives tickets from servers that are in this situation and he currently spends a fair amount of time working on the ticket(s) until he finds out that the ticket(s) from that server can be disregarded because they are "in project".

Use Case 2 describes a scenario where a sysadmin needs to find out whether a particular server is being changed or not, since (s)he has been assigned a ticket in that server. Currently, BSF employees have two non-exclusive options. First, they can look at the change database that describes all planned changes for a server in a given day. This database contains information about who performs the changes and the exact time they were supposed to start and finish, among other pieces of information. However, unplanned changes are fairly common because of the complexity of customers' IT environments. The second option is to ask the CE of the customer to which the server belongs. During the focus group, we learned that a CE for a particular customer might change in a one or two-month period[3]. In short, finding out whether a particular server is being changed or not is a complex task that requires sysadmins to inspect databases and interact with a couple of people. In *Live Corkboard*, this situation could be handled in at least two different ways. First, a user could simply

---

[3] The reasons for changing a CE are diverse. For instance, a customer might decide to upgrade its IT environment. In this case, a more experience CE might be assigned to that customer to help with this transition.

visit the community area to find out who the CE of a particular customer is and then contact her. Second, a user could post a question on *Live Corkboard* about possible changes taking place in the servers of a customer. This question will be visible for all sysadmins interested in the customer independently of their departments. In any case, our solution was evaluated by the study participants as very useful and better than the approaches they adopt today.

Sysadmins who are CEs envisioned another advantage of *Live Corkboard* that could facilitate their work. In our survey, we learned that it is not unusual for a sysadmin to have to interact with employees from the customer organization. CEs, because of their constant interactions with customer organizations, are familiar with their technical personnel. Hence, when the sysadmins need to interact with them, they have to ask the CEs for the contact information. According to the CEs, if this information were already available in the community area, this would reduce the number of requests they have to answer on a daily basis.

Furthermore, CEs answer other types of questions and that, often, disrupt their work. Because of the problems on the current BSF tools, CEs might even have to answer the same questions over and over again. Accordingly, the CEs in the study saw *Live Corkboard* positively (Use Case 3) as a way to implicitly, by providing answers to questions, store information that is useful for other sysadmins and, consequently, reduce the burden on them. Moreover, given the frequency of changes in CEs, the study participants saw the storage aspect of the prototype as a way to understand and bring them up to speed whenever they change from one customer to another. It should be noted that CEs already write some documentation about the customers they are responsible for. This is part of their work, so they saw *Live Corkboard* as a way to actually making such information useful to others, in contrast to the current state of affairs where this does not happen. In short, we have evidence that *Live Corkboard* should help BSF employees store and share information about customers.

An interesting theme that emerged from the focus groups was the integration of the prototype with BSF tools and having IT components as first class objects. As indicated in the survey, one of the problems in the BSF organization is the large number of tools used by sysadmins, each one storing different pieces of information about the customer. In using our social tool as the focal point for a customer, to integrate information from other tools was seen as a major improvement in sysadmins' work. The downside of the integration was the scalability of the tool. Given the large number of tickets and changes handled per day per sysadmins, the Live Corkboard might not scale properly. Another aspect of the scalability was the number of customers handled by sysadmins: more than 20. In this case, this would mean more than 20 instances of *Live Corkboard* (one per customer) open at the same time, something that the participants did not see as practical.

Integration of current tools and having IT components as first class objects also mean that it is possible to look at the "history" of a server, i.e., the set of the previous tickets and changes that took place on it, as well as all the fixes and maintenance/improvement procedures performed on it. This was regarded as very relevant since problems on a server often lead to more than one ticket. By looking at a server's history, it would then be possible to find solutions performed by other sysadmins in the past to the tickets they are handling. Furthermore, as we learned in the field study and heard again in the focus groups, a relevant number of tickets result from mistakes or failures

occurred during the processing of a change. Thus, changes performed on a server might lead to tickets on that same server.

6. DISCUSSION

In general, researchers in organizational theory and computer supported cooperative work (CSCW) have long recognized the difficulties of coordinating work across boundaries. Geographical boundaries, for instance, reduce informal communication and, as a consequence, coordination becomes more difficult [26]. Organizational boundaries are by no means different; they require additional effort from actors [3]. Especially in highly dynamic and interdependent environments, *"lateral connections"* [3, 4, 5] need to be established among actors so that they work properly. As we discussed before, the BSF organization recognized this situation as problematic and had been adopting solutions to deal with that.

We designed *Live Corkboard* exactly to address this need of cross-boundary information, keeping in mind the dynamism and complexity of IT service delivery work. Accordingly, one of the important aspects of our design is to facilitate the identification of people associated with the customers, i.e., expertise location and finding [28]. While social networks have been explored to help this task [28, 29], we adopted a simpler approach based on a question and answer paradigm, because it is already employed in the organization. Our approach has the additional advantage of allowing storage and reuse. In fact, the feedback we received from the CEs indicates that this is an appropriate approach. Despite that, we plan to explore automatic approaches like mining the content of tickets [30].

As Grudin pointed out [31], the motivation for using collaborative systems relies on a complex trade-off between the extra-work that collaboration requires and the benefits it provides. Since our prototype is customer-centric, i.e., addresses the customer aspect of the BSF organization, CEs who are "theoretically" the experts in a customer, play an important role in this case. Results from our focus groups suggest that CEs would *carry out* the extra work (posting information on *Live Corkboard*), because they would benefit from doing so by not being disrupted as often by the other sysadmins as they are today.

In hindsight, it is not surprising that the main concern raised in the focus groups was the scalability of our approach, since in IT service factories hundreds, or even thousands, of tickets and changes might be handled daily, in contrast to dozens of surgeries in a hospital [4, 18, 33]. The reason for the smaller number of events in a hospital is the smaller scale when compared to an IT service factory. In general, recent research has shown that scalability is mostly ignored in the design of collaborative tools [34]. There are different ways to address this. For instance, a zoom feature was planned for the Live Corkboard. So, the board area could be much larger than the screen. Another possibility is to augment the tickets with "social information" about other BSF employees who, for instance, have worked with the ticket or who could potentially be impacted by the ticket. In general, we are exploring possibilities to improve the scalability of our approaches according to our context.

7. CONCLUSIONS AND FUTURE WORK

Cross-boundary communication, coordination, and information sharing has been proving to be a major challenge for organizations of all sizes in their quest for a more integrated and holistic performance. By combining qualitative and quantitative studies followed by an iterative, user-centric design process we were able to develop a social media tool that was positively evaluated by BSF employees. This is our most important contribution: the presentation of the design of a novel social tool, hardly ever found in the literature. Furthermore, we believe that our study presents compelling evidence for the adequacy of this social tool. Currently, we are improving the functionalities of the tool and preparing a pilot deployment to support the BSF employees in the context of a couple of customers. Key issues we are planning to study involve not only the impact of the tool on cross-boundary communication and coordination, but also how to effectively measure this impact. We also plan to explore other contexts where the Live Corkboard can be used as a community platform.

It is important, however, to qualify our contribution considering both the context and the limitations of the studies. First, IT service factories are a relatively new domain area for research, with a very particular, high-tech population in daily contact with end-users and sales people, so we are still experimenting with and learning about the best tools to apply in this context. Second, cross-boundary communication and coordination are considered in the context of customer knowledge, which adds significant external, uncontrollable elements to the problem.

REFERENCES

[1] Palmisano, S. F. The Globally Integrated Enterprise. Foreign Affairs 85, 3 (2006), 127-136.

[2] Thompson, J. D. (1967): Organizations in Action. New York: McGraw-Hill.

[3] Scott. R. W. Organizations: rational, natural, and open systems. 5. ed. New Jersey: Prentice Hall, 2003. 430 c.

[4] Faraj, S., & Xiao, Y. (2006). Coordination in Fast-Response Organizations. *Management Science*, *52*(8), 1155-1169.

[5] Kellogg, K. C., et al. (2006). Life in the Trading Zone: Structuring Coordination Across Boundaries in Post-bureaucratic Organizations. *Organization Science*, *17*(1), 22-44.

[6] Zhao, D., Rosson, M. B. 2009. How and why people Twitter: the role that micro-blogging plays in informal communication at work. In Proc. of GROUP 2009. ACM, New York, NY, USA, 243-252.

[7] Haber, E., et al. (2011). Collaboration in system administration. *CACM*, 54(1), 46.

[8] DiMicco, J. et al. Motivations for social networking at work. In Proc. of *CSCW*. ACM, (2008), 711-720.

[9] http://www.itlibrary.org/index.php?page=Incident_Management ITIL Incident Management - The ITIL Open Guide.

[10] George, M. Lean Six Sigma for Service: How to Use Lean Speed and Six Sigma Quality to Improve Services and Transactions. McGraw-Hill (2003).

[11] McCracken, G., *The Long Interview*. 1988, Thousand Oaks, CA: SAGE Publications.

[12] Jorgensen, D.L., *Participant Observation: A Methodology for Human Studies*. 1989, Thousand Oaks, CA: SAGE publications.

[13] de Souza, C. R. B., et al. Information needs of system administrators in information technology service factories. In Proc. of CHIMIT, ACM, 2011.

[14] Wild, C., Seber, G. Chance Encounters: A First Course in Data Analysis and Inference, John Wiley & Sons, 1999.

[15] Gutwin, C., et al. 2004. Group awareness in distributed software development. In Proc. of *ACM CSCW 2004*. ACM, New York, NY, USA, 72-81.

[16] Bardram, J. E., Bossen, C. A web of coordinative artifacts: collaborative work at a hospital ward. In Proc. of GROUP. ACM, (2005), 168-176.

[17] Whittaker, S. Schwarz, H. Meetings of the Board: The Impact of Scheduling Medium on Long Term Group Coordination in Software Development. *Journal of CSCW, vol.* 8, 3, 1999, pp. 175-205.

[18] Branham, S. et al. Let's Go from the Whiteboard: Supporting Transitions in Work through Whiteboard Capture and Reuse. In Proc. of CHI. ACM, Atlanta, GA, (2010), 75-84.

[19] Ishii, H. TeamWorkStation: towards a seamless shared workspace. In Proc. of CSCW. ACM, New York, NY (1990), 13-26.

[20] Ju, W., et al. Where the wild things work: capturing shared physical design workspaces. In Proc. of CSCW. ACM, New York, NY (2004), 533-541.

[21] Mynatt, E. D. The Writing on the Wall. In Proc. of INTERACT '99, IOS Press, Edinburgh, UK (1999), 196-204.

[22] Voida, S. et al. Integrating virtual and physical context to support knowledge workers. IEEE Pervasive Computing, 3 (2002) 73-79.

[23] The Agile Manifesto.

[24] Krueger R. A., M. A. Casey, Focus Groups: A Practical Guide for Applied Research, Sage, 2008.

[25] Strauss, A. L.; Corbin, J. *Basics of Qualitative Research* (1990), SAGE Publications.

[26] Kraut, R. et al. Patterns of contact and communication in scientific research collaboration. In Proc. of *CSCW*. ACM, New York, NY, USA, 1-12, 1988.

[27] McDonald, D. W., Ackerman, M. S. Just talk to me: a field study of expertise location. In Proc. of *CSCW*. ACM, New York, NY, USA, 315-324, 1998.

[28] McDonald, D. W., Ackerman, M. S. Expertise recommender: a flexible recommendation system and architecture, In Proc. of *CSCW*, 2000, Pennsylvania, PA, USA

[29] Ehrlich, K., Shami, N. S. Searching for expertise, In Proc. of *CHI*, Florence, Italy, 2008.

[30] Anvik, J., Murphy, G.: Determining Implementation Expertise from Bug Reports. MSR Workshop, 2007.

[31] Grudin, J. 1988. Why CSCW applications fail: problems in the design and evaluation of organizational interfaces. In Proc. of *CSCW 1988*. ACM, New York, NY, USA, 85-93.

[32] Dourish, P., Bellotti, V. 1992. Awareness and coordination in shared workspaces. In Proc. of *CSCW 1992*. ACM, New York, NY, USA, 107-114.

[33] Xiao, Y., et al. 2001. Cognitive properties of a whiteboard: a case study in a trauma centre. In Proc. of *ECSCW 2001*. Kluwer Academic Publishers, 259-278.

[34] Costa, J. M. R, et al. (2011). The Scale and Evolution of Coordination Needs in Large-Scale Distributed Projects: Implications for the Future Generation of Collaborative Tools. In Proc. of *CHI*, Vancouver, Canada.

[35] Hurlock, J. and Wilson, M. L. (2011) Searching Twitter: Separating the Tweet from the Chaff. In: *5th International AAAI Conference on Weblogs and Social Media*. AAAI Press.

[36] Chakrabarti, D. and Punera, K. (2011) Event Summarization using Tweets. In: *5th International AAAI Conference on Weblogs and Social Media*. AAAI Press.

[37] Horowitz, D. and Kamvar, S. D. (2010). The anatomy of a large-scale social search engine. In Proc. of *WWW*. ACM, New York, NY, USA, 431-440.

How Accessible are the Voice-Guided Automatic Teller Machines for the Visually Impaired?

Sushil K. Oswal
University of Washington
oswal@u.washington.edu

ABSTRACT

This experience report presents the results of a preliminary user study of the accessibility and usability of a set of automatic teller machines. The purpose of this study was to evaluate the voice directions for operating the machine for their accuracy, completeness, and functionality. A salient feature of the study was that the testing was conducted by a blind user with training in Information Design, Technical Communication, and Accessibility. The qualitative data gathered in this study suggests that the accessibility and usability in the present time voice-retrofitted ATM systems leaves much to desire. In fact, this researcher failed to accomplish most of the planned banking tasks on the four ATM systems tested in this study. The researcher recommends that disabled users must be engaged in the initial stages of designing such support systems so that the accessibility features could be built into the machine interface and less than satisfactory retrofits could be avoided.

Categories and Subject Descriptors

A.0 [**General Literature**]: General – *conference proceedings;* E.m: miscellaneous

Keywords

Accessible design, user testing, usability, automated support systems, visually impaired users.

1. INTRODUCTION

This experience report presents the results of a preliminary study of the accessibility and usability of four automated teller machine (ATM) systems manufactured by the same company to the blind. One purpose of this testing was to evaluate whether or not the voice description of the ATM matched the actual machine because blind users face considerable problems during ATM transactions if they cannot locate various parts and controls of the system. A second purpose was to test whether or not the voice directions for operating the machine were accurate, complete, and functional. In their discussion of online support systems, Selber, et al. (1996) argue that "Evaluating the usability of online support systems should be a central component of the development process..." [14]. According to them, "Usability testing measures user effectiveness and efficiency. At a secondary level, it checks accuracy, consistency, and completeness" [14].

Automatic teller machines are interactive computerized devices for providing customers with an opportunity to conduct basic banking transactions without a human teller in public locations around the clock. Like most other computer devices, they have a graphic user interface for interacting with customers via text and images [3]. At this stage of digital developments, voice-guided systems are considered most appropriate for blind users since many blind adults have no knowledge of Braille. With this limitation in mind, to provide access for a broad section of visually impaired population to the automatic banking services, some providers have retrofitted existing ATM terminals with interactive, voice-guided systems and tactile labels in Braille and raised print. Although automated speech input can provide access to many disability groups, including the elderly and users with limited body movement, who cannot avail the affordances of a voice-guided system alone, such systems have not yet gained purchase in banking business because of their unacceptable accuracy rates for speech recognition and lack of privacy in the public environments in which most ATM transactions take place (Hone, et al 1998 [7]; Noyes 2001 [13]).

This study tested each of the four machines for the commonly performed ATM tasks employing voice guidance and using 11 questions for testing ATM systems from the NFB website:

1. Are you able to locate the headphone jack?
2. Did voice guided information begin upon plugging in the headset?
3. Are areas such as the headset jack, card insertion slot, cash retrieval slot, and receipt printer marked with tactile signage?
4. Are brief instructions provided regarding the location of these items?
5. Do the audible instructions and descriptions match the layout and functions of the machine?
6. Using voice guidance, are you able to verify dollar amount to be withdrawn before continuing the transaction?
7. Using voice guidance, are you able to verify dollar amount to be transferred from one account to another?
8. Using voice guidance, are you able to verify balance status for the desired account?
9. Are error messages spoken?
10. Using voice guidance, are you able to complete your chosen transaction?
11. Please give any comments that you have about the voice guidance system, the ability to verify the transactions or dollar amounts, and/or your experience as to the ATM's usability [12].

The data from this questionnaire is displayed in 4.0 Table 1.

2. REVIEW OF ATM LITERATURE

Researchers in Information Design, Technical Communication, and Human-Computer Interaction fields have emphasized the importance of participatory design, and at times it is almost considered synonymous with user-centered design (Sullivan and Porter 1998 [17]; Spinuzzi 2005 [15]; Johnson, Salvo and Zoetewey, 2007 [8]; Sun, 2012 [18]). Likewise, a body of research exists on ATM system design dealing with issues of access for the disabled from a range of disciplines, ergonomics, software design, and cognitive psychology; however, none of them specifically talk about the application of participatory design approaches (Baber and Noyes, 1996 [1]; Manzke, 1998 [10]; Stern, 1984 [16]).

Small scale studies have been conducted with blind and partially sighted users to test the accessibility and usability of automatic teller machines (ATMs) both in simulated and real life environments. In a study of nine blind and partially sighted users, van Shaikh, et al. simulated a PC equipped with voice as an ATM terminal to test the usefulness of voice messages with and without visual messages on three variables: perceived performance, attitude towards using a voice ATM and attitude towards the concept of a voice ATM [20]. While their blind users found the voice messages helpful, the Chi square tests of the data from the partially sighted users capable of reading 24 point size on a computer screen had neither a negative nor a positive attitude towards the addition of voice messages to visual messages.

Kobayashi, Iwazaki, and Sasaki (2000) conducted a test on their sound-based prototype with eight blind persons; however, their study does not provide exact details of the voice or sound-guided messaging system they employed in this prototype [9]. They also mention that Braille-guided ATM terminals had been tested in Japan but had been rejected because of some mechanical problems. Coventry, Johnson, and de Angeli start their article with the title, Achieving Accessibility through Personalization [5], but finish it with Vanderheiden's (2000) more problematic universal usability dictum which states that designers should "focus on designing products so that they are usable by the widest range of people operating in the widest range of situations as is commercially viable" [21]. We know that meeting the needs of the widest range of population does not mean that all of the features of a system are usable for all people with disabilities. The point is that if a system is not usable by a certain population, it cannot be considered accessible irrespective of whether or not it has all the elements of accessibility or usability required by la or professional standards. In most of the ATM accessibility-related research, it is also not clear to what extent the blind were involved in the testing of devices in design process. Only the Kobayashi, et al. study indicated that they planned to improve their prototype based on the feedback provided by their testers [9].

Similarly, methodological literature about conducting usability studies on human-device interactions in digital environments with blind users is hard to come by at this time. The published accessibility studies referenced above provide little information about the methods employed for gathering user data and the actual role played by the blind. In their article entitled, Methodology and guidelines for the evaluation of accessibility of public terminal devices by people with visual or hearing disabilities: Sound, audio and speech design considerations, Vasiliadis and Angelidis (2005) present the results of their research on the acceptable levels of ambient noise in the vicinity of card-reading devices, such as ATMs and ticketing machines [22]. Though they take human-device interactions involving speech and/or sound into consideration, their method is limited to the study of ambience noise levels and their effects on the user interactions with the accessible terminals. In short, methodological guidelines on the testing of accessible design of digital devices for the blind remain at best scanty. The way twenty years ago, usability engineers had to insert themselves in the software development cycle to regularize the process of designing user interfaces, there is need for accessibility specialists to actively participate in the digital design process from the beginning of the product cycle so that methods for inclusive design and design testing could be developed (Mayhew 2008) [11]. These specialists could also give attention to inclusivity and participation of disabled users in this process.

In the United Kingdom, Royal National Institute for the Blind published a booklet with guidelines on the design of accessible public terminals back in 1997 which has not been updated since 1998 (Gill) [6]. None of the U.S. organizations of or for the blind engaged in research activities have yet published formal guidelines for conducting research on public terminals, such as, ATMs, ticket vending machines, and the electronic kiosks ubiquitous at most U.S. airports. However, National Federation of the Blind website offers a set of questions for an ATM accessibility testing program related to one of its earlier settlements with a manufacturer [12]. This study, in addition to employing these questions, adapted some of the guidelines for designing accessible websites provided by Theofanos and Redish (2003) [19]. They suggest 32 guidelines for designing accessible web pages and at least four of their guidelines are pertinent to the evaluation of the accessibility of interactive public terminals with some contextual modifications: 1) the blind users must understand the voice browser, 2) the commands should be mnemonic and intuitive, 3) provide one website for all instead of offering two separate websites, and 4) use recognizable key words and labels.

The text should be in two 8.45 cm (3.33") columns with a .83 cm (.33") gutter.

3. TESTING STUDY METHOD

The testing was conducted by a blind user accompanied by a sighted assistant. The blind tester sought no sighted assistance until he had made at least three attempts at performing the planned tasks. All the four machines were tested on the same day. Only totally dysfunctional machines were tested on a second day to provide a second chance. A pair of standard headphones was used for following the voice messages from the ATM. The blind user, an expert keyboardist and an average Braille reader, entered his requests manually. Since the user's bank does not offer a voice-guided, accessible ATM location in his area, third party ATM systems were used for this testing. The user had used such machines in the past although this was his first attempt at using a voice-guided ATM in the current residential location. While the blind user tested these machines, the sighted assistant took detailed notes. The user employed the think-aloud protocol as he went around conducting transactions on these machines. Later, these notes were typed into the blind user's laptop the same day. As a back up mechanism, all the think-aloud discourse and the assistant's follow up remarks were also recorded on a pocket-size digital recorder. The assistant's typed up notes were further expanded with the help of the recording to fill in the missing details.

To follow a standardized procedure, once the user and his assistant arrived at their testing location, the tester first examined the surface of the ATM system to determine whether there were Braille labels, tactile icons or graphics which would help him locate items such as headphone jack, card insertion slot and cash and receipt dispensers. Once he found the headphone jack, he plugged in his headphones and tried to follow the instructions consistently.

4. DATA FROM USER TESTING

The following Table presents the complete data from the testing of the four ATMs. All the voice guided ATM machines were supposed to start speech automatically as soon as the headphones were plugged in to the socket. When an ATM did not start voice guided instructions after plugging the headphones into the socket, further testing was abandoned.

Table 1. ATM Data from User Testing

TEST QUESTIONS	ATM Location 1	ATM Location 2	ATM Location 3	ATM Location 4
Can locate headphone socket?	Yes	Yes	Yes	Yes
Did voice guidance start?	Yes	No	Yes	No
Tactile marks on slots?	Yes but not helpful	Yes but not helpful	Yes somewhat helpful	Yes but not helpful
Instructions about slot locations?	No	Not Applicable	No	Not Applicable
Do descriptions match ATM layout?	No	Not Applicable	No	Not Applicable
Can confirm amount before completing transaction?	No	Not Applicable	No	Not Applicable
Can make transfer between accounts?	No	Not Applicable	No	Not Applicable
Can verify account balance?	Yes	Not Applicable	No, not very well	Not Applicable
Are error messages spoken?	No	Not Applicable	No	Not Applicable
Can complete desired transaction?	No	Not Applicable	No	Not Applicable
Comments on overall user experience...	See 5.1	See 5.2	See 5.3	See 5.4

5. QUALITATIVE COMMENTS FROM USER TESTING

Because every one of the ATM machines performed at different levels, the qualitative data from their testing varies in detail.

5.1 ATM Locations

This ATM was located in a noisy bar and restaurant. Even at 1:00 P.M., the place was crowded and many customers participated in rather loud conversations.

As the tester performed a preliminary survey of the ATM, he noticed that the Braille label for the cash dispenser was located on a vertical panel below the waist level. An average height adult had to bend down to touch the text, a highly difficult position for finger reading. The headphone jack, although located in a slightly indented space, was still hard to detect. The numeric key pad was wobbly (probably because of its age) and #5 key had a tiny dot to help in positioning fingers on the pad. ENTER or OK key button had a tiny circle for a "0" which looked more like a degree sign. The CLEAR button had a tiny raised, left arrow which was hard to decipher. The "X" on the CANCEL key was equally hard to read because of its small size.

The card reader slot was hard to locate because of the complicated design of the surrounding space. The two banks of buttons on both sides of the display screen had no Braille or raised print identifiers. Inserting the plug in the headphone jack was difficult because of its location in a tiny slanted well. Only after repeated attempts the headset could be made to function. Even then, the low volume level could not be raised because of the wobbliness of the keys on the overall worn out numeric pad. Because of the barely inaudible speech of the response system no attempt was made to transfer funds from one account to another.

By pressing the arrow buttons at the bottom of the keypad, the user successfully raised the volume but it did not remain stable for the duration of the actual transaction. The volume level went down while ATM checked balance and printed receipt. While the display screen reported that the audio transaction was in progress, the voice directions told the blind user to remove the headphones. In short, the two user interfaces were not in sync with one another. It is also important to note that a display screen would usually prompt the sighted user to decide whether or not they desire another transaction but the speech interface in this context offered no opportunity for another transaction. At this point the display screen continued to function as expected and offered the options of: inquiry, transfer, withdrawal. Upon another attempt, this machine did provide the blind tester an opportunity to make a *balance inquiry* but the volume went down during this operation.

To summarize, it was impossible to hear because of the low volume of the voice guiding system and the high noise level in the establishment. Despite repeated efforts, the volume up button failed to respond. Likewise, it was difficult to read the Braille label for the cash dispenser because the cash dispenser was located below waist level. Besides the low volume, the synthesized voice was also of a low quality, and the robotic enunciation was hard to interpret. The instructions about how to insert the card into the reader slot were themselves poorly worded and difficult to follow.

As a cultural aside, during these multiple attempts, the bar owner came over to the ATM machine and looked over the blind user's shoulder while he was testing the ATM. According to the sighted assistant, the bar owner could see the display screen on the ATM and inquired if the machine was working.

5.2 ATM Locations #2
During the first visit, this ATM terminal was totally Out of Order although the owner had stated otherwise over the phone the same afternoon. At second visit, the machine was functional with the visual display screen but the voice-guided system did not go beyond the headphone insertion stage.

5.3 ATM Locations #3
This ATM machine was located inside a Veteran's facility and the user had to walk approximately one block through a corridor to reach the bar and cafeteria located in the rear of the building. The machine itself is located in one of the back rooms of the cafeteria. The user inquiries revealed that it was a general purpose ATM and none of the Veterans using this machine were blind.

The Braille labels were difficult to read because they were below waist level. The headset jack was not labeled but was located in an indented space. The user could not locate the card slot because of its location in a highly uneven surface design with various curvatures, nooks, and dents. Sighted help was required for this purpose after the first attempt. The audio description of the machine was incomplete. As the user tried to withdraw $40.00, the display screen read "Temporarily unable to process transaction" but no information was provided by the voice messaging system.

In the second attempt the user was able to withdraw $20.00. The cash dispenser on the machine was really quiet and the user did not hear the machine dispensing cash. The audio system provided no prompt for removing the cash, nor did it give a message about the completion of the transaction.

Overall the speech was difficult to understand and the volume was also low even when raised to the highest level. The user was able to conduct some business in this location because the bar and cafeteria were relatively quiet at this time. Again, the blind user had difficulty inserting the card with "stripe up" as prompted. This problem might have something to do with the differing layout and task design of the various hardware pieces of the two ATM Systems. While the ATM machine at Location #1 prompted the user to insert the card with embossed numbers facing to the left down, this machine asked for the magnetic strip right side up; however, the word, "magnetic" was very poorly pronounced by the voice system which added to the confusion. Only after five or six attempts, the user was able to follow the voice system's pronunciation of this word and understand the direction. While the user was successful in making a balance inquiry at the second attempt, he failed to transfer funds from one account to another even after four attempts. During these four attempts, the blind user followed the voice directions meticulously and the sighted assistant monitored the operation closely. The negative outcome in this case was the result of repeated malfunction by the machine. The machine did prompt the user to choose appropriate accounts for transaction and also prompted for a transfer amount

but once the amount was entered the machine did not complete the transaction. It displayed the message, "temporarily unable to process this transaction" but no audible message was provided. The CANCEL key on this machine also failed to respond.

When the user tried to conduct a withdrawal, this machine did alert the user that a fee would be charged for the transaction and processed the request for $40.00 correctly. The machine did not provide any feedback about whether or not the transaction was complete and the user had to depend on his ears when the cash was dispensed. At the end of this withdrawal transaction, the system also did not ask if the user would like another transaction.

The overall voice response to user commands from this system also had considerable lag ranging from two to five seconds. This ATM system was also in poor physical condition. The top half of the ATM tended to slide backward when buttons were pressed on the keypad. The keys on the numeric pad were overly sensitive on this machine and the speech interface provided little feedback. The voice system did not call numbers as they were entered and therefore the user could not determine if the PIN# had been entered accurately. On the other hand, all the information entered by the user was presented on the display screen even when the machine was being used by a blind person with a headset. Generally, the ATM system in this situation, should not display the numbers a user enters on the keypad to protect the customer PIN number from an unauthorized disclosure.

5.4 ATM Locations #4
This ATM was located in an old strip mall with many corridors and poorly designed store fronts in rather confusing hallways. The machine itself was located way deep in the center of the mall.

In terms of the working status of this machine, the visual interface was functioning but the voice-guided system was totally dysfunctional during this visit. No speech was possible even after multiple attempts at inserting the headphone plug in the port. During the second visit, again the visual interface of the ATM was functioning but the audible interface was still not functional enough to permit a transaction. No speech was possible beyond the headset connecting stage even after the headphone plug was inserted in and removed from the port several times.

6. DISCUSSION AND IMPLICATIONS OF THE TESTING RESULTS
A uniform design for all machines can help blind users orient themselves a great deal faster and without a struggle. Unnecessary nooks and corners on the machine surface misguide these users to unusable surface areas. None of the machines followed the Braille labeling conventions applied by the organizations such as, American Foundation of the Blind, American Printing House for the Blind, National Federation of the Blind, and Royal National Institute for the Blind in their devices developed for the blind. Following the standard labeling conventions can also facilitate the training process for new users. This study covered only four ATMs and yet it discovered three different voices in these tests. Since most blind consumers are avid screen reader users, they are adept at following artificial speech but deployment of different speech engines with poor voice quality makes it difficult to

become familiar with any of the ATMs. Use of standardized speech engines and voices can foster better recognition and comprehension of artificially generated speech. Another major discrepancy noticed was with the quick keys for Fast Cash housed in a separate panel located above most of the ATM display screens. None of the machines had voice response systems to interact with these quick keys although they would be quite handy for novice blind users. Both for the sake of equity and convenience, these quick keys also need to be accessible to the blind just the way they are available to the sighted customers.

Every one of the four machines tested also failed to describe one or more physical characteristics, or functions of the system. With one exception, all the other descriptions included some inaccurate or incomplete information. For instance, none of the machines had a Braille label next to the receipt dispenser and the blind user had to depend on the receipt printer's noise to find the printed receipt as a guide. Only one machine had a Braille label for the deposit slot. Since these Braille labels and audio descriptions are central to a blind person's ability to orient one's self in relation to the machine, these descriptions should be designed by a professionally trained technical communicator. All such descriptions also require systematic testing by more than one blind user because different blind users have different skill levels. The sighted testers cannot always be depended upon for accessibility testing because they can unknowingly overlook certain missing or inaccurate details. Their familiarity with the visual design of the equipment and the procedure for operating it can make them perform even poorly or incorrectly stated instructions correctly.

Further, design of standardized layouts akin to telephone keypads, QWERTY keyboards and light switches on set spots, can be quite helpful in assisting the blind users acclimate themselves to these ATM systems. Such layouts will reduce the frustration many visually impaired customers experience when they cannot locate one or the other slot on these machines.

Equally annoying were the different settings for inserting the ATM card into the reader slot for each of the four machines. Considering the difficulty many people with or without sight have in inserting the card correctly in the reader slot, it's curious that no manufacturer has yet employed the automatic image technology common in scanning software systems. While the current scanning software systems are fixed imaging devices, they can be replaced with more up to date, automatic rotation technology. Such an improvement would eliminate the need for a unidirectional insertion of these cards and save the user from multiple attempts.

A standardized overall exterior design for these ATM machines will also go far towards their accessibility to the blind. For example, each of the machines stood at a different height. Likewise, the speakers on each of the machines were located on different spots and none of them were at the face level of an adult user. Their sound quality left something to be desired even for public terminals.

Besides an accessible machine design, the actual location of these ATM terminals in easy to access spots can further promote disabled access. None of the business locations for the four

machines studied had an easy to detect sign with the street address.

7. CONCLUSION

The Cognitive Ergonomist and Engineering Psychologist, Harmut Wandke, (2005) claims that some of the devices and techniques originally developed for disabled users have proven useful for others [23], implying that an average user's needs are not always being met by the assistance built into the standard design for all. While designers discuss a large number of problems responsible for ineffective human-machine interaction including the need for tutorials, explanations, and appropriate language, but rarely do they directly discuss the problems caused by faulty communication or information design whether it is textual, graphic, or voice guided [2] and [4]. It could be asked how an effective design concept is possible without direct input from the disabled users whose needs might be markedly different from an average, able-bodied designer or the composite user persona created by the designer. Even more significant is to build that communication bridge between the user and the digital machine.

8. REFERENCES

[1] Baber, C., & Noyes, J. (1996). Automatic Speech Recognition in Adverse Environments. *Human Factors*, 142-155.

[2] Barnum, C. (2010). *Usability testing essentials: Ready! set! test!* New York: Morgan Kaufmann/Elsevier.

[3] Bowen, J. (n.d.). *How ATMs Work*. Retrieved from http://money.howstuffworks.com/personal-finance/banking/atm6.htm

[4] Butler, K., Esposito, C., & Hebron, R. (1999). Connecting the design of Software to the design of work. *Communications of the ACM*, 38-46.

[5] Coventry, L., Johnson, G., & De Angeli, A. (2002, September 1). Achieving accessibility through personalisation. *Proceedings of the 16th British HCI conference Volume 2 . 2*, p. http://www.antonella_de_angeli.talktalk.net/files/Pdf/Achieving%20Accessibility%20through%20Personalisation.pdf. London: Springer Verlag

[6] Gill, J. (1998). Access Prohibited? Information for Designers of Public Access Terminals. London, UK: Royal national institute for the blind.

[7] Hone, K., Graham, R., MaGuire, M., Barber, C., & and Johnson, G. (1998). Speech Technology for Automatic Teller Machines: An investigation of user attitude and performance. *Ergonomics*, 962-981.

[8] Johnson, R., Salvo, M., & Zoetewey, M. (2007). User-Centered Technology in Participatory Culture: Two Decades "Beyond a Narrow Conception of Usability Testing". *IEEE Transactions on Professional Communication*, 320-332.

[9] Kobayashi, I., Iwazaki, A., & Sasaki, K. (2000). An inclusive design of remittance services for the blind user's operation of Automatic Teller Machines. *Proceedings of the 2000 conference on Universal Usability* (pp. 153-154). New York: ACM.

[10] Manzke, J. (1998). Adaptation of a cash dispenser to the needs of blind and visually impaired people. *Proceedings of*

the third international ACM conference on Assistive technologies (pp. 116 - 123). New York: ACM.

[11] Mayhew, D. J. (2008, May). User experience design: Evolution of a multi-disciplinary approach. *Journal of Usability Studies, 3*(3), 99-102.

[12] National Federation of the Blind. (n.d.). *ATM testing questions.* Retrieved July 10, 2012, from nfb.org: www.nfb.org/atm-testing

[13] Noyes, J. (2001). Talking and Writing-How natural in human2machine Interaction? *International journal of Human Computer Studies*, 503-518.

[14] Selber, S. A., Johnson-Eilola, J., & Mehlenbacher, B. (1996, March). Online Support Systems. *ACM Computing surveys*, 197-200.

[15] Spinuzzi, C. (2005, May). The methodology of participatory design. *Technical Communication, 52*(2), 163-174.

[16] Stern, K. R. (1984). An evaluation of written, graphics, and voice messages in proceduralized instructions. *Proceedings of the Human Factors and Ergonomics Society Annual Meeting*, (pp. 314-318).

[17] Sullivan, P., & Porter, J. (1997). *Opening Spaces: Writing Technologies and Critical Research Practices.* Greenwich, CT:: Ablex Publishing.

[18] Sun, H. (2012). Future directions. In H. Sun, Cross-cultural technology Design: Creating Culture Sensitive Technology for Local Users (pp. 237-270). New York: Oxford UP.

[19] Theofanos, M. F., & Redish, J. (. (2003, November-December). Guidelines for accessible and usable web sites: Observing users who work with screen readers, Reprinted and expanded. *Interactions, X*(6), 38-51.

[20] van Schaik, P., Petrie, H., & Japp, J. (1997). The ATM speaks: the design and evaluation of an automatic teller machine with voice output. In e. a. Anogianakis (Ed.), *Advancement of Assistive technology, (AAATE) Fourth European conference. 3*, pp. 223-227. Burke, VA: IOS press.

[21] Vanderheiden, G. (2000). Fundamental principles and priority setting for universal Usability. *CUU '00 Proceedings of the 2000 conference on Universal Usability* (pp. 32-37). New York: ACM.

[22] Vasiliadis, T. and Angelidis, P. (2005). Methodology and guidelines for the evaluation of accessibility of public terminal devices by people with visual or hearing disabilities: Sound, audio and speech design considerations. *Technology and Disability* 17 11–24.

[23] Wandke, H. (2005). Assistance in human-machine interaction: a conceptual framework and a proposal for taxonomy. *Theoretical issues in Ergonomics Science*, 129-155.

Stitchtures: Interactive Art Installations for Social Interventions in Retirement Communities

Claudia B. Rebola
Georgia Institute of Technology
247 4ᵗʰ St NW
Atlanta, GA 30332 USA
crw@gatech.edu

Patricio A. Vela
Georgia Institute of Technology
247 4ᵗʰ St NW
Atlanta, GA 30332 USA
pvela@gatech.edu

Jorge Palacio
Georgia Institute of Technology
247 4ᵗʰ St NW
Atlanta, GA 30332
palacio.jorge@gmail.com

Gbolabo Ogunmakin
Georgia Institute of Technology
247 4ᵗʰ St NW
Atlanta, GA 30332 USA
gogunmakin@gatech.edu

Chauncey Saurus
Georgia Institute of Technology
247 4ᵗʰ St NW
Atlanta, GA 30332 USA
casaurus@gmail.com

ABSTRACT

The purpose of this paper is to describe the design and development of an interactive art installation, Stitchtures, for retirement community shared common areas. Physical and digital co-design activities are described in the development of an interactive art piece inspired by biological systems and collective behavior. Vision systems are also described for data gathering during implementation. The combined methodologies respond to the specific aims of the project, which investigates the effects of design and technology interventions on aiding interactions among older adults in retirement communities.

Categories and Subject Descriptors

H.5.2 [User Interfaces]: *User-centered design*; H.5.3 [Group and Organization Interfaces]: *Collaborative computing*; I.4.8 [Scene Analysis]: *Tracking*, I.5.4 [Applications]: *Computer Vision*; J.5 [Arts and Humanities]: *Arts, fine and performing*

General Terms

Design, Human Factors, and Performance

Keywords

Design, installation, sensing technologies, social interaction, older adults, retirement communities

1. INTRODUCTION

Addressing interaction in retirement communities' shared areas might bring us closer to understanding and preventing social isolation and loneliness among older people. Interaction with other individuals seems to be a simple activity, but may represent a challenging task for older adults. Shared common areas in

retirement communities are great opportunities for interaction with other individuals. Yet, they are highly underutilized, lacking designs and technologies to promote socialization.

Designing interactive art installations for shared common areas in retirement communities can help older adults counteract loneliness and lack of human interaction. Moreover, they can encourage individuals to more fully utilize their environment and promote interactions with other individuals. An interactive design that benefits and grows from the involvement of multiple people may allow individuals to connect through interactive creation. The purpose of this paper is to describe the design and development of Stitchtures for shared common areas in a retirement community. The specific aim of the project is to investigate the effects of design and technology interventions in aiding interactions among older adults in retirement communities. The significance of this project is to encourage wellness in retirement communities might as a vehicle for promoting independence and quality of life among older adults.

2. BACKGROUND

2.1 Interactions in Retirement Communities

Depression is a growing health concern among the aging population affecting nearly 7 million aging adults in the United States [16]. Data suggests that social isolation and loneliness are the major causes of depression and one of the major factors influencing premature death among elders [2]. As such, depression has been identified by the Centers for Disease Control as one of four areas that should be addressed to improve older Americans' health and quality of life. Several studies have linked depression to two types of experiences: (a) loneliness, which can be defined as emotional isolation and subjective unwelcome feelings of lack or loss of companionship and (b) social isolation, which can be defined as the objective absence of contacts and interactions with a social network [7,17,20].

The Quality of Life-AD (QoL-AD) is a 13-question assessment, which is regularly used to determine an individual's quality of life. It has been found that meaningful activities and relationships were two of the top four factors in residents' assessment of the quality of life in nursing homes [11]. Most retirement communities offer a variety of activities organized by dedicated event managers to improve the quality of life among residents. Even though these facilities afford social exposure, loneliness may still be experienced among older adults [1]. However, Fiveash [9] found that residents are rarely alone yet they feel boredom is a major issue in their daily lives.

2.2 Technologies for Healthy Aging

Nehmer *et al* [13] proposes that older adults can benefit from technologies as much as younger generations so long as certain criteria are fulfilled, such as appropriate cognitive and physical cost correlation to results. These technologies can include devices that require no direct effort from older adults, such as wrist bands that track GPS coordinates to help caretakers locate dementia patients [10]. Novelty is also relevant when addressing technologies. Daffner *et al* [8] found that interest and exposure to novel environments and stimulation can sustain and possibly delay mental decline.

Nature can have a significant impact on aging. Gardening is a common activity considered relaxing and enjoyable for older adults. It has been found that 20 minutes of visiting a garden in a group everyday can drastically increase older adults feelings of self worth and social integration [4]. Ulrich [19] showed that exposing people to unthreatening natural environments could have a positive effect. The study suggests that exposure to natural environments leads to greater recovery of physiological stress indicators compared to those exposed to urban environments.

Additionally, nature serves as a unique source of inspiration. Looking at nature and biological systems in design has led to the development of new practices like bio-inspired design and biomorphism. Santulli [15] distinguishes these two practices by explaining that biomorphism aims at mimicking functions and morphologies of natural structures while bio-inspiration focuses on transferring qualities and strategies inspired by nature through an abstraction process. For example, Pax Technologies used the shape of Calla Lilies to create an impeller that mixes liquids more efficiently and with less energy or WhalePower which designs turbine blades with a leading edge shaped like a Humpback Whale's fin to combat wind turbulence [18].

3. STITCHTURES FRAMEWORK

The overall goal of the project is to investigate the effects of design and technology interventions among older adults in retirement communities, more specifically in common shared areas (see figure 1). With the aforementioned literature, we identified different motivations to develop Stitchtures. One is related to increasing interactions among older adults. As previously described, one of the major problems in retirement communities is a lack of active interaction with other members. Another motivation is related to bringing older adults closer to nature and art. Given older adults lack of engagement with natural environments, the main interest is to develop bio-inspired art as a vehicle for interaction. Lastly, motivating older adults to move is of central importance, as older adults tend to remain in their rooms.

Stitchtures is an interactive art installation for older adults. It is a dynamic piece that encourages older adults to interact with it. As the interaction occurs, the art installation evolves. Consequently, evolution of the art installation is dependent on the interaction of individuals with both single (one individual) and multiple (multiple individuals) contacts. The installation consists of a series of overlapping three-dimensional patterns inspired by older

adult's everyday objects. Interactions with the art piece occur via sensing technologies inspired by biological systems. As individuals approach and interact with the art installation, visual feedback of differing modalities invite, motivate and engage users.

Designing an art installation that operates within this framework responds to specific goals, primarily related to reducing the sense of depression/isolation and facilitating social interactions among older adults in retirement communities. It is hypothesized that designing interactive technologies will facilitate communication among older adult in retirement communities, more specifically common shared areas. The next sections describe the design and development of Stitchtures. Physical and digital co-design activities are described in the development of an interactive art piece inspired by biological systems and collective creativity.

4. PHYSICAL AND DIGITAL CO-DESIGN

Designing an interactive art installation encompasses design in the physical and digital realms. These realms cannot be separated. Instead of foregrounding the creation of interactions and interfaces that map onto and access digital information, there is a need to explore when and how digital computational media can be drawn back to the physical environment and how physical interactions can model digital behaviors [12]. This practice can be referred to as physical and digital co-design. Co-design requires a collaborative and interdisciplinary team. As such, different disciplines including industrial design, human computer interaction, and computer vision were brought together to respond to the needs of designing an interactive art installation.

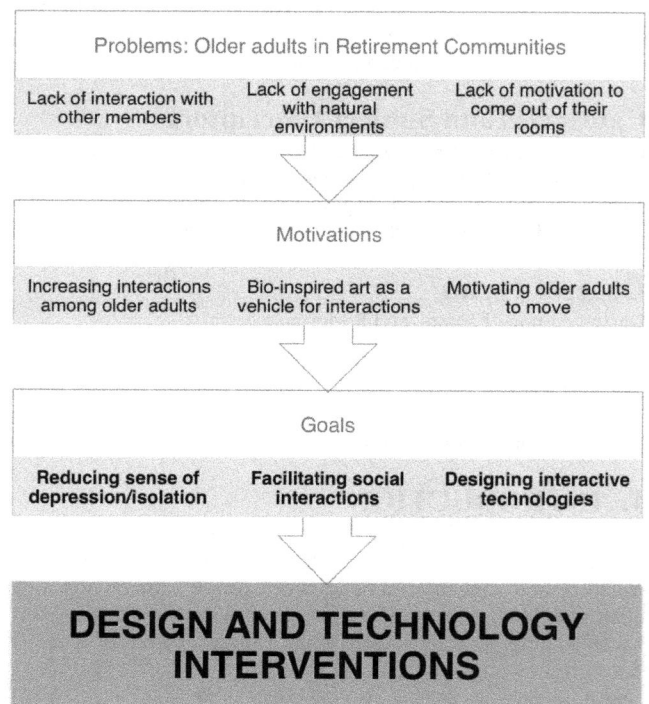

Figure 1. Stitchtures framework

4.1 Conceptual Design Development

Early explorations involved studying how to materialize interactions and how those physical representations can coexist with digital interactions. Initial explorations included developing concepts that addressed the ability for technology and design to contextualize users withdrawn from their surroundings. The focus was on bringing attention to the effect of self-isolation on one's surroundings and helping contextualized users in their environment. During this phase, the team focused on studying examples of interactive art installations that were interactive and reactive. Examples included the *Aperture* facade installation with interactive and narrative displaying modes consisting of an iris diaphragm matrix, whose variable diameter is the main interaction with the piece [14]. Other examples included the *Living Wall* project [5], which aims to create electronically enhanced wallpaper with touch sensors, LED's, and Bluetooth technology, allowing users to touch decorative elements of the wall to turn on lamps, adjust heating, or activate a stereo. Lastly, the interactive wall *Mes Etoiles* was explored as interactivity is triggered by proximity of people to the art piece. The closer one gets to the wall, the larger the number of lit LEDs on the surface, as activated by embedded proximity sensors [3]. All these examples represent a way of using designed surfaces for people to communicate or to build collective creations using their bodies as instruments.

Having examples of interactive art installations, Stitchtures iterations focused on surfaces development. During this phase, patterns were studied to frame the project. Investigation of patterns included developing a moodboard containing references to older adult's everyday objects such as clothing, linens, upholstery, décor, and jewelry (see figure 2). The goal was to lead design decisions around familiar forms while avoiding the presence of obtrusive devices that may intimidate or discomfort the users. This approach responded to the need of bringing about a physical design that was familiar to our end user, older adults.

As the refinement phase of the pattern progressed, a repetitive floral motif emerged, similar to a quilt. Quilts are physical comforters made of repetitive patterns traditionally composed of three layers of fabrics combined using the technique of quilting. Meaning, the joining at least two fabric layers by stitches. This allowed the design be inspired not only to develop a layered three-dimensional pattern (see figure 4) but also to use conductive thread for *stitching* the pattern as a unified installation. Quilts also evoke the idea that users are building this piece by stitching together the sections of a whole. Simultaneously, it also allows the design to be linked to nature by emphasizing the plant and floral aspects of the form.

Digital interactions were also biologically inspired. By looking at nature as a source of inspiration and innovation, the art piece's core idea was framed on behaving like a living plant that requires care and attention (interaction). Through different versions, formal designs were simplified, abstracted and molded individually from natural variations of the Clematis flower (Clematis Vitalba, Clematis Jackmannii, and Clematis Stans respectively). As an integrated pattern, forms were refined by looking at the behavior of the liana. The liana vine uses trees and other vertical support to climb canopies to reach sunlight. This intertwining concept was adopted. The art piece was the designed with growing sections that permanently light up and, like the liana, they go from piece to piece and connect all the pieces as the art piece grows.

Figure 2. Pattern moodboard

4.2 Final Design

The final design consists of several layers containing a total of 52 modular pieces and distributed in a designated area of 97.25x84.50x10 inches from the actual retirement community common shared space (see figure 3). There are three different types of layers, which have a distinctive pattern designs (see figure 4). One of the layer designs covers a grid area of 4x4 modules with 16 modules. Each module is 21.75 x 21.75 inches. Additional layers cover a grid area of 4x8 modules with 28 modules. Each module is 21.75 x 14.75 inches. All modules are cut from transparent acrylic, of which two of the three distinctive designs are white fabric backed. These are attached by architectural aluminum rods, which allow the hard wiring to run throughout the piece. All modules are hand stitched with conductive thread to bring power to LEDs. Each modules hold white colored LEDs.

Figure 3 Stitchtures Art Installation

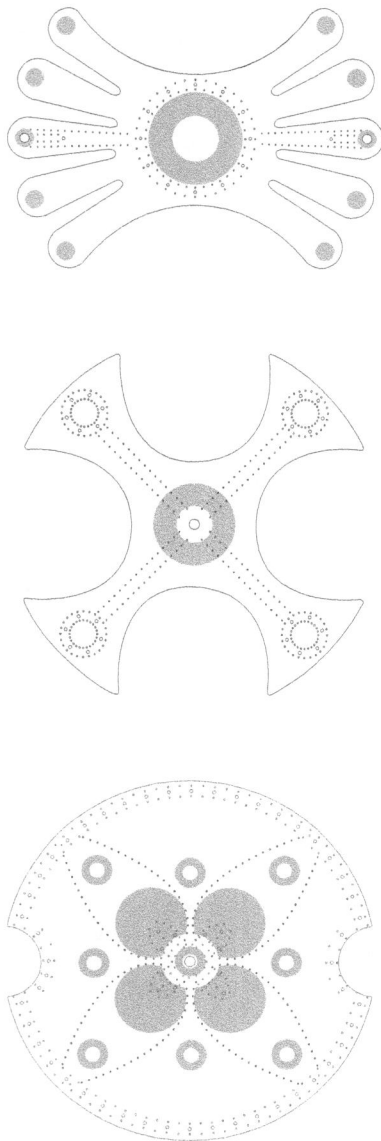

Figure 4. Stitchtures patterns # 1, 2 and 3

4.3 Interactive Technologies Development

To promote a more natural form of interaction with the art installation, the interactive technologies development phase was based on behavioral patterns found in nature connected to communication. For example, behavioral communication patterns were noted in how animals interact at close proximity. As input mechanisms with the art installation, proximity patterns were defined to provide an active area large enough for two or more people to interact with the piece and prevent situations where users get drawn too close to each other that it repels them or too far from each other that they don't interact.

In terms of output mechanisms in the art installation, there was a need to provide an unspoken language that is easy to recognize to the users. Blinking was defined to lure users closer to the piece. Fireflies and how they use blinking lights to lure their mates inspired the design decision. Additionally, the monochromatic

white light and fabric mimics species without defenses that need to blend with the environment [6]. This mimicry creates a more relaxed invitation that uses the idea a defenseless animal to make the piece approachable instead of using the shocking invitation of bright colors to bring users into interacting with the art installation.

The result is an interactive art installation where the only form of feedback is through the use of monochromatic light. Sets of white LEDs accentuate sections of individual modules becoming the voice of the piece. Approximately 2000 LEDs create a series of organic patterns in three types of interactions: *invite, engage,* and *motivate.* Each interaction has its own method of communication (see figure 5).

For the *invite* interaction, blinking is used to attract users to the art installation. Once an infrared range finder detects a user in its 5-meter sensing range, the LEDs on the outermost layer starts blinking (pattern #1). As the user gets closer, the blinking slows down until the LEDs become permanently on.

At close proximity, the piece focuses on the *engage* interaction. This form of interaction is centered on real time feedback that responds directly to users' actions. Phototransistors detect shadows cast by users and immediately respond to the user's actions by creating dynamic light patterns in the back layer of the piece (pattern #2). The more users simultaneously interact with the piece, the more patterns become lit up.

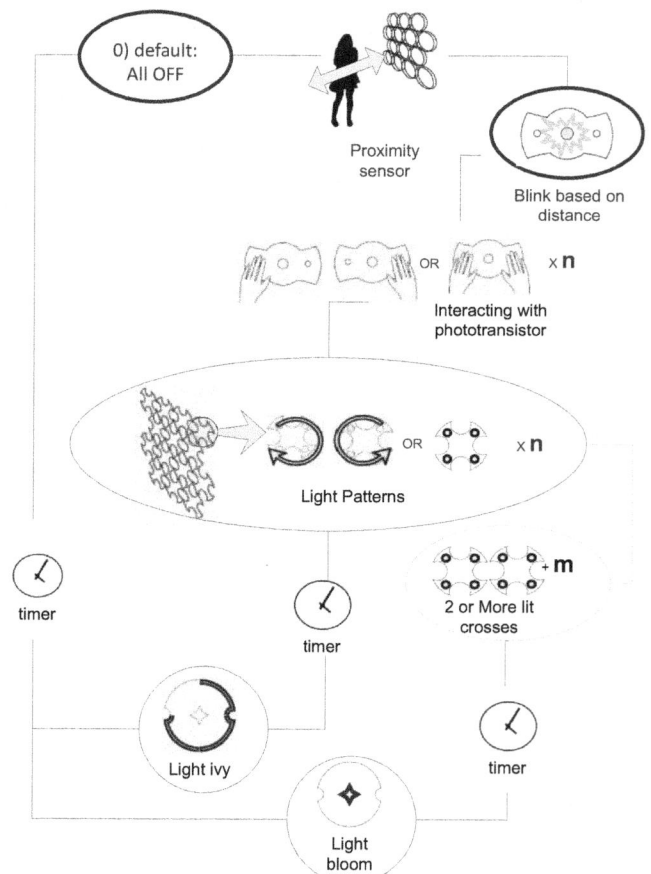

n = number of crosses

m = number of additional cross fully lit

Figure 4. Stitchtures Interaction Map

Finally, to encourage users to continue interacting with the piece, the *motivate* interaction is implemented. Inspired by plant growth, the motivate interaction is based on the amount and type of user input. As users interact with the piece by activating the phototransistors, sections of the last layer (pattern #3) light up. This lit state represents the growth of the plant with ivy like shape. The more users interact with the piece, the more the plant grows and the more sections of the piece light up. To control the growth rate, a timer determines when the next piece should light. The count is renewed when a new section is lit. Conversely, a second timer initiates to control the to decay of the plant, turning off sections when no interactions occur. Additionally, the piece accounts for collaborative actions in the motivate interaction mode by only lighting the center sections of the circles when two or more people interact with the piece. These center sections symbolize the blooming of the flower, a final maturation state that can only be achieved through the concerted efforts of two users.

4.4 Stitchtures Implementation

For the next step of the project, the interactive art piece will be installed at a local independent living retirement community. A vision system will be developed and installed in order to gather data to answer the following questions: *Foremost* is: what are the patterns and communication interaction changes of older adults in retirement communities' common areas under the conditions of the Stitchtures' art piece intervention? *Subsequent* questions are: 1) what is the number of older adults present in retirement communities common areas? The purpose of this question is to understand if- and how many- older adults come out of their rooms; 2) what patterns do older adults follow in retirement communities' common areas? The purpose of this question is to understand how older adults use or locate themselves in retirement communities' common areas; and 3) what is the number of communication interactions of older adults in retirement communities' common areas?

Data collection will be executed in different common shared spaces in different floors of the community. One floor will be used as a control group and another a test floor where the art installation will be installed.

5. VISION DEVELOPMENT

The effect of the interactive art installation will be monitored using video cameras. Cameras will be mounted in positions that allow observation of the area surrounding the art piece. A computer will be placed at the common area location. Additionally, a microphone will be mounted in the ceiling in the center of the common area. All equipment will be used to record, analyze and visualize user behaviors in the environment (see figure 6).

Data from the cameras will be processed using computer vision algorithms. People will be automatically detected by using background subtraction and foreground detection methods. The method used in this case will be a Gaussian Mixture Model (GMM). The background will be modeled statistically using multiple Gaussian distributions. Objects will be declared as foreground if they do not match the distributions of the background. This will create a binary mask that outlines the silhouette of the people in the scene. The foreground detection will be used to create a heat map, which shows where people spent most of their time in the room (see figure 7). Detected people will be tracked using computer vision algorithms. Tracking will allow measurement of how many people are in the scene and

whether they are interacting to quantify the effect of the art piece. Tracking provides the people's trajectories in time, which will provide a count of how many people walk by the art piece without stopping versus how many people stop, plus a count of how many people interact in response to the piece's feedback modalities.

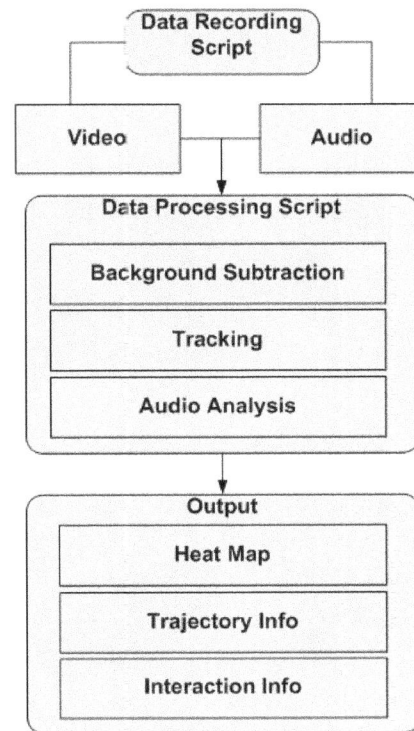

Figure 5. Vision System Overview

Comparison of the count data will measure the impact of the art on interactions. The recorded audio will provide confirmation of the visually estimated interactions. Periods of silence and periods of voice activity will be correlated with the tracking results to determine if there are interactions going on. To do so recorded audio will be coded in terms of presence of sounds or presence of silence. Detection of sound will indicate interaction correlated to visual analysis. Periods of silence and periods of sound activity will be combined with the tracking results to determine the type of interactions occurring on account of the art installation.

5.1 Data Analysis

Collected data will be analyzed to respond to the aforementioned questions. Data analysis will be reported visually (see figure 7). Data analysis will involve detecting the presence of people in the scene so as to give the number of those using the common shared area in the retirement community. Also, the trajectory people use in the scene will be analyzed. The trajectory analysis will answer the question of what patterns older adults use in the community shared space. Heat maps will be generated to understand what areas are most frequently used in the shared space. Lastly, audio information will be analyzed to count the number interactions in which tow or more people involved with in the common shared area. Analysis will be completed in common shared area where the art installation is not present and compared to the shared area where the art installation will be installed.

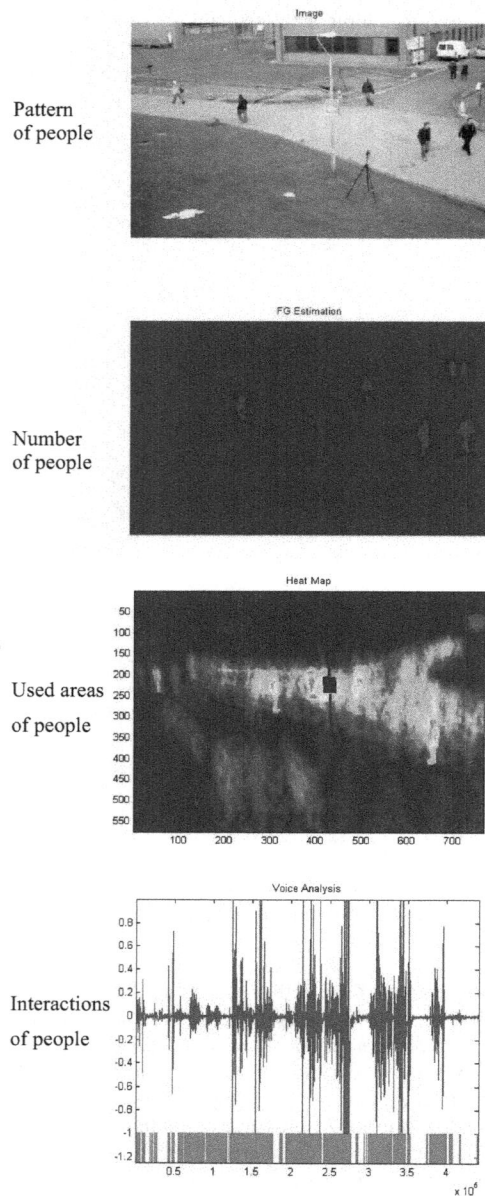

Pattern of people

Number of people

Used areas of people

Interactions of people

Figure 6. Data Analysis

6. CONCLUSION

Bringing design and technology to retirement communities may be a step towards getting closer to improving the quality of life among older adults. Designing art installations for retirement communities to aid social interaction remains to be explored. This paper described the physical and digital co-design of an art piece inspired by nature with older adults in mind. Also, vision systems were specified for measuring user interactions in retirement communities. Collected data with the aforementioned designs will allow researchers and practitioners to understand the role of design and technology in promoting social interaction. More specifically, it will allow them to understand how to motivate older adults to move and socialize in shared environments and communities.

7. ACKNOWLEDGMENTS

This study has been funded by the RIM Seed grant Program at Georgia Tech. We are grateful for their support. Also, we would like to acknowledge the School of Industrial Design at Georgia Tech that partially funded the materials to develop the art installation. Lastly, special thanks to the Calvin Court facility that has been kind to grant us access to the community.

8. REFERENCES

[1] Adams, K.B., Sanders, S. & Auth, E.A. 2004. Loneliness and depression in independent living retirement communities: Risk and resilience factors. *Aging & Mental Health*, 8(6), 475–485.

[2] Alpass, F.M. & Neville, S. 2003. Loneliness, health and depression in older males. *Aging & Mental Health*, 7(3), 212–216.

[3] Barragan, H. & Aitken, A. 2007. Pared interactiva/Interactive Wall. Retrieved April 29, 2011, from http://barraganstudio.com/projects/mes-etoiles/

[4] Brown, V.M., Allen, A.C., Dwozan, M., Mercer, I. & Warren, K. 2004. Indoor gardening and older adults: effects on socialization, activities of daily living, and loneliness. *Journal of Gerontological Nursing,* 30(10), 34-42.

[5] Buechly, L., Lovell, E., Mellis, D. & Perner-Wilson, H. 2009. Living Wall. Retrieved April 29, 2011, from http://hlt.media.mit.edu/?p=27

[6] Caro, T. 2009. Contrasting coloration in terrestrial mammals. *Philosophical Transactions of the Royal Society B: Biological Sciences* 364(1516): 537-548.

[7] Cattan, M., White, M., Bond, J. & Learmouth, A. 2005. Preventing social isolation and loneliness among older people: A systematic review of health promotion interventions. *Ageing & Society*, 25, 41–67.

[8] Daffner, K. R., Ryan, K. K., Williams, D. M., Budson, A., Rentz, D. M., Wolk, D. A. & Holcomb, P. J. 2006. Increased responsiveness to novelty is associated with successful cognitive aging. *Journal of Cognitive Neuroscience* 18(10): 1759-1773.

[9] Fiveash, B. 1998. The experience of nursing home life. *International Journal of Nursing Practice* 4(3): 166-174.

[10] Joore, J. 2007. Improving independence of elderly people by introducing smart products: the guide me localization case. *Knowledge, Technology & Policy* 20(1): 59-69.

[11] Kane, R. A., Kling, K. C., Bershadsky, B., Kane, R. L., Giles, K., Degenholtz, H. B., Liu, J. & Cutler, L. J. 2003. Quality of life measures for nursing home residents. *The Journals of Gerontology: Series A Biological sciences and medical sciences* 58A(3): 8

[12] Mazalek, A., Winegarden, C., Al-Haddad, T., Robinson, S. J. & Wu, C.-S. 2009. Architales: physical/digital co-design of an interactive story table. *Proceedings of the 3rd International Conference on Tangible and Embedded Interaction*, Cambridge, United Kingdom.

[13] Nehmer, J., Lindenberger, U. & Steinhagen-Thiessen, E. 2010. Aging and technology - friends, not foes. *GeroPsych: The Journal of Gerontopsychology and Geriatric Psychiatry* 23(2): 55-57

[14] Ryl, F. 2009. Appeel. Retrieved April 29, 2011, from http://www.thegreeneyl.com/appeel

[15] Santulli, C. 2010. Introducing students to bio-inspiration and biomimetic design: a workshop experience. *International Journal of Technology and Design Education*. DOI: 10.1007/s10798-010-9132-6.

[16] Steinman, L. E., Frederick, J. T., Prohaska, T., Satariano, W. A., Dornberg-Lee, S., Fisher, R., Graub, P. B., Leith, K., Presby, K., Sharkey, J., Snyder, S., Turner, D., Wilson, N., Yagoda, L., Unutzer, J. & Snowden, M. 2007. Recommendations for treating depression in community-based older adults. *American Journal of Preventive Medicine, 33*(3), 175–181.

[17] Townsend, P. 1957. *The Family Life of Older People*. London: Routledge and Kegan Paul.

[18] Treehugger. 2011. Retrieved April 29, 2011, from http://www.treehugger.com/galleries/2009/01/nature-inspired-innovation-9-examples-of-biomimicry-at-work-image-gallery.php?page=7

[19] Ulrich, R. S. 1991. Stress recovery during exposure to natural and urban environments *Journal of Environmental Psychology* 11(3): 201-230.

[20] Weiss, R. 1982. Issues in the study of loneliness. In Peplau, L. & Perlman, D. (eds.). *Loneliness: A Sourcebook of Current Theory Research and Therapy* New York: John Wiley and Sons, 71–80.

Help Features in Community-based Open Innovation Contests. Multimodal Video Tutorials for the Elderly

Claas Digmayer
Department of Textlinguistics and Technical
Communication
RWTH Aachen University
52062 Aachen
+49 241 80-93565
c.digmayer@tk.rwth-aachen.de

Eva-Maria Jakobs
Department of Textlinguistics and Technical
Communication
RWTH Aachen University
52062 Aachen
+49 241 80-93563
e.m.jakobs@tk.rwth-aachen.de

ABSTRACT

This paper deals with the question of how multimodal video tutorials can help the elderly to understand and use new digital genres, like community-based open innovation contests. The paper presents results of an empirical study focusing on initial contact situations and typical user tasks, like acquiring an overview of main portal functions and using toolkits for idea creation. The study is part of the interdisciplinary project OpenISA (Open Innovation Portals for Innovative Products and Services addressing the Elderly). The aim of the project is to adapt the concept of open innovation contests for the elderly (age group 65+) by creating open innovation portals for the target group and analyzing their use. Based on one of these portals, a multimodal video tutorial has been created and tested with older users.

Categories and Subject Descriptors

H 5.2 [**Information Systems**]: User Interfaces – *evaluation/methodology, graphical user interfaces, training, help and documentation, user-centered design*

Keywords

Video Tutorial, Multimodal Help Feature, Web Usability, Web Design for Older Users, Open Innovation, Innovation Contest, Toolkit for Idea Creation.

1. INTRODUCTION

The landscape of digital genres is changing rapidly. On an almost monthly basis Internet users are confronted with new communicative formats, which require special abilities. If users want to participate in this fast changing world, they constantly have to learn new use patterns or to re-think common use patterns. In this paper, we discuss how users can be helped in initial contact situations to understand the functional design of a certain digital artifact, e.g. a community-based open innovation contest (COIC) [13], and genre-specific features, like toolkits [28]. COIC are used by companies to develop innovative products and services. Within COIC, toolkits for idea contests (TIC) are frequently implemented. They enable users to generate ideas interactively

from predefined graphical modules. Interactivity with COIC and TIC, however, is not self-evident and must be learned.

In our study we investigate the use of COIC by the elderly (as part of the project OpenISA[1]). Older Internet users represent a fast growing target group with high relevance for companies, not only because of a global ageing demographic change, but also with respect to their knowledge, their experience and their interest in sharing the digital world. Older users are often confronted with digital media late in their professional or private life, partly after retirement. A key issue is how this particular target group, especially users of the age group 65+, can be supported by design decisions with regard to participatory design (cf. [35]).

Web design and usability for older users are frequently analyzed topics in the field of human-computer interaction research. The results are used for the development of age-related guidelines and heuristics (e.g., [7], [21], [23]). Unfortunately, many of these recommendations are based on an undifferentiated concept of age and aging, often focusing on age-related degradation processes. They neglect that aging is a highly differentiating factor – the elderly represent a highly diverse user group ([6], [39]). Many age-related guidelines and heuristics do not take into account differentiating attributes, like experience and frequency of use or spectrum of familiar digital genres. Other factors, that are rarely considered, concern specifics of a digital genre or design strategies, such as the transfer of application-specific procedural knowledge and related patterns, e.g., the transfer of the "drag&drop" strategy from window-operating systems on websites.

Complex websites, like COIC not only combine common functions and use patterns, but also they often establish new ones. In first contact situations users need to be enabled to understand these new features. One solution to support the process of understanding and learning may be integrated help features, e.g. multimodal video tutorials. In our study we investigate the following research questions (RQ):

RQ1: Do older people use video tutorials? How do they use them? For which tasks?

RQ2: Are video tutorials appropriate to teach older users the structure of a COIC portal and action sequences in TIC in first contact situations?

---
[1] Third party funded by the European Union (European Regional Development Fund (ERDF) 2007–2013 – 'Investition in unsere Zukunft").

RQ3: Do video tutorials support older users in general or only a certain user type?

RQ4: Which help feature modalities do older users prefer for which kind of task?

2. RELATED WORK

2.1 Awareness of New Digital Media

In recent years, the Internet and related digital genres have undergone great changes. They can be described by terms like media convergence, media differentiation, multi-channeling and cross-media [3]. Another phenomenon is the trend towards scenario-based portals and websites [16]. This type of digital genre refers to the psychological insight that our knowledge of the world is partly organized as "scenario-knowledge" [32]. We expect certain areas of our lives, like a contest, to (generally) proceed according to a kind of script. Our knowledge of scenarios (like contest, auction, restaurant visit) comprises the knowledge of social situations and their components, knowledge of the expected participants, their roles, forms of behavior, social relations, and typical actions. Scenario-based website genres draw on the participant's verbal knowledge of such scenarios, which, by providing patterns and metaphors for action (e.g., the shopping basket metaphor in Amazon) thus assist users in negotiating (or navigating) their way through the website [16]. Without this kind of knowledge certain portals like Ebay (as virtual auction house) would not function.

COIC are examples of scenario-based portals. Their production and reception presupposes the knowledge of two different scenarios: how contests function and how online communities interact. The design of the COIC portal www.einfachtelefonieren.de establishes the scenario of an open idea contest [27], which allows participants to submit contributions (for instance with a TIC) as well as to comment on other submissions, to contact other participants and even to cooperate with them.

With the emergence of new digital genres, first time users need to adopt them step-by-step. Research on initial contact situations shows that users tend to perceive new media formats by using established communicative formats as reference objects [38]. In first contact situations they form the basis for an ongoing process of comparing new design solutions (e.g., the naming of functions) with existing design solutions. Problems arise if the design of the scenario-based portal does not fit the expectations of the users or if users are not familiar with parts of the scenario or the scenario as a whole. In this paper, we assume that help features, such as multimodal video tutorials can help first time users to understand the scenario-based organization of a COIC portal.

2.2 Help Features

In HCI research literature different types of help features are mentioned: About the site, E-Mail us, FAQ, feedback, index, search, site map, user tip [36], tutorial, animated demonstration, pop-up help, wizard, help community, newsgroup, chat, instant messaging [33], phone support [9] and animated assistance [26].

Video tutorials in particular appear to be a natural way of showing users how to interact with an interface [29]. Research on drawing and 3D applications showed the usefulness of short segmented video tutorials ([12], [10], [30]). Other investigations question the value of video tutorials with respect to textual help features ([15], [11]). In a study on a programming environment, graphical help (picture or video) was rated as more helpful than textual instructions [14]. In another investigation on the same topic users

completed tasks faster and more accurately with the help of video tutorials than with textual help [25]. The same study indicated that video tutorials alone are not sufficient for retention and transfer of interface procedures – one week later the participants achieved poorer results on the same tasks. An investigation of a spreadsheet application showed the helpfulness of video tutorials compared to textual help [34]. Few investigations focus on the use of video tutorials on websites for older users: A study investigating short video help features for Internet and E-Learning portals showed that this feature supports senior students [19]. The findings reported above raise the question of whether short video tutorials are suited to assist older first contact users in executing tasks on scenario-based websites (e.g., gaining an overview of the structure of a COIC portal, performing action sequences in TIC).

2.3 Older Internet Users

Studies in different western countries indicate that older users often show a lack of understanding concerning Internet technologies and related technical terms. This may result in cautious use of websites and long processing times ([5], [24], [4]) or in an interest not only to use but also to understand the given digital format (e.g., the offered content, purposes of the format, how to navigate) [18]. Recommendations for the design of websites for older users often focus on ways to lower barriers resulting from age-related degenerative changes in physical as well as mental capabilities and are therefore based on a faulty image of old age (e.g., [7], [21], [23]). Many heuristics seem to focus on people's disabilities rather than people's abilities. But "not everyone over 50 has eyesight poor enough to require maximizing the size or contrast of text of a web page. Not every person over 50 has problems with motor control or significant short term memory loss. The diversity of this demographic group is stunning" [6].

The present study relies on a differentiated view of older users: We see ageing as a complex process, which results in various outcomes and is affected by multiple factors, like personal abilities, life course and lifetime experiences, gender, education and socio-economic contexts [1]. How human beings use and experience technologies depends not only on their interests, skills and knowledge (e.g. computer literacy), but also on their early socialization with technology [31] and their use profile.

In consequence, older users should not be categorized exclusively by their biological age. In this study, other relevant factors are used to characterize older Internet users more appropriately. These factors are frequency of use, variety of use and activity preferences [2]. Using this framework, (older) users can be classified as sporadics (low frequency and variety of Internet use for private purposes), debaters (medium frequency and variety of Internet use for discussion and information exchange), entertainment users (medium frequency and variety of Internet use for hedonic purposes), socializers (medium frequency and variety of Internet use for connecting with other people), lurkers (medium frequency and low variety of Internet use for leisure activities), instrumental users (medium frequency and variety of Internet use for utility-oriented activities) and advanced users (high frequency and variety of Internet use for various activities).

2.4 Multimodality

Digital genres are designed multimodal. With respect to the representation of content and the communication between human and computer, language is the most important modality – written or spoken [37]. Video tutorials combine spoken and written language with other communicative resources, like graphics and animations to create a multiply meaningful ensemble, in which each mode supports the user in certain ways to achieve a goal (e.g., gaining an overview of a website or using a TIC): "image shows what takes too long to read, and writing names what would be difficult to show. Color is used to highlight specific aspects of the overall message" [20]. Speech does not occupy the visual channel and therefore provides additional information to the visually perceived [9]; animation is used to show the dynamic behavior of a system [22]. The possibility of combining multiple dynamic modalities distinguishes new multimodal media from static text-based media (cf. [9]), which can also be applied for textual help features (e.g., tooltips or FAQ) and video help features (e.g., video tutorials).

In respect of the topic of this paper, relevant questions are which modalities are suitable for which kind of task (gaining an overview of the structure of a COIC portal, performing action sequences in TIC) and/or user (all users or a certain user type). Which modality or combination of modalities do users prefer?

3. CASE DESCRIPTION

3.1 The Community-based Open Innovation Portal www.einfachtelefonieren.de

The COIC www.einfachtelefonieren.de was designed to develop innovative ideas for the next generation of mobile phones for the elderly. The winners of the competition were awarded with prizes (trips to Berlin and mobile phones). The portal supports different functions (see figure 1).

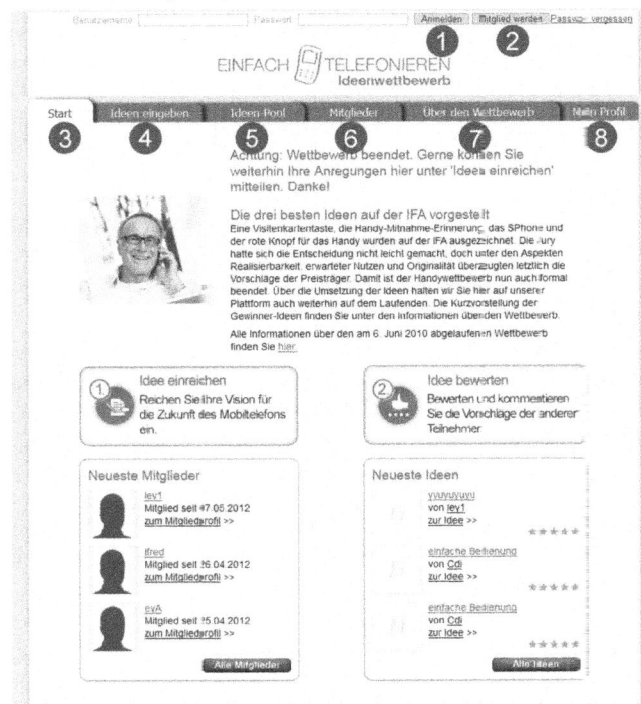

Figure 1. The Homepage of the COIC including the functions login (1), registration (2), start of the COIC (3), submission of ideas (4), commenting on and evaluating submitted ideas (5), members (6), information about the contest (7) and user profile (8).

The participating users can submit ideas as text (with additional pictures, videos or other documents) or with the help of an integrated toolkit (TIC). The TIC requires users to select one of four types of mobile phones (see figure 2). Subsequently, the

outlines of front and back of the chosen type are displayed and can be used as a basis to place given design elements, such as display, keypad, single keys, decoration elements and text engravings. Modification functions allow users to scale, color and rotate design elements. Functions of the mobile phone can be defined by dragging given or self-composed icons into a separate selection box.

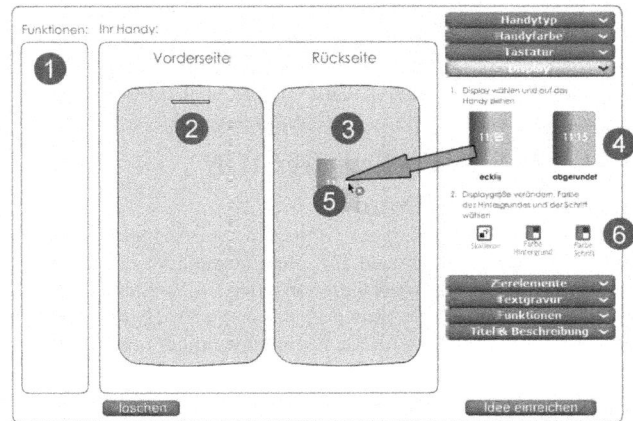

Figure 2. The toolkit for idea creation with the selection box for functions (1), outlines of the selected mobile phone type: The front side (2) and the reverse side (3), design elements (4) and modification functions (6). Design elements must be dragged of the phone outline (5).

Additionally, users are required to enter a title and a description for their idea. Submitted ideas can be evaluated and commented on by other users. Users need to register and login in order to submit, evaluate and comment on ideas.

3.2 Usability Problems of the Open Innovation Portal

In a first study, the COIC portal was evaluated in three test series (methods: single user test, co-discovery tests, teach-back tests) with 21 test persons (age: between 60 and 75 years; gender: 4 female, 17 male) [17]. Two main problems were identified: Users struggled to get an overview of the website (main functions) and to use the TIC.

Overview problem: The overview problem was caused by missing explanations on the homepage. The test persons could not build up a mental representation of the overall website structure and had problems understanding the goals of the COIC portal and how to use the portal. The problem prolonged the orientation phase and the time it took to find functions.

Problems handling the TIC: Difficulties in using the TIC were caused by three design flaws:

(1) Low perceptibility of required entries: Each design process must start with the selection of one of four mobile phone types. The selection is an obligatory condition for all following design steps. If a user fails to start with this task, all further actions and entries are not accepted by the TIC. The test persons struggled to manage this task because of missing information (e.g., missing visual cues, instructions and feedback if no type had been selected). The problem caused long processing times and the submission of incomplete ideas (e.g., a textual description without a toolkit design).

(2) Inconsistent input methods: The TIC requires the user to combine and modify design elements with a mixture of clicking,

dragging, dragging and dropping as well as text entries. Because of underspecified, incomplete or missing instructions the test persons had serious problems identifying and using the right input method. The problem prolonged processing times, caused the submission of incomplete ideas and led to task abortions.

(3) Low perceptibility of placement locations for design elements: Users can place each design element on just one of three possible locations – on the front of the outline of a phone type, on its reverse or on the selection box for functions. The correct location is hard to identify because of missing visual clues as well as inconsistent, underspecified, false and missing instructions. This led to long processing times and submission of incomplete ideas.

4. EXPERIMENTAL DESIGN
4.1 The Video Tutorial
To overcome problems of the COIC www.einfachtelefonieren.de, a video tutorial was created [8]. Nine segments explaining both contest and main functions were uploaded on Youtube and linked via a menu, which was shown at the end of each segment. The tutorial was evaluated with six test persons (age: between 61 and 74 years, gender: one female and five male) and found to be helpful. However, the tests indicated some problems with the tutorial (lengthy segments, small and vanishing player elements, difficult menu handling).

In this study, an optimized version of the video tutorial for www.einfachtelefonieren.de was tested. All subordinated instructions were deleted with the aim of achieving a maximal segment length of one minute [29]. The menu was removed. In the first version the tutorial could only be used as a whole. In the optimized version, the user can access the video segment directly she or he needs to use the main functions of the COIC (total number of segments: six). The video segments were embedded in Flowplayer, which allows the enlargement of interactive elements. Different modalities were combined to guide users: Speech for instructions, text to inform users about the super ordinated goal of each segment (e.g., submitting an idea) and to state input methods, images to enlarge referenced interactive elements of the website and to show arrows pointing to referenced elements, animations to exemplify the implementation of instructions on the website, visual highlighting to mark referenced interactive elements (see figure 3).

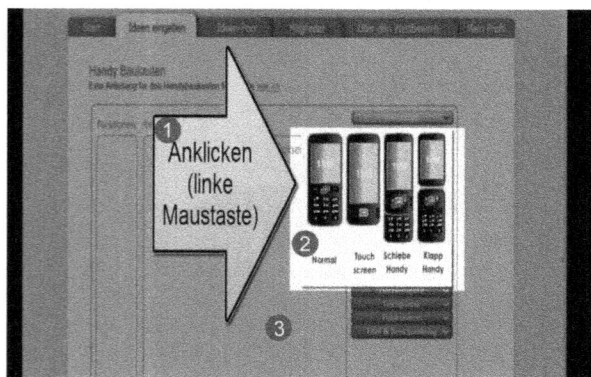

Figure 3. The video tutorial including arrows with short instructions (1), enlarged interactive elements (2) and non-referenced elements shown grayed out (3).

4.2 Test Design
The video segments were embedded as a list in a test environment including a copy of the original COIC www.einfachtelefonieren.de and evaluated in a test series with single users. Before the tests, the participants filled out a questionnaire (items: spectrum and frequency of their Internet use, classification as novice, advanced user or as expert). At the beginning of the tests, the participants received a short introduction to the use of the videos. The test persons were instructed to comment upon the course of the test. In the test, the participants had to accomplish a list of seven tasks (login, gain an overview of the website structure, watch ideas of other users, submit a freely formulated idea, submit an idea with the TIC, comment on an idea of another user, logout). The tasks were embedded in a realistic scenario (initial contact situation). Before the execution of tasks, users were informed that they could use the video segments as help feature. After each test, a retrospective interview was carried out.

In the study 17 people participated (gender: 13 males, 4 females; age: 60 to 77 years, on average: 66,5 years). None of them were experienced in using COIC portals. Most of the participants were inexperienced in using video tutorials. Based upon the questionnaire three test persons were classified as sporadic users (one female), nine as instrumental users (one female) and five as advanced users (two female). The tests were conducted in April 2012 and recorded with a video camera, screen recording software (activities onscreen) and a dictating machine (retrospective interview). The participants were instructed to comment spontaneously on what they were thinking and doing. Their verbal comments were transcribed and anonymized. All participants consented to the recording of audio and video data and the use of the anonymized data for research purposes only.

The analysis is guided by the research questions stated in the introduction. Because of the explorative character of this study, the data is analyzed qualitatively. The number of participants is small, so the findings cannot be presented be generalized.

5. RESULTS
5.1 Use of the Video Tutorial
The tests showed that older users apply different strategies in utilizing a video tutorial in a first contact situation with a COIC. Use frequency varied depending on the participants and the problems they encountered during the tasks.

5.1.1 Use of the video tutorial
88.2% of the participants used the video tutorial (n=15). The majority of them used a video tutorial for the first time (n=12).

Two participants did not use the video tutorial. In the retrospective interviews they stated that they did not encounter any problems during the tasks and thus did not need the help feature. Nevertheless, both participants submitted incomplete ideas via the TIC, but did not notice this problem due to missing feedback from the toolkit.

5.1.2 User strategies
The six video tutorial segments were used in three different ways: (1) The test person watched the video segment at the beginning of a task in order to gain an overview of what he or she was required to do (n=2). (2) The test person used a video segment only if he or she encountered problems during the execution of a task (n=3). (3) 66.6% of the test persons combined strategy 1 and 2 (10 of 15 persons).

Some participants watched a certain video segment multiple times during a test to solve different problems (n=3). To receive certain information, some participants watched one and the same video segment multiple times in a row (n=5) or used the timeline to jump to certain points in a video segment (n=4). Some participants paused video segments to keep the pace (n=4) or to skip the video when they found the required information (n=2).

5.1.3 Frequently used video segments

The video segments were used with varying frequency. A frequently used video tutorial segment was the 'Introduction to the website' (n=10). The participants accessed this video segment for different tasks: to gain an overview of the website structure and its functions (n=3), to locate the login function (n=4), to find ideas submitted by other users (n=3), to locate submission possibilities for ideas (n=3) and to find the commenting function (n=1).

Another frequently used video segment was the 'Introduction to the TIC' (n=11). The test persons used this segment at the beginning of the TIC-related test task (n=7) or watched the video segment to solve problems during the execution of this task (n=4).

Other video segments were watched less frequently like the segments 'Evaluating and commenting on ideas' (n=8), 'Watching ideas of other users' (n=5), 'The selection between the two idea submission possibilities' (n=5) or 'Submitting freely formulated ideas' (n=4).

5.1.4 Task-related assistance

The video segments were used for all tasks except the logout task (login: n=4, gain an overview of the structure n=3, watch ideas of other users: n=7, submit a freely formulated idea: n=7, submit an idea with the TIC: n=11, comment on another idea: n=8).

In the interviews the participants were asked which tasks and problems are mainly supported by the video tutorial. They named four task and problem areas: understanding the structure of the website (n=11), the usage of the TIC (n=10), submitting freely formulated ideas (n=5) and commenting on other ideas (n=2).

Understanding the COIC structure: Concerning the structure of the COIC, the test persons stated that the video tutorial was helpful with regard to two major problems: Gaining an overview of the basic structure of the COIC (n=9) and locating certain functions (e.g., login, TIC, comment function; n=9).

The participants described the structure of the COIC as confusing and full of unnecessary information (n=9). Others stated that they needed time to get used to the structure (n=3). Only a few participants encountered no problems (n=3). The video tutorial shortened the orientation phase and reduced attempts of *trial and error* at the beginning of the test as the following quotation illustrates:

TP 12[2]: "The structure is complicated without videos. Without videos you need to read everything and try to click everywhere."

For some participants the tutorial was a prerequisite to solve a certain task successfully:

TP13: "At first I sat helplessly in front of the website and could only continue after having watched the video. It was like a flash of recognition or an eye opener."

The video tutorial assisted the participants to understand the order of necessary steps. They were guided successfully through the website. Furthermore, the locations of main functions of the COIC were shown. This facilitated the participant's orientation to the website structure:

---

[2] "TP 12" stands for "test person 12".

TP 15: "At first I jumped back and forth and did step three before step two. After I had watched the video I went back and saw where I needed to go."

Use of the TIC: Regarding the use of the TIC, participants mentioned different problems that were resolved by the tutorial: Confusing input methods (n=5), the incomprehensible structure of the TIC (n=3) and imperceptibility of areas to place design elements (n=2). In the video segments, spoken instructions were offered to overcome the mentioned problems:

TP 11: "It was helpful. After listening I knew exactly what to do."

The video tutorial showed users how to perform action sequences with exemplary demonstrations which were perceived as being helpful:

TP9: "Things are visualized, like the movement of the cursor and that is easy to memorize."

In the demonstrations, the user does not only hear the instruction, he or she also sees arrows pointing at interactive elements of the TIC completed by short written instructions. These elements of the video tutorial were evaluated positively:

TP 17: "The instructions with arrows are quite helpful."

As earlier studies have shown [17], the use of the TIC is one of the most critical points of the COIC portal. In this study, the tutorial enabled the participants to handle the TIC successfully. Eleven participants used the tutorial, 81.8% of them submitted a complete idea with the help of the tutorial (n=9). One participant did not recognize that he had followed the first instruction (selection of the phone type) successfully and aborted the task. Another participant watched the TIC tutorial segment but could not use the toolkit due to technical problems.

Participants who did not rely on the TIC-related video segment (n=6) were less successful in terms of task completion: Only 50% of them accomplished the TIC task successfully (n=3). The other test persons confused input methods and were therefore not able to place design elements on the outline of the selected phone type. Thus they submitted incomplete ideas. One of them stated in the retrospective interview that it should be mandatory to watch the tutorial before starting to work with the TIC to be informed about the rules of the toolkit.

5.2 Evaluation of the Video Tutorial

The participants were asked to evaluate the tutorial (benefits and shortcomings). The overall evaluation was positive. However, some participants had problems with layout and content of the video segments. Furthermore, they made recommendations for improving the tutorial.

5.2.1 Benefits and shortcomings

Helpfulness: 15 of the 17 participants evaluated the helpfulness of the tutorial. 86.6% of them stated that the segments assisted them in using the website (13 of 15 persons). Participants commented on the help feature as follows:

TP 11: "You get the information you need in a relatively short time. The information you need to accomplish tasks. That was helpful. You don't need to click through lengthy explanations."

Two users did not want to rate the videos because they had not used the segments frequently during the tests. Two participants said that the videos were not helpful.

Amount of given information: The participants were asked whether the amount of information given in the video segments was adequate. 13 participants answered this question. 84.6% of them responded positively (n=11). Two participants stated that the amount of information was (slightly) too much.

Logic of sequencing: The participants were asked to evaluate the logic of the sequencing of instructions provided in the video segments. 13 participants responded to this question. 84.6% of them evaluated the sequencing positively (n=11). One participant stated that the concurrent use of written and spoken instructions confused him. Another participant found the sequencing comprehensible, but complained about the playback speed.

Shortcomings: The participants encountered different problems during the use of the tutorial. Some participants mistook the tutorial for the website and tried to execute instructions in the videos (n=5). Other participants stated that they had problems to find the subpages of the COIC referenced in the video segments (n=3). Two test persons criticized the fact that an enlargement of the videos to full screen covered the website: They were thus not able to carry out the instructions step by step.

The amount of information given in the TIC segment was criticized as too extensive (n=1) with too short pauses (n=1), which required participants to concentrate (n=1) or distracted them from using the website (n=1). One participant stated that the videos do not provide any additional information to the website. Seven participants did not encounter any problems with the video tutorial at all.

5.2.2 Suggestions for improvement

The participants were asked how to optimize the video tutorial. Seven participants stated that the tutorial could not be improved. Two test persons suggested that the video segments should be accessible via a search function:

TP 8: "I think that it should be possible to enter a keyword in the help feature, mobile phone toolkit for example. And then it should take me there and tell me what to do."

Five participants suggested that the video segments should be embedded in the website itself instead of being offered additionally as a list. One test person recommended shortening the segments; others demanded more information in the TIC segment about basic functionalities (n=1) and about pitfalls of the toolkit (n=1). One participant demanded that the TIC-related video segment should be shown automatically if the user makes mistakes. Visual elements of the videos should be reduced to avoid the concurrent presentation of different information (n=1). One participant suggested that the videos should be maximized to full screen automatically and minimized again when the video is over.

5.3 User Type-related Support

Based upon the questionnaire, the participants were classified as sporadic users (n=3), instrumental users (n=9) and advanced users (n=5). The classification shows that the participants were predominantly experienced users. The data show that the use of the video tutorial differed depending on the user type. In summary, the tutorial helped all types of users, but was accessed for different purposes.

Sporadic users: The sporadic users accessed the video tutorial frequently to understand the COIC structure and to gain an overview before using a certain function (e.g., login and commenting function). One participant used the tutorial to solve a problem with the placement of design elements in the TIC. The tests showed that the sporadic users encountered more problems with the handling of the video player than the other groups, such as maximizing a video or switching between video and website.

Instrumental users: The instrumental users accessed only few video segments to execute tasks. One participant used no segment at all, four accessed one segment, two used two segments, one test person watched three segments and another one four segments. The video segments were mainly used to locate certain functions and to solve action-related problems, like the use of the TIC by learning more about related functions like drag&drop of design elements. In the interviews, instrumental users stated that they accessed the tutorial to find and to understand functions. Concerning the handling of the video player, they encountered fewer problems than the sporadic users.

Advanced users: The advanced users accessed the video segments more frequently than the instrumental users (one used three segments, two accessed four segments and one used five segments, only one used no segments). The video segments were used for different purposes: to learn about the structure of the COIC, to find functions and to solve problems while using functions. They handled the video player confidently. Nevertheless, two participants stated that they do not normally use help features on websites. In their daily Internet use they try to solve problems using the trial-and-error strategy.

5.4 Representation Modes

In the tested video tutorial, information was presented in different ways: as written information, spoken information, image, visual highlighting and/or animation. The users *hear* a certain instruction, they *see* a video sequence at the same time (or a static video picture) with arrows or visual highlighting that marks elements on the video (or picture). The arrows are exclusively used to point at interactive elements. The retrospective interviews indicate that the combination of representation modes is evaluated in different ways. Some participants appreciate the *combination* of modalities; others prefer special means of representation, like animation, arrows and highlighting.

These preferences seem to be applicable to other situations of the participant's Internet use. The retrospective interviews indicate three groups with different preferences for help feature representation modes: users who prefer video instructions (verbally and visually represented information), users who prefer written instructions and users who prefer the combination of both representation modes depending on tasks, e.g., video for the representation of declarative knowledge (like the explanation of a website structure) – written information for the representation of procedural knowledge (like instructions to use functions). Generally, video tutorials were evaluated as a helpful feature of websites. The perspective on representation modes is influenced by experiences with help features of other communicative formats (like print manual for mechanical devices).

5.4.1 Representation modes of the video tutorial

In order to gain an insight into how users experience representation modes, the participants were asked which modality they found helpful (written information, spoken information, images, visual highlighting, animation).

One group of participants (n=5) stated that they appreciated the combination of different representation modes:

TP 6: "I regard the modalities as one unit. It all fits together. There was none that I would have wanted to do without."

They argued that the combination of different modalities supports different kinds of users:

TP 12: "Instructions need to take into account aural as well as visual learners. Both types need to be guided."

Other arguments concerned the form of combination: Different modalities should be used for different purposes to avoid redundancy of information – spoken and written instructions should not be identical word for word. Instead, written instructions should be short and offer keywords. One participant mentioned the condition of bad eyesight and – in this case – the benefits of spoken instructions. In general, spoken instructions were well liked and described as easier to understand and to memorize than written instructions. One participant appreciated the tone of voice (speaker), which gave him the impression that the users were taken seriously.

Another group of participants stressed the potential of visual means (n=5), like arrows, visual highlighting of interactive elements and animation.

TP 9: "These big arrows that point to the target are nice. You can understand really well what is shown on screen."

Some test persons referred positively to the possibility of emphasizing interactive elements (e.g., links and buttons) by visual highlighting (n=2). In the video tutorial visual highlighting is used to mark elements of great importance, elements of minor importance are shown grayed out. This technique guides the user through the website – especially the type of learner who relies on visual clues. One participant recommended that visual highlighting should be used carefully. It should be applied only for elements of high relevance:

TP 9: "One always needs to ask oneself: What will the user actually do in ninety-five percent of all cases on the website? And these things need to be shown. I really liked this interactive feature."

Three participants referred positively to animations in the video tutorial. They used the animated demonstrations to correct errors. The animation allows the users to compare the current state of the system (e.g., the TIC) with the target state.

TP 15: "I could see and compare what I had done wrong."

One participant said that the animation of interactions (like dragging objects) is more understandable than written descriptions.

5.4.2 Preferences for help feature modalities on websites in general

In the retrospective interviews, the participants were asked which representation mode they prefer to be assisted on websites (written instructions, written instructions with pictures, spoken instructions, videos with written instructions, videos with spoken instructions or videos with both written and spoken instructions).

The answers indicate three user types: users who prefer text-based assistance (n=7), users who prefer video assistance (n=5) and users who prefer – depending on the task to be solved – an alternation of both (n=5).

Preference for text-based help features: The participants who prefer text-based features stated different advantages of this option: Written information can be printed on paper, can be skimmed, read repeatedly and at one's own pace. Some participants also stated that written instructions should include pictures (n=4).

The interviews indicated that the preference for text-based features on websites is partly based on experiences with other topic-related communicative formats, like print manuals for technical products (n=3):

TP 6: "If I make a directed search on the Internet, I usually find what I am looking for. That is why I do not necessarily need video instructions. It is just like with manuals: I download them to my hard disc for some device. Then I look for short instructions and sketches."

Another mentioned feature is the combination of text and pictures:

TP 8: "I would prefer text with pictures from habit. I come from a generation in which people experienced using the phone in their youth, and television perhaps. To me new technologies are not really prevalent."

Participants also argued for the use of text-based help features by naming possible disadvantages of video tutorials: They assume that video demonstrations are too time-consuming.

TP 5: "Video help is perhaps too time-consuming. If I visit a website, I do not want to watch a video demonstration, I need to see directly on the website where to go."

Preference for video-based help features: Participants who prefer video help features on websites addressed the demonstration effect:

TP 4: "Video demonstrations show what needs to be executed."

One participant stated that he liked video help without audio output; preferring to read the required information and thus preferred video tutorials with textual instructions. Another test person prefered videos with only textual and audio output in order to read and hear instructions simultaneously. One participant saw video help features as the future of web help feature design.

Preference for an alternation of text-based and video-based help features: One participant favored video help features as well as text-based features (flow charts). In his experience, flow charts proved to be effective. Some participants favored a mixture of text-based and video-based help features depending on the task to be solved (n=4). They stated that video tutorials should be used for declarative knowledge (e.g., to explain the structure of a website) and written instructions for procedural knowledge (e.g., instructions on how to execute functions) (n=3):

TP 7: "At the beginning, a descriptive video is necessary. Afterwards, textual help is sufficient to accomplish tasks."

One test person preferred videos to gain an overview of the website structure and spoken instructions explaining functions.

The usefulness of video tutorials in general: The participants were asked if they regard video tutorials as a useful feature on websites in general. 70.5% of the participants evaluated video help features as useful (n=12). Nevertheless, some requirements were stated: Video tutorials should be short, build up systematically and be offered on complex websites or for complex functions which are not self-explanatory for first time users (e.g., home-banking sites, tax web applications and extensive forms). 17.6% of the participants rated video tutorials as not helpful (n=3) for the following reasons: Reading is more comfortable than watching videos. Video tutorials are usually too long to be used efficiently. If websites are self-explanatory, video tutorials are not needed.

6. DISCUSSION

This study shows how video tutorials can be a useful feature for older users in handling complex websites in a first contact situation. The test data indicate that a video tutorial can support the usage of community-based open innovation contests and complex functions like toolkits for idea creation.

With regard to **RQ1**, the tests showed that a vast majority (88.2%) of the participants used video tutorial segments to solve tasks. Nevertheless, we see a need for further research concerning the question if the high use frequency of the tutorial was influenced by the test setting (participants were instructed to use the tutorial in case of problems) and may vary in real use situations.

Furthermore, the test data showed that the tutorial was used for all tasks except the logout task. The last finding indicates that the test persons needed help in nearly all steps of the contest. The reasons for this may be different. We assume that in some cases (e.g., the login task) the video tutorial was helpful to compensate shortcomings of the tested website. This assumption is supported by the fact that the participants of this study as well as the participants of a previous study, which used the same website [17], criticized design problems, such as a confusing website structure. Another argument for this assumption is the fact that no participant of this study needed the help of the video tutorial to solve the logout function. All of the participants were familiar with the common design pattern to locate the login and the logout function at the same place. Those who found the login function (with or without the help of the video tutorial) were also able to find the logout function.

Other reasons for using video segments may be related to the complexity of scenario-based portals. The tested COIC portal combines two scenarios: an open contest scenario and an online community scenario. The participants were not familiar with these scenarios. The portal feature with the highest complexity is the TIC. The TIC offers a wide variety of design possibilities; its usage requires complex action sequences. Nearly all participants who used the TIC-related video tutorial segments were successful in terms of task completion, participants who did not rely on the help feature were clearly less successful.

Regarding **RQ2**, most of the participants evaluated the video tutorial as helpful. The amount of information offered in the tutorial was rated as appropriate. In the optimized version the video segments were not longer than one minute. The data indicate that a short duration has a positive impact on the usefulness of the segments (see also [12], [10], [30]). The comparison with findings of a previous study [8] shows that short video segments are better suited to support older users than longer video segments.

As mentioned above, the video tutorial helped resolving flaws of the website design in many cases (see also [8], [17]). Although it helped participants to handle design flaws, help features should generally not be used for this reason. Instead, websites and their functions should be as self-explanatory as possible.

Concerning **RQ3**, the tests revealed that video tutorials are helpful for different types of older users: sporadic, instrumental and advanced users. Furthermore, they show that these three user groups apply different use strategies. Sporadic users accessed the tutorial frequently for orientation-related tasks (e.g., gaining an overview of the website structure) and action-related tasks (e.g., dragging objects in the TIC). Their frequent use of video segments can be explained by a lack of web experience and a resulting uncertainty in the handling of the COIC. Therefore, sporadic users may rely more on help features. Instrumental users accessed only few video segments. They used the tutorial for one special reason: to identify and understand functions that are helpful to solve a certain action-related problem. The interview data indicate that this user group profit from their utility-oriented behavior. Advanced users accessed the video segments more frequently than the instrumental users. Nevertheless, their

comments in the interviews indicate that they may not rely on video tutorials during their everyday use of the Internet and prefer to solve problems on their own. This is maybe due to their high web experience.

Furthermore, the tests showed that previous web experience influenced the handling of the tutorial's video player: Participants who had no experience with web videos encountered more problems than experienced participants. These findings indicate that short video demonstrations are best suited for instrumental users, who are used to handle web video players and who are not yet sufficiently advanced to use the web without help features.

Concerning **RQ4**, the retrospective interviews showed that the participants differ in their general preferences for representation formats: some appreciate text-based help features (in some cases combined with pictures), some favor video-based help without written information, some prefer – for different tasks – a mixture of both. This finding confirms the heterogeneity of the target groups of older users.

The retrospective interviews indicate that preferences can be influenced by positive experiences with other types of supporting communicative patterns like print manuals for technical products. Some users expected the video tutorial to be designed in the same way as these communicative patterns. If other communicative patterns are functioning as reference objects for video tutorials on websites this insight should be used for their design (see also [38]).

For function-related instructions most participants preferred text-based help features over video-based assistance. A previous study showed that users like to watch video demonstrations instead of reading textual instructions [25]. As the present study shows, this finding may not be generally applicable to the group of older users.

There is still need for research to gain more insights into the utilization of video tutorials for websites: Are video tutorials only useful in first contact situations or can they be adapted for websites users frequent regularly? If this is the case, the question is for which type of website are they best suited (e.g., scenario-based, action-oriented or other websites types). Furthermore, different types of help features (like avatar-based animated assistance [26]) need to be compared to draw conclusions which type of help feature is suited best for older users with respect to a certain topic, a certain information type (declarative or procedural knowledge) or a certain purpose like to promote a website by having fun.

7. REFERENCES

[1] Baltes, P.B. and Baltes, M.M. 1990. Psychological perspectives on successful aging: The model of selective optimization with compensation. In *Successful aging: Perspectives from the behavioral sciences.*, P.B. Baltes and M.M. Baltes Eds. Cambridge Universal Press, New York, 1-34.

[2] Brandtzaeg, P.B. 2010. Towards a unified Media-User Typology (MUT): A meta-analysis and review of the research literature on media-user typologies. *Computers in Human Behavior 26*, 5, 940-956.

[3] Bucher, H.-J. 2010. Multimodalität - eine Universalie des Medienwandels: Problemstellungen und Theorien der Multimodalitätsforschung. In *Neue Medien - Neue Formate. Ausdifferenzierung und Konvergenz in der Medienkommunikation.* Campus Verlag, Frankfurt, 41-79.

[4] Chadwick-Dias, A., Bergel, M., and Tullis, T. 2007. Senior Surfers 2.0: A Re-examination of the Older Web User and the Dynamic Web. In *Proceedings of the 4th International Conference on Universal Access in Human-Computer Interaction (UAHCI)* (Beijing, China, July 22 - 27, 2007), Springer, Berlin.

[5] Chadwick-Dias, A., McNulty, M., and Tullis, T. 2003. Web usability and age: how design changes can improve performance. In *Proceedings of the 2003 Conference on Universal Usability (CUU)*. (Vancouver, BC, Canada, November 10 - 11, 2003), ACM, New York, NY, USA, 30-37. DOI= http://dx.doi.org/10.1145/957205.957212.

[6] Chisnell, D.E. and Redish, J.C. 2005. *Designing web sites for older adults: Expert review of usability for older adults at 50 web sites.* http://assets.aarp.org/www.aarp.org_/articles/research/oww/AARP-50Sites.pdf.

[7] Coyne, K.P. and Nielsen, J. 2002. *Web Usability for Senior Citizens. Design Guidelines Based on Usability Studies with People Age 65 and Older.* Nielsen Norman Group, Fremont.

[8] Digmayer, C. and Jakobs, E.-M. 2012. Interactive Video Tutorials as a Tool to remove Barriers for Senior Experts in Online Innovation Contests. In *Proceedings of the 6th International Technology, Education and Development Conference (INTED)* (Valencia, Spain, March 05 - 07, 2012).

[9] Dix, A., Finlay, J., Abowd, G., and Beale, R. 2004. *Human-Computer Interaction.* Pearson Prentice Hall, Harlow.

[10] Fernquist, J., Grossman, T., and Fitzmaurice, G. 2011. Sketch-Sketch Revolution: An Engaging Tutorial System for Guided Sketching and Application Learning. In *Proceedings of the 24th ACM Symposium on User Interface Software and Technology (UIST).* (Santa Barbara, CA, USA, October 07 - 10, 2011), ACM, New York, NY, USA, 373-382. DOI= http://dx.doi.org/10.1145/2047196.2047245.

[11] Grabler, F., Agrawala, M., Li, W., Dontcheva, M., and Igarashi, T. 2009. Generating photo manipulation tutorials by demonstration. *ACM Transactions on Graphics 28*, 3

[12] Grossman, T. and Fitzmaurice, G. 2010. ToolClips: An investigation of contextual video assistance for functionality understanding. In *Proceedings of the 28th International Conference on Human factors in Computing Systems (CHI).* (Atlanta, GA, USA, April 10 - 15, 2010), ACM, New York, NY, USA. DOI= http://dx.doi.org/10.1145/1753326.1753552.

[13] Hallerstede, S.H. and Bullinger, A.C. 2010. Do you know where you go? A taxonomy of online innovation contests. In *Proceedings of the 21st International Society For Professional Innovation Management Conference (ISPIM)* (Bilbao, Spain, June 07 - 09, 2010).

[14] Harrison, S.M. 1995. A comparison of still, animated, or nonillustrated on-line help with written or spoken instructions in a graphical user interface. In *Proceedings of the SIGCHI conference on Human factors in computing systems (CHI)* (Denver, CO, USA, May 07 - 11, 1995), ACM Press/Addison-Wesley Publishing Co., New York, NY, USA, 82-89. DOI= http://dx.doi.org/10.1145/223904.223915.

[15] Hategekimana, C., Gilbert, S., and Blessing, S. 2008. Effectiveness of using an intelligent tutoring system to train users on off-theshelf software. In *Proceedings of the 19th Society for Information Technology and Teacher Education*

International Conference (SITE) (Las Vegas, NV, USA, March 03 - 07, 2008), AACE, Chesapeake, VA, USA.

[16] Jakobs, E.-M. 2009. The Evolution of Web-Site Genres. In *Language and New Media: Linguistic, Cultural, and Technological Evolutions.* Hampton Press, Cresskill, NJ, 349-365.

[17] Jakobs, E.-M. and Digmayer, C. 2010. *Usability für Ältere. Internal Report*, Department of Textlinguistics and Technicla Communication, RWTH Aachen University.

[18] Jakobs, E.-M. and Ziefle, M. 2008. What's the problem: Age or technology? In *Proceedings of the International Conference on Health Care Systems, Ergonomics and Patient Safety (HEPS)* (Strasbourg, France, June 25 - 27, 2008).

[19] Kocejko 2011. The influence of multimedia based e-learning techniques for the capability of adopting the knowledge by senior students. In *Proceedings of the 14th International Conference on Interactive Collaborative Learning (ICL)* (Piestany, Slovakia, September 21 - 23, 2011). DOI= http://dx.doi.org/10.1109/ICL.2011.6059582.

[20] Kress, G. 2010. *Multimodality: A social semiotic approach to contemporary communication.* Routledge, Taylor & Francis Group, London.

[21] Kurniawan, S.H. and Zaphiris, P. 2005. Research-Derived Web Design Guidelines for Older People. In *Proceedings of the 7th International ACM SIGACCESS Conference on Computers and Accessibility* (Baltimore, MD, USA, October 09 - 12, 2005), ACM, New York, NY, USA, 129-135. DOI= http://dx.doi.org/10.1145/1090785.1090810.

[22] Narayanan, N.H. and Hegarty, M. 2002. Multimedia design for communication of dynamic information *International Journal of Human-Computer Studies 57*, 4, 279-315.

[23] National Institute on Ageing and National Library of Medicine 2001. *Making your Website Senior friendly.* . http://www.nih.gov/icd/od/ocpl/resources/wag/documents/checklist.pdf.

[24] Newell, A.F., Dickinson, A., Smith, M.J., and Gregor, P. 2006. Designing a portal for older users: A case study of an industrial/academic collaboration. *ACM Transactions on Computer-Human Interaction 13*, 3, 347-375.

[25] Palmiter, S. and Elkerton, J. 1991. An evaluation of animated demonstrations of learning computer-based tasks. In *Proceedings of the SIGCHI Conference on Human Factors in Computing Systems (CHI)* (New Orleans, LA, USA, April 27 - May 2, 1991), ACM, New York, NY, USA, 257-263. DOI= http://dx.doi.org/10.1145/108844.108906.

[26] Perera, N., Kennedy, G.E., and Pearce, J.M. 2008. Are You Bored? Maybe an Interface Agent Can Help! In *Proceedings of the 20th Australasian Conference on Computer-Human Interaction (OZCHI)* (Cairns, Australia, December 08 - 12, 2008), ACM, New York, NY, USA. DOI= http://dx.doi.org/10.1145/1517744.1517760.

[27] Piller, F. and Ihl, C. 2009. *Open Innovation with Customers. Foundations, Competences and International Trends. Trend Study within the BMBF Project "International Monitoring".* RWTH Aachen University, Aachen, Germany.

[28] Piller, F. and Walcher, D. 2006. Toolkits for Idea Competitions: a Novel Method to Integrate Users in New Product Development. *R&D Management 36*, 3, 307-318.

[29] Plaisant, C. and Shneiderman, B. 2005. Show me! Guidelines for producing recorded demonstrations. In *Proceedings of the 2005 IEEE Symposium on Visual Languages and Human-Centric Computing (VLHCC)* (Dallas, TX, USA, September 21 - 24, 2005), IEEE Computer Society, Washington, DC, USA, 171-178. DOI= http://dx.doi.org/10.1109/VLHCC.2005.57.

[30] Pongnumkul, S., Dontcheva, M., Li, W., Wang, J., Bourdev, L.D., Avidan, S., and Cohen, M.F. 2011. Pause-and-play: automatically linking screencast video tutorials with applications. In *Proceedings of the 24th ACM symposium on user interface software and technology (UIST)* (Santa Barbara, CA, USA, October 16 - 19, 2011 2011), ACM, New York, NY, USA, 135-144. DOI= http://dx.doi.org/10.1145/2047196.2047213.

[31] Sackmann, R. 1996. Generations, Inter-Cohort Differentiation and Technological Change. In *Elderly People in Industrialised Societies.*, H. Mollenkopf Ed. Edition Sigma, Berlin, 289-308.

[32] Sanford, A.J. and Garrod., S.C. 1981. *Understanding written language: Exploring of comprehension beyond the sentence.* John Wiley & Sons, Chichester.

[33] Shneiderman, B. and Plaisant, C. 2010. *Designing the User Interface: Strategies for Effective Human-Computer Interaction.* Addison Wesley, Upper Saddle River.

[34] Spannagel, C., Girwidz, R., Lothe, H., Zendler, A., and Schroeder, U. 2008. Animated demonstrations and training wheels interfaces in a complex learning environment. *Interacting with Computers 20*, 1, 97-111.

[35] Spinuzzi, C. 2005. The Methodology of Participatory Design. *Technical Communication 52*, 2, 163-174.

[36] Stowers, G.N.L. 2002. *The State of Federal Websites: The Pursuit of Excellence.* Public Administration Program, San Francisco, CA.

[37] Strong, G.W. 1995. New Directions in Human-Computer Interaction: Education, research, and practise. *Interaction 2*, 1, 69-81.

[38] Wirtz, S., Jakobs, E.-M., and Beul, S. 2010. Passenger Information Systems in Media Networks - Patterns, Preferences, Prototypes. In *International Professional Communication Conference (IPCC)*, Enschede, Netherlands, 131-137.

[39] Ziefle, M. and Jakobs, E.-M. 2010. New challenges in Human Computer Interaction: Strategic Directions and Interdisciplinary Trends. In *4th International Conference on Competitive Manufacturing Technologies (COMA)*, Stellenbosch, South Africa, 389-398.

Doing Multimodal Research the Easy Way:
A Workflow for Making Sense of Technologically Complex Communication Situations

Guiseppe Getto
SUNY Cortland
114C Old Main
Cortland, NY 13045-0900
011-1-517-574-8965
guiseppegettoatwork@gmail.com

Mary Lourdes Silva
Ithaca College
953 Danby Rd.
Ithaca, NY 14850
011-1-607-269-5359
msilva@ithaca.edu

ABSTRACT

In this paper, we describe the methodology known as Systemic Functional Multimodal Discourse Analysis (SF-MDA), as well as how it can be easily paired with a variety of technologies and research methods to successfully analyze and make sense of any combination of communicative modes, while leaving plenty of room for tailoring data visualizations for a variety of audiences, both scholarly and professional. Our ultimate goal is to provide researchers and practitioners with a simplified workflow of this methodology for employment in a variety of contexts.

Categories and Subject Descriptors

K.4.3 [**Computers and Society**]: Organizational Impacts – *Computer-supported collaborative work.*

General Terms

Documentation, Design, Human Factors, Theory

Keywords

Research, Multimodal Discourse Analysis, Data Visualization

1. INTRODUCTION

Several new technologies allow researchers to represent multiple modes of communication in their original form and to collect, analyze, and visualize research data in easily accessible formats. These technologies include log files, keystroke software, eye-tracking software, video recording, screen capture software, and screen-shot capture; and are often paired with more traditional research methods such as surveys, interviews, focus groups, field observations, think-aloud protocols, and textual analysis. Although there have been advancements made by academics and industry professionals in computer science and related fields in the use of these new technologies to visually represent large and complicated data sets, disciplines like technical communication, digital humanities, and professional writing have fallen behind. Despite the plethora of tools available to both capture and display multiple modes within a research setting, representations of research in the humanities have been predominantly communicated in a reductive manner. The classic example is research on several different modes of digital communication (i.e.

image, video, hypertext, text) that predominantly uses only two modes to code that data (textual analysis) and communicate the findings (a text-based article or an oral conference presentation).[1] In order to bring the practices of digital humanists, technical communicators, and professional writing researchers more into line with their counterparts in computer science and the private sector, this paper draws on a methodology known as Systemic Functional Multimodal Discourse Analysis (SF-MDA) as well as the experiences of two writing researchers' who have used SF-MDA to examine digital communication in educational contexts. We hope to present a workflow for conducting research via SF-MDA, a workflow usable by not only academic researchers, but also by any professional tasked with accounting for multiple modes of communication within a single study or project. We begin by introducing the theoretical orientation of SF-MDA, and then move into how it can be easily paired with a variety of technologies and research methods to successfully analyze and make sense of combinations of communicative modes, while leaving plenty of room for tailoring data visualizations for a variety of audiences, both scholarly and professional.

2. SF-MDA AND SOCIAL SEMIOTIC THEORY

Systemic functional multimodal discourse analysis (SF-MDA) is a research approach that involves the cross-examination of multiple modes of communication (e.g., language, visual representations, symbols, gestures, sound, interactive hypermedia, video) situated in their social contexts. It is predicated on the theory that a given mode of communication affects the delivery of a particular message, even if the same content is represented in different modes. For instance, the specifications for a new piece of software that an engineer communicates to a technical writer will differ significantly if they are delivered via e-mail as opposed to via video chat. In the recent past, the problem with SF-MDA research of more dynamic modes, such as video and hypermedia, as O'Halloran [1] argues, is that analysis has often focused on static images of video or screenshots of web text, thus rendering very dynamic modes as static for the purposes of analysis. Digital technologies, however, allow researchers to analyze dynamic modes of communication, also referred to as semiotic resources, in more dynamic innovative ways. The theory that houses SF-MDA is known as social semiotics.

---

[1] Though there are certainly researchers in these fields who have made use of a plethora of modes for reporting results, the scenario we present has largely been the norm, in our collective experience.

Derived from Halliday [2], social semiotics holds that any act of meaning-making is a social practice that must be situated in context. In the study of semiotics, scholars borrow from Halliday's systemic functional linguistic theory, which views grammar not as a system of rules but as a resource to make meaning. The resources communicators use in a given communication situation, or semiotic resources for short, are thus thought of as the choices available to communicators within that situation. These choices are also profoundly social, however: people learn to mobilize semiotic resources in order to communicate via acts of communication with other people. Thus, all the semiotic resources available to a given communicator can be thought of as vast network of interconnected communication options, some learned from past communication situations, and some observed as readily available in the present one.

Systemic functional multimodal discourse analysis (SF-MDA), as a methodology derived from social semiotics, focuses on how people make meaning via a variety of distinct modes, with a mode defined, as Bezemer and Kress argue [3], as a semiotic resource used for the purposes of representing meaning within a given culture (i.e., video, graphics, sound, speech, writing, gestures, music) within a larger medium, or channel of communication (i.e. television, radio, Internet, mobile). The interconnected nature between multiple modes of communication, and between the people who utilize those modes for communication, is at the heart of systemic functional multimodal discourse analysis (SF-MDA). As people use and adapt modes in response to specific communication situations, and as audiences consume them via a variety of media, their conventions change over time.

3. A WORKFLOW FOR USING SF-MDA

Though this theory may be familiar to academics, it is probably unfamiliar to computer scientists and industry professionals operating outside the academy. The question arises: why should technical communicators working within industry or computer scientists developing new technologies care about SF-MDA? Or, perhaps a better question is: how should such professionals use SF-MDA? Our answer to this question is simple: because communication is complex and becoming more complex, largely due to increased reliance on Information and Communication Technologies (ICTs) and, as Slattery [4] argues, due to the embeddedness of ICTs within the social networks that make up the modern workplace, the ability to utilize a flexible methodology in order to understand how communicators and their audiences assemble meaning is invaluable. SF-MDA can thus be used for more than generating interesting academic publications; it can be used to improve communication within a professional organization, for usability testing on a new product or service, or as a way for designers to adequately describe products-in-development to prospective clients.

In order to make SF-MDA usable in all these contexts, as well as to improve its usage within academic contexts, we present below a workflow for moving through an entire study using SF-MDA. We operationalize the stages of a study as data collection, analysis, and reporting of results, but recognize that certain disciplines may describe the research process very differently. For each stage we provide grounded explanations of how SF-MDA can be used, as well as issues that may arise.

3.1 Data Collection

At the same time that digital technologies make it easier for researchers to collect nearly any kind of data, these advancements have presented researchers with different challenges when

attempting to conduct SF-MDA research. First, the sheer amount of data that can be collected and stored is astronomical. For instance, screen capture can be used to record hours of online and offline computer activity in video format. The next challenge is finding the most efficient tools to analyze the layered and interconnected relationships between individual modes of communication and the media they contribute to. In order to deal with challenges like these, we present the following heuristics, which are meant less as stepwise lists, and more as key considerations when approaching a technologically complex research situation.

3.1.1 Bounding

The first step is for researchers to "bound" what counts as data (i.e., what modes communicators are using as resources for making meaning) and what does not. As Witte [5] has noted, bounding this kind of interpretive research can be problematic at best. When approaching our running example—a software engineer communicating design specifications to a technical communicator—if either party uses a productivity tool such as Google Calendar or Trello.com to manage their workflow, should those tools be counted as modes used for communication? Based on our own experiences, it is impossible to collect and analyze all the modes of communication being used by a communicator who is proficient in a variety of ICTs. In our own research, we have had to account for communicators interacting with video software, online search engines and databases, web browsers, digital video cameras, video-based social media platforms like Youtube and Vimeo, etc., and the variety of communicative modes entailed by these technologies.

Deciding what is important can be very difficult in such a complex research situation, even in a relatively straight-forward study, where the research question is something like: during communication between a software engineer and tech writer, at what point does miscommunication negatively impact the productivity and efficiency of both parties? In order to answer such a question, bounding such a study should involve an active process of winnowing down to essential data that begins the moment the study starts. We suggest a simple method for doing so. As researchers plan for and begin to enact their study, they should: 1) follow technologies. Technologies are often the tool by which communicators utilize modes and so can often help a researcher decide which modes are important, based on which technologies communicators employ. 2) Researchers should ask participants what they consider to be some of the essential modes of communication they are utilizing, and 3) should decide, based on their growing understanding of the research situation, which modes and media seem to be most important to participants as they communicate. So, in our running example, if Google Calendar was frequently used by both communicators to organize their communication, was considered important by both communicators, and was frequently returned to as a central hub of communication during research, it is probably important to focus on.

3.1.2 Collecting

Returning to the components of a communication situation that we inherit from SF-MDA: modes utilized as basic semiotic resources and media or channels by which they are communicated, it can also be incredibly difficult to decide which of these components need to be collected for a sound analysis to take place, not to mention the decision of which methods and technologies to use for data collection. These decisions will also impact the modes in which the research can be reported. To begin to deal with these challenges, consider the following tables:

Table 1. Data Collection Methods

Method	Mode(s)
Survey	Textual
Interview	Sound and/or Video
Think-aloud protocol	Sound and/or Video
Textual analysis (collecting documents from participants)	Textual, Hypermedia, Graphic/Visual (depending on the type of document)
Field observations	Textual, Sound, and/or Video

Table 2. Data Collection Technologies

Technology	Mode(s)
Log file analysis software	Textual, Graphic/Visual
Keystroke software	Textual, Graphic/Visual
Eye-tracking software	Textual, Graphic/Visual, Video of eye-paths forming
Video recording	Sound, Video
Screen capture software	Textual, Graphic/Visual, Video
Screen-shot capture software	Textual, Graphic/Visual

We present these tables as by no means an exhaustive list of the various methods and technologies available to researchers, but more as a guide for thinking about the modes that various methods and technologies allow researchers to collect. Once a researcher has an orientation to a study, or in other words has begun to bound a data set and is ready to start collecting data in earnest, a game of mix-and-match must ensue in which the researcher decides which technologies and methods will render the best data.[2] Again we provide a simplified answer to this issue. Researchers should ask themselves: 1) which modes do I need to collect to answer the questions I am trying to answer about this communication situation? 2) Which modes will best help me track the ways communicators are making the meanings I most care about? 3) Which modes are most important to the *systemic function* of communication in the particular communication situation I am investigating? 4) Which digital technologies do I have access to that will best represent results within the actual modes I will be collecting data?

Obviously, the third and fourth questions above bear some explanation. We will deal with the third now, and the fourth when we discuss reporting of results. We recommend focusing on modes as the main objects of inquiry when conducting SF-MDA

---

[2] We highly recommend doing pilots for SF-MDA studies in order to help with the bounding process. Doing a pilot or even practicing data collection and analysis in a mock manner will often teach a researcher which technologies, methods, and types of data are needed.

research. Once modes are collected, the media or channels of communication by which communicators send messages become easily discernible. That being said, it is important not to lose sight of the forest for the trees: when bounding a study and choosing a method and technology for data collection, it is paramount not to isolate the modes of communication being studied from their social contexts. Remember that the SF-MDA methodology holds that beyond the individual modes communicators use in a given communication situation lies a network of knowledge about modes, composed of the knowledge that communicators bring from past experiences communicating with others, and the knowledge that they develop together in the present situation. Here are some questions to help researchers avoid eliding the social context of the modes they are studying: 1) what are the basic building-blocks of communication that communicators are employing? 2) How do communicators define these building-blocks? Do their definitions of them change at all as they communicate? 3) What part does the social interaction of the communicators play in their process of mobilizing particular modes?

The workflow for our example situation would go as follows. If our research question has to do with finding instances of miscommunication, we would want to bound our data set broadly, so as not to miss a mode that could be important later. Thus, we would want to start by interviewing both communicators and maybe even observing them communicating a few times. If we were looking for miscommunication, we might focus more on their "on-task" activities such as conducting business-related meetings, collaborating, and writing. We might further winnow this down by only focusing on tasks that involve both communicators, such as e-mails they send to each other, video chats they conduct, and files they send to one another. So our central modes would be video, e-mail, and computer files. Capturing these modes would be easy as many video chat programs include a record button, and e-mails and files could simply be cc-ed to us, or collected later. The video footage would also give us a good sense of the types of interaction the two communicators were engaging in. We might finish up our study with a member check in which we show some video footage to our participants and ask them about moments we felt they were miscommunicating. We might also do some preliminary analysis on the other modes and check out tentative findings with them to get a fuller picture of their communication.

Ultimately, we suggest identifying easily discernible modes to collect, but also trying to capture as much ancillary data regarding the usage of these modes in context as possible. In our own research, for instance, we have paired video recording with field observations of users utilizing video editing and web design software, and think-aloud protocols with having participants engage in active Internet browsing. These types of pairings avoided divorcing the modes we were investigating from the social contexts in which they were being used, as well as making analysis much simpler. In order to demonstrate why investigating modes in their social context makes analysis simpler, we turn now to the analysis portion of the workflow.

3.2 Analysis

Analysis can also be tricky when balancing a variety of communicative modes, for, as Flewitt [6] states, "[a]ny kind of transcription, whether of audio or video data, is by definition a process of transformation, where complex, richly situated phenomena are reduced for the purpose of analysis" (34). In other words, not only is an SF-MDA researcher collecting a variety of modes, but analysis will then reduce these modes into *another*, more simplified mode, so that the researcher can begin to make sense of his or her data. Because of this, it is essential to foreground the decisions one makes when doing analysis. These decisions fall into two categories for us: 1) creating bins, and 2) turning bins into codes.

3.2.1 Creating Bins

A nice way to begin to analyze data is simply to put data into bins that represent the primary patterns that are recognizable and that interest the researcher. This is a process that should start as soon as data collection starts, and these bins should, of course, be heavily influenced by the intended audience. To again draw on our running example: if researching the collaborative communication practices of a software engineer and a technical writer, these participants would be an important audience for the analysis of data collected. They may even suggest bins that they care about, either explicitly, by naming a pattern they see in their own communication during an interview or member check, or implicitly, by engaging often in a specific type of communicative activity. Though the names for these bins (e.g., from our own research: "moments of collaboration," "usage of modes," "summarization," "discussion of paper") can be largely arbitrary, they should also be informed by any professional audiences the research will be reported to. In our other running example, then, if we were looking for moments of miscommunication between our software engineer and technical writer, our bins should evolve from an informed understanding of what best practices of communication are from our given discipline. Terms often do not travel well between disciplines; therefore, it's important to work with participants in a language they will understand, but also to classify data in a way that members of one's own discipline will understand. This is part of the process that turns these bins into codes.

3.2.2 Turning Bins into Codes

As Blythe would have it [7], what we are calling bins, or the initial categories that enable a researcher to make sense of his or her data, are public evidence of analysis. Though some researchers choose to reveal the nitty-gritty details of their research, such as hand-written notes they scrawled during particularly interesting moments of data collection, it is understood that large portions of data will not be publicly available, except to officiating agencies (like an Institutional Review Board) and to research participants. This is particularly true in the private sector where easily scanned reports are often the only public artifacts to come from research.

At the same time, it is important to be able to explain one's process of reducing a technologically complex communication situation into codes, which can be thought of as verifiable patterns within data. So, if a researcher decides to use an Excel spreadsheet to code data, as we have both done in our own research, it is important to be able to explain why data existing in the form of several different modes (e.g. documents, video, e-mail) was reduced to this simpler form. Because any method of transcription used will reflect the values of the researcher, it is key that researchers make transparent their theoretical biases during the interpretive process. For instance, as illustrated in Figures 1 and 2 below, Silva's Excel spreadsheet organizes different forms of data (e.g., visual description, codes, transcript, time stamp) into

rows and utilizes the hyperlink and comment features in Excel as a way of mapping the total communication situation.

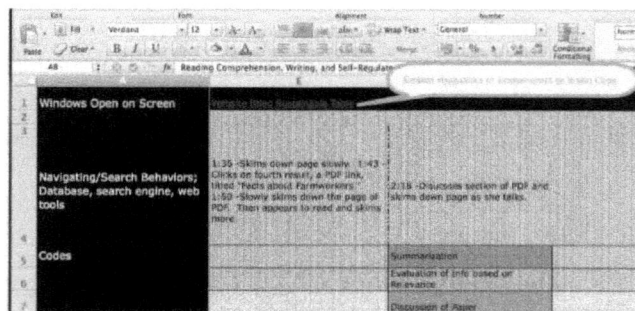

Figure 1. Sample Excel spreadsheet of coded data showing hyperlink to other modes of data

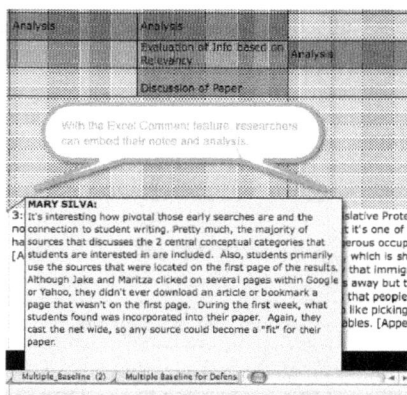

Figure 2. Sample Excel spreadsheet of coded data showing comments feature

The biases of SF-MDA researchers, for instance, are that meaning is situated and localized and is comprised of the interconnected relationships of multiple modes. As a result, the generalizability of the claims we make are limited and claims made about a single mode in isolation are short-sighted because modes always depend on one another for meaning. However, we also accept the fact that all modes within a given communication situation can not possibly be reviewed due to the sheer amount of data required, and that the way one defines a "mode" in a given communication situation is highly contextualized as well. Thus, the specific modes data gets reduced to during analysis, in SF-MDA, are less important than the reasons why it was reduced in this manner. It is imperative for researchers to explain why they made the choices they made during analysis. This is the difference between bins and codes: bins become codes when they become verifiable representations of data, and verification is an iterative process. Codes must be checked and rechecked against samples of the entire data set. We have both spent countless hours placing portions of data in bins only to find that this original characterization of our data was off, and that we thus had to try a different characterization and reclassify our data, over and over again until we were sure the pattern held.

Thus, in our fictional example, though we may originally classify particular moments of our data as examples of miscommunication, during a member check our participants may disagree, or may feel that those moments didn't negatively impact their productivity and efficiency. It may turn out that our participants felt that they were not miscommunicating in the video footage snippets we show to them. After a discussion with them about why, we should go back to our data to make sure that we stand by our definition of "miscommunication" and the portions of our data we have coded as being "miscommunication." If we find slippages in our logic for coding any of our data, we should go back to the total data set and recode it. As can be seen by this example, it pays to communicate preliminary findings to participants early to avoid having to recode entire portions of our data.

As can also be seen, this can be an overwhelming process, and represents a huge portion of the workload in SF-MDA research. Here are some questions to help make sense of this process: 1) why are these bins/codes the most interesting? What values do they represent? 2) Do my participants equally value these means of interpreting their communication? Why or why not? 3) What meaning am I losing by translating my data into a particular mode for analysis? How will I account for this loss of meaning? 4) How will I keep data intact in its original context for later reporting? 5) How can I lessen loss of meaning by doing coding in multiple modes?

As we will discuss in the next section, question numbers four and five are key when doing SF-MDA research, as many rich possibilities exist for not only interpretation, but for reporting. At the level of analysis, however, it is vitally important that researchers preserve modes in their original format as much as possible. If modes are always used in social contexts, it holds that the actual format they are used in within these contexts also matters. There are probably reasons why our fictional software engineer uses a particular program for video chat, for instance, and the clues to why may be within that very mode of communication itself as well as within the context in which it is used. In addition to doing some transcription and coding in spreadsheets, for instance, we have also preserved video data in its originally captured form and built the sorting of this data into our analysis process. We now turn to why this is important for the final state of our workflow: reporting results.

3.3 Reporting of results

The format in which results are reported, in our experience, is one of the most neglected aspects of multimodal research. We have each read and listened to many research reports in which researchers simply described the data they had collected without providing any account of the data in its original form. So, whereas some aspects of the analysis process, such as categorizing data into bins, does not need to be made public, we would argue that the original formats of all data collected *should* be made public. Not only is this imperative due to the contextual specificity of SF-MDA that we mentioned above, but also: professional and participant audiences deserve to see and hear, and thus to be able to more easily conceptualize the complexity of a multimodal research situation. If we again return to our fictional example, and add that our job as researchers is to improve the workflow between the software engineer and technical communicator, and that we had additionally used screen capture software to collect video of each participant's workflow on their individual computers during communication with each other, it would only make sense to represent key snippets of this data to our participants so that they, themselves, could see, and perhaps even contest, issues we saw with their workflow. Imagine coming to these professionals with findings that they are supposed to take for granted and which we provide no evidence for outside of our own

words of description in a textual report, especially when evidence for our claims exist in easily-displayed modes like video.

Not only is this unfair to participants and professional audiences, but it is unnecessary as well. And though we don't have data to back up this claim, we suspect that this lack of transparency has to do with two key factors that can severely impact the reporting of SF-MDA research: 1) the overwhelming amount of data that this methodology requires, and 2) the media by which much research is reported, both in the private sector and within the academy. We have each spent hundreds of hours within our own data sets puzzling over the patterns we had named, and asking ourselves and members of our research team if these patterns were, indeed, representative. The thought of having to conduct a secondary interpretive process in which we then render dozens of hours of video data into some kind of visual representation of these patterns is anathema for most researchers, including us.

This is why we urge researchers to *embed* these secondary forms of interpretation into their data collection and analysis. Getto, for instance, while watching his videotaped data of participants using various communication technologies, recorded time codes as part of his coding scheme. His transcription process, in other words, left data intact in its original form while allowing him to make sense of it. It was easy for him to then go back later to select key snippets of video, and to edit these snippets together into a kind of member check video which he used to present codes to his participants by showing them footage he had recorded that he had labeled as that code. Participants were then able to increase the validity of his codes by critiquing them, or by adding new insight into what was going through their minds when they were performing the type of activity that code represented. Silva completed a similar process while analyzing screen capture videos of her participants online search activities, embedding markers or captions as codes into the video timeline as well as field notes in the form of pop-up comments. Video editing software like Camtasia, Adobe Premiere, iMovie, or Final Cut Pro make it easy for researchers who are using video as a method of data collection to work within the modes of interest during analysis as well as to present results using those same modes.

When making the decision about what modes to preserve data in, one should consider the following: 1) what modes do primary audiences prefer for research reporting? 2) Are there ways to embed secondary modes within a report, when the conventions of that report limit it to a particular mode, so that readers can see data for themselves? 3) In general, what combination of modes best represents the communicative function being investigated?

As for the second issue we raised with data reporting above, the limitations of media within professional and academic settings, we have no quick solution to this problem. We have struggled to represent our research at conferences and other professional venues when not provided with adequate technologies to display impressive data visualizations we had spent hours creating. And with the prevalence of the whitepaper as a method of reporting research in the private sector, we wonder what limitations researchers within industry face when reporting results to busy clients and colleagues, when those results are rendered from technologically complex communication situations. We can only advise to push against modal conventions in these situations, and to present data in as many modes as a given reporting venue allows.

4. IMPLICATIONS

Within this short report, we have barely scratched the surface of the implications of doing multimodal research via this robust methodology. Since SF-MDA was first introduced in publication in the mid 90s by O'Toole [8] and Kress and van Leeuwen [9], usage of it has exploded within fields like technical communication, professional writing, and digital humanities. Other disciplines seem much slower to take it up, or, as we have claimed, use it as a method of data collection and analysis only, rendering technologically complex data sets into unified modes, usually textual ones, for dissemination to larger audiences. We hope that this workflow has demonstrated that not only is this a robust methodology for research in a variety of communication situations, but also that it holds great potential for increasing understanding about and proficiency in the technologically complex communication situations we face on a daily basis as professionals.

5. REFERENCES

[1] O'Halloran, K. 2009. Multimodal analysis and digital technology. In A. Baldry and E. Montagna, Eds., *Interdisciplinary Perspectives on Multimodality: Theory and Practice*. Retrieved from http://courses.nus.edu.sg/Course/ellkoh/docs/O'Halloran%20(2008)%20-%20edited.pdf.

[2] Halliday, M. 1978. *Language as Social Semiotic: The Social Interpretation of Language and Meaning*. University Park Press, Baltimore, MD.

[3] Bezemer, J., and Kress, G. Writing in multimodal texts: A social semiotic account of designs for learning. *Written Communication*. 25, 2 (April. 2008), 166-195.

[4] Slattery, S. Undistributing work through writing: How technical communicators manage texts in complex information environments. *Technical Communication Quarterly*. 16, 3, (December. 2007), 311-325.

[5] Witte, S. Research in activity: An analysis of speed bumps as mediational means. *Written Communication*. 22, 2 (April. 2005), 127-165.

[6] Flewitt, R. Using video to investigate preschool classroom interaction: Education research assumptions and methodological practices. *Visual Communication*. 5, 1 (February. 2006), 25-50.

[7] Blythe. S. 2007. Coding digital texts and multimedia. In H. McKee and D. DeVoss, Eds. *Digital Writing Research: Technologies, Methodologies, and Ethical Issues*. Hampton, Cresskill, NJ, 203-228.

[8] O'Toole, M. 1994. *The Language of Displayed Art*. Leicester University Press, London.

[9] Kress, G., and van Leeuwen, T. 1996. *Reading Images: The Grammar of Visual Design*. Routledge, London.

Articulating Everyday Actions: An Activity Theoretical Approach to Scrum

Brian J. McNely
University of Kentucky
Writing, Rhetoric, and Digital Media
1315 Patterson Office Tower
Lexington, KY 40506

brian.mcnely@uky.edu

Paul Gestwicki
Ball State University
Department of Computer Science
Robert Bell 455
Muncie, IN 47306

paul.gestwicki@gmail.com

Ann Burke
Ball State University
Department of English
Robert Bell 297
Muncie, IN 47306

acburke@bsu.edu

Bridget Gelms
Ball State University
Department of English
Robert Bell 297
Muncie, IN 47306

bcgelms@bsu.edu

ABSTRACT

In this paper, we detail findings about the use of Scrum—a widely adopted agile software development framework—among a student game development team. Looking closely at six weeks of Scrum practices from a larger fifteen-week ethnography, we describe how Scrum strongly mediates everyday actions for the thirteen participants we studied. In analyzing our data, we deployed activity theory in concert with genre theory to better understand how participants repeatedly articulated and coarticulated finite, goal-directed, individual actions in the service of a broader, ongoing, shared objective. We offer, therefore, a way of understanding the Scrum process framework as a powerful orienting genre that facilitates collective development practice by stabilizing and intermediating a host of related, dynamic genres and artifacts.

Categories and Subject Descriptors

K.6.3 [**Management of Computing and Information Systems**]: Software Management — *software development, software process*

General Terms

Management, Documentation, Theory.

Keywords

Scrum, activity theory, writing, mediation, orienting genres

1. INTRODUCTION

How do cross-functional teams of game developers design communication experiences to effectively shepherd cyclical individual goals in the service of larger team objectives? Moreover, how might such effective communication design

experiences be taught to emerging software developers and user experience designers? We explored both questions simultaneously during a fifteen-week ethnographic study of a unique experiential learning seminar that, by its completion, cultivated a working game development studio. This team of developers and user experience designers prototyped, iterated upon, and eventually shipped a dynamic, web-based learning game. As we discuss in this paper, participant actions were strongly mediated by the Scrum process framework [31], a widely adopted method of agile software development.

For the team of thirteen, this intensive seminar was their only course during the semester, comprising fifteen credit hours and ongoing interactions with a professional partner—a major children's museum in the participants' state. For the large research university where this study was conducted, the seminar embodies a unique approach to experiential learning that is *immersive*—it takes place away from the main campus and must be conducted in concert with a professional partner. In these ways, the everyday environment of the development team resembled that of a working studio and looked almost nothing like a traditional learning space. Indeed, participants typically arrived each day by 8 AM, and worked together—on just this one development project—until 4 or 5 PM. Led by a professor of computer science (Gestwicki, who was not involved in data collection), the team employed the process management framework of Scrum within the larger context of agile development [cf. 6, 13, 21, and 30].

Our analytic approach and understanding of Scrum practices is informed by activity theory. Davydov notes that within the consciousness of a given individual are reflections and representations of "the needs, interests, and positions of other people involved in certain social relations and participating together with this individual in some kind of joint activity" [8, p. 51]. This social understanding of individual consciousness in the context of joint activity is central to our explorations of Scrum's role in mediating everyday actions. Based on our systematic analysis of six weeks of qualitative data, we argue that the Scrum process framework acts as a powerful orienting genre assemblage that facilitates collective software development practice by stabilizing and intermediating a host of related, dynamic genres and artifacts. Through their intentional, ongoing orientation to

Scrum artifacts, therefore, participants: 1. mediated their own daily actions; 2. held each other accountable for cyclical team actions; and 3. frequently considered the "needs, interests, and positions" [8] of other team members as they verbally articulated and then *coarticulated* particular goal-directed actions in the service of the broader ongoing activity.

In a similar study of student development teams, Holland and Reeves [15] note that teams actively construct understandings about themselves and their work relative to the specific contexts in which they are positioned. They contend that programming "takes place within socially produced activities by means of historically derived artifacts and technologies" [15, p. 275]. In the remainder of this paper, we explore the active constructions and understandings of our participants through the historically derived genres and artifacts of Scrum and agile methods. Our activity theoretical approach to artifacts and tools focuses on *mediation*, and how through such mediation artifacts may "qualitatively change the types of activities in which subjects engage" [25, p. 9]. We begin by providing an overview of Scrum practice and details about the immersive learning environment that we studied. We then detail our methods and describe our activity theoretical framework. Finally, we describe our key findings, exploring Scrum as an orienting genre assemblage that mediates day-to-day goal-directed actions in powerful, yet often subtle ways.

2. SCRUM OVERVIEW AND LOCAL IMPLEMENTATION

Scrum is a team management framework designed to "address complex adaptive problems, while productively and creatively delivering products of the highest possible value" [31, p.3]. It operationalizes the principles articulated in the Manifesto for Agile Software Development [4], and as such, it is commonly used on agile software development teams. Scrum was designed for industrial practice, but it has also been adopted for and adapted to higher education, particularly computer science education [11, 28, 40]. Continuous improvement through learning is explicitly valued in agile software development [7], which makes Scrum a natural fit for teaching reflective practice [10, 28, 29].

Previous studies of Scrum from a design of communication perspective have focused on local adjustments to Scrum practice for documentation teams [1] and the perceived value of documentation within agile approaches [38]. Stettina and Heijstek note that Scrum does not rely on traditional forms of documentation, but it does rely on "constant collaboration" [38, p. 159] within Scrum teams, ideally through face-to-face interactions. The authors point out that, in addition to a preference for face-to-face collaboration, Scrum teams also typically favor physical artifacts (such as a Scrum wall with user cards and sticky notes) [38, p. 161]. This echoes the practice at our research site; the Scrum Board, as we discuss below, was the most significant material genre mediating participant practice, pulling together a constellation of related artifacts and genres. Stettina and Heijstek contend that "Documentation seems neglected by original Scrum literature" [38, p. 164]. But as we discuss below, from a genre and activity perspective, documentation of Scrum practice may occur through a variety of genres—both traditional and hybrid [34], both official and ad hoc. An activity perspective helps us see the role of these various Scrum communicative genres as they mediate work practices.

Contextualizing our study, therefore, requires understanding critical aspects of Scrum, and we provide a summary here; for the authoritative definition of Scrum, please refer to Schwaber and Sutherland [31]. The team we studied worked in two-week increments called "sprints." At the beginning of each sprint, the team selected a set of user stories and committed to their completion. The team was responsible for articulating the tasks necessary to satisfy the user story, and for tracking these tasks throughout the sprint. User stories and tasks were given material, written representation through large index cards and smaller sticky notes, respectively. These artifacts were placed on the Scrum Board and thus served as continuous reminders of task progress during a given sprint. Note that there are no traditional managers in Scrum; instead, a Scrum Team is characterized by its ability to self-organize [14]. At the end of a sprint, the potentially shippable products are reviewed by the Product Owner (in our study, the instructor acted as Product Owner). During the course of our participant team's seven sprints, these products included paper prototypes, concept art, design documentation, event plans, digital prototypes, and the final, shipped software.

A software development methodology describes and defines all of the tools, processes, and interactions of a software development team. Scrum was a cornerstone in the methodology used by our participants, with many of the specific implementation details—including balancing pre-production and production, story point assignment via planning poker, and asset tracking boards—taken from recommendations provided by Keith [18]. Central to our study were observations of the Daily Scrum (referred to at our research site and hereafter as the daily "stand-up"), a 15-minute daily event where team members verbally and gesturally articulate their actions from the previous day, their plans for the coming day, and any impediments they might encounter. As a whole, the stand-up meetings are designed to "synchronize activities and create a plan for the next 24 hours" [31, p. 10]. The other primary source for agile methodology at our research site was *Clean Code* [22], which the team decided to adopt early in the project. Pair programming—where two developers work side-by-side at one workstation [3]—was used for nearly all programming tasks. The team used test-driven development when it was not made impractical by user-interface concerns; following the advice of Beck [2], pairs used hand-written, personal, ad hoc task lists for tracking immediate future tasks.

Hoda, Noble, and Marshall's [14] research represents perhaps the most in-depth qualitative study of Scrum, exploring the work of 24 participants—12 in New Zealand and 12 in India—from 14 different software organizations over two years. The key finding of their study was that "team members adopt one or more of 6 informal roles to facilitate their team's self-organization" above and beyond typical, pre-defined roles like Scrum Master [14, p. 288]. However, because their focus was on the self-organization of teams, they did not closely investigate *member-to-member interactions*; in other words, they did not explore in much detail the ways that one developer's daily practice influences another's—irrespective of the Scrum Master, Product Owner, or someone assuming one of their 6 roles—and how that member-to-member interaction shapes the ongoing organization and work of teams. Instead, the authors focused much more on the facilitating roles played by agile coaches. Their work, while important, does little to shed light on how the daily actions of developers in teams *mediate each other's actions* in the service of broader activity. Moreover, since their work did not collect or account for the many artifacts central to Scrum practice, they perhaps overlooked the role that these artifacts and communicative genres play in the organization of teams. Our study helps explain how members of a Scrum team mediate one another's everyday work, attending in particular to the role of Scrum genres in such mediation.

3. THE IMMERSIVE LEARNING ENVIRONMENT

Our research was conducted at a large university in the Midwestern United States that privileges high impact educational practices [19] through unique experiential learning opportunities. Our research site embodies these unique experiences, known officially as *immersive learning*. The physical research site, about one mile removed from campus, was a three-story mansion on a large, wooded lot in a residential neighborhood. In this idyllic location, two different fifteen credit seminars run during the fall and spring semesters each year, literally immersing students in an extended, interdisciplinary project led by a dedicated faculty member whose sole commitment is to the seminar that he or she leads. As a research team, our efforts were guided by a simple line of inquiry: what do students "get out of" immersive learning experiences, and how are these experiences qualitatively different from traditional learning environments? We were particularly interested in the role of writing, communication, and collaboration in such experiences, with this paper serving as an apt example of how our research focus was attuned to our site.

As an educational philosophy and approach, immersive learning is characterized by academic-professional partnerships that fuse traditional academic content and skills development with real societal needs, typically within the U.S. state where this research was conducted. In this way, immersive learning curricula always results in a tangible, actionable deliverable, which may range from a business plan or policy recommendation to a web-based learning game, as was the case at our research site. Immersive learning experiences are student-directed and faculty-mentored, and they are strongly focused on student learning outcomes. By design, these experiences often serve as entry points into a student's chosen profession. Finally, immersive learning projects always involve interdisciplinary teams. It is within this context, therefore, that we explored the lived experience of our participants over a full semester.

While our overarching research questions focused on the unique affordances of the immersive learning environment, our ethnographic methodology gave us a fine-grained understanding of learning and collaborative development at our research site. We are able to document, therefore, not only what participants learned, but *how* they learned. In the remainder of this paper, we foreground the *how* of participant collaborative development by exploring their everyday actions as mediated by the Scrum framework. The intensive, everyday nature of the immersive learning environment mirrors industrial practice, where, as the originators of Scrum have argued, the framework "bind[s] together the events, roles, and artifacts, governing the relationships and interaction" of software development [31, p. 3]. It is in this sense that Scrum acts as a powerful orienting genre assemblage mediating the work of our participants. In the following section, we describe our methods before moving on to a discussion of our theoretical frame and key findings.

4. METHODS

Following Smagorinsky [32], in this section we detail our research questions, discuss our methodological approach, describe our participants, and provide details about our data collection, reduction, and analysis procedures. Working with a mature, selective population of students involved in the immersive learning project described above, our Scrum-related research questions were exploratory:

- How do participants use Scrum to manage the collective work of software development on a daily basis? *and,*

- What genres and artifacts mediate such work, and how?

In order to answer these questions—and the broader, immersive learning oriented research questions that served as the primary impetus for our work—we deployed an ethnographic methodology designed to capture the rich details of lived experience for our participants. Four researchers spent almost 135 collective hours in the field, across 83 separate observations over 15 weeks. This level of *in situ* observation led to the collection of multiple forms of data across multiple instances with each participant, giving us both a robust qualitative dataset and strong tacit understanding of everyday practices from which to base our claims. Discussion of the full dataset is beyond the scope of this paper; as we describe below, our investigation of Scrum practices is limited to six weeks of data collection focused on daily stand-up meetings, sprint planning sessions, sprint reviews, and sprint retrospectives.

As we noted above, our findings about Scrum practices are based upon the work of thirteen student participants, 6 of whom were female and 7 of whom were male (to protect their identities, we refer to participants as V-01 through V-13). Our youngest participant was 19 years of age during the study, while the oldest was 26. The average age of participants was 22, and for 4 participants, this project was to be their last academic work before graduation. Seven participants were computer science majors, while the remaining participants listed animation, visual communication, theatre studies, history, accounting, and music technology as their first major. The overall maturity and earnestness of this group of participants was, we believe, a key factor in their ability to coordinate complex, interdisciplinary work using agile software development methods. Indeed, an outside observer might assume that participants comprised a professional software development team, since neither the daily practices nor the learning environment resembled any kind of traditional classroom.

Overall, our 83 site observations resulted in many individual data events across six major types:

- *Fieldnotes and Analytic Memos*: our observations produced nearly 170,000 words of fieldnotes that were focused on both individual and collaborative practices, tool mediation, and participant lived experience. We produced analytic memos frequently, generating 24 reflections and syntheses of observed practice during the collection period.

- *Audio Recordings*: we gathered 45 audio recordings of daily stand-up meetings, sprint reviews, sprint retrospectives, ad hoc collaboration sessions, and impromptu interviews.

- *Interviews*: we conducted three rounds of semi-structured interviews with participants; these interviews focused on how participants viewed their own practices and those of others, how they viewed their work in relation to traditional curricula, and how they used a variety of mediating tools and artifacts in their everyday practice.

- *Photographs*: we collected over 400 photographs during our study; these photographs were primarily used to document ephemeral and ad hoc writing practices (such as those on the Scrum board or on whiteboards, for example).

- *Videos*: we collected two videos of stand-up meetings and one video of pair-programming practices.

- *Artifacts*: we collected over 150 participant-produced artifacts (written documents, design objects, and images).

This level of data collection allows us to triangulate insights across multiple data events and multiple instances.

Our focus on Scrum practices relies on data collected across five of these six categories during a six-week period that began one month into the semester. We chose this time frame for two reasons: first, participants were mostly acclimated to Scrum practices by this time, and over the following six weeks they deepened their understanding of the framework in concert with meaningful prototyping and development; and second, this time frame was long enough—covering three full sprints—to determine general patterns of Scrum's role in managing and mediating participant work at our site. The reduced dataset under consideration, therefore, is detailed in Table 1.

Table 1. Reduced 6-week dataset.

Data Type	Instances	Analytic Segments
Fieldnotes	21	312 paragraph-separated units
Stand-up Audio	14	[triangulation]
Transcribed Interviews	14 (1 impromptu)	271 paragraph-separated units
Photographs of Scrum Board	19	[triangulation]
Videos	2	[triangulation]

Given our reduced dataset, our primary analytic focus was trained on fieldnotes generated by three different researchers combined with transcripts from the first round of semi-structured interviews, which included three questions related to Scrum:

- Tell me about your experience with Scrum for this project.

- How are you personally using things like the User Stories and other organizational notes (burndown chart, etc.)?

- How are you personally keeping track of things related to the project (example? where?)?

Audio recordings and videos of daily stand-up meetings, sprint reviews, sprint retrospectives, and photographs of the Scrum board were used as triangulation measures to increase the reliability of fieldnote observations; these audio and video recordings were not transcribed for this study. 13 semi-structured interviews and one impromptu interview were transcribed, forming 271 paragraph-separated units for analysis.

We coded fieldnote units and interview units deductively, applying a three code qualitative schema that was initially developed inductively from observations, analytic memos, and tacit understanding of our research site. As we coded, however,

we remained open to further inductive insights; indeed, we generated additional perspectives from this inductive analysis through the emergence of "accountability" as a related participant concern. Since Scrum is specifically designed to encourage participants' articulation of goals and actions, our final coding schema revealed relationships among the closely related everyday practices detailed in Table 2.

By applying our coding schema while remaining open to new, inductively-derived codes, we systematically analyzed and triangulated six weeks of Scrum practice across multiple forms of data, across 13 participants, and across 21 observations from 3 different field researchers. In this process, we've developed three key insights about Scrum practice that were prevalent across participants, and that shed light on how software developers used agile methods and genres to mediate their work. In the following section, we describe our activity theoretical framework for understanding Scrum's role in the particular assemblage of intermediated genres central to this form of agile software development practice. For our participants, the Scrum Board acts as a powerful and ever visible stabilizing and *orienting genre* that pulls together and mediates clusters of other related genres for individual participants working in the service of a shared objective. In this way Scrum mediates participants' daily articulations and coarticulations of finite, goal-directed actions that comprise their collaborative activity. This data, therefore, helps explain intersubjective participant mediation.

5. ACTIVITY THEORY, GENRE, SCRUM

In this section we provide details on our theoretical and analytic framework for understanding our participants' practices with Scrum. Nardi argues that activity theory is "a research framework and set of perspectives" rather than a methodology or single theory [23, p. 7]. Activity theory is rooted in the phenomenological facets of lived experience: "consciousness is located in everyday practice: you are what you do" [23, p. 7]. And what you do, as Vygotsky [39], Lave and Wenger [20], Nardi and O'Day [24], and Kaptelinin and Nardi [17], have demonstrated, is "firmly and inextricably embedded in the social matrix of which every person is a part," a matrix composed of people, histories, genres, and material artifacts [23, p. 7]. Activity theory, therefore, "incorporates strong notions of intentionality, history, mediation, collaboration and development in constructing consciousness" [23, p. 7]. Most importantly, Nardi contends that human activities "cannot be understood without understanding the role of artifacts in everyday experience, especially the way artifacts are integrated into social practice" [23, p. 14]. Indeed, Kaptelinin argues that "Human activity is mediated by a number of tools, both external (like hammers or scissors) and internal (like concepts or heuristics)" [16, p. 109]. Such mediating tools or artifacts are, crucially, laden with social and cultural norms and histories—they carry "cultural knowledge and social experience" [16, p. 109].

Activity is a broad construct that is comprised of concrete, everyday *actions* and *operations*. Activities, Bødker argues, are conducted "through the *actions* of individuals, directed toward an object or another subject" [5, p. 149; emphasis in original]. Activities, in fact, give meaning to our various actions, she contends. And each action, as Kaptelinin [16] suggests, is itself composed of a series of often unconscious operations. Bødker argues that "We can analytically separate the categories of activity, action, and operation by asking why something takes place, what takes place, and how it is carried out" [5, p. 149]. In order to explore the whys, whats, and hows of collaborative software development work, we carefully and systematically

Table 2. Coding schema, instances by data type, and illustrative examples.

Code	Description	Fieldnote Instances	Interview Instances	Example
Self-mediation [SM]	Code as [SM] any instances of participants using external artifacts (sticky notes, mobile devices, notebooks) to mediate their articulation of actions and goals	57	40	V-01 is reading from her notes on a post-it note. She's waiting on a response from the museum. V-07 reads from a post-it note, he wants to determine in his group if what they've been developing is successful.
Accountability [ACC]	Code as [ACC] instances where a participant notes a sensitivity to their actions and how they impact others; code as [ACC] instances where a participant notes the need for others to complete work that affects the team	51	32	V-08: "I think the biggest thing that bothers me sometimes is that ... I feel like people don't always hold themselves accountable." V-09: "We need to be better, I mean, people start saying more often like, well I can't start programming this until somebody has this UI thing, you know."
Coarticulated Actions [CA]	Code as [CA] instances where one participant verbally or gesturally references their work in relation to another's, or when a participant verbally articulates a shift in their planned work because of something that another participant has articulated	80	52	V-04: "I know multiple times where someone said, you know, 'I'm going to be working on this today,' it's like okay, 'well that means I probably should go over there and work on it too.'" V-11: "specifically today V-06 and I were gonna work on tasks ... that I mentioned [in the stand-up]. I didn't have a whole lot of other stuff that I needed to be working on ... Since V-06 was ready to move on to [another task], I was able to know that, like, I get to work on that today."
Orienting [OR]	Code as [OR] any instances of verbal, gestural, or written reference to the Scrum Board, Burn-down Chart, or related artifacts (e.g., specific user stories, tasks, backlogs, documents, etc.)	433	53	V-10: "Well I definitely interact with the Scrum board multiple times a day. At any point when I don't know what to be working on I'll just go check [it] out, see what all is being worked on and what hasn't started."

traced the artifacts and genres of Scrum and their role as mediators of actions and activity within a specific context of use. As Raeithel and Velichkovsky argue, such actions represent our everyday work, "corresponding to a variety of verbal or otherwise symbolic prescriptions called tasks" [26, p. 219]. Indeed, Scrum places a continual emphasis on task completion and resolution. Raeithel and Velichkovsky add that they "recognize goal directedness as a specifically human type of intentional, object-related, joint activity" [26, p. 220]. Actions are thus goal-directed and finite; they are typically orchestrated in multiple, complex, often overlapping formations (the *what*) in the broader service of the *why*—of activity.

And activities, fundamentally, are object-oriented. In this way, objects define the character of collective activities, since objects carry motive and meaning for a given individual or group. Engeström and Escalante illustrate how human activities are always "oriented toward something and driven by something. This something—the object—is constantly in transition and under construction, and it manifests itself in different forms for different participants of the activity" [9, p. 360]. In this way, we can see the distinction between activities and actions; Engeström and Escalante point out that objects must not be confused with goals or aims, since in activity theory "conscious goals are related to discrete, finite, and individual actions; objects are related to continuous, collective activity systems and their motives" [9, p. 360]. Activity theoretical studies must balance this relationship carefully while also recognizing that defining the shared objects of collective activity can be especially difficult [cf. 37]. Individual participants may have slightly different objects in mind as they go about their work; we argue, however, that the Scrum framework stabilizes and orients participants toward a shared object (defined through the collective work of Sprint planning) around which individual participant actions may coalesce.

Scrum, as we have argued, serves as a powerful *genre assemblage* that mediates activity. As Russell [27] and Spinuzzi [36] have argued in their discussions of writing, activity, and genre research (WAGR), activity theory and genre theory are complementary approaches that have been used together productively. Written communication genres, Russell contends, are "arguably the most powerful mediational means for organizations and institutions" [27, p. 40]. Genre, therefore, is a unit of social action; "the object of activity," Russell argues, "can be seen to attain its stability, reproduction, and continuity through genres," such that genres then serve as "crucial links between subjects, tools, and objects" [27, p. 45]. Indeed, Spinuzzi persuasively demonstrated how genres represent "the traces of an ongoing activity, represent problem solving in that activity, and thus tend to stabilize the activity in which they are used" [34, p. 39].

Finally, Spinuzzi [35] has shown how genres do not simply communicate, but strongly *mediate* actions: "mediating artifacts [and genres] qualitatively change the entire activity in which workers engage" [34, p. 38]. His genre ecologies framework [34, 34], like WAGR, synthesizes the complementary approaches of activity and genre theories to see genres as representing "distributed cognition in the sense that cognitive work is spread among the genres and artifacts that belong to them" [35, p. 114]. "Since genres are contingent on each other," he argues, "the success of any given genre depends on its interconnections with other genres and how those genres jointly mediate a given activity" [35, p. 114; see also 32]. From a genre ecology perspective, then, "genres are not simply performed or communicated, they represent the 'thinking out' of a community as it cyclically performs an activity" [35, p. 114]. Mediating genres may potentially change participant actions on a moment-by-moment basis. Such genres are therefore fundamentally involved in shaping practice itself. The WAGR and genre ecology approach thus highlights genres and artifacts that may be invisibilized by other frameworks, genres and artifacts that support daily self-mediation, for example, and unofficial, ad hoc, and ephemeral genres that go missing in approaches trained strictly on sequences of official genres like software documentation [cf. 12].

Our study of Scrum specifically sought out and accounted for many of the ephemeral, ad hoc, often invisibilized genres and artifacts central to the everyday actions that comprised our participants' collective activity. Informed by writing, activity, and genre research and Spinuzzi's genre ecologies framework, we are able to describe how Scrum pulls together the many different genres and artifacts of software development to mediate and direct activity. Specifically, we can see how Sprint Planning, Reviews, and Retrospectives involve a host of ephemeral communicative genres (many of which are informal, verbal, gestural, or only temporarily written on whiteboards) that are then made visible and concrete through written user stories and tasks that become displayed and manipulated on the Scrum Board. In this way, Scrum helps orient participants around shared objects that are temporarily stabilized (for the duration of the sprint, for example).

In the following section we describe key findings about participants' use of Scrum artifacts and genres.

6. FINDINGS

Spinuzzi describes genres as "instantiated solution[s]" to recurrent situations [36, p. 367]; genres thus carry the "residue of past problem-solving" [36, p. 367]. Genres, he argues, "develop through repeated cycles in which they progressively orient (or reorient) to the repeated situations to which they respond" [36, p. 367]. In this way, he argues, "genres come to embody a given logic or tradition: a frame within which activity is interpreted" [36, p. 367]. Certainly, Scrum acts as a specific frame through which software development activity is interpreted. But just as genres orient and reorient to particular and recurrent social situations, the work of genres themselves helps to orient and reorient the actions of people who use them. And as Spinuzzi points out, "genres are rarely deployed alone: They interact in *genre assemblages* to collectively address complex cyclical activities," leading to a situation where "many genres shape the cyclical activity within which they are mobilized" [36, p. 367]. Finally, just as genres shape cyclical activity, they also foster improvisation and development [36, p. 368], especially when they are formed of complex assemblages of less frequent genres that may have different histories of use.

In this section we present three interrelated findings about the use of Scrum artifacts and genres among our participants. First, we describe how the Scrum framework provides software development teams with a ready-made genre assemblage to which individuals adapt during the course of their daily work via *self-mediation*. In this way, participants bring with them a host of idiosyncratic and often ad hoc genres that help them mediate their own work within the broader context of ready-made genres from the Scrum framework [cf. 12]. Second, we detail how development teams jointly accomplish daily actions by making micro-level adjustments that we describe as *coarticulations*. These practices support Scrum's larger emphasis on accountability. Participants, therefore, both self-mediate and co-mediate each other's actions as a part of working within the Scrum genre ecology. Finally, as a powerful *orienting genre assemblage*, Scrum has a palpable centripetal velocity that pulls together a host of related genres and artifacts, helping to stabilize and shape shared (activity theoretical) objects over time.

6.1 Self-mediating Actions

As a process framework, Scrum is typically implemented with a series of interrelated, ready-made genres and artifacts. These include often tangible items such as the Product Backlog and Scrum Board and communicative and process genres such as daily stand-up meetings and Sprint Reviews. Our research suggests that developers who are new to Scrum (like many of the participants in our study) will use personal writing work to reconcile existing, often idiosyncratic ways of tracking actions with the Scrum framework. Moreover, our study suggests that, even as developers acclimate to Scrum and become more familiar with its genres, they may *continue to use* existing, idiosyncratic modes of tracking (to-do lists, sticky notes, etc.) within the context of Scrum's ready-made genres.

Indeed, we observed some of the most experienced Scrum developers (notably, the Product Owner, and V-07, who had previous Scrum experience) continually drawing on both established and ad hoc personal genres to mediate their own articulation of actions in the daily stand-up meetings. These self-mediating strategies helped many (but not all) participants manage day-to-day reporting to verbally articulate their personal involvement in the project. Despite Scrum's richly textured group of genres, artifacts, and processes, participants often mediated their own actions by deploying personal hybrid genres [34] that helped them orient to Scrum processes.

For example, V-03, a visual communication major new to Scrum and software development, used a personal moleskin notebook to keep track of daily planning items that eventually became fodder for stand-up reporting to her team. We repeatedly observed her reading from her notebook during stand-up meetings, mediating her own reportage by way of tools that were not ostensibly a part of the Scrum genre assemblage. V-10 and V-11, both of whom had previous experience with Scrum, and both of whom were computer science majors, often mediated their day-to-day actions by way of a whiteboard. This form of self-mediation was ephemeral—since their little task lists and notes were often erased shortly after they appeared—but substantial in directing their actions and reports nonetheless.

6.2 Coarticulating Actions and Accountability

Even as participants deploy often ad hoc and idiosyncratic self-mediating strategies, the Scrum framework explicitly fosters developer-to-developer co-mediation. While a participant might use an idiosyncratic self-mediating genre just prior to a stand-up meeting (e.g., by jotting down her most important actions for the upcoming day on a throw-away sticky note), they also frequently rearticulated actions on the fly, usually in response to a colleague's report. We describe this practice as *coarticulating actions*, since a participant's report of upcoming tasks was often doubly mediated and articulated—initially by their own "thinking out" of upcoming actions, and then as an agile response to other, more pressing needs verbally articulated by a colleague during a stand-up. In this way, micro-level, everyday developer-to-developer coarticulations fostered collaborative work in meaningful ways—ways that, we contend, directly support Scrum's ideal of self-organization [cf. 14].

These coarticulated actions were frequently traced through our *in situ* observations of daily stand-up meetings and then corroborated in participant interviews (see Table 2). The format of the Scrum stand-up meetings asks participants to explicitly articulate their work; but in doing so, a given developer's articulations can cause ripples that affect other members of the team. Such ripples are often reconciled through *coarticulations*—micro-level, on the fly adjustments and reframings of actions in response to team needs. In this way, daily actions are often coarticulated and jointly mediated, thus (often) supporting the team's expressed desire for accountability. In other words, as the team coarticulates daily actions they express support for, and accountability to, the most pressing project needs, fomenting a shared objective.

In the following excerpt from fieldnotes generated near the midpoint of our reduced 6-week dataset, we can see both self-mediation and coarticulated actions in detail:

> V-03 begins the stand up meeting, reading from her notebook [SM]. V-11 reports briefly and is followed by V-10 who wants to tackle a to-do list with V-05 [CA]. V-06 echoes V-11 [CA]. V-08 reports and plans to finish up the main parts of the design doc. V-05 echoes V-10 [CA]. V-07 follows reports on the success of Friday's playtest. ... V-04 worked on the playtest and plans to work with V-07 [CA] to see what they need to do with the design doc and work with the challenges.

Here we can see how much intersubjective work is facilitated through micro-level coarticulations. Participants share ongoing work, often with another participant in mind; in other scenarios (see Table 2), participants redirect future work in response to a colleague's articulated needs. These micro-level adjustments substantially mediate everyday intersubjective practice.

6.3 Orienting Genres and Shared Objects

To a significant extent, Scrum is effective in managing the work of agile teams because of the centripetal force it exerts on a host of complex genres and artifacts mediating the practice of software development. The Scrum Board and its related artifacts—user stories, tasks, columns—is the key *orienting genre* in the Scrum assemblage; in this sense, most of the related artifacts, genres, and practices (those that are ready-made and those that are idiosyncratic) are *oriented to* the Scrum Board. The Scrum Board pulls in these other genres and artifacts and allows them to coalesce, temporarily, in an ever-visible and stable way, thus shaping daily actions. The Scrum Board, it must be said, is in turn *shaped by* the daily actions (and articulations of those actions) of the team.

To better understand just how practices are oriented toward the Scrum Board (and thus how it generates centripetal force on the actions of development teams), it is useful to closely examine Sprint Planning and Review sessions. In a two-hour observation of one of the team's Sprint Planning meetings we generated 2,800 words of fieldnotes in 14 paragraph-separated units. This observation was notable, though, because of the many instances of verbal and gestural interactions with the Scrum Board that could be identified and traced. During just this one observation, for example, we identified 33 clear instances of orienting moves, as team members and the Scrum master discussed user stories, voted on their priority, moved individual tasks to the board, and generally oriented their work in and through this important central genre of activity. The team members constantly referenced the constellation of artifacts that comprise the Scrum board during this meeting, highlighting the important role that the board plays in orienting follow-on actions. In our observation of the subsequent Sprint Review, this effect is even more pronounced; in 2,100 words of fieldnotes over 28 paragraph-separated units, we identified 62 separate instances of participants orienting to the Scrum Board and related artifacts through verbal, gestural, and written actions.

The centripetal force generated by the Scrum Board as an orienting genre, we argue, plays a crucial role in generating and stabilizing a shared object for the development team. This is significant, since delimiting the objects of shared activity can be particularly difficult [cf. 37]. In agile software development, Scrum helps participants jointly construct and attune their everyday actions around shared objects, even if only temporarily (for the life of a sprint, or, more likely, for the life of a given development project). While individual team members bring different perspectives (and indeed, different objects) to the activity of software development, the Scrum Board, as an orienting genre, fosters the coalescence of a shared object by providing a visible and material space of collective orientation.

7. CONCLUSION

In this paper, we have argued from rich empirical data that the Scrum process framework strongly mediates the activity of software development by providing a means for articulating, coarticulating, and executing actions in the service of a shared objective. Scrum helps facilitate this work through its powerful orienting genre—the Scrum Board—and the communicative and mediational practices that are pulled together and intermediated through such orientation. We've described how participants in our study orient to Scrum through self-mediating strategies and ad hoc, idiosyncratic hybrid genres; we've detailed findings about the articulation and coarticulation of actions deployed in the service of collective development activity; and we've argued that Scrum is crucially important in helping agile teams generate and manage their work around a shared object.

Our study is necessarily limited: we explored the work of one development team over 15 weeks, and the practices of this team, comprised of undergraduate students in a unique immersive learning seminar, surely differs in certain ways from professional development practice. We would argue that these differences are perhaps best measured in levels of experience rather than in the shaping and coordinative properties of Scrum. We believe, therefore, that these findings contribute new insights into the role that Scrum plays in software development, and more importantly, how Scrum is directly relevant to professionals in design of communication fields. In future work, we plan to expand our analysis to include the full 15 weeks of data we collected, exploring in particular the ways in which Scrum facilitates the agile response to a major, sudden change in the object of activity.

8. ACKNOWLEDGEMENTS

This study was funded through a Ball State University Provost's discretionary research grant. We are grateful for this generous support. We also wish to thank our participants—insightful and dedicated emerging professionals—and the Virginia Ball Center for Creative Inquiry.

9. REFERENCES

[1] Baptista, J. (2008). Agile documentation with uScrum. In *Proceedings of the 26th Annual ACM Conference on Design of Communication (SIGDOC '08)*. ACM, New York, NY, 275–276.

[2] Beck, K. 2002. *Test Driven Development by Example.* Addison-Wesley, Boston, MA.

[3] Beck, K., and Andres, C. 2004. *Extreme Programming Explained: Embrace Change* (2nd edition). Addison-Wesley, Boston, MA.

[4] Beck, K., Beedle, M., van Bennekum, A., Cockburn, A., Cunningham, W., Fowler, M., Grenning, J., Highsmith, J., Hunt, A., Jeffries, R., Kern, J., Marick, B., Martin, R.C., Mellor, S., Schwaber, K., Sutherland, J., and Thomas, D. 2001. *Manifesto for Agile Software Development.* http://agilemanifesto.org.

[5] Bødker, S. 1996. Applying activity theory to video analysis: How to make sense of video data in human-computer interaction. In *Context and Consciousness: Activity Theory and Human-Computer Interaction*, B. Nardi, Ed. MIT Press, Cambridge, MA, 147–174.

[6] Cockburn, A., and Highsmith, J. 2001. Agile software development: The people factor. *Computer* 34(11), 131–133.

[7] Cockburn, A. 2006. *Agile Software Development: The Cooperative Game.* 2nd edition. Addison-Wesley, Boston, MA.

[8] Davydov, V.V. 1999. The content and unsolved problems of activity theory. In *Perspectives on Activity Theory*, Y. Engeström, R. Miettinen, and R.L. Punamäki, Eds. Cambridge University Press, Cambridge, UK, 39–52.

[9] Engeström, Y. and Escalante, V. 1996. Mundane tool or object of affection? The rise and fall of the Postal Buddy. In *Context and Consciousness: Activity Theory and Human-Computer Interaction*, B. Nardi, Ed. MIT Press, Cambridge, MA, 325–373.

[10] Gestwicki, P., and Morris, R.. 2012. Social Studies Education Game Development as an Undergraduate Immersive Learning Experience. In *Handbook of Research on Serious Games as Educational, Business and Research Tools.* IGI Global, Hershey, PA, 838–858.

[11] Hanks, B., Wellington, C., Reichlmayr, T., and Coupal, C. 2008. Integrating agility in the cs curriculum: practices through values. In *Proceedings of the 39th SIGCSE technical symposium on Computer science education (SIGCSE '08)*. ACM, New York, NY, USA, 19-20. DOI=10.1145/1352135.1352145 http://doi.acm.org/10.1145/1352135.1352145

[12] Hashimov, E., and McNely, B. 2012. Left to their own devices: Ad Hoc genres and the design of transmedia narratives. In *Proceedings of the 30th Annual ACM Conference on Design of Communication (SIGDOC '12)*. ACM, New York, NY.

[13] Highsmith, J. 2004. *Agile Project Management: Creating Innovative Products.* Addison-Wesley, Boston, MA.

[14] Hoda, R., Noble, J., and Marshall, S. 2010. Organizing self-organizing teams. In *Proceedings of the 32nd ACM/IEEE International Conference on Software Engineering (ICSE '10)*, Vol. 1. ACM, New York, NY, 285–294. DOI=10.1145/1806799.1806843 http://doi.acm.org/10.1145/1806799.1806843

[15] Holland, D., and Reeves, J. R. 1996. Activity theory and the view from somewhere: Team perspectives on the intellectual work of programming. In *Context and Consciousness: Activity Theory and Human-Computer Interaction*, B. Nardi, Ed. MIT Press, Cambridge, MA, 103–116.

[16] Kaptelinin, V. 1996. Activity theory: Implications for human-computer interaction. In *Context and Consciousness: Activity Theory and Human-Computer Interaction*, B. Nardi, Ed. MIT Press, Cambridge, MA, 103–116.

[17] Kaptelinin, V., and Nardi, B. 2006. *Acting with Technology: Activity Theory and Interaction Design.* MIT Press, Cambridge, MA.

[18] Keith, C. 2011. *Agile Game Development with Scrum.* Addison-Wesley, Boston, MA.

[19] Kuh, G. D. 2008. *High Impact Educational Practices: What They Are, Who Has Access to Them, and Why They Matter.* AAC&U, Washington, D.C.

[20] Lave, J., and Wenger, E. 1991. *Situated Learning: Legitimate Peripheral Participation.* Cambridge University Press, Cambridge, UK.

[21] Martin, R. 2002. *Agile Software Development: Principles, Patterns, and Practices.* Pearson, Upper Saddle River, NJ.

[22] Martin, R. 2008. *Clean Code: A Handbook of Agile Software Craftsmanship.* Prentice Hall, Upper Saddle River, NJ.

[23] Nardi, B. 1996. Activity theory and human-computer interaction. In *Context and Consciousness: Activity Theory and Human-Computer Interaction*, B. Nardi, Ed. MIT Press, Cambridge, MA, 7–16.

[24] Nardi, B., and O'Day, V. 1999. *Information Ecologies. Using Technology with Heart*. MIT Press, Cambridge, MA.

[25] Propen, A. D., and Schuster, M.L. 2010. Understanding genre through the lens of advocacy: The rhetorical work of the victim impact statement. *Written Communication* 27(1), 3–35.

[26] Raeithel, A., and Velichkovsky, B. M. 1996. Joint attention and co-construction: New ways to foster user-designer collaboration. In *Context and Consciousness: Activity Theory and Human-Computer Interaction*, B. Nardi, Ed. MIT Press, Cambridge, MA, 199–233.

[27] Russell, D. 2009. Uses of activity theory in written communication research. In *Learning and Expanding with Activity Theory*, A. Sannino, H. Daniels, and K. D. Gutiérrez, Eds. Cambridge University Press, Cambridge, UK, 40–52.

[28] Schild, J., Walter, R., and Masuch, M. 2010. ABC-Sprints: adapting Scrum to academic game development courses. In *Proceedings of the Fifth International Conference on the Foundations of Digital Games (FDG '10)*. ACM, New York, NY, USA, 187-194. DOI=10.1145/1822348.1822373 http://doi.acm.org/10.1145/1822348.1822373

[29] Schön, D. A. 1984. *The Reflective Practitioner: How Professionals Think In Action*. Basic Books, New York, NY.

[30] Schwaber, K., and Beedle, M. 2001. *Agile Software Development with Scrum*. Prentice Hall, Upper Saddle River, NJ.

[31] Schwaber, K., and Sutherland, J. 2011. The Scrum Guide: The Definitive Guide to Scrum: The Rules of the Game. Scrum.org.

[32] Smagorinsky, P. 2008. The method section as conceptual epicenter in constructing social science research reports. *Written Communication* 25(3), 389–411.

[33] Spinuzzi, C. 2002. Compound mediation in software development: Using genre ecologies to study textual artifacts. In *Writing Selves/Writing Societies: Research from Activity Perspectives*, C. Bazerman and D. Russell, Eds. WAC Clearinghouse, Fort Collins, CO, 97–124.

[34] Spinuzzi, C. 2003. *Tracing Genres through Organizations: A Sociocultural Approach to Information Design*. MIT Press, Boston, MA.

[35] Spinuzzi, C. 2004. Four ways to investigate assemblages of texts: Genre sets, systems, repertoires, and ecologies. In *Proceedings of the 22nd Annual ACM Conference on Design of Communication (SIGDOC '04)*. ACM, New York, NY, 110–116.

[36] Spinuzzi, C. 2010. Secret sauce and snake oil: Writing monthly reports in a highly contingent environment. *Written Communication* 27(4), 363–409.

[37] Spinuzzi, C. 2011. Losing by expanding: Corralling the runaway object. *Journal of Business and Technical Communication* 25(4), 449–486.

[38] Stettina, C. J., and Heijstek, W. 2011. Necessary and neglected? An empirical study of internal documentation in agile software development teams. In *Proceedings of the 29th Annual ACM Conference on Design of Communication (SIGDOC '11)*. ACM, New York, NY, 159–166.

[39] Vygotsky, L. 1978. *Mind in Society: The Development of Higher Psychological Processes*. Harvard University Press, Cambridge, MA.

[40] Wallace, C., Mohan, S., Troy, D. and Hoffman, M. E. 2012. Scrum across the CS/SE curricula: a retrospective. In *Proceedings of the 43rd ACM technical symposium on Computer Science Education (SIGCSE '12)*. ACM, New York, NY, 5–6. DOI=10.1145/2157136.2157142 http://doi.acm.org/10.1145/2157136.2157142

QualiCES, A Method for Verifying the Consistency Among Documents of the Requirement Engineering Phase

Luã Marcelo Muriana
Federal University of Mato Grosso
UFMT
Cuiabá, Mato Grosso, Brazil
luamarcelo17@gmail.com

Cristiano Maciel
Federal University of Mato Grosso
UFMT
Cuiabá, Mato Grosso, Brazil
cmaciel@ufmt.br

Fabiana Freitas Mendes
University of Brasilia
UnB
Brasilia, Brazil
fabiana.mendes@unb.br

ABSTRACT
During the initial software specification phase, requirement document, use cases description and interface prototypes can be generated as a way to aid in the construction of system data. The consistency among these documents is a quality attribute which must be emphasized at this phase of the software development process. The QualiCES method is presented herein; it allows assessing the consistency among these software documents, and is supported by a checklist and by a consistency metrics developed to this end. As benefits, there is defect detection and a software quality warranty from the beginning of software development. The method was executed in a case study. Based on the results, the viability for applying the method can be verified, as well as the proposal innovation degree.

Categories and Subject Descriptors
D.2.4 [**Software/Program Verification**]: *Model checking, validation*; D.2.8 [**Metrics**]: *Performance measures;* D.2.9 [**Management**]: *Software quality assurance (SQA)*

Keywords
Software Quality; Software Inspection; Requirement Engineering; Consistency.

1. INTRODUCTION
Software development is a process that has gained increasing importance in the pre-sent society. As software development has grown, so has the complexity of clients' specifications. Thus, development costs, production time and maintenance difficulties increase, and the finished products are also subjected to different kinds of problems.

So that these problems do not last, there is a series of software validation and verification activities, such as the software inspection techniques that help to discover problems and, as a consequence, cooperate towards attaining software quality. Software quality is understood as the degree at which a system, component or process complies with the specified requirement, and/or with the end user's expectations [7].

Studies such as [15] and [11] show that conducting this validation and verification process from the very beginning of the software lifecycle reduces the costs and efforts spent to repair errors that may occur, besides ensuring that software quality is present since the beginning of a software lifecycle process. For this, it is important for quality assurance techniques to be used. In this study, this is obtained by means of a validation and verification method proposed for the requirement engineering phase, which is supported on the application of a checklist and on a consistency analysis metrics among documents generated in the initial phase of the software development process; the method was named QualiCES (Quality via Consistency in Software Specifications). Therefore, our aim is to define, to develop and to analyze a method that helps with the perception of consistency among software documents.

Faced with the existence of other works that verify the quality of a particular artifact in software design, this research focuses on the analysis of the consistency among three types of documents still at the requirement engineering phase: requirement document, use case description, and interface prototypes, viewing problem detection. Added to the motivation of this work is the fact that works with this research focus have not been found.

After the development of the QualiCES method, it was tested in the "Social eGov" design [9] allowing the verification of its documentation quality by means of the consistency among artifacts. .This research can be seen completely in [17].

The following Sections will detail this method. Initially, issues related to requirement engineering and to software quality are approached in Section 2. In Section 3, studies related to this research are presented. In turn, Section 4 presents the QualiCES method developed in this study. Section 5 reports the case study conducted as a way of verifying the viability of the method proposed. Lastly, Section 6 provides the final considerations.

2. THEORETICAL REFERENCES
According to [14], software development is composed of four basic and fundamental stages: requirement engineering, development, software validation and evolution.

During the requirement engineering phase, the needs and functionalities to be met by the software are identified and formalized in different documents. Despite being such an initial phase, quality must be taken into account, since requirements are the software foundations.

When the phase is conducted having quality in mind, it results in complete, clear, non-ambiguous requirements that follow the industry standards. Yet, for this to be attained, a lot of effort is necessary [8; 2].

During the requirement engineering phase, different software documents are generated, among which the following may be detached: requirement document, description of use cases, and interface prototypes.

The requirement document serves as a reference for the next phases in the software development process. If an error is not detected at the very beginning of this process, it may propagate and thus affect the other artifacts to be developed. Hence, finding and correcting errors in the requirement artifacts early in the software development process prevents future rework.

The use case description may derive from a requirement document, or may be developed so as to represent the system requirements. However, when building a use case model from the requirements, [3] says that the developer must be very aware as there will be defects deriving from previous phases, even if they have been inspected.

Another way to obtain requirements and/or verifying them is by means of prototyping the desired software. [14] says that a prototype may be used in a software process in several ways, and within requirement engineering, a prototype may aid the discovery and verification of the system requirements.

Dealing with requirements also involves their management, that is, once defined, they have to be made stable enough to ensure an adequate execution in later phases. If changes are necessary, they have to be adequately controlled. A tool used to this end is traceability, which usually denotes the degree at which a relation can be established among different development artifacts [11], i.e., traceability defines the relationship among the different parts of a system. [11] also says that the information obtained from traceability may help to ensure quality.

The QualiCES method analyzes the consistency among requirement documents and, as a consequence, assumes they are related. Hence, in case there is any inconsistency among them, they must be corrected. Therefore, requirement management and especially traceability are not directly related to this study; however, the method contributes to a correct traceability among the requirement documents.

Another stage of software development is validation, also known as Verification and Validation (V & V). However, "the term 'validation' is used inconsistently, both in the literature and in practice" [11]. Therefore, the definition by [16] is adopted herein, for both validation and verification. [16] says Validation means to analyze whether or not the right system is being built. On the other hand, [16] says Verification analyses whether or not the system is being built correctly. Therefore, this study is concerned with verifying if there is consistency among the documents of the requirement engineering phase so as to build the right system with quality.

[11] believes that software validation at initial phases of the software development process reduces the costs and the effort for correcting errors in phases following the development process. Detecting defects in the requirement document is seen as one of the most efficient and effective techniques of quality assurance in software engineering [12].

Within the V & V process, there are several approaches such as software inspection, software test, walkthrough and peer review [13]. We conducted a more in-depth study when approaching software inspection, seeing that this is currently one of the most common ways of software quality assurance [4]. Thus, this work is restricted to the software specification and software validation phases, considering that the latter should occur all along the development process.

Software inspection is defined as a formal assessment technique in which requirements and software design and even the program code are thoroughly examined by a person or a by a group of people aiming to detect defects, development standard violations and other problems [1]. [10] generalizes saying that software inspection is a specific type of revision which may be applied to all software artifacts and has a strict and well defined defect detection process, as can be seen in Figure 1 as follows.

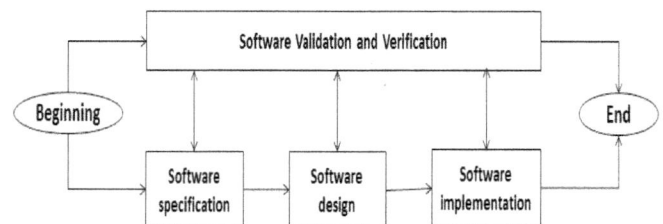

Figure 1. The software development process adopted for this work.

So as to improve understanding and the search for defects, there are different revision techniques in the software inspection process, among which the Checklist-Based Technique (CBT). This technique creates a guide (the checklist) which reminds the tester of the topics to be analyzed in the artifact and hence also helps to search for defects or deficiencies. "Individual items in a checklist may enumerate, prioritize or propose questions to help the reviewer to discover defects" [10].

Checklist use is considered a standard software inspection technique in many companies, as stated by [15]. This may be justified, as CBT may be applied as a complement in any other validation and verification technique [11]. For this reason, CBT was chosen as the base for this study.

Therefore, assuring software quality is ensuring that there is coherence in the ideas and information presented by the requirement documents, use cases and interface prototypes by the detection of problems, thus assuring that documents are consistent.

3. RELATED WORKS
In this work context, several studies were conducted in order to obtain software quality from the very beginning of the software development process.

Table 1. A summary of the focus of the studies.

Approach	Focus	Author
Requirement	Requirement quality.	Jani (2010)
	Validation and verification of requirements by means of a more interactive process.	Gusev (2010)
Use case	Construction of use cases for detecting defects in the requirement document.	Belgamo et al. (2005)
	Defects detection by the application of a checklist.	Anda, Sjøberg, (2002)
	Quality of the description of use cases.	Aurum *et al.* (2004)
	Quality of the description of use cases, and Quality of the use cases representation.	Gregolin (2007)
Software inspection	Comparison between software inspection techniques.	Thelin et al. (2003)

[8] conducted a study which analyzed the software specification requirement quality to assure that the quality is acceptable. A software quality assurance technique, a checklist was applied to the study to determine whether the requirement standards and procedures were or not being followed along the requirement specification phase. For this, the author identified quality attributes expected from a requirement specification document: complete, consistent, correct, modifiable, relevance rating, traceable, non-ambiguous, understandable, testable, verifiable, validable.

[6] goes further and proposes a more iterative verification and validation way. The author states that a way of obtaining a better quality not only in requirement specification, but all along the software development process, is to verify and validate all the artifacts generated all over the software process. The author says that, when the option is to work with an activity flow in which an activity will only be started after the previous activity is fully completed and approved, some defects will not be detected once they will only appear when tested in other phases of the software development process. Hence, the author proposes that other artifacts are generated for requirement verification and validation, such as prototypes, and that verification is not limited to the checklist alone, for example. To conclude, the author stresses that this activity flow does not assure that requirements are error-free, but assures that potentially critical defects affecting the implementation are identified.

In [15] study, two software inspection techniques are compared: the use-based one, and the checklist-based one. The authors say that the use-based technique is better than the checklist-based one in terms of effectiveness and efficiency, as it is capable of finding the defects that most affect users, besides its application being faster.

Both [6] and [15] criticize the checklist-based software inspection technique in their studies. However, the comparison proposed by the authors analyzes the detection of the most serious defects in the user's perspective, and the method proposed here analyzes more comprehensive problems such as the detection of lack of requirements, and inconsistency among software documents and artifacts.

[3] compare the checklist efficiency and effectiveness with the tool developed in their study: TUCCA (Technique for Use Case Model Construction and Construction-based Requirements Document Analysis). TUCCA is composed of two inspection techniques: AGRT (Actor Goal Reading Technique) which views determining the system actors and their goals, and UCRT (Use

Case Reading Technique) which aims to determine the use case model. Jointly, these techniques collaborate with the construction of the use case besides revising the requirement specification document. With the study and the experiment conducted, the authors showed that TUCCA is effective in building the use case and in defects detection, once the technique developed obtained results as good as the checklist-based technique. The authors consider that there are always defects in an artifact developed and that the requirement engineering phase is essential for the success of the software development next phases. Nevertheless, the method proposed by the authors is driven towards defect detection during the use cases building process; in turn, the method proposed herein is guided towards the identification of incoherence problems among use cases, requirement document and prototypes.

Once the use case is built, [1] say that its quality in terms of correctedness, completion, consistency and good understanding of the functional requirement are important to the final quality of the software product. Thus, [1],[2] and [5] developed, in each of their studies, a checklist that sought the identification of defects in the use cases. Some of the items analyzed by their respective checklists were considered in the elaboration of the QualiCES method checklist, as a dependence among use cases, actors and the lack of functionalities, for example. Yet, the method here proposed adapts these items so that a more interactive analysis can be performed, as proposed by [6] and thus not being limited to a single software document or artifact at a time.

[6] showed that when the validation and verification process occurs since the initial phase of the software development, more defects are likely to be detected. Hence, the author proposes a more interactive inspection process. The method developed herein considers as documents to be analyzed: requirement specification document, description of use cases and interface prototypes. That is, a method that analyzes the consistency between documents and artifacts generated during the requirement engineering process is proposed, not being limited to the quest for use case quality or requirement quality alone.

Therefore, as in the studies aforementioned, the QualiCES (Quality de Consistency in Software Specification) method proposed here is supported on the use of the checklist technique and, at the end of its application, quality attributes are expected to be attained as proposed by [5] and [8]. A summary of the focus of the studies aforementioned is shown in Table 1.

4. QualiCES METHOD

QualiCES (Quality via Consistency in Software Specifications) is a method that aims to assess the consistency among software documents, especially among requirement specification, use cases and interface prototypes. For this reason, it is a quality assurance method that can be used at the very initial phases of software development, contributing to reducing design costs.

QualiCES is a method that does not aim to analize the quality or content of documents; instead, it deals with the consistency among documents. It is assumed that the documents have been developed in a high-quality manner, and that possible problems have already been checked.

For the QualiCES method to be applied, the documents to be verified must be *frozen*, i.e., the documents assessed cannot undergo any kind of alteration during the application of the method proposed.

The method is composed of five stages, described as follows:

1. **Identification of quality needs:** this stage consists of identifying the needs of the software development team to assure software quality, as for example, efficiency in the delivery of services or products, a fact that represents quality improvement; or dissemination of good practices related to improvement in the organization as a whole and not in specific projects. Having in mind the importance of software quality from the very beginning of the software development process, detecting problems still at the requirement engineering phase cooperates towards the final efficiency of products delivered, for example. Thus, for applying the QualiCES method, requirement documents, description of use cases and interface prototypes have to be available;

2. **Analysis of the necessary documents**: this stage accounts for gathering the necessary documents for analyzing and for verifying whether:

   - The requirements of the requirement document are correctly identified; and
   - Each use case has an interface prototype related to it or the other way round.

Use cases that do not have a corresponding interface prototype, or vice versa, cannot be analyzed. The method proposed requires that all the use cases and prototypes necessary are developed so as to have an analysis and a greater quality assurance. This stage is composed of the following activities:

a) Obtaining the necessary documents for the method application;
b) Analyzing the documents, verifying whether there is a use case and a prototype or a set of corresponding prototypes, as well as verifying whether the requirement document is complete.

3. **Checklist application:** The checklist proposed by the method has to be filled separately for each use case having its respective prototype, so as to detect defects among the documents and artifacts of the requirement engineering process. Section 4.1 details the checklist of the method created. The following activities compose this stage:

a) Choosing a use case and its corresponding prototype and filling in the checklist heading, so as to identify the application made;

b) For each of the checklist questions, analyzing the rule and providing the final analysis report; and

c) If some defect is detected, filling the fields directed to identifying defects.

4. **Consistency metrics application:** With the checklist application, defects are detected, and from them, it is possible to apply the consistency metrics for analyzing the quality of the artifacts and documents inspected. The metrics description can be found in Section 4.2. For that, conducting the following activities is made necessary:

a) After answering the whole questionnaire, collecting data for applying the metrics, i.e., adding the points of each group of defects, per items, and obtaining the total valid questions; and

b) Applying the consistency metrics according to the formulas defined in Section 4.2.

5. **Analysis of results:** the results obtained from the consistency metrics application should be analyzed according to the parameters defined in Section 4.3. The following activities compose this stage:

a) Analyzing the result obtained and recording it;

b) Going back to stage 3 and conducting the other subsequent activities and stages until all the use cases and their prototypes are inspected; and

c) Reporting to those responsible for the software specification so that the due corrections can be made, when necessary.

The QualiCES method execution flowchart can be seen in Figure 2. The numbering of the activities refers to the numbers of each stage of the method, as well as the activity to be conducted at each stage (Table 2).

The following sections will describe the three last stages of the method. Stages 1 and 2, respectively, are assumed not to require specific procedures for being carried out. Stage 1 requires the application of the method. In Stage 2, in turn, the existence of all the necessary documents for applying the method is verified, as previously described in item 2 of this section.

4.1 Stage 3 – Checklist

A checklist was developed to help to perceive inconsistencies among software documents, guiding the search for defects among documents.

In the checklist construction, questions were generated to analyze the documents, as well as the consistency among them. The questions were separated into five items to be considered during the inspection process. Each checklist question is composed of an assessment rule, which is found with the question, and the purpose of which is to help to fill in the checklist. As an alternative to answering the questions, four op tions are proposed. Whenever a problem is detected, the checklist provides the analysis of the problem identified in 3 different perspectives which have to be compulsorily filled in. The checklist proposed is composed of four parts, as depicted in Figure 3, which are: i)

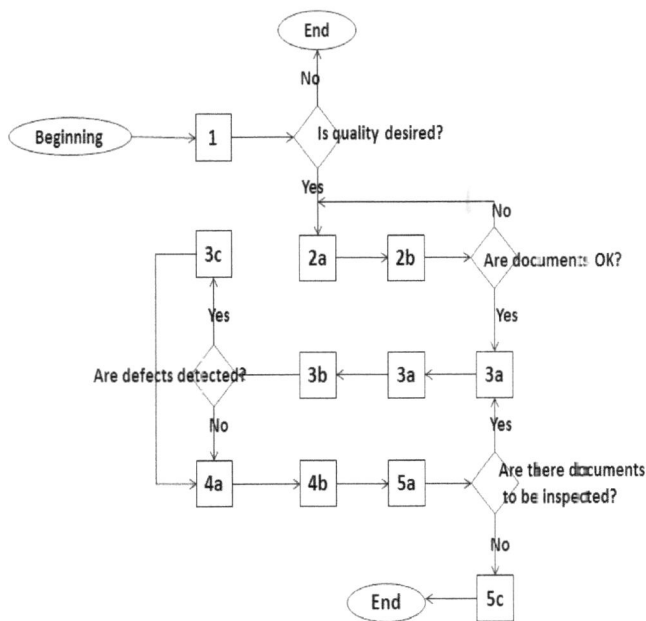

Figure 2. QualiCES method flowchart.

Table 2. Flowchart activities

Activity ID	Activity Description
1	**Identification of quality needs**
2	**Analysis of the necessary documents**
2a	Obtaining the necessary documents for the method application
2b	Analyzing the documents.
3	**Checklist application**
3a	Choosing a use case and its corresponding prototype and filling in the checklist heading.
3b	Analyzing the rule and providing the final analysis report
3c	Filling the fields directed to identifying defects.
4	**Consistency metrics application**
4a	collecting data for applying the metrics.
4b	Applying the consistency metrics
5	**Analysis of results**
5a	Analyzing the result obtained and recording it;
5b	Going back to stage 3
5c	Reporting to those responsible for the software specification.

items analyzed/questions/rules; ii) conclusion, that is, a response given to the question; iii) classification of the problem found; and iv) justification and/or observations concerning the item analyzed.

4.1.1 Items analyzed.

The checklist contains 28 questions, divided into five items to be simultaneously analyzed among the requirement document, use case description document and interface prototype. They are:

- **Content:** includes four questions analyzing the use case general description, verifying the reach of the objective proposed and of the functionality provided in the requirement document, both by means of the use case, and by means of the

prototype. Furthermore, it groups items analyzing the data dictionary, as well as the terms used to identify the functionality objective;

Functionality: counts on seven questions analyzing if both the use case and the prototype consider all the functional requirements related to the functionality described in the use case. Moreover, they aim to detect the omission of a requirement and/or of a requirements that does not apply to the use case or to the prototype inspected;

- **Functionality execution:** so that a certain system functionality is attained, some steps have to be followed, some restrictions and/or alternatives also have to be considered. Therefore, this section counts on questions analyzing whether the major and alternative flows, as well as the restrictions of a use case, can be followed in the interface prototype. Again, the existence of missing or spare steps in both artifacts is verified. There is also an analysis of whether the pre and post conditions of the use case are perceived in the prototype. This Section contains nine questions;

- **Dependence between functionalities:** some use cases need another one to complete a certain functionality in a system. Hence, this item accounts for analyzing whether the use case description and the prototype consider an include and exclude relationship among the use cases. This item is composed of four questions;

- **Users:** any system developed may have several types of users classified according to their function within a system. This item thus analyzes whether all the users/actors have been modeled both in the use case and in the prototype, besides analyzing whether roles and responsibilities were respected within the functionality proposed. This item is composed of four questions.

Figure 3. Structure of the checklist proposed.

4.1.1.1 Questions assessments rules

So that each of the questions related to each item analyzed could be correctly interpreted, validation rules were defined, as in the examples as follows:

- **Rule 2.1** – The use case should describe all the functionalities desired for it and for the related functional requirements. Related question: 5;

- **Rule 3.2** – The use case description should specify the main and alternative flow as completely as possible, allowing each of the flow steps to be executed by means of the prototype. Related questions: 13 and 16.

The purpose of the validation rules is to aid the one applying the method during the inspection process. The rules defined for each question show what and how it can be analyzed so that a problem is/is not identified.

4.1.2 Possible conclusions for the questions

By means of the validation rules of the questionnaire, it is possible to have four response options:

- **Yes/No:** for some questions, *yes* refers to situations in which the rule defined for a certain question analyzed is fully complied with, whereas *no* refers to situations in which the rule defined is not complied with. Yet, depending on the question, the opposite will also be possible for both possibilities.

- **Partly:** when the rule defined is partly complied with, i.e., when it is complied with, but some information lacks to complete it;

- **Not applicable:** when it is not possible to respond to a question or when it is impossible to analyze the request, or because some other issue has not been met and, therefore, the related questions cannot be answered. Attention must be given to this report, as it will be important for the consistency metrics application.

4.1.3 Classification of the problems detected

The aim of the QualiCES method is to identify problems by filling in the checklist developed herein. For this, the validation rules defined for each of the 28 questions composing the checklist must be taken as a base for interpretation. Thus, whenever a rule fails to be fully or partly complied with, a problem is detected, and therefore, the problem has to be analyzed in three different ways:

1. **Hinders the objective:** a defect may or not affect the implementation of a functionality. When a problem is perceived, the reviewer may therefore say whether it affects (*yes* or *no*) the use case objective and its functionality.

- **Yes:** When the objective affects the user, preventing him/her from using the functionality analyzed. Examples: a functional requirement is missing, some characteristics of the role of a system user are not considered;

- **No:** When the defect does not affect the reach of the functionality objective. Example: difference between the attributes of a data dictionary and the attributes identified in the prototype.

2. **Correction urgency:** a defect differs from another in several items, and one of them is related to correction urgency. Thus, when a problem is detected, the correction urgency should be analyzed. The urgency can be classified into three levels, as follows:

- **Short term:** When the defect detected has to be corrected before starting the software design phase. Example: missing requirements;

- **Medium term:** When the software design process can be followed, but the defect has to be corrected before the implementation. Example: adding a missing key in the prototype because the use case failed to foresee this action.

- **Long term:** When the defect can be corrected during or after the software implementation. Example: alteration in the name of the fields.

3. **Functionality importance:** Based on the user's perspective, the defect detected should be classified considering the importance of the functionality to the user, which may be:

- **Very important:** if the defect found prevents the user from executing a functionality. Example: the lack of a requirement;

- **Important:** if the defect found partly affects the user's interaction with the system. Example: the lack of a "cancel" key;

- **Not very important:** if the defect found does not at all affect the user's interaction with the system. Example: name divergence between the data dictionary of the use case description, and the name used in the prototype.

Hence, after filling in the checklist, and with the defects detected, the QualiCES method recommends the generation of indicators by means of the consistency metrics. The metrics details are presented in the next section.

4.2 Stage 4 – Consistency metrics

The consistency metrics was developed to support the QualiCES method so as to cooperate with a faster visualization of the number of problems detected once the metrics proposed specifically points to where the greatest problems lie. Therefore, the consistency metrics is a simple way of verifying the presence of quality as early as in the requirement engineering phase.

The consistency metrics is composed of three stages: data collection, data analysis and result presentation. The subsections as follows detail each of these stages.

4.2.1 Data collection and data tabulation .

At this stage, the data necessary to generate each of the indicators proposed by QualisCES are presented and described. This stage is composed of the following steps:

a) For each question answered in the checklist in which a problem is found, the *poX* scoring obtained is added in relation to the attributes "hinders the objective", "correction urgency", and "functionality importance", in which X is the number of the question being considered. This scoring is given considering Table 3.

Table 3. Definition of values for the possible answers.

Hinders the objective	Correction urgency	Functionality importance
Yes = 1	Short term = 3	Very important = 3
No = 0	Medium term = 2	Important = 2
	Long term = 1	Not very important = 1

b) For each item (content, functionality, functionality execution, dependence between functionalities, and users), the X scoring (*poX*) of the questions composing it is added, thus obtaining the scoring of the questions related to the content item (poC), the scoring of the questions related to the functionality item (poF), the scoring of the questions related to the functionality execution item (poEF), the scoring of the questions related to the dependence between functionalities item (poDF) and the scoring of the questions related to the user item (poU). The scorings are recorded in a checklist as that illustrated in Figure 3.

c) Each item scoring previously obtained is multiplied by its corresponding weight; for this, consider Table 4.

Table 4. Weights concerning each item analyzed.

Item	Weight (P)
Content (C)	PC = 0.1
Functionality (F)	PF = 0.3
Functionality execution (EF)	PEF = 0.4
Dependence between functionalities (DF)	PDF = 0.1
Users (U)	PU = 0.1

The weights defined in the previous table were obtained by means of the number of questions existing in each item analyzed. For this, the total questions in each item analyzed was divided by the total questions in the checklist. The results obtained were approximated and thus the values in Table 3 were obtained

$$PC = 4 \text{ questions} / 28 \text{ questions} = 0.14$$
$$PF = 7 \text{ questions} / 28 \text{ questions} = 0.25$$
$$PEF = 9 \text{ questions} / 28 \text{ questions} = 0.32$$
$$PDF = 4 \text{ questions} / 28 \text{ questions} = 0.14$$
$$PU = 4 \text{ questions} / 28 \text{ questions} = 0.14$$

It is worth stressing that, in case there are modifications in the checklist so that it can be adapted to other applications, such as the number of questions to be considered; for example, it will be necessary to make alterations in the values in Table 3.

d) The scoring obtained between the items and their respective weights are added, and the result obtained is divided by the total valid questions (TPV), thus obtaining the consistency quality coefficient (QC), as can be seen at number 1, in which TPV is the total number of valid questions (number 2), TP is the total number of questions in the checklist, and TPNA is the total non-applicable questions.

$$QC = (poC*PC + poF*PF + poFE*PFE + \\ poDF*PDF + poU*pU)/TPV \qquad (1)$$

$$TPV = TP - TPNA \qquad (2)$$

4.3 Stage 5 – Analysis of results

After the application of the consistency metrics for each checklist filled in, the method proposed expects the results to be analyzed. Hence, this study considers that the consistency among the documents analyzed during the requirement engineering phase is given by using the following values:

- **Consistent:** when the result of the metrics application (QC) yields results smaller or equal to 0.199;

- **Not very consistent**: when the result of the metrics application yields results greater than 0.,3 and smaller than 0.699;

- **Inconsistent:** when the result of the metrics application yields results greater than 0.7.

The values defined for rating the results obtained were chosen based on the average of the results obtained with the application of QualiCES in the case study described in Section 5. Hence, more tests with these values are necessary.

4.3.1 Presentation format

For presenting the data collected, tabulated and analyzed, the tabular format was chosen. The table should have the following columns: use case, items, scoring of each item, total non-applicable questions (TPNA), consistency quality (QC), and final rating. Every time the checklist is filled in, an input is generated in the Table with sublines containing the name of the use case or of the prototype and each of the items analyzed. For each item, the scoring obtained is placed beside it, along with the TPNA, QC and the rating obtained. Observe Table 5.

5. CASE STUDY

The software design chosen for applying the method is described in this Section, as well as the results attained with the verification.

The case study was carried out with the verification of the documentation in a software development design being implemented by the 'Social eGov" research project, which is currently composed by 14 researchers, comprising undergraduate students, master's candidates and professors of the Computer Science course. So far, the project has produced the following documents: requirement specification, use cases and interface; and artifacts such as modeling entity-relationship. The purpose of the "Social eGov" design is to cooperate and to expand the citizens' participation in the Government-related issues. For this, the group has developed a component framework, which has allowed the customization of resources during the e-participative systems development [9].

As determined by stage 2 of the QualiCES method, it is necessary to analyze the documents to be inspected. In this project, the following were documented:

- In the system requirement document, 23 functional requirements;
- In the requirement document, as well as in the use cases description document, four classifications of users for the system;
- 42 use cases;
- 17 interface prototypes.

Table 5. Model for tabulating the result obtained from the QualiCES method.

Identification	Item	Scoring	TPNA	QC	Rating
<name of use case or of prototype>	Content	<poC>	TPNA	QC	<Consistent or not very consistent or Inconsistent>
	Functionality	<poF>			
	Functionality execution:	<poEF>			
	Dependence between functionalities:	<poDF>			
	Users	<poU>			

After the documents analysis, it was possible to apply the checklist (stage 3), thus obtaining the necessary data for the application of the consistency metrics provided in stage 4 of the method proposed.

After the documents analysis, it was possible to apply the checklist (stage 3), thus obtaining the necessary data for the application of the consistency metrics provided in stage 4 of the method proposed.

As a result of the application of the checklist and of the metrics, it was possible to detect inconsistencies in all of the documents analyzed. The items that most presented defects were "functionalities" and "functionality execution".

According to the consistency metrics proposed herein, the checklist application showed that the documents and artifacts analyzed are: consistent, not very consistent or inconsistent. As from the values obtained with the QualiCES method application, it was possible to elaborate Table 6, which contains the rating of the results analyzed, as well as the number of defects found overall at every consistency level possible.

Table 6. Number of defects found for each final rating of the metrics.

Consistency level	Final classification	Number of problems detected	Percentage
Consistent	6	12	32.73%
Not very consistent	7	54	43.63%
Inconsistent	4	44	23.64%
TOTAL	17	110	100%

6. QualiCES METHOD ANALYZIS

The method QualiCES' aplication in the project "Social e-Gov" allowed to realize the lack of consistency among documents analyzed. As can be seen in Table 6, the results show that eleven documents were either not very consistent or inconsistent, totaling 98 defects detected. These problems could represent a loss to the quality of the system longer. Therefore, detection of them at this point of software development as stated [11] will reduce the cost and effort need for future corrections.

Based on the results obtained with this research, the QualiCES method showed to be viable for applications. The method viability is due to the advantages it presents:

- During the method application, three software documents are concurrently and interactively analyzed, allowing problems to be detected in any of them;

- The method proposed presents a metrics that analyzes the consistency among these documents according to the amount of problems detected;

- The way the results obtained are presented with the application of the checklist (see Table 4), facilitates the perception of where the greatest problems lie.

Therefore, as can be analyzed, the QualiCES method goes beyond the studies mentioned in Section 3. A large share of the studies conducted is supported on a single document for analysis so as to detect problems, such as [1], [2] and [5]. This study, in turn, as suggests [6], uses several documents simultaneously.

The V & V process is a way of assuring software quality. In this sense, with the QualiCES method application, some quality attributes could be analyzed, identified and verified, such as: completeness, internal consistency, reachability, traceability, correctedness and accuracy. While [5] adapts these attributes to the use cases quality, [8] adapts them to requirement quality. Here, quality attributes are adapted so as to verify the consistency among the requirements and use cases and prototypes. Therefore, in the requirement engineering phase, the QualiCES method allows for:

- **Completeness:** all the functionalities described by the use cases and represented in the prototypes are specified in the requirement document;

- **Internal Consistency:** functional requirements, use cases and prototypes are not conflicting among themselves;

- **Reachability:** the prototype related to the use case represents the description and the functional requirement specification, also meeting possible non-functional usability requirements;

- **Traceability:** being each requirement and use case duly identified, it is possible to trace the consistency among them;

- **Correctedness:** being the functionality correctly described by the use case and represented by the prototype, their definition in the requirement document describes their objective accurately;

- **Accuracy:** once accurately described, functional requirements and use cases assure the prototype reachability.

7. FUTURE WORKS AND CONCLUSIONS

The QualiCES method (Quality via Consistency in Software Specifications) proposes a sequence of steps aligned with the software development phases and may be applied in the requirement engineering phase, by analyzing the consistency among software documents by means of problem detection.

For this, the method proposes a checklist, which supports the analysis of content. functionalities, functionality execution, the dependence between functionalities and the role of users by verifying the requirement document, description of use cases and prototypes. The problems detected by the checklist application are classified, and are then analyzed by means of a consistency metrics which allows classifying the documents analyzed into consistent, not very consistent and inconsistent. The method also proposes a way of syntactically presenting the inspection results.

Besides problem detection, the method proposed showed to support the quality assurance process. Thus, by means of the checklist developed, several software quality attributes are contemplated: completeness, internal consistency, reachability, traceability, correctedness and accuracy. For these attributes to be attained, the work proposed presented a set of assessment rules for the checklist questions, which serve as design guidelines in the software engineering area, independently of the checklist. The rules defined in the QualiCES method provide important recommendations concerning content, functionality, functionality execution, dependence between functionalities and the role of system users.

However, the focus of the method proposed lies on the analysis of the functional requirements; hence, non-functional requirements are not considered during the checklist application. Yet, as future works, we intend to use usability and accessibility factors.

Also, the method is limited for requiring that only use cases that have their respective prototypes, or vice-versa, may be inspected. Furthermore, only inspecting use cases that have their respective prototype constrains the method, once prototypes are not always produced as a detailing of use cases. For this, as a future work, the suggestion is that the method be able to adapt to situations in which not all the requirement documents are available.

For being a use case model, the method proposed was based on the case model by the "Social eGov" research team, which was used as a case study for this work. Thus, as future work, our intention is to make the method adequate to internationally acknowledged use case templates.

Moreover, this study needs further tests so that both the checklist and the consistency metrics may be validated and proved, thus improving them. The other studies may allow calibrating the consistency metrics QC developed herein, since all the values suggested are considered suggestions that may be adapted at each design, and are referred to in Tables 1 and 3.

Again, the method proposed was applied by a single tester and it is thus necessary for other testers to use the method as a way of verifying its behavior in other designs, along with analyzing testers' understanding in the application of the checklist and of the metrics developed.

The method is still limited to requiring the tester that applies the method to know software engineering; he/she is also recommended to know the design to which the method is applied. Thus, as future works, refining and optimizing the questions of the checklist proposed are also suggested.

Besides the suggestions considered, the following works may evolve from the present study: experiments and comparatives of software inspection of the method proposed with the existing ones; comparison and comparatives of applying the method proposed with methods that separately consider the requirement document and the description of use cases; and, along the software development process, assessing the decrease in implementation errors due to the application of the method.

8. REFERENCES

[1] B. Anda, D. I. K. Sjøberg.: Towards in the Inspection Technique for Use Case Models. In SEKE'02 -14th IEEE Conference on Software Engineering and Knowledge Engineering, Ischia, Italy, July 15-19, 2002, pp 127-134.

[2] Aurum, K. Cox, R. Jeffery.: An Experiment in Inspection the Quality of Use Case Descriptions. In Journal or Research and Practice in Information Technology, 2004, Vol. 36, No. 4.

[3] Belgamo, S. Fabbri, J. C. Maldonado.: TUCCA: Improving the Effectiveness of Use Construction and Requirement Analysis. In Empirical Software Engineering, 2005 International Symposium, 2005, vol., no., pp. 10 pp., 17-18.

[4] F. Elberzhager, J. Münch, B. Freimut.: Optimizing Cost and Quality by Integrating Inspection and Test Processes. Waikiki, Honolulu, HI, USA, 2011.

[5] R. Gregolin.: "Uma proposta de inspeção de em modelos de caso de uso." São Paulo, 2007. Dissertação de mestrado. Instituto de Pesquisas Tecnológicas do Estado de São Paulo.

[6] G. Gusev.: Practical Review of Software Requirements. In Software Engineering Conference (CEE-SECR), 2010 6th Central and Eastern European, 2010, pp.185-188, 13-15.

[7] IEEE, IEEE Std 610.12-1990.: IEEE Standard Glossary of Software Engineering Terminology. Corrected Edition, in IEEE Software Engineering Standards Collection, The Institute of Electrical and Electronics Engineers, New York, 1991.

[8] JANI, H. M.: Applying Case-Based Reasoning to Software Requirements Specifications Quality Analysis System. In Software Engineering and Data Mining (SEDM), 2010 2nd International Conference on, 2010, vol., no., pp.140-144, 23-25.

[9] Maciel, C. SLaviero, P. C. Souza, M. A. D. CAMPOS, E. C. SANTANA.: Platform design details to support eparticipation environments deployment. In: Third IFIP WG 8.5 International Conference on eParticipation (ePart 2011), Delf. Electronic Government and Electronic Participation. Osterreich : Trauner Verlag, 2011. v. 37. p. 382-391.

[10] S. M. Melo.: "Inspeção de Software". University of São Paulo: São Carlos, SP, 2009. Available at: <http://moodle.stoa.usp.br/file.php/559/InspecaoArtigo.pdf?forcedownload=1> [Accessed 15 September 2011]

[11] K. Pohl.: Requirement Engineering. Springer – Verlag Berlin Heidelberg, Springer, 2010.

[12] A.A. Porter, L. G. Votta Jr., V. R. Brasili.: Comparing Detection Methods for Software Requirements Inspections: A replicates Experiments. 1995 Available at < http://ieeexplore.ieee.org/xpl/freeabs_all.jsp?arnumber=391380> [Accessed 09 octover 2011]

[13] SOFTEX, "MPS. BR – Guia de Melhoria de Processo do Software Brasileiro", 2011. Available at: <http://softex.br/mpsbr/_guias/guias/MPS.BR_Guia_de_Impl

ementacao_Parte_4_2011.pdf>, [Accessed 10 November 2011]

[14] Sommerville.: "Engenharia de Software São Paulo". Pearson Adisson-Wesley. Brazil, 7th edition, 2007.

[15] T. Thelin, P. Runeson, C. Wholin.: An Experimental Comparison of Usage-Based and Checklist Reading. In IEEE Transictions on Sofware Engineering, 2003, vol.29, no 8.

[16] Boehm, B. W.: Verifying and Validating Software Requirements and Design Specifications. Reprinted in Boehm, B. W. (ed.), Software Risk Management, pp. 205 - 218, IEEE Computer Society Press, 1989.

[17] Muriana, L. M. : Um Metódo para Garantia da Qualidade de Software na Fase de Engenharia de Requisitos. Cuiabá, Mato Grosso, 2011. Trabalho de Conclusão de Curso apresentado ao Instituto de Computação da UFMT.

Understanding Social Media Advertising in Higher Ed:
A Case Study from a Small Graduate Program

Laura Palmer
Southern Polytechnic State University
1100 South Marietta Parkway
Marietta, GA 30060
1-678-915-7203
lpalmer2@spsu.edu

ABSTRACT

This paper describes how a small academic program used social media marketing—specifically, a Facebook advertising campaign and a Facebook page—to attract prospective students. From the results obtained, the design and deployment of Facebook as part of a strategic departmental communication and marketing plan requires more study. While advertisements brought users to the page, the conversations and engagement typically expected in a social network site did not materialize. In the end, the online advertising and promotion resulted in no new student applications to the graduate program.

Categories and Subject Descriptors

H.5.3 [**Group and Organizational Interfaces**]—web-based interaction, synchronous interaction, theory and models

General Terms

Documentation, Design

Keywords

Social media, higher education, social media advertising, Facebook, communication

1. INTRODUCTION

The English, Technical Communication, and Media Arts (ETCMA) department at Southern Polytechnic State University (SPSU) offers an online graduate degree called the M.Sc. in Information Design & Communication (IDC). Faced with increased competition and waning applications, the graduate faculty in ETCMA sought new ways to promote the degree and attract more applicants to the program. Social media advertising seemed to be a logical and cost-effective choice. As an online program, recruiting through a channel like a social network site (SNS) would be a way to capture individuals who were digitally literate and possibly interested in pursuing distance education. Additionally, it was thought that this group would be willing to enquire about the program and share information through an SNS due to their familiarity with online interactions. Yet, the design of

social media communication as a way to reach and recruit these students for a small program within a university was unfamiliar territory for the IDC graduate faculty.

At educational institutions across the country, social media marketing is gaining ground. It provides a viable opportunity for marketing higher education offerings [1], p. 15. With the ability to reach an ever-growing online market easily and with a financial outlay measuring as fractional compared to traditional advertising mediums, targeted social media advertising is a logical choice.

What follows is our experience of creating a Facebook presence for the purpose of promoting our graduate degree offering via Facebook advertisements. Specifically, this research focuses on the design and targeting of the ads deployed through Facebook's advertising feature. It also examines how the page functioned as a site of engagement for promoting the graduate program. The results, as assessed by Facebook interaction metrics, web site traffic statistics from analytics, and applications to the program, define our limited understanding of the design of social media communication for marketing small programs in higher education. This study makes a strong case for further research.

2. BACKGROUND

The IDC program experienced a drop in applications starting in the fall semester of 2010. The program—formerly a Master of Science in Technical Communication—traditionally had solid application and enrollment statistics; however, the recent decline in applicants meant it was time to reconsider our marketing efforts. Print ads in professional societies' magazines, once the bread and butter of the advertising plan, were not yielding results. Changes in professional societies' membership significantly decreased the number of people who saw the ads. As these societies moved their professional publications from print to digital-only formats, our opportunities for visibility also dropped.

Radio spots, another tried and true tactic in our advertising arsenal, were also losing ground as a marketing initiative. While the Gordian knot of metropolitan traffic practically guaranteed a captive radio audience, changes in technology reconfigured the drive-time audience base. MP3 players, satellite radio, and GPS systems with real-time traffic information meant drivers selected media other than radio. Print, radio, and other traditional outbound advertising media were also becoming more costly and proving to be the least effective means available to reach potential students [2], p. 30. Overall, relying on these outbound marketing channels was not serving the program well.

Inbound marketing, as measured by visitor traffic to the IDC program web site, was gaining ground. The web site's analytics, which we tracked with some regularity, indicated a robust number of hits to the site each month—around 1,000, on average.

Additionally, the analytics revealed that the organic hits to the site were good; in other words, the major search engines were bringing people to the web site.

However, the web site had its limitations. While it was a digital, inbound marketing asset, its function after a certain point was similar to brochureware—it was static. Informational gaps arose for students as the site could not answer every question a prospect might have [3], p. 8. Additional questions required a phone call to the department or an email—an outmoded form of communication for many younger people [2], p. 36. The web site failed to leverage interactive communication, harness the increased credibility of online word-of-mouth marketing [1], p. 15 and capitalize on user-generated testimonials for decision-making [3], p. 9. Common sense and the wild successes of the business world led us to believe that social media advertising could increase awareness about the program, and ultimately, our application numbers [3], p. 8. Thus, we began a process that would lead to marketing the graduate program through Facebook advertisements and, in turn, a Facebook page.

3. OUR PROCESS

The design of communication—as both content and advertising—for a SNS such as Facebook required a multi-phased approach. The initial start of the Facebook advertising campaign lagged due to an unexpected but necessary internal learning curve. While the IDC graduate faculty were enthusiastic about beginning our online marketing campaign, actually carrying it out was significantly more challenging. The very ease of using social media, as a casual, conversational activity, belies the complexities of using it as a medium for professional communication, interaction, and promotion.

Our development process prior to launching advertising included:

- Page setup
- Content and audience
- Page management
- Engagement metrics

3.1 Page Setup

At the outset, we learned setting up the correct category of Facebook page was vital. Categorizing it under the "Company, Organization, or Institution" heading for page type was important—launching a personal page for a business entity is an all-too-common "rookie" mistake. The correct page type and a relevant page name, along with completing the "About" information, is vital for the findability of the page via searches within Facebook or through other popular search engines. Additionally, including the IDC program's URL is critical for referring visitors to more information about the graduate offerings. While requiring some concerted thought, these setup tasks proved some of the simplest processes we would encounter in the early phases of our campaign.

3.2 Content and Audience

Once the page was set-up, the two most challenging questions were *What content would we put on our Facebook page?* and *Why would people come here to read it?* An early thought about content was to make the Facebook page private—that is, make it non-viewable to the public. This would mean content would not be a concern. We could then use the advertising mechanism and

link from the ads to the web site's IDC graduate program information.

However, with further consideration, we felt this would violate user expectations for the channel. Additionally, as the real power of Facebook for brand awareness is conversational and interactive communications among people, having a page that was both private and inactive would not serve us well. From this discussion, we moved forward with making the page public under the name *Information Design & Communication: SPSU.*

Our original questions about *What content?* and *Why would people come?* still lingered. We needed to consider user engagement and the value-proposition in what we were communicating. Now, however, we also had the question of *Who will manage the page?* to resolve. Our initial idea of merely advertising via social media now meshed with problems ranging from the ambiguous to the complex. At times, the initiative felt like the *ready-fire-aim* model of strategy and less like an intentional plan.

Because social media is about people and relationships as they interact to share meaning, we did not want to aggressively promote brand awareness on the Facebook page [1], p. 14. As we were unsure about exactly what content we would generate and who would generate it, the most expedient solution was to post brief prefatory comments with links to material relevant for an IDC graduate student—current or prospective. The *Why would people come?* portion of our two initial questions would be tangentially answered, we hoped, from our content links.

For current students, the material would engage them with broad ideas in the fields related to IDC and provide them with a springboard for online discussion. For prospective students, the link to current students and the opportunity to exchange ideas about the program and the profession were obvious. As well, the linked material would help demonstrate the breadth of our program from its roots in technical communication to its expansion into other disciplinary areas. In short, the material might help a potential student understand the program and determine if it would be a good fit with their goals. For both cohorts, we thought this material would be good starting points for on-the-page interactions and exchanges.

3.3 Page Management

With the *What* and *Why* of content answered, the issue of page management and oversight required our attention. Someone would need to post content, monitor responses, reply to queries, create/manage the advertising, and be "the voice" of the page. Per industry wisdom, that person should not be a student intern or anyone unfamiliar with the details of the program [4], p. 217-218. Ultimately, the page manager would be a current member of the IDC graduate faculty[1].

As this faculty member had experience with a personal Facebook page, some of the basic functions of a SNS were understood. However, performing those functions through a personal Facebook account was a less-than-optimal solution; conflating personal and professional social media identities is fraught with problems. Thus, a second Facebook account was created solely for generating a generic profile called "IDC Pagemanager." The profile allowed the faculty member to manage the page and post; additionally, a department admin also had access to see the

---

[1] This individual is also author of this experience report.

weekly billings and reconcile advertising expenses with credit card changes.

3.4 Engagement Metrics

In order to understand the page's user activity—that is, to see the day-to-day metrics called "Insights" in Facebook's nomenclature—we had to have "Likes" in excess of 30. We announced the creation of the page to our graduate students and faculty; a few new Likes appeared but not nearly enough for our goal of seeing the Insights. We learned that most of the faculty and graduate students were not Facebook users—the myth of ubiquity was shattered. Yet, we needed Likes for a variety of reasons. Insights data was one of the reasons, but we also wanted to leverage user interaction to increase search engine ranking [5], p. 171. An increased ranking, we thought, might be another way to capture organic search users—a significant cohort, according to our analytics. Hearing our plight, one of our graduate students convinced several of his Facebook friends to "seed" our page with Likes, and soon we hit the magic number of 30.

4. ADVERTISING WITH FACEBOOK

With the issues of deployment, content, management, metrics, and initial user base now considered, we could turn our attention back to our initial goal of advertising. Facebook's interface for creating online advertising was relatively straightforward—we needed artwork, a text-based call-to-action, a budget, an idea of our target population's demographics, and a method of payment. Some internal processes came into play again and deferred our initial effort once more. Encumbering our $350 budget to the department's credit card, as a weekly charge-per-click on the ad, was initially challenging because the business model did not mesh with established university processes. We also needed to be sure the credit card information would be secure on Facebook's back end. With these administrative issues managed, we moved forward.

4.1 Campaign #1: March and April

Our first ad launched in March of 2011 (Figure 1) and represented a cautious step into the world of Facebook advertising. For artwork, we followed examples of other higher education advertisers and used the university's logo. The call-to-action asked users to learn more about our programs.

SPSU SOUTHERN POLYTECHNIC STATE UNIVERSITY

Information Design & Communication

Learn about our Master of Science in IDC degree or our Graduate Certificate in Technical Communication

This ad targets 427,840 users:
- who live in the United States
- age 18 and older
- who like illustration, information architecture, graduate school, graphics, master's degree, technical communication, graphic design, usability, multimedia design, information design, instructional design, design, content developer, graphic designer

Figure 1: Initial Facebook advertisement for the program.

Using Facebook's demographic targeting selectors to reach a relevant audience, the ad delivered to adult residents of the US who listed interests broadly related to graduate school, design, and/or communication in their Facebook profile. With a target base of 427,840 users, it was easy to assume we would get hits—even one-tenth of 1% would be admirable.

At the end of April—two months after the start of the campaign—the results were compelling. The ad received two clicks, resulting in an expenditure of $1.41 of our $350 budget. Our website's analytics reported Facebook had been responsible for five visitors to our site. This number represented 0.24% of all the visits to the site for the two-month period. Of those five visits, the analytics indicated Facebook visitors had an Average Visit Duration (AVD) of 35 seconds and a 2.8 average of Pages/Visit (P/V) viewed. The analytics' statistics for the site as a whole showed the AVD to be 2.54 minutes and P/V to be 3.59. Our limited results via these engagement metrics were perplexing [5], p. 259.

We did not see a significant uptick in page Likes during this first campaign—only a few current graduate students and one or two additional faculty members Liked the page. Other measures of interaction beyond Likes, such as comments on posts and shares, were negligible. Potential students were not asking questions via the page, and current students were silent. Our content, as a starting point for user engagement, lacked buoyancy.

4.2 Campaign #2: May and June

Our second round of advertising—a May 15th to June 30th campaign—required a different approach. Launching more ads, per Facebook's recommendation, was one tactic employed. As this author was teaching a special topics summer course on content strategy, adding a module on Facebook advertising was a natural fit. Certainly, current students would have insight into reaching their peer cohort and the assignment would be an interesting addition to their course work. They would create the artwork, determine the demographic targeting, and write the microcopy for their individual Facebook advertisements.

Two instructor caveats, taken from the text *The Facebook Marketing Book*, informed the students' work for this assignment. First, they needed to design ads that would provide a "seamless user experience" [5], p. 225. The click-through must take users to the Facebook page. Second, the ads needed to reflect "user-generated content" rather than the high production values of professional graphics and "polished stock photography" [5], p. 227. Following the recommendations in *The Facebook Marketing Book*, other contextual information about best practices in ad composition was included. These best practices discussed using photos of people, considering the color-palette surrounding the ad, and deploying special graphical effects sparingly [5], p. 227.

On May 15th, the nine students in the content strategy graduate class launched their ads. Of the nine student ads launched, five received no clicks during the duration of the campaign. The results that follow focus on the outcomes from the successful ads.

4.2.1 Ad #1: Wide Targeting

One student presumed that playing the numbers might be the best method for gaining hits to the page and encouraging interaction and engagement such as Likes, Shares, and conversations. Keeping with a staid design (Figure 2), the targeting demographics cast a wide net to over 47 million Facebook users by not restricting the ad's distribution via the use of terms related to profile interests. This ad received three clicks and depleted our $350 advertising budget by $2.25.

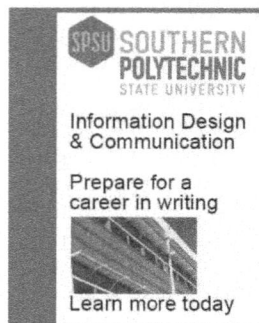

This ad targets 47,534,460 users:
- who live in the United States
- age 18 and older
- who graduated from college

Figure 2: Reaching potential users through a wide targeting strategy

4.2.2 Ad #2: Relating to People

As best practices indicated that a photo of a person in the ad design would engage users, another student tried this approach. We did not see person/photo prediction bear out in our results. Our most popular ad with a picture of a person (Figure 3) yielded only five clicks and diminished our $350 budget by a scant $4.00.

Evolve your career through SPSU's online Information Design & Communication program now!

This ad targets 420,600 users:
- who live in the United States
- exactly between the ages of 25 and 40 inclusive
- who like writing, documentation, networking, career change, grammar, journalism, graphic design, language, design, building websites, technology or editing
- who graduated from college

Figure 3: Ad with a person

4.2.3 Ad #3: Into the Ephemera

As with many studies, outliers are not uncommon—our Facebook advertising experiment was no exception. The student-generated ad that garnered the most click-throughs surprised us (Figure 4). Targeting just over 600,000 users through age, education, and interests targeting, this ad consumed $330 of our $350 advertising budget with 397 clicks. It also resulted in the page gaining more than 156 new Likes.

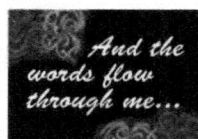

Are you a writer or designer or both? Take your talent to a new level with SPSU's online Information Design & Communication program.

This ad targets 637,630 users:
- who live in the United States
- exactly between the ages of 24 and 64 inclusive
- who like writing, creative writing, graphic design, design or communication
- who graduated from college

Figure 4: The most successful ad in our campaign.

The ad was visually both artistic and evocative, but graphically it did little to define that we were promoting an academic program at a state university. The question then became *Why are people clicking on this ad?* In order to determine if we might be reaching a pool of prospective students, we reviewed every new Like of the IDC Facebook page to learn more, where possible, about the people who clicked through. While some profiles were fully private, many individuals had open access to their personal "About" information, and Wall postings. It was possible from the new Likes to view the profiles (partial or full) of two-thirds of our respondents.

5. RESULTS

The results of our second Facebook advertising campaign can be broken down into what we saw in the following four categories: New Likes, User Interactions, Web Site Analytics, and Applications Received.

5.1 New Likes

An analysis of profiles revealed a strong surge of Likes from people using Facebook to market and cross-promote their moneymaking ventures. Every day, Likes came from would-be music moguls and wrestling promoters to artists of all kinds including a painter of unicorn fantasy murals. Non-fiction writers and literary creatives looking to freelance or sell their poetry collections selected Like, as did others for whom an academic program's Facebook page had seemingly no relevance based on their profile information. It was not possible to parse out who might be a good prospect for our graduate program from this cohort.

5.1.1 The Artwork

Our new Likes came almost exclusively from the artistic ad design. One hypothesis about the success of this artwork with respect to Facebook users and Like relates to the esoteric ad design; the high contrast and warm colors, combined with the artful script text of "And the words flow through me," captured users' imagination and struck a chord. It embraced the ephemera and mystery of the creative process. Another hypothesis about the high instance of Like responses may relate to confusion about the function of the "thumb up" icon and Like notation (You like this) under the ad. We wondered if the meaning was unclear to users and if they perceived the "You like this" to be an endorsement of the artwork rather than of the entity (business, institution) behind the artwork.

One assertion we felt confident in making was the following: The text beside the artwork was not meaningful. It may be that Facebook users do not read this text. Another possibility is that our text did not clarify we were an academic program; perhaps we were a vocational or continuing education program in the minds' of users. Either way, it suggested our new Likes might be wholly uninterested in the program.

5.2 User Interactions

It was not possible, from the Likes we received in the second campaign, to parse out who might be a good prospect for our graduate offerings. Thus, we chose to examine if our new Likes were interested in our program as measured by how they interacted with our Facebook page [5] p. 63. User interactions were, unfortunately, sparse. Two new Likes indicated that they Liked a link on our page; otherwise, there were no user-generated posts or conversations. This finding lent support to the idea that most people who clicked through on the ad and Liked the page had no stake in learning about the graduate program.

5.3 Web Site Analytics

The web site's analytics program revealed that our second advertising campaign resulted in some small, but positive trending. Our first campaign, with only one ad, resulted in five Facebook visitors coming to our web site. The second campaign—where four ads were running successfully—resulted in 39 visitors to our web site.

Pages/Visit (P/V), as an engagement metric, did not change significantly between the two campaigns—2.80 versus 2.77. Both campaigns P/V from Facebook referrals were below the average of 3.66 P/V from direct traffic to the site. The most interesting finding for us was on the engagement metric of Average Visit Duration (AVD). In the first campaign, the five hits spent an average of only 35 seconds on the web site; in the second campaign, there was a notable rise in the AVD time to 1.43 minutes. It may be that some of our new Likes were reading the pages more carefully.

5.4 Applications Received

July 1 marked the application deadline date for Fall 2011 admission. Each application packet received was compared to the list of new Likes achieved during the second advertising campaign. Unfortunately, not one of the Likes from the page was in the pool of potential new admits for the Fall 2011 semester.

Once the semester began, we polled new admits to determine if they had seen the Facebook ads or found the IDC Facebook page through any form of search. Students indicated they found the program through the state database of institutions/programs or through search engines and organic searches. No one had seen the ads or come directly to Facebook via a search.

6. CONCLUSIONS

Social media advertising with Facebook did not function as we expected; increased interest in our program and a robust pool of applicants did not materialize. It may be safe to say, at this time, that small academic programs will see few to no benefits from advertising through Facebook until additional research provides a deeper understanding of the strategies and tactics necessary for this new medium.

First, we did learn that the design and targeting of Facebook ads is both an art and a science. Results suggest users like attractive ads—and they will click on those ads without much regard for the accompanying text or business behind the ad. What remains unknown are the elements of good ad design for an academic program. School logos and official-looking ads did not, as we now know, work well.

Yet, esoteric designs that omit the visual identity of the institution/program pose other problems. First, these ads invite click-throughs that, while usually inexpensive, can quickly decimate a small budget. Second, there is the question of ethical design; there is an obligation to be upfront about the business behind the ad. Piquing users' interests with blurred, suggestive images or emotional appeals of puppies and babies is not desirable.

Next, with respect to page engagement, it may be that Facebook functions differently for a small academic program. The conversations and interactions commonly seen on consumer sites were not, in any way, replicated on our program's Facebook page. On our page, current students rarely posted or interacted and none of our new Likes engaged in any conversation whatsoever. This "low degree of content contribution" has been seen in other research about students and social media use in higher ed [3], p. 21. While this research focused on an undergraduate population, our results suggest graduate students may be no different.

One thought on why prospective graduate students do not engage on a Facebook page centered on the size of the program and the lack of interactivity from existing members. Prospective students may feel a small community is either unwelcoming or exclusive when interactions are low; therefore; they might believe that crossing the threshold will not result in useful information. Thus, it could be suggested here that Facebook is a not channel for recruitment; it may be better suited to retention as recent research suggests [2], p. 36.

Third, budgets may be a significant problem for small programs in higher education when it comes to promotion through Facebook advertising. Across both of our campaigns, there was only $350 available. It may be that we need to significantly up the ante to market ourselves and, in turn, attract more potential students.

It is important to note that engaging in social media marketing is more costly, in terms of time, than expected. Advertising campaigns and the page itself require monitoring, review, and adjustment; there needs to be "a voice" of the page and that voice needs to post relevant information on a regular basis. Getting the message to be both right and meaningful takes more experience than most interns can provide; thus, it is a question of who, among the faculty, could take on this role.

More research on social media marketing/advertising in higher education is required. Little exists on how social networking sites like Facebook function for the purposes of reaching potential new students. These are still very early days in our understanding of social media; there are countless opportunities for exploration. It is, without a doubt, an excellent time to move forward into what promises to be a rich area of study for the design of communication.

7. REFERENCES

[1] Leng, H. K. The use of Facebook as a marketing tool by private educational institutions in Singapore. *International Journal of Technology and Educational Marketing*. 2, 1 (January-June, 2012): 14-25. DOI=http://10.4018/ijtem.2012010102

[2] Rekhter, N. Using social network sites for higher education marketing and recruitment. *International Journal of Technology and Educational Marketing.* 2, 1 (January-June, 2012): 26-40. DOI=http:// 10.4018/ijtem.2012010103

[3] Constantinides, E., and M. Zinck Stango. Potential of the social media as instruments of higher education marketing: A segmentation study. *Journal of Marketing for Higher Education.* 21, 1 (June-July, 2011): 7-24. DOI=http://10.1080/08841241.2011.573593

[4] Falls, J., and E. Deckers. *No Bullshit Social Media.* Indianapolis: Que Publishing, 2012.

[5] Zarella, D, and A. Zarella. *The Facebook Marketing Book.* Sebastopol, CA: O'Reilly Media, Inc., 2011.

Sharing Time: Engaging Students as Co-Designers in the Creation of an Online Knowledge Sharing Application

Michael Gilbert
University of Washington
Human Centered Design & Engineering
00-1-206-354-3741
mdg@uw.edu

Mark Zachry
University of Washington
Human Centered Design & Engineering
00-1-206-543-6429
zachry@uw.edu

ABSTRACT

This paper introduces the peer-supported design process undertaken in the creation of a novel online knowledge sharing application called the Haystack Exchange. Along with seven undergrad and graduate students involved in a course research group, the authors of this paper presented a fully functional online prototype of an application designed to connect those seeking knowledge work with those willing to do that work, creating an outlet for knowledge workers to share and contribute effort. Students were engaged as active co-designers in the system, examining existing applications online offering similar services, discussing relevant research in building online communities, and ultimately re-designing the system to make it context-appropriate for different deployment scenarios. This paper reports on the details of this unique design process, discussing its merits, implications, and the prototypes that resulted. The paper concludes with a discussion of the peer design process as an instructional approach that promotes student engagement.

Categories and Subject Descriptors

H.5.2 [**User Interfaces**]: *Evaluation/methodology, Prototyping*

Keywords

Student engagement, design evaluation, co-design in practice, knowledge sharing, system design.

1. INTRODUCTION

Technology is frequently seen as simply the mediator for well-defined and constrained interactions in collaborative systems. But, as technology progresses, so too does the potential for collaborative systems to both direct the activities of participants as well as to allow those activities to shape what the systems are capable of, their design, their intent, and the means by which they inspire collaboration within target populations. In this way, the focus in developing a collaborative system is not only on the system itself, but on the entire community that the system is intended to serve, allowing for emergent interactions to shape the functionality provided in an online application.

Accordingly, in this project the stakeholders can be distinguished among three groups. The first group is comprised of the students

involved in the research group, utilizing a practical application as a pedagogical tool for describing the complex interactions inherent in online communities. The second group includes the community that the application is intended to support, those under-served or under-employed willing to share their talents or interests with others. The final group includes the primary researchers involved in organizing the research group with the goal of achieving a better understanding in how online communities are formed and maintained, and how collaboration can best be enabled between remote or disparate individuals.

In the sections that follow, we will first describe the background research relevant to the design of the system itself and the introduction the students were given to the problem space. After, we will describe our process in introducing the students in the research group to the Haystack Exchange system, involving them in its design and operation. Finally, we will describe the lessons learned during the course of the research group, including what factors led to successfully engaging the students, how that engagement took form, and what discussion may arise as a result of that engagement.

2. BACKGROUND

The driving idea behind the creation of the Haystack Exchange was the notion of the Time Bank, first created in the early 1980s by Edgar Cahn as a potential solution to growing inequality and a sense of social exclusion in society [3], social exclusion here defined as the inability to "earn income from engaging in productive work", to "take part in community-building and social networks for friendships and mutual support," and to "influence decisions which affect one's life, and to join in collective effort to challenge inequitable social structures," [11]. Time Banks provide a framework of reciprocal exchange where time, or effort, is a unit of currency in which one hour of service, any service, is equal to one hour of any other service available by those in the time bank [13]. Cahn states that these Time Banks and their currency-in-trade, Time Dollars, are not an alternative economy but something quite different. He argues that Time Dollars are "designed to rebuild a fundamentally different economy, the economy of home, family, neighborhood, and community... They are the Core Economy. The Core Economy exists side-by-side with the world of commerce – regardless of the medium of exchanges used to consummate transactions in that world" [2].

This ideal—that of creating an exchange system that does not detract from a traditional economy but instead adds to the local, neighborhood and community economies—is not one that has been ignored in the commercial sector. Many other companies have recognized that there is value in individual engagement, in peer-to-peer service exchange, and have created applications attempting to create value with this latent skill. Among them, Coffee & Power, a marketplace for skill-based jobs, recently raised $1 million dollars from venture capitalists [10]. Zaarly, a proximity based real-time buyer powered market, has so far received $15.1 million in seed and series A funding [16]. Gigwalk, a non skill-based work exchange, has received $1.7 million in seed funding [6]. And TaskRabbit, a portal to support errand outsourcing, has so far received over $6.8 million in seed and series A funding [12]. Each of these companies has a unique approach to serving the communities that they aim to represent, but they largely share one common goal: to harness the efforts of individuals and to create value, whether community-based, service-based, or product-based, where there had been none before.

The background given above is relevant as it not only represents the genesis of an idea that led to the creation of the Haystack Exchange, but the description (albeit abbreviated) given to the participants in the Haystack Exchange research group to introduce them to the problem space that the application was meant to occupy, to describe the problems that the application was meant to ameliorate, and to show the potential that such an application may have in a commercial or industry context.

The team of co-designers in this project were members of a for-credit research group in Human Centered Design & Engineering at the University of Washington [14]. The Haystack research group, constituted in spring 2012, aimed to evaluate and design a fully functional online prototype application called the Haystack Exchange, which would allow knowledge workers to share their interests and talents with a broad community. The authors created this research group following two assumptions about the potential value of co-designing an application with students. First, that students' experience would be more salient if they were interacting with a working prototype of an interaction type with a history of enabling development in real communities. And second, that feedback gained from individuals actively involved as members of the community that the application was intended to support would be more valid, allowing for more effective improvements in the system itself.

3. DESIGN PROCESS
The design approach used for this project was somewhat unconventional, engaging students as co-designers in order to foster a new approach to design learning and innovative work, a paradigm being explored by other educators in varied technology-focused learning contexts today (e.g., [7]). In the process of putting together the Haystack research group we hoped to pose three primary questions to those involved. First, what is the system and what were the sociological underpinnings of its creation? This includes understanding where the original idea for the time bank came from, what some of the shortcomings of early implementations are, and how the industry has attempted to adopt those early ideals in commercially successful applications. Second, what extant research exists that could inform the design of an online community intended to serve as an electronic mediator in a time bank scenario? This would include identifying factors that impact the success or failure of online collaborative communities, including issues of membership, motivation, rewards, and group identification. And third, how could a better understanding of the research around building successful online communities be best utilized to re-design the Haystack Exchange system, allowing for evolution from its genesis as an online

implementation of a time bank coordinator towards a design that would be most engaging to a target population? In other words, how may the system have the greatest impact on an online community even if that system would no longer adhere to the strict methodology behind the creation and maintenance of the time bank? Time with the Haystack research group was roughly split to answer these three questions and it included activities related to system introduction, relevant research, and re-design prototyping.

3.1 Conceptual Introduction
To ensure that students were familiar with the origin of the motivating idea for an exchange system and the time banks on which such a system would be based, the initial phase of research group activity was focused on becoming familiar with past research on Time Banks [2,3,11], related Local Exchange Trading Schemes [11], and potential shortcomings of both approaches [1,11]. Additionally, research group contributors were tasked with exploring each of the industry examples of peer-to-peer production described above and identifying the target audience, the services offered, the means of executing those services, and potential motivating factors that exist in each to encourage a lively online community.

Starter system. During the time group participants were being introduced to the conceptual ideas motivating the authors, they were also introduced to a fully functional, though rudimentary, working prototype of the Haystack Exchange system. All members of the group were given accounts on the system and asked to actively use it to exchange simple services (such as "take a photograph of the cherry trees on campus" or "write me a haiku") and to reflect on how the system aligned with traditional views of time banking and peer-to-peer service exchanges. Figure 1 shows an example of the Haystack Exchange system as it was initially presented to the research group.

3.2 Relevant Research
The next major phase of research group activity was dedicated to identifying and discussing existing research around the larger issues of building successful online collaborative communities. This included literature on identifying development strategies that lead to successful implementation of design goals [5], encouraging commitment and motivation in online communities [4], and encouraging participation in communities once brand commitment is achieved [8,9]. Additionally, research group participants continued their use of the system during this time, actively reflecting on and discussing how the design practices stated in the above literature could be implemented to encourage commitment, participation, and to increase motivation in our system.

3.3 Re-Design Prototyping
The final phase of research group activity focused on ideation and development of a suggested re-design of the Haystack Exchange system. These re-design proposals were intended to allow group participants to take the idea of the original Haystack Exchange peer-to-peer service exchange application, identify a context in which that application may be most suitable, and create a high fidelity prototype of a new product.

Figure 1: Index view of the original Haystack Exchange, showing recently created offers and requests by research group members.

By allowing group participants to select their own context for deploying a future application we were hoping to encourage a wider breadth of finished prototypes. For instance, the original stated context for the application was to provide neighborhoods and communities a novel means of establishing peer-to-peer service exchanges in a free and open manner. Suggested alternative contexts included creating a for-profit model, in which services were exchanged for real currency targeting industry professionals in knowledge working fields, focusing on physical goods exchanges between two-parties similar to a barter exchange, or creating a social network game in which points were rewarded for successful service exchanges.

All group members participated in the above progression, researching, planning, designing, building, and demonstrating their high fidelity prototypes in front of the entire research group. The next section discusses our findings throughout this process, followed by the concluding discussion and the implications of those findings.

4. LESSONS LEARNED

Through this experience, we learned that student engagement and accomplishment can be broken down into three separate categories, enumerated here and described in more detail below. First, initial design choices strongly shape the functionality and usability of the system once it is deployed (so such choices must be made cautiously to avoid constraining creativity prematurely). Second, student engagement early on in the design process, and accordingly their familiarity with the background that informed the design of the prototype system, provides them with a valuable insight into evaluating the tool and allows them to incorporate more informed feedback into the discussion sessions. And third, allowing the students to choose the context in which their system would act allowed initial ideas to transform, allowing for

divergent and creative approaches to be explored despite the shared goals and shared experience exploring the relevant literature.

Design choices constrain moving from an ideal system to a deployed system. In evaluating factors that may impact individual motivation to participate in an online community, we intentionally delayed implementing key motivational interactions in our prototype application. For instance, adopting motivational interactions involving in-application currency may constrain development in directions in which currency diminishes the goals of the online interaction. Similarly, adopting a point-based system of rewards for system involvement (so called gamification of the application) constrains system development by requiring additional motivational factors and design decisions to not create a negative effect among system participants by conflicting approaches not working in tandem in a final deployed application.

As a result of this design decision to avoid implementing motivators for online collaboration, student contributors were able to more directly tie design suggestions in existing motivational research [5] to possible improvements in the system itself. Without constraining possible design interventions that the students may suggest, research discussions were able to be more expansive in scope and the potential utility of such an application for target populations was more fully explored.

Student engagement at an early stage in the design process provide a unique lens to evaluate the system prototype. Beyond simply using the system and verifying intended functionality, by leading students through the early stages of system design, from conception through research and prototype development, our initial assumptions regarding the utility of an online tool for open collaboration were challenged by their involvement with it in real-world scenarios. For example, where the initial time bank model focuses largely on peer-to-peer interactions, student

123

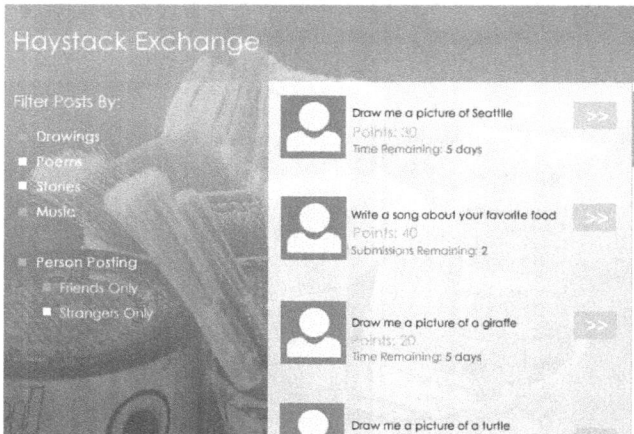

Figure 2: Re-designed task search page.

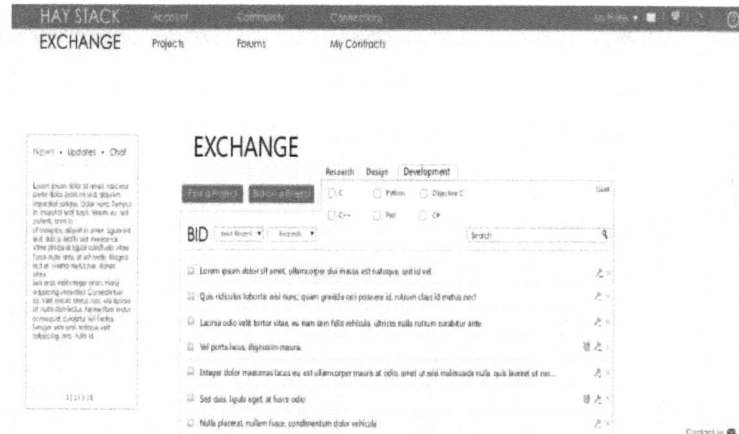

Figure 3: Alternative re-designed task search page.

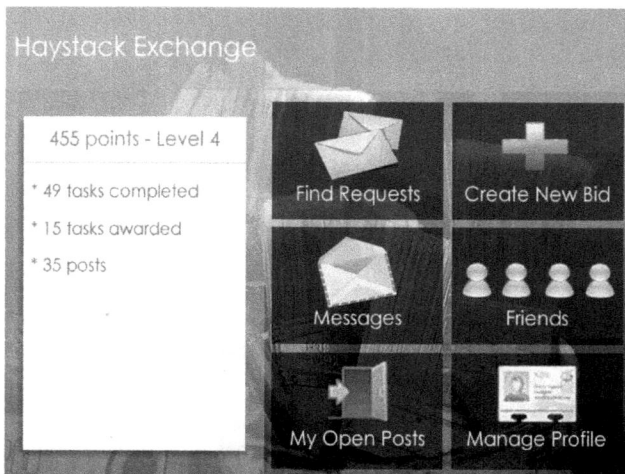

Figure 4: Re-designed user profile page.

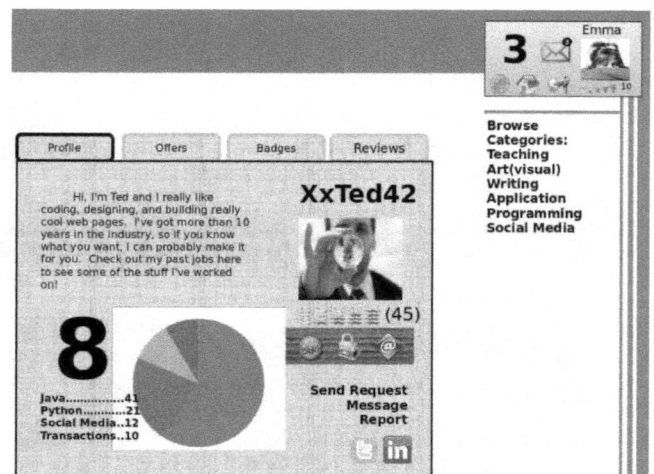

Figure 5: Alternative re-designed user profile page.

involvement highlighted the potential for group formation and network interactions beyond what the original model that inspired the project was intended to support. Further, incorporating existing literature on motivation and online community participation allowed the student contributors to ground observation in current theory, solidifying suggestions that they may have been otherwise less able to articulate.

Additionally, their preconceptions regarding what a system similar to ours should be capable of and in what context such a system would exist led to widely divergent ideas about how Haystack should be designed, what the expected audience of such a system would be, and how motivation will be addressed in attempting to engage a large, remote group of individuals interacting with one another towards specific ends.

Student designs diverged despite shared goals and experience. Expanding on number two above, engaging the students as co-designers in the system, despite participating in shared team research and discussions regarding application design and motivating factors, led to widely divergent approaches in the students' suggested re-designs of the application. Opening the opportunity for student contributors to identify the context in which their re-designs would exist led to a diverse collection of use scenarios for the system, including as a for-profit application exchanging real currency, as a tool to mediate technological interactions for the under-served or under-employed, and as a

point-based game in which players earn experience through system interaction. Consequently, the end products of the re-design assignment covered a broad spectrum of potential approaches to engage potential end-users. Conversely, if design convergence had been desired, dictating the context of the application would have constrained suggested re-designs allowing for a more narrow scope of potential approaches in the re-design process.

To provide an example of the design divergence, Figures 2 and 3 above show two different interpretations of the task search page, the design in Figure 2 emphasizing a point-based system of task exchange where more tasks completed allows the user to "level up", whereas the design in Figure 3 is intended to address the needs of knowledge professionals seeking paid collaborators for service exchanges. Figures 4 and 5 both show re-designed profile pages for Haystack users; however as Figure 4 approaches the page from a point-based perspective, Figure 5 focuses on the analytical representation of previous work to inform users of their current state within the system. Each approach, all equally valid, was inspired by research group members' interpretations of a unique context in which the system could most effectively exist.

Regarding the design of the Haystack Exchange system itself, many contributor observations during research discussions in the course of the research group led to direct improvements of the system. Based on their direct involvement in the system, student contributors originated many design ideas to advance system development, including:

- The need to support instant communication among service members (i.e., a chat interface) to facilitate a more open exchange of ideas.

- The need to support automatic group formation so that service members engaged in similar activities over the course of time can more easily find one another.

- The need to support an online portfolio system so that work registered in the Exchange could be directly used to supplement online resume materials, and a rewards system to increase motivation to participate in the Exchange.

As co-designers of a preliminary system in which they could claim involvement [15], all research group participants seemed to have a vested interest in not only understanding how the system could work, but *how to make it better*.

5. CONCLUSION

As stated above, the goals of this project were two-fold: to both create a system that would enable peer-to-peer service exchange, and to create a tool that would allow for direct student engagement in the design and deployment of that system. What we experienced is that by involving students in the research group from an early stage of development, and by allowing them the freedom to directly impact the design and nature of that system, we have been able to receive a level of feedback and a breadth of ideas that would have been difficult had their interactions been abstract, based only on readings and third party software.

Student engagement was predicated on two factors. First, the design practice they were involved in was perceived to be meaningful, as their designs were towards the improvement of an existing system and had the potential to impact something real and tangible. Secondly, the goal of the system was meaningful to the student co-designers in that the system was intended to help individuals connect to others in novel ways. This flexibility allowed students with varied interests to still contribute in unique ways, some opting for increasing participation through gamifying interactions, others choosing to create a system more similar to a for-profit contractor-for-hire service. Student direct involvement with an active system in development over which the group had complete control allowed for a level of contribution and input that would otherwise not have been achievable.

As the Haystack Exchange system progresses, so will the nature of student's involvement with that system. Future steps will include implementing design interventions suggested by students and supported by research as explored in earlier stages of the project, and deploying the system more widely to better measure its impact and effects on more disparate populations. Throughout this process, student engagement has been critical to the continued evolution of the system itself, their participation and enthusiasm driving future iterations of the application, peer production in practice.

6. ACKNOWLEDGMENTS

Many thanks to Kim Sophia Brown, Ashkaan Khatakhotan, Dharma Dailey, Jonathan Lee Russo, Thomas Stanton, Christopher Le Nguyen, Jake Landry, and the Human Centered Design & Engineering department at the University of Washington for supporting this ongoing research.

7. REFERENCES

[1] Aldridge, T. J., & Patterson, A. (2002). LETS get real: constraints on the development of Local Exchange Trading Schemes. *Earth*, 370-381.

[2] Cahn, E. (2001). On LETS and time dollars. *International Journal of Community Currency Research*, 5, 2-5. Retrieved from http://ijccr.net/IJCCR/2001_(5)_files/IJCCR Vol 5 (2001) 2 Cahn.pdf.

[3] Cahn, E. (2004). *No More Throw Away People*. Washington, DC: Essential Books.

[4] Farzan, R., Dabbish, L., & Kraut, R. (2011). Increasing commitment to online communities by designing for social presence. *Proceedings of Computer Supported Cooperative Work (CSCW) 2011*. Retrieved from http://dl.acm.org/citation.cfm?id=1958874

[5] Kraut, R. E. & Resnick, P. (2012). *Building successful online communities: Evidence-based social design*. Cambridge, MA: MIT Press.

[6] Gigwalk. (2012). Retrieved from http://www.crunchbase.com/company/gigwalk.

[7] Lee, J., Vaajakallio, K., & Mattelmäki, T. 2011. Tracing situated effects of innovative design methods: inexperienced designers' practices. In *Proceedings of the Second Conference on Creativity and Innovation in Design (DESIRE '11)*. ACM, New York, NY, USA, 103-113.

[8] Ling, K., Beenen, G., Ludford, P., Wang, X., Chang, K., Li, X., Cosley, D., et al. (2005). Using social psychology to motivate contributions to online communities. *Journal of Computer-Mediated Communication*, 10(4), 00–00. Wiley Online Library. Retrieved from http://onlinelibrary.wiley.com/doi/10.1111/j.1083-6101.2005.tb00273.x/full

[9] Ludford, P. J., Cosley, D., Frankowski, D., & Terveen, L. (2004). Think different: increasing online community participation using uniqueness and group dissimilarity. *Proceedings of the SIGCHI conference on Human factors in computing systems* (Vol. 6, pp. 631–638). ACM. Retrieved from http://portal.acm.org/citation.cfm?id=985772

[10] Rao, Leena. (2011). Second Life Founder Launches Coffee & Power, A Jeff Bezos-Backed Marketplace for Skill-Based Jobs. Retrieved from http://techcrunch.com/2011/11/01/second-life-founder-launches-coffee-power-a-jeff-bezos-backed-marketplace-for-skill-based-jobs/.

[11] Seyfang, G. (2002). Tackling social exclusion with community currencies: learning from LETS to Time Banks. *International Journal of Community Currency Research*, 6, 1-11. Retrieved from http://www.ijccr.net/IJCCR/2002_(6)_files/IJCCR Vol 6 (2002) 3 Seyfang.pdf.

[12] Taskrabbit. (2012). Retrieved from http://www.crunchbase.com/company/taskrabbit.

[13] Time Banking. (n.d.). In Wikipedia. Retrieved July 7, 2012, from http://en.wikipedia.org/wiki/Time_banking.

[14] Turns, J., & Ramey, J. (2006). Active and Collaborative Learning in the Practice of Research: Credit-based Directed Research Groups. *Technical Communication*, Vol. 53, No. 3. pp. 296-307.

[15] van Rijn, H. & Strappers, P. J. 2008. Expressions of ownership: motivating users in a co-design process. In Proc*eedings of the Tenth Anniversary Conference on Participatory Design 2008 (PDC '08)*. Indiana University, Indianapolis, IN, USA, 178-181.

[16] Zaarly. (2012). Retrieved from http://www.crunchbase.com/company/zaarly.

Communication Patterns for a Classroom Public Digital Backchannel

Honglu Du, Mary Beth Rosson, John Carroll
College of Information Sciences & Technology
Pennsylvania State University
{hzd106, mrosson, jcarroll}@ist.psu.edu

ABSTRACT

Digital backchannels have become an increasingly important field of study for researchers investigating educational technologies. We designed and deployed one such backchannel integrated with a public display – ClassCommons – in a 15-week field study that took place in a university classroom. We extracted and analyzed the communication patterns that emerged in the use of Class-Commons. In this paper, we use these data to address the following research questions: how do students appropriate public digital backchannels in classrooms, what communication patterns are typical in classroom digital public backchannels, how if at all do students' participation in the digital public backchannels evolve over an extended period of time and what are the characteristics of the messages that get more responses from other students?

Categories and Subject Descriptors

H.5.3 [**Information Interfaces and Presentation**]: Group and Organizational Interfaces – *computer-supported cooperative work, web-based interaction.*

Keywords

Public digital backchannel, computer mediated communication, E-learning, social media.

1. INTRODUCTION

In many college classrooms, students are passive spectators. The professor arrives, gives a lecture and students learn individually, listening and taking notes. This model of teaching in classes is called the transmittal model in which students learn by passively receiving knowledge from the teacher. However, according to social-constructivist theories of learning[1], knowledge cannot be simply pulled from textbooks or be poured from teachers' heads into students' heads. Instead knowledge is constructed by engaging individual learners to actively bring their prior knowledge to make sense of the new information which will further be constructed as knowledge embedded in their minds. In these theory views, knowledge construction is influenced by its surrounding community (the social context). In contrast to the transmittal model in which students are passive information recipients, the social constructivist model emphasizes the importance of placing

students at the center of the learning process – that is by becoming active learners. Currently, active learning has been recommended as one of the seven principles for good practices in undergraduate education[2].

In this paper, we present communication behavior associated with use of a public digital backchannel discussion tool – ClassCommons – that aims to promote active learning in classrooms for college students. In particular, we describe conversational patterns that emerged over a 15-week deployment of the tool in a mid-size university class (50 students). A related paper [3] reports other aspects of ClassCommons use and impacts during the field study, but does not analyze the participants' communication behaviors when using the backchannel.

2. RELATED WORK

The term "backchannel" is used to describe a non-primary communication channel between the speaker and the listeners, in which feedback is given to the speaker in un-intrusive ways from the listeners to show their interest, attention and provide feedback [4]. Examples of face-to-face backchannels are short utterances like "uh-huh", "yeah", "right", "okay", or spontaneous longer feedback and body language like head nods, eye gaze or facial expressions. Research has shown that backchannels are important for maintaining communication efficiency[5].

In classrooms, backchannels are an efficient and un-intrusive way for students to interact with the teacher. For example students use backchannels when they nod their heads to show they understand a topic being discussed, and the teacher may adjust his or her communication based on such feedback. However as the size of the audience increases, backchannels are harder to establish and communication between the speaker and the audience loses quality. It is hard for a speaker to make sense of multiple simultaneous feedback from different listeners; visual signals are quickly lost in a crowd [6]. As a result, speakers tend to focus only on a few audience members and the individual backchannels of those few. In situations with a large audience (e.g., a large lecture class), it is common that just a few individuals engage actively in backchannel communications with the speaker.

Researchers and educators have explored various options for technology interventions that can facilitate interaction between teachers and students in classrooms. For instance, classroom response systems allow the teacher to present multiple choice or true/false questions; students can then respond to these with specialized handheld "voting" devices, perhaps resulting in a public display of aggregated results [7-10].

Other text-based classroom technologies offer students an opportunity to engage in richer interactions with the instructor. Active Class uses PDAs for classroom communication: Students can post text questions to the teacher during lectures, using a handheld device. A teaching assistant (TA) may respond to these questions during class, or the teacher may choose to address some questions. When this system was used in undergraduate computer sciences classes, researchers find that it helped teachers get timely feedback from the students, overcame student apprehension in large classes, and enabled multiple students to ask questions at the same time[11].

Classroom Presenter extended the concept of a backchannel by allowing students to annotate a slide being discussed by the teacher; the resulting notes are publicly displayed in the classroom. A trial of this system suggests that it increase class participation in classes from multiple disciplines [12, 13]. The Harvard Live Question Tool allows students to submit answers to questions that are raised by the teacher; the answers are displayed publicly in the class. No formal evaluations have been conducted to study the impact of this tool, although Educause has recommended it as an effective way to encourage students' participation and students-teacher interaction[14]. Similar results have been found in ClassCommons and Fragmented Social Mirrors [6, 15, 16]. Most recently, McNely[17] theorized the potential of using digital backchannels in classrooms to assist collaborative mean-making.

Previous studies have focused on evaluating whether these technology interventions increase students' participation in class. In our prior study, we reported the factors that influence students' and teachers' adoption of digital backchannel tools, and their impacts on students' sense of community[3]. In this paper, based on the same set of data we collected in [3], we investigated the concept of digital backchannel from a communication perspective with a focus on analyzing the communication patterns in digital backchannels and how students would use public digital backchannels. In addition to that, the previous studies have evaluated the effects of classroom backchannels only for a limited period of time (usually 1-2 class sessions). Although students' participation was high in these short trials, it was not clear what the participation would be like through an extended period of use. More specifically, in this study we seek to answer the following research questions:

RQ1: How can students appropriate public digital backchannel tools in classrooms?

RQ2: What communication patterns occur in classroom digital public backchannels?

RQ3: How do students participate in a public classroom backchannel over an extended period of time?

RQ4: What are the characteristics of the backchannel messages that evoke more responses from other students?

3. CLASSCOMMONS SYSTEM

The design of ClassCommons is drawn from a general design concept wherein people are offered a common interaction space to interact with one another virtually while in a shared physical environment. Thus the design requirements for ClassCommons are relatively simple: accept input from students, present students' submitted content in a controlled fashion, and manage the display of this input. The ClassCommons system accomplishes this with three basic components; there is a client device (any device with web browsing capability can be used, e.g., web-enabled mobile phones, laptops), a server and a large public display.

Any device with access to the Internet can be a client. To contribute, students log in to a posting website (Figure 1) with their uni-

versity account and credentials. Students can post text messages, images and Youtube videos using the client interface. Students can choose to post with their real name or to enter an alias when posting. The messages students post are shown on the public display in the front of the classroom. Students can reply to messages already posted on the client interface and can "like" individual messages. The number after *Like* in Figure 1 indicates how many students have liked that message and the number after *Replies* indicates how many replies that message has evoked.

Figure 1. Client Interface of ClassCommons

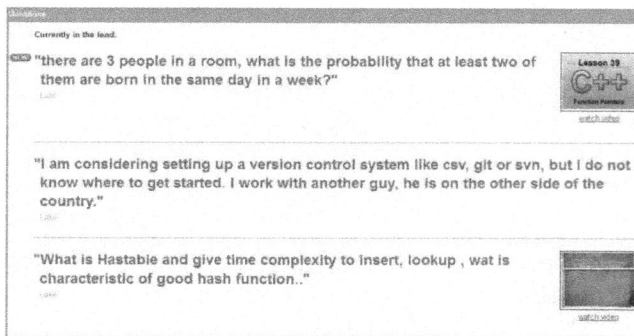

Figure 2. Public display view of ClassCommons

The messages are displayed in real time on the public display, viewable to all the students as well as the teacher in the classroom. In the current version, messages are displayed in a "First In First Out" (FIFO) fashion; the messages posted earlier are displayed first. The most recent message appears at the top the public display with a red new icon in the front. Whenever a new message is posted, older messages will be pushed downward. If a video or image is posted, a thumbnail of the video/image will be displayed at the right side of the display. The instructor can then decide whether or not to play the video in the class. Figure 2 shows the layout of the public display.

The goals of ClassCommons are similar to the impromptu backchannel activity studied by Yardi [18] , but the tool differs in in that the backchannel discussion is *public*, presented on a large display visible to all, whereas in the Yardi study students engaged in side chat conversations not seen by the teacher. ClassCommons makes the chat channel a shared resource for all class members. The system used in this study is an improved version of an earlier prototype [16]. Usability bugs (e.g., display readability) were addressed and new features were added, including: a) options to post emoticons, videos and photos; b) a liking function c) threaded interaction; and d) public anonymity and private accountability (PAPA).

Public Anonymity and Private Accountability (PAPA): The system implements a policy known as public anonymity and private accountability (PAPA). Students can choose whether to use their real name or enter an alias when posting a message. However if a student uses an alias, the teacher can still discover the identity of the sender. This was implemented because findings from a previous study [16] indicated that students who are shy are concerned about having their real name displayed on the public display. But on the other hand, complete anonymity could lead to more mischief. The PAPA feature allows students to choose public anonymity with respect to their classmates but still be held accountable by their teacher. Students were aware of this PAPA feature.

4. THE FIELD STUDY

The data analyzed in this paper were obtained through a field study of ClassCommons in a Human Computer Interaction (HCI) class for sophomores, juniors and seniors; the study took place over the Fall 2011 semester (15 weeks), in a large university in Northeast America. Because there was a one-week semester break in November, the actual period of system use was 14 weeks. There were 50 students in the class, 7 females and 43 males. HCI met three times a week on Mondays, Wednesdays and Fridays for 50 minutes each time. The instructor of this course was a junior instructor teaching HCI for the first time.

Students were offered up to two extra credit points for participating in the study; this offer was made at the start of the semester when they were invited to complete a background survey. At the end of the semester, the instructor awarded extra credit based on levels of participation (the number of messages posted). Students were not required to participate in the research study to gain access to ClassCommons.

Figure 3 shows the physical setup of ClassCommons in the class. The larger public display on the left is used by the teacher to project lecture slides; the second smaller public display on the right contains the content posted through ClassCommons. The public display was 5' (width) x 6' (height); pilot testing ensured that the font size used was legible from every location in the class.

The instructor did not put any constraints on what students should and should not post in ClassCommons; he welcomed any content. In addition to collecting log data and survey results (these are reported in [3]), the first author came to every class throughout the semester, observed what happened, and took notes.

5. RESULTS

To investigate the appropriation and use of ClassCommons, we analyzed the log data collected by the system; each contribution was logged and included its content (or that it was a "like"), the date and time it was posted, and the author. The first class session was used for familiarization with ClassCommons, so messages posted on that day were eliminated from the analysis. In total, 42 of 50 students (84%) contributed to ClassCommons discussions; 517 messages were posted. Of these, 75 messages contained an image and 5 contained a video.

To answer the question about how students appropriated public digital backchannels, we conducted a qualitative analysis of the messages posted. One researcher read each message and grouped the messages that were in the same thread as a *conversation*. The researcher decided whether messages belonged to a conversation by determining whether they addressed the same topic or whether one message was a reply to another. Note though that topic relatedness was enough to form a grouping; we did not require that a "conversation" be comprised of back-and-forth exchanges from two or more participates.

The researcher referred to notes taken during class observations to better understand the contexts in which the messages were posted and to parse the messages into conversations. If a message was posted but it did not evoke any responses, it was coded as a conversation with length of 1. One researcher developed the initial parsing and coding; two other researchers reviewed it and refined the coding later.

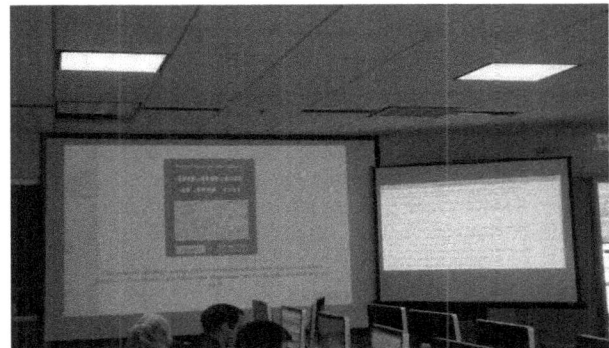

Figure 3. ClassCommons in the HCI classes, the larger screen on the left displays the teacher's slides, and the smaller screen on the right displays messages in ClassCommons

The 517 individual messages were parsed into 265 conversations. We focused on conversations as the unit of the analysis instead of individual messages because a) conversations can provide more context information about each individual message, based on which the qualitative analysis would be more accurate; and b) communication patterns, the focus of analysis in this paper, are instantiated in conversations rather than in individual messages.

5.1 Conversations Overview

For each conversation, its length (the number of messages in that conversation), the number of participants involved in that conversation, and the average number of messages posted by each participant in a conversation were calculated. Table 1 shows the details of the statistics of these variables.

Variable	Statistics (mean, s.d)	Max
Thread Length	1.95(1.90)	17
Participants	1.72(1.33)	9
# of Messages /participant	1.08(0.24)	2.5

Table 1. Statistics of thread length, # of participants and the # of contribution per participant in a thread

The most salient communication pattern in these data is that most of the groupings are not conversational interactions at all: (60.4%) consisted of only 1 message. For the groupings of size larger than

1, about 20.4% of the conversations had 2 messages and 19.2% had 3 or more messages. The distribution of the number of participants in each conversation showed an analogous pattern. Most of the conversations had only 1 participant (63.4%), 19.4% of the conversations had 2 participants and 16.98% of conversations had 3 or more participants. See Table 2.

# of msgs in a conversation	%	# of participants in a thread	%
1	60.38	1	63.4
2	20.38	2	19.6
3	8.3	3	8.68
>3	10.94	>3	8.3

Table 2. Distribution of # of messages and # of participants in a thread

5.2 Trends in Conversation Characteristics

In other studies, public digital backchannels tools have been used in classroom settings, but in general these have investigated only short periods of time (e.g., 1-2 class sessions). As a result we know little if anything about how students would use such a service over an extended period time. The semester-long data collection in this study provides the perfect opportunity to examine participation trends over several months of use.

We began this analysis by grouping the conversations according to their length (length =1, length =2 and length >=3). We did this because our preliminary summary analysis (Table 2) had revealed that very few conversations had more than three posts, but a number were of length two, perhaps a basic conversational interaction (e.g., question-answer or comment-reaction). After grouping them thusly, we examined the number falling into each conversation length over the 15-week period. Figure 4 shows these data.

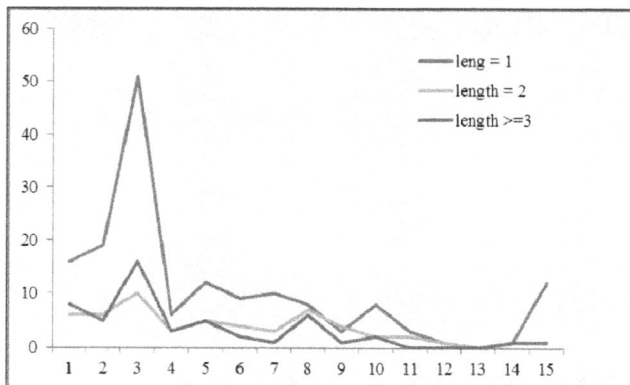

Figure 4. The number of conversations of different length over the 15 weeks

Overall, conversations in ClassCommons were more frequent in the earlier part of the semester; participation declined gradually over time.

Of note for the current analysis, conversations of different length showed similar patterns. The initial high usage could be attributed to a novelty effect. When it was first introduced, students were more curious about it and would like to try it. Later on students' participation stabilized after the initial novelty.

Note the two peaks in ClassCommons conversation activity along the semester – weeks 3 and 15 (Figure 4). In Week 3, the number of conversations is much higher than the other weeks. In Week 15, the number of non-conversations (i.e., those of length 1)

jumped relative to earlier weeks. Review of class observation notes revealed that those two weeks corresponded to periods when the students gave presentations about their group projects. In the HCI class, students were divided into 10 teams and each team's term project was to design a new system. Week 3 was the week that they presented their ideas and week 15 was the week that they presented their prototype systems. This team presentation activity seemed to be particularly evocative with respect to commenting. The relatively high levels of participation during these weeks (i.e., in contrast to weeks when the teacher was lecturing) may indicate that students feel more comfortable commenting on their peers but not on the instructor. Unfortunately we did not recognize these peaks until after the data were analyzed so the interview questions were not designed to shed light on this possibility.

Week 8 also displays a local maxima for the longer threads. Week 8 is when the results of the mid-term exam came out and students used ClassCommons to ask questions regarding the mid-term results, leading to more conversations of this kind appearing in week 8. As more students started using ClassCommons for this purpose, other students contributed miscellaneous content (e.g., for entertainment purposes). Both of these factors led to a rise in conversation frequency for week 8.

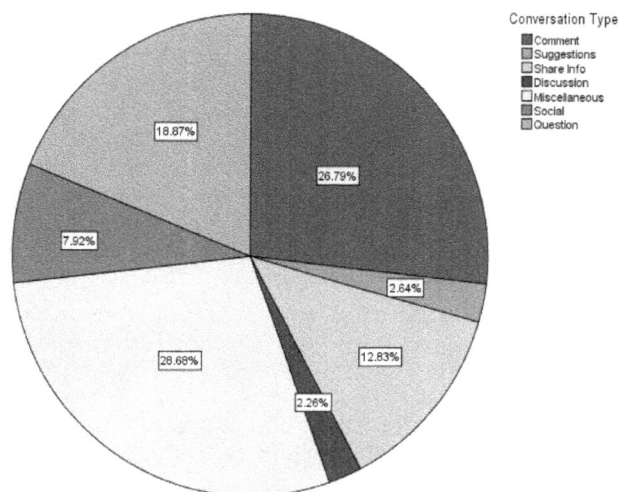

Figure 5. The distribution of different types of conversations in ClassCommons in HCI class

5.3 Conversations in ClassCommons

We used a card-sorting technique to categorize the main topic type of each conversation. To do this we read the post comprising each conversation, noted its topic, and assigned a descriptive label. The conversations were then iteratively clustered into similar groups. In the end, we identified seven types: comments, suggestions, information sharing conversations, discussion conversations, question conversations, social and miscellaneous conversations. Figure 5 shows the distribution of these conversations types. Comments and miscellaneous messages were most common, followed by questions, information sharing, social conversations, suggestions and discussions. We now consider in more detail the nature of each of these categories.

No.	Poster	Content
#1	Anony-mous 36	*"confused about question"* (The student was confused by the teacher's question.)
#1	Jack	*"depth inception. Depth within depth!"* (The teacher was talking about "inception" in the class.)
#3	Anony-mous 132	*"The lecture is good! I like that usually the professor involves the students during the lectures using games and discussions."* (Comment on the lecture.)
#4	GoState-BeatBama	*"look at the audience, not your slides"* (Comment on other students' presentation.)
#5	BigLuigi	*"don't overclock your system if you don't know what you r doing, you can do some serious damage to system :/."* (Comment on one team's project idea)
#6	BigLuigi	(Comment on another's team's presentation slides.)

Table 3. Examples of Comments Conversations

5.3.1 Comments

In many conversations, the students simply commented about things or activities ongoing in the classroom. In this sense the ClassCommons backchannel can be seen as a sort of "digital utterance" as students are thinking aloud about their current class experience. Various kinds of comments were made, including reactions to the lecture, the quiz or other students' presentations. Most of these comments were of length 1; that is they were an individual student's thought about some topic or issue. Table 3 contains examples of the comments category.

As we reported earlier, team presentations were heavily commented. In fact 75.4% of the comments (49/65) were in response to other students' presentations; many of these had a kidding or sarcastic aspect to them (see, e.g., the last comment in 3). Students were less likely to comment on the instructor's lecture. Again, we speculate that this is due to students' greater comfort teasing other students, rather than the instructor.

5.3.2 Questions

Students used ClassCommons to ask questions. Most of these questions addressed issues with assignments, quizzes and grades. A few of them were questions about a topic currently under discussion (#1 in Table 4). All of these questions were answered, either by the instructor (who at times addressed ClassCommons question in the class orally), by the TA or by other students who answered by posting in the system. Table 4 shows examples of the question-based conversations.

One benefit of using ClassCommons is that students can easily ask question in the class and get timely responses, either from the instructor, TA or other students. In the course exit survey, in response to the question about what they liked about ClassCommons, students commented that *"You can ask quick questions to other people and get a timely response"*; *"I like the ability to post a question and have it answered immediately by my peers who have the extremely unique perspective of being in the exact same position in the course"*.

No.	Poster	Content
#1	Mr. Mackey	*"Unjustified claims are bad, mmmkay?"*
	TA	*"Right. The challenge is how to justify the claims. Any thoughts?"*
	Mr. Mackey	*"Research. Could be surveys, studies of other products and their sales, features, etc."*
#2	Jason	*"Anybody here able to access their u drive?"*
	Jack	*"NOPE"*
	TA	*"@Jason: I have access."*
	Jason	*"it's frustrating, i can't open any documents from my desktop or drives."*
	Blaine	*"@ Jason: Go to my computer, then the U drive, then the folder with your first initial, then the folder with your middle initial. You should be able to get to your documents there"*
#3	BigLuigi	*"soooooooooo. anyone know if we are choosing something, or making something entirely new?"*
	Anony-mous28	*"Do we create something or use something that already exists?"*
	BigLuigi	*"ahhhh, ok. so, we choose something that is already there, and just propose a way to enhance or add to it... i think"*
	TA	*"Both options are acceptable. Designing something completely new, or improving an existing system."*

Table 4. Examples of Question Conversations

5.3.3 Share Information

Another use of ClassCommons was the sharing of information among peers. This usually happened when the teacher was talking about something in the class, and the students posted additional information that was related to what was being talked about. Messages of this kind usually contained an image or a link to an external webpage. These postings enriched the course content and made the course subject more vivid. See Table 5 for examples.

This type of usage emphasizes that teachers are no longer a *"sage on the stage"*. In traditional classrooms, it is just the teacher who does the talking during the class and students rarely have opportunities to speak up, even when what the teacher says is controversial. ClassCommons gave students another channel for speaking up. See example #4 in 5: prior to this post, the teacher was talking about the tongue map, showing large regional differences in sensitivity across the human tongue, which was commonly produced in textbooks and often cited. Parallel to the lecture, the student found an article showing that this traditional view of tongue sensitivity is in error, according to latest research; the student shared this article with the whole class. The instructor noticed that particular post in ClassCommons and acknowledged its relevance. He said that he would look into this later after class.

No.	Poster	Content
#1	Greg	*"mr sketch"* (In response to the instructor's question about whether there is any design example that integrates scent.)
#2	BigLuigi	*"You know what's really interrupting? When I'm playing a video game, and I cannot pause it, and my mom or significant other calls."* (When the teacher was talking interruption in the class.)
#3	Ben	*"Piano stairs! Persuasive technology! http://www.youtube.com/watch?v=2lXh2n0aPyw"* (Share an example of persuasive technology)
#4	trollface	*http://www.scientificamerican.com/article.cfm?id=the-taste-map-all-wrong* *sorry, that picture was false* (The teacher was talking about the tongue map, a student found an article that showed that that map was wrong)

Table 5. Examples of Sharing Information Conversations

5.3.4 Discussion

Although students used ClassCommons primarily to make spontaneous digital comments and ask questions as reported above, at times they used it to discuss class-related topics. In one example, the instructor was talking about the pros and cons of two designs of the vending machine in the class. He put the pictures of the vending machines on his power point slides (Figure 6) and asked for students' opinions. Students started posting their thoughts in ClassCommons (#1 in Table 6). Some of the messages were quite insightful; others were intended to be humorous. After all, ClassCommons makes it possible for students to further discuss topics of interests and the *"unique perspectives"* offered by students amplify the course material and enrich the course content. In the #2 example in Table 6, students were discussing color and how it is related to words, and one student shared with the whole class a Wikipedia article that explains it.

Figure 6. The two vending machines discussed in class

Discussion conversations only account for about 2.26% of all the conversations in ClassCommons. In our interviews with students, we asked students why there were relatively few discussions taking place in ClassCommons. Students told us that a) *"not all students were scholars who have the best attentions in discussing course subjects"*, and *"students are motivated by grades. If they*

are not being graded on something, probably they won't spend much time on it" and b) to encourage students to involved in more course related discussions, the instructor should provide some form of scaffolding. For examples, *"having the professor pose questions, and having people like post answers on it would be effective in having more students participate in the discussion"*.

No.	Poster	Content
#1	David	*"Can't see the stock on the left machine"*
	Jordan	*"You're able to roundhouse the left machine more efficiently."*
	Chuck Norris	*"I fully endorse the machine on the left."*
	David	*"Also the left one leaves a small margin for error. One mis-step and you're getting a diet soda instead of a delicious normal one"*
	David	*"....I meant the right."*
	BigLuigi	
	HeHateMe	*"@bigluigi...well said"*
#2	Ben	*"Some people think certain words have certain colors"*
	Tom	*"In all seriousness, I have heard people associate certain types of music with color"*
	Anonymous112	*"@Thomas. Totally agree.. colors and music can bring out certain moods for sure"*
	alias	*"http://en.wikipedia.org/wiki/Synesthesia"*

Table 6. Examples of Discussion Conversations

5.3.5 Suggestions

A small number of the conversations (2.64%) contained suggestions. For example, students posted messages to make suggestions about improving the design of a system being used in the class. Another interesting observation was that in one case students used it to suggest something that might be challenging to voice in a normal fashion, for instance, submitting a suggestion that the quiz should be open notes. See Table 7.

Although suggestion conversations were not common, the appearance of such postings can still be seen to have important implications. ClassCommons empowers students. It opens another channel for students to negotiate with the instructor regarding class logistics and organization; this is less likely to happen in traditional classrooms and typically would happen in private if the student goes to the professor during office hours or has a brief conversation after class. ClassCommons makes it easier for students to speak up about things that they might be shy about raising in person; the fact that students can post messages under an alias ameliorates concerns about asking something that is otherwise difficult to broach. At the same time, it makes the suggestion public, so if it has broad consequences (e.g., the request for open notes on the quiz), all students can appreciate and benefit from the post. Interestingly, the instructor may be more likely to accommodate requests that are made in public forum like ClassCommons – it is easy enough to deny or postpone a private request from a single student, but a suggestion that is viewed and implicitly "seconded" by many others who are also in the room would be harder to ignore.

No.	Poster	Content
#1	Jim	*"Looks like strip_tags() needs to be applied to aliases as well."*
	TA	*"You are right. Thanks!"*
	Tom	*"Jim is awesome!"*
#2	VIP Lounge	*"This quiz should be open note - WAY too much material."*
	Sidthekid	*"Agree with VIP..open note team quiz"*
	Teacher	*After seeing this on the public display, the instructor agreed to make the quiz open note.*
	Trollface	*"I LOVE xxx (instructor's name), not trollin".*
	VIP Lounge	*"This professor is my hero".*
#3	Trollface	*"Wow this looks a lot harder, partners should be allowed"*

Table 7. Examples of Suggestion Conversations

5.3.6 Social Conversations

Conversations happening at the beginning of the class (5 minutes or less after class begins) function as ice-breaking messages (#3, #4 in Table 8); conversely, conversations at the end of the class (5 minutes or less before class ends) are to say Goodbye to the class (#2 in Table 8). These postings were coded as social purpose conversations and this category accounts for about 7.92% of all the conversations in ClassCommons.

No.	Poster	Content
#1	Anonymous100	*"Nice haircut"* (The instructor had a haircut)
#2	BigLuigi	*"Have a great weekend folks!!: stay dry, and GO STATE!!!"*
#3	trollface	*"Good Morning Minions"*
#4	d-(^-^)z	*"Class is starting! IM SO EX-CITED"*
	trollin	*"We so excited"*
#5	Dr. Toboggan	*"Happy birthday ^_^"* (It was the instructor's birthday)

Table 8. Examples of Social Purpose Conversations

5.3.7 Miscellaneous

At times, incidental and non-class-related conversations were messages posted during the class. Such postings were actually quite common, comprising 28.68% of the conversations. They included students chatting with each other, messages to share something funny, and talk about sports, etc. (see Table 9). Within this category, Internet memes were common (#2, #3 in Table 9). The goals for this type of posting are simple – they were intended to entertain the class. However, it is less clear whether there were negative impacts, for example distraction away from class topics or teasing that made a student or group feels bad.

5.4 Characteristics of Long Conversations

One goal of the public backchannel was to involve more students in class discussion. However, the majority of "conversations" in ClassCommons had one or two messages only. Essentially, one

No.	Poster	Content
#1	BigBen	*"In other news the Steelers will go 15-1 this year."*
	Anonymous69	*"Doubtful"*
#2	GotSWAG	(funny picture)
#3	BigLuigi	*"You did so well, here is one schrute buck :D"*
#4	Kid in the Red Polo	*"I am the coolest cat in class"*
	Zoidberg	*"Why not Zoidberg?"*
	kid in the pink polo	*"I'm even cooler than kid in the red shirt, I also go by vip lounge. I like to pretend im anonymous, but I sit in the back corner"*

Table 9. Examples of Miscellaneous Conversations

person would post something and no one would react at all, or one person would post and one other person would react. To explore the characteristic of the conversations that have more participants and a longer length, we collected all the conversations that have a length of more than 3 exchanges and analyzed their characteristics.

We found that only 17 conversations had a length that is greater than 3, with a maximum of 17 messages and a minimum of 4 messages. A researcher read through all of these conversations, considering carefully how each of the conversations was initiated and developed over time and different participants. We found three general patterns: **a)** questions that were open ended and no one is able to provide a definitive answer; **b)** topics that were controversial and that provoked debate; and **c)** topics that were interesting enough to invite further expansion. We now consider each of these in turn.

5.4.1 Open ended questions

In ClassCommons, questions that were open ended were likely to attract more students to the issue. For instance, in the #1 example in Table 6, the teacher asked students to discuss the pros and cons of two different vending machines. Six students participated in the discussion with 7 messages posted. Another example is that a student was trying to ask whether other students are currently able to access a specific resource (their u-drive) on their computer. No one had a definitive answer, so different students posted related information trying to help that student solve the problem. Table 10 shows all the messages that were posted by students on this topic.

5.4.2 Controversial Topics

Not surprisingly, controversial topics attract more students to a discussion. Conversations of this kind usually start with one student posting a message in ClassCommons. In that message, something is mentioned or some point is made. If other people hold different opinions, they will start posting messages debating and arguing. The initiator of the thread may feel compelled to comment on the differing points of view, and others may weigh in to support one or the other perspective.

Poster	Content
Tom	"Anybody here able to access their u drive?"
Jansen	"NOPE"
TA	"@Thomas: I have access."
TA	"I don't know if undergrad students have different restrictions."
wharrgarbl	"@Thomas i can access mine too"
Tom	"It's frustrating, i can't open any documents from my desktop or drives."
MICHAEL	"@Tom: Go to my computer, then the U drive, then the folder with your first initial, then the folder with your middle initial. You should be able to get to your documents there."
HeHateMe	"@Tom my computer is the same way...have of these computers don't work."

Table 10. Students offering information to help a student with a problem

Poster	Content
VIP Lounge	"We already have assignments out and pending. why are you assigning more?????"
Mike	"Wayyy too many assignments at once."
Dr. Toboggan	"It's called work. They tend to assign it in classes. Get over it."
VIP Lounge	"It's called senioritis. just because you like being a prude doesn't mean i want to stay away from the bars."
Dr. Toboggan	"So you're lazy, a drunk, and not able to complete assignments unless eschewing a social life?"
alias	"mantis, mantis toboggan"
VIP Lounge	"Nope, i'm a well-rounded college student with a life. sorry you never get out, bucco. plus, i've already accepted a full-time job. good luck getting one with your lack of social skills."
Alias	"Well said VIP"
Dr. Toboggan	"Just make sure to bring up to your boss at your new job that you can't have too much work as you need to hit up the bars."
Sidthekid	"classcommons heating up, loving the animosity. Hatersgonnahate"
ALL_CAPS_G UY	"SO SOUR."
Skynet	"The negative energy is killing this discussion."
VIP Lounge	"Just make sure to bring up to your interviewer while stressing over the job that you can't go out to lunch to chat because you have to read national geographic's article about queen bees"
VIP Lounge	"By the way, i'm the guy that got the first quiz to be open notes"
Kip Drordy	"Nose clams"
Trollface	"MINIONS MINIONS, umadbros?"
Trollface	"Also i apologize for not attending this INTER-WEBS BATTLE sooner..."

Table 11. An example of student debating on a controversial topic

Table 11 shows an example of this, a conversation in which students were debating the importance of being assigned many demanding class assignments versus having a social life. Initially

the student with the alias "VIP Lounge" complained that there were too many assignments. In response, "Dr. Toboggan" (another student) suggested that "VIP Lounge" should *get over it*. A debate then ensued, at times even including some personally demeaning commentary, but with several other students also contributing to the debate occasionally. It is not clear whether the discussion "settled" anything about this topic, but presumably the two main contributors felt that they had succeeded in expressing their personal views. It is interesting to see a values-oriented debate of this sort, even under the PAPA policy, because the anonymity is only approximate. Many students "knew" who was contributing under the different aliases and yet in this case two of them were willing to engage in a public disagreement. It may be that even the feeling of anonymity allowed by PAPA is enough to release inhibitions that might otherwise be felt.

5.4.3 A Topic Worthy of Expansion

Another situation where conversations might be developed is when something is posted that is of particular interest to another student, who then chooses to expand on the topic. Table 12 shows an example of this: BigBen posted a message commenting that the team who was making the presentation put too many words on their slide and Skynet Lounge made a similar point. Next a third student was inspired to post another funny image related to this. In conversations of this kind, students were building a conversation using some vivid examples to amplify content suggested in a previous message. To a great extent, conversations of this kind seemed to develop opportunistically, depending on whether there is more to be said, and particularly whether any student has an entertaining contribution to share.

Poster	Content
BigBen	"they should put more words on the slides(Joke)"
trollface	"oh i forgot"
Skynet Lounge	"can you guys fit MORE words on this slide?"
Anony-mous36	"BOOM!"
Sidthekid	"haha bigluigi well said"

Table 12. Students expand a conversation

6. DISCUSSION

Overall ClassCommons was popular with the students. In the class exit survey, we asked students whether they would like to use ClassCommons in future classes, 92.68% of the respondents (38 out of 41) indicated that they would like to do so.

Our analysis of the communication patterns has revealed a number of ways in which students appropriated the ClassCommons tool. Some of these were clearly for entertainment purposes, but even when entertaining many of the conversations contained course-relevant comments or expansions of what was taking place in class. We did observe relatively high proportion of conversations that were used for social or incidental entertainment. We cannot conclude that these are "bad", because they may be helpful in raising feelings of sociality amongst the students [GROUP]. At the same time, from the active learning perspective that motivated this work, we would hope to see more use of ClassCommons for learning-related communication. With that in mind, we suggest design attention should be paid to two issues: helping students to use ClassCommons for communication that engages higher-order thinking and reducing the amount of random messages.

6.1 Promote Higher-Order Thinking

In the current trial, the instructor played a relatively passive role in use of ClassCommons. He encouraged students to initiate their own interaction, and students were allowed to post anything they wanted. Perhaps partially as a result of this, many of the questions asked in ClassCommons were "housekeeping questions", about assignments, quizzes and class presentations. Only a few were explicit questions or elaborations of course concepts.

Instead of just letting students post messages in the system, the instructor could play a more proactive role. According to Vygotsky [1], in students' learning processes, there is a Zone of Proximal Development (ZPD), that refers to the potential knowledge and skill space students can reach when they are properly engaged and guided by the teacher or in collaboration with other more capable peers. Teachers can help students achieve the ZPD by providing scaffoldings for students.

Several possible scaffolding approaches might be used in conjunction with public digital backchannels: the instructor might post a question in ClassCommons and ask students to respond. The teacher might also focus on open-ended questions to attract more participants in a discussion, or he or she might raise a topic expected to be controversial and encourage students to freely express their opinions, as reported in Section 5.4. The instructor might follow through by reviewing students' input and summarizing, commenting, or providing other feedback to the class or to individuals. In this way, the teacher would be using question asking as a deliberate strategy to promote discussions over the backchannel.

6.2 Reduce Miscellaneous Conversations

In the current study, about 28% of the conversations included incidental content that had nothing to do with the class. Miscellaneous conversations added little or nothing of value to the content being conveyed in the course, although they may have ed to some feelings of enjoyment. However, we worry that such conversations may distract students from the class lecture. Indeed, in a class exit survey, when students were reporting what they liked the least about ClassCommons, one complaint concerned irrelevant content of this sort. For example: *"Sometimes people posted irrelevant pictures or had irrelevant conversations." "Sometime, people posted things that were not relevant to the course on the display, which in some cases were a distraction."*

There are at least two techniques that teachers might use to decrease the tendency for these course-irrelevant postings. One of these would be to encourage contributors to use their real names.

In the course exit survey, students also mentioned that *"A lot of anonymous posts were off-topic."* Further, *"having an alias didn't allow others to get to know names in class"* which would not be helpful in facilitating community building in classrooms.

Second, teachers have an opportunity to set the norm and expectations when introducing the tool into the class. In this study, when introducing ClassCommons, the instructor did not specify the expectations for its use. Instead students were simply encouraged to participate and post messages freely; any content was welcomed. If an instructor knows in advance what kind of content he or she wishes to see, appropriate norms and expectations can be set in advance, possibly reducing the amount of random conversations.

7. Conclusions

In this study, we investigated the use ClassCommons, a public digital backchannel tool in an undergraduate class of moderate size. Generally, the concept of public digital backchannel was well accepted by students, as indicated by the high percentage of students who would like to use ClassCommons in the future. We analyzed the communication patterns of public digital channels and reported how student appropriated public digital backchannels in the class. The results demonstrated the potential of public digital backchannels in classrooms to actively engage students to make comments, ask questions, discuss class subjects, offer and ask for help for each other. We conclude with discussions that aim to help educators and researchers along this line of research.

8. ACKNOWLEDGMENTS

We would like to thank the instructor Shaoke Zhang and students in IST331 for their participation in this study and we would like to thank our colleague Stuart Selber for the comments and feedback on the earlier draft of this paper.

9. REFERENCES

[1] Vygotsky, L. S. *Mind in society: The development of higher psychological processes.* Harvard University Press, Cambridge, MA, 1978.

[2] Boyle, J. T. Using classroom communication systems to support interaction and discussion in large class settings. *Association for Learning Technology Journal,* 1, 3 2003), 43-57.

[3] Du, H., Rosson, M.B. and Carroll, J.M. Augmenting Classroom Participation throughPublic Digital Backchannels. To Apear in Proceedings of the ACM GROUP, 2012. ACM.

[4] Yngve, V. On getting a word in edgewise. *In Proceedings of the The Sixth Regional Meeting of the Chicago Linguistic Society.*

[5] Krauss, R. M. The role of audible and visible back-channel responses in interpersonal communication *Journal of personality and social psychology*, 35, 7 1977), 523-529.

[6] Bergstrom, T., Harris, A. and Karahalios, K. Encouraging initiative in the classroom with anonymous feedback. *In Proceedings of the 13th IFIP TC 13 international conference on Human-computer interaction* - Volume Part I (Lisbon, Portugal, 2011). Springer-Verlag.

[7] Dufresne, R., Gerace, W., Leonard, W., Mestre. J. and Wenk, L. Classtalk: A classroom communication system for

active learning. *Journal of Computing in Higher Education*, 7, 2 1996), 3-47.

[8] Robertson, L. J. Twelve tips for using a computerised interactive audience response system. *Medical Teacher*, 22, 3 2000), 237-239.

[9] Miller, R. G., Ashar, B. H. and Getz, K. J. Evaluation of an audience response system for the continuing education of health professionals. *Journal of Continuing Education in the Health Professions*, 23, 2 2003), 109-115.

[10] Fies, C. and Marshall, J. Classroom Response Systems: A Review of the Literature. *Journal of Science Education and Technology*, 15, 1 2006), 101-109.

[11] Ratto, M., Shapiro, R. B., Truong, T. M. and Griswold, W. The ActiveClass Project: Experiments in encouraging classroom participation. *In Proceedings of the CSCL* (2003). Kluwer Academic Publishers.

[12] Anderson, R., Anderson, R., VanDeGrift, T., Wolfman, S. Y. and Yasuhara, K. Promoting Interaction in Large Classes with Computer-Mediated Feedback. *In Proceedings of the CSCL* (2003). Kluwer Academic Publishers.

[13] Linnell, N., Anderson, R., Fridley, J., Hinckley, T. and Razmov, V. Supporting classroom discussion with technology: A case study in environmental science. *Frontiers In Education Conference Global Engineering Knowledge Without Borders Opportunities Without Passports*, 2007.

[14] EDUCAUSE 7 Things You Should Know About Live Question Tool. EDUCAUSE, 2011.

[15] Du, H., Rosson, M. B., Carroll, J. M. and Ganoe, C. I felt like a contributing member of the class: increasing class participation with classcommons. In Proceedings of the ACM GROUP, 2009. ACM.

[16] Du, H., Jiang, H., Rosson, M. B. and Carroll, J. M. Increasing Students In-Class Engagement through Public Commenting: An Exploratory Study. In Proceedings of the 2010 10th IEEE International Conference on Advanced Learning Technologies (2010). IEEE Computer Society.

[17] McNely, B. Backchannel persistence and collaborative meaning-making. *In Proceedings of the 27th ACM international conference on Design of communication* (Bloomington, Indiana, USA, 2009). ACM.

[18] Yardi, S. The role of the backchannel in collaborative learning environments. *International Confrence on Learning Sciences*, 2006.

Meta-Design and Cultures of Participation: Transformative Frameworks for the Design of Communication

[Keynote Presentation]

Gerhard Fischer
Center for Lifelong Learning & Design (L3D)
Department of Computer Science and Institute of Cognitive Science
University of Colorado, Boulder USA
1-303-492-1502
gerhard@colorado.edu

ABSTRACT

Meta-design (transcending other design disciplines such as user-centered design and participatory design) is focused on "design for designers". It provides foundations for a fundamental shift from *consumer cultures* (specialized in producing finished goods to be consumed passively) to *cultures of participation* (in which all people are provided with the means to participate actively in personally meaningful activities). These frameworks explore and support new approaches for the design, adoption, appropriation, adaptation, evolution, and sharing of artifacts by all participating stakeholders. Meta-design and cultures of participation are not dictated by technology alone: they are the result of incremental shifts in human behavior and social organizations.

Categories and Subject Descriptors
H.5.2 User-Centered Design, H.5.3 Theory and Models

Keywords
cultures of participation, meta-design, socio-technical environments, rich ecologies of participation, design trade-offs

BIOGRAPHY

Gerhard Fischer (http://l3d.cs.colorado.edu/~gerhard/) is a Professor of Computer Science, a Fellow of the Institute of Cognitive Science, and the Director of the Center for Lifelong Learning and Design (L3D) at the University of Colorado at Boulder. He is a member of the Computer Human Interaction Academy (CHI) and a Fellow of the Association for Computing Machinery (ACM). His research is focused on new conceptual frameworks and new media for learning, working, and collaborating; human-computer interaction; design; domain-oriented design environments; distributed cognition; universal design (assistive technologies); and socio-technical environments. His recent work has focused on social creativity, meta-design, and cultures of participation.

30 Years of Documentation and the Design of Communication

Scott Tilley

Department of Computer Sciences
Florida Institute of Technology
stilley@cs.fit.edu

ABSTRACT

This special panel session celebrates the 30th edition of the ACM SIGDOC conference. The panelists and moderator are all SIGDOC Chairs representing different eras in SIGDOC's rich history, from its humble beginnings in 1975 to the present. The panel session represents a unique opportunity to hear from experts who have the ability to place new developments in the design of communication in a historical context.

Categories and Subject Descriptors

D.2 [**Software Engineering**]; D.2.7 [**Distribution, Maintenance, and Enhancement**] – Documentation; D.2.10 [**Design**]; H.1.2 [**User/Machine Systems**] – Human Factors.

General Terms

Documentation, Design, Human Factors

Keywords

SIGDOC, documentation, design of communication, 30th anniversary, panel

1. BACKGROUND

2012 marks the 30th edition of the ACM SIGDOC conference. SIGDOC was originally known as the ACM's Special Interest Group on Computer Documentation. It's now known as ACM's Special Interest Group on Design of Communication. This broader interpretation of the DOC acronym affords members the ability to examine the design of communication as it is taught, practiced, researched, and conceptualized in the fields of user-centered design, technical communication, software engineering, information architecture, and usability.

SIGDOC *Special Interest Group on Design of Communication*

SIGDOC was founded in 1975 by its first Chair, Joe Rigo, with the help of many enthusiastic supporters, including two other early Chairs, Tom D'Auria and Diana Patterson. This special panel session celebrates SIGDOC's many accomplishments over the years and the people who helped create and shape its role in the DOC community.

The panel has representatives from different eras in SIGDOC's rich history, from its humble beginnings to the present. The panelists have all been SIGDOC Chairs. They will present a brief position statement on their experience with the conference, and express their view on how the field has changed over time.

There will also be a moderated discussion with all participants, focusing on some of the future challenges facing the field in the coming years. The panel session represents a unique opportunity to hear from experts who have the ability to place new developments in the design of communication in a historical context.

2. PANELISTS

Rob Pierce is the current SIGDOC Chair. He is an Advisory Information Developer for IBM and the user assistance team lead for the Watson Core Technology group. Rob previously worked as an information developer for Digital Equipment, Compaq, and Rational Software. Rob enjoys the intellectual vitality of SIGDOC and the active participation of its members. His interests in software development best practices, along with the design, development, and presentation of technical content, are aligned with what he does for IBM. He enjoys the synergy between the academics and the business professionals that comprise the SIGDOC membership as well as the breadth of topics that are relevant to SIGDOC. Rob has contributed to past SIGDOC conferences as a committee member, a panelist, and as a presenter. He was also the SIGDOC newsletter editor from 2001-2009 and 2011-2012.

Kathy Haramundanis was SIGDOC Chair from 1997-2003. She has been in the technical documentation field for 38 years, at Wang Laboratories, Digital Equipment Corporation, Compaq Computer Corporation, and Hewlett-Packard Company. She has a BA in Russian from Swarthmore College and an MS in

Computer Science from Boston University. She is the author of *The Art of Technical Documentation* (1992, 1997) – an early introduction to the field for new practitioners, used in college classes. She has been a member of the STC Executive Council (1993-95), recipient of the STC Merit award in 2003, and an STC competition judge from 1989-2000. She was also SIGDOC Treasurer (1993-2003) and a member of the ACM SIG Governing Board Executive Council (2001-2003). She publishes in the field, is a reviewer for AAAS Science Books and Films, and cited in Who's Who in America.

Nina Wishbow was SIGDOC Chair from 1993-1997. She has been a technical writer, instructional designer, usability tester, and interaction designer, and has managed teams in each of these areas. She also has written style guides for technical publications and user interfaces, and recently wrote a hybrid style guide for user interface content for Symantec Corporation. She is currently a Principal User Experience Writer at Symantec. Her previous experiences include Senior User Experience Manager at Openwave, User Experience Manager at Collabnet, Lead and Principal writer roles at Citrix and Oracle, respectively. Nina earned a Ph.D. in Rhetoric and Document Design from Carnegie Mellon University in 1988.

Diana Patterson was SIGDOC Chair from 1980-1989. She is an Associate Professor of English at Mount Royal University in Calgary, Canada, where she has been since 1991. She helped to develop their degree in Information Design. She currently teaches composition, the survey courses, and research methods.

Tom D'Auria was SIGDOC Chair from 1977-1980. He is Chairman and CEO of Information Methods Incorporated (IMI). He is a consultant to most NYC agencies, the LAPD, and the public safety agencies in Raleigh, NC. Tom has over 40 years experience in information technology with more than 20 years in the public and university sectors having worked and taught at Carnegie-Mellon (Pittsburgh) and Columbia Universities. He held a senior management position in New York City's data processing community for almost 10 years helping to create the city's technology and telecommunications agency. He hosts a weekly technology radio show that airs each Sunday on KFNX. He is a Fellow of the ACM. He is currently on the boards of the Mount Vernon (NY) Police Foundation, the Hudson River Museum, the New York Law Enforcement Foundation, the BraveKids Foundation, and the Daytop Village Foundation.

3. MODERATOR

Scott Tilley was SIGDOC Chair from 2003-2005. He is a Professor of Software Engineering in the Department of Computer Sciences at the Florida Institute of Technology, a Professor of Information Systems in the College of Business, and an Associate Member of the Harris Institute for Assured Information. He is a Visiting Scientist at Carnegie Mellon University's Software Engineering Institute. He is Chair of the Steering Committee for the IEEE *Web Systems Evolution* (WSE) series of events. He was General Chair for the 24th *IEEE International Conference on Software Maintenance* (ICSM 2008), which took place in Beijing, China. He writes the weekly "Technology Today" column for the *Florida Today* newspaper (Gannett).

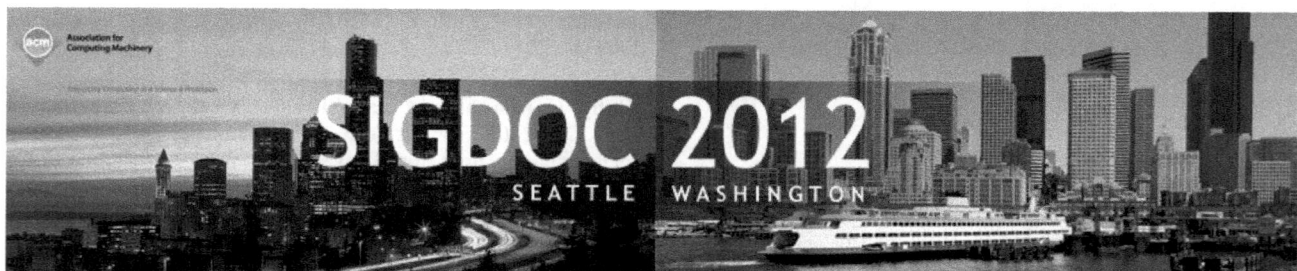

Collaborative Systems: Characteristics and Features

Manuela Aparicio
ADETTI-IUL/ ISCTE-IUL
IADE
UNL/ISEGI
manuela.aparicio@iscte.pt

Carlos J. Costa
ADETTI-IUL/ISCTE-IUL
University Institute of Lisbon

carlos.costa@iscte.pt

ABSTRACT

This work identifies some of the most significant advantages of collaboration systems as well as key features of these systems.. This study identifies the most preferred sytsems, as well as factors that influence its acceptance. In order to identify the main dimensions influencing collaborative system acceptance was used the TAM Model (Technology Acceptance Model). Then it was conducted an empirical study: collaboration systems were analysed, a blog systems was evaluated using TAM and blog systems group of users were identified.

Categories and Subject Descriptors

K.4 [**Computer and society**]: Organizational Impacts, Computer-supported collaborative work

Keywords

Collaborative systems, TAM, Technology acceptance model, Blog Systems

1. INTRODUCTION

Group work can be accomplished in several ways: cooperative group, coordination at work and individual work independently.

In the case of cooperative group, there are concerted efforts. The work of each of the elements of the group is closely related. For example, when a group of rowers are in a race, they must develop effort of coordination in order to pursue the best place. If the coordination is necessary there are a set of contact points. But the effort is mostly individual. For example a race is done independently, only when the baton is exchanged do the runners meet. There are groups in which the effort is made predominantly by an individual. The result of the group will be the sum of individual results.

Collaborative software is technology designed to facilitate group work, thus contributing to this increase in productivity.

In fact, collaborative software are computer systems that support people engaged in tasks (and targets) and they provide common inter-face-shared environment [7]. Collaborative systems are tools

used to facilitate the implementation of group work. These tools must be specialized enough in order to offer users forms of interaction which facilitate the control, coordination, collaboration and communication among users. It can be seen from this that the aim of the Collaborative Systems is to reduce the barriers imposed by physical space and time [9].

Computer Supported Collaborative Work is an interdisciplinary scientific field considers how teamwork can be supported by information and communication technologies. Examples of aspects studied include improving the performance of groups, in carrying out its tasks.

2. TYPOLOGY OF COLLABORATIVE SYSTEMS

There are some taxonomies for Collaborative Systems [1].

Collaborative Systems can be classified according to interaction and communication. Collaboration tools (collaborative systems) may be classified according to the place of interaction (face or distance) and time (synchronous or asynchronous). There are synchronous and asynchronous collaborative systems.

The asynchronous tools do not require a short or immediate response time. The e-mail and discussion forums are great examples of asynchronous tools. Tools workflow and calendars (Groupware) are also considered asynchronous tools. The asynchronous collaborative systems include Email, Newsgroups and mailing lists, workflow systems, hypertext, group calendars, and collaborative writing systems. Synchronous tools are those that require immediate response time (for example, instant messaging (ICQ, Messenger), conferences and video conferences). Examples of synchronous collaborative systems or real-time as follows: Table sharing (eg Smartboard), Video Communication Systems, Chat Systems, Group Decision Support Systems (GDSS) or multi-player games.

3. COLLABORATIVE SYSTEMS MAY IMPROVE GROUP PERFORMANCE

Several collaborative tools may be used to improve group performance, like agendas, chat or messaging systems, document repositories, audio and video conferencing, electronic meeting systems, workflow systems and authoring document systems

Agenda allows the creation of individual schedules for teams or corporate, including options for reserving rooms, scheduling and resources required for the interaction between the team.

Chat or messaging lets you exchange instant messages across the network to which the collaborative system is connected. It allows quick and low cost to people who are geographically distant. Electronic mail has become a basic tool of communication, virtually all organizations have already adapted to the use of this technology. It is considered a collaboration tool for groups, if necessary, however, take some care, because improper use may cause serious problems, such as the reception of unwanted messages, which can pose risks to the system and the overhead generated by the sending and receiving these types of messages.

Document Repository is a central repository of files, which provides security in storage, data access, version control, and facilitates the use and manipulation by multiple users.

The audio and video conferencing are ways to establish a synchronous communication (real time) to persons or groups of people who are geographically distant. The conference call can be accomplished through audio systems, such as handset speakerphone or network connection via the VOIP technology (Voice communication over the IP protocol). The video conference is a group formed by the transmission of audio and image synchronously, which can also allow the sending of data. Collaborative Systems must allow the use of these two forms of communication. Using the resources of audio and video conferencing is possible to meet with a group of people geographically far apart, share the contents of the presentation speech for all members present, with transmission of voice along with data displayed on the screen simultaneously. It allows the build of virtual meetings.

Electronic meeting systems provide knowledge resources and intelligence that can be easily accessed, (since the available information is well structured) and provide agility in decision making. Electronic Brainstorming Systems (rapid generation of multiple ideas for solving a given problem), polls and electronic voting are examples of resources that support the decision process.

Discussion forums are tools that give users the possibility of group discussions on particular issues and linked asynchronously.

The collaborative systems have the ability to control and manage the workflow, i.e., those that require the need of legal cases, or any other type of bureaucratic process. This procedure consists of a set of possible states of the process, together with the transition rules between states.

Authoring documents solve the need for multiple users to work on the same document. Most collaborative systems have been designed to meet this need. They allow a control of document editing, once a user has edited a file, it had been unavailable to other users to edit, until the user releases it for approval or editing by others.

It is common to provide resources for collaborative systems assembly forms. This is a form of standardization in the provision of information, where users, rather than produce a new document, fill out a form predetermined. This functionality promotes gains in quality and time in workflow processes.

4. CHARACTERISTICS OF COLLABORATIVE SYSTEMS

In the information economy, obtain, distribute knowledge and intelligence and enhance group collaboration have become vital not only to innovate but also to to survive[10]. Companies are increasingly dependent on Collaborative Systems, due to

excellent performance, which, coupled with the use of consciously has provided good results in business and business processes [10]. It is believed that collaboration systems facilitate the use of information and knowledge management, serving as support to information and knowledge work. This knowledge base consists of structured internal knowledge or explicit, product manuals and research reports; external knowledge, competitors, products and markets, including competitive intelligence; and informal internal knowledge: one that is in the minds of employees [10].

TABLE 1- Collaborative Systems grouped and categorised in time and space

	SPACE- Face	SPACE- Distance
TIME- Synchronous	Synchronous conferencing Video-conferencing Web conferencing	Document sharing Electronic meeting systems (EMS) Evaluation and survey Instant messaging Online chat Online spreadsheets Project management systems Rating and Comments Social software Surveys Synchronous conferencing Video-conferencing Web conferencing
TIME- Asynchronous	Workflow system XML Forms Management and workflow.	Application sharing Blogs Bookmarking, Business Intelligence Calendaring software Data conferencing Document Management Document repository Document sharing Document versioning E-mail Electronic calendars Evaluation and survey Knowledge management List Management Office suite Online spreadsheets Prediction markets Project Management Project management systems Rating and Comments Resource Management Revision control Social Software Surveys Tagging Time and cost management Time Tracking voice mail Web publishing Wikis Workflow systems XML Forms Management and workflow

The main purpose of a collaborative system may have the following definitions [10]:

- Management and coordination of work in a team of handlers of data and knowledge; .
- Integrating the work of the manipulators of information at all levels and functions of the organization, customization and distribution as defined by the user;
- Integration with the organization's external environment, such as customers, suppliers, government agencies, public and regulators, etc.;
- Management, creation, storage, retrieval and dissemination of documents;
- Definition of programming tasks/ appointments for individuals and groups;
- Facilitate the communication of voice and data to individuals inside and outside the organization;
- Management of contacts and relationships internal / external and information about users, customers and suppliers.

Features and tools of Collaborative System are often mixed and it is often difficult to separate them. Several researchers that study this field identify the following features (that are related to corresponding tools).

5. INTENTION TO USE COLLABORATIVE SYSTEMS

What are the most used? Most preferred? What influence their acceptance? In order to answer those question, a survey was conducted. The conducted study aimed to understand in which extent students intended to use collaborative systems and tools to accomplish their work. The survey was made with undergraduate students from different programs as a reason that students usually have many working groups in their multiple courses. A list of well known applications was made according to the tools functionalities and regarding the place interaction and time characteristics, from the table 1. Questions were formulated having the TAM – Technology e Model [6], as base. The figure 1 exemplifies the grouping of questions as part of the main variables of the model, such as perceived usefulness (PU), perceived easy of use (PEOU) and use (USE).

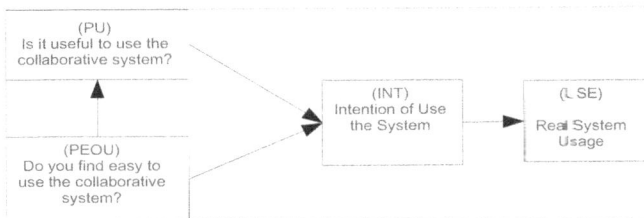

Fig 1 - Type of questions according to TAM model

Venkatesh and Davis [13], proposed an extension of TAM, the TAM2. TAM2 includes social influence process such subjective

norm, and cognitive instrumental process such as job relevance, output quality and result demonstrability.

TAM has been applied in numerous studies testing user acceptance of information technology. Just for example, TAM was applied to study the following technologies: word processors , spreadsheet applications , e-mail , web browser , telemedicine , websites , e-collaboration , elearning , ERP and Mindstorms .

The collaborative systems analysed are result of previous research ([3], [4], [5], [2], [12], [11]).

Supported in the previous dimension were derived Three hypotheses:

H1) Perceived ease of Use will have a positive effect on the perceived usefulness.

H2a) Perceived usefulness will have a positive effect on the users behavioral intention of use.

H2b) Perceived ease of Use will have a positive effect on the user behavioral intention of use

H3) Users behavioral intention will have a positive effect on actual use.

6. EMPIRICAL STUDY

In order to evaluate research hypothesis, an empirical study was conducted. In this study, a sample composed of students answered a questionnaire.

The study was composed of a general survey including several collaborative tools. Then, the blog was analyzed in detail.

The collaborative systems included in the survey covered the main characteristics of the working group tools. In the following table a list of the collaborative systems in the survey is included.

Table2- Collaborative Systems

Tools	Share Files	Work on the same Files	Voice & Video	Distance Interaction	Sync	Async
Wiki	√	√		√		√
Blog	√			√		√
E-mail	√			√		√
CMS	√	√		√		√
e-learning	√		√	√	√	√
Social Networks (Facebook & Tweeter)				√	√	√
Chat (Facebook, Messeger, Gmail)			√	√	√	
Google Docs	√	√		√	√	√
DropBox	√	√		√		√
Multi-player online Games			√	√	√	√

This study was carried out during October and November of 2011. The number of students answering questionnaires was 98.

These students belonged to the program of management and computer science. The range of age was from 18 to 36 years old. 66% of these students were full time students and the rest were part-time students. The following table shows the results of the survey. It was used a 7 point Likert scale, scale 1 was a totally disagree up to scale 7 – completely agree.

Supported in the TAM conceptual framework we analyze the level of acceptance of Blog Systems. We started by analyzing perceived usefulness (PU), perceived ease of use (PEO) and Intention to use the system (INT) and effective use (USE)

In order to validate research hypothesis, regression analysis was used as data analysis tool.

Table 3- Survey Results

		PU	INT	PEOU
Multiplayer Games	mean	4,01	3,42	5,11
	std. Dev.	1,69	1,96	1,75
Blog Systems	mean	4,6	4,06	5,36
	std. Dev	1,24	1,66	1,36
CMS	mean	4,27	3,87	3,96
	std. Dev	1,23	1,64	1,41
DropBox	mean	4,89	4,76	5,22
	std. Dev	1,75	1,8	1,66
e-Learning	mean	6,47	6,21	5,85
	std. Dev	0,81	1,18	1,22
e-mail	mean	6,64	6,35	6,44
	std. Dev	0,69	0,98	0,96
Facebook	mean	5,32	5,36	6,17
	std. Dev	1,51	1,77	1,25
Google Docs	mean	5,62	5,06	5,68
	std. Dev	1,25	1,6	1,21
chat Systems	mean	5,25	5,01	6,18
	std. Dev	1,4	1,69	1,32
Tweeter	mean	3,28	2,59	4,45
	std. Dev	1,61	1,92	1,73
Wiki	mean	5,12	4,84	5,68
	std. Dev	1,45	1,78	1,43

Note: PU – Perceived usefulness

  PEOU – Perceived ease of use

  INT – Intention to use the system

  Values presented: Average and Standard Deviations

H1) Perceived ease of Use will have a positive effect on the perceived usefulness.

In order to test this hypothesis it was performed a regression analysis, where Perceived usefulness (PU) is the dependent variable and perceived ease of use (PEOU) is the independent variable.

Table 4- Regression Analysis - H1)

SOURCE	DF	SS	MS	F	Prob.>F
Regression	1	.600	7.600	4.989	0.028
Residual	96	146.247	1.523		
Total	97	153.847			

R	R2	F	Prob.>F	DF1	DF2
0.222	0.049	4.989	0.028	1	96

Adjusted R Squared = 0.039

Std. Error of Estimate = 1.234

Variable	Beta	B	Std.Error	t	Prob.>t	VIF	TOL
PEOU	0.222	0.203	0.091	2.234	0.028	1.000	1.000

Constant = 3.515

Results presented in the table suggested a limited correlation between the variables. Even if there is a relation of causality between the two variables, there is no linear relation between the behaviour of those variables.

H2a) Perceived usefulness will have a positive effect on the users behavioural intention of using an blog.

H2b) Perceived ease of Use will have a positive effect on the user behavioural intention of using blog.

In order to test this hypothesis a regression analysis was performed, where behavioural intention of use (INT) is the dependent variable and perceived usefulness (PU) and perceived ease of use (PEOU) are the dependent variable.

Table 5- Regression Analysis - H2)

SOURCE	DF	SS	MS	F	Prob.>F
Regression	2	125.951	62.976	28.921	0.000
Residual	95	206.865	2.178		
Total	97	332.816			

Dependent Variable: "Blog_INT"

R	R2	F	Prob.>F	DF1	DF2
0.615	0.378	28.921	0.000	2	95

Adjusted R Squared = 0.365

Std. Error of Estimate = 1.476

Variable	Beta	B	Std.Error	t	Prob.>t	VIF	TOL
PEOU	0.511	0.687	0.111	6.164	0.000	1.052	0.951
PU	0.247	0.363	0.122	2.974	0.004	1.052	0.951

Constant = -0.965

Results presented in the table suggested that we could have an acceptable model. On the other hand, perceived usefulness (PU) have a more reduced impact that perceived ease of use (PEOU) on the intention of use of the system.

H3)   Users behavioral intention will have a positive effect on actual use of a blog.

In order to test this hypothesis it was performed a regression analysis, where actual use (USE) is the dependent variable and behavioural intention of use (INT) is the independent variable.

Table 6-Regression Analysis - H1)

SOURCE	DF	SS	MS	F	Prob.>F
Regression	1	92.727	92.727	57.878	0.000
Residual	96	153.803	1.602		
Total	97	246.531			

Dependent Variable: "Blog_USE "

R	R2	F	Prob.>F	DF1	DF2
0.613	0.376	57.878	0.000	1	96

Adjusted R Squared = 0.370

Std. Error of Estimate =   1.266

Variable	Beta	B	Std.Error	t	Prob.>t	VIF	TOL
INT	0.613	0.528	0.069	7.608	0.000	1.000	1.000

Constant =   0.605

In order to identify specific group of users it was used Weka to perform the cluster analysis. Simple EM (expectation maximization) class Cluster was the technique used.

The variables used in the cluster analysis were the following:

- INT – Intention of using the blog system
- OB – feel obliged to use the blog system
- PEOU – Bog system perceived ease of use of the
- PU – Perceived Usefulness of the blog
- PU1 – Perception that the system will increase own productivity
- USE – Actual usage
- Age – Age

As it was presented, two groups were identified. One group of blogger (30%) and another group of non-bogglers (70%). The non bloggers only uses blog system if they think are obliged.

Results presented in the cluster analysis may complement results of the TAM model. In fact, the variables follow normal distribution and may be estimated the parameters of the model, other information may be extracted from the data. The rational is that in fact when we are analysing a sample (from a specific universe) groups of specific elements of this sample may have specific characteristics. In this case, we may find group of users that have specific behaviours towards blog usage.

Table 7- Cluster Analysis

Number		Group 1	Group 2
Number	Number	29	69
	Percentage	(30%)	(70%)
INT	mean	5.8177	3.3781
	std. Dev	1.2908	1.2198
OB –	mean	2.0865	2.532
	std. Dev	1.5392	1.5544
PEOU	mean	6.2113	5.0916
	std. Dev	1.0206	1.298
PU	mean	5.4499	4.2079
	std. Dev	0.8765	1.2045
PU1	mean	5.6282	2.9634
	std. Dev	1.1014	1.1425
USE	mean	4.427	2.2106
	std. Dev	1.4458	1.1047
Age	mean	21.2789	20.1939
	std. Dev	4.4615	3.0015

Log likelihood: -12.9338

7.   CONCLUSIONS

In this paper we identified key characteristics of collaborative systems. Then, we identified which are the most preferred and what factors influenced their acceptance. To answer this question we used TAM (Technology Acceptance Model). According to our survey, perceived usefulness is connected to the intention of use. Other statistical analysis suggested that other dimensions must be identified to explain the intention of use of collaborative systems. Blog was analysed in detail. It was possible to identify two groups of users. One it is composed of students that intent to continue using the blog system and another that is not so interested. Empirical research was generically coherent with studies performed previously. Specially in what concerns the intention to participate actively in collaborative systems, writing posts , messages or any other type of intervention.

8.   ACKNOWLEDGMENTS

Research presented here was partially supported by FCT – Fundação para a Ciência e Tecnologia.

9.   REFERENCES

[1]   Colleman, D. (1997) Groupware: Collaborative Strategies for corporate LANs and Intranets – Prentice Hall .

[2]   Costa, C. J. & Tavares, M. (2007).Knowledge management process in the local government. Proceedings of the 25th annual ACM international conference on Design of

communication, SIGDOC '07 (pp 182–188). New York, NY, USA: ACM.

[3] Costa, C. J., & Alturas, B. (2010). Social networks and design of communication. Proceedings of the Workshop on Open Source and Design of Communication, OSDOC '10 (pp 11–14). New York, NY, USA: ACM. 9

[4] Costa, C. J., & Costa, P. (2010). Wemoga: walking through a map. Proceedings of the Workshop on Open Source and Design of Communication, OSDOC '10 (pp 61–63). New York, NY, USA: ACM.

[5] Costa, C. J., Nhampossa, J. L., & Aparício, M. (2008). Wiki content evaluation framework. Proceedings of the 26th annual ACM international conference on Design of communication, SIGDOC '08 (pp 169–174). New York, NY, USA: ACM.

[6] Davis, F. (1989), "Perceived usefulness, perceived ease of use, and user acceptance of information technology", MIS Quarterly 13(3): 319–340

[7] Ellis, C. , Gibbs , C & Rein. G. (1991), Groupware: some issues and experiences, Communications of the ACM, v.34 n.1, p.39-58.

[8] Guzdial, M., Rick, J., & Kerimbaev, B. (2000). Recognizing and supporting roles in CSCW. Proceedings of the 2000 ACM conference on Computer supported cooperative work, CSCW'00 (pp 261–268). New York, NY, USA: ACM.

[9] Johansen, R. (1988) Groupware: Computer Support for Business Teams The Free Press

[10] Laudon, K. Laudon, J. (2004). Management Information Systems, 11 edition, Prentice Hall.

[11] Pena, J., & Costa, C. J. (2010). Open source isometric browser games framework. Proceedings of the Workshop on Open Source and Design of Communication, OSDOC '10 (pp 51–54). New York, NY, USA: ACM.

[12] Sousa, F., Aparicio, M., & Costa, C. J. (2010). Organizational wiki as a knowledge management tool. Proceedings of the 28th ACM International Conference on Design of Communication, SIGDOC '10 (pp 33–39). New York, NY, USA

[13] Venkatesh, V. and Davis, F.D. (2000). "A Theoretical Extension of the Technology Acceptance Model: Four Longitudinal Field Studies". Management Science, 46 (2), pp. 186-204.

Instant Annotation: Early Design Experiences in Supporting Cross-Cultural Group Chat

Na Li[1], Mary Beth Rosson[2]
College of Information Sciences and Technology
The Pennsylvania State University
329B IST Building, University Park, PA 16802
[1]nzl116@psu.edu, [2]mur13@psu.edu

ABSTRACT
Cross-cultural group chat is an important option for supporting communication in both industry and education settings. However, studies of such interactions have reported persistent communication problems that appear to be due to mismatches in non-native and native speakers' language proficiency. With this problem in mind, we have been exploring a conceptual design called Instant Annotation. Our design concept supports a kind of threading in chat using annotation, thus offering para-communication support in cross-cultural group chat. As part of this design investigation, we studied native and non-native speakers in a group chat activity, shared the new design concept, and interviewed users to gather their feedback about the Instant Annotation concept. The results pointed to three different design use cases and led us to envision four general design features that we will explore in our ongoing work. We discuss the cross-cultural communication problem, findings from the interview study, the current design and future directions.

Categories and Subject Descriptors
H.5.2. [Information interfaces and presentation (e.g., HCI)]: User Interfaces - *User-centered design*; H.5.3. [Information interfaces and presentation (e.g., HCI)]: Group and Organization Interfaces - *Synchronous interaction*.

Keywords
Cross-cultural, native speaker, non-native speaker, scenario-based design, CSCW, group discussion, online chat, annotation, tagging.

1. INTRODUCTION
Cross-cultural communication is taking place everywhere as the world is getting flat. It happens in working places, classrooms, international conferences, online chat boards, emails, and more. Research conducted across many disciplines (e.g. education, psycholinguistics, sociology, HCI and CSCW) shows that language proficiency plays an important role in cross-cultural communication. In particular, non-native speakers often suffer from communication problems caused by language proficiency issues both in face-to-face communication and distributed online communication [6,18].

Non-native speakers receive and understand information more slowly; they need more time to organize expressions; and they frequently make grammatical errors, due to an increase in cognitive load when processing a second language [8]. In this context, comparison studies have found that text-based computer-mediated communication (CMC) can be beneficial to non-native speakers [24]. Text communication typically requires less immediacy in response than face-to-face or oral communication, thus alleviating the cognitive burdens of non-native speakers. With CMC tools, non-native speakers have more time to read others' expressions and generate their own expressions. Nonetheless, studies show that there are communication problems caused by non-matching levels of language competence in text-based CMC [7]. Many such problems have been reported in classroom or group studies [4,6,7], perhaps indicating that they are particularly prominent in multi-person communication settings.

A common problem found in those studies is a disruption in turn-taking, a flaw in existing text chat systems that has been identified in the literature [22]. Because there are no social cues indicating start and end of speaking as in face-to-face communication, speakers may send messages at the same time. Therefore, any given message may not be a response to the most recently received message but rather refer to a point made several messages earlier. This disruption of the sequential turn-taking system may generate communication confusions, particularly when overlapping threads are semantically related. The disruption might arise more easily in cross-cultural group chat due to the unmatched levels of language proficiency and differences in general communication styles.

Although researchers from different areas have noted communication problems in cross-cultural group chats, there is a relatively little research that articulates users' needs and requirements in these settings; there are few examples of CMC tools that have been designed to support cross-cultural communication. Given these gaps in research and tool development, we have begun to explore the needs and requirements of mixed groups of non-native and native speakers, drawing from these studies to design new tools that can help them to communicate better with one another. Our work has been inspired by two streams of design research - threaded chat [22] and collaborative annotation [12]. In particular, we have designed an enhancement to group chat called Instant Annotation (IA) – a conceptual design in which participants use a parallel channel to annotate or otherwise comment on an ongoing discussion. We believe that IA might assist information retention and conversation management in cross-cultural communication.

In this paper, we report our initial exploration of the design space with an eye on cultural differences in participants' reactions to the IA concept. We hope by doing this that we can tailor the design concept to the different needs of non-native and native speakers. We first used a warm-up task to immerse our participants' into the experience of cross-cultural group chat; we next presented the IA conceptual design and asked our participants to reflect on its usefulness. We show that by offering an early design concept for feedback, and asking users to weigh pros and cons of the conceptual design, we were able to learn about users' needs, enabling us to refine the design. In the balance of the paper we describe the communication problem we are addressing, the IA design concept, the methods we used to introduce this concept to users, our findings and the implications we drew for continued work.

2. BACKGROUND

Text-based instant communication tools have been studied for many years. Both their drawbacks and their benefits are well known. On one hand, text chatting affords a level of reviewability and revisability [2] that is difficult to match with audio or video channels. On the other hand, taking turns in text chat can easily be disrupted by overlapping threads of multiple topics. Several qualitative studies have reported participants' frustrations in online group discussion; in these cases the frustration seems to be directly linked to the frequent and flexible turn-taking common in text-based CMC [4,6,7]. These facts motivated our interest to explore new design features that could possibly solve the problem. In this section, we briefly review the disrupted turn-taking problem and two streams of designs in the literature that inspired our work.

2.1 Disrupted Turn-taking

Turn-taking has been studied for some time in oral conversations; it is seen as a vital component in the construction of any spoken interaction [20]. Turn-taking is accomplished through the dynamic collaboration of interlocutors, who exchange cues about whether they plan to hold a turn, start or end a turn, or interrupt a turn. Schegloff pointed out that turn-taking also occurs in text-based conversations but with slightly different dynamics than spoken conversations [21]. Due to the common lack of nonverbal social cues (e.g., seeing that someone is preparing to "speak"), several interlocutors may enter a conversation at the same time. As a result, even though utterances appear one at a time on the screen, and thus may seem to be sequential [25], there is no necessary logical linkage between each turn. In addition, in contrast to spoken conversations where utterances are produced and heard at the same time, an expression in a text chat is often seen by others only after the user finishes typing all the words and sends it to the system. Therefore, a given conversational turn may actually respond to a turn several turns before it. This difference disrupts the sequential nature inherent in face-to-face conversation [9].

The problems emanating from disruptions in turn-taking are exacerbated in group chat, because there are more interlocutors competing for turns. Gonzalez [6] found that people often introduce new topics without finishing previous ones and they only selectively attend to the topic that is of most interest to them. Therefore, some participants may feel overwhelmed and even lost in parallel and fast-flowing discussions, especially speakers who have slow keyboarding skills, slow reading/writing skills, or different cultural backgrounds [17].

Asymmetrical relationships are often formed on the basis of language competency, similar to the asymmetrical relationships built upon expertise or authority [26]. When a native speaker perceives that a non-native speaker has language deficiencies that interfere with communication, the native speaker may then assume control of the conversation [5]. This language competency imbalance may then affect turn-taking: Native speakers are likely to take over most of the turns, whereas non-native speakers have fewer opportunities. When this imbalance is severe, non-native speakers may simply refrain altogether from participating in the conversation, even if they have great ideas and are eager to participate at the beginning.

2.2 Threaded Chat

Threaded chat helps people to organize their chat logs into threads. This design feature can be integrated into chat systems or other tools for different purposes, such as managing conversation structure or supporting side chat. Smith et al. [28] proposed an IM tool that supports threaded chat, in which the threaded structure is integrated in the main chatting window thus making it a primary element in such communication. To initiate a new topic, a speaker clicks the "root" of the conversation tree to create a new thread. To respond to an existing thread instead, the speaker clicks on that thread to create a turn placeholder for editing. Although this method makes the relationships between turns clear, it interrupts the flow of the conversation quite a bit, such that it "hops around" and feels unnatural. As a result, users' satisfaction rates are low compared to standard chat.

Threaded chat can also be found in other tools but integrated as a more peripheral element of the design. The primary activity those tools support is not chatting; however chatting is included to assist the primary activity. For example, some anchored discussion boards designed to support students' collaborative learning have offered threaded chat on a sidebar next to the discussion window.

A representative example is WebAnn [1], used by students to discuss specific points in a digital document. To create a discussion point in WebAnn, a user selects the text snippet in the document to be annotated, causing a new thread to be created in the sidebar for editing. Other users can reply by clicking on that thread. Conceptually, the selected text snippet becomes the thread's anchor and the central point of the on-the-side discussion thread. A study of WebAnn showed that positioning threaded discussions next to the anchoring text raises people's awareness of others' interests and activities [16]. Two other studies with similar designs showed that people are motivated to participate after seeing others joining the activity [11,12].

2.3 Collaborative Annotation

The idea of collaborative annotation is similar to the anchored discussion boards in that it also provides peripheral spaces for anchored points. In fact, researchers at times have referred to designs like WebAnn as collaborative annotation tools. The reason for this is that the sidebar is not exclusively used for chatting; sometimes it is used for annotating the anchored content. This means that the thread does not represent a conversation but rather one or more notes or tags about the anchor. In this case, the structure of the "conversation" space is flat compared to the tree-like structure of a threaded chat.

Studies of collaborative annotation tools suggest that serious challenges arise for designers when the annotation features must be integrated with real-time communication and collaboration [12]. Because synchronous interaction is usually attention demanding, adding a subtask such as annotating points could be

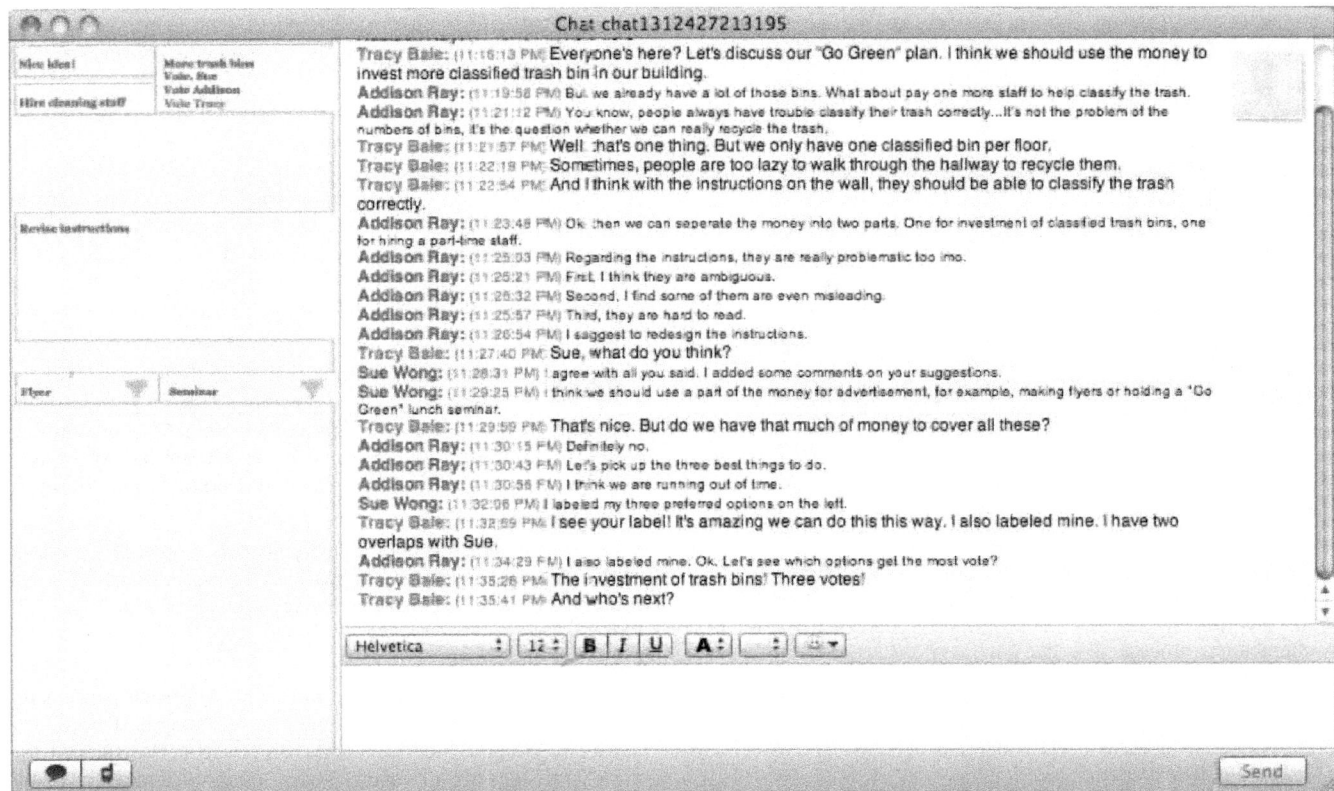

Figure 1. A mock-up of the Instant Annotation design concept.

difficult. Kelkar et al. [12] described a "live" collaborative tagging system for real-time audio meetings. Their system allows users to annotate utterances that are indexed by a timeline. However, their system did not support replying or otherwise elaborating an existing annotation. They found that users could not multitask well between tagging and active participation in the meetings.

3. INSTANT ANNOTATION

Inspired by threaded chat design and collaborative annotation design, we developed a conceptual design – Instant Annotation (IA). It supports conversation management and information summarization through an annotation space that is positioned near the main chat area (see Fig. 1 the light gray rectangular "tabs" in the left subpane hold annotations related to the text chat in the right). For convenience, in the paper we will refer to the right subpane as the "IM" window, and the left as the "IA" window).

To start a new annotation, a user clicks on a line of text in the IM window; this will generate an annotation tab in the IA window. The user can then add text to that tab. Other interlocutors will see the annotation as soon as the user clicks the comment button at the bottom left. The annotation tabs are tied to their anchoring line(s) of the chat log and will scroll up with that content. If more than one annotation is created for the same line(s) of text chat, they will appear side by side as shown in the top and bottom annotations in Fig. 1. To reply to an annotation, a user double clicks the annotation; when this happens a reply tab is created under the original annotation. In this way we are able to

distinguish threaded chat and unrelated annotations of the same chat content.

Our design concept differs from prior work in several ways. We are the first to apply annotation tools to real-time text chat. Our design also supports a mix of threaded chat (i.e., comments and replies) and general annotation (i.e., multiple unrelated notes). As a result, users can seamlessly transition between threaded side conversations and simple annotations. Finally we have as a primary design goal to display and support the sidebar communication in as non-invasive a fashion as possible, so as to minimally disrupt the flow of the main conversation. We expect that users will only use it when they have a particular need in managing their conversations. We turn now to the methods we used to introduce and to gather feedback and design directions for the IA conceptual design.

4. METHOD

Early in design, when designers are still exploring the problem space, the emerging design concept may not have been specified well enough to create an interactive prototype for user evaluation. Nonetheless, it can be very beneficial to gather feedback and suggestions at this time, particularly if the concept is novel; users' input can help in formulating more detailed requirements as the design work continues. Often such input is gathered through field studies, with the goal of learning about users' needs in the real world. However, because the scope of the IA project is small and focused on a particular set of concerns related to language proficiencies, fieldwork was not a practical option. Instead we sought to engage participants in a familiar usage experience in a lab setting (a group chat) where we could closely observe their behavior; with the group chat experience fresh in their minds, we then injected the IA design concept as an object of inspiration and reflection.

The lab-based method we used can be viewed as an adaptation and merging of scenario-based design (SBD) [19] and technology design probes [10]. In SBD, hypothetical users are envisioned as they interact with novel technology features in a familiar activity context and the ideas evoked by this exploration are used to transform the current activities. When using design probes, a novel technology concept is introduced into an ongoing activity or situation, usually for some period of time, so that the designers can observe what sorts of reactions or new behaviors it evokes in users. Our approach was to ask users to first enact a familiar activity (providing a personal usage scenario), and leverage that usage context to gather reactions to a novel technology concept.

More specifically, we engaged native and non-native speakers in an online group chat using technology familiar from their everyday lives – AOL Instant Messenger (AIM). Following this experience, we presented the IA design concept (Fig. 1), and gathered feedback using one-on-one semi-structured interviews. In the interviews we asked participants to reflect back to the group chat experience and to consider whether and how they might incorporate the IA concept into this cross-cultural communication process. We had intensive discussions with our participants, encouraging them to voice both pros and cons about their reactions to the design concept.

4.1 Participants

Over a two-month period we assembled five groups for study, each with two native speakers (Americans) and two non-native speakers (Chinese). After each session and set of interviews we did an initial coding of the participants' reflections and concluded the study after reaching the point of theoretical saturation [23], when themes were repeated in the data and no new themes were emerging.

We chose to study Chinese as the representative samples of non-native speakers because both their language and culture are very different from the western world; therefore they are likely to experience communication problems when communicating with people from the western world. We do not expect that our findings will be specific to Chinese non-native speakers, but future work will be needed to determine whether they apply to other non-native speaker populations.

The participants were undergraduate and graduate students majoring in information science or psychology from a large university in the Northeast United States; students' ages ranged from 20 to 43. There were 8 females and 12 males. Because we are not interested in gender effect in our study, and to avoid gender-related social and communication dynamics, we ensured that all groups were of the same gender. Most of the native speakers had some experience in collaborating with non-native speakers as part of group work (two Americans had not had this experience). Some of them had studied with non-native speakers in course projects in the past, and some of them worked closely with non-native speakers every day.

For the Chinese participants in our study, all had been living in the U.S. for less than four years, and all reported an advanced English proficiency (indicated in their pre-task survey). Advanced English proficiency was described as "I can carry on a conversation with a native speaker of the language, although it is highly evident that I am not a native speaker of the language." Thus any difficulties observed should be seen as persisting even once a non-native feels relatively comfortable conversing in a new language.

4.2 Task

We set a simulated group task that could stimulate participants' thoughts about cross-cultural group chat. The task was adapted from a study of second language learners' communication media preferences [4]. Each participant was asked to assume the role of a "Go Green" team member and to discuss with their group members how to spend $5000 to support environmental sustainability.

Four participants chatted about the sustainability topic in AIM for 15 minutes. They were asked to generate at least eight ideas and to decide on the best three. This combination of brainstorming and decision-making within the task make it similar to the real world situations where formal discussions occur (e.g. in business or academic settings).

Before entering the group chat, participants completed a pre-task survey; they also completed a post-task survey. Our analysis and discussion of these survey results is reported elsewhere [14].

4.3 Interviews

We conducted a semi-structured interview with each participant, spending approximately 30 minutes in discussion. During the interview, we presented the IA design concept: We showed the mock-up images to participants. Using the mock-up image we did a walkthrough to "demo" basic functions the IA could provide. We then asked several open-ended questions as described below; in this paper we focus particularly on answers to the second and third question. The open-ended question format allowed us to pursue other points that came up in each participant's response.

1. What was the participant's experience in this cross-cultural group discussion, especially their experience communicating with people from other countries?

2. Will a chat client featuring Instant Annotation help him/her in cross-cultural group discussions and if so how? Providing use cases if possible.

3. What are the limitations of Instant Annotation? Or, what other features can he/she imagine to assist cross-cultural group discussions?

Each interview was recorded and transcribed to text. Participants were interviewed in their first language. For interviews with Chinese participants, the transcriptions were translated back to English by the first author.

The transcripts were analyzed informally to discover themes related to cultural differences and communication difficulties. Specifically, we informally coded the transcripts with descriptive words, such as "tagging topics", "taking notes of important contents", and "side chat", etc. And then we sort through similar codes and merge them into higher-level concepts. We searched for themes that could cover the full range of concepts.

5. DATA ANALYSIS

Although we also collected and analyzed the chat logs of the five groups, the analysis of those data are reported elsewhere [14]; our focus in this paper is the participants' reactions to the IA design concept *after* experiencing the group chat. In general, we found that most participants (18 out of 20) expressed an interest in using an IM tool that included an IA space, and they voiced many ideas about how they would use it based on the experiences they had just has as well as their more general experiences using group chat tools and interacting with speakers from different cultures. Collapsing across these various ideas, we have organized their ideas into three high-level categories: tagging, side chatting, and other concepts.

5.1 Tagging

Many participants envisioned that they could use an IA space for tagging; that is, to provide a conceptual level description of a piece of text. They also indicated what they would use the tags for; these more specific ideas led to three sub-themes in our discussion of tagging as a design direction. We refer to these subthemes as *use cases* by analogy to the hypothetical uses that are often generated during requirements engineering [13]. Of interest to our general research project, these use cases suggested that the non-native and native speakers differed in how and why they would incorporate tagging into their cross-cultural communication.

One common use case for tagging in the IA space was to quickly retrieve earlier discussion points. Participants indicated a need to remember these discussion points when a discussion went for a long time or when it became complex with a number of rich ideas. We noticed that one participant had noted his group's ideas on a piece of paper, and all five groups had at least one member who summarized the emerging ideas in the chat window during the chats.

Going beyond the general need to manage a long and complicated discussion, two of the non-native speakers envisioned a more specific scenario: They would use the tags to help reveal the structure of a conversation. In these cases, they said they needed a clearer view of the flow of a conversation because of disruptions in turn-taking. As one interviewee said:

"The discussion of a topic may be disrupted by other discussions, the tags will help you to follow a topic more easily. When a conversation goes really long, discussions of several topics may be mingled together, the tags will make the structure of the conversation clearer. " (Interviewee 1, Chinese)

Only non-native speakers suggested the use of tags for capturing conversation structure. In this sample at least, native speakers seemed not to have comprehension problems caused by disruptions in turn-taking, perhaps because they are quite familiar with this from their everyday online chatting activities.

A second use case for tagging was to make a note of points that have not yet been shared, so that they can be discussed later. One surprise was that it was native speakers who repeatedly mentioned this possible use, not the non-native speakers. Some native speakers tended to speak less, giving the non-native speakers more chances to talk. Such a strategy might reduce their chances of introducing new ideas while they promote the non-native speakers' opportunities to contribute:

"I had a couple ideas but I tried to only kind of go in turn as much as possible so that everybody had a chance." (Interviewee 4, American)

"Sometimes I waited to give everyone else time to type, because I typed faster than some people, I was trying to not say anything." (Interviewee 12, American)

Although not explicitly calling out the cross-cultural demands of the conversation, we speculate that it was at least partly the native speakers' awareness of the culture difference – and the accommodations they made in response – that led to production loss [3] in these groups. It is interesting to consider whether and how often such accommodation happens in cross-cultural communication. It suggests a social sensitivity along with finely tuned cross-cultural communication skills, perhaps a function of the prior experience many of the native speakers had in working with student peers from other countries. Interestingly for our design project, this use case could be supported by the same IA affordance as the more general tagging goal (i.e., a place to hold "extra" ideas). In this case though, we can hypothesize that a side conversation space might be at least as important to native speakers who are being considerate as to non-native speakers who are feeling stressed by the pace of the conversation.

Two native speakers also suggested the use of tags as a temporary reminder for ideas that they wanted to express but that would not have let them "keep up with the flow of the current chat" (Interviewee 13, American). In this case, it was not so much that they wanted to give their non-native counterparts a chance to contribute but rather than they judged that this was not the right time to change a topic. Thus they elected to wait for the next turn because they did not want to "completely ruin someone's thought" (Interviewee 4, American). When asked to compare using tags as a reminder versus paper and pencil, they said the tags would be used as "visual markers" that were easy and convenient to access, whereas paper and pencil might not be always available.

The third use case of tagging was to promote awareness of a discussion point. In two different groups, the two Chinese participants' ideas were at times ignored, apparently due to the overwhelming and parallel discussions taking place. These two Chinese speakers were significantly less talkative than the other three participants in their groups and their expressions tended to be short and simple, making them easy to miss.

One of the Chinese participants made several efforts to re-raise or re-address the ignored ideas from her Chinese group member. This caused her to be seen as a coordinator who organized and shifted topics back and forth in her group. She later provided a compelling scenario of using collaborative tagging to replace her role: *"If we missed an idea and we all wanted to catch it up, we would all annotate that idea. Then we would easily shift back to that idea and further discuss on it. " (Interviewee 15, Chinese)*

Another Chinese participant expressed similar ideas about collaborative tagging as a way to raise awareness of others' contributions. On the other hand, the native speakers voiced no concerns about the highly parallel and disrupted communication style, taking it as "a common feature that all chatting systems have".

5.2 Side Chatting

Another general design scenario that many participants envisioned was using the IA space for a side conversation. A common need recognized by both native and non-native speakers was to easily comment about earlier discussion points. As stated by the interviewees below,

"Because each tab corresponds to a topic, if I comment there, they can easily see it. If I respond to an earlier point in the main window, then you have to search above to anchor the point. With the IA window and maybe a bright alert sign when new comments are added, it's easily for people to see what they say, what others respond, and what others respond to those response." (Interviewee 16, Chinese)

"Sometimes I don't know how to say it in English, especially when many people are discussing, I miss the chance to speak out, after a while, I forget it myself. ... With the IA space, I can make up the discussion points I missed." (Interviewee 1, Chinese)

The side chat feature provides users an alternative way to communicate, one that requires little extra effort to foreground an earlier discussion point before commenting on it. Furthermore, other users do not need to search through the complex chat record to access the point. It is as easy as going right to the point, clicking to expand the comments and reading them. Non-native speakers saw this as a chance for them to jump into a conversation at a later point, for example after they had a chance to process and reflect on what others were saying. Interestingly, they felt that they would only respond to ideas in the IA space when a discussion of the idea was over, because responding while a topic was still in discussion "would interrupt the flow of the main chat too much" (Interviewee 8, Chinese).

The only time that the interviewees predicted that they might respond to currently active ideas in the IA space is when several parallel discussions were taking place. In this case, the rationale for responding next to a piece of text was similar to the one above, in that it would save effort to foreground which point was the target of the new response.

As an example, this functionality was achieved in a different way in group 5's discussion. The conversation of Group 5 had many cases of disruption, for example one parallel discussion that involved eight out of the ten ideas proposed through the whole discussion process. However, group 5's members thought their conversation was clear, because they successfully developed a communication protocol within the group: Adopting a practice often seen in microblogs, they used @groupmember's name to direct responses to the right person. The following snippet from their chat log showed how this worked for them (participants' screen names have been replaced by letters).

A: I have one idea.

B: @A: yes?

C: We can set up a group to collect student, staff, and faculty's address and then make the carpool assignment.

D: Note to tall: we are at 12 minutes of discussion so far.

B: @C: We kind of already have that.

A: We can purchase some cloth bags and distribute them among the students.

This spontaneous practice is similar to making a comment to the side of a piece of text, which is also able to direct attention of the right person to the right place. One of the participants of group 5 also offered a compelling scenario that uses the IA space to organize a major discussion and a sub-discussion in his lab meeting: *"If you are on a task where some people are worrying about when we are gonna schedule things versus how do we organize logistics for something else, people who are scheduling things can have their own discussion about something versus this general conversation about logistics."* (Interviewee 17, American)

This scenario also applies to the case of native speakers placing tags as reminders for ideas to discuss later. They could chat on these ideas while waiting for the non-native speakers to input their ideas in the main chatting window.

Some interviewees suggested that the IA space could serve as a convenient mechanism to express agreement/disagreement (e.g. Nice idea!) and other quick opinions for that matter. For example, one interviewee said, *"Because the normal chat does not hold a lot of ways for you to kind of make different expressions unless you use the happy faces or those kind of things. But I think this is a much better way to do it."* (Interviewee 3, American)

5.3 Other Use Cases
Besides tagging and side chatting, interviewees offered several other use cases of the IA space. They could use it to note down important facts, such as phone numbers, people's names, and addresses, etc. This is similar to Micronote [15], which provides a temporary note for fast retrieval. Inspired by the decision making task, participants also mentioned that they might use the IA space to vote for the three best ideas. Although this use case is specific to the task they were given, it might generalize to other decision-making tasks, especially those tasks requiring majority vote of ideas for the final decision.

One participant suggested adding the IA feature to chat tools used for larger groups. He provided an example of annotating in a chat room: Many online live sportscasts provide a chat channel next to the video, so that fans can express opinions, reactions or converse with other fans. Fans from the two sides often debate for their team, which generates some discussion points. Because there are hundreds of fans in the room, the screen updates very rapidly, which makes these conversations severely disrupted.

In this situation the IA space could help to organize discussions by allowing responses next to a piece of text. It also helps to remind people of important contents. In fact, this scenario also incorporates tagging and side chatting. However, an interesting point raised by this scenario was the scale of the chatting activity. The IA feature may be even more useful in chatting contexts that involve many people as opposed to the small groups we studied.

6. DESIGN CHOICES
We have shared users' reactions to and reflections about uses of the IA design concept, after first being primed with an experience in online chat among native and non-native speakers. We turn now to a set of design implications that are entrained by the range of usage ideas and that we are now considering in the elaboration and realization of the IA design concept.

6.1 Tag Access Control
The interviewees were sensitive to the tags' access rights, though they differed in whether they believed tags should be used for private or public purposes. Although their interview comments did not elaborate this issue enough to clarify the distinction, they asked questions like "Who will see my tags?" and "What does others' IA space look like?" This suggests that tag ownership and control will be an important issue as we elaborate our design.

When talking about use cases for the IA space, at times participants distinguished between personal versus others' chat content. For example, *"I will definitely tag others' ideas, so that I can review them easily."* (Interviewee 2, Chinese) This participant also said that he would not tag his own ideas. Another participant also saw tagging as a communication tool with public access, *"I will tag something when I want to emphasize it to others."* (Interviewee 10, Chinese) In contrast, interviewee 3 only thought about tagging his own content, *"If you don't want to express yourself in this group chat, so if you want to hold something and send it as a sidebar to somebody outside the chat. You could take that idea offline and hold it there for yourself for later."* (Interviewee 3, American)

These different views of the tags lead to the general design question, "Who will see what in the IA space?" The simplest option is to make the side pane entirely public or entirely private. However, such a design might only satisfy one portion of users' needs. A second option is to give users the right to decide what access mode they want for each tag. However, this extra operational cost may add considerable burden to users who do not want to worry about access for each comment. A better compromise might be to make the IA window entirely public but give users the opportunity to "hide" any tags they wish. Yet another option is to have two side panes, one private and one public. The worry there is that users might be more distracted by a two-part IA display, or by navigating between them if they were layered using tabs.

6.2 Notifications
While sharing their thoughts about using a side chat to raise awareness of a discussion point, several interviewees asked how other users would be notified of new contents. Because the annotations are anchored by a piece of text, a natural design is to display annotations next to the text as the main chat proceeds. But will users notice a new annotation or a response to an annotation if it is not shown in the current window to which they are attending? As the chat continues, earlier comments scroll up out of sight; this means that a new annotation intended for public viewing might be missed by other users.

With this concern in mind, one participant proposed to include a dashboard at the top of the IA pane. When new content is added, the dashboard could display a hyperlink that other users can click on to go to the content, somewhat like the function of an anchor link in an html page. The dashboard would be updated whenever new annotations are posted. An alternative design would be to have a pop up window at the right bottom corner (i.e., in the IM window). When new content is added, it could pop up for a few seconds and then provide a hyperlink at the corner until the user clicks it. We think that both of these designs could have a positive effect on raising awareness. If new contents about the same discussion point occur often, it indicates a general interest of that discussion point; people may be attracted to see what others say in this hot topic. A history pane containing the recent annotations the user visited may also be useful for the user to quickly revisit the tags or side conversations that are emerging.

6.3 Annotation Ownership
In the side chatting scenarios described earlier, users communicate under an annotation tab. One issue that arose was how to distinguish among different annotation contributors, so that the participants can communicate unambiguously. One simple design is to color-code each annotation, so that they represent the color of the user. However, when many users are participating in a chat, there may be too few colors to be distinctive. Another design is to automatically add users' names or icons as a prefix to an annotation. However, because the IA

space may be small relative to the main chat window (implying that it should be used for concise expressions), the addition of user information may overfill the space. This may be an issue that is best left to a group, for example depending on how many participants it includes.

6.4 Operational Cost
Finally, two interviewees expressed concerns about the extra cognitive costs of the IA features. Reading and contributing to an online group chat is already demanding; they wondered about the effort required to also attend to and contribute to an IA pane. We also have had this concern from the beginning of this research program. While we have proposed a mechanism for annotation creation in our design scenario, we recognize that we may not have yet found a good solution. For example, we may replace the action of right clicking on a text line with a hot key, to see whether it reduces the interaction costs, and there may be other keyboard shortcuts that could simplify navigation among lines of text in the chat log as well as navigation to and from the IA window. These will be an important focus in our iterative design process as we prototype, evaluate and refine the IA concept.

7. REFLECTIONS ON THE STUDY METHODS
This ongoing project is an exploratory project stemming from the first author's doctoral research. We found the design method we have described here to be very useful for exploring the design space from the users' perspective very early on in the design process. Thus one goal of this paper is to share our experience of using the method with others in the HCI and CMC design community, so that projects with similar characteristics could benefit from our experience.

From the start, our over-arching goal has been to design a new technology that could assist cross-cultural group communication. A traditional design approach would be to carry out fieldwork to understand target users, develop the technology and then evaluate it to see what the users like or dislike [19]. At that point, the design may be revised and reevaluated. However, in our research project, time and labor are limited. We wanted to use a lightweight method that could quickly reveal some specific and useful implications about our design ideas. So we started with a lab task instead of fieldwork. The task in our study was carefully plotted, so that it could mimic situations that might happen in the real world. This allowed us to investigate users' problems and needs in-situ, even though the "in-situ" was a simulated communication situation. In fact, we observed many expected user behaviors, such as non-native speakers whose comments were ignored, parallel discussions in the chat, listing things to remember, and so on. These observations confirmed that the design scenario we had developed was realistic. We found that our participants were fully engaged in this process, as revealed both by the active discussions during the task, and the many creative reactions and reflections they provided in their interviews.

Because we only have one developer in the project, we cannot afford to spend significant time in iterative tool development. To accelerate the work of this one developer, we emphasized the development and evaluation of a conceptual design at the start of the project. After a recent experience with online group discussion, in combination with any relevant past experience, our participants were able to provide many inspiring but also feasible suggestions for how the conceptual design might be integrated into their online group discussion behaviors. We believe that this lightweight approach may be useful to other design research projects that are limited in time and labor. The combination of a realistic task followed by an interview about a design concept has provided a way to gather rich and useful information from participants.

Thinking more broadly, the approach could be used in many rather different projects. For example, suppose a designer envisions a bike-route application for a town. Residents who ride bikes could be asked to first finish a route-planning task using Google Maps; with that in mind the designer could seek feedback for an early idea about the route-mapping project. Because participants would have just practiced route-planning, their experiences of the problems and processes of this task are fresh, and they are motivated to think seriously about the novel design concept. Because they were recently "contextualized" by a concrete route-planning experience, they are tuned to think as bike-riders who need to plan routes.

The benefit of providing a conceptual design for evaluation (i.e. versus thinking more abstractly about design features) is that it creates a specific base from which to form reactions and new ideas. At the same time, it may limit the ideas possible because participants will focus on what has been presented rather than totally new concepts.

One limitation of design concept interviews is that problems that users foresee may arise from lack of experience with the task or the technology rather than the design itself. Therefore, it is important to choose participants who have the right kinds of technology and task experience (in our case, text chat, including groups and including cross-cultural groups). If we had recruited less experienced chatters or chatters without cross-cultural experience, the chats and subsequent interviews would likely have been much less rich. Similarly, in the bike-route example, if participants are not familiar with Google Maps or riding bikes, their experiences of the task and design ideas may be dominated by frustrations of learning these things, and the post-task interviews would be less valuable. We suggest screening participants to select those experienced with the task and the technology.

A more general limitation of the work reported here is the nature of the study and data analysis. We observed and interviewed five groups, each composed of two native and two non-native speakers; all were university students. Our focus throughout has been on understanding users' ideas; in this we have relied very much on the comments offered by individual participants rather than attempting to draw conclusions about general populations. This is appropriate for the phase of design research currently in focus – our current goal is to acquire as rich as possible an understanding of design opportunities and challenges for the IA concept, not to formally test hypotheses or to generalize our findings to other groups or communication tasks.

In the next design iteration, we plan to explore some of the more unexpected communication patterns we observed, such as the tendency for some native speakers to hold back in deference to non-native speakers. We will also revise our conceptual design in consideration of the design implications we have presented. Following this iterative process, we will prototype and evaluate an operational tool (i.e., once we no longer find new useful suggestions from users about the conceptual design). In summary, the point of our method is to closely integrate our ideas about IA design and possible use scenarios, so that representative users can participate in each iteration of the design process.

8. CONCLUSIONS

Online cross-cultural group chat has many communication problems. Prior work has shown that non-native speakers are frustrated by their lower language competencies and disruptions in turn-taking. Inspired by the literature and related work of threaded chat tools and collaborative annotation tools, we proposed a novel conceptual design, Instant Annotation. We conducted a qualitative study to understand the communication problems between native and non-native speakers in a group chat setting that used a text-based communication tool, and solicited feedback and ideas about the IA concept. A data analysis of the chat log and the interviews showed several communication problems in this setting. Some of them were predicted by our theoretical analysis, while others were unexpected. One interesting phenomenon we found was that being aware of the language differential, native speakers at times hold back their ideas in order to give non-native speakers more chance to talk.

Our analysis of users' suggestions led us to three classes of design scenarios for IA. The users thought they might use IA for tagging, side chatting, and several other more specific use cases. However, they differed in their intentions of using these features. Some of the differences seem to be due to culture or language proficiency differences; these point to interesting research directions for our future work. For example, we plan to implement an IA prototype and run the experiment again. We will log users' behavior using the IA pane during the chats, and compare their behavior to confirm our findings in this paper. We generated four design choices from users' feedbacks to revise our design. We also reflected on our experience of using a "naturalistic" warm-up task as a method for engaging and contextualizing users' reflections and ideas about a novel design concept. We offer this as a general method that can be used in a variety of exploratory design efforts.

9. REFERENCES

[1] Brush, A. J. B., Bargeron, D., Grudin, J., Borning, A. and Gupta, A. Supporting interaction outside of class: anchored discussions vs. discussion boards. In Proc. Proceedings of the Conference on Computer Support for Collaborative Learning: Foundations for a CSCL Community, International Society of the Learning Sciences.

[2] Clark, H. H. Using language. Cambridge University Press, 1996.

[3] Diehl, M. and Stroebe, W. Productivity loss in brainstorming groups: Toward the solution of a riddle. Journal of Personality and Social Psychology, 53, 3 (1987), 497-509.

[4] Freiermuth, M. R. Native speakers or non-native speakers: Who has the floor? Online and face-to-face interaction in culturally mixed small groups. Computer Assisted Language Learning, 14, 2 (2001), 169-199.

[5] Gaies, S. J. Modification of discourse between native and nonnative speaker peers. In Proc. TESOL '82.

[6] Gonzalez, D. Teaching and learning through chat: a taxonomy of educational chat for EFL/ESL. Teaching English with Technology, 3, 4 (2003), 57-69.

[7] Hara, N. and Kling, R. Students' frustrations with a Web-based distance education course. First Monday, 4, 12 (1999).

[8] Harrington, M. and Sawyer, M. L2 working memory capacity and L2 reading skill. Studies in Second Language Acquisition, 14(1992), 25-38.

[9] Herring, S. C. The rhetorical dynamics of gender harassment on-line. Information Society, 15(1999), 151-167.

[10] Hutchinson, H., Mackay, W., Westerlund, B., Bederson, B. B., Druin, A., Plaisant, C., Beaudouin-Lafon, M., Conversy, S., Evans, H., Hansen, H., Roussel, N., Eiderback, B., Lindquist, S. and Sundblad, Y. Technology probes: inspiring design for and with families. In Proc. CHI '03, ACM

[11] Kalnikait, V. and Whittaker, S. Social summarization: does social feedback improve access to speech data? In Proc. CSCW 2008, ACM, 9-12.

[12] Kelkar, S., John, A. and Seligmann, D. D. Some observations on the "live" collaborative tagging of audio conferences in the enterprise. In Proc. CHI '11, ACM, 995-998.

[13] Kulak, d. and Guiney, E. Use Cases: Requirements in Context. Addison-Wesley Professional, 2000.

[14] Li, N. and Rosson, M. B. At a Different Tempo: What Goes Wrong in Online Cross-Cultural Group Chat? In Proc GROUP '12, ACM.

[15] Lin, M., Lutters, W. G. and Kim, T. S. Understanding the micronote lifecycle: improving mobile support for informal note taking. In Proc. CHI '04, ACM.

[16] Marshall, C. C. and Brush, A. J. B. Exploring the relationship between personal and public annotations. In Proc. JCDL '04, ACM, 349-357.

[17] Mynard, J. Introducing EFL students to chat rooms. The Internet TESL Journal, 8, 2 (2002).

[18] Neeley, T., Hinds, P. J. and Cramton, C. Walking through jelly: Language proficiency, emotions, and disrupted collaboration in global work. SSRN eLibrary(2009).

[19] Rosson, M. B. and Carroll, J. M. Usability engineering: Scenario-based development of human-computer interaction. Morgan Kaufmann, 2001.

[20] Sacks, H., Schegloff, E. and Jefferson, G. A simplest systematics for the organization of turn-taking for conversation. Language, 50, 4 (1974), 696-735.

[21] Schegloff, E. Discourse as an interactional achievement: Some uses of 'uh huh' and other things that come between sentences. Georgetown University Press, 1982.

[22] Smith, M., Cadiz, J. J. and Burkhalter, B. Conversation trees and threaded chats. In Proc. CSCW '00, ACM.

[23] Strauss, A. L. and Corbin, J. M. Basics of Qualitative Research: Techniques and Procedures for Developing Grounded Theory. Sage Publications, 2008.

[24] Wang, H.-C., Fussell, S. F. and Setlock, L. D. Cultural difference and adaptation of communication styles in computer-mediated group brainstorming. In Proc. CHI '09, ACM.

[25] Werry, C. C. Linguistic and international features of internet relay chat. John Benjamins Pub Co, 1996.

[26] Woken, M. D. and Swales, J. Expertise and authority in native-nonnative conversations: The need for a variable account. Multilingual Matters, 1989.

The Rat City Rollergirls and the Potential of Social Networking Sites to Support Work

Toni Ferro

University of Washington
428 Sieg Hall
Seattle, WA, 98195
503-360-7226
tdferro@uw.edu

ABSTRACT

Increasingly, researchers and organizations are interested in the potential for social networking sites to support the day-to-day tasks of workers. This study examines the way the Rat City Rollergirls (RCRG), a roller derby team, communicates using social media to support the business of their organization. While the RCRG is a volunteer organization, their use of social media to support their day-to-day business demonstrates the potential of social networking sites to support organizational work in ways beyond marketing and customer communication and exposes design considerations for implementing social networking sites.

Categories and Subject Descriptors

H.5.3 [Information Systems]: Group and Organization Interfaces--- Computer-supported cooperative work

General Terms

Management, Design.

Keywords

Social media, collaboration, social networking site, SNS

1. INTRODUCTION

The significance of social networking sites (SNSs) in the workplace is a growing area of study. Research suggests that SNSs such as Facebook and Twitter have the potential to support some day-to-day workplace tasks by allowing employees to leverage information and resources from a growing number of sources both inside and outside of their companies. However, so far, there is little consensus on the value of SNSs for work and many companies restrict the use of such systems, arguing that they reduce employee productivity [7]. In addition, companies that have deployed enterprise-proprietary SNSs for workplace use have reported relatively low adoption and use rates [1, 4, 12].

This study examines how the roller derby team, the Rat City Rollergirls (RCRG), uses an online forum to run their day-to-day business. Though the RCRG is a volunteer, non-profit

organization, the organizational use of their forum illustrates how SNSs can provide business value for organizations beyond marketing and customer communication. Though an online forum is not typically considered a "social networking service," the RCRG manages their forum such that it functions in much the same way an SNS does. An examination of the use and management of the RCRG forum suggests design and implementation considerations for SNSs to support business.

Previous studies on SNS use in businesses include studies of systems that are deployed internally by a specific company as well as the business use of publicly available online sites such as Facebook and Twitter. Previous studies have also examined the use of social media by non-profit organizations.

This study is a departure from the previous literature on for-profit and non-profits using SNSs, because it does more than examine the value of an SNS within a specific company or study the marketing value of SNSs for non-profits. The intent of this study is to first illustrate the variety of uses of the RCRG forum, then to examine the design elements of the forum that have the potential to improve business implementations of SNSs. Few previous studies of SNSs in the workplace have included discussions of specific features or system configurations and their impact on system adoption.

Therefore this research examines the use of the RCRG forum in supporting the day-to-day business and social interaction of the RCRG and then identifies design implications by comparing the design of the RCRG forum with SNSs as previously defined in the literature. The following sections review the previous literature regarding SNSs and their uses in the workplace.

1.1 Social networking sites

Social networking sites (SNSs) have been defined by boyd and Ellison as allowing individuals to 1) create a profile, 2) create and share a list of other users they are connected to and 3) visit the profiles of their connections. Boyd and Ellison also argue that SNSs are centered on individuals instead of topics [3]. However, previous researchers have argued that the way a service is used is more important than its technical features when it comes to identifying its "genre" [5]. In addition, boyd and Ellison's feature-based definition has become problematic as more and more sites implement these features while having primary uses that are quite different than those of an SNS. For example, YouTube and Flickr have the three features defined by boyd and Ellison, however, are more commonly thought of as media sharing sites instead of SNSs.

Approaching the definition of SNSs through the use of these systems instead of through their technical features provides new ways to envision the design and implementation of SNSs to support day-to-day business operations. Specifically, in this study the RCRG forum does not meet the feature criteria set forth by boyd and Ellison, however, as will be discussed in subsequent sections, the RCRG has implemented their forum in such a way that it closely resembles an SNS in the way that it is used.

1.2 Business uses of social networking sites within organizations

Researchers have studied the use of publicly available SNSs, such as Facebook, Linked In, and Twitter for business. Many companies discourage the use of such sites and research has shown that as many as 50% of workplaces completely prohibit their use at work [7]. However, the value of publicly available SNSs to connect employees to a growing number of resources leads researchers to predict that SNSs will become as valuable to workers as email and instant messaging [13].

Archambault and Grudin conducted a longitudinal study within Microsoft that showed an increased use of Facebook, Linked In, and Twitter by participants over the four years of the study (2008-2011). However, the authors found no consensus among the participants about whether or not these systems were valuable for conducting day-to-day business [1].

Ferro and Zachry looked at the business use of publicly available online services (PAOSs), such as SNSs, along with other types of services such as media sharing tools like Flickr and social marking tools like Delicious. The study surveyed knowledge workers who are members of technology-oriented online groups such as Meetup or Google groups. Each year, participants were asked to report the PAOSs most valuable to them for work purposes. In 2008 more participants reported Wikipedia than any other site and Wikipedia was the only site reported as valuable by more than 20% of participants. Linked In was second, reported by 14% of participants. However, starting in 2009 SNSs were reported as valuable for work by more participants than any other PAOSs. In 2009, Twitter, Linked In, and Facebook were reported as valuable for work by more participants than any other sites and over 25% of participants reported each of them as valuable for work. Google Docs was fourth and was reported by over 15% of participants. In 2010, Twitter was again reported by more participants than any other site (more than 20% of participants), followed closely that year by Google Docs and Linked In [6].

Several companies have deployed enterprise-proprietary SNSs and have reported professional benefits. For example, Beehive is a Facebook-like site that was created and deployed within IBM. DiMicco et. al., found that participants used Beehive to "advance their career within the company," and "campaign for projects and ideas within the company." The authors conclude by suggesting that SNSs inside a company will become increasingly important due to the fact that the workforce of the future will expect to do business using SNSs. And, more importantly, companies will prefer to have ownership of the data in SNS systems as opposed to the data being owned by another company [4].

Richter and Reimer examined three different SNSs deployed within specific companies: IBM's Bluepages, Accenture Ltd.'s People Pages, and SAP's Harmony. The researchers found that participants used the SNSs inside their companies for "identifying experts," "building personal context," and "fostering existing relationships" [12].

Holtzblatt et. al., conducted a study at the MITRE Corporation on their SNS called Handshake, which is available to invited participants outside of MITRE as well as to the company's employees. Therefore, while the system is not publicly available,

it allows employees to invite collaborators from outside of the corporation (for example, suppliers and customers) to participate in the SNS. Frequent users reported that the system "supports collaboration, strengthens social connections, and facilitates knowledge management" [8].

Similarly, Zhang et. al., studied Yammer, an enterprise-proprietary system similar to Twitter, at Pitney Bowes and found that participants most value "staying aware of what others are working on," as well as "making new connections" [16]. However, only 30.1% of users answered Strongly Agree or Agree when asked if they felt Yammer was useful and 26% answered that they felt neutral about Yammer's usefulness [16].

1.3 Social uses of social networking sites within organizations

Several companies have reported social benefits related to interpersonal communication as a result of SNS implementations. For example, DiMicco et. al. found that participants used Beehive to "connect on a personal level," as well as the professional benefits reported [4]. And Steinfield et. al. found a correlation between high uses of Beehive and high amounts of social capital. The authors argue that SNSs can make it easier to socialize new employees as well as employees that are geographically distant from their teams [15].

Zhao and Rosson interviewed 11 Twitter users at a large IT company and framed their findings on previous research that has shown the value of informal communication at work. The benefits of informal communication include "relational benefits" such as "person perception, common ground, and connectedness" and "personal benefits" related to acquiring information that is "beneficial for one's personal work goals" [17]. The researchers found that participants reported relational and personal benefits from using Twitter. For example, participants reported having a better understanding of people they followed on Twitter, because they had a view into "all sorts of aspects of their personality." One participant also noted that Twitter acted as a "people-based RSS feed" and that he trusted the information received through his network on Twitter more than information from crowdsourced systems such as social bookmarking or other tagging systems [17].

1.4 Non-profit organizations and social media

Previous research on how non-profit, volunteer-based organizations use social media has focused on how these groups use or could potentially use technology for activities such as communicating with their constituents, fundraising, marketing, and community building [2, 14]. And while these are important capabilities for a non-profit organization, this study focuses instead on how the organization uses social media internally to manage their day-to-day business.

Other studies about non-profit groups and their use of social media have focused on groups where the members meet online, interact online to accomplish their goals, and have an end result that is an entirely online product, including for example, studies of the interactions of contributors to Wikipedia [9] and open-source software development [10]. This study focuses on the RCRG, whose members all live in the same metropolitan area (Seattle, WA), have face-to-face business meetings and practices, and conduct online collaborations that result in physical events.

2. METHODS

Twelve members of the RCRG were interviewed about their roles in the league and their use of the online forum. The interviews were semi-structured and took between 30 and 60 minutes, resulting in more than ten hours of taped interviews and over 200 pages of transcriptions. In addition, quantitative information about the forum (for example, number of users, number of posts, etc.) was gathered.

2.1 Participants

Ten of the twelve participants are women. All are between the ages of 23 and 45. The participants have a variety of educational backgrounds and work experiences and have been part of the RCRG for varying amounts of time. For example, three participants have been with the organization for less than a year, and two participants were involved in founding the RCRG seven years ago. Seven of the participants are active skaters, three are alumni skaters who continue to help with the organization, one is a referee, and one is a non-skating official.

3. RESEARCH SITE

The RCRG is a business organization as well as a social organization. This section provides a brief history of the organization as well as some basic information about the size of the organization and its structure. In addition, this section discusses the structure of the forum, the moderation of the forum, and the number of forum users and posts.

3.1 The RCRG

The term "roller derby" dates back to the 1920s. Team competition and physical contact defined roller derby by the 1930s. On-and-off revivals of roller derby took place through the 1970s and 1980s when roller derby teams were managed and sponsored by promoters with a focus on spectacle and profit.In 2003, women in Austin, Texas formed the first flat track derby league, the Texas Rollergirls. They coined the term, "by the skaters for the skaters," which has become the philosophy of the flat track derby movement. That year, several other teams were formed across the country and in 2004 a group of women in Seattle decided to start a league. In 2005 the RCRG was launched.

The Women's Flat Track Derby Association (WFTDA) formed in the fall of 2005. The WFTDA maintains the official flat track derby rulebook, sanctions tournaments, and certifies teams. Over 80 WFTDA flat-track leagues now exist in the United States.

The RCRG also has support staff such as referees, non-skating officials (who track penalties, track skater statistics, and keep score), as well as photographers, mascots, and other volunteers (for example, medics, members of the production crew, and a music DJ). The skaters number about 80-90. With support staff, the RCRG numbers roughly 120-130 people. As shown in Figure 1, the RCRG conducts bouts in Seattle's Key Arena where in June 2010 the RCRG set a modern derby record for attendance with over 6000 spectators [11].

The RCRG is a highly distributed organization. Though the members of the RCRG all live in the Seattle, WA area, at the time of this study, the organization had no permanent physical space that they rented or owned. Team members see each other frequently at practices; however, members of different teams may see each other only at monthly league meetings or at bouts.

3.2 The RCRG Forum

The RCRG forum is based on the free, open source bulletin board software phpBB (www.phpbb.com). The forum has 14 sections that contain 50 parent boards and 60 child boards. Most of these sections are not available to the public and instead are only available to skaters. The public is able to see only 2 sections that contain 13 parent boards and 9 child boards.

The RCRG forum is set to automatically delete posts after twelve months with the exception of some posts like policies and photos. At the time of the study, the forum had 4917 topics and 50,525 posts. Again, most of these posts are not available to the general public. Only 1315 (27%) of these topics and 8340 (16.5%) of the total posts are viewable by the public and about 5000 (60%) of the publicly available posts are related to photos of the events.

The RCRG forum has 1335 registered users. Most of these users are fans with only about 300 of the users being support staff, active skaters, alumni, or retired skaters. Many of the RCRG forum users actively post on the forum. At the time of this study, the posts on the forum were written by 478 different users. And 159 of those users wrote 100 or more posts. Figure 2 shows the distribution of the number of users and the number of times they have posted.

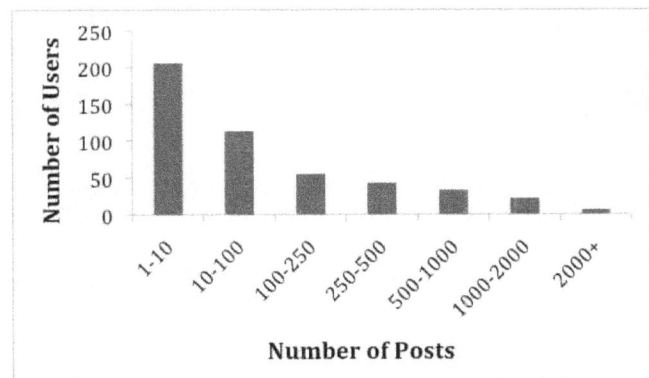

Figure 2. The number of RCRG members who have posted to the forum and the number of posts

The RCRG IT team that supports the forum consists of 1 IT manager, 2 forum administrators, and 14 forum moderators. The IT manager provides support to the administrators and moderators and troubleshoots major issues. The administrators approve the initial posts from public users and fix posts that have problems. The forum moderators are team members and officials who are also responsible for adding and removing members from the access control lists in their groups.

As previously noted, the RCRG forum does not meet the feature definition of an SNS developed by boyd and Ellison in [3], however, the uses of the RCRG forum are similar to the uses of SNSs. Creating a profile and connecting to others is required in boyd and Ellison's definition, and the RCRG forum users have profiles and are connected to other users. However, the connections to other users are pre-set through the forum administration by configuring the access controls to the system. For example, the RCRG is a league that consists of multiple teams. When a new member is drafted into a team in the RCRG she is put into a group with the other members of her team. If she joins a committee she may also be in a group with the other members of the committee. She may then post information to the forum that is restricted to the members of her team or to the members of her committee. In addition, members are able to create posts that are available to all of the members of the organization (including referees and staff) as well as posts that are available to the general public. Functionally, users can create posts that are visible only to select others in the same way they can when using Google+ "circles" or Facebook "lists." In the case of

Figure 1. An RCRG bout in Seattle's Key Arena (photo copyright: Jules Doyle)

the RCRG, however, the circles or lists are pre-defined for the users by the system administrators.

And as this study will show, participants reported interacting with the forum in the same way users interact with SNSs. For example, the participants interviewed as a part of this study used a streaming view of unread topics that showed them the latest post at the top of their screen and previous posts lower on the screen. This view resembles the streaming feeds available through Twitter, Facebook or Google+. In addition, many of the types of posts on the RCRG forum are typical of the types of posts seen on publicly available SNSs, such as birthday wishes and photos. The types of posts in the RCRG forum are discussed in later sections.

In summary, the RCRG forum does not strictly meet the feature definitions as described by boyd and Ellison – participants do not create and manage their own connections, and the forum is primarily topic-centered (though participants do create profiles). However, the use of the forum is very similar to the use of SNSs and the way the organization has leveraged the technology can be instructive to organizations designing and implementing SNSs.

The following sections describe the business of the RCRG to demonstrate that the business of the RCRG is much the same as the business of for-profit organizations. The ways in which the day-to-day business of the RCRG is conducted through the forum are then illustrated through specific examples. Then, because the previous literature on the uses of SNSs in business has shown the social importance of the systems, this study illustrates the social aspects of the RCRG and how these social aspects are enacted through the online forum. Finally, the study derives implications for the design and implementation of SNSs in other organizations based on the implementation and use of the RCRG forum.

4. RESULTS

This section demonstrates that the work of running the RCRG is similar to the work of running any other organization with distributed employees whether for profit or not for profit. In addition, the way the RCRG uses their forum to manage their day-to-day business is shown through specific examples of league members using the forum to aid in project management, organizational awareness, and policy development.

This section also illustrates the social aspects of the RCRG and how they are enacted through the forum. The examples provided show that the RCRG uses the forum to fulfill similar social functions as those you would expect to see in a workplace, for example, planning team building events or recognizing the work of other team members. The examples show that team members use the RCRG forum much the same way that individuals use publicly available SNSs such as Facebook.

These descriptions of the RCRG and the forum provide researchers and practitioners examples of the uses of SNSs within organizations. An examination of the RCRG forum and its configuration and deployment has implications on other business implementations of SNSs as well as implications for future research.

4.1 The business side of the RCRG

The large amount of work necessary to manage a sports league the size of the RCRG (for example, event coordination, sponsorship coordination, and volunteer coordination), requires the RCRG to be run like any other business. Some participants referred to the RCRG as "the company."

The responsibilities the participants have as members of the RCRG illustrate the business-like nature of the organization. Participants reported holding the following RCRG positions: Facilities Manager (schedules practice times with all of the teams and the league and rents their space to other groups), IT manager, HR Ombudswoman (mediates grievances), Member of the Board of Directors, Director of Business Operations (oversees HR, finances, taxes, and facilities), WFTDA representative, insurance lead, forum administrator, and committee chair (policy committee, volunteer committee, community care committee, and spirit committee). Figure 3 shows the organization chart of the RCRG.

Like most businesses, the league and its committees have regularly scheduled business meetings. Skaters are required to attend a league meeting once a month that lasts about four hours. Members of the board of directors meet twice a month, once in person and once on the phone. Some of the committees also have set meeting schedules (for example, the policy committee meets once a quarter, HR meets monthly, ombudswomen meet monthly, and bout production meets once a week). Other committees have work that is cyclical and so meet on an ad-hoc basis whenever meetings are needed. And teams hold strategy meetings before or after some practices. Some participants referred to their membership in the RCRG as a second full-time job and one stated, "It's another 40-hour-a-week non-paid volunteer happy job. I love it."

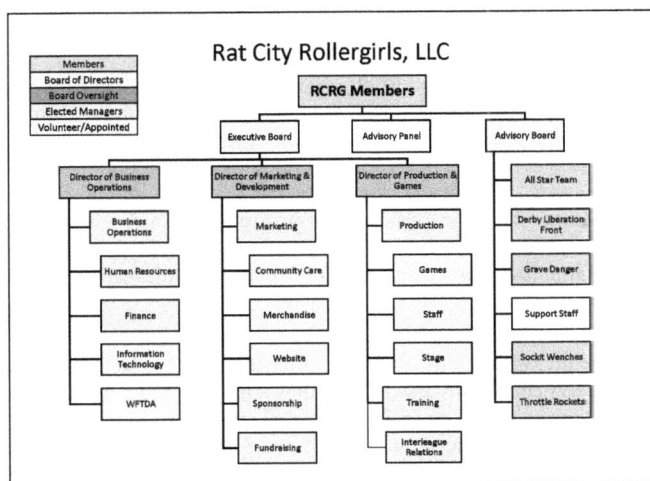

Figure 3. The Rat City Rollergirl's organizational structure

In addition, to being a demanding business to run, the RCRG is a highly distributed organization. At the time of this study, the RCRG had no permanent space for practices or meetings (since these interviews, they have rented a permanent space). Members of the same team see each other the most frequently because of their frequent practice schedule. As one participant noted, "Yeah, we all see each other several times a week, because we practice so often." However, the members on one team do not necessarily see the members of another team in person frequently. Members of different teams may only see each other at league meetings, bout practices and actual bouts. One participant referred to the members of the league as "ships that pass in the night."

4.2 Business uses of the forum

Many of the participants noted that a large part of the work of the RCRG is done on the forum. One participant stated that "Everything is done on the forum," and another participant explained it a little differently by saying that "Everything is on the forum or accessible through the forum." The main business uses of the forum are project management, awareness, policy revision, discussions, and voting.

4.2.1 Project management – "Who is responsible for this project and where are you at?"

The work of the league includes many projects and many of the project management tasks are handled through the forum. For example, participants reported doing or seeing the following types of tasks on the forum: identifying resources, assigning tasks to resources, approving budget changes, tracking hours worked, holding people accountable for their work, and scheduling.

Teams use the forums to identify who is available to participate in specific bouts (identifying resources). One participant described her most recent activity on the forum like this,

> "The team that I'm on were deciding whether to play in a game at the end of February. You had to post if you'd paid your registration, what positions you want to play and whether you're OK with paying an extra five bucks for a t-shirt to play in."

Also, the work members are responsible for at bouts is hashed out on the forum. One participant described it like this, "for bout production we all sign up for our jobs on the forum, for what we're going to do at the bouts, whether it's sell merch or, you know, pass out stuff at the entrance."

Members are required to contribute six non-skating participation hours to the organization per month. Members that need more participation hours post on the forum that they need more hours and are looking for opportunities to help with a bout or with another committee. One participant noted that "people will go to that section and post, 'hey, I need three hours to meet my participation for the month, what can I do for you, how can I help you out?'"

The number of hours worked and the number of practices attended is important to each member, because it indicates whether or not she is eligible to compete in bouts. Therefore, participation and attendance hours are tracked on the forum so the skaters can both keep tabs on their status in terms of participation hours and attendance and so they can verify that their hours are being tracked correctly. One participant is responsible for tracking the attendance for her team and describes it like this, "It's not an official league position... I track every person on my team... And I just post it on a thread on the forum." Another participant explained that it is important that the information is posted on the forum, because "you go on the forum and check to make sure that they saw, that they got your attendance, because attendance is important for eligibility to skate."

The RCRG budget is also available on the forum and in some cases committees will use the forum to approve budget changes. One participant noted that, "If something is out of budget, you need to post a poll to make sure it gets approved by the majority of the league."

One participant also noted that she uses the forum to hold people accountable for the work that they are responsible for. She stated that she sometimes posts requests for status updates like the following question,

> "We agreed that x, y, z needed to be done and agreed to this deadline and we are coming very close to this deadline and I haven't seen any updates. Who is responsible for this project and where are you at?"

The participant stated that posting this kind of question to the forum reminds the whole league that they are owed some information, which makes the person responsible feel some pressure to get their work done on time.

Many participants discussed the ways that meeting, practice, and bout scheduling take place on the forum. One participant stated that, "if we're going to have a meeting with Community Care, then you would post to the forum a comment like this one, 'A meeting for Community Care is going to be here,' and then post the dates." After the meetings, meeting minutes are also posted on the forum.

4.2.2 Awareness – "The forum is the main venue through which all the information regarding everything we do passes"

A common theme participants referred to when talking about the forum was the idea that the forum is necessary for "staying on top of things." Most participants reported using the forum multiple times a day and some reported having the forum open on their computer all day. Participants felt that if they did not look at the forum frequently they would be missing out.

One participant explained that she goes on the forum every day, because "there is too much stuff that goes on on the forum to not." Another participant explained that she feels she has to go on the forum daily because, "whole giant discussions can go past and if you aren't able to get on the forum for a couple of days you can just be completely oblivious to something really important that is going on." Another participant illustrated the importance of the forum by explaining that on the rare occasions the forum is not working, the league members get upset, "if the forum goes down then you get a million emails, 'The forum's down!' You know, people just freak out."

Participants also identified the forum as the key place for finding and disseminating information. Some participants reported using the forum primarily to get information. One participant stated, "I don't say a lot, but I use it to get a lot of information." Another participant stated, "everything will be on there; all the information about events, if practice schedules get changed," and also, "the forum is the main venue through which all the information regarding everything we do passes."

4.2.3 Policy and rules revisions – "Our consensus opinion ... will return back to the national level as our league vote."

One specific business use that many participants mentioned was using the forum for policy revisions. During the time the interviews were taking place a policy committee had recently been formed to update out-of-date policies as well as write new policies. One of the study participants was the new chair of the policy committee and described that she was currently responsible for updating a policy. To do so she had gathered input about the problems with the policy from the other members of the policy committee and other people who felt strongly about the policy, then she updated the policy and sent the changes via email to the team captains (in this case the captains would be responsible for enforcing the policy). After getting feedback from the captains and making changes to the proposed new policy she posted it to the forum. She then described the interaction going on once the proposed changes were posted, "There were whole discussions." She noted that league members went back and forth about some confusing wording and in the end, "I chimed in and I said, 'Yeah, OK, I'm gonna change it that way, that's a good idea'."

The officials also provide feedback to the WFTDA about proposed rules revisions and they use the forum to collect feedback from all of the RCRG officials. One participant described the process as starting when one of the officials posts the recommended changes to the official's section of the forum. Then each official goes through the changes line by line and votes yes or no or abstain and provides feedback about their vote directly on the forum. Then the officials discuss the votes online as a group and finally, "our consensus opinion on each question ends up being what our representative will return back to the national level as our league vote."

In summary, the RCRG operates like a distributed organization and uses their online forum extensively to coordinate their day-to-day work. The forum is used for project management tasks including identifying resources, tracking contributions, approving budget changes, holding people accountable for their commitments, and scheduling meetings. The forum is also used as a way to stay on top of current organizational issues. And finally, the forum is used to propose, discuss, and approve policy and rules changes. These uses of the RCRG forum to conduct day-to-day business demonstrate potential uses of SNSs within other organizations. The next sections illustrate the social aspects of the RCRG and the social uses of the forum.

4.3 The social side of the RCRG

Though the work of the RCRG is much the same as a for-profit business, it is important to note that, as a volunteer-run, non-profit, organization, the RCRG in many ways is also a social organization. The WFTDA website states that the "founding tenets of the sport" are "by the skaters for the skaters, with democratic representation, skater-owners, and a strong commitment to our local communities." The organization of the RCRG and their decision-making processes illustrate their commitment to these values.

In addition to being a successfully run business with strong democratic values, the RCRG is fundamentally a social group. When someone joins the RCRG they know they are joining an organization with a specific social makeup. Many of the league members join not because they are great skaters (many have not been on skates since they were kids) but because they want to be a part of this unique organization. As a result of members self-selecting into the roller derby subculture and seeing each other frequently at practice, the members are not just on a sports team and not just managing a non-profit business, they are participating in a social organization.

The importance of social interaction is openly acknowledged by the league and is integrated with the business of managing the league. For example, the Spirit Committee is dedicated to maintaining the morale of the league. The Spirit Committee organizes a vote for the "Rollergirl of the Month," and, as one participant told us, helps "put together parties and all the fun things that just keep people remembering why they like each other."

In many cases the participants talked about the social activities they did with friends they made in the RCRG. One participant explained, "every Wednesday after practice we always go to a bar close to our practice facility." The same participant also noted, "we have little get togethers at least several times a year, typically around someone's birthday." Also, this participant noted, "there's this thing called derby prom... the league has a prom for itself and most of us show up at that."

4.4 Social uses of the forum

While a lot of work gets done on the RCRG forum, the forum is not just for business. Participants reported using the RCRG forum socially as well. The main social uses of the forum participants reported were planning events, communicating to a social network, and posting classifieds.

4.4.1 Event planning - "What kind of beer do you want to have at the official's party this month?"

Organizing offline social events was one of the most frequently reported social uses of the RCRG forum. One participant noted that the individual teams,

> "...use team sections to organize any event that we're having as a team. Whether it's team night or practice or we're just, you know, getting together, or we're having a bar night – all of that planning is done on the forum."

She also stated that after the event members then post messages to each other, for example, "oh thank you so much for coming." Another participant noted that the use of the forum "can be around either team-sanctioned or non-sanctioned events" like a "craft night with booze." Another member noted that they sometimes use the polls feature of the forum to organize parties, for example, he noted "sometimes the vote will be, 'What kind of beer do you want to have at the official's party this month'."

Sometimes the social event that is organized is a surprise party for someone's birthday or bachelorette party. In the case of a surprise party, forum administrators have occasionally created unique sub-sections of the forum with their own access lists that include everyone except for the league member who is being surprised. Other event-related posts participants mentioned seeing on the forum were things like, "hey my husband's in a really great band and they have an event going on," or, "hey let's do something," or even, "hey let's think of something to do and do it together."

4.4.2 Social network communication - "oh look at this moustache I was wearing at a party the other night…"

The RCRG forum has designated sections that are specifically for non-RCRG business. A participant noted, "we have several sections that are, you know, designed for kind of shooting the shit and telling us random things." She explained that one of the sub-sections is titled, "Stuff you want to tell us." Participants reported that some of what goes in these sections is similar to the type of postings people post to Facebook. Primarily, the types of interactions participants reported included posting status updates to the other members of the league, wishing other members happy birthday, posting photos of bouts, and posting kudos to other members.

Some participants expressed the positive effect of members posting status updates on the forum. For example, one participant noted, "sometimes people will post that they are really bored at work and they want to know what other people are listening to via streaming media." This participant also noted that after something like that is posted, a lot of people quickly post responses and that posts like those "really bring out the friendly instincts in people."

Another participant felt the same way about these status updates and stated, "once someone starts getting crazy like 'oh look at this moustache I was wearing at a party the other night' then we all get in a better mood." The same participant noted, "it's fine by me if people get a little silly, because like I said this is a hard job, and I like it when people tell what they did on the weekend or post a YouTube clip that is just for no intents and purposes, it's just funny." This participant even directly noted that she does not use SNSs like Facebook or MySpace and instead uses the RCRG forum.

Many of the participants noted that birthdays are always posted on the forum. And one participant stated that after a birthday topic is posted, "there'll be 30 Happy Birthday posts right after that." Posting kudos is also common on the forum. One participant stated, "I have really been trying to make sure that I profusely thank people that kick ass, so I do a lot of kudos."

Many of the participants noted that a number of photographers support the league and post links to pictures (typically linked to Flickr or their own personal photography pages). One of the participants noted, "after the bout or competition the photos slowly come up from the different photographers, I spend a lot of time looking at those." The section of the forum that is dedicated to pictures is available to the public and is the most popular section of the public forum.

4.4.3 Classified ads, "Hey, I'm selling my couch."

Dedicated non-business sections are used for the types of posts that are posted on craigslist or other classified ads sites. One participant described such a section and its posts, "there is one, for instance, that's called "Non-RCRG." He explained that this section is used "if you're trying to sell your car or if your job is hiring or something like that."

Another participant noted that she had recently written a post in one of these sections that said, "my son's preschool is selling See's candy to raise money to buy chicken eggs and an incubator and an egg turner so if you want some See's candy let me know." The same participant read us some of the titles of the posts in the "Help wanted and services available" section. Examples of the titles are, "Need plumbing work," "Anyone have a noisy old typewriter," and "I'm going out of town and need someone to water my plants and watch my cat." Another participant gave an example post title as "Hey I'm selling my couch, I'd rather sell it to you guys than put it on craigslist."

In summary, while the forum is used extensively to conduct the business of the RCRG, it is also used socially. Participants use the forum to plan social events like team building events and bar nights as well as posting birthdays, kudos, and bout photos. Participants also reported using the forum to post status updates like those posted on SNSs like Facebook or MySpace. In addition, some sections of the forum are used like a private Craigslist available just to the members of the league.

These social uses of the forum demonstrate potential uses of SNSs implemented in distributed organizations. While many organizations may not have the same high levels of social participation that are seen here, many businesses do many of these things such as plan team buildings and celebrate birthdays. The next section discusses the implications of this study for SNS deployments in organizations and suggests considerations for SNS design for corporations.

5. DISCUSSION

Examining systems like the RCRG forum allows us to think about the implementations of SNSs in organizations in new ways. The RCRG is a non-profit, volunteer run, distributed organization that uses a forum to manage their day-to-day business as well as to keep connected socially. And while the RCRG forum does not strictly meet the definition of an SNS put forth by boyd and Ellison [3], the RCRG uses their forum in much the same was as SNSs such as Facebook are used. The RCRG members share photos, they wish each other happy birthday, they post information about their days, they get recommendations, and they sell their old furniture through their forum.

Because the RCRG forum is widely adopted and extensively used, the differences between the RCRG forum and typical enterprise-proprietary and publicly available SNSs foreground important elements of SNS design and implementation. Three areas for consideration that are raised by this study are social uses of SNSs in organizations, pre-set network connections, and individually-centered or topic-centered systems.

5.1 Social uses of SNSs in organizations

A feature of the RCRG forum that stands out as different from the business-oriented SNS implementations previously discussed is the overt social use of the forum. Some participants noted that social use of the forum was not necessarily encouraged; however, it was not discouraged and some participants reported enjoying seeing the personal posts of others.

Findings from previous studies have illustrated the social value of SNSs in the workplace. For example, at IBM researchers found that participants valued "connecting on a personal level" [4] and socializing new and distributed team members [15]. Other studies showed that SNSs have value for "building personal context" and "fostering existing relationships" [12]. At the MITRE Corporation frequent users of Handshake reported that it "strengthened social connections" [8]. And Zhao and Rosson specifically found informal communication benefits from Twitter use in the workplace [17].

The high levels of social use of the RCRG forum and the social value of SNSs found in previous studies raises questions about the value of an overt acceptance of social posts in SNSs for business use. Does including social topics as well as business topics in a system have an impact on whether or not employees will participate actively in the system? It may be that including social topics alongside work topics contributes to keeping people engaged with the RCRG forum. In the case of RCRG, the nature of the volunteer organization as a unique subculture indicates that many people join to make friends and so integrating social topics alongside the business ones makes sense where this may not be as true in for profit businesses. However, a level of tolerance of social topics may make SNSs effective tools for recruiting, retaining, and motivating employees.

Much of the social interaction of the members of the RCRG is similar to the social interactions that take place in any other type of business. Coworkers often plan happy hours, have team lunches, go on teambuilding outings, give kudos, celebrate birthdays, and share photos. It is plausible that if social postings such as these were encouraged (or not discouraged) on a business SNS, individuals would contribute and possibly become more interested in the other aspects of the system that relate directly to their work. In this way, having birthday wishes and budget approvals show up in an SNS feed one after the other may benefit the organization.

Access control, security, and privacy are certainly important issues when it comes to social postings. An individual may feel comfortable posting a goofy picture of herself for her team members to see, however she might not want the CEO to see the same photo. Members of the RCRG, do not have to worry about privacy settings, as the access control is centrally managed and limited to the members of the league. Therefore, members do not have to worry that their boss or the CEO of their company is going to see anything embarrassing that they post. Therefore, social postings on an enterprise-proprietary SNS would require special privacy and security considerations.

The success of the RCRG at balancing the business and social aspects of their organization through a single system also points to the importance of overcoming the belief that social sharing at work through an SNS is a productivity killer. The sentiment that time spent in an SNS is time wasted may make it hard for employees to feel comfortable posting socially oriented information (or any information) to a workplace SNS. And while the members of the RCRG often join the team for social reasons, the expression of the social aspects of their organization on the forum does not make team members less effective in their work for the organization. Instead, as one participant noted, she works very hard for the RCRG and social postings put her in a better mood.

Finally, the question of whether or not people will be willing to use multiple SNSs (one that is proprietary to their company and one that is publicly available such as Facebook) remains an open question. Numerous news articles frame discussions of Facebook, MySpace, Google+, and Twitter as a heated competition for unique users indicating that currently users are unlikely to be active users of all of these systems. One member of the RCRG noted that she used the RCRG forum instead of Facebook, however, many RCRG members also have accounts on other SNSs. In the future, it is not clear how willing people will be to maintain multiple SNS profiles and accounts in different settings.

Archambault and Grudin note that the rise of Linked In use they saw at Microsoft may indicate that employees are increasingly using multiple SNSs for different purposes [1]. However, in the same study Archambault and Grudin noted that some participants reported wanting to ask a question of a colleague using Facebook, but, they did not want to go through the work of creating Facebook groups with access controls so that they could discuss work issues. And participants considered creating multiple Facebook accounts (for example, one for work and one for personal use); however, only one participant reported actually trying it [1].

5.2 Pre-set network connections

Another feature of the RCRG forum that is different than that of SNSs is that system administrators manage the access control settings and therefore the network of each user. Members of the RCRG do not have to take the time to create and manage groups. Instead their network structure is built into the system and managed by administrators. Previous studies have addressed the issue of SNS users having such a broad range of people in their network that it becomes difficult to post anything that would be appropriate or interesting to everyone [1]. In the case of the RCRG forum, this issue is resolved by the administration of the system. Members are able to post to only their team or only their committee without having to do the work of group setup or maintenance.

Having pre-set groups or circles not only eliminates the need for individual members to manage their groups, but also eliminates the need for network building itself. A member's social network is effectively constructed in the network when the user is created and added to the various access control lists for their team and their committees. This aspect of the forum raises questions about business deployments of SNSs. For example, is it better for employees who are members of the same team at work to have to go through the effort of connecting with each other or is it better for the system to automatically acknowledge that relationship? And does the notion of having to connect online to someone who is on your team have an impact on the cohesiveness or effectiveness of the team? It seems reasonable, that for some team members (especially new ones) there may be a level of social awkwardness that would have to be overcome before feeling comfortable connecting to their coworkers through an SNS.

The size of the RCRG, roughly 120 people, makes it both possible to manage the access control of the forum at an administrative level and to create a network structure where everyone is connected to everyone else. In a company of 1000 employees, it is harder to imagine a system where everyone is connected, much less in a company as large as Microsoft or IBM. However, the notion of pre-set groups and connections could still have value in a large company made up of divisions, departments, groups, and teams.

5.3 Individually-centered or topic-centered systems

Part of boyd and Ellison's definition of SNSs included the notion that they are centered on individuals instead of centered on topics. However, the RCRG forum, which participants use as an SNS, has pre-set connections and pre-set groups, and therefore the RCRG forum users do not spend time managing their personal networks or viewing the personal networks of their connections. Instead, the primary activity on the forum is centered on the topics.

The topic-centered nature of the RCRG forum raises more important questions for business implementations of SNSs. For example, is a focus on topics or individuals better for business SNS systems? Are there team types or situations where a topic-centered system is more effective than an individual-centered system (or the other way around)? It may be the case that without the work of managing their networks, users spend more time reading and responding to the issues raised on the system. Or it may be that topic-centered systems counter some of the other benefits of SNSs such as "connecting on a personal level" [4] or "building personal context" [12].

6. CONCLUSION

Though the RCRG is a non-profit, volunteer organization, it functions very much like a medium-sized business with distributed teams. As this research shows, examination of technology use in non-profit organizations like the RCRG can foreground design questions for business implementations of SNSs and other social media services.

The RCRG members use their forum in much the same way that individuals use SNSs. And the RCRG relies heavily on the forum to conduct their everyday business through project management, awareness, and policy and rules revisions. In addition the RCRG uses the forum for social purposes such as event planning, social network communication, and classified ads.

Because the RCRG forum has been broadly adopted and is heavily used, the unique nature of the forum implementation can provide insight into the design and use of SNSs within businesses. Examination of the RCRG forum shows that allowing overt social uses of the system may engage employees more fully with the organization and with their work. In addition, it may be valuable to have team structures be pre-set in a business SNS, eliminating the need for individuals to seek each other out or set up and maintain their own groups. Finally, there may be situations where it is beneficial to create systems that are topic focused instead of individually focused.

7. ACKNOWLEDGMENTS

Many thanks to the members of the RCRG as well as Alena Benson, Malinda McRae, Sudha Bhat, and James Humphrey.

Additional thanks to Dr. Charlotte Lee, Dr. Mark Zachry, and the SIGDOC blind reviewers for their support and thoughtful feedback.

8. REFERENCES

[1] Archambault, A. and Grudin, J., "A longitudinal study of Facebook, Linked In, & Twitter use," *CHI*, pp. 2741-2750, 2012.

[2] Boeder, P., "Non-Profits on E: How Non-Profit Organisations are Using the Internet for Communication, Fundraising, and Community Building." *First Monday* 7, 7 (2002).

[3] boyd, d. m., and Ellison, N.B., "Social Network Sites: Definition, History, and Scholarship," *Journal of Computer-Mediated Communication*, vol. 13, no. 1, pp. 210-230, Oct. 2007.

[4] DiMicco, J. et al., "Motivations for Social Networking at Work," in *CSCW* 08, 2008, pp. 711-720.

[5] Divine, D., Ferro, T., and Zachry, M. "Work through the Web: A Typology of Web 2.0 Services." *SIGDOC*. 2011. 121-127.

[6] Ferro, T., and M. Zachry. "Networked knowledge workers on the web: An examination of trends 2008 - 2010." *Handbook of Research on Business Social Networking: Organizational, Managerial, and Technological Dimensions*. Ed. M. M. Cruz-cunha. Business Science Reference, 2011.

[7] Half, R., "Whistle-but don't tweet-while you work," Robert Half Technology, 2009. [Online].

[8] Holtzblatt, L.J., Drury, J., Weiss, D., Damianos, L., and Cuomo, D., "Evaluation of the Users and Benefits of a Social Business Platform," in *CHI*, 2012.

[9] Krieger, M., Stark, E., and Klemmer, S.R., "Coordinating Tasks on the Commons:Designing for Personal Goals, Expertise and Serendipity," in *CHI*, 2009, pp. 1485-1494.

[10] K. R. P. M. and S. K. G., "Empirical studies of global volunteer collaboration in the development of free and open source software," *ACM SIGSOFT Software Engineering Notes*, vol. 37, no. 2, p. 1, Apr. 2012.

[11] H. Reynolds, "Rat City Breaks Modern Attendance Record," *Derby News Network*, 2010. [Online].

[12] A. Richter and K. Riemer, "Corporate Social Networking Sites – Modes of Use and Appropriation through Co-Evolution," in *ACIS*, 2009, no. Schooley 2005, pp. 1-10.

[13] M. Skeels and J. Grudin, "When social networks cross boundaries: a case study of workplace use of facebook and linkedin," *GROUP*, pp. 95-103, 2009.

[14] T. Spencer. The Potential of the Internet for Non-Profit Organizations. *First Monday* 7, 8 (2002).

[15] C. Steinfield, J. M. DiMicco, N. B. Ellison, and C. Lampe, "Bowling Online: Social Networking and Social Capital within the Organization," in *C & T*, 2009, pp. 245-254.

[16] J. Zhang, Y. Qu, J. Cody, and Y. Wu, "A case study of micro-blogging in the enterprise: use, value, and related issues," *CHI*, pp. 123-132, 2010.

[17] D. Zhao and M. B. Rosson, "How and Why People Twitter: The Role that Micro-blogging Plays in Informal Communication at Work," in *GROUP* 04, 2004, pp. 243-25

Applying User Research, Usability Testing and Visual Design Techniques to a Printed Publication Targeted at Teenagers

Joe Welinske
Blink Interactive
1011 Western Avenue Suite 810, Seattle, Washington 98104
1-206-304-1687
jwelinske@yahoo.com

ABSTRACT
The ACT testing service had suspicions that their 16-page booklet, "Using Your ACT Results" was not well suited to today's high-school seniors. They enlisted the Seattle-based consultancy Blink Interactive to conduct user research with high school students in three cities. It was determined that (1) the students resisted the text-intensive design and that (2) there were nuggets of information that the high-school students would have found valuable, if they had found them.

The study prompted a redesign in which expository text was in large part replaced by infographics and a narrative focused around the experience of an individual student. This project recommends ways in which information will need to be communicated to future generations of young readers.

ACM Categories & Subject Descriptors
A.2 General Literature: REFERENCE

Keywords: Visual design, Infographics, Usability testing, Documentation design, User research

PROJECT SCOPE
Blink helped ACT in evaluating the expectations for and effectiveness of an important ACT customer-facing publication: "Using Your ACT Results" (UYAR). The information provided by that publication is extremely important to the examinees of the ACT Test. The document, in conjunction with the ACT score report help students understand what their scores mean and how to benefit from this knowledge.

The UYAR is presented to the students as a sixteen-page printed booklet and also as web-site text. The booklet is provided to the student along with their score report.

The first phase of the project consisted of a general review of the content and design of the existing publication. It also included a review of similar publication offerings from ACT competitors.

The second phase was a series of interviews with ACT stakeholders regarding the nature and objectives of the various publications and customer types. Information from the stakeholder interviews was used to inform the specific project approach for the user research interviews and the redesign of the targeted publications.

The third phase was a detailed study of customers to better understand their needs and expectations. We examined their workflow, interaction with the publication, working environment, relationships with other customers, and satisfaction with the publication.

The final phase was to review and analyze the information gathered from the participants and make recommendations for improving the design and usability of the publication.

STUDY OVERVIEW
During the period of March 18 through April 4, 2012, Blink conducted user research with the goal of gaining insight into how students used the "Using Your ACT Results" (UYAR) booklet.

Blink worked with a recruiting vendor to arrange interviews in Seattle, WA and Lincolnshire, IL. ACT arranged interviews in the Iowa City area. Interviews were also conducted remotely via a variety of communication methods. A total of 16 students participated in the study. Participant characteristics included: male and female; public, parochial, and private; sophomores, juniors, and seniors. Table 1 shows a sample of the collected data.

USER RESEARCH FINDINGS AND RECOMMENDATIONS

1. The students had little or no memory of even seeing the UYAR booklet.
All the students needed time during the interview to acquaint themselves with the information in the booklet.

- The focus on the student report when the scores arrived rendered the booklet "invisible."

- The small, dense text and newsprint stock were a deterrent to the students wanting to explore the booklet.

✓ **Recommendations.** The text, layout, and production of the booklet should be designed to have a more accessible, more visually interesting style.

2. The students have a wide-range of interests with respect to the UYAR content.
During the course of the interviews, students were asked to review a copy of the printed UYAR booklet and highlight the areas that interested them. Table 1 summarizes the interests of individual students with respect to the various sections of the booklet.

Table 1. Student Areas of Interest for the UYAR, based on data from Blink's User research.

Which sections students picked as most relevant (sorted by total (Tot.) selections)																	
UYAR sections	**Individual student selections (with initials)**																**Tot.**
	C A	S L	J M	A T	K Y	R B	A B	K G	M B	M W	A W	H O	T T	V V	T C	C O	
Should You Test Again		*		*		*	*	*	*				*	*			**8**
How Colleges Use Your Results					*	*	*	*		*		*				*	**7**
How We Compute Your Scores…	*		*	*	*				*		*						**6**
Your College Readiness				*		*	*	*	*			*					**6**
Your ACT Scores…	*			*											*	*	**4**
Your College Reports				*					*			*					**3**
Requesting a Copy of Your Test Questions					*							*					**2**
Which Colleges Meet Your Needs											*	*					**2**
Paying for College											*		*				**2**
Planning Your Education and Career		*										*					**2**
See How Your Scores Compare											*						**1**
Understanding and Using Your ACT Scores				*													**1**
Career Area List										*							**1**
Comments On Your Essay																	**0**
A Note About Test Scores																	**0**
Ordering Additional Score Reports																	**0**
Scholarships																	**0**

Each column represents a student. Each row represents a section of the brochure. An asterisk indicates that the student selected that section of the brochure as of **high interest** to them. The total number of students selecting a certain section is listed in the far right column. Student initials are listed in the first row of data.

- There is a wide range of interest levels for the UYAR topics. A few of the topics were of high interest to most of the students. Others were of no interest.

- For the topics of interest to individual students, they generally wished they had known that the information was available close at hand.

✓ **Recommendations.**
-The best approach would be to integrate the highest interest topics directly into the student report. Explicit references could be made from the student report to the topics remaining in the booklet.
-Alternatively, the booklet might be discontinued and replaced with a web-based version.
-If the booklet is kept intact – not replaced or merged – it should be reorganized to have the topics of highest perceived value up front. A redesign of the layout could improve the usability of the document.

IMPLEMENTATION OF DESIGN

Blink implemented the recommendations with adjustments to the text, images, and overall page design. Sample pages from the original publication (See Figure 1) and the new design (See Figure 2) are available as PDFs here:

http://www.blinkux.com/sigdoc/

The elements of high interest to the students have been given a more prominent position toward the front of the publication. Items of lesser interest have been relegated toward the back or eliminated.

A significant amount of text has been replaced with several infographics designed to tell the story visually. It is possible to understand the key elements of the score report just by reviewing the graphics. The infographics can also be converted to animated images for the web site version.

Much of the text was revised to tell a similar story with more focus and fewer words. The page count was reduced in half without affecting the objectives of the publication. Savings in printing and mailing costs are being partially diverted to a higher-quality, more attractive paper stock.

The page design uses a more contemporary design through the selection of typeface, line-spacing, and gradients. The landscape orientation provides improved reading with a two-page spread for the content of companion pages 2/3, 4/5, and 6/7.

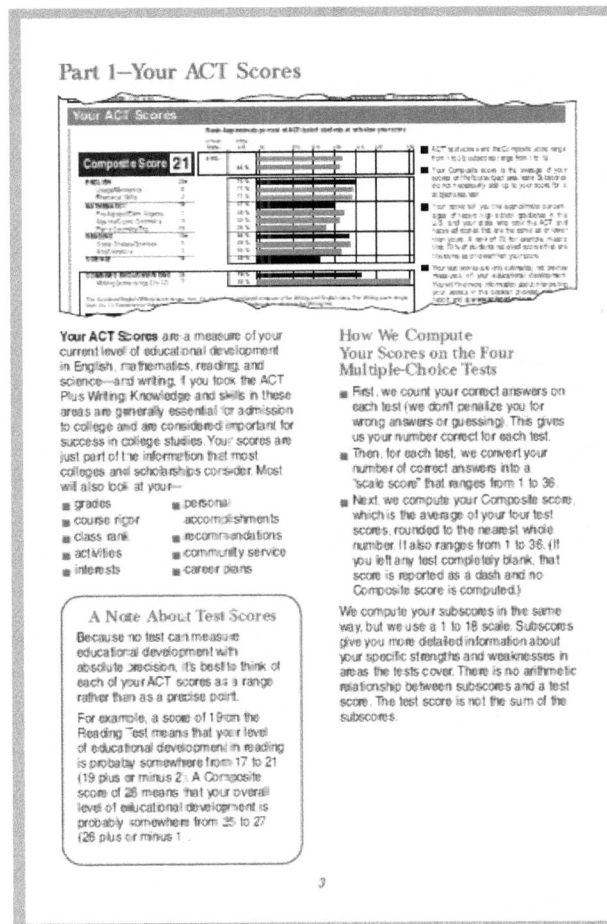

Figure 1. Sample page from original ACT publication.

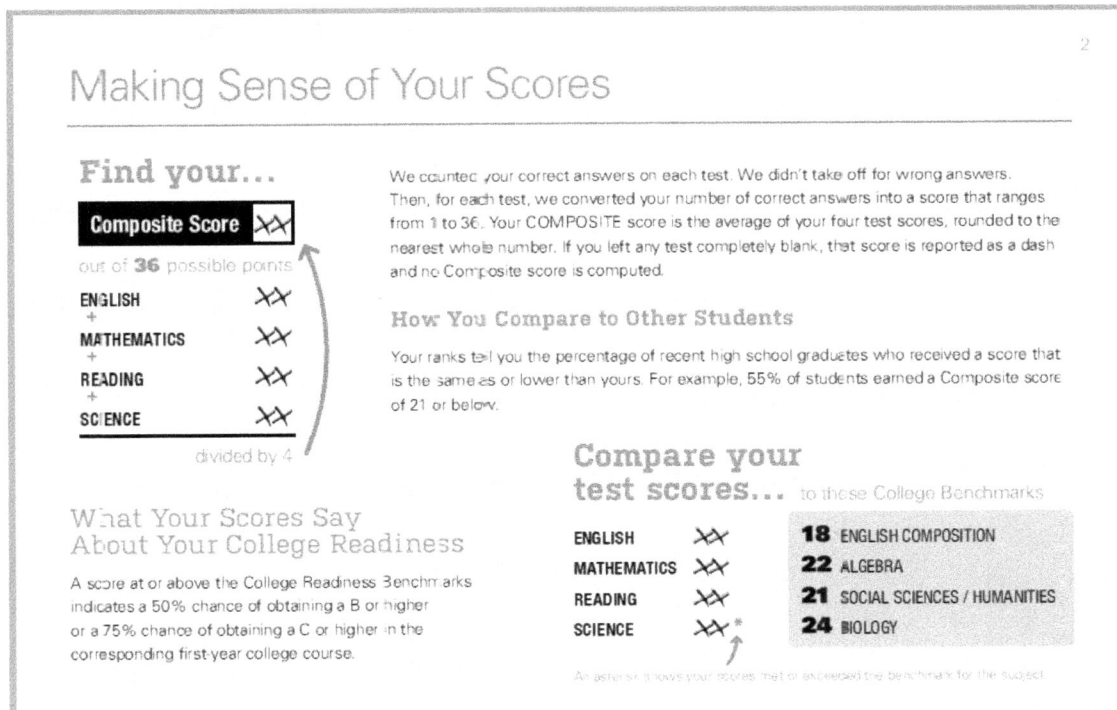

Figure 2. Sample page from Blink's recommended design.

Reading to Decide

Michael J. Albers

East Carolina University

Department of English

Greenville, NC 27858

252-328-6374

malbers@acm.org

ABSTRACT

Many communication situations have shifted to complex situations where people read information and make decisions (they *read to decide*). With reading to decide, information needs revolve around information seeking and decision making After finding information, people need to interpret and apply it. Writing documents focused on reading to decide means shifting from creating texts about how to perform tasks to creating texts with an understanding people's information needs and how they interact with information.

Categories and Subject Descriptors

H.0 Information Systems: General

General Terms

Documentation, Design, Human Factors, Theory

Keywords

Reading to decide, decision making, contextual awareness, complex information, information relationships

1. INTRODUCTION

"Traditional minimalist and task documentation works well for teaching the basic use of the tools, but at some point, many users need more information to help them make complex decisions about using the *tool*" [my italics] [16, p. 19] to accomplish a task or achieve a goal. Historically, a technical writer's focus was on how to use a tool. Writing instructional material about how to use a tool or other variations of step-by-step processes was the norm in 1988 when Redish [38] wrote "Reading to Learn to Do" and that tool-focus continued past 1997 when Esler wrote the sentence which opened this article. Since then, many technical communicators have shifted from step-by-step instructions to writing content (typically web-based) aimed at communicating concepts and ideas to be used for decisions. The rise of the huge amount of information available on the World Wide Web and the increasing development of complex reports within corporations, have moved many technical communicators away from writing instructions and toward informational content. Information which a reader uses to develop an understanding of a situation and to make decisions about that situation and not as a source for how to perform a sequence of steps [4, 31].

From the reader's viewpoint, one fundamental purpose of accessing an informational system (used very loosely here to include any applicable collection of documents, including web pages, reports, manuals. etc.) is to collect sufficient information to make a decision (which can run from "now I know enough about this topic" to "ok, our plan is…"). Rather than reading to learn, reading to do or reading to learn to do, they are *reading to decide*. That is to say, readers need to obtain information that allows them to develop a clear understanding of what is currently happening, what information relationships exist, and to use that to predict what may happen in the future. They then use this information to make decisions; decisions which influence the future development of the situation.

From the design team's viewpoint when creating informational content, a reader's efficient and effective decision making ability is driven by the design and content.

The previous paragraph should not be construed as saying that all content is now reading to decide. That is not close to reality. Technical communicators are still creating a wide range documents that meet readers needs which do not focus on decision making. There is still a need for instructions, informational material, learning material, etc. and this still forms the bulk of many writers' work. But there is a growing number of writers who focus on content creation focused on the reader's need for decision making material; this paper only considers that section.

This paper first takes a deeper look at what is meant by reading to decide and provides some examples. It then gives a brief overview of two decision making models and considers how design teams can apply them to reading to decide information. It then presents a methodology, contextual awareness, which can assist a design team in formulating how to effectively present reading to decide information. Finally, it concludes with two examples.

2. READING TO DECIDE INFORMATION

A design team's development of reading to decide information forms a continuum. It can span from a formal business report (Do we expand into area X? or The cause of the accident was Y and do Z to prevent a reoccurrence) to a web-based mix of static information and highly dynamic values (a store manager making inventory placement choices) to content describing complex situations (which healthcare treatment option is best for me). In all these situations, readers need information which they must mentally interpret and integrate to arrive at a decision point. Design teams must ensure readers are aware of the salient information and gain a coherent mental picture of the situation to support making decisions. Doing so is essential because of people's tendency to only look at local issues when making a decision, but any decision has global implications for the entire situation [14]. A decision that makes things easier today, but complicates matters for the rest of the week gives a short-term gain that becomes a long-term loss. High quality reading to decide information will help avoid a short-term focus by making people aware of longer-term and bigger picture effects.

Some examples of complex situations in which people are concerned with reading to decide include:

- Patient healthcare decisions. Research on healthcare information provided to patients consistently finds many information sources provide good information, but fail to explain it in context (often even in a generic context) and fail to relate it to understanding treatment options and associated quality of life issues. See Michie, Dormandy, and Marteau [28] for research on medical procedure decisions.

- Business analysis and problem-solving, such as store managers evaluating inventory against future needs [31]. The failure of many business reports can be traced to providing an abundance of data with the expectation that readers would somehow be able to reorganize and understand all of the information and apply it to their specific situation [40].

- Project managers evaluating information. Corporate and government project managers evaluate information and allocate resources among many projects [31]. These decisions involve a trade-off between production time and development needs. Interrelationships between projects can result in decisions made for one project rippling outward to negatively affect others.

- Educational problem-solving. Case studies or extended problems are typical in upper-division physical sciences, engineering, and business courses. With case studies, the issue could be reframed as "learning to read to decide," but the student is reading a collection of material and making decisions. The how to read and analyze the case material exists outside of the case itself. The pedagogical reasons exist on top of the actual reading/decision process.

A common factor across all of these situations is they lack highly structured information that can be presented with clearly defined end points; none of the situations have clear start and stop points or even a clear point of completion at which either a design team or a reader can declare "*all* of the information is here" (or even "all of the important information is here to make a good decision"). Instead, the necessary information revolves around a shifting mix of information seeking, problem-solving, and decision making. The design problem expands to require active involvement of all areas of the design team to fulfill the user experience goals. Supporting Information seeking requires solid information architecture, while supporting decision making require more than just the basic content, but the content placed within the business context and business rules.

In these complex reading to decide situations, design teams must give primary consideration to the interrelations of information and the environment within a situation's context [7]. In a complex or ill-structured problem-solving situation, people are better viewed, not as someone with clear goals moving from a defined start point to a defined end point (an often unstated assumption of task analysis), but as someone with fluid, ill-formed goals constantly dealing with ambiguous information and multidimensional processing strategies [4, 7, 29, 31, 33]. In reading to decide situations, a person's goal shifts from efficiently completing a task to reading and analyzing information to understand the situation and to act on it [46].

For example, consider a website helping people plan a vacation. Whether or not to rent a car can have a major effect on how much can be done during the vacation. Factors of price, parking issues,

attraction accessibility, and car rental factors all come into play. But these are related to what the person wants to do during the vacation. If the hotel provides a shuttle to/from major attractions, then a car might be an unnecessary expense. However, a person who eats at the hotel versus a person likes to eat at small local diners have different needs. Even people who intend to take the shuttle to major attractions may need a car for other purposes. The decision to rent a car is not a simple yes/no, but one that involves multiple, interrelated factors closely tied with other vacation choices.

Understanding a situation requires mentally integrating many pieces of information with respect to the user goals and the current context. It requires understanding that the information exists, how it is related to the situational context, and the relationships between the information elements [7]. The design team's task is to minimize the mental effort required for readers to gain that understanding. On the other hand, the design team cannot make the decision for the reader; reading to decide should not be considered some sort of wizard that asks questions and pops out a solution. Instead, it provides the information that people need and supports them in evaluating it to arrive at an appropriate decision.

3. DECISION MAKING

Most decision making situations which design teams must deal with are a mix of conceptual and informational content which a person needs to understand. Information needs within complex situations applicable to reading to decide documents never exist in isolation. Instead, they are embedded in the larger tasks and goals that the decision maker is trying to accomplish. For example, Dicks [15] looked at how people interact with a genomics research software system designed to help analyze genome sequencing. He found they needed more than button pushing information, but instead they needed to know how to integrate information from different modules within the system.

Decision making occurs as a result of comparing what is perceived in the environment and what is known by the decision maker [27]. Even in what is typically perceived as a simple information look up, the reality can be complex. In a study about using a handbook to format a citation for a research paper, Howard and Greer [19] found students made an extensive number of decisions as they interacted with the handbook to create a citation. Poor design frequently caused the students to create incorrect citations which they believed were correct. Orasanu and Connolly [34] discuss how most of the research on decision making has focused on two different conditions.

- Control situations, where people are dealing with a physical system such as a power plant. The studies examine how people maintain situation awareness and make decisions when the system moves away from a nominal state.

- Lab-based studies that typically dealt with A/B choices. People have a choice to do A for a reward X or choice B for a reward of Y. Unfortunately, this studies rarely move beyond making the decision and having to deal with any ramifications. As such, they lack the complexity of real-world situations.

Although research often looks at decision making in isolation, in reality decision making occurs as part of larger tasks and is only a single part of achieving a larger goal of interacting with a situation. A study may isolate the situation by presenting a person with three choices and letting them select one. But then the study stops and does not explore the affects the decision has on the evolution of the situation or how people interact with the information to track the results of the decision. Orasanu and Connolly [34] place decisions within a cycle which "consist[s] of defining what the problem is, understanding what a reasonable solution would look like, taking action to reach that goal, and evaluating the effects of that action" (p. 6).

Dekker [14] considers how all decisions are made based on local conditions, but that they have global ramifications. Managers make decisions which are optimized for their division, but may have a negative impact on other divisions or the company as a whole. People often make a choice to go with the lowest cost option (short term gain), even when they admit that it means replacing the item in a few years, rather than a higher cost option that will last longer. Dekker explains how the information supporting decisions must consider the global situation, but that the definition of global is highly flexible. This flexibleness appears in decisions such as buying a product where the person tries to look past cost and consider the environmental impact, distance of shipping, work conditions of overseas labor, etc. Clearly, what is meant by "global" can grow exponentially and must be defined for each situation.

3.1 Review of Two Decision Making Models

This paper briefly reviews two major decision making models. The classical model is often the only one taught or that people have heard mentioned, but it fails to reflect how people operate in real decision making situations [43]. Instead, the recognition primed model is the one commonly accepted as how people actually go about making decisions.

3.1.1 Classical decision-making model

The *classical decision-making model* attempts to quantitatively arrive at the optimal solution to a problem. Often, this is the only decision making model taught or discussed in textbooks. In theory, it is very simple. All of the possible choices/solutions are determined, the factors or criteria which influence the solutions are determined, and weighting values are assigned to each of the criteria. In this model, people are expected to evaluate all the various alternative solutions with respect to the factors that influence the solutions. The result is a matrix with factors across the top and possible solutions down the side. By assigning weighting functions to each factor, the optimal solution can be found by simply summing over the factors; the solution with the highest value is the optimal solution. Figure 1 shows a hypothetical example for evaluating PCs.

Classical decision making assumes people define a complete set of relevant criteria and evaluate all possible valid solutions against the criteria, and then make the optimal choice. While looking nice from a theoretical viewpoint, research has shown that people simply don't evaluate situations in this manner [25]. Some obvious problems with the classical model [23, 24]:

- Determining all the alternative solutions in advance
- Determining the factors which influence them
- Setting the weighting factors

	Speed (.2)	Memory (.3)	Drive (.1)	Cost (.4)	Total
PC 1	10	7	7	8	8.0
PC 2	10	6	6	6	6.8
PC 3	12	6	6	7	7.6
PC 4	8	9	8	8	8.3
PC 5	11	6	7	9	8.3

Figure 1. Example of classical decision matrix. This matrix shows the evaluation of 5 PCs based on four criteria. The numbers under the criteria name are the weights assigned to each. By multiplying each value by the weight and adding the resulting scores, the best choice can be determined. In this example, there is a tie between PC 4 and PC 5.

There is no way to ensure that any of these three factors have been fully and properly identified. In addition, most real-world situations are not analytic in nature, thus not lending themselves to classical decision analysis. In addition, situational complexity results in more data than can possibly be handled or broken down into effective criteria. The crux of the problem is that the classical decision making model assumes people start with a planning segment where they carefully plan out their course of action. When decision making situations are viewed in this way, the problems of the classical model become apparent; there is rarely adequate time or no method to methodically analyze the information efficiently.

3.1.2 Recognition-primed model

Research into how people actually make decisions reveals a different picture from the classical model. Decision-making is rarely the logical process design teams would like it to be [43]. Hollnagel [18] and Klein [24, 25] have been highly critical of the classical model. Mentally constructing the situation model requires integrating information from multiple sources, different modalities, and different times. In additions, there can be ambiguous or conflicting information. Klein [24] has advanced a *recognition-primed model* which more closely describes real-world decision making. The recognition primed model fits the real-world process of people quickly looking at a situation and almost immediately knowing what to do based on past experience. Based on how they view the situation, they rely on intuitive thinking, which rapidly leads to an answer [37, 25].

The recognition primed model assumes that people perform assessments of situations based on experience and that they attempt to make satisfactory, rather than optimal, decisions. For example, when people search for information, they suffice rather than attempt to find all or the best information [34, 42]. People often settle for less than optimal performance; instead of maximizing output, they economize on cognitive resource allocation and attempt to produce a satisfactory output with minimal effort.

3.2 Decision making in reading to decide situations

Most complex decision-making situations, the kind relevant to reading to decide, revolve around people obtaining an understanding of the situation and doing something with that understanding. Design teams need to move away from a "rational and logical view of decision-making and focus instead on such things as problem structuring/framing, creativity and idea processing, post-decision, and feedback analysis" [11, 35, p. 450]. In fact, additional research into how people make decisions has found several factors which must be considered when developing reading to decide content.

- People use their prior knowledge to fill in any unexplained concepts or unclear causal relationships. The accuracy of filling in that information depends on the person's knowledge. People often do not realize they lack all of the information they need and are far less likely to try to find information when it requires effort to search for it [26].

- People process information in ways that fits the presentation without restructuring it [12] and adjust and create the strategies they use for making decisions opportunistically, based on information they interact with [36].

- Salience of information must reflect its importance. A common source of error is when the information has been correctly perceived, but its relative importance has been misinterpreted [22], often because the information did not receive a proper salience that matched the person's current goals [5]. Dumping information with the assumption the reader will sort it out violates information salience considerations.

- People want to use all of the available information and mentally process the most salient information as the most important. When the most salient information is not the most important/relevant, then poor decisions can result, although people believe they made a good choice.

- People evaluate information based on the order in which they receive it. The first option people evaluate becomes the anchor against which future options are evaluated [25]. A presentation order relevant to the situation coupled with information salience drives the decision making process.

- Under time pressure (real or perceived), people jump to a conclusion before seeing all of the information, much less taking the time to interpret it [47].

- People try to distinguish relevant from irrelevant information and to group information elements together. Although this sounds obvious, relevance and proper grouping are situation-dependent and not a function of the information itself. Irrelevant information strongly affects decisions even when people consciously admit the information is irrelevant. Chinander and Schweitzer [13] explain this finding as arising from the ease of manipulating the information, which creates an input bias.

- People engage in what is called an "effort-accuracy tradeoff framework"[36]. They balance the effort/cost of a particular course of action against the benefits of taking that action. Interestingly, people focus more on reducing the cognitive effort than on maximizing decision quality. Gregor and Benbasat [17] found the "effort-accuracy tradeoff" applies to how people use explanatory text. People would ignore explanatory information unless they felt it was worth the effort to read and interpret it.

- Framing (presenting the information from different viewpoints) affects the factors people consider when analyzing a situation and making decisions. How the information gets framed has a strong effect on the decision. Framing takes one or more aspects of a situation and increases the relative salience of those common and distinctive features, even when they don't necessarily deserve that increase [44].

- Preference reversals can occur in which, depending on the presentation, people consistently pick option A or B and believe they made the best choice [21, 45].

A formal business report may attempt to follow the classical model and develop a matrix of the major factors, but most decision making does not occur in such a formal way. People making vacation decisions or healthcare decisions do not attempt to create a matrix. They mentally evaluate choices and jump to conclusions. Reading to decision information must be developed with the acknowledgement that decisions are made following the recognition primed model.

4. CONTEXTUAL AWARENESS AND READING TO DECIDE

The recognition-primed model discussed in the previous section was developed based on studies of people which required rapid decisions, such a fire commanders or pilots. This section extends its concepts to reading to decide information and provides a basis on which to evaluate audience information needs and content analysis.

Anytime people work with information to make decisions they attempt to build a story and make decisions that make sense with respect to that story. Or, to rephrase the sentence, document content must help readers mentally develop a coherent story that presents an integrated and connected flow of information about their current situation.

Thus, helping a person build that clear coherent story should be a major goal of design teams when developing information for reading to decide. Creating a coherent story requires information presentation that enables clear comprehension of the situation. In addition, more than the information itself, it is the relationships within the information that drive how well a person understands it and builds a coherent story [7].

Understanding a situation and building a coherent story requires mentally integrating many pieces of information with respect to the reader's goals and the current context. The design problem of not fully understanding a situation was difficult when the task was writing procedures, which had defined start and end points, and where the text was either right or wrong. The design problem is magnified with reading to decide information. As Mirel says [30, p. 233], "complex tasks and problem solving are different in kind not just degree from well structured tasks." The information needs found in these situations differ from the information needs of well-structured tasks:

- "Information overload is endemic. People must sift through more information than they can deal with. They must figure out how to allocate attention efficiently among an overabundance of information and information sources.

- Data analysis and recursive decision-making are cognitively very burdensome; people have little cognitive workload available for dealing with unusable interfaces [or poor information presentation] regardless of format of presentation" [39, p. 103].

Rather than a lack of information, the failure to anticipate people's needs forms the basis of most information problems and poor decision making; an issue design teams must explicitly address.

Developing Contextual Awareness

Information about the situation

→

Person develops contextual awareness

Prior knowledge and mental models →

→ Makes decisions

Stages of Contextual Awareness

Knows nothing about the situation

↓

Knows the individual data points

↓

Understands how the information fits within the *current* situation

↓

Can make informed predictions about the *future evolution* of the situation

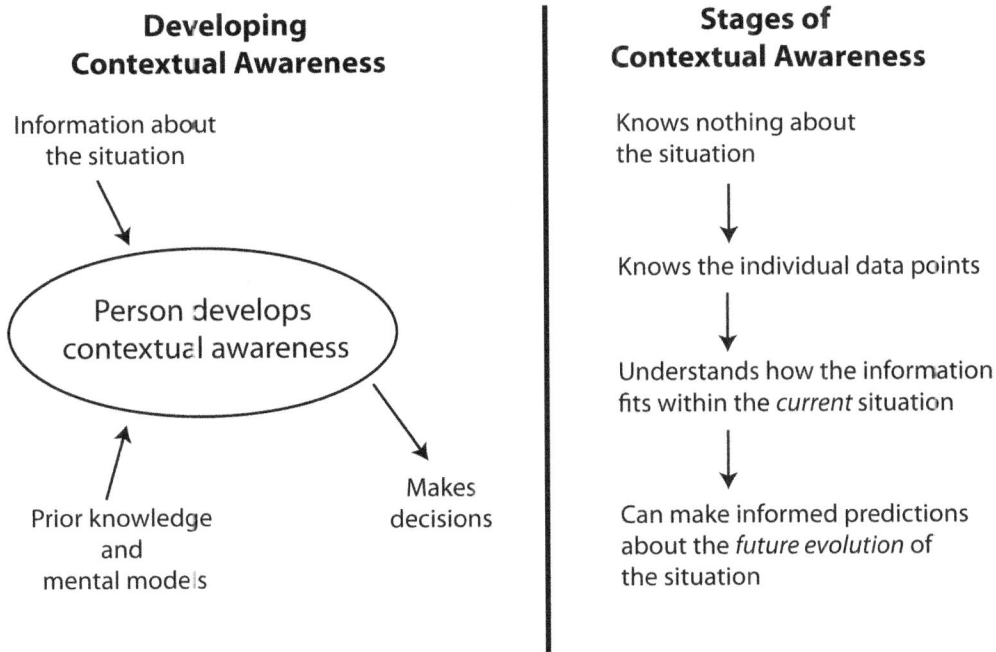

Figure 2. Developing contextual awareness. A person's understanding moves from knowing specific facts to being able to predict future developments. The design and quality of the information provided to them directly affects how easily they can develop this understanding.

Overall information content (whether printed documentation or web-based systems) is often high, but poor organization and design destroys the content's ability to communicate that information [2]. Ackoff [1] suggests that managers typically suffer from a shortage of decision-relevant information and a simultaneous overabundance of irrelevant information

Design teams must confront the issue that, as people evaluate complex information to gain knowledge, they do not follow a clean linear path as found in a typical procedural text. In reading to decide situations, rather than looking up single elements, a person needs to find and integrate several pieces of information. A business analyst trying to figure out why regional sales are dropping will rarely find the answer in a single factor. Instead, they need to figure out how multiple factors, which may be rather insignificant alone, are working together to cause the drop in sales. Morrison, Pirolli, and Card [32] found only 25% of the people they studied searched for something specific; looking for a clearly defined X. Rather than needing single pieces of information, they found 71% searched for multiple pieces of information. Plus, more than just having multiple pieces of information, they must understand the relationships between those pieces of information. In a study where the task was to compare features of cars so they could make a purchase recommendation to their boss for new company cars, most people gave up on using a car corporation web site and simply said they would go talk to a dealer. While the site provided abundant information on individual models or to easily answer some of the boss's specific questions [3]. The problem found in the study was not difficulty in finding single pieces of information, but integrating them into a usable form.

When creating texts that will be used for reading to decide, design teams need to consider how people interact with and manipulate the information. It is clearly not enough to simply provide the information; it must be organized and presented in a way that lets readers fit that information into their background knowledge and build up a coherent understanding of the entire situation. It must support high quality human-information interaction. The readers need to develop *contextual awareness* (figure 2) [6, 9, 10].

This section takes the ideas of contextual awareness as developed in the early references and builds on how to apply them to reading to decision situations. The informational needs of reading to decision situations are the ones where contextual awareness is most relevant, but also the ones where many design teams have difficulty focusing on meeting those needs.

Building contextual awareness can be considered as having built a logical story where people can be confident of their future development predictions. Obviously this story is not a good murder mystery with multiple plot twists, but like the mystery detective, people must deal with an overabundance of information (often conflicting and/or irrelevant) and must figure out how to fit the pieces together. Unlike the mystery novel, high quality reading to decide information works as a plot spoiler and clearly lays out how the pieces fit together at the beginning.

Contextual awareness is the understanding of the information and relationships within a situation which forms the basis for:

- How to interpret new information.
- How to make decisions for interacting with that situation.

Contextual awareness is about a person's state of knowledge about the situation and not about the process they use to obtain that knowledge. Different people will use different methods and approaches to gain contextual awareness. The goal is to ensure people obtain the information they need and not force them to first look at source A and then source B.

Elements of good contextual awareness shown in figure 2 are:

- Understands how the information fits within the current situation. The reader understands the information which describes what is happening now. They exhibit deep knowledge rather than surface knowledge about the situation.

- Understands the information relationships [7]. Fully grasping information lies not in knowing the information itself, but in how it relates to other information. The person understands the cause and effect relationships and the correlation relationships within the situation. They can describe these relationships as well as how changes will ripple through the entire situation.

- Understands the future development of the situation. They are able to make predictions about the effects of different decisions on the situations. Situations are dynamic; any decision/intervention results in some of the information changing. Decisions are made from a local viewpoint, but they tend to affect a much wider area. The reader needs to understand how a decision and its resulting effects will ripple through the situation; ripples that typically extend well beyond the area of immediate concern and can cause undesirable results in non-immediate areas [14].

Contextual awareness fits into the cyclic nature of understanding a situation and decision making (Figure 3). A person starts with very low contextual awareness and it builds as they interact with the reading to decide information.

4.1 Contextual awareness as a design tool

Contextual awareness gives the design team a filtering tool which can be used to judge how the information fits within the reader's needs for reading to decide information. Any potential content or design choice can be viewed within the framework of how it helps a reader develop contextual awareness. The information design and content drives how easily and how completely people can construct a story and map it back onto the actual situation.

Situations which require design teams to consider contextual awareness are those which contain complex information that must fit within a situation and be presented to meet a reader's information needs [4, 8]. Basing the analysis around contextual awareness gives the design team a method on which to base the content analysis as they develop and organize reading to decide information. It also provides a basis on which to structure both early prototyping and usability testing.

A significant part of the design analysis (figure 4) can be considered as defining the information needs that help readers develop contextual awareness. A design team needs to define information that people need to build a coherent story and to map that story onto a situation timeline. The design analysis works to ensure people receive the information they need at the proper time and that it properly relates to other information. With good contextual awareness, people will understand both the information and the relationships between information, as well as how both fit into the current and the future evolved situation [7].

Designing with a goal of enhancing contextual awareness focuses early design efforts on developing an awareness of the pertinent factors which an audience group needs to know and the order in which they must be presented to maximize comprehension (figure 5). Based on those information needs, the information requirements, presentation, and the flow of information can be developed. The goal is to allow a design team to create a structure which meets those information needs across all design personas (audience members). For example, the information needs of junior and senior technical people are different. They need different levels of detail and may need information presented in different order to best understand the situation.

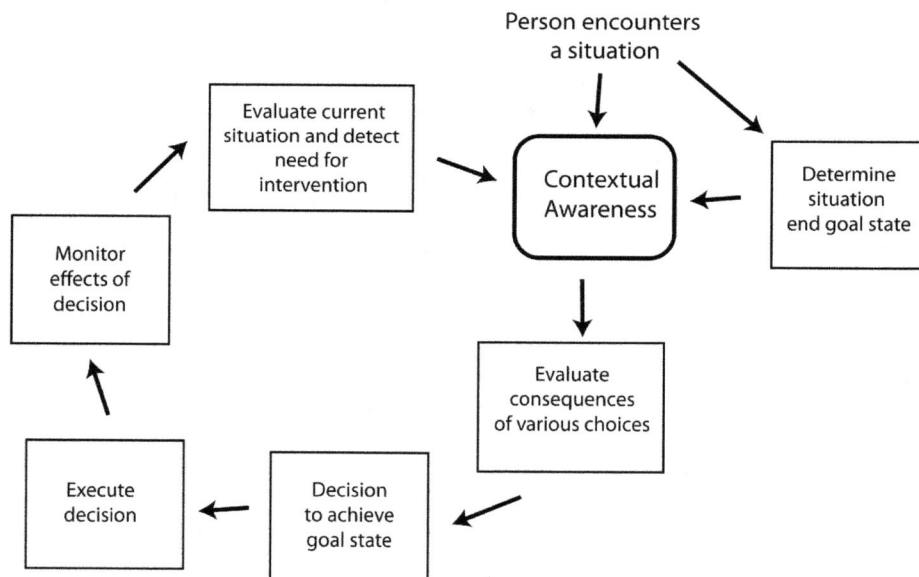

Figure 3. Reading to decide decision process. A person enters the cycle with low contextual awareness. Each cycle increases their contextual awareness as they makes decisions and monitor the situation as it responds to the decision.

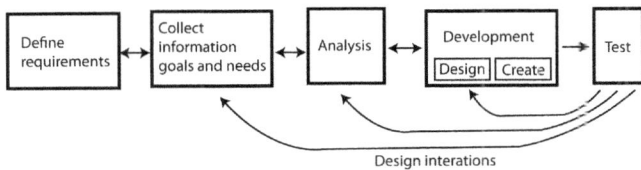

Figure 4. Typical design and development flow diagram.

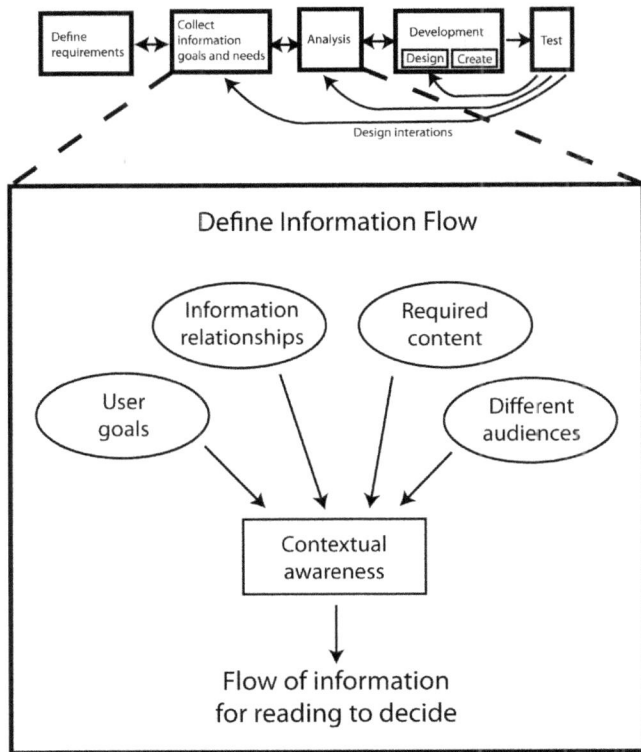

Figure 5. Information analysis and contextual awareness. During the analysis, how the information must flow to the reader must be created based on the audience's information needs and the required information relationships.

5. BRIEF EXAMPLES

Example #1

When purchasing new equipment, many people try to use classical decision making methods. They create a table with the different equipment models across the top and the criteria down the side. Then each of the criteria is assigned a weight. The intent is that the equipment will be evaluated by just those criteria and the one with the highest total value will be picked.

Unfortunately, this approach assumes that all of the criteria have been defined, that they have been assigned the proper weights, and that the evaluation is unbiased. Human nature tends to result in a highly biased evaluation with the preferred option getting higher marks or the weights getting adjusted until it shows the preferred choice is best.

This approach fails to build contextual awareness because it stops at the low levels. It has the basic facts (the criteria) but fails to consider how different values of those criteria cause different responses to the equipment. In other words, this approach ignores soft values that can strongly affect the future use of the equipment. Factors such as how people will react to the new machine (they

might see it as threatening their job), might have unintended consequences such as extra noise in the work place or tax the air conditioning units, space requirements, etc. These soft factors are all part of the global aspects of the new equipment that should considered when building the contextual awareness before making a purchase decision. High quality reading to decide information would contain this information so the reader to consider it.

Example #2

A typical method of presenting complex information on a website is with a question and answer format. A list of questions is asked with answers provided for each one. For example, many healthcare sites use this format to provide information about a specific disease or treatment option.

A problem with this approach is that it tries to convert a complex information situation into a simple one [4]. An underlying assumption is that all of the reader's information needs can be stated as single questions and that the design team can define all of those questions.

Developing contextual awareness and using it to support reading to decide information means going beyond giving people answers to specific questions. Even if we assume the design team is presenting the proper questions, the reader's contextual awareness is still in doubt without significant testing. Many readers like the Q&A format and a test of fact acquisition after reading the website will probably show good results. People will know the answers for the individual questions. However, if the test focuses on overall comprehension of the information and if the person can use it for making decisions, then the usability test questions would also include how well the person can predict future developments and how well they understand the information relationships (typically relationships which cross two or more questions). When this level of question is asked, the design team may find the readers can recite the facts (answers that reflect a single question/answer), but don't understand how they connect to other facts and can't apply them to make an informed decision.

6. CONCLUSION

Traditionally, technical communicators addressed highly structured situations, with a basic goal of efficiently completing a task. But many communication situations are no longer highly structured; instead, they have shifted to complex situations revolving around information seeking, problem-solving, and decision making. The communication needs have shifted to complex situations where people read information and make decisions; they *read to decide*. In these situations, finding the information is but a first step; after it is found the person needs to interpret it and decide if and how it applies to their situation. Even if they get presented with information which is accurate and reliable, that information is essentially useless unless they are able to interpret it and apply it to their current situation. These complex informational situations require that people develop *contextual awareness,* which gives design teams a foundation from which to perform the analysis, design, and testing that ensures a person can relate information to the current situation.

For technical communicators, writing documents focused on reading to decide means a shift from thinking about documenting how to perform tasks. Instead, the design team needs to understand what information people need to make decisions and how they interact with that information in the process of reaching a decision. Creating reading to decide content moves the technical communicator to the center of fulfilling the design team's responsibilities of providing a high quality user experience.

A complex situation's context is external to and outside the writer's control. Instead, it only exists within the reader's world; an understanding of a situation depends on the reader comprehending the available information and interpreting it properly. A design team's job is to ensure reader comprehension and interpretation occurs efficiently and effectively. The previous two sentences are, of course, obvious statements to any experienced technical communicator. However, it is an extremely difficult task to perform, especially when, to achieve the goal, readers' must interact with complex information contained within a reading to decide context.

Developing content for a complex system must be regarded as fundamentally different from simple systems. Accordingly, we must rethink how we develop and test the information, we must consider new ideas and employ new methods [29, 39, 41]. There are no single answer, no simple answers, and the situation contains a dynamic set of relationships which change with time and in response to decisions/actions [4, 20].

Within these complex situations, people are reading to decide. They are taking information and building a coherent story based on the information relationships, and attempting to influence a situation via their decisions. Design teams can use contextual awareness as an element in designing the text and as a basis for testing the material to determine if people understand it and can use it to make decisions.

7. REFERENCES

[1] Ackoff, R. (1967). Management misinformation systems. *Management Science, 14*, 147–156.

[2] Albers, M. (1996). Decision-making: A missing facet of effective documentation. *Proceedings of the 14th Annual International Conference on Computer Documentation.* Raleigh NC. October 21–22, 1996.

[3] Albers, M. (2000). Information design for web sites which support complex decision making. *Proceedings of the STC 2000 Annual Conference.* Orlando FL. May 21–24, 2000.

[4] Albers, M. (2004). *Communication of Complex Information: User Goals and Information Needs for Dynamic Web Information.* Mahwah, NJ: Erlbaum.

[5] Albers, M. (2007). Information salience and interpreting information. *Proceedings of the 27th Annual International Conference on Computer Documentation.* El Paso TX. Oct 22–24, 2007.

[6] Albers, M. (2008). Human-information interaction. *Proceedings of the 28th Annual International Conference on Computer Documentation.* Lisbon Portugal. Sept 22–24, 2008.

[7] Albers, M. (2010). Usability and information relationships: Considering content relationships when testing complex information. In M. Albers & B. Still (Eds.), *Usability of Complex Information Systems: Evaluation of User Interaction.* (pp. 109–131). Boca Raton, FL: CRC Press.

[8] Albers, M. & Still, B. (2010). *Usability of Complex Information Systems: Evaluation of User Interaction.* Boca Raton, FL: CRC Press.

[9] Albers, M. (2009). "Design for effective support of user intentions in information-rich interactions. *Journal of Technical Writing and Communication. 39.2*, 177–194.

[10] Albers, M. (2011). Contextual awareness as measure of human-information interaction in usability and design. Poster presented at *HCI International.* Orlando, FL. July 12-14, 2011.

[11] Angehrn, A. & Jelassi, T. (1994). DSS research and practice in perspective. *Decision Support Systems, 12*, 267–275.

[12] Bettman, J. & Zins, M. (1979). Information format and choice task effects in decision making. *Journal of Consumer Research, 6.2*, 141–153.

[13] Chinander, K. & Schweitzer, M. (2003). The input bias: The misuse of input information in judgments of outcomes. *Organizational Behavior and Human Decision Processes, 91*, 243–253.

[14] Dekker, S. (2011). *Drift into Failure: From Hunting Broken Components to Understanding Complex Systems.* Burlington, VT: Ashgate.

[15] Dicks, S. (2010) Designing usable and useful solutions for complex systems: A case study for genomics research. In M. Albers & B. Still (Eds.), *Usability of Complex Information Systems: Evaluation of User Interaction.* (pp. 207–222). Boca Raton, FL: CRC Press.

[16] Esler, A. (1997). "Complex problems: What's the next step?" *SIGDOC Asterisk Journal of Computer Documentation , 21.1* 19–22.

[17] Gregor, S. & Benbasat, I. (1999). Explanations from intelligent systems: Theoretical foundations and implications for practice. *MIS Quarterly 23.4*, 497–530.

[18] Hollnagel, E. (1993). Decision support and task nets. In G. Klein, J. Orasanu, R. Calderwood, & C. Zsambok (Eds.), *Decision Making in Action: Models and Methods.* (pp. 31–36) Norwood, NJ: Ablex.

[19] Howard, T. & Greer, M. (2010) Innovation and collaboration in product development: Creating a new role for usability studies in educational publishing. In M. Albers & B. Still (Eds.), *Usability of Complex Information Systems: Evaluation of User Interaction.* (pp. 67–86). Boca Raton, FL: CRC Press.

[20] Janke, N. (2010). Language complexity and usability. In M. Albers & B. Still (Eds.), *Usability of Complex Information Systems: Evaluation of User Interaction.* (pp. 47–66). Boca Raton, FL: CRC Press.

[21] Johnson, E., Payne, J., & Bettman, J. (1988). Information displays and preference reversals. *Organizational Behavior and Human Decision Processes, 42*, 1–21.

[22] Jones, D. & Endsley, M. (2000). Overcoming representational errors in complex environments. *Human Factors, 42.5*, 367–378.

[23] Klein, G., Orasanu, J., Caldewood, R., & Zsambook, C. (1993). (Eds.), *Decision Making in Action: Model and Methods.* Norwood, NJ: Ablex.

[24] Klein, G. (1993). A recognition-primed. decision (RPD) model of rapid decision making. In G. Klein, J. Orasanu, R. Calderwood, & C. Zsambok (Eds.), *Decision Making in Action: Models and Methods.* (pp. 138–147) Norwood, NJ: Ablex.

[25] Klein, G. (1999). *Sources of Power: How People Make Decisions.* Cambridge, MA: MIT.

[26] Mao, J. & Benbasat, I. (2001). The effects of contextualized access to knowledge on judgment. *International Journal of Human-Computer Studies, 55*, 787–814.

[27] Mason, R. & Mitroff, I. (1973). A program for research on management information systems. *Management Science 19*, 475–487.

[28] Michie, S., Dormandy, E., & Marteau, T. (2003). Informed choice: Understanding knowledge in the context of screening uptake. *Patient Education and Counseling, 50*, 247–253

[29] Mirel, B. (1998). Applied constructivism for user documentation *Journal of Business and Technical Communication, 12.1*, 7–49.

[30] Mirel, B. (2003a). Dynamic usability: Designing usefulness into systems for complex tasks. In M. Albers & B. Mazur (Eds.), Content and Complexity: Information Design in Software Development and Documentation (pp. 233-261). Mahwah, NJ: Erlbaum.

[31] Mirel, B. (2003b). *Interaction Design for Complex Problem Solving: Developing Useful and Usable Software.* San Francisco: Morgan Kaufmann.

[32] Morrison, J., Pirolli, P., & Card, S. (2001). A taxonomic analysis of what world wide web activities significantly impact people's decisions and actions. Presented at the *Association for Computing Machinery's Conference on Human Factors in Computing Systems*, Seattle, March 31 - April 5, 2001.

[33] Mumby, D. (1988). *Communication and Power in Organizations: Discourse, Ideology, and Domination.* Norwood, NJ: Ablex.

[34] Orasanu, J. & Connolly, T. (1993). The reinvention of decision making. In G. Klein, J. Orasanu, R. Calderwood, and C Zsambok (Eds.), *Decision Making in Action: Models and Methods*, (pp. 3–20). Norwood, NJ: Ablex.

[35] Parker, C. & Sinclair, M. (2001). User-centred design does make a difference. The case of decision support systems in crop production. *Behaviour & Information Technology, 20.6*, 449–460.

[36] Payne, J., Bettman, J., Coupey, E., & Johnson, E. (1992). A constructive process view of decision making: Multiple strategies in judgment and choice. *Acta Psychologica, 80*, 107–141.

[37] Rasmussen, J. (1986). *Information processing and human-machine interaction: An approach to cognitive engineering.* New York: North-Holland.

[38] Redish, J. (1988). Reading to learn to do. *The Technical Writing Teacher, 15.3*, 223–233.

[39] Redish, J. (2007). Expanding usability testing to evaluate complex systems. *Journal of Usability Studies 2.3* 102–111.

[40] Rude, C. (1995). The report for decision making: Genre and inquiry. *Journal of Business and Technical Communication, 9*, 170–205.

[41] Scholtz, J. (2006) Metrics for evaluating human information interaction systems. *Interacting with Computers, 18*, 507–527.

[42] Simon, H. (1979). *Models of Thought.* New Haven, CT: Yale UP.

[43] Stewart, J. (1994). The psychology of decision making. In D. Jennings, (Ed.), *Decision Making: An Integrated Approach*, (pp. 54–95). London: Pitman Publishing.

[44] Tversky, A. (1977). Features of similarity. *Psychological Review 84*, 327–352.

[45] Tversky, A., Slovic, P., & Kahneman, D. (1990). The causes of preference reversals. *The American Economic Review, 80*, 204–217.

[46] van den Haak, M.J., Jong, de, M. & Schellens, P. (2007). Evaluation of a municipal website: Three variants of the think-aloud method compared. *Technical Communication, 54.1*, 58–71.

[47] Wright, P. (1974). The harassed decision maker: Time pressure, distractions, and the use of evidence. *Journal of Applied. Psychology, 59.5*, 555–561.

Navigating by Index and Guided Tour for *Fact Finding*

Tao Yang, Mexhid Ferati, Li He, Davide Bolchini
Indiana University
School of Informatics at IUPUI
535 West Michigan Street
Indianapolis, Indiana 46202
{taoyang, mferati, lh6, dbolchin}@iupui.edu

ABSTRACT

The primary mechanism for navigating a website consists of pages with lists of links (or *indexes*). Such indexes are most effective when they convey the necessary hint (or *scent*) to anticipate the content they point to. When indexes fail to do so, users who are seeking specific information need to click on a link just to explore where it leads to, and then go back to the index to select another item. In a study with 150 participants, we explored whether *guided tour navigation* – which enables users to linearly *browse* items *without* going back to the index – could outperform scentless indexes in fact-finding tasks. Our results suggest that indexes remain a better solution than guided tours, even when lacking information scent. Guided tours, however, improve user's performance when the target content is found in the first half of collection with 20 items. Implications for designing effective navigation patterns are discussed.

Categories and Subject Descriptors

H5.m. Information interfaces and presentation (e.g., HCI): Miscellaneous

Keywords

Index, list page, information scent, guided tour, fact-finding.

1. INTRODUCTION

On Best Buy's website, a user looks for a laptop with 9-hour battery life. On NBA.com, a fan looks for players with a three-point field goal percentage above 40%. On a university website, a student looks for a 1.5 credit class offered in the Summer term.

These three scenarios illustrate common types of tasks that can be characterized as *fact-finding* [9]: users look for a specific piece of information based on a prior knowledge they possess. In the Best Buy scenario, users are trying to locate a laptop with a long battery life; and in the NBA.com scenario, the basketball fans look to find players who can shoot three-pointers well. "Long battery life" and "three-point field goal percentage above 40%" are the respective *cues* that users utilize to locate information items that match the sought criteria (i.e., the models of the qualified laptops or the names of the qualified players).

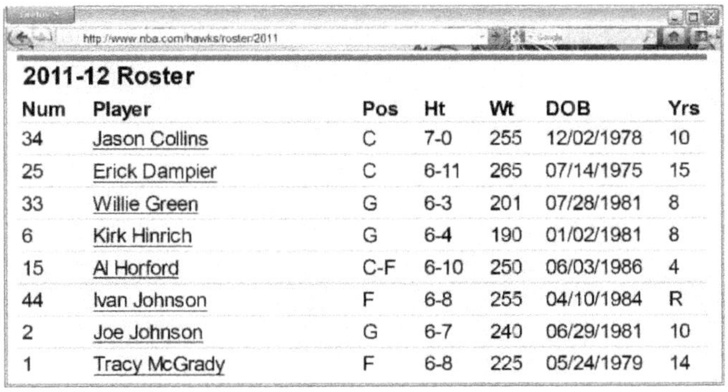

2011-12 Roster

Num	Player	Pos	Ht	Wt	DOB	Yrs
34	Jason Collins	C	7-0	255	12/02/1978	10
25	Erick Dampier	C	6-11	265	07/14/1975	15
33	Willie Green	G	6-3	201	07/28/1981	8
6	Kirk Hinrich	G	6-4	190	01/02/1981	8
15	Al Horford	C-F	6-10	250	06/03/1986	4
44	Ivan Johnson	F	6-8	255	04/10/1984	R
2	Joe Johnson	G	6-7	240	06/29/1981	10
1	Tracy McGrady	F	6-8	225	05/24/1979	14

Figure 1. Conveying the appropriate information scent on *list pages* is critical (http://www.nba.com/hawks/roster/2011).

To accomplish such fact-finding tasks, users may need to browse a large collection of information items (e.g., a group of basketball players). To organize collections of website content, "list pages" [5][21] are typically used. For example, a list of NBA players provides access to detailed profiles of each player (Figure 1). A list page, however, is more than a list of access points for each list item; it also anticipates several attributes of the content items to help users better identify them. In the NBA.com example, not only are the names of the players listed, but other additional information, including their positions and age, are shown as well. Each of these attributes acts as a useful *scent* that may lead users to their *food* (i.e., the target information), as information foraging theory [14][16] suggests: fact-finding can be seen as analogous to the behavior of animals going after their prey.

Lists, however, do not always feature the right "scent" that users expect. For example, in the NBA.com scenario, if the "three-point field goal percentage" attribute is shown on the list page, users can easily locate on the list shooters that match the criteria without exploring the player's detail page. But if this attribute is absent (as it is in Figure 1), users will need to access each player's detail page to find if any of the players has achieved that score. In other words, a list page that offers the scent matching the *cue relevant to a particular task* enables users to find information very quickly.

On the one hand, from the designer's standpoint, it is highly impractical to include in a list *every attribute* for each content item. In fact, the purpose and the challenge of designing an effective index is exactly to anticipate *selected* relevant information to support users in identifying and locating the content of interest. On the other hand, from a user's perspective, ***index navigation*** (Figure 2A) *that fails to provide the sought-after scent* forces users to go back and forth between the list page

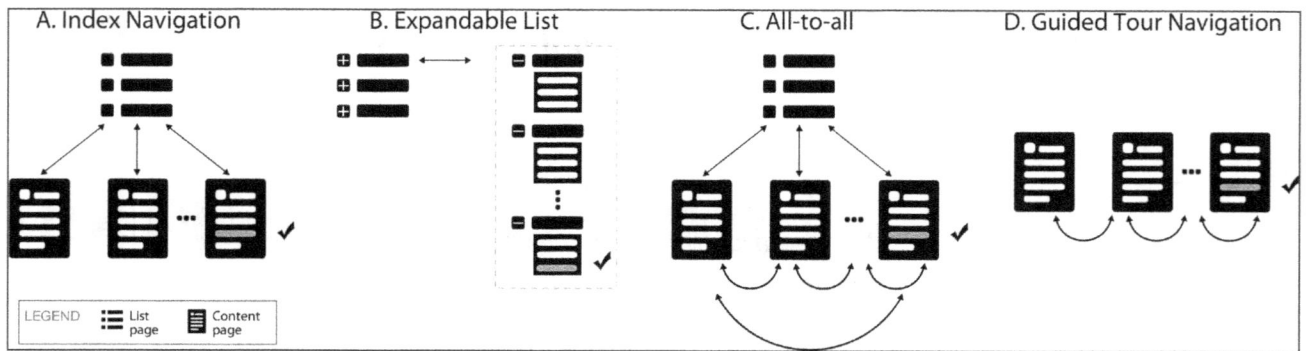

Figure 2. Four commonly-used web navigation patterns [5].

and list item page until the fact is found [5]. This process could be cumbersome and time-consuming, especially in large collections.

One solution to this problem is to use an *expandable list*, in which each list item can be expanded to reveal the complete content (Figure 2B). This feature enables users to simply unfold and review each item without navigating outside the index, even if the original list does not contain a useful scent. Expandable list, however, suffers from a scalability problem. For example, a product on Best Buy typically contains several screens of detailed content, including product description, technical specifications, and photo galleries as well as editorial and customer reviews. Packing such a large amount of content for all products into a list page will cause two issues to arise. First, the layout design for such a rich, expandable list becomes extremely challenging; second, the loading time of the list page may increase significantly and may negatively impact users' experience.

Another solution to facilitate navigation when an index has poor scent is to adopt an *all-to-all* pattern (Figure 2C). This strategy embeds a list in each item page so that users can access any content item from any other item without navigating back to the index. Like the expandable list, this solution may not be scalable. As the number of items in the collection grows to hundreds, designing and maintaining such lists becomes impractical.

We could argue that, instead of browsing, having an *advanced search* could be a practical solution. Users can input the keywords along with specific search conditions based on their fact-finding cue. This, however, would require building an expensive and

Figure 3. Guided tour navigation on Google mobile to preview search results (2012).

highly accurate and precise *site* search engine. Additionally, users' fact-finding cues can be vaguely articulated, which can cause search results to be inaccurate. In any case, even with the best search, users will still need to review a *list of items* as search results, thus bringing us back to the problem of index navigation. Another common design strategy to support "search by navigation" is *faceted browsing* [6]. This technique enables users to select an attribute of interest first (e.g., the "score" of the player) and then browse a collection "filtered" by that attribute, or facet. This solution is promising to accelerate fact finding, but still poses to the problem of sorting through a list of items, which can also be long and poorly designed even when filtered by "facets".

A radically different, yet common, navigation pattern is the *guided tour* [5]. This pattern sequentially links the items of a collection to support linear navigation (Figure 2D), and it is extensively used for purely *browsing purposes*, i.e., when users are not looking for any specific information. For example, Google recently featured a *guided tour* navigation for *search results* to browse the thumbnails of the target websites (Figure 3). As a more traditional example, browsing photo albums on Flickr relies on a guided tour pattern (the photo slideshow). Similarly, as Adobe launches a new animation product, a guided tour of the five most important features might be used to educate users on the key enhancements of the new tool. In the guided tour pattern, there is *no index*, but only linear navigation (back and forth) through the content items of the collection. Therefore, the guided tour allows users to move through a collection of list items without going back to a list page. This pattern also seems to provide a scalable solution (it might work for several items), and it is much cheaper to implement than an accurate, state-of-the-art search engine.

Intrigued by the characteristics of the guided tour, we wondered whether it could also benefit *fact-finding* scenarios, specifically in those situations in which the index lacks the appropriate scent. We then set out to explore the following research question: *Can guided tour navigation improve the efficiency and user experience when an index does not provide the scent that matches users' fact-finding cue?*

Addressing this question can shed new light on novel designs for existing web applications, and introduce low-cost solutions that may substantially improve user experience.

2. RELATED WORK

In web and hypermedia design, using guided tours is a common navigation strategy that is adopted in a variety of design contexts and domains. We could argue that even Bush [2] with his Memex

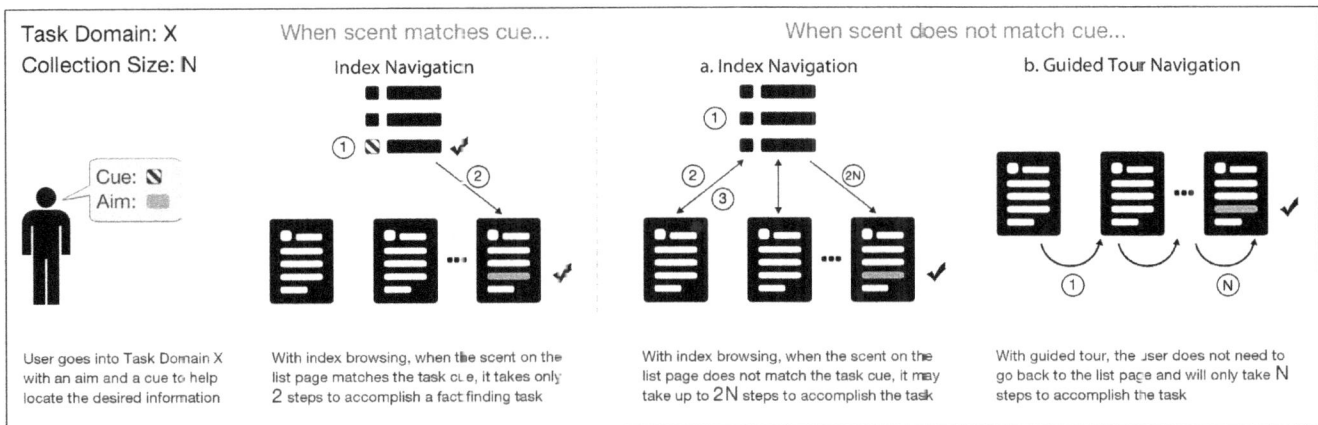

Figure 4. Modeling the key task and design factors for index and guided tour in fact-finding scenarios.

envisioned trails of linked documents that subverted the traditional navigation by index with a more linear, on-the-fly organization. Trigg [18] further explored this idea with Web documents. Functioning as an idea management system, a collection of cards called tabletops were interconnected as a way of communicating the organization of NoteCards. The tabletops were connected using path mechanisms called guided tours. Similarly, Furuta [4] designed a system called Walden's Paths to be used in education. Using this system, teachers could generate sequential trails that guide students in their learning process. Ariadne [8] is another guided tour interface, which provides a way to browse and edit guided tours through learning material.

The guided tour is also used as a technique to order independently linked documents, such as chapters of an online book [1]. The goal is to provide a clear start and an end to a chain of documents through an interface. Such interfaces also enabled the combination of individual guided tours into one, more complex, guided tour which also featured a clear start and an end point.

According to Zellweger [22] predefined paths or links in a hypertext help orientation. When users follow a predefined path they are less likely to feel lost compared to when browsing freely. The guided tour path is typically pre-defined by the designer, and curated from an initially unordered set of items. Zellweger [22] describes two ways that users could experience the guided tour: single-stepping and automatic. The single-stepping method allows users to progress through the tour by engaging a "next" command throughout the entire path. The automatic method enables a fully pre-programmed experience, in which the system moves through the items by following a predefined timing.

Xu et al. [19] present an implementation of trails to enable students to learn a course. Students initially choose their goals, and then the system creates a trail that guides students' learning processes with the least amount of time and effort. The students are also given the option of specifying trail units to suit their needs. The benefit of guided tour interfaces in the process of education is also pointed by Steinacker et al [17]. In order to evaluate the learning outcomes, the system provides a structure that will guide students through all required units to cover all the needed information Thus, the system needs to provide guidance to users, to prevent them from being confused and lost. Kreutz et al. [11] describe a tool that defines a trail of documents in the form of a guided tour. The tool enables the users to choose among several guided tours. Upon choosing a tour, an introduction about the tour is provided. If users select the tour, they can then navigate through it by engaging the next and previous buttons to move

forward or backward, respectively. Users have the ability to abandon the tour and browse elsewhere, though the system enables users to return to the last visited tour and resume it with a click of a button. Garzotto et al. [5] discuss the guided tour navigation as a design pattern for the Web. According to this study, guided tour provides easy-to-use access to a small group of objects, assuming that the user has no particular reason or criteria to choose one of them. The guided tour navigation identifies an order among a collection of items and creates sequential links among them. Links could be only forward (e.g., next) or forward and backward (e.g., next and previous).

This rich body of knowledge on guided tour navigation shows the proven potential of this strategy to support *browsing* scenarios. The navigational properties of the guided tour, however, have never been explored to benefit the more pervasive and critical needs of *fact-finding tasks*.

3. MODELING THE PROBLEM SPACE

To operationalize and empirically investigate our research question, we introduce here key concepts to characterize the factors involved in index and guided tour for *fact-finding* tasks. We model a fact-finding task into three components: *task domain*, *aim*, and *cue*. These terms are defined as follows.

- **Task domain:** a curated collection of information items relevant to a user's fact finding need. A task domain X is characterized by collection size N.
- **Aim:** the target information item that users want to find.
- **Cue:** an attribute of the aim which is known by the user.

For example, for the task "find the NBA players who have a three-point field goal percentage of over 40%," the *task domain* is the set of basketball players in the National Basketball Association; the *aim* is the name(s) of the player(s) who meet(s) the *cue*: "a three-point field goal percentage of over 40%."

We model as follows the key components of an *index navigation* strategy.

- **Content page** refers to each individual web page that contains the overall content of an information item of the website, e.g., the profile page of an NBA player.
- **List page** refers to actual *index* that lists the links to the information items of the task domain, e.g., a list page of all the best shooters in the NBA. Note that a list page is an essential component of index navigation strategy, but it is not offered in guided tour navigation.

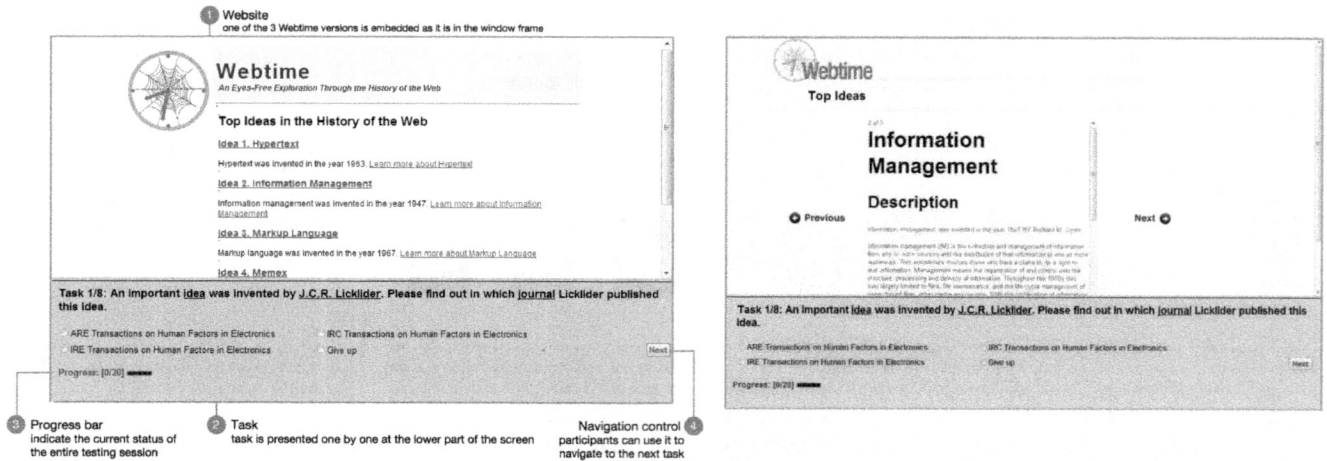

Figure 5. Online Field Testing Environment (OFTEN) used in the study and linked from the crowdsourcing platform [20]. Webtime with Index condition (left) and Webtime with Guided Tour condition (right) embedded in OFTEN.

- **Scent** refers to the selected attributes on a list page that describe the characteristics of the list items. For example, on the list page of NBA players, the scents are the players' *names*, birth *dates*, and *positions*. Scents may make it easier for information-seekers to locate the information they need from the list page.

With these simple modeling elements, we are able to characterize three types of fact-finding scenarios that (Figure 4) can support a user who approaches task domain X with an aim and a cue in mind.

(a) *When scent matches the cue.* In the first situation, the cue is shown on the list page as a scent that helps users to sense the aim. Therefore, the users can simply follow this scent and find the aim in merely two steps. This process, however, is usually too ideal. Many times, list pages are not so effective.

(b) *When scent does not match the cure.* When the cue is not shown on the list page, users cannot get any hint about where to go. Hence, they may need to check the content pages one by one to find the cue and the aim. If the aim is on the Nth content page, it may take the user up to 2N steps to accomplish the task.

Taking a closer look at the second situation, we may find that the list page can only complicate the browsing activities because it requires users to go back to it each time they navigate to an undesired content page. At this point, we propose that guided tour navigation can be a more convenient strategy because it allows the user to move through all the content pages without going back to the list. In terms of navigation mechanics, the guided tour would require N steps at the most to accomplish the same task, which would save about 50% of the navigation steps.

4. Hypotheses

Based on the modeling of the research problem, we propose the following hypotheses:

H1: In a fact-finding task, when the *scents on a list page match the task cue*:

- H1.1. index yields higher success rate than guided tour navigation
- H1.2. index is more efficient than guided tour navigation

- H1.3. index yields better navigation experience and lower cognitive effort than guided tour navigation.

Our rationale is that if a list page happens to contain the fact-finding task cue, users are less likely to give up on their task and may spend much less time to find the aim using index than guided tour navigation. In this situation, index navigation provides users a better navigation experience and reduces their cognitive effort.

H2: In a fact-finding task, when the *scents on a list page do not match the task cue*,

- H2.1. guided tour yields higher success rate than index navigation
- H2.2. guided tour is more efficient than index navigation
- H2.3. guided tour yields better navigation experience and lower cognitive effort than index navigation.

Our rationale is that if a list page does not contain the fact-finding task cue, users are more likely to give up and may spend much more time to find the aim using index than guided tour navigation. In this situation, guided tour provides users a better navigation experience and reduces their cognitive effort.

5. Study Design

"Even when we have correct premises, it might be very difficult to discover what they may imply" – Herbert A. Simon [15]

We could well stop our investigation to the detailed modeling of the various navigation solutions. This would clearly identify "*guided tour*" as a superior solution than "index without useful information scent" during fact finding tasks. However, we are aware of the limitation of our modeling, which considers mainly the mechanics of the design features and is not able to anticipate *all* the behavioral factors in place in complex human-computer interaction. For this reason, we set out to empirically verify our hypotheses by planning and conducting a large-scale, online experiment, which is described in the following sections.

5.1.1 Experiment Stimuli

According to the research hypotheses, we needed three versions of the same website (example shown in Figure 5). Both of the first two versions adopted an index navigation strategy. The difference was that the list pages in the first version contained the scent matching the task cues of the experimental tasks (see Appendix). In contrast, the list pages in the second version did not convey

Study Variables: 3 website versions x 3 collection sizes x 2 aim locations

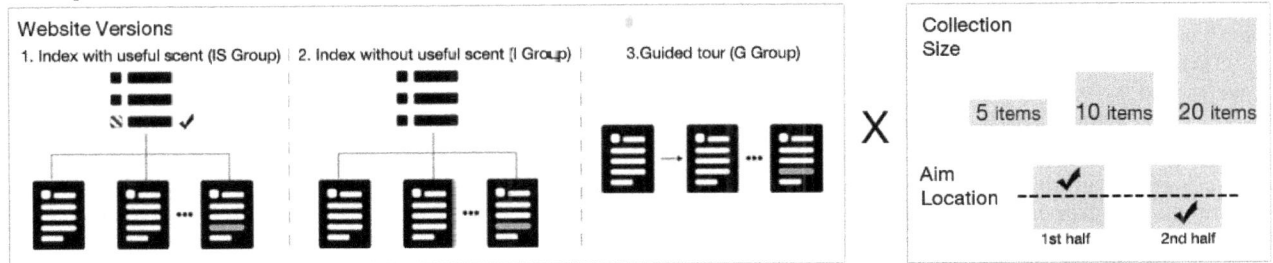

Experiment Procedure:

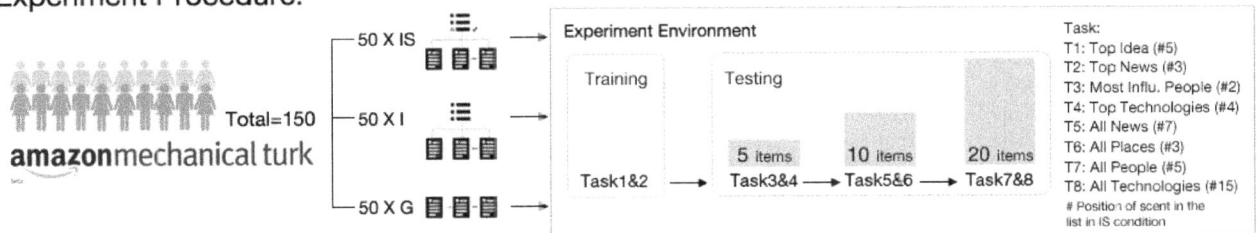

Figure 5. Study variables and experiment procedure.

those cues. Accordingly, the first version was named as Index-with-useful-Scent version (IS). The second was named as Index-without-useful-scent version (I). The third version used guided tour navigation (G). Therefore, hypothesis 1 (H1) was tested by comparing version IS and G, while hypothesis 2 (H2) was tested by comparing version I and G. [1]

The sample website we created is called Webtime. The aim of this website was to serve as an experimental test bed for several navigation strategies developed in a current NSF-funded project. In terms of sample content, Webtime contained five categories of content pages: people, places, technologies, ideas, and news stories. The content pages under each category were accessed through various list pages. For example, there were four list pages in the "people" category: most influential people, visionaries, followers, and all people. We also determined the attributes which were shown on the list pages as scents (see Table 1). For example, on the IS version of Webtime, the list pages in the "people" category presented people's name, birth date, and the institution where s/he worked as scents.

Table 1. Attributes shown on the list pages (IS version).

Category	Scents on List Pages
People	Name; Birth date; Institution
Place	Name; Location
Technology	Name; Year of Invention; Inventor
Idea	Name; Year of Invention; Inventor
News	Title; Date of Publication; Publication Outlet

---

[1] Examples of the experimental stimuli can be accessed at:
Index-with-useful-Scent:
http://discern.uits.iu.edu:8670/NSF_WEB_FastBrowsing-with-scent/-small-collection-1-influential-people-with-scent.html
Index-without-useful-scent:
http://discern.uits.iu.edu:8670/NSF_WEB_FastBrowsing-no-scent/-small-collection-1-influential-people-no-scent.html
Guided tour:
http://discern.uits.iu.edu:8670/NSF_WEB_FastBrowsing-guided-tour/4-inf-people-1.html

The I version of Webtime was created by removing from the list pages the scents which corresponded to the cues of the experimental tasks (see Appendix).

All list pages were removed from the G version but the collections were kept; for instance, a collection of the most influential people or a collection of visionaries. Users could access the content pages in each collection by moving from the first to the last item.

5.1.2 Collection Size, Tasks, and Aim Positioning

By analyzing the research problem, we also found that the sizes of the content page collections can have an influence on how much guided tour navigation can *save* an ineffective list page (Index-without-useful-scent). For example, if there are only five content pages in a collection, even if the list page is ineffective, users may still be able to find the aim in a very short time because there are not many things to browse. However, if the collection contains 20 items, the users may spend a longer time to find the aim or they may even give up due to the inconvenience of going back and forth for several times during a task. In this situation, guided tour may substantially reduce users' frustration and the amount of time they spend. Based on this assumption, we created experimental tasks for various collection sizes. The small collection consisted of five items, the medium collection 10 items, and the large collection 20 items. Although a real-world large collection may contain hundreds of items (e.g., an ecommerce catalogue), we set the maximum size to 20 for two reasons. First, our collection size was limited by the practical availability of content for the experimental prototype; second, we did not want to disrupt the user experience during the experiment by assigning to online users (not as fully controlled as in a lab environment) too long or too frustrating tasks.

The tasks were created based on the three components of typical fact-finding tasks: task domain, aim, and cue. The task domains corresponded to the content page categories: people, places, technologies, ideas, and news stories. The aims of the tasks were located only in the content pages, and were not disclosed in the list pages. So, users must access the content pages to find their aims, which guarantees that users will navigate into the website. The task cues were selected from the attributes listed in Table 1.

This makes sure that users can always find the task cues on the list pages in the IS version. But, whenever an attribute is used as a task cue, it is removed from the corresponding list pages in the I version. Therefore, users who use the I version are not able to match the cues to the scents on the list pages. The full list of all tasks can be found in the appendix.

While creating the tasks, we found that the locations of the task aims may also greatly affect performances. For example, if the aim is located in the first item of a collection, even if the list page is ineffective and the collection is large, users can still find it easily. In contrast, even in a small collection, if the aim is in the last item, it might still take users a longer time to find. To investigate the effect of this variable, for each collection size, we put the task aims in two typical locations: middle of the first half and middle of the second half of a collection. For example, for the two small collection tasks (5 items), one of them had its aim in the 2nd item of the collection (middle of the first half), while the other had its aim in the 4th item of the collection (middle of the second half). The detailed arrangements can be found in the appendix. These arrangements allowed us to compare how effectively the guided tour can save an ineffective list page when the aim is located either at the front or the end of a collection.

5.1.3 Study Variables and Experiment Procedure

A $3 \times 3 \times 2$ mixed-modality experiment was conducted (Figure 6). The between-subject independent variable was website version, which had three levels: IS, I, and G. The within-subject independent variables were: collection size (small, medium, and large) and location of task aim (first half or second half of a collection). The dependent variables were: task success rate, time-on-task, and self-reported navigation experience and cognitive effort. The self-reported navigation experience and cognitive effort were captured using the navigation experience and cognitive effort modules of the DEEP usability questionnaire [20].

The experiment was conducted using *crowdsourcing*, which refers to solving problems or gathering ideas by assigning tasks to people around the globe [3][12]. We used a popular online platform for crowdsourcing called Amazon Mechanical Turk [7][10][12][13]. Amazon Mechanical Turk supports two roles: requesters and workers. The requesters can post task assignments online, which are called HITs, and promise a certain amount of payment to each worker. The requesters also have the right to reject paying a worker if s/he does not provide valid responses. On the workers' end, they can access the HITs, perform the tasks, and receive the payment.

There have been many discussions concerning the advantages and disadvantages of using online crowdsourcing and Amazon Mechanical Turk [7][13]. The main advantage is the convenience in recruiting a large sample of participants with broad demographic backgrounds. In particular, university researchers no longer need to only rely on student participants [7]. The main disadvantage, however, is the bias caused by the workers' intentions in accomplishing the tasks quickly [13]. For example, a worker may start performing tasks without reading instructions. Therefore, researchers need to find effective ways to identify the invalid responses. In this study, we detected invalid responses by applying three criteria: (1) a worker finished all tasks in an *extremely* short amount of time (through statistical distribution) relative to the average; (2) a worker gave up or failed significantly more tasks than most of the other workers (i.e., a sign of trying to *game* the system); (3) a worker selected the same answer to all the

Likert scale questions (i.e., a sign of not reading the tasks and question and answer randomly).

Since web browsing is a common activity for all Internet users, the crowdsourcing technique can help us access a broader user profile and elicit more generalizable trends. We opened one HIT on Amazon Mechanical Turk, which was accessed by 150 participants. Participants who provided valid responses were rewarded $2. Inside the HIT, there were some brief instructions, a link, and a textbox (to submit a reward code). Based on the pre-test, the entire test could be finished in around 10 to 15 minutes. Therefore, we warned the users that if they finished everything in a very short time (e.g., less than 5 minutes), they would not be paid. The provided link led participants to an online field testing environment (introduced below). Upon finishing the test, the environment automatically generated a reward code. The participants were instructed to submit the reward code in the textbox to receive the reward.

To flexibly deploy and control the WebTime study prototypes on the crowdsourcing platform, we linked a HIT from Amazon Mechanical Turk to a custom Online Field Testing Environment (OFTEN), which we developed in previous work [20][2]. With OFTEN, researchers can easily control, compose and publish online a task-based, website-related experiment. As shown in Figure 5, the OFTEN interface used in our study consists of two parts: the upper part embeds one of the three website versions of WebTime, while the eight fact-finding tasks were shown one after another in the lower part. The tasks were all multiple choice questions. For each question, there were one correct answer, two interference answers, and the option to give up.

To systematically expose users to the designed experimental conditions, OFTEN used a simple a PHP program to show the three website versions alternatively to the crowdsourcing participants. For example, if the first participant was shown the IS version, the second was shown the I version, and the third the G version. This guaranteed that the three versions were tested by different participants (a between-subject design). The experiment procedure is illustrated in Figure 6. First, the participants performed eight tasks using one of the website versions assigned by the OFTEN engine. The first two tasks were considered training tasks for users to get familiar with the corresponding navigation strategy. The other six were formal tasks. The small collection tasks were always presented at the beginning, while the large collection tasks were always presented in the end. This allowed users to gradually get adjusted to performing tasks on larger collections. Second, the participants filled out a questionnaire regarding their navigation experience and cognitive effort in performing the tasks. Last, we gathered the participants' demographics including sex, age, and Internet usage.

6. RESULTS

We pruned the collected data (150 responses) by removing 15 incomplete responses or outliers. Among the 135 valid responses, 45 belonged to the IS (Index-with-useful-Scent) group, 46 to the I (Index-without-useful-scent) group, and 44 to the G (Guided tour) group. Overall, 76 of our participants were male and 59 female. All participants were at least 18 years old: 6 were 18-20, 72 were 21-30, 26 were 31-40, and 31 were over 41 years old. Most of the

---

[2] The OFTEN environment and the experiment can be accessed through: http://discern.uits.iu.edu:8670/FB_IS/Consent.php

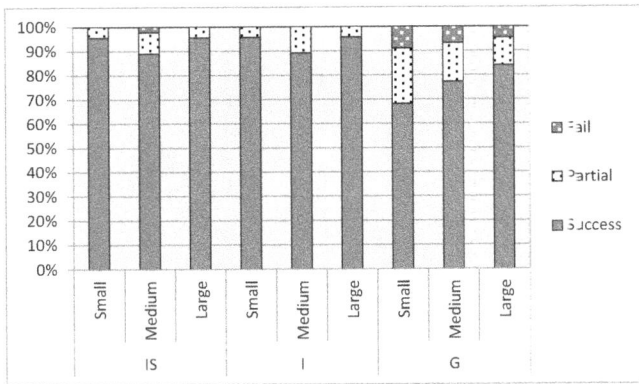

Figure 7. Guided tour decreases success rate in all conditions.

participants (N=129) used the Internet "several time a day" and the rest (N=6) used it at least 1-2 times a week. This ensured that participants were familiar with regular web browsing. We also checked the main effects and interactions of the participants' demographics on the outcome measures (e.g., time-on-task). No significance was found.

Overall, the experimental results surprised us because they show that guided tour, by removing the need of using the index, *did not outperform* ineffective indexes (Index-without-useful-scent). In the following sections we will illustrate the results in detail and discuss possible explanations of this interesting phenomenon.

6.1 Overall Performances

6.1.1 Lowest Success Rate Yielded by Guided Tour
One-way between-subject ANOVA was conducted to compare the average success rates of group IS, I, and G. The average success rates were calculated by averaging the binary success scores (0 = fail; 1 = success) across six tasks. Levene test for homogeneity of variance was significant ($p < .01$), which indicated that the variances across the three groups were not equal. Therefore, Welch's adjusted F value was used to test for significant effects of the three website versions.

The overall ANOVA showed that there were significant differences among the three groups: Welch's F(2, 79.22) = 4.64, $p < .05$, $\omega^2 = .05$. Tukey HSD tests revealed that guided tour yielded significantly lower success rate (M = .85, SE = .04) than both IS (M = .96, SE = .01, $p < .01$) and I (M = .97, SE = .01, $p < .01$). IS and I had no significant difference in regard to success rate ($p = .99$), indicating that removing useful scents did not prevent users from finding the aim.

Task success rates were compared within each collection size. Since each collection size included two tasks, we defined success rate in three levels: fail (failed in both tasks), partial success (succeeded in only one of the two tasks), and success (succeeded in both tasks). Chi-Square independence test was conducted to make the comparisons. The Chi-Square test was significant in the small collection condition ($\chi^2_{(4, N = 135)}$ = 20.46, $p < .01$, Cramer's V = .28), indicating that task success rate significantly correlated with website version. In particular, the G group yielded many more failures (failure rate = 9.09%) and partial success (partial success rate = 22.73%) than the IS group (failure rate = 0%; partial success rate = 4.44%) and the I group (failure rate = 0%; partial success rate = 4.35%).

In medium and large collection conditions, task success rate did not significantly correlate with website version. However, as

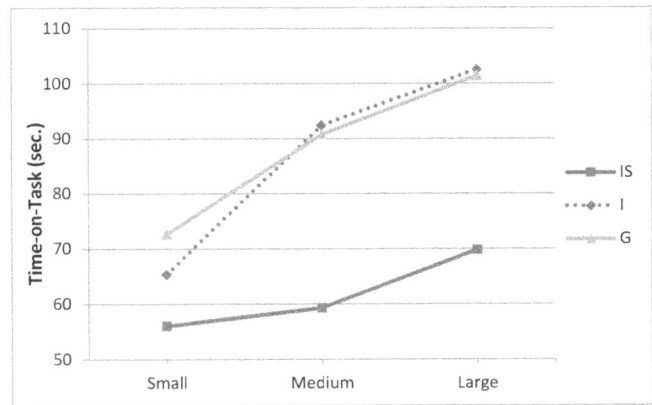

Figure 8. No significant difference between guided tour (G) and a scentless index (I) on time-on-task.

illustrated in Figure 7, guided tour still yielded the lowest success rates in these two conditions compared to IS and I.

6.1.2 No Significant Reduction on Time-on-Task
The average time-on-tasks of groups IS, I, and G were compared using one way ANOVA. The three groups were not homogeneous according to the significant Levene test for homogeneity of variance ($p < .01$).

Overall, there were significant differences among the three groups: Welch's F(2, 80.85) = 17.18, $p < .01$, $\omega^2 = .19$. Tukey HSD tests indicated that the IS group spent significantly less time (M = 61.69 sec., SE = 2.83) than group I (M = 86.77 sec., SE = 3.75, $p < .01$) and G (M = 88.27 sec., SE = 6.66, $p < .01$). This confirmed that index navigation was more efficient than guided tour when scent matched cue, as hypothesized. No significant difference, however, was found between groups I and G ($p = .97$) and the average time-on-task for group G was even higher.

A two-factor mixed-model ANOVA was conducted with website version as the between-subject factor and collection size as within-subject factor. The main effect for collection size was significant (F(2, 131) = 28.56, $p < .01$, $\eta_p^2 = .30$). The larger the collection, the more time was needed to complete the tasks. When the assumption of homogeneous covariance (Sphericity) was not considered, the multivariate statistic suggested that there was a significant interaction effect caused by collection size and website version (F(4, 262) = 2.77, $p < .05$, $\eta_p^2 = .04$). As shown in Figure 8, the possible interaction was found from the intersection of I and G. In the small collection condition, G (M = 72.61 sec., SE = 7.53) was more time-consuming than I (M = 65.35 sec., SE = 4.97), but in the medium collection condition, G (M = 90.77 sec., SE = 8.15) became less time-consuming than I (M = 92.42 sec., SE = 6.50). This interaction effect, however, became insignificant when the assumption of Sphericity was considered: F(3.77, 248.51) = 2.15, $p = .08$, $\eta_p^2 = .03$. Also, one-way ANOVAs showed that, in each of the three collection size conditions, I and G had no significant difference in terms of time-on-task.

6.2 Overall Perceptions

6.2.1 Slight Improvement on Navigation Experience
The navigation experience questionnaire we used [20] was reliable in all experimental conditions (Cronbach's Alpha > .731), indicating that all its items were measuring the desired concepts.

One-way ANOVA showed that there was no significant difference among groups IS, I, and G in terms of navigation experience (F(2,

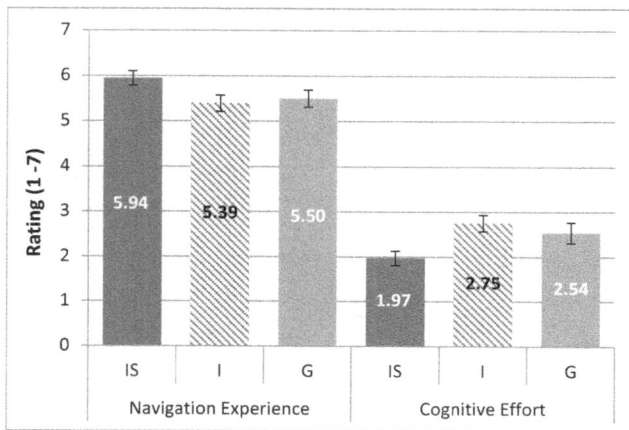

Figure 9. Guided tour (G) improves but does not significantly outperform a scentless index (I) on navigation experience and cognitive effort.

132) = 2.74, p = .07, η^2 = .04) (Figure 9). Nevertheless, Group G had slightly better navigation experience (M = 5.50, SE = .19) than group I (M = 5.39, SE = .18), as hypothesized. Group IS had the best navigation experience (M = 5.94, SE = .16) among the three groups.

6.2.2 Slight Improvement on Cognitive Effort

The cognitive effort questionnaire was also reliable in all experimental conditions based on Cronbach's Alpha (> .721). One-way ANOVA showed that there were significant differences among groups IS, I, and G (Welch's F(2, 86.08) = 5.52, p < .01, ω^2 = .06) (Figure 9). Tukey HSD tests suggested that group IS needed least cognitive effort (M = 1.97, SE = .16) compared to group I (M = 2.75, SE = .18, p < .05) and G (M = 2.53, SE = .23, p = .10). Guided tour reduced users' cognitive effort only slightly compared to index-without-useful-scent, and this difference was not significant (p = .71).

Besides the overall performances and perceptions, we also examined how user performance was influenced by the locations of the task aims. Several interesting patterns were found.

6.3 Aim Location: First Half of the Collection

This section reports the analysis of user performance in the situation when the task aims were located in the *first half of the collections*. For small collections, group G had significantly more

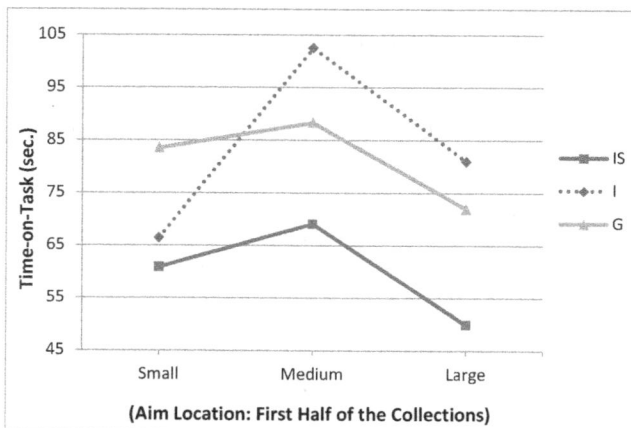

Figure 10. When the aim is in the first half of a collection, guided tour is more efficient than an ineffective index in the medium and large collection conditions.

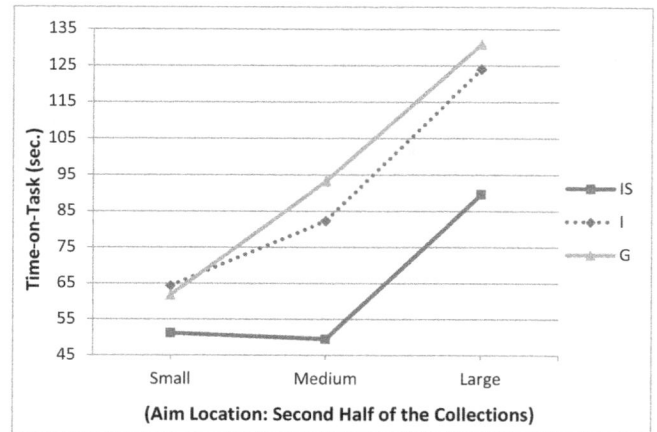

Figure 11. When the aim is in the second half of a collection, guided tour requires more time than an ineffective list in the medium and large collection conditions.

failures (failure rate = 18.18%) than group IS (failure rate = 2.22%) and I (failure rate = 0%) ($\chi^2_{(2, N = 135)}$ = 14.09, p < .01, Cramer's V = .32). No significant difference was found in the medium and large collection conditions.

The trend of time-on-task across collection conditions was somewhat contradictory with the overall time-on-task. As shown in Figure 10, the time spent decreased in the large collection condition (the decrement was statistically significant in group G) compared to the medium collection condition.

Similar to the overall time-on-task, there was no significant interaction between collection size and website version (F(4, 264) = 1.93, p = .11, η_p^2 = .03), although there was an intersection between I and G in Figure 10. The pattern in the medium and large collections is consistent with our hypotheses: guided tour requires less time than an ineffective list.

6.4 Aim Location: Second Half of a Collection

When task aims were positioned in the second half of the collections, group G yielded significantly more failures than group IS and I in both small (failure rate of group G = 22.73%; IS = 2.22%; I = 4.35%; $\chi^2_{(2, N = 135)}$ = 12.99, p < .01, Cramer's V = .31) and medium collection conditions (G = 20.45%; IS = 4.44%; I = 0%; $\chi^2_{(2, N = 135)}$ = 13.81, p < .01, Cramer's V = .32).

Although not statistically significant, the pattern of time-on-task contradicts our hypothesis. As shown in Figure 11, users spent more time using guided tour in the medium and large collection conditions than using an index without useful scent.

To sum up the findings, guided tour did not prove to be a good alternative to scentless indexes in terms of navigation efficiency and effectiveness. Guided tour only slightly reduced the time-on-task of an ineffective list when the collection size was relatively large and the task aim was in the first half of the collection. When the task aim was located in the second half of the collection, however, it increased the time spent on a task.

7. DISCUSSION

7.1 Guided Tour ideal for *browsing*, but not for *fact finding*

By solely relying on the analytical modeling of the navigation mechanics (Section 3) we had clearly anticipated that Guided Tour navigation would be significantly more efficient than indexes without cues during fact-finding. However, given the complexity of the factors involved in real life scenarios, we decided to run a controlled experiment to put to test our reasoning and verify the anticipated outcome (hypotheses) in a large-scale, "live" situation.

Interestingly, and *contrary to our expectations* (Hypothesis H2), our experimental findings reveal that guided tour does not support effective and efficient navigation for *fact-finding tasks*. On the one hand, index navigation still performs better than guided tour when users are seeking specific information from a collection, and even when indexes lack the cue that would facilitate the identification of content. This indicates that the mechanism of the index, even when poorly designed, is still better than not having an index to support retrieval. On the other hand, guided tours seem ideal for *browsing* tasks, i.e., when users are not seeking for specific information, and have no reason or will to pick a specific item out of a collection [5].

Specifically, our study confirms hypotheses H1.1, H1.2 and H1.3, as it shows that index navigation is more efficient and it yields higher success rate than guided tour when the scents on a list page match the task cue. Additionally, index yields better navigation experience and cognitive effort than guided tour. Our study *does not confirm* hypotheses H2.1, H2.2 and H2.3, as it shows that index navigation is more efficient and it yields higher success rates than guided tour even when the scents on a list page *do not* match the task cue. Moreover, even when the information scent is missing, index yields similar navigation experience and cognitive effort with guided tour. This shows that our analytical modeling (Section 3) was not able to anticipate important factors that in fact emerged during the online experiment. These factors, discussed in the next sections, include *control*, *direct navigation* and *familiarity* with the index navigation pattern.

7.2 Indexes and the Sense of Control

A possible explanation for the success of index navigation (regardless of the scent) is that the index structure *per se* provides to the user a sense of control over the collection. In fact, index navigation provides an important *communicative function* by helping users get an overview of the content collection. This helps users keep a sense of the *whole* to be controlled during navigation, and this helps anticipate their actions and plan resources for the information quest. In contrast, by using a guided tour, users lack to form an at-a-glance awareness of the collection and must blindly follow the items one by one in the sequence that designers have decided and users cannot control or anticipate. This may be ideal for browsing but is inefficient for *fact-finding tasks*, due to information retrieval pressure.

7.3 Indexes Enable Direct Navigation

Indexes provide also a critical *navigation* function. By enabling users to directly select and access the details of *any item* of a collection at any time, index is a highly flexible structure that supports multiple retrieval strategies. With an index, users can navigate directly to a list item they desire based on a scent information, intuition or best guess (when a scent is not provided). This factor can explain the superiority of scentless indexes, which enabled users to adopt a *trial and error* strategy to complete the tasks. Thus, even if it takes several trials (depending on the availability of the scent) to find the desired fact, generally index is still faster than guided tour.

From this perspective, guided tour proves to be a *very rigid* structure, because the collection has to be browsed linearly, by following a pre-defined sequence that cannot be changed by the user. Interestingly, the exception to this is when users are browsing a large collection of items collection and the aim is located in the first half of the set. In this condition, our findings suggest that guided tours can be more efficient and yield better navigation experience than indexes. Such a trend is particularly evident for medium and large collections. This finding also indicates that when designing a guided tour, the order of the items in the collection is *critical*: as intuition would suggest, the items placed early on in the sequence are *found* much more quickly than others.

7.4 Familiarity with Index Navigation

With respect to users' expectations, the guided tour might be a non-familiar (unexpected) modality to *retrieve information* from a collection. On the one hand, guided tour is commonly associated with browsing, when users can sit back, relax and enjoy the content (e.g., a photo album), rather than hunting for critical information. On the other hand, web users are so used to navigate to content by index (even when are poorly designed) that facing a guided tour for these tasks may seem awkward, and would require more time to adjust to it. Therefore, the familiarity of web users with indexes is a powerful motivator for quickly becoming efficient with this pattern. Being used to navigate back and forth from an index makes users overcome the difficulties posed by the lack of scent.

8. CONCLUSIONS

This paper makes three contributions to the design of interactive communication:

(1) Models the key task and design factors that structure fact-finding with index and guided tour navigation, and provides the conceptual framework to empirically examine their dynamics;

(2) Investigates the novel hypothesis that guided tour, traditionally and extensively used to support browsing-oriented navigation, can benefit *indexes* lacking information scent during *fact-finding*.

(3) Presents a crowdsourced, large-scale empirical study that furthers our understanding of the navigation effectiveness, efficiency, and user experience of indexes and guided tours for fact-finding scenarios. By contradicting our initial hypothesis, our results suggest that even *scentless* indexes still possess communicative and navigational functions that make them generally better candidates than guided tours to support *fact finding by navigation*.

Based on the results of this study, we are advancing this line of work in two directions. First, we aim at understanding the benefits and limitations of *mixed navigation pattern* (index and guided tour together) [5], to support fact-finding tasks. This combination will hopefully leverage the benefits of both navigation patterns, index and guided tour. Essentially, the navigation pattern will provide users with an overview of the collection and direct navigation to any of the list items. From that point, users can go directly to any of the list items and then continue browsing the content linearly without being forced to go back to the list page.

Second, we are demonstrating and testing a variety of navigation patterns to improve the user experience of *screen reader users*, who are able to *listen to* content and navigation prompts, but cannot rely on the visual channel to navigate large collections of items. This aural navigation research is conducted in collaboration with the Indiana School for the Blind and Visually Impaired in Indianapolis. Our rationale for this work is that *index navigation* can cause a detrimental waste of mechanical and cognitive effort for screen reader users. In fact, blind users are not able to get an at-a-glance *overview* of the list because index items are read aloud in strictly linear sequence. A guided tour pattern could thus provide a faster and more natural browsing alternative in aural scenarios.

9. ACKNOWLEDGMENTS

This research material is based on work supported by the National Science Foundation (NSF) under Grant #1018054. Any opinions, findings and conclusions or recommendations expressed in this material are those of the authors and do not necessarily reflect those of the NSF. We thank all the study participants for their contribution. We also thank Lindsay Kaser and Callie Archibald for their revisions of the paper, and Jason Eggert for the co-design and development of the Webtime prototype.

10. APPENDIX: Experimental Tasks

Tasks for Small Collections (5 items)	Aim Location
Task #3*: An important <u>person</u> (**Domain**) in the history of the web was born on <u>March 11, 1890</u> (**Cue**). Please, find out the <u>number of scientists</u> (**Aim**) he or she used to coordinate.	2nd out of 5 (middle of 1st half)
Task #4: An important <u>technology</u> (**Domain**) was invented by SoftQuad Software (**Cue**). Please, find the year (**Aim**) in which this technology was released.	4th out of 5 (middle of 2nd half)
Tasks for Medium Collections (10 items)	
Task #5: An important <u>news story</u> (**Domain**) was published by <u>Atlantic Monthly</u> (**Cue**). Please find out which <u>concept</u> (**Aim**) was mentioned in the story.	7th out of 10 (middle of 2nd half)
Task #6: A company plans to create a new headquarters campus in the <u>Silicon Valley</u> (**Domain**). Please find the <u>name of the company</u> (**Cue**).	3rd out of 10 (middle of 1st half)
Tasks for Large Collections (20 items)	
Task #7: An important <u>person</u> (**Domain**) in the history of the web was born on <u>January 30, 1925</u> (**Cue**). Please, find out what organizing <u>principle</u> (**Aim**) he or she has implemented in his or her lab.	5th out of 20 (middle of 1st half)
Task #8: An important <u>technology</u> (**Domain**) was invented by <u>Ray Tomlinson</u> (**Cue**). Please, find the <u>model</u> (**Aim**) this technology is based on today.	15th out of 20 (middle of 2nd half)

*Additional training tasks (T1 and T2) of similar structure were provided before the tasks.

11. REFERENCES

[1] Bry, F., Eckert, M., (2005). Processing Link Structures and Link Bases in the Web's Open World Linking. In Proceedings of Hypertext'05, 135-144.

[2] Bush, V. (1945). As we may think. Atlantic Monthly, 176 (1), pp. 101–108.

[3] Chia, P. H., & Chuang, J. (2012). Community-based Web Security: Complementary Roles of the Serious and Casual Contributors. In Proceedings of CSCW'12, 1023-1032.

[4] Furuta, R., Shipman III, F. M., Marshall, C. C., Brenner, D., & Hsieh, H-W. (1997). Hypertext Paths and the World-Wide Web: Experiences with Walden's Paths. In Proceedings of Hypertext' 97, 167–176.

[5] Garzotto, F., Paolini, P., Bolchini, D., & Valenti, S. (1999). "Modeling-by-Patterns" of Web Applications. Workshop on the World Wide Web and Conceptual Modeling, 293-306.

[6] Hearst, M.A. (2009). Search User Interfaces. Cambridge University Press.

[7] Jacquet, J. (2011). The Pros & Cons of Amazon Mechanical Turk for Scientific Surveys. Scientific American.

[8] Jühne, J., Jensen, A. T., and Grønbæk, K. (1998). Ariadne: A Java-based Guided Tour System for the World Wide Web. In Proceedings of the 7th International World Wide Web Conference, 131-139.

[9] Kellar M., Watters C., and Shepherd M. (2006). A Goal-based Classification of Web Information Tasks. In Proceedings of SIGCOMM, 101-112.

[10] Kittur, A., Chi, E., & Suh, B. (2008). Crowdsourcing user studies with Mechanical Turk. In Proceedings of CHI 2008.

[11] Kreutz, R., Euler, B. & Spitzer, K. No Longer Lost in WWW-based Hyperspace. In Proceedings of Hypertext'99, 133-134.

[12] Kulkarni, A., Can, M., & Hartmann, B. (2012). Collaboratively Crowdsourcing Workflows with Turkomatic. In Proceedings of CSCW'12, 1003-1012.

[13] Nelson, E. T., & Stavrou, A. (2011). Advantages and Disadvantages of Remote Asynchronous Usability. In Proceedings of Human Factors and Ergonomics Society 55th Annual Meeting, 1080-1084.

[14] Pirolli, P. L. T. (2007). Information Foraging Theory: Adaptive Interaction with Information. Oxford: Oxford University Press.

[15] Simon, H.A. (1999). The sciences of the artificial. MIT, p15.

[16] Spool, J. M., Perfetti, C., & Brittan. (2004). Designing for the Scent of Information. Middleton, MA: User Interface Engineering.

[17] Steinecker, A., Seeberg, C., Reichenberger, K., Fischer., & Steinmetz, R. (1999). Dynamically Generated Tables of Contents as Guided Tours in Adaptive Hypermedia Systems. In Proceedings of World Conference on Educational Multimedia, Hypermedia and Telecommunications, 640-645.

[18] Trigg, R. (1988). Guided tours and tabletops: tools for communicating in a hypertext environment. ACM Transactions on Information Systems (TOIS), 6 (4), 398-414.

[19] Xu, H., Zhou, X., Ni, J., & Zhao, Z. (2000). Adaptability in KDAEHS: an Adaptive Educational Hypermedia System Based on structural Computing. In Proceedings of Hypertext' 2000, 250-251.

[20] Yang, T., Linder, J., & Bolchini, D. (2012). DEEP: Design-Oriented Evaluation of Perceived Usability. International Journal of Human-Computer Interaction, 28(5), 308-346.

[21] Yang, T., Ferati, M., Liu, Y., Rohani, R., & Bolchini, D. (2012). Aural Browsing On-The-Go: Listening-based Back Navigation in Large Web Architectures. In proceedings of CHI 2012, 277-286.

[22] Zellweger, P. T. (1989). Scripted Documents: A hypermedia Path Mechanism. In Proceedings of Hypertext'89, 1-14.

Designing and Evaluating the Mobile Experience Through Iterative Field Studies

Robert Racadio, Emma Rose, Suzanne Boyd
Anthro-Tech, Inc.
1107 Harrison Ave NW
Olympia, WA 98502

{robracadio, emmarose, suzanneboyd}@anthro-tech.com

ABSTRACT

This experience report describes using iterative field studies to design and evaluate the mobile experience of soundtransit.org. One study aimed to evaluate the design of paper prototypes early in the design process and another study was conducted to test the implementation of an interactive prototype. In this report, we share our experience to provide readers with lessons that can be applied to conducting their own mobile field studies. Finally, we describe some of the broader impacts that have resulted from this work.

Categories and Subject Descriptors

H.5.2 [INFORMATION INTERFACES AND PRESENTATION]: User Interfaces – *evaluation/methodology, mobile input devices and strategies, prototyping, user-centered design*

General Terms

Design, Human Factors

Keywords

User experience, mobile, field studies, paper prototyping, mobile user testing, user-centered design, usability testing, transit, government

1. INTRODUCTION

Creating a mobile experience has become crucial for most web sites. This was especially true for Sound Transit, a regional transit authority in the Puget Sound region that plans, builds, and provides transit services including commuter rail, light rail, and buses. Sound Transit's riders expect information resources that they can consult on the go.

This experience report details how Anthro-Tech designed and evaluated a mobile experience by conducting a series of field studies. Readers of this report will learn how field studies for mobile designs need to be adapted to acknowledge the context of the mobile experience. We provide details about conducting two field studies at different times in the user-centered design lifecycle. Finally, we share lessons learned from the experience that offer guidance to others planning their own field studies of

mobile products. The experience report concludes with broader impacts of the work.

2. BACKGROUND

2.1 Field Studies

Field studies are a collection of research methods adapted from anthropology and the social sciences. Field studies are useful because they help researchers collect more naturalistic data since they observe users in their context-of-use instead of in a lab.

Rosenbaum and Kantner describe field studies on a continuum with exploratory methods on one end, such as ethnography to more structured methods on the other, such as contextual inquiry and field usability studies [7]. The User Experience Professionals' Association's Body of Knowledge defines field studies as a method "for gathering user requirements" or "for studying currently executed tasks and processes" [3]. In these definitions, field studies are characterized typically as a tool for early ideation or understanding existing designs and practices, typically in a workplace setting.

2.2 Investigating Mobile in the Field

Mobile experiences add additional challenges and opportunities for field studies because the context-of-use is not a static location like a workplace, but instead is wherever a user happens to be with his or her phone. Researchers may consequently avoid studying the mobile context because it is often thought of as being logistically complex and resource intensive. However, as we demonstrate in this report, field studies can be well suited for investigating the mobile experience. They allow researchers to go to where the users are, understand how that context impacts their experience, gather design and technical feedback from realistic situations, and learn things that may not be apparent in a more controlled environment. Field studies are beneficial throughout the design lifecycle and not just during ideation, and, if well organized, are comparable to lab-based methods in terms of the resources needed to conduct them.

2.3 SoundTransit.org: The Need for a Mobile Experience

Sound Transit is a regional transit authority in the Puget Sound region of Washington State. As part of a larger effort to improve service for its riders, Sound Transit engaged Anthro-Tech to lead a user-centered redesign of their web site to make their site more rider-focused [10]. Usability studies provided evidence that users were more successful and satisfied with the redesigned site and the redesign was heralded as a success.

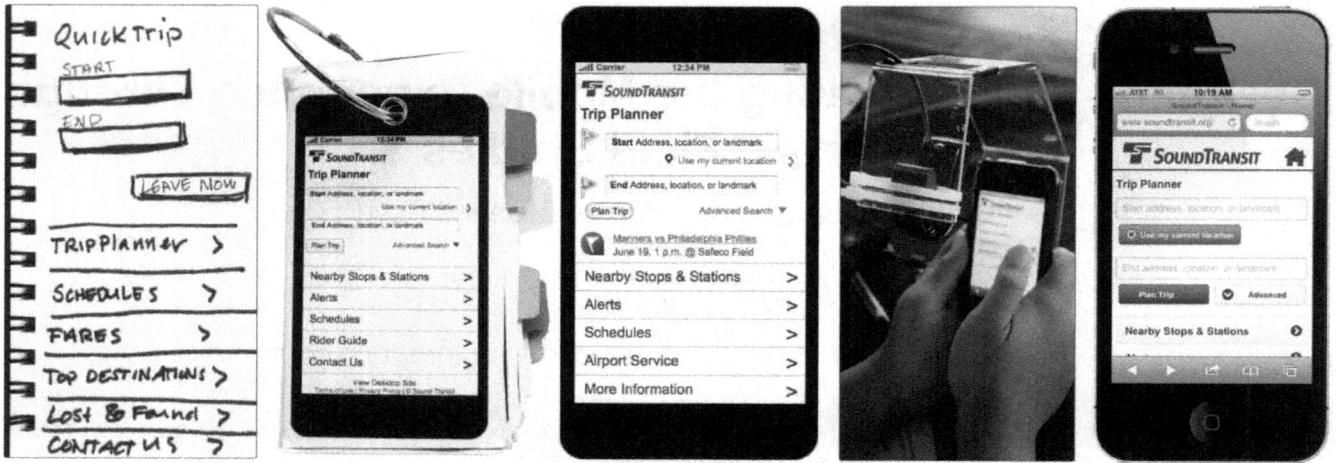

Figure 1 Iterative field studies of the paper prototypes and the interactive prototype shaped the final design of the soundtransit.org mobile site.

After redesigning the desktop site, it was clear there was a need for a mobile-specific experience, which is a natural extension for a transit site since users need to access information while on the go. Analytics of the site showed a 119% increase of mobile users accessing the site between March 2010 and March 2011. Interviews with riders and calls to the customer support line provided additional evidence that users required more information on their mobile devices.

Prior to the design of the mobile experience, smartphone users had to view the full desktop site on their mobile while feature phone users could not access the site at all.

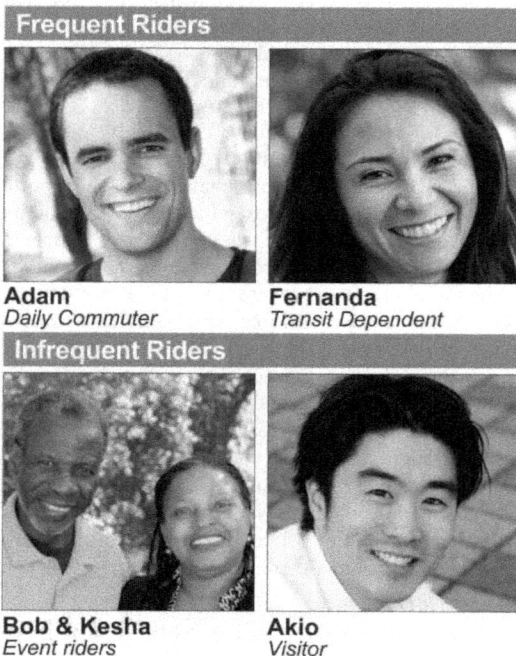

Figure 2 Sound Transit Rider Personas used for the desktop and mobile design of soundtransit.org

2.4 Following the User-Centered Design Process

Following the successful user-centered redesign of the existing desktop web site the Sound Transit mobile site was developed with the same approach by starting with understanding users and their needs.

Anthro-Tech helped Sound Transit research its users during the redesign of the desktop site, including gathering information about users' top tasks and personas. Given the ubiquity of internet-enabled mobile devices across many demographics [9], it was reasonable to repurpose that data and assume that those who were using the desktop site might also have access to a mobile phone. The mobile design needed to include the needs of *frequent riders*, such as daily commuters and those without personal vehicles (transit dependent), and *infrequent riders*, such as visitors and those who use transit to attend special events. Figure 2 shows the four personas that were the target of the design.

Following the user-centered design process, we iteratively designed and evaluated a concept for the mobile design, starting with low fidelity sketches, creating a paper prototype, and finally creating an interactive prototype (see Figure 1). During each iteration, a team of Anthro-Tech researchers and Sound Transit staff gathered feedback from stakeholders and users. This experience report focuses on the two field studies the team conducted on the paper prototype and the interactive prototype.

3. STUDY 1: PAPER PROTOTYPE

The objective of the first field study, conducted early in the design process, was to evaluate paper prototypes with users. Anthro-Tech created digital prototypes in Axure RP [1], using the list of users' top tasks. These tasks guided the decision about which pages of the mobile prototype to develop. Using a digital tool like Axure RP to create the prototype had several advantages over using pen and paper. First, it allowed us to create templates that could be re-used across the different pages of the site. Second, it streamlined keeping track of different versions of the prototype to test with users. Third, it made it easier to make changes to the prototype. Finally, it allowed team members to collaborate on the design of the prototype without having to be co-located.

3.1 Prototype Design Considerations for the Field

Based on conducting similar studies in the past, the Anthro-Tech team of researchers knew the materials needed to be designed to be suitable for a field study. First, we wanted the prototype to be *portable* so that it would be easy for facilitators to carry. Second, the prototype needed to be *usable* so that participants could easily understand how to interact with it and the researchers could easily facilitate it during the study. Third, it needed to be *durable* to withstand use by multiple people throughout a day of studies

To meet these considerations, the prototypes were printed on cardstock – making them durable – and cut to the size of a medium-sized iPhone – making them portable. We also bound them together using a large binder ring and marked off the different sections of the prototype using binder tabs. These made it easy for the facilitator to change the order of the prototype and flip through to the correct page as participants "tapped" through the prototype. We also adapted our pre- and post-study questionnaires, the list of scenarios, consent forms, and honoraria receipt forms to be portable, durable, and usable as well. The research team stowed the materials in the pockets of the Sound Transit-branded aprons we wore in the field. The aprons not only turned our researchers into roving self-contained usability testing units, but also helped us appear "official" and trustworthy when we interacted with participants.

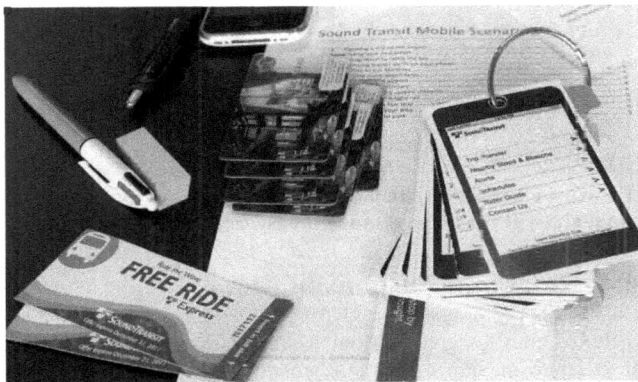

Figure 3 Study materials were developed and selected for being portable, durable, and usable in the field.

3.2 Creating Scenarios

The study scenarios selected represented users' top tasks and focused on ones that were particularly relevant to the mobile setting. These included tasks such as planning a trip, finding out when a bus will arrive, and looking for transit alerts that could impact travel plans.

3.3 Study Planning and Preparation

To make the best use of our limited time in the field (approximately two hours), our research team consisted of five researchers total from Anthro-Tech and Sound Transit. Having multiple facilitators helped us evaluate the prototype with more participants. The lead researcher developed the study materials and the rest of the team piloted the materials to refine them. This also gave the team a chance to familiarize themselves with the prototype and customize the ordering of the pages if needed. Additionally, official clearance from Sound Transit was arranged in advance of the study date so that we could conduct the study at transit stations and on Sound Transit vehicles.

3.4 Field Site

The field study took place in the morning to include representation from daily commuters. Field sites included a transit station in downtown Seattle, and riding different modes of transit, including buses, light rail, and a commuter train. Conducting studies while riding transit posed challenges, but it also ensured that we could recruit actual Sound Transit users.

3.5 Conducting the Study

Participants who consented to take part in the study were asked questions on demographics, transit use, usage of the Sound Transit website either on their desktop or mobile. We presented the prototype to participants and asked them to complete scenarios using think-aloud protocol [2]. Each researcher took detailed notes during the sessions. We found that taking notes while in transit was challenging. Findings that emerged across our participants were documented as we moved page-by-page through the prototype. Following the study, we asked participants questions about their experience with the prototype. Participants were offered coffee shop gift cards and transit passes as honoraria. For more information about who participated in the study, see Table 1.

Table 1 Breakdown of participants in the paper prototype field study (*n* = 33)

	# of Participants
Male	16
Female	17
Phone Ownership	
Owns smart phone	17
Owns feature phone	4
Does not own a mobile phone	2
Transit Use Frequency	
More than 1 time a day	8
Daily	8
Weekly	4
Less than once a month	2

3.6 Analyzing the Data

Immediately following the field research, the team met with the Sound Transit project sponsor to debrief on the study findings. Scheduling the debrief session immediately after being in the field enabled us to document findings while they were fresh. This was important due to the difficulty of taking detailed notes while on transit. The final deliverable from this research activity was a detailed list of findings and recommendations for improving the next versions of the prototype.

4. STUDY 2: INTERACTIVE PROTOTYPE

We iterated the digital prototype based on the feedback from the paper prototype field study. Based on this design, the development team from Sound Transit and OpenPlans.org then built a functional, interactive prototype that used live data. We conducted a second set of field studies to observe how riders would interact with a live site and understand how the site performed on riders' own phones.

4.1 Creating the Mobile Sled

For the second field study we wanted to be able to record the study sessions with mobile users and allow them to use their own devices. To do so we decided to build a mobile test sled for the interactive prototype study. The set-up had several requirements.

First, the set-up needed to allow users to hold their phones as naturally as possible. Second, it needed to support a web cam that could be angled to observe and record the user's screen. Several options existed, ranging from do-it-yourself mobile testing sleds [5, 6, 8] to more fully-featured kits that included custom cameras [4]. Third, the testing set up needed to leverage the existing equipment we used for usability testing (including cameras and usability testing software). Finally, the testing solution needed to look professional. Since participants would be using their own phones we wanted to ensure the testing solution wouldn't damage their devices and would accommodate a variety of phone form factors (including flip phones). This requirement led us to conclude that DIY solutions would not work for our needs.

The solution we chose was a mobile testing sled design adapted from a design from the California Digital Library [6]. The modified design was then professionally fabricated at a local plastic shop. The design of the sled supported different kinds of web cameras and accommodated different mobile phone form factors. Because it was made from plastic, it was light enough for participants to hold in their hands.

4.2 Mobile Testing Configuration

To conduct the study, we set up two stations, each consisting of a mobile testing sled, a laptop, and a web camera. The cameras were secured to the sleds using zip ties. The web camera was connected via USB extension cords to a laptop running Morae Recorder to record the sessions. Extension cords were important to give participants more freedom to move their phones and interact with them more naturalistically. The facilitators secured the participants' phones to the sled using rubber bands, which could be easily adjusted and removed without risk of damaging a participant's phone. An example of this set-up can be seen in Figure 3.

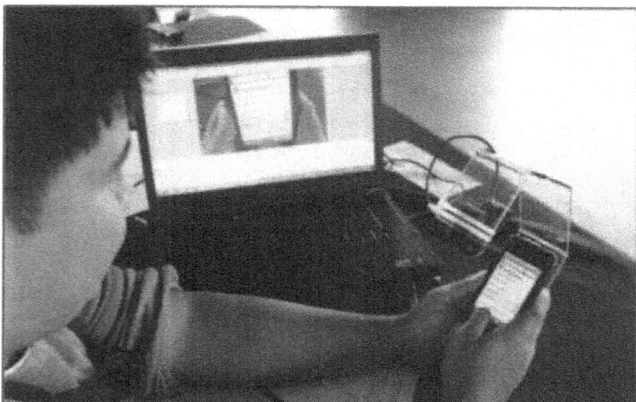

Figure 3 Interactive prototype field study included a mobile sled to record participants using their own mobile phones.

In order to get clear video, it was important to be able to adjust the cameras' brightness settings and focus manually. At the beginning of each session, we adjusted the camera settings to optimize the recordings of the mobile phone.

4.3 Field Site

We conducted the field study of the interactive prototype at the Sound Transit Link Light Rail station at Sea-Tac International Airport. We chose this location because it allowed for recruitment of target users of Sound Transit. Specifically, it helped us to reach

visitors, who are traditionally harder to recruit since they are typically in the area only temporarily. This location also helped us recruit locals who were traveling or going to work at the airport. Similar to the paper prototype study, we received permission and support from Sound Transit prior to conducting this study.

The study station was in an area next to the light rail ticket vending machines, which made us highly visible, but out of the way of those who would not want to participate, see Figure 4.

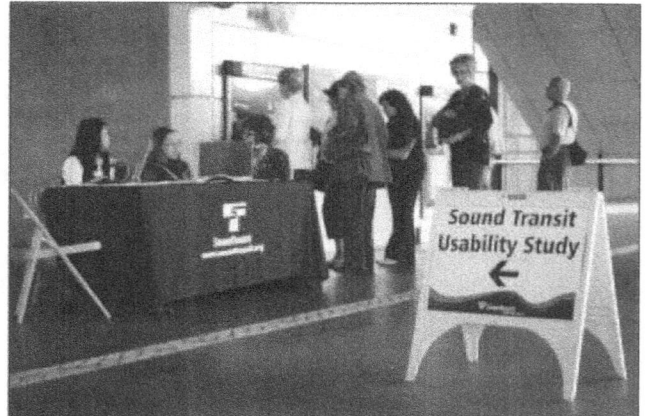

Figure 4 Choosing a site located next to transit ticket vending machines at the airport made it easy to recruit participants.

4.4 Roles and Responsibilities

Like the paper prototype study, the research team for this study included both researchers from Anthro-Tech and Sound Transit. In order to maximize our time, conduct sessions with as many participants as possible, and capture data efficiently, we divided the responsibilities of recruiting, facilitating, and note taking between the four-member research team. Three of the four team members facilitated the studies with users, while the remaining team member acted as a dedicated note taker who would record notes relayed to them by the facilitators into a spreadsheet.

Having a dedicated note taker was beneficial because it maximized efficiencies. In between sessions, each facilitator could debrief and share their findings with the note taker, who would then record the information and start to analyze the data. Then that facilitator was free to prepare for the next participant. Meanwhile the other facilitators were recruiting users or conducting sessions.

4.5 Recruiting

We recruited participants by directly approaching people in the station and by asking those who came to us to ask for information (sometimes about the study, but more often about trip or fare information). We asked participants if they had a mobile phone with Internet access and screened out those who did not. For their participation, we offered all-day light rail passes as honoraria.

4.6 Conducting the Study

After consenting to participate and be recorded, participants completed a written pre-test questionnaire while the facilitators set-up the participant's phone on the testing sled and adjusted the cameras to record the session. During the study, the participant was asked to complete several scenarios similar to the ones used in the paper prototype study. They were asked to complete the scenarios on their phones using think-aloud protocol. For more information about the participants, see Table 2 below.

Table 2 Breakdown of participants in the interactive prototype field study (*n* = 13)

	# of Participants
Male	7
Female	6
Phone Ownership	
iPhone	10
Android	1
Other smartphone	2
Transit Use Frequency	
More than 1 time a day	2
Daily	2
Weekly	3
Less than once a month	2
Less than once a year	4

4.7 Analyzing Data

Between sessions, the note taker conducted preliminary analysis and grouped similar findings and themes. At the end of the day, the team debriefed to review the preliminary analysis, generated additional findings, and developed a prioritized list of changes that needed to be made to the site. This list was shared with the development team to review, prioritize, and implement.

5. LESSONS LEARNED

The two field studies were critical to the design and development of the new mobile site. Each study had different goals and designs, but together they provide several key takeaways that can be helpful for others conducting field studies.

5.1 Field Studies Can Make Recruiting Easier

Conducting research in the field made it easier to recruit participants. Being at stations and on transit ensured that we could find participants who were actual users of Sound Transit's services. Had we conducted only a lab study, our visitor user group would have been challenging to recruit, not because they're rare, but because they're only temporarily in the area. In the field we were easily able to find visitors to recruit for our studies.

Choosing an appropriate site to conduct field studies was key to the success of our studies. Since participants were recruited opportunistically and not scheduled in advance, we needed to design a study that would maximize our chances of finding willing participants. We chose sites where we could recruit a captive audience, i.e., an audience who had the ability and opportunity to participate in a study and did not have competing obligations. People at the airport and riding on buses had free time and were willing to take part in a study.

5.2 Combine Field Studies with Lab Studies to Leverage the Recruiting Strengths of Both

The recruiting criteria for the field studies included finding participation across the user groups, but also across types of phones. We anticipated that it would be difficult to find users with internet-enabled feature phones in the field. Therefore, we complemented the fieldwork with one day of lab usability testing to recruit and schedule these users in advance.

5.3 Careful Planning is Key to Success

Field studies can be logistically complex, which is why careful planning and preparation is key. The success of these studies hinged on careful logistical planning, preparing the research team, and developing tools that were suitable for the field.

We needed to plan time to get the appropriate clearances to conduct studies on Sound Transit property, have the client approve study materials, and obtain honoraria. Staying on top of these administrative details ahead made sure we could conduct the studies as planned.

Also, both of our studies needed to take place in half of a day, so the research team needed to be well prepared. Preparation included getting everyone on the research team familiar with the prototype, walking through a full study, and making changes to the materials based on feedback from the walkthroughs.

We spent time developing study materials and creating research tools for the field. Creating paper prototypes are beneficial for trying out a design and iterating it based on user feedback prior to moving forward with coding and development. However, creating a paper prototype that was field-friendly required additional assembly and preparation. For both studies, we developed alternative, shorter consent forms and questionnaires to allow more time to evaluate the prototype. For the interactive prototype study, we researched, designed, iterated, and fabricated the mobile testing sled. For this study, we also created a note taking spreadsheet that would make it easy for our dedicated note taker to catalog and analyze findings as the study progressed.

5.4 Provide Different Options to Participants

In our paper prototype study, we presented potential participants with two options to participate: a short five minute study with fewer questions and scenarios in exchange for a transit ticket, or a longer 15-minute study in exchange for a gift card. We provided two alternatives to acknowledge that while we may have a captive audience on transit, some people may only have a short amount of time to participate. Presenting two study options allowed us to reach more participants than we might have otherwise.

5.5 Involve Clients as Researchers

Anthro-Tech helps organizations embrace user-centered design and bring these techniques into their existing processes. Including clients in research is key. Sound Transit staff played a critical role on the research team. They provided subject matter expertise on the intricacies of transit, provided input and feedback on design concepts and helped design the scenarios and study materials. Being involved with the research, helped Sound Transit staff effectively communicate design decisions to the development team and advocate for user-centered design to project stakeholders. The staff were also key in helping to execute the recommendations and make decisions about implementing the mobile experience of the site.

5.6 Collect Feedback on the Broader Rider Experience

Though the field studies focused on the design of the mobile web site, the research yielded many findings about the broader transit experience. Findings included users impressions about the experience of riding the bus or train, what information they seek when they first arrive at the airport, and how they experience transit and transit tools in their hometowns. We may not have learned about these things if we only conducted lab studies. Ultimately, the field studies broadened the focus of inquiry to look at the end-to-end experience, not just the online experience. These findings are helping the organization look beyond the online experience and consider the impact of their stations, signage, vehicles, and beyond.

6. IMPACT BEYOND MOBILE

While the results of both field studies helped to validate and refine the mobile design concepts, the studies had additional impact beyond the mobile site.

First, the studies helped uncover design opportunities for the desktop site in addition to mobile. We learned that users of the mobile site use and value location-based and context-aware transit information, such as stop-specific information and trip planning. Users were also interested in having location and context aware features on the desktop site. As a result, Sound Transit is in the process of porting some of the features developed for the mobile experience back to the desktop site.

Second, the studies have helped the Sound Transit understand the broader transit experiences of their riders. Involving employees in the research and sharing rider experiences have encouraged Sound Transit to include user-centered design in additional areas such as signage and ticket vending machines.

Finally, the results of these studies have helped Sound Transit become recognized as a leader and model for other government organizations in the region in employing user-centered design methods to create better experiences for their customers.

7. CONCLUSION

Many organizations share Sound Transit's goal to create a compelling mobile experience that complements the experience of their desktop site. With the increasing ubiquity of mobile devices and applications, designers and researchers need methods that help them create products for mobile users, and in particular, methods for studying mobile use in the field. Our experience report shows how Anthro-Tech uses field studies to drive mobile product development and create lasting impacts.

8. ACKNOWLEDGMENTS

We are grateful for the opportunity to collaborate with the Sound Transit team on this research especially De Meyers and Jaime Vogt. Their involvement in these studies and commitment to making data-driven and customer-centric improvements led the way.

9. REFERENCES

[1] Axure: Interactive Wireframe and Software Mockup Tool: *http://www.axure.com*. Accessed: 2012-07-12.

[2] Boren, T. and Ramey, J. 2000. Thinking aloud: Reconciling theory and practice. *Professional Communication, IEEE* .... (2000).

[3] Field Study: *http://www.usabilitybok.org/field-study*. Accessed: 2011-07-12.

[4] MOD 1000: Measuring Usability: *http://www.measuringusability.com/products/mod1000*. Accessed: 2012-07-12.

[5] Making an aluminum mobile device camera sled: 2011. *http://gwdesign.tumblr.com/post/5019128889/making-an-aluminum-mobile-device-camera-sled*. Accessed: 2012-07-12.

[6] Mobile Usability Testing Rig for m.cdlib: 2011. *http://www.cdlib.org/cdlinfo/2011/02/15/mobile-usability-testing-rig-for-m-cdlib/* . Accessed: 2012-07-12.

[7] Rosenbaum, S. and Kantner, L. 2007. Field usability testing: method, not compromise. *International Professional Communication Conference 2007* (Seattle, WA, 2007).

[8] Schusteritsch, R., Wei, C.Y. and LaRosa, M. 2007. Towards the perfect infrastructure for usability testing on mobile devices. *CHI '07 extended abstracts on Human factors in computing systems - CHI '07* (New York, New York, USA, Apr. 2007), 1839.

[9] Smith, A. 2012. *17% of cell phone owners do most of their online browsing on their phone, rather than a computer or other device.*

[10] Sound Transit: *http://www.soundtransit.org*. Accessed: 2012-07-12.

Adapting Grounded Theory to Construct a Taxonomy of Affect in Collaborative Online Chat

Taylor Jackson Scott, Katie Kuksenok, Daniel Perry
Michael Brooks, Ona Anicello, Cecilia Aragon
University of Washington
423 Sieg Hall
Seattle, WA 98195
{omni at, kuksenok at cs., dbperry at, mjbrooks at, oanicell at, aragon at}uw.edu

ABSTRACT

Distributed collaborative teams increasingly rely on online tools for interaction and communication in both social and task-oriented goals. Measuring and modeling these interactions along different dimensions can help understand, and better design for, distributed collaboration. Affect is one such dimension that can play a crucial role in the dynamics, creativity, and productivity of distributed groups. We contribute an adaptation of the grounded theory methodology as a flexible and extensible means for constructing a taxonomy of affect in text-based online communication. Such a taxonomy can serve as an analytic lens for the continued investigation of the role of affect in creative collaborative endeavors as mediated by communication technology. We describe our modified grounded theory approach and then validate our method by constructing a taxonomy with data from chat logs collected during a longitudinal study of a multi-cultural distributed scientific collaboration.

Categories and Subject Descriptors

K.4.3 [**Computers and Society**]: Organizational impacts – *Computer-supported collaborative work.*

General Terms

Human Factors, Theory

Keywords

Grounded theory, affect, collaboration, taxonomy, text-based communication, computer-mediated communication

1. INTRODUCTION

In a variety of both personal and work settings, communication technologies support distributed groups that rely heavily on text-based forms of communication to achieve their collective goals [3, 5, 12, 17, 22]. As a result of the widespread adoption of these ubiquitous and rapidly changing communications tools, a significant portion of research in related fields has focused on their design and usage.

Mehlenbacher's assessment and history of ACM SIGDOC has noted that the field of communication design has expanded to include numerous diverse research areas such as human-computer interaction, computer-mediated communication, interaction design, and collaborative systems. These areas are "united by a common interest in the relationship between text and technology" [20].

The role of communication technologies in creative, distributed collaborations has been of particular interest in creativity research [3, 9, 13]. Recently, Aragon et al. investigated how to foster collaborative creativity in diverse online communities such as scientific researchers and children learning to program [2]. *Affect*– the experience of feeling or emotion–plays a crucial role in these types of creative collaborations, especially influencing communication between group members [3, 12, 15, 17]. As groups work, conversations can range from excitement and confusion to frustration and annoyance, as well as a wide range of other affective states. To investigate this link between affect and the rapidly evolving communication-supporting technologies that shape social dynamics, we have developed a method for constructing a taxonomy of affect to be used as an analytic tool to investigate online text-based communication.

First, we will discuss the increasingly pervasive presence of text-based forms of communication in work practices, as well as the role of affect in the way that this communication is carried out. Second, we will provide an overview of the traditional Strauss and Corbin method for construction of grounded theory that is widely used in the fields of human-computer interaction and design of communication, often in adaptations of grounded methods to alternative analytic ends. This will provide the necessary background for presenting our own adaptation of this method in order to develop a taxonomy of affect in text-based communication. As additional validation of the adapted grounded theory method presented, we will discuss how our taxonomy has been deployed for the coding of chat log data, and how this will support our future research in this area.

2. BACKGROUND

During face-to-face meetings in which the members of a collaborative team are co-located in both space and time, both verbal and nonverbal physical cues play an important role in the way that communication is carried out and processed by the members of the group [16, 17]. However, with the widespread growth in the last few decades of technologies that enable new and increasingly robust modes of remote communication, collaboration is now just as likely to take place between members of a distributed group that do not benefit from the affordances of face-to-face communication [17]. A large portion of this communication takes the form of text, including emails, text messages, and instant messaging chats. These online, text-based forms of communication have become ubiquitous and constitute one of the most important means of contact between members of many distributed groups.

Synchronous online chat differs from other online text-based communication media, such as email, in several significant ways. Since conversations can take place in real time, they capture some of the synchronicity that is associated with face-to-face or voice communication. This synchronicity can greatly enhance the effectiveness and efficiency of this mode of communication by allowing for real-time interaction. However, unlike other real-time modes of communication, text-based chat also has benefits associated with asynchronous communication. Messages can be replied to at the convenience of the correspondents or as dictated by the circumstances of the tasks being performed. Additionally, all of the messages can be logged, providing a persistent record of the conversation. In these regards, this kind of text-based online chat can offer positive aspects of both synchronous and asynchronous forms of communication.

The trace created by using text-based chat communication to mediate creative problem solving can be studied to better understand collaboration. Affect and mood influence creative performance both in individual and collaborative environments [1, 13, 26]. Here, we use Russ's definition of *affect*, 'a feeling or emotion as distinct from cognition' [26]; affect is thus more pervasive than the interrupting neurophysiological experiences of emotions [21]. The expression of affect still plays an important role in these text-based forms of communication, but it takes on forms that are distinct from those found in face-to-face communication [22]. Affect-laden words, emoticons, special abbreviations, deformed spellings, punctuation, and interjections are just a few of the many ways in which the expression of affect has been adapted to text-based forms [15, 17, 18]. These signals, embedded in a detailed trace over time, can help measure the quality and quantity of affect expression in text-based communication between members of a distributed group. The utility of this measurement for further analyses depends on how robust the analytic lens is to the effects that the specific communication medium has on the character of affect expression.

Existing taxonomies of affect and emotion focus primarily on classifying psychophysiological responses to internal states and environmental factors [4, 11, 22]. There are several conflicting theoretical models of affect and emotion in multiple fields. Examples include the dimensional models of Russell [27], the emotion wheel of Plutchik [22], and the distinction between basic and complex emotions [4, 11]. Emotion is often measured via facial expression, vocal features, and body posture as the physical *expression* of emotion (rather than focusing on internal *state*) [10].

Researchers interested in understanding how we express and perceive emotions rely primarily on analyzing these physical forms of expression [10]. This is not possible when attempting to measure the expression of affect in text-based communication from a chat log; furthermore, the affordances of the medium can lead to individuals adjusting communication practices to express affect via text in ways that they would not do using the spoken word and thus are not well-accounted for in existing taxonomies. Our work bridges the gap between research that considers the measurement of affect, and the design of communication media that can fundamentally shape human expression.

3. OVERVIEW OF GROUNDED THEORY
The grounded theory (GT) method is traditionally described as "a qualitative research method that uses a systematic set of procedures to develop an inductively derived grounded theory about a phenomenon" [8]. The goal of this method is to generate a theory that emerges from the data being comparatively analyzed, rather than the application of an existing theory to answer a research question [8, 14]. The method is especially well suited to producing theories of interactions between different social units, and is widely used in many social science fields [6].

In order to analyze the data and build a theory that is grounded in it, Strauss and Corbin suggest three types of coding activities – open, axial, and selective [8]. While they are generally carried out in sequence, they are also often used iteratively as the research progresses, taking advantage of the emergent and reflexive properties of this method [6]. These procedures form the core of this methodological approach and are the main processes by which the data is used to generate a theoretical framework.

3.1 Open Coding
During open coding, text data, such as field notes or interview transcripts, is examined line by line, the main concepts and categories are identified, and their properties and dimensions are initially captured through the use of memos that discuss the researchers' ideas behind the codes. The concepts captured in these memos can be seen as the core units of the theory being developed. The similarities and differences between data points are examined, then named and recorded in the memos. This phase of coding is an open process during which all pieces of data are of interest to the researcher, and few if any restrictions are placed on what data gets coded and how it is conceptualized.

3.2 Axial Coding
During axial coding, categories, concepts, and codes are related to one another by linking them around the axis of a single category at the level of their properties and dimensions. In order to understand how these categories and codes relate to one another, Corbin and Strauss suggest the use of a "paradigm model" that takes into consideration the relationships between conditions, context, actions/interactions, and consequences. The basic idea of this model is to systematically propose linkages between these aspects and then look back to the data for validation. This paradigmatic model is then used to link sub-categories with their respective categories in a way that reveals an underlying structure of the codes produced during open coding. Generally, axial coding proceeds until a level of "theoretical saturation" is reached whereby gathering or examining new data does not lead to the emergence of substantially new structure.

3.3 Selective Coding
The first major goal of selective coding is the formulation of a core variable or category to which all other categories and codes can be related. At this point, open and axial coding processes cease, and only those categories and variables that can be related to this core variable continue to be coded as the formulation of the theory proceeds. Strauss and Corbin point out that this core category should be able to explain variation as well as contradictory evidence found in the data. The core variable represents a type of narrative that is grounded in the data by which the categories identified during axial coding are linked.

Finally, as a means of refining the theory produced through the selective coding process, Strauss and Corbin suggest that the researcher review the theory to check for internal validity and logic; attempt to account for underdeveloped categories; eliminate any excess categories; and to validate the theory (as might be accomplished through a high-level comparison with the original data).

3.4 Grounded Theory in Context

Qualitative data analysis methods grounded in data enable the discovery of emergent themes, rather than focus empirical investigation on pre-specified hypotheses. These methods have been critical in constructing and refining theories of social phenomena, including in human-computer interaction topics. Schoonewille et al. used GT to better model and understand developer comprehension of software documentation and then validated their model using a cognitive theory of multimedia [29]. Power and Moynihan used an adapted GT approach in constructing a framework to explain the situational variety of styles of requirement documentation, as well as a three-part scheme for classifying these requirements that was a direct result of their GT coding [24]. Finally, Razavi and Iverson produced a theory of end-user information sharing behavior in a personal learning space using grounded theory methods that were enacted in a similar fashion to our own [25].

In research of human interaction with information systems, grounded theory methods are used not only for construction of a theory, or as part of a mixed-method case-study approach, but also as a means to refine an initially hypothesized theory [19, 28]. In this case, the initial theory can be modified, refined, or further informed by themes that emerge from the application of open, axial, or selective coding to qualitative data. Our adaptation of this approach, on the other hand, takes the route of treating GT as an intermediate analytic step that results in a taxonomy to be used in subsequent analyses. Our expectations for this taxonomy extend beyond the construction of a theory, including, for instance, the need to automatically detect instances of codes in a large-scale dataset and perform statistical analyses. The goal of using this taxonomy for a purpose not typically part of the GT method led to the adaptations we propose.

The primary characteristic of the analytic processes of GT is closeness to the data. In studying affect in text-based communication, nuanced means of communicating and expressing affect are of key interest to research, and pose challenges to existing taxonomies of affect which are not amenable to the peculiarities of text-based, distributed expression [4, 10, 11, 22]. Not only do these taxonomies rely on implicit physical characteristics not present in text for classification, they are also not ideal for capturing subtle affective states such as confusion or agreement. These other forms of affect are just as important as classical categories of emotion when attempting to account for all of the factors contributing to the dynamics of the group. The capacity to systematically extract previously unacknowledged themes is inherent in the GT methodology and is crucial in this task. Nevertheless, the direct application of GT traditionally results in a theory or model of the data, which is not the purpose for which we want to use these methodologies.

4. CONSTRUCTING OUR TAXONOMY

Our dataset is comprised of four years of chat logs created by the cross-cultural collaboration among members of the Nearby Supernova Factory (SNfactory), an astrophysics collaboration of approximately 30 core members; about half of the scientists are located in the U.S. and the other half in France. These scientists are studying Type Ia supernovae, a specific type of stellar explosions that have a consistent brightness, allowing their

distances to be effectively measured over time and thus trace the expansion history of the universe. The group operates their telescope remotely three nights per week; during such operation, numerous decisions must be made quickly and collaboratively despite the fact that many of the team members have never met each other and come from differing cultural backgrounds. Chat is the team's primary means of communication during telescope operation [2].

These situational factors shape the team members' expression of affect as they carry out their work and communicate with each other. Over the four-year span of our chat log, conversations range over excitement at new findings, frustration with faulty software or hardware, confusion with incoming data, and many other affective states. There are a total of 485,045 chat messages, many produced by automated programs ("bots") using the chat protocol to relay changes in the state of the world (sunrise/sunset; weather; telescope settings, etc.). One of the primary concerns when developing our taxonomy was to account for the nuanced and specific ways that affect is communicated and expressed in a text-based medium. We found that many existing taxonomies were created to characterize affect predicated on implicit physical representations such as facial expressions or tonal inflection [4, 10, 11, 22]. This stands in stark contrast to much of the expression of affect in text-based communication which relies heavily on explicit statements of emotion and text features such as emoticons and punctuation [15, 22]. Our application of GT was specifically intended to develop and refine a taxonomy that captured these types of affective expressions. Although this construction of a taxonomy for coding is not a typical use of GT, an appreciation for the method's closeness to the data as well as the method's ability to identify and group themes made it an ideal candidate for adaptation to our needs. Whereas the codes generated and applied during grounded theory are generally used to provide structure and inform the development of a theory, we were specifically refining these codes into a taxonomy that could be used as a coding scheme in its own right for the further analysis of our data.

During traditional open coding, data is initially organized into concepts and themes [3]. Using this approach, we explored the data in an unrestricted manner through a careful line-by-line reading of portions of the chat logs. Given that this stage of the GT method is specifically geared towards openness, the need for adaptation was minimal. We initially coded anything and everything that was of interest, not just affect, but also accounted for instances of creativity, collaboration, and other events significant to the group. Due to the scale of our data, it was not possible to perform open coding on the entirety of the data set, so we strategically sampled areas that contained high volumes of interaction between the participants in order to maximize our chances of finding significant and interesting phenomena.

Axial coding enabled us to focus the scope of what we would account for in our taxonomy. In addition to this substantive dimension, we also began to explore the inclusion of two other separate axes. As we related the instances of affective expression to one another, we found it useful to note their intensity (high or low) as well as their valence (positive, neutral, or negative) as is commonly done in sentiment analysis. These measures provided an additional fine-grained characterization of our substantive codes as well as a means to resolve ambiguities when applying codes that were not explicitly positive or negative depending on the context. Along with the substantive axis, the intensity and valence axes formed the overall paradigmatic model by which the codes produced during open coding were grouped and refined around a central set of codes.

Selective coding involves the formulation of a core variable or category to which all other categories and codes can be related to in a sufficiently significant way to be considered a substantial part of the final theory being developed [8]. For us, this core variable took the form of an 'affect' category to which all of our codes in the taxonomy were being related. One primary difference between the traditional GT approach and ours was that we still continued an iterative approach to open and axial coding during our selective coding. This was done because through our selective coding process, we continued to encounter new and significant points of interest in our data. As these new codes were identified and defined, they were combined into the selective coding process as part of our attempt to reach the theoretical saturation that generally signifies the completion of this phase in traditional GT [14]. This selective coding process was also an opportunity to explore the internal validity of our taxonomy by evaluating how well it accounted for affective expressions in our data.

4.1 Plutchik's Wheel of Emotion

After selectively coding our data, we were left with a core category (affect) to which we had related all of our other variables in order to form a theoretical framework that could account for affective expression encountered during open coding. We had also begun the process of validating, expanding, and trimming our codes through the iterative application of our categories to the data in order to check the internal validity of our coding scheme and the resulting taxonomy. At this point in the grounded theory process, it is generally accepted that relevant literature will be reviewed in order to better situate the emerging theoretical model within the existing body of research in that area [14]. This step in the grounded theory method was well suited to the creation of a taxonomy of affect without replacing or reinventing existing taxonomies. We hoped to account for the shortcomings of taxonomies that were not specifically capable of addressing the variations of affect expression that are present in text-based communication mediated by online chat.

Through our review of existing taxonomies of affect and emotion, we found that Plutchik's Wheel of Emotion was closely aligned with what we had been seeing and coding for in our data. Although we have been careful to make a distinction between affect and emotion, they are still closely related. In fact, not only were there numerous codes in our taxonomy that were not present in the Plutchik wheel, there are several emotions from Plutchik that were not in the taxonomy we had created but were still found to be applicable to our own data. Additionally, the inclusion of the Plutchik emotions also ensures that our own work builds on and extends existing theories of affect and emotion.

Ultimately, the application of this adapted grounded theory approach was our solution to the problem of attempting to translate a very large body of work on affect and emotion into a more appropriate and useful analytic lens. This lens can then be used to examine the specific types of affective expression present in our data because it accounts for the distinct ways in which these expressions are molded by the text-based medium.

5. RESULTS

5.1 Taxonomy in Use

During several months, five members of our research team iterated on developing a coding scheme as part of the adapted grounded process we have described. The resulting taxonomy includes substantive codes reflecting affect state expression (listed in Figure 2 below), as well as valence codes relating to how

time	speaker	message
05:58:41	Alice	ok, so where was the f***ing SN on the image? #1: interest / anger / high / negative #2: annoyance / confusion / low / negative #3: interest / frustration / high / negative
05:58:55	Alice	was it the bright blob? #1: interest / anger / high / negative #2: considering / low / negative #3: interest / neutral
05:59:03	Ben	5876 absorption is much wider than the H alpha in v space #1, #2, #3: no affect
05:59:18	Ben	Oh hmmm. #1, #2, #3: considering / neutral
05:59:28	Ben	Lemme see what [the] coordinates were... #1, #2, #3: no affect
06:13:07	Charlie	is it "well-developed"? #1: interest / neutral
06:13:18	Alice	Should be an interesting experiment. #1, #2: anticipation / low / positive #3: interest / neutral
06:13:19	Dana	yes #1, #3: agreement / neutral #2: no affect
06:13:20	Dana	big!! #1: excitement / agreement / high / positive #2, #3: excitement / low / positive

Figure 1. Two examples of conversations from our dataset, with anonymized speaker names and excluding any identifying detail. Each segment was coded by three members of the research team; their annotations are shown below each line.

positive, negative, or neutral a message is overall, and intensity codes for low or high expression intensity (where 'neutral' valence does not call for an intensity code). Substantive codes are not mutually exclusive, and can be combined with valence and intensity labels for greater flexibility. For example, a sarcastic comment can express nuanced affect in this context, including "frustration/negative/high" during particularly stressful periods, and "amusement/positive/low" during less demanding times (see Figure 1 above for examples).

Messages could also be coded as "no affect" to systematically distinguish messages that had been coded and identified as expressing no identifiable affective state, and those which were yet to be coded. We coded approximately 5% of the total chat log data with the final taxonomy, utilizing a team of three primary coders and five additional coders, all part of the research team. For several weeks, coders focused on applying substantive codes and 'no affect,' and then the additional intensity and valence axes were added to the affective coding scheme. A summary of how many messages were coded, and by how many coders, is shown in Table 1. Of 35,614 messages coded, 15,942 (45%) were coded as 'no affect' by at least one person – although, as the second example in Figure 1 shows, 'no affect' can be plausibly incident with more neutral affect codes, depending on interpretation.

In many cases, multiple substantive codes, those codes which capture the nature and meaning of a message, may apply, such as annoyance and frustration applying to these three messages, sent by the same person: "Did I see a bunch of = vs == in there??? / WHAT / WHO DID THAT". The theoretic basis of the Plutchik taxonomy includes relationships between codes that are more or

Figure 2 taxonomy table:

Less Intense → More Intense		
pride / serenity	amusement / joy	ecstasy
agreement / acceptance	supportive / trust	gratitude / admiration
tired / distraction	disbelief / surprise	amazement
considering / interest	relief / anticipation	excitement / vigilance
apologetic / pensiveness	embarrassment / sadness	grief
apathy / boredom	disgust	frustration
disagreement / apprehension	confusion / fear	terror
annoyance	impatience / anger	rage

Figure 2. Our taxonomy, arranged from less to more (left to right) intense affect expression, and with more typically positively-charged instances at the top and more typically negatively-charged at the bottom, with many in the middle, such as 'interest,' capable of being expressed in a positive as well as negative context.

less intense variants of one another (e.g. apprehension/fear/terror). Additionally, multiple substantive codes can be used simultaneously, such as "anger / confusion / low / negative" expressed in a conversation about error-prone software Example messages where this expressiveness is especially useful are included in Figure 1. Of the messages coded, 1,599 were coded with multiple substantive codes simultaneously by at least one coder (129 were coded with more than two substantive codes by at least one coder).

This process took several months, and leveraged a tool for coding chat logs that was developed within our team (shown in Figure 3). The tool was developed over the course of a year, simultaneously with the creation of the taxonomy, to make the coding of chat logs faster and easier, and coded data more accessible for analysis (via storage in a central relational database and a carefully designed user interface). We plan to release this tool to the public in the near future.

Table 1. Summary of coding progress using the included taxonomy. This table shows the number of messages coded with substantive affect codes only, the number of messages coded along all three axes, and the distributions of coding across different numbers of independent coders.

#coders	#messages coded with substantive codes or 'no affect'	#messages coded with substantive codes, valence, and intensity
1	18,843	8,399
2	5,274	1,073
3	2,704	403
>3	537	17
all	27,344 (5.64%)	9,892 (2%)

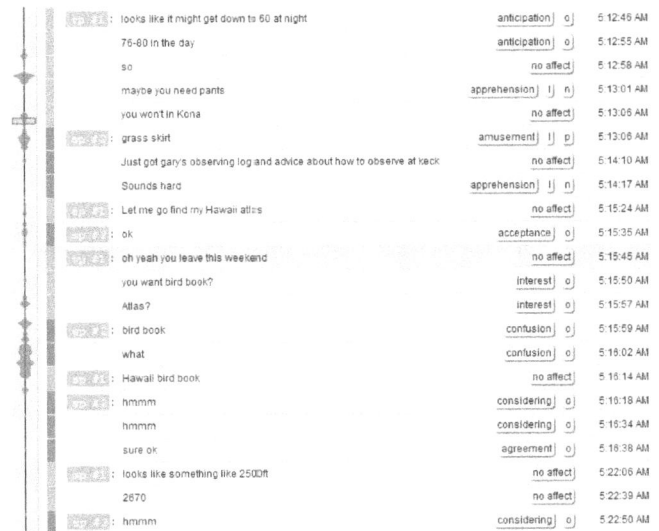

Figure 3. A screenshot of the coding tool, developed by the team, as seen by an individual coder applying codes. ("o" is neutral, "l" and "h" are low and high intensity, and "n" and "p" indicate negative and positive valence)

5.2 Inter-Rater Reliability

Although the grounded methodology itself does not always call for the calculation of inter-rater reliability, verifying that human annotators can reliably apply codes validates the use of a grounded taxonomy for further analytic steps. However, the construction of this taxonomy does not necessarily produce one that is non-exclusive. Applying multiple codes at once, while necessary for capturing nuanced dimensions of affect expression, for example, violates one typical assumption of reliability metrics: the exclusivity of codes.

Cohen's kappa [7] and other widely used reliability metrics that calculate the reliability based on *observed agreement* to *chance agreement* tend to assume exclusive application of codes. The main problem with such an application is that when coders can apply multiple codes per item, the standard estimate of the probability of chance agreement becomes erroneous (underestimating the true probability). We analyzed our coded data using a modified version of the kappa statistic, which overcomes the problem of non-exclusive code application through a Monte Carlo simulation

We first extended the *observed agreement* term to work for non-exclusive codes. We defined agreement about a particular code on a single chat message in the following way: if more than half of the people who coded the message said that the code was present, then they agree. If all of them said that the code was absent, then they also agree. Any other combination is disagreement. For comparison, traditional kappa calculations, which deal with only two coders, also consider the coders to be in agreement when they chose the same rating. We used this definition of agreement because our coders had many non-exclusive codes available, and because *not* using a code on a specific message does not strongly imply that the coder disagrees with that code, only that it was less appropriate than other codes available (e.g. *rage, annoyance,* and *fear* may co-occur).

Estimating the probability of coders agreeing by chance is more complex. Since chat messages may have variable numbers of coders, and coders may choose to apply variable numbers of codes, it is difficult to compute the probability of chance agreement directly. We developed an estimate of the probability of chance agreement based on a Monte Carlo method. We first calculate the probability of choosing each code for each individual coder, and the probability of applying specific numbers of codes for each individual coder. This gives us a profile of each coder's general behavior, independent of which chat message is being coded.

Next, we randomly simulate ratings for a very large number of messages. For each message we are simulating, we decide which coders are going to rate it, based on the proportion of messages rated by those coders in the dataset. Then, for each of those coders, we randomly choose a number of codes to apply, sampling from the distribution we already calculated for that coder. Each of these codes is randomly selected from the coder's prior distribution of code choices. Counting the number of these simulated messages where agreement occurred allows us to estimate the probability of random agreement. This approximates the typical measure of chance agreement in the two-rater exclusive-code case, but generalizes to our more heterogeneous data. The Monte Carlo simulation continues until all probability estimates are stable to within 0.0001, generally requiring about 2 million messages to be simulated.

To finally calculate this modified kappa, we divide the difference between the rates of observed and chance agreement by the difference between one and the rate of chance agreement [7]. Some example reliability measures over our own data are shown below in Table 2.

Table 2. The observed and chance agreements, and resulting modified-kappa reliability scores, for 6 of the most common codes in our taxonomy over a 35k message dataset

Code	Obs. % Agreement	Prob. Chance Agreement	Kappa
interest	0.925	0.609	0.808
amusement	0.933	0.827	0.611
considering	0.931	0.864	0.490
agreement	0.954	0.909	0.491
confusion	0.906	0.755	0.615
annoyance	0.929	0.693	0.770

6. DISCUSSION

The method that we have applied to this specific problem area and data set is based on embracing the qualitative process. The validation or evaluation of this method poses several key limitations that we hope to address. We also frame the work that we have completed thus far in the context of a larger research agenda, with the possibility of extending our method to account for other data sets and phenomena not specific to affect.

6.1 Limitations

Given the size of the data set that we are coding (485,045 messages), it is reasonable to assume that there could very well be unique instances of affective expression that we have not yet encountered during the grounded theory coding process itself, or the subsequent coding of our data with the resulting taxonomy. Although we have tried to anticipate and account for this not only through rigorous sampling of the data, but also through the integration of the Plutchik taxonomy with our own in order to make it more robust and flexible; we acknowledge that there may be affect in the data that is not specifically accounted for in our taxonomy. Therefore, we do not claim that our taxonomy is

exhaustive, but only that it has thus far successfully accounted for the affective content we have encountered.

In both formulation and application, the coding scheme is not comprised of mutually exclusive codes. While it is often the case when creating or using a coding scheme to have only one specific code that is applicable to any given piece of data, we found this restriction too limiting in effectively capturing the variety and subtlety of the affective content that we sought to identify in our data. The flexibility of combining concepts afforded by non-mutually-exclusive coding, such as in open coding, is in tension with analytically-motivated exclusive coding along each dimension, typical to axial coding. The decision to favor the flexibility of non-mutually-exclusive codes influences the interpretation of coded data. For instance, for a given line of chat, if code A is applied, but not code B, code B might still have been justifiable, but subjectively less than A. If one coder applies A and B, and another only A, it is a different sort of disagreement than if one of the coders only applied code C. There are also consequences for the measurement of inter-rater reliability. Standard formulations of reliability metrics are not strictly applicable in this case; a modified kappa methodology appropriate here was detailed in section 5.2.

Despite the difficulties introduced by foregoing exclusivity in coding, this decision grants the taxonomy more expressive power. There are instances when a single line might share two or more codes (such as anger, frustration, and annoyance all occurring simultaneously). Because these affective states often co-occur, we find it valuable from an analytical standpoint to retain access to this granularity of coding. We deliberately chose to avoid flattening the instances of codes occurring in our data by collapsing several co-occurring codes into a single unified code. It was more practical to allow the co-incidence of codes, such as anger and frustration, or surprise and frustration, rather than increasing the taxonomy, potentially combinatorially, in response to the complexities of affect expression in chat.

Finally, we constructed this taxonomy to answer specific questions about the role of affective expression in the dynamics of a particular distributed collaborative team (SNfactory). Thus far, we have not attempted to apply it to another corpus of chat logs or other forms of text-based communication. We plan to address these limitations through our future research which will explore the usefulness of this taxonomy for other chat data sets.

6.2 Future Work

The method described here resulted in the construction of a robust taxonomy of affect that is firmly grounded in our data set and builds on a large body of related work. Unlike traditional grounded theory approaches, our method focuses on using aspects of the methodology that maintain closeness to emergent themes in the data to construct an analytic lens both sufficient for our data and flexible enough to be used in other types of investigation. As Charmaz notes, even finished grounded theories are somewhat open-ended and the constructions of concepts are able to shape both the process and the final product [6]. We expect that this will be reflected in the ongoing construction and refinement of this taxonomy as we continue to apply it to our data; not only through our own reflexive engagement with our taxonomy, but also through the dialectic relationship between the taxonomy and the data it was derived from.

We intend to further validate our approach by utilizing the taxonomy to code other data sets for affective content. This would provide the opportunity to see how well it captures and accounts for this property more generally. We can then compare inter-rater reliability scores to address performance between the two corpora. It would be particularly interesting to investigate how appropriate this taxonomy is for a wider variety of text corpora. Additionally, since affect is only one example of the phenomena that play an important role in collaborations, it would also be appropriate to apply the same methodological approach to the construction of a taxonomy for some property other than affect. This could be achieved through a reiteration of the adapted grounded theory approach to our own data set, or to some other unique data set.

Understanding affect in collaborative work is an important topic that can reveal much about how communication is conducted via these types of real-world exchanges, as well as how we might design new technologies to support them. This work can also further the development of a model of how collaborative communication takes place and how it impacts group dynamics. The development of this adapted grounded theory approach and the construction of our taxonomy are not ends in and of themselves, but are rather first steps in a more comprehensive understanding of how the affective states of participants in distributed collaborations are related to the dynamics and productivity of these teams.

7. CONCLUSION

Our ongoing research on the role that affect plays in distributed group collaborations motivated the development of a taxonomy that accounts for the distinctive expression of affect that takes place in text-based online communication. We drew upon existing bodies of research on both emotion and computer-mediated communication to inform our approach, and ultimately used a novel adaptation of the grounded theory method to construct an appropriate taxonomy. We wanted to account for the nuanced and specific ways that affect is communicated and expressed in a text-based medium, and existing taxonomies of emotion were found to not be a good fit for this goal. This adapted grounded theory approach was our solution to the problem of attempting to translate a very large body of work on affect and emotion into a more appropriate and useful analytic lens that accurately reflected the phenomena of affect found in our data. The resulting taxonomy has been used to code a large corpus of chat logs collected during a longitudinal study of a distributed scientific collaboration. We hope that other researchers in this area will find both the method and the taxonomy we have presented to be of use in their own studies.

8. ACKNOWLEDGMENTS

We deeply appreciate the reviewers' careful reading of our work which greatly strengthened this paper, and we thank the scientists of the SNfactory collaboration. This work was funded in part by an NSF Graduate Research Fellowship in Computer Science.

9. REFERENCES

[1] Amabile, T.M., Barsade, S.G., Mueller, J.S., and Staw, B.M. 2005. Affect and Creativity at Work. *Administrative Science Quarterly 50*, 3 (September 1, 2005). 367-403.

[2] Aragon, C. R., Poon, S., et al. 2009. A tale of two online communities: fostering collaboration and creativity in scientists and children. In *Proceedings of the Seventh ACM Conference on Creativity and Cognition* (Berkeley, California, USA, 2009). C&C '09. ACM, New York, NY, 9-18.

[3] Aragon, C.R. and Williams, A. 2011. Collaborative creativity: a complex systems model with distributed affect. In *Proceedings of the 2011 Annual Conference on Human Factors in Computing Systems* (Vancouver, BC, Canada, 2011). CHI '11. ACM, New York, NY, 1875-1884.

[4] Barrett, L.F. 2006. Solving the Emotion Paradox: Categorization and the Experience of Emotion. *Personality and Social Psychology Review 10*, 1 (February 1, 2006). 20-46.

[5] Bullinger, A.C., Hallerstede, S.H., et al. 2010. Towards research collaboration – a taxonomy of social research network sites. In *Proceedings of the Sixteenth Americas Conference on Information Systems* (Lima, Peru, August, 2010). AMCIS '10 12-15.

[6] Charmaz, K. 2006. *Constructing grounded theory: A practical guide through qualitative analysis.* Sage Publications.

[7] Cohen, J. 1960. A Coefficient of Agreement for Nominal Scales. *Educational and Psychological Measurement 20*, 1 (April 1, 1960). 37-46.

[8] Corbin, J.M. and Strauss, A.L. 2008. *Basics of qualitative research: Techniques and procedures for developing grounded theory.* Sage Publications.

[9] Csikszentmihalyi, M., 1997. *Creativity: Flow and the psychology of discovery and invention.* New York: Harper Collins Publishers.

[10] De Silva, L.C., Miyasato, T., and Nakatsu, R. 1997. Facial emotion recognition using multi-modal information. In *Proceedings of 1997 International Conference on Information, Communications and Signal Processing.* ICICS '97. 397-401.

[11] Ekman, P. 1992. An argument for basic emotions. *Cognition & Emotion 6*, 3-4 (1992/05/01), 169-200.

[12] Fitzpatrick, G., Kaplan, S., and Mansfield, T. 1996. Physical spaces, virtual places and social worlds: a study of work in the virtual. In *Proceedings of the 1996 ACM Conference on Computer Supported Cooperative Work* (Boston, Massachusetts, USA, 1996). CSCW '96. ACM, New York, NY, 334-343.

[13] George, J.M. and Zhou, J. 2002. Understanding when bad moods foster creativity and good ones don't: The role of context and clarity of feelings. *Journal of Applied Psychology 87*, 4, 687-697.

[14] Glaser, B.G. and Strauss, A.L. 1967. *The discovery of grounded theory; strategies for qualitative research.* Aldine Pub. Co., Chicago.

[15] Hancock, J.T., Landrigan, C., and Silver, C. 2007. Expressing emotion in text-based communication. In *Proceedings of the SIGCHI Conference on Human Factors in Computing Systems* (San Jose, California, USA, 2007). CHI '07. ACM, New York, NY, 929-932.

[16] John-Steiner, V. 2000. *Creative collaboration.* Oxford: Oxford University Press.

[17] Kraut, R., Egido, C., and Galegher, J. 1988. Patterns of contact and communication in scientific research collaboration. In *Proceedings of the 1988 Conference on Computer-supported Cooperative Work* (Portland, Oregon, USA, 1988). CSCW '88. ACM, New York, NY, 1-12.

[18] Liu, H., Lieberman, H., and Selker, T. 2003. A model of textual affect sensing using real-world knowledge. In *Proceedings of the 8th International Conference on Intelligent Sser Interfaces* (Miami, Florida, USA, 2003). IUI '03. ACM, New York, NY, 125-132.

[19] Matavire, R. and Brown, I. 2008. Investigating the use of "Grounded Theory" in information systems research. In *Proceedings of the 2008 Annual Research Conference of the South African Institute of Computer Scientists and Information Technologists on IT research in Developing Countries: Riding the Wave of Technology* (Wilderness, South Africa, 2008). SAICSIT '08. ACM, New York, NY, 139-147.

[20] Mehlenbacher, B. 2011. The evolution of communication design: a brief history of the ACM SIGDOC. In *Proceedings of the 29th ACM International Conference on Design of Communication* (Pisa, Italy, 2011). SIGDOC '11. ACM, New York, NY, 249-256.

[21] Moore, B.S. and Isen, A.M. 1990. *Affect and social behavior*. Cambridge [England]: Cambridge University Press.

[22] O'Neill, J. and Martin, D. 2003. Text chat in action. In *Proceedings of the 2003 international ACM SIGGROUP Conference on Supporting Group Work* (Sanibel Island, Florida, USA, 2003). SIGGROUP '03. ACM, New York, NY, 40-49.

[23] Plutchik, R. 1980. A general psychoevolutionary theory of emotion. In *Emotion: Theory, Research, and Experience: Vol. 1. Theories of Emotion*, R. Plutchik and H. Kellerman Eds. Academic press, 3-33.

[24] Power, N. and Moynihan, T. 2003. A theory of requirements documentation situated in practice. In *Proceedings of the 21st Annual International Conference on Documentation* (San Francisco, CA, USA, 2003). SIGDOC '03. ACM, New York, NY, 86-92.

[25] Razavi, M.N. and Iverson, L. 2006. A grounded theory of information sharing behavior in a personal learning space. In *Proceedings of the 2006 20th Anniversary Conference on Computer Supported Cooperative Work* (Banff, Alberta, Canada, 2006). CSCW '06. ACM, New York, NY, 459-468.

[26] Russ, S.W. 1993. *Affect and creativity: the role of affect and play in the creative process*. L. Erlbaum Associates, Hillsdale, N.J.

[27] Russell, J.A. 1980. A circumplex model of affect. *Journal of Personality and Social Psychology 39*, 6, 1161-1178.

[28] Sarker, S., Lau, F., and Sahay, S. 2000. Using an adapted grounded theory approach for inductive theory building about virtual team development. *SIGMIS Database 32*, 1, 38-56.

[29] Schoonewille, H.H., Heijstek, W., et al. 2011. A cognitive perspective on developer comprehension of software design documentation. In *Proceedings of the 29th ACM International Conference on Design of Communication* (Pisa, Italy, 2011). SIGDOC '11. ACM, New York, NY, 211-218.

[30] Zhou, L. and Dongsong, Z. 2005. A heuristic approach to establishing punctuation convention in instant messaging. *Professional Communication, IEEE Transactions on 48*, 4, 391-400.

Short-Term Methodology for Long-Term Usability

David G. Novick, Baltazar Santaella, Aaron Cervantes, Carlos Andrade
Department of Computer Science
The University of Texas at El Paso
El Paso, TX 79968
+1 915-747-5480

novick@utep.edu, bsantaella@utep.edu, arcervantes@miners.utep.edu, candrade@gmail.com

ABSTRACT

Approaches to understanding usability of computer interfaces over the long term typically rely on longitudinal studies, which are limited in scope to the period of the experiment. In this study, we explore whether a non-longitudinal, cross-sectional approach can reliably detect useful differences in usability between novices and experts. Our approach takes a "snapshot" of usability problems and behaviors across a heterogeneous sample of users, ranging from novice to expert. Our analysis suggests that a cross-sectional methodology can distinguish between less experienced and more experienced users with respect to the kinds of applications that cause frustration, frequency of use of help, and whether the problem was solved. Our analysis also suggests that the method is poor at distinguishing causes of frustration and the overall distribution of types of solutions tried. The data also suggest that three months of use of an application is the most useful point at which to distinguish less-experienced from more-experienced users.

Categories and Subject Descriptors

H.5.2 [**Information Interfaces and Presentation**]: User Interfaces – *Evaluation/methodology, training, help, and documentation.*

Keywords

Usability, time, methodology

1. INTRODUCTION

In the last five years, the research community has turned increasing attention to the issue of usability over time, based on the insight that the problems encountered by experienced users of a user interface may not be the problems discovered by the new users who typically serve as subjects in usability tests. A special interest group at CHI 2007 [13] on capturing longitudinal usability was followed by a panel presentation at CHI 2008 [15] on the methodology of longitudinal usability data collection. CHI 2010 hosted a special interest group on best practices in longitudinal research [2]. And this year brought a workshop on theories, methods and case studies of longitudinal research [4]. Longitudinal studies have shown that, as users gain experience with a computer program, they encounter

different kinds of problems and try to solve these problems in different ways. And longitudinal methodologies address significant shortcomings relative to other methodologies for understanding usability over time. But they are inherently limited in scope, so to speak, to no more than the length of each study's period [16]. How, then, can people looking at longitudinal issues break past the time limits of longitudinal methodologies to study users' experiences over much longer periods of time?

In this paper, then, we review the development of methodologies for studying usability over time, looking at both longitudinal and cross-sectional methods. We review analytical frameworks for the study of long-term usability and discuss objections to cross-sectional approaches. We propose a methodology that uses a cross-sectional design and contemporaneous evaluation. We test this "snapshot" methodology using the natural experiment produced by people using computers in their everyday lives. We analyze the results of the study, with particular attention to seeing if the snapshot method can find differences between less-experienced and more-experienced users with respect to interaction behaviors such as use of help and abandonment of tasks. Finally, we discuss the implications of our results for understanding the time period in which users change from novices to experts and discuss the study's methodological limitations.

2. BACKGROUND

Longitudinal studies, which take place over time, contrast with cross-sectional studies, which take place at one point in time but with participants with different levels of experience. In other words, longitudinal studies can be seen as a within-subjects methodology and cross-sectional studies as a between-subjects methodology. With respect to longitudinal methodologies, two different methodological paradigms have been proposed. One paradigm [16] distinguishes: *micro* studies, which are typically short-term usability tests; *meso* studies, which look at users over a period of weeks or months; and *macro* studies, which look at users over years or even the program's entire life-cycle. An alternate paradigm [5] differentiates methodologies in terms of when the data are collected relative to the users' experience: repeated sampling studies, which use a pre-and a post-test; longitudinal studies, which collect multiple user experiences as they occur; and retrospective studies, which collect multiple user experiences from memory at the end of the study's period.

2.1 Medium-term studies

Researchers have reported successful several meso studies in recent years. The modern line of longitudinal research into usability of user interfaces begins with Mendoza and Novick's 2005 research on usability over time [7], which addressed the issue that usual usability testing may actually reveal problems of novice users and of learnability than of underlying problems that would frustrate experienced users. The study examined usability issues among middle-school teachers creating Web sites, for both the use of documentation and the underlying software, tracking the causes and extent of user frustration over eight weeks. The authors found that, over the eight weeks, the users' level of frustration dropped, the distribution of causes of frustration changed, and the users' responses to frustration episodes changed. These results suggested that the sorts of errors that are most prominently featured in conventional usability testing may not be significant over longer periods of time.

Subsequent meso studies included iPhone usability over a period of five weeks [3] and Web-based homework application over a semester [6]. The results of these studies reinforced the conclusion that that users' initial experiences with an application may not reliably predict their experiences in prolonged use.

2.2 Longer-term studies

But what about usability over longer periods of time? The necessary limitations of time and resources mean that few if any macro studies have been conducted [16]. Repeated sampling studies would be impractical, as researchers would have to conduct pre- and post-tests years apart, and would have data for only two time points for their efforts. Longitudinal studies would be equally impractical, as the researchers would have (a) to support a cohort of subjects over years, while the subjects may want to change to a different version or a different program, and (b) to continue the single study for years, perhaps with negative results. And retrospective studies, despite some evidence of effectiveness for medium-term time frames [16, 5, 12], are either relatively short-term or suffer from the distance of memory to the extent that the study seeks longer-term results. A study of the relative reliability of usability observation methodologies suggested that that retrospective approaches, such as interviews and surveys, provide less reliable views of users' problem-solving behaviors than do contemporaneous approaches such as participatory evaluation and direct observation [9].

Two proposed approaches attempt to address the problem of creating short-term methodologies for long-term usability. The Always-On+Adoption approach [1] in effect aims to reduce the time needed for a longitudinal study by speeding up the rate of initial use. While likely a useful technique for many applications, Always-On+Adoption can only reduce the overall time of the longitudinal study to the extent that it shortens the time of the users' early use. As a result, it may not produce enough speed-up to be practical for years-long macro studies, and results from this approach have not yet been reported. A second approach, UX Curve [11], is a retrospective methodology in which the user draws a curve that describes how the program's user experience has changed over time; while drawing the UX curve, the user explains the reasons behind the changes in the curve. UX Curve is similar to critical incident analysis but focuses explicitly on the temporal progression of the user experience. Using this approach enabled researchers to obtain qualitative experience data in two hours for six months of use of a program. But like critical incident analysis, UX Curve is limited by the effectiveness of the users' recall. Salience of memory may reflect the importance of incidents, but retrospective techniques appear to be less reliable than contemporaneous techniques [9] and, for really long-term studies, users may not be able to recall incidents that were truly critical from a design standpoint.

2.3 The "Snapshot" Approach

Given the impracticality of traditional longitudinal methodologies for macro-scale studies of usability, and given the relative reliability of contemporaneous methodologies over retrospective methodologies, a practical methodology for the study of long-term usability would be a cross-sectional methodology with contemporaneous recollection.

Cross-sectional methodologies have been criticized as vulnerable to under-controlled variation among users, leading to false attributions of effects to the variation in time rather than variation among users [5]. This criticism relies principally on the work of Prümper et al. [10]. While Prümper et al. observed that changes in the definition of experience (e.g., overall experience with computers vs. specific experience with a program) led to different usability results, their study nevertheless showed that it would be possible, given a particular definition of experience, to derive meaningful results with a cross-sectional methodology. And in fact, Prümper et al. relied on such a methodology to report the substantive results of their study. This suggests less that cross-sectional methodologies are inherently unreliable and more that researchers should take care to specify the experience perspective through which they interpret their results.

Actually, longitudinal studies suffer from exactly the same problem identified by Prümper et al. because the studies' subjects do not remain constant with respect to use characteristics. That is, it is true that the subjects gain experience over time with respect to the application that is the target of the study, but it is also true that they gain experience with computers generally, too. Along the same lines as Heraclitus's observation that no-one steps into the same river twice, one can note that no longitudinal survey samples the same users twice. Moreover, longitudinal studies are inherently subject to this problem, because the researcher cannot control for the experience perspective.

Longitudinal studies track the same individuals, across common stages of experience, while cross-sectional studies look at different individuals over different stages of experience. Longitudinal studies track use of the same application, while cross-sectional studies can look at use of multiple applications. Indeed, one can view the whole world of computing as a natural experiment using a cross-sectional design. That is, at any moment in time, for almost any given application there are many—possibly millions—of users, each of whom has his or her own level of experience with that application. This level of experience could range from a few minutes to several decades, which would enable macro-scale studies. So instead of tracking users over time and waiting for years, one could take advantage of the world's natural experiment to gather data on a set of users who, right now, have different levels of experience.

Accordingly, we implemented and used such a technique, which effectively takes a "snapshot" of use by multiple users of different levels of experience, with their frustration episodes reported through contemporaneous participatory evaluation rather than retrospection. This method is between-subjects and asks the users to report frustration episodes at the time the episodes occur. In this way, we suggest, researchers looking at longitudinal issues can break past the time limits of longitudinal methodologies to study users' experiences over much longer periods of time. In the sections that follow, we describe our approach, report results of an initial study, and discuss whether this technique for looking at usability over longer periods of time usefully adds to the understanding of usability issues.

3. METHODOLOGY

The key idea of our approach is that users self-report (via Web-based surveys) their experiences with computer technology as these experiences occur. Subjects fill out an initial survey with demographic and experiential information, and then fill out incident surveys when they encounter frustration with computer programs.

Thus we asked users first to fill out an initial survey online about themselves and their experience with technology. This survey included information about varieties of experience with computers and programs, along the lines studied by Prümper et al. Pre-testing suggested that the initial survey took less than ten minutes to complete.

We solicited subjects via social networking and asked subjects to recruit their acquaintances. Over a period of 25 days, 71 subjects (excluding apparent duplicates) completed the demographic survey. The subjects lived in ten U.S. states and two other countries, with most subjects from the area of El Paso, TX, other areas of Texas, and the Pacific Northwest. As indicated in Table 1, subjects' median age was 30-39.

Table 1. Age of subjects.

N	Age
1	18 to 24
4	25 to 29
32	30 to 39
14	40 to 49
13	50 to 59
5	60 to 69
1	70 +

The subjects' experience with computers ranged from 8 to 40 years, with a median of 20 years. Their self-evaluated proficiency ranged from our scale's minimum (1) to the maximum (5), with a mean self-evaluated proficiency of 3.93.

Subjects were then asked to fill out at least one, and possibly more, incident reports during the next three days, each time they encountered a frustrating experience in using computer technology, using a Web-based form. The incident report form included questions about the user's specific extent of experience with the program involved in the report. Pre-testing suggested that the experience report also took less than ten minutes to fill complete. Each demographic survey had a unique 3-digit identifier that was the only way to connect demographics to incident reports, thus guarding anonymity of the subjects.

The experience report comprised an introduction and seven main questions. The categories of solution methods in Question 7 were based on the twelve categories reported in [8], although as noted in Section 4, our analysis collapsed these to four categories. The experience report asked these questions:

Below please describe a frustrating experience that you had recently in using a computer. We will combine this information with that of others to aid us in designing and improving future technology help systems for users like you.

Now think about a recent experience using a computer that frustrated you.

In your own words please share the experience.

1) What software or application were you using that caused the frustration?
   - Approximately for how long (days, months or years) have you been using this application?
   - On average, how many days a month do you use this application?
2) Please explain what you were attempting to do.
3) What caused your frustration?
4) Could you identify the problem?
   - Yes
   - No
   - Unsure
   - Do not remember
   Please explain.
5) Were you able to solve the problem?
   - Yes
   - No
   - Unsure
   - Do not remember
   Please explain.
6) Could you identify other possible solutions?
   - Yes
   - No
   - Unsure
   - Do not remember
   Please explain.
7) What tools or options did you use in trying to solve the problem?
   - I read the printed manual
   - I used the electronic manual
   - I used the help feature in the application/program
   - I searched the web for a solution
   - I searched the online knowledge base of the application/program
   - I asked someone I know for help
   - I asked for help online
   - I found a workaround or alternative method
   - I found a solution via trial and error
   - I talked with the technical support department for the application/program
   - I gave up
   - Other:

Do you have any additional comments on the frustrations you have experienced with technology or help systems?

Do you have any comments on this survey?

4. RESULTS

The study's subjects reported 41 unique frustration episodes. The subjects reported experience levels with the application that ranged from two days to eleven years. Figure 1 presents the distribution of experience levels with the application. The x-axis is the upper limit of the time interval, in years, for the episodes, and the y-axis is the number of episodes for that time interval. For example, there were six episodes where the subjects had more than four and up to eight years of experience with the application.

We now examine the time-series results for the kind of software the subjects used, the nature of the frustration episodes they reported, the solution methods they tried, and the extent to which they used help resources.

4.1 Software Involved in Frustration Episodes

As the study's subjects reported frustration episodes that occurred with the software they were using, we first examined differences between less-experienced and more-experienced users with respect to the kind of software they used and which, because of the study's design, led to the frustration episode. We defined less-experienced as having three months or less experience with the software. As indicated in Figure 2, the less-experienced users experienced problems with different kinds of software than did experienced users, and this difference in software was significant (ChiSq < 0.001).

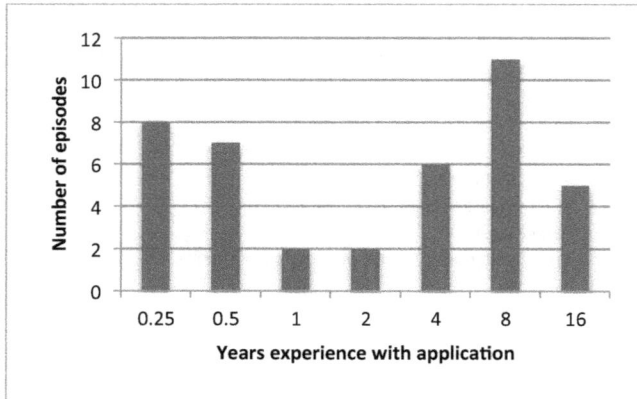

Figure 1. Distribution of self-reported experience levels with the application involved in users' frustration episodes.

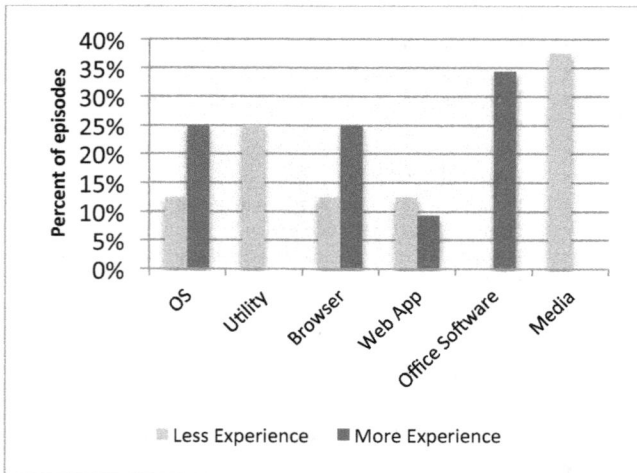

Figure 2. Differences between less-experienced and more-experienced users with respect to software involved in frustration episodes.

Less-experienced users had more problems with utility and media software, and more-experienced users had more problems with operating systems, browsers, and office software.

4.2 Nature of Frustration Episodes

Earlier studies (e.g., [8]), reported changes over time in the relative frequencies of different kinds of frustration episodes. These kinds of results are perhaps the primary goal of studies of usability over time: what caused the users' problems as a function of experience.

While the data from our study do show changes over time, the trends are not as clear as those reported in [8]. Figure 3 shows the changes in relative distributions of frustration causes as a function of time. The y-axis is the percentage of episodes of a frustration type for a particular level of experience with the software, and the x-axis is the experience level ("0" is the interval of experience from none to less than three months, etc.). The lack of a clear overall trend may be due to the heterogeneous software used by the subjects. Some of the kinds of frustration causes did appear to have interesting trends, though. Figures 4 and 5 show the trends for "App behavior" and "Freeze/crash," respectively.

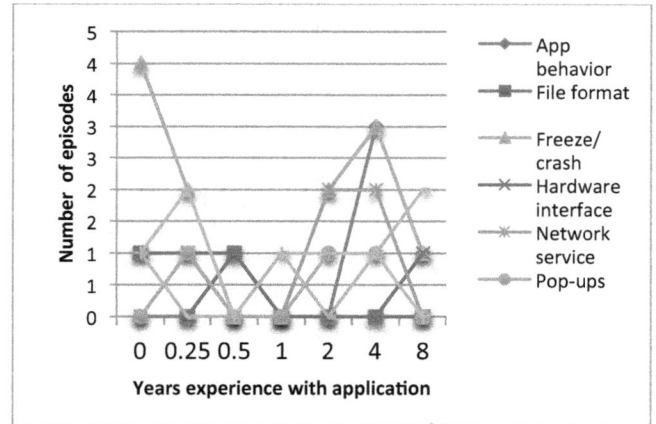

Figure 3. Relative frequencies of frustration causes as a function of experience with the software.

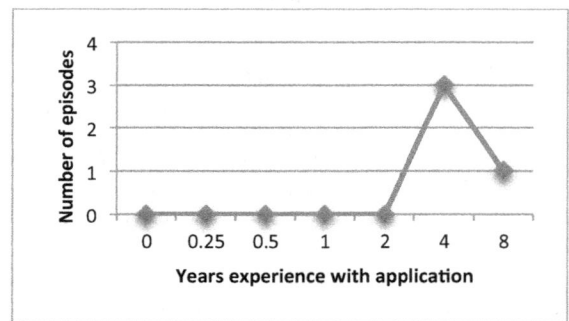

Figure 4. Absolute frequency of frustration episodes caused by "Freeze/crash" as a function of experience with the software.

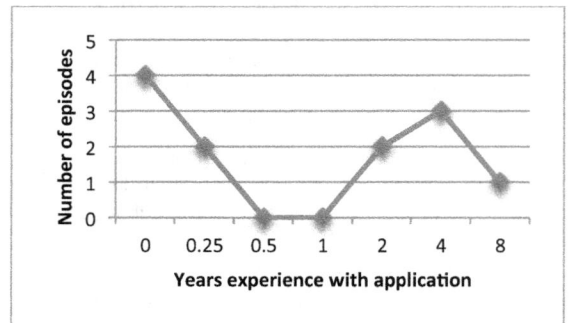

Figure 5. Absolute frequency of frustration episodes caused by "App behavior" as a function of experience with the software.

The results for "Freeze/crash" seem counterintuitive, in that the more-experienced subjects reported greater use of office software and lower use of media software, in that office applications would seem less likely to freeze or crash than media applications. The results for "App behavior" may suggest that novice users do have a greater frequency of usability problems with an application's user interfaces, which trends down until the point when, as the users gain more than a year's experience, they begin tackling more advanced tasks, leading again to usability problems with the interface. In other words, some of the differences between less- and more-experienced users may be due to the more-experienced users trying to accomplish more with the application: attempts at tasks with greater complexity lead to greater frustration. The actual problems reported by the users tend to support this conjecture. For example, experienced users of office applications had problems generating a table of contents in Microsoft Word or creating a function in Microsoft Excel to select unique numbers in a column.

We also looked at the relative frequencies of causes of frustration episodes not as a time series but rather distinguishing between less-experienced users (zero to three months of experience with the software leading to the frustration episode) and more-experienced users (more than three months of experience). This analysis is shown Figure 6. Again, no clear relationship is evident, which was confirmed by statistical analysis (ChiSq > 0.57).

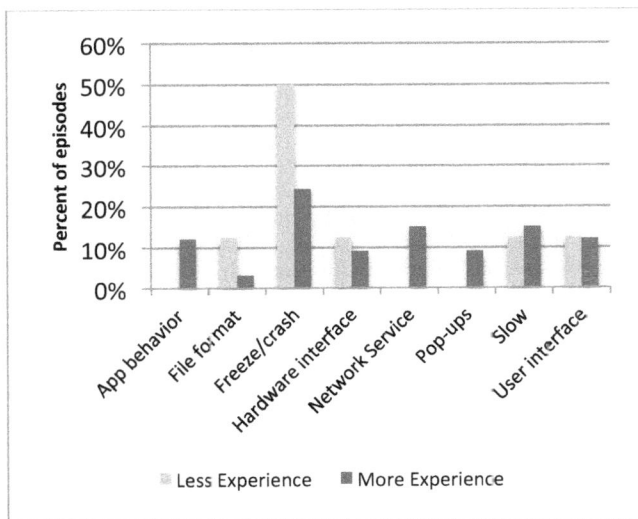

Figure 6. Relative frequencies of frustration causes as a function of less or more experience with the software.

4.3 Solutions Tried

For each episode, the users reported all of the methods with which they tried to solve (or abandon) the problem. The questionnaire used the twelve categories (plus "other") reported in [8], but for purposes of analysis we collapsed the responses into four categories:

- Using help from a manual, on-line help, or Web pages
- Asking someone, such as a colleague, a help desk, or a stranger via the Internet
- Using a workaround, which produces the appearance of a solution, or trial and error exploration of the interface
- Rebooting the computer or giving up.

Subjects could report more than one solution method for a frustration episode (e.g., used help system, asked someone I know, gave up). The distributions of the subjects' reported

solution methods are show in Figure 7, distinguishing less-experienced users (zero to three months of experience with the software leading to the frustration episode) and more-experienced users (more than three months of experience). Analysis of these data suggests that there is not a clear overall relationship between level of experience and choice of solution method (ChiSq > 0.29). In only one episode did a subject report using a printed manual.

However, relative greater numbers of more-experienced users than less-experienced users actually solved their problem (ChiSq < 0.05), as could be surmised from Table 2, where less experience means zero to three months of experience with the software leading to the frustration episode and more experience means more than three months of experience.

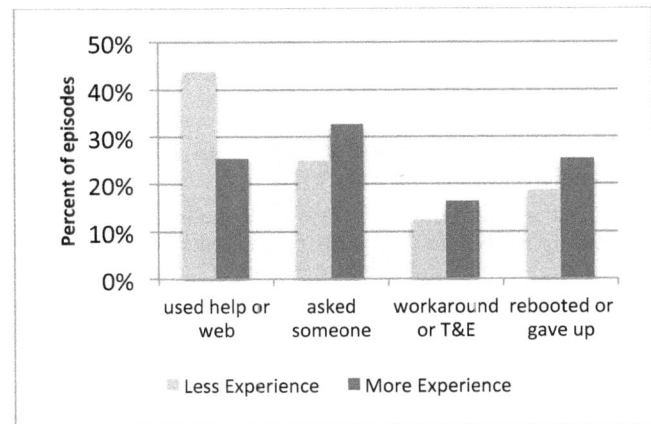

Figure 7. Distribution of solution methods as a function of experience.

Ironically enough, the experienced users achieved this success while using help significantly less than less-experienced users, as shown in Table 3, where "used help" means used help from a manual, on-line help, or Web pages, or asked someone, such as a colleague, a help desk, or a stranger via the Internet. This difference was significant (ChiSq < 0.001).

Table 2. Problem solution as a function of experience.

Solved problem	Inexperienced	Experienced
Yes	0	12
No	6	9

Table 3. Use of help as a function of experience.

	Less Experience	More Experience
Did not use help	1	14
Used help	11	6

These results are consistent with those reported in [8], which suggest that people using help are no more likely to achieve task success than people not using help, and that use of help tends to fall off as function of experience, even when people encounter novel problems.

5. DISCUSSION

In the course of our analysis, we tried distinguishing less-experienced and more-experienced subjects with different break points. That is, we tried a series of analyses where more-experienced meant more than three months, more than six months, and equal to or more than four years of experience with the software with which the user had a frustration episode. These analyses suggest that the greatest changes in users' experiences come early. For example, we looked at the significance of the chi-square test for whether subjects used help. As indicated in Figure 8, Chi-square increases, and thus significance falls off, as the break-point between experience levels increases.

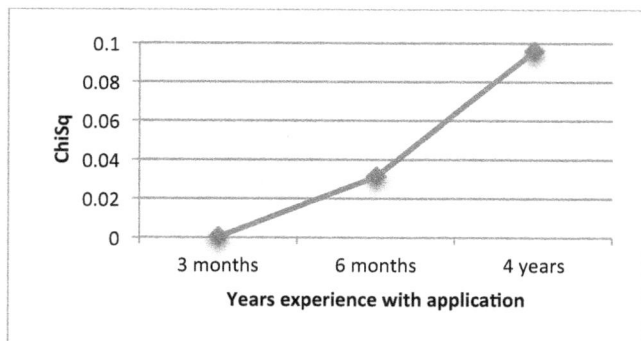

Figure 8. Chi-square of test of use of help as a function of break-point between experience levels.

We found a similar result in looking at the kinds of software reported by subjects in their frustration episodes as a function of experience. As indicated in Figure 9, again Chi-square increases, and thus significance falls off, as the break-point between experience levels increases.

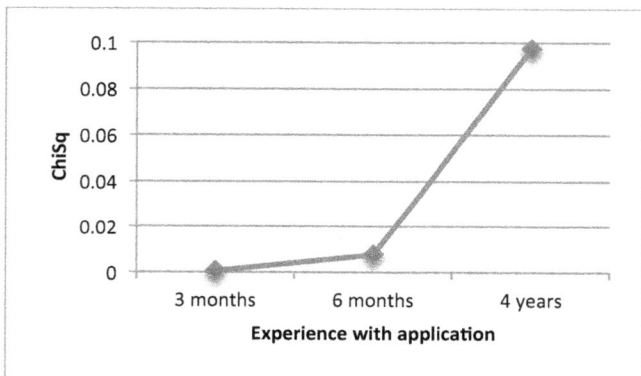

Figure 9. Chi-square of test of type of software used as a function of break-point between experience levels.

This analysis suggests that macro-longitudinal studies beyond perhaps a year may not be particularly useful for many kinds of applications, as most of the observable differences in use appear to occur within three to six months of initial use. Because we had only eight experience reports with application use less than or equal to three months, we were not able to explore whether an even lower break-point for experience would be useful.

6. CONCLUSION

This paper explored whether a non-longitudinal, cross-sectional approach could reliably detect useful differences in usability between novices and experts.

Our results suggest that it is possible to study long-term usability with a methodology that combines a cross-sectional approach with contemporaneous evaluation. This "snapshot" methodology avoids potential problems with retrospective evaluation, while, as we have argued, being no worse off than longitudinal methodologies with respect to variability among subjects. The snapshot methodology

enables researchers to look at usability over much longer periods of time than would be practical with longitudinal methods.

Our analysis suggests that a cross-sectional methodology can distinguish between less experienced and more experienced users with respect to the kinds of applications that cause frustration, frequency of use of help, and whether the problem was solved. Our analysis also suggests that the method is poor at distinguishing causes of frustration and the overall distribution of types of solutions tried. This latter result is frustrating, so to speak, because understanding these differences is a principal goal of studies of usability over time, and the results of the longitudinal studies discussed in Section 2 suggest that these differences across time do, in fact, occur. It may be that the heterogeneous collection of software used by our study's subjects contributed to this problem and that applying the snapshot approach to a single application would yield more useful results. It is also possible that clearer results might be produced by collecting more than 41 experience reports.

The data also suggest that three months of use of an application is the most useful point at which to distinguish less-experienced from more-experienced users.

6.1 Limitations

While the study did yield useful results with respect to kinds of applications that cause frustration, frequency of use of help, and whether the problem was solved, with only 41 experience reports, it seems clear that a greater number of reports would be highly useful.

More fundamentally, our results may reflect a self-selection bias among the subjects who participated in the study. This possible bias may be seen, for example, in the distribution of experience for the software used, which is weighted toward multi-year use, and in the subjects' overall experience with computers, which had a median value of 20 years. Thus our results should be interpreted as reflecting the usability experiences of relatively sophisticated users of computers.

Along similar lines, the extent of experience with applications may be a function of when the applications became available. Users may have some number of years experience with an application because it was launched that many years ago; other applications, more recently launched, will not have any users with longer experience. As a result, trends for causes of frustration may conflate newness of the application and lack of experience with the application.

The relatively high experience levels of our subjects also meant that we had fewer low-experience frustration reports than we had hoped to obtain. Consequently, our analysis could not reliably distinguish experience levels below three months.

7. ACKNOWLEDGMENTS

This work was supported in part by an endowment from AT&T. The authors thank the study's participants for their time. The authors also thank Nigel Ward and the conference's reviewers for their helpful comments, which markedly improved this paper.

8. REFERENCES

[1] Jacobsson, M. and Nylander, S. (2012) Always-On + Adoption – a method for longitudinal studies. CHI 2012 Workshop on Theories, Methods and Case Studies of Longitudinal HCI Research, May 5, 2012, Austin, TX.

[2] Jain, J., Rosenbaum, S., and Courage, C. (2010). Best practices in longitudinal research, *Proceedings of the 28th International Conference Extended Abstracts on Human Factors in Computing Systems (CHI '10)*, April 10-15, 2010, Atlanta, GA, 4791-4794.

[3] Karapanos, E., Hassenzahl, M., and Martens, J.-B. (2008). User experience over time: An initial framework. *Proceedings of the 26th International Conference on Human Factors in Computing Systems (CHI '08)*, Florence, Italy, 3561-3566.

[4] Karapanos, E., Martens, J.-B., and Hassenzahl, M. (2012). CHI 2012 Workshop on Theories, Methods and Case Studies of Longitudinal HCI Research, May 5, 2012, Austin, TX, http://longitudinalusability.wikispaces.com/CHI2012Worksh op.

[5] Karapanos, E., Martens, J.-B., and Hassenzahl, M. (2012). On the retrospective assessment of users' experiences over time: Memory or actuality? In: CHI 2012 Workshop on Theories, Methods and Case Studies of Longitudinal HCI Research, May 5, 2012, Austin, TX.

[6] Khanlarian, C., 2010, A *Longitudinal Study of Web-Based Homework*, Ph.D. Dissertation, University of North Carolina at Greensboro.

[7] Mendoza, V., and Novick, D. (2005). Usability over time, *Proceedings of SIGDOC 2005*, Coventry, UK, September 21-23, 2005, 151-158.

[8] Novick, D., Andrade, O., Bean, N., and Elizalde, E. (2008). Help-based tutorials, *Proceedings of SIGDOC 2008*, Lisbon, Portugal, September 22-25, 2008, 1-8.

[9] Novick, D., Elizalde, E., and Bean, N. (2007). Toward a more accurate view of when and how people seek help with computer applications, *Proceedings of SIGDOC 2007*, El Paso, TX, October 22-24, 2007, 95-102.

[10] Prümper, J., Zapf, D., Brodbeck, F.C., and Frese, M. (1992). Some surprising differences between novice and expert errors in computerized office work, *Behaviour & Information Technology* 11(6), 319-328.

[11] Roto, V., and Kujala, S. (2012). Studying six months in two hours. In: CHI 2012 Workshop on Theories, Methods and Case Studies of Longitudinal HCI Research, May 5, 2012, Austin, TX.

[12] Szóstek, A., and Walo, K. (2012). Prospective Day Reconstruction method: a way to validate service design concepts. In: CHI 2012 Workshop on Theories, Methods and Case Studies of Longitudinal HCI Research, May 5, 2012, Austin, TX.

[13] van Lumig, C.J.L. (2009). *The influence of user expertise on the usability experience: Interfaces for different users at Vodafone call centers*. Master's thesis, Eindhoven University of Technology.

[14] Vaughan, M., and Courage, C. (2007). SIG: Capturing longitudinal usability: what really affects user performance over time?, *CHI '07 extended abstracts on Human factors in computing systems*, April 28-May 03, 2007, San Jose, CA, 2149-2152.

[15] Vaughan, M., Courage, C., Rosenbaum, S., Jain, J., Hammontree, M., Beale R., and Welsh, D. (2008). Longitudinal usability data collection: art versus science?, *CHI '08 extended abstracts on Human factors in computing systems*, April 05-10, 2008, Florence, Italy, 2261-2264.

[16] von Wilamowitz Moellendorff, M., Hassenzahl, M., and Platz, A. (2006). Dynamics of user experience: How the perceived quality of mobile phones changes over time. User Experience - Towards a unified view, Workshop, *4th Nordic Conference on Human-Computer Interaction*, October 14 - 18, 2006, Oslo, Norway, 74-78.

Data Visualization for Psychotherapy Progress Tracking

Kelly Koerner
Evidence-Based
Practice Institute, LLC
206.265.2507
k.koerner@comcast.net

Dharma Dailey
University of
Washington HCDE
dharma.dailey@gmail.com

Mike Lipp
University of Washington HCDE
mikeli77@uw.edu

Heidi Connor
University of Washington HCDE
hidcon@uw.edu

Rohit Sharma
University of Washington HCDE
rohitsh@uw.edu

ABSTRACT

In this experience report, we recount how we designed and built data visualization tools for clinical decision making in psychotherapy. We describe how a combination of three factors enabled us to build a high-fidelity prototype within eight-weeks: 1) a multi-disciplinary team; 2) an agile methodology that incorporated participatory user-centered research into the design approach; and 3) a coherent conceptual framework for designing data visualization for decision making [1]. Elements of our approach and the lessons learned may be useful to others who must design tools to display multivariate data for users who work under tight time constraints and high cognitive loads, and whose skills using data visualization vary widely.

Categories and Subject Descriptors

H.5.2 [Information Interfaces and Presentation]: User Interfaces—User centered design, Graphical user interfaces (GUI); I.3.6 [ComputerGraphics]: Methodologies and Techniques—Interaction Techniques; H.4.8 [Information Systems Applications]: Types of Systems—Decision Support

Keywords

Data Visualization, Agile User Research

1. INTRODUCTION

In this case study, we describe our experience designing and building a data visualization tool for clinical decision making in psychotherapy. We describe how our multi-disciplinary team successfully combined agile methodology with participatory user-centered design to understand and address the needs of users who vary widely in their ability to use data visualizations and who make decisions under tight time constraints and high cognitive-loads. We used a conceptual framework that maps decision makers' tasks onto the data visualization tasks [1], giving us a model that conceptually directed not only development but also our strategy for evaluating the prototype's efficacy. These combined factors allowed us to design and build a working experiment-ready prototype within eight weeks.

The final data visualization prototype features two components: an individual client view (Client Dashboard, Figure 1) and a

caseload view (Multi-Client Dashboard, Figure 2). Each dashboard helps the therapist rapidly interpret scores from patient reported symptom measures and compare those scores to relevant benchmarks to aid clinical decision making. In both dashboards, heads up displays and filters appear on the left side. Graphical displays of symptom monitoring for an individual patient over time (Figure 1) or a population of patients and therapists (Figure 2) appear to the right. The prototype we built is part of a larger performance monitoring and feedback system, Online Progress Tracking (*OPT-beta*, [2]), that helps mental health therapists systematically monitor the progress of patients in psychotherapy while they learn and use evidence-based mental health care practices. Monitoring patients' progress is important as it has been demonstrated that therapists who do so have improved client outcomes [3].

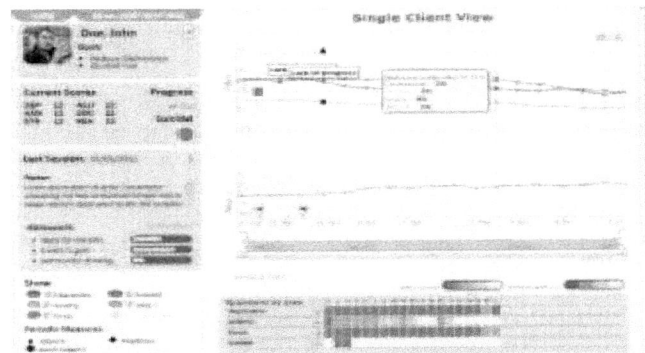

Figure 1. Client Dashboard

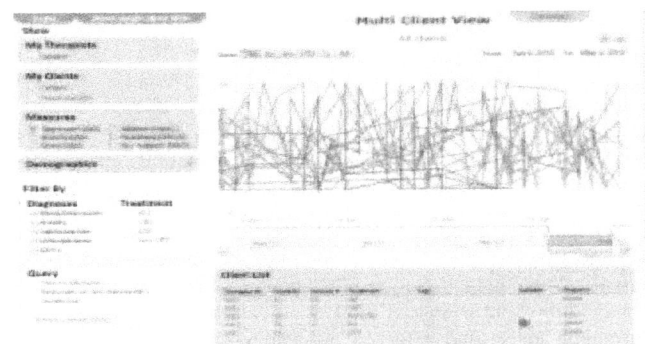

Figure 2. Multi-Client Dashboard

1.1 Our Team

Our five-member team divided responsibility for the design process into primary roles with two programmers (Sharma and Lipp), one designer (Connor), one user experience researcher (Dailey) and one domain expert and data collector (Koerner). But in practice, each took on secondary roles as described below. The clear yet overlapping skills and frequent communication made for a strong agile process.

1.2 A Conceptual Model for Decision Making Guides Our Design

The purpose of our visualization design is to aid decision making. To help us think categorically about how to design for decision making, we used a heuristic framework devised by Bautista and Carenini [1] for designing visual interfaces. This framework integrates task analysis of the general decision-analysis process with task taxonomies for data visualization, making it more likely that a visualization supports the user's efforts to make good decisions from the data. It also conceptually divides decision making interactions into three separate, yet interwoven elements: construction, inspection and sensitivity analysis.

Our user research and testing focused on application of these elements as follows. In keeping with Bautista and Carenini's concept of *construction*, our user tests evaluated whether our visual displays supported users ability to quickly yet accurately *construct* data models that readily aid the most common clinical decisions. In keeping with the concept of *inspection*, we tested if the user could easily retrieve details on demand that facilitate forming and testing hypotheses relevant to their work. Along these lines, we also evaluated whether our displays reduced ambiguity and the likelihood that users would misinterpret data. Finally, in keeping with Bautista and Carenini's concept of *sensitivity analysis*, we tested if the therapist can use our tool to easily explore various "what if..?" scenarios to better understand patients' progress. Because users often quickly transition through these aspects of decision making, our design aims to support fluid movement between them. For example, if a user discovers new data that might alter their working hypothesis on the treatment course for a patient, our design should readily support a flow from inspection of current data to sensitivity analysis exploring alternative hypotheses to construction of a new working hypothesis of the best treatment options for that patient.

Following Bautista & Carenini, we then mapped key decision making tasks to specific visualization techniques. When a user selects a single patient or a group of patients, urgent status indicators are clearly distinguishable based on their color, shape and location. Preattentive attention grabbing helps users to rapidly recognize the most important information on the screen. For example, we used a red dot to signal when a patient's symptom scores indicate that they are suicidal. Once alerted to such information, we support a therapist's ability to construct decision models by employing zoom and filter interactions that afford users the ability to explore the details behind alerts.

Our visual design supports the decision making task of inspection with details-on-demand and focus-plus-context interactions. These visualization interactions help therapists rapidly form hypotheses about the client's status, find multivariate explanations, and formulate cause and effect relationships among variables over time. During inspection, data visualization must expose uncertainty. For example, when the therapist sees scores with large variability from week to week, the data visualization tool should help the therapist to discern whether the pattern observed is clinically relevant or due to normal score fluctuations. Finally, upon seeing data that informs choice, therapists will want to add or modify their objectives as well as add or modify the alternative actions about which they want information (sensitivity analysis). For example, after identifying a recent relapse in symptoms, the therapist may change the selected time period to scan across the entire course of treatment looking for other times where the patient has relapsed or explore how this patient's course in therapy compares to other patients with similar characteristics.

To adapt the conceptual decision making framework for usability testing, we designed questions directly based on each of its three components: construction, inspection, and sensitivity analysis. For construction, we tested if our tool can enable users to quickly find the individual or group of patients, or variables relevant to construct models of the most common clinical decisions. In addition, we tested if the therapist could rapidly gain needed information under strict time constraints. For inspection, we tested if the user could easily retrieve details on demand that facilitate forming and testing hypotheses. In addition, we presented tasks that include 'traps' where the therapist may be prone to misinterpret data, and tested whether the data visualization tool provided sufficient help to expose uncertainty. Finally, for sensitivity analysis, we tested whether the therapist could use our tool to easily explore various "what if..?" scenarios to better understand patients' progress. We also tested if the transition between all three phases was sufficiently fluid and if the user could change objectives upon discovering new data and easily pursue the next hypothesis.

1.3 Challenges Our Users Face

Our users face several challenges that constrained our preliminary design. First, therapists must fill each work day with as many sessions as possible, with 5-10 minutes between sessions to document the last session and then prepare for the next. Therapists work under high cognitive load as they manage multiple tasks, under time pressures, with frequent interruptions.

Second, therapists vary widely in their ability to correctly read and interpret graphically displayed data. For some, interpreting basic line graphs is challenging. For most, general concepts about reliable change are unfamiliar. For example, when asked to read patients' graphically displayed data, most therapists do not consider how clients' ratings on symptom measures can vary by chance without actually representing reliable change and end up incorrectly assuming that changes are significant when they are not. Tight workflow, high cognitive load, and low data interpretation skills can make therapists prone to dismiss emotionally challenging information. For example, therapists may be prone to incorrectly deduce that a particular patient is making progress when in fact he is not.

Finally, therapists need to quickly and accurately analyze both episodic and weekly measurements relative to benchmarks. The user needs to understand symptom severity and see patterns across different measures easily, with a single glance. The challenge is that each measure has its own scoring system, with different norms and cutoffs. This makes it difficult to display all measures on the same graph while simultaneously providing visual cues that quickly indicate clinical norms (e.g., how severe the symptom score is).

2. USABILITY RESEARCH AND DESIGN PROCESSES

2.1 An Agile Methodology

Our team employed aspects from agile software development around teamwork and rapid iterations. We averaged two design iterations per week. This quick pace provided a constant stream of incremental feedback that we used to validate our design or make adjustments to improve observed issues. In terms of teamwork, we shared information and sought out each other's input. Perhaps, most helpful was that tasks were assigned to small groups rather than individuals, and therefore every task afforded collaboration. Because our team was interdisciplinary this assured that knowledge was shared across roles.

Each design iteration consisted of these components:
1. usability research and evaluation
2. regular consultations with domain experts as needed to resolve questions
3. confirm or improve design (and prototype) based on findings.

In tandem with early design iterations, we also built use cases, a simulated data set, and selected a visualization library.

2.2 Usability Research and Evaluation

Typically, to facilitate rapid design iterations, we conducted tests and interviews with one participant at a time, enabling us to incorporate any changes into the design prototype before the next session. One of our priorities was to quickly verbally report the take-aways and subsequent designs with the entire team. Research notes and design iterations were also available to the whole team via shared online folders. This constant communication enabled us to absorb user research findings and consider design options as a team.

Usability testing included both formal and informal components. Formal components included structured usability evaluations which presented therapists with realistic tasks, such as using the graphical display to explain how well a patient is doing. Similarly, to test the intuitiveness of individual components, we asked therapists to tell us the meaning of several unlabeled design elements presented within the dashboard. These more formal evaluations were followed by informal semi-structured interviews, which involved returning to the same users with new iterations and asking for additional feedback and input. Because of the ongoing participatory nature of the testing, users could quickly tell us if our design was improving or getting worse.

2.3 Regular Consultations with Domain Experts

For this design cycle, user research was conducted with domain experts who had specific and complementary knowledge on aspects of the type of decision making we are trying to represent. For example, we conducted a user test with a domain expert who was both a therapist and a statistician, followed by a semi-structured interview. We were then able to circle back later, with specific questions about our design, through email on an ad-hoc basis. One of our team members was a domain expert herself and had access to a number of other domain experts. These experts were all trained in the best practices of progress monitoring but had various degrees of experience with the system in development. The diversity of these users gave us a nice combination of opinions and experiences to evaluate our designs. This rich pool of experts worked well with our rapid iteration

technique as it provided a nearly continuous feedback into our design iterations, keeping our agile process user-centered throughout development.

2.4 Confirm or Improve Design (and Prototype) Based on Findings

User testing results either confirmed the design or led to better definition of problems with the design. Problems were identified and shared back to the full team, and all team members sketched possible solutions. Because our designer sat in on most user tests and interviews, she could rapidly translate the team's sketches into new design options. This helped build a shared understanding of general user experience and consensus on specific solutions. This process typically resolved some design questions, but led us back to user research and testing for others.

2.5 Supporting the Prototypes with Use Cases and Data Set

Concurrent with the development of the interactive prototypes, we created two use cases. These were used for formalized scenario based user testing and a cognitive walkthrough, emphasizing anticipated interactions with the two dashboards. In concert with these narratives, a sample data set was created to populate the prototypes, ensuring that key analytical and visual elements of our design would be evaluated.

2.6 Criteria and Process for Selecting a Visualization Library

To guide the selection process for a visualization library we would use to build our prototype, we established a set of criteria to describe important elements. These criteria proved valuable, serving as common points of evaluation from which we could make our final choice. The criteria consisted of the following items:
1. easy enough to learn and implement by novice programmers over a period of eight weeks, but robust enough to handle the requirements laid out in our user research
2. flexible enough to be expanded and used in an actual clinic
3. free to use for a non-profit

Utilizing the selection criteria, we conducted an informal survey of available visualization platform and narrowed our choices down to the D3 or HighStock JavaScrip libraries. While both platforms satisfied our criteria, we decided to use HighStock because of its relative ease of use, and a wide variety of sample visualizations provided, which were similar to what we intended to build.

3. LESSONS LEARNED

3.1 Displaying Multiple Measures with Different Norms is Challenging

We faced one particularly tough design challenge due to the users' need to see multiple measures on the same graph while indicating symptom severity. Each of the measures used has different norms and cut offs for mild/moderate/severe. For statistical reasons, normalizing all measures to the same scale so that the measures could be displayed against a common severity range was not possible without distorting the underlying data. Additionally, we needed to display both weekly and periodic measures. In the inspection phase, our users wanted to quickly see two types of data: the range in which the score falls and the individual question responses that make up each score. At first, we created a simple table that displayed the actual scores in each cell. This displayed the data clearly, but took up a lot of space. Additionally, our time constrained users had difficulty quickly identifying critical issues and patterns, since they had to read and interpret values from each cell individually.

To reduce the footprint required to present these two types of data and to make the data easier to scan and interpret, we decided to use a two tiered expanding/collapsing heatmap (Figures 3 and 4).

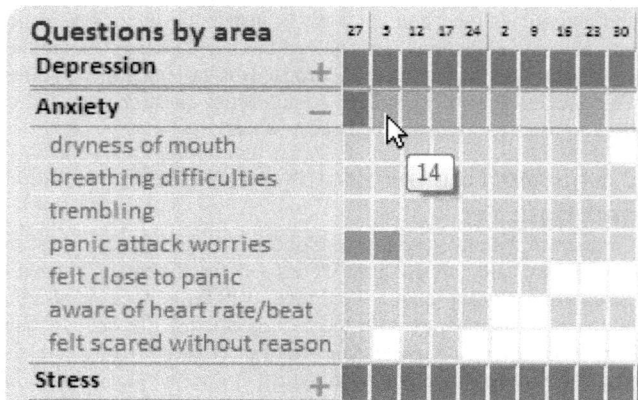

Figure 3. Heatmap expanded to show Anxiety scores

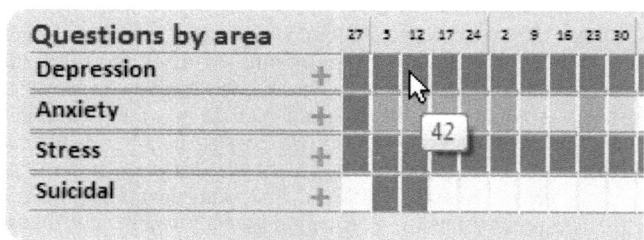

Figure 4. Collapsed heatmap showing symptom categories

The heatmap solution offered a number of improvements over the simple table including:
1. encoding numeric values into colors that could be mapped to severity and that were easier and quicker to analyze by the user
2. implementation of collapsed/expanded modes, the heatmap displays key information without cluttering the UI
3. making scores for individual questions were available as details on demand by expanding rows of the heatmap or on mouseover.

3.2 Select a Visualization Platform with an Established User Base

One thing that we did not anticipate was the time it would take for us to become familiar enough with JavaScript to utilize our selected visualization platform HighStock. To quickly learn JavaScript, CodeAcademy proved to be a great resource. We also did not realize that the number of current users of a platform is an important selection criterion. We learned that this is the case, as more users result in a richer user community and better support mechanisms. In this way, it may have ended up being easier to debug our code if it were created using D3 instead of HighStock,

since the former is a more popular platform. However, there were ample resources available that enabled us to tackle each HighStock programming challenge and achieve the goals laid out by our design.

3.3 Simulating Data is Harder than You'd Think

We created a dataset that would allow us to test key analytical and visual elements of our design. Data from real patients were used (with personal details removed) as the basis for the creation of fictitious cases. Cases were then replicated for a final 86 x 1881 matrix of 30 therapists and 200 clients assessed with multiple measures and seen for differing lengths of treatment. The end result accurately represented the distribution of treatment response rates and typical missing data rates. What proved difficult, however, was that when therapist users explore, they very rapidly begin moving between construction, inspection and sensitivity analysis, and expect the data to yield a deep and coherent backstory for any case they choose to examine. For these users, realistic simulation is critical to creating a high-fidelity interactive prototype. As we attempted to build out our data set, we realized how difficult and time consuming it is to create a large simulated multivariate data set.

3.4 Users Need a High-Fidelity Prototype to Conceive of How to Use Big Data

Even though the users we worked with when developing the visualization prototypes were all domain experts in progress monitoring, data visualization of big data is new to them. They had a hard time conceiving of what they would want to do if they could explore hundreds or thousands of cases of multivariate data. Low fidelity prototypes did not provide enough interactivity for them to imagine what they might be able to do with such data. It became clear that users require a high-fidelity prototype with realistic data to explore before they begin to understand what is possible. We expect it will take several more iterations with high-fidelity prototypes before we can confidently understand users' needs when exploring big multivariate data for clinical decision making.

3.5 Agile User Research and Rapid Prototyping Worked Well for Us

We had eight weeks to create a functioning prototype and each of us had limited hours per week for project development. We balanced the workload across the team on the front end by learning each other's schedules so that we timed the handoff of tasks to team mates' availability. Individual team member's responsibilities were clear, but flexible. We informally defined and refined goals and milestones by consensus, with each team member taking on some of the project management work. Where possible we shared functionality. For example, the designer was present for all user research interviews and the developers contributed drawings based on user research during the ideation phase. The incremental and participatory user-centered design approach resulted in a nearly continuous pipeline of feedback from users and domain experts. The agile team work, with multiple disciplines and overlapping responsibilities let us maintain a rapid pace and come in with a working high fidelity prototype on deadline.

In retrospect, we could have benefited from more structured project management and monitoring of schedules and progress. Half way through the project we ran into some challenges including those mentioned in previous sections. Our team was able to leverage our experience by making good decisions on how to spend our remaining time, but we were still rushed at the end and making last minute adjustments and finishing touches. Paying closer attention to actual progress and schedules may have allowed us to recognize the impact of unforeseen challenges and recognize we would need to adjust future commitments in order to stay on track with the originally scheduled delivery date.

4. CONCLUSION

It was a rewarding experience to collaborate as a multi-disciplinary team and, in eight weeks, successfully design and build a data visualization prototype for clinical decision making. A key learning from this experience was that it is possible to adapt a particular framework for understanding decision making - the conceptual decision making framework of Bautista & Carenini - in order to design a visualization tool that supports better decision making. This framework usefully focused our initial design and user research, and provided a heuristic standard against which to test design decisions—all elements should strengthen the user's ability to complete decision tasks and result in a smooth flow between construction, inspection, and sensitivity analysis phases of the decision making process. Our work now is to assist the Evidence-Based Practice Institute in experimentally evaluating whether the prototype works as intended. We will be releasing our code publicly via GitHub and then assisting the team at the EBPI by sharing our knowledge and helping them to deploy the tool.

5. REFERENCES

[1] Bautista, J., & Carenini, G. (2006) An Integrated Task-Based Framework for the Design and Evaluation of Visualizations to Support Preferential Choice. AVI '06, May 23–26, 2006, Venezia, Italy.
http://www.cs.ubc.ca/~carenini/PAPERS/AVI06.pdf

[2] Koerner, K. & Persons, J. P. (2010-12) National Institute of Mental Health, 2010. Project title: Online Platform to Help Mental Health Practitioners Implement EEPs (1R43MH093993 – 01).

[3] Shimokawa, K., Lambert, M. J., & Smart, D. W. (2010). Enhancing treatment outcome of patients at risk of treatment failure: Meta-analytic and mega-analytic review of a psychotherapy quality assurance system. *Journal of Consulting and Clinical Psychology, 78*(3), 298-311.

6. ACKNOWLEDGMENTS

This research was partially supported by National Institute of Mental Health (1R43MH093993-01) to Kelly Koerner and Jacqueline B. Persons. We gratefully acknowledge Cecilia Aragon, PhD, for her mentorship and expertise during this project.

Designing Hospital Metrics:
Visual Analytics and Process Improvement

Brenton Faber
Worcester Polytechnic Institute
Salisbury Labs 19
100 Institute Rd, Worcester, MA
508-831-4930
bdfaber@wpi.edu

Adhish Rajkarnikar
Director, Decision Support & Finance
Kennedy Health Alliance
205 E Laurel Rd. Stratford NJ 08084
856-83-1016
a.rajkarnika@kennedyhealth.org

ABSTRACT

This paper describes the creation, development, and introduction of two new visual analytic tools documenting a process improvement project within a hospital-based medical system. After situating the project within "Visual Analytics" and the Design of Communication, we show hospital performance in these two activities before and after the introduction and dissemination of the visual tool. The paper argues that visual analytics are rhetorical practices merging data with strategic argumentation. As such, visual analytics used in process improvement activities must be supported with system accountability. The project encourages researchers and practitioners to see value in visual analytics as new forms and rhetorical applications of data mining. At the same time we offer that the relationship between analytics, designing communication, and organizational performance is complicated and nuanced with significant issues beyond information and knowledge transfer.

Categories and Subject Descriptors

H.5.3 [**Information Systems**]: Information Interfaces and Constructs; Group and Organization Interfaces; Organization Design.

General Terms

Management, Measurement, Documentation, Performance, Design, Human Factors, Theory.

Keywords

Health Care, Metrics, Visual Analytics, Data Mining, Process Improvement, Average Length of Say, Continuity of Care.

1. Visual Analytics & The Design of Communication

This paper presents a case study and findings from our efforts to design and introduce two new visual communication metrics within a hospital process improvement effort. "Visual Analytics" is a term recently given to the study, design, and use of visuals to record, interpret, and describe data. As Heer and Agrawala write, "visualizations leverage the human visual system to support the analysis of large amounts of information" [15 p. 49]. Kleim et al.,

situate "visual analytics" within the current need for "the right information being available at the right time" and we would add, in the right form [17, p.155].

Citing Thomas and Cook [28], Kleim et al., define visual analytics as "the science of analytical reasoning facilitated by interactive visual interfaces" [17, p. 157]. Kleim et al. note the acquisition of raw data is no longer an issue for organizations or researchers. Instead, it is the ability to make these vast amounts of information meaningful that challenge information developers, architects, and other data-focused professionals. They write, "the overarching driving vision of **visual analytics** is to turn the information overload into an opportunity: Just as *information visualization* has changed our view on databases, the goal of visual analytics is to *make our way of processing* data and information transparent for an analytic discourse (emphasis in original) [17, p. 155]. The visual design of analytics is important to the design of communication as it integrates decision-making, human factors, interactive visualization, data analysis, and sense making [15, 17, 20].

Visual data and its applicability to usability [7], education [4], information conceptualization [23], aesthetics [16], and real-time data analysis [18] are well-established themes in technical communication research. This historic grounding provides obvious advantages for studying visual analytics. For example, Heer and Agrawala situate their "design considerations" for visual analytics within discussions of appropriate divisions and allocations of work; processes of information foraging and schematization; and linguistic principles for meaning making including grounding, deixis, and ambiguity [14, pp. 51-55], all topics well established within technical communication research.

While visual metrics have been prominent in transportation [25] and telecommunications [26] research, the combination of visual communication, data mining, and analytics for organizational change and process improvement efforts are relatively new methods and correlative issues for our field. As a way to introduce these themes and problems to technical communication research we now turn to our case study, the design and introduction of two visual metrics within a hospital. We initially present our research context and design imperatives. We then introduce the metrics and visuals used to communicate hospital performance. We show the performance of both activities before and after the introduction of the metric in order to evaluate the relative impact of the visual tool.

2. Designing Visual Data to Guide Hospital Activities: Research Context

As Berger notes, American hospitals typically operate through "gut feel" or "seat of the pants type of management" which emphasizes experience, hierarchy, and tradition [3 pp. xiv, 23]. Despite the strong scientific education required for clinical leadership positions within healthcare (mostly physicians), scientific tools and methods largely have not crossed-over into administration and operations. Most hospital managers have risen from line positions and have little formal managerial training. Most problematically, while health systems have used some form of electronic data collection since the 1980s, these systems are notoriously difficult and poorly designed for providing current, relevant, analytical data for clinical and financial managers. As a result, healthcare organizations are awash in data but do not have adequate systems, tools, or expertise for measuring, interpreting, evaluating and acting on that data.

Incentives built into the American Recovery and Reinvestment Act (ARRA) have meant that health systems are quickly updating electronic medical systems to comply with Centers for Medicare and Medicaid Services (CMS) "meaningful use" requirements. While some of the more advanced systems provide analytical capacities for assessing productivity, performance, quality, and finance, simply installing a new computer system will not transform a hospital into an information-driven culture. Obstacles persist in the ways that an information-driven culture threatens existing experience and tradition-based hierarchies. Hospitals have strong and protective administrative and cultural silos in which information reports vertically with few opportunities for sideways integration [3; 12, p.44; 22]. Finance is bracketed from clinical practice and quality, performance improvement, case management or other areas of administrative oversight have few points of leverage within clinical areas. Further, medical data is highly restricted and its use regulated by federal Health Insurance Portability and Accountability Act (1996). While administrative and financial data does not include patient-specific personal health information, dissemination of any hospital data is often subject to similar protections and restrictions. As a result, there exists a tremendous need within healthcare organizations for useful, relevant, proactive information that can be successfully integrated into day-to-day practice.

Our research takes place in an early effort toward implementing an "information-driven" culture within a small community hospital [3, p.4]. Here, we will briefly review the current resurgence of analytics and how the practice has been used in Health Care management. Next, we introduce two new measures we introduced at the hospital: Current Length of Stay (CLOS) and Patients without Primary Care Providers (NoPCP). As noted above, we demonstrate hospital performance in these two activities before and after the introduction and dissemination of the metric. We then conclude by returning to the context of visual analytics and the design of communication to argue that despite various strong claims about metrics, their integration with a change management plan needs to be supported with system accountability.

3. Publicly Reported Healthcare Data

The U.S. Department of Health & Human Services has recently made available Medicare quality, performance, and cost data of hospitals, physicians, nursing homes, home health agencies, and dialysis facilities (http://www.healthcare.gov/compare). The hospital-specific site (available at http://hospitalcompare.hhs.gov/)

allows visitors to compare hospitals' process of care measures, outcomes, use of medical imaging, patients' experience, patient safety, volume, and overall Medicare spending. Hospitals can be compared on general characteristics, specific diseases, and specific surgical procedures. This resource, along with other publicly-available sites such as the Dartmouth Atlas of Health Care (http://www.Dartmouthatlas.org) and The Leapfrog Group (http://www.leapfroggroup.org) have challenged the traditional restrictions applied to healthcare data. Theoretically, publishing a particular hospital's surgical infection rate, readmissions rate for specific diseases, or mortality rates creates more informed patients, insurance payers, and physicians and creates greater imperatives for improvement.

3.1 Data Mining for Hospital-Specific Events

Whereas these large public data sites provide healthcare consumers new levels of transparency and accountability, the data presented here represents large aggregate outcomes of thousands of day-to-day processes. For example, it is difficult to use a hospital-wide readmission rate for Congestive Heart Failure as a proactive management metric. The number may be useful as a descriptive account and may suggest but not illuminate any number of inadequacies (improper discharge instructions, poor medication reconciliation at discharge, inadequate case management or clinic follow-up). As such, a much more micro level of granularity is needed to enable those within a health system to manage toward more macro measurements.

Berger uses the term "information-driven hospital" to describe "an organization that uses a group of numbers (metric indicators), which represent key success factors, to set goals derived through benchmarks" [3, p.4]. By monitoring each individual metric, managers can identify areas for improvement, anticipate and ideally manage to large-scale aggregate outcomes like those published by HospitalCompare or Leapfrog. Such metrics can be operational, financial, or clinical. For example, though actual causation is difficult to ascribe, hand-washing compliance is an operational metric that can influence hospital acquired infection rates, readmission rates, and length of stay. Physician chart turn-over (number of iterations until a visit can be billed) can influence financial metrics. Clinicians can be more accustomed to this associative logic since indicators such as a patient's vital signs often stand-in as a proxy for other diagnostic indicators (infection, internal bleeding). Berger writes that metrics are not developed in isolation but the process often entails benchmarking against best practices among peer institutions. Table 1 diagrams the pragmatic system Berger recommends for managing by metrics [3, p.5].

Table 1. Berger's steps toward an information-driven hospital

Toward an Information-Driven Hospital
Employ Benchmarking as directional marker for goal setting
Develop accountability to ensure that the goals are met
Adopt consequences, both positive and negative, as an accountability response

The systematic development, tracking, reporting and reinforcement of granular quantitative performance objectives has more recently been popularized as business analytics [2,10,11]. Davenport and Harris define analytics as "the extensive use of data, statistical and quantitative analysis, explanatory and predictive models, and fact-based management to drive decisions and actions" [10, p.7]. They cite what they call a "competitive advantage scale" which creates a vertical continuum among related business intelligent resources. At the most basic level they position descriptive reports. Scaling up from here, they list ad hoc reports and queries, alerts, statistical analysis, forecasting, predictive modeling, and ultimately optimization (at the highest level) [10, p.8; see also 9]. As Corne, Dhaenens, and Jourdan note, the explosion of digital data has seen a correlating level of interest in developing tools for deeper analysis and methods that are not available from classical database management systems [9, p.469]. This has certainly been the case in health care as the growth of electronic data systems, either in electronic health records (EHRs) or electronic health systems (EHS) simultaneously record and store data from each event within and across a patient visit. Data from a single visit can then be joined to similar data from other visits and other patients to map and potentially predict things like disease progression, utilization, patient compliance, cost and quality events, and variability in care standards.

Ideally, all of this data cumulates in proactive process improvement efforts targeted to large-scale hospital wide goals. Process Improvement efforts initially may simply recognize bad data, poor data entry processes, or activities that are not occurring. In more advanced systems, various process improvement efforts can be tied to metrics in anticipated "continuous improvement" efforts [8, 27, p. 358] guided by strategic monitoring through visual dashboards or other displays of key indicators [19, p. 264-265]. Whereas typical business intelligence reporting systems emphasize on after-the-fact analysis, the goal of new techniques for data analysis is predictive modeling, proactive identification of problems, and in some cases, preventative metrics – metrics that anticipate and avoid patient harm such as central line infections, [see e.g., 24], falls, infections, and readmissions.

4. Creating Proactive Metrics

In late 2010 and early 2011, we began reporting two new metrics as part of a daily report produced by the Data Analysis department at Community Hospital (a pseudonym). Community is a small 100-bed hospital located in the mid-Atlantic region of the US. Data Analysis was a new department initiated in 2009 to provide analytics support to Hospital Senior management. The department reported to the CEO and produced reports for strategic planning, a daily dashboard of key performance metrics, and other ad hoc reports for hospital planning and management.

The daily dashboard reported typical health care management metrics: Capacity by service group, admissions by major disease, length of stay averaged across all patients during the month, readmission rate averaged by month, number of patients who returned to the Emergency Department within 72 hours, surgical start time accuracy, and turnover times between surgeries.

We were concerned that these metrics were retroactive and descriptive rather than proactive and potentially predictive. In other words, knowing that the Average Length of Stay (ALOS) was increasing was useful but the metric itself was not operational, tied to an activity that could be accomplished to improve performance. Similarly, we may know that readmissions were increasing or that patients were returning to the Emergency Department within 72 hours but these metrics on their own were not strategic or to tied to a more granular system that could address root causes for these events.

We called the two new metrics we introduced "Current Average Length of Stay" and "No PCP". In what follows we will describe the two metrics, show their performance, describe their effect on larger hospital operations, and finally their limitations as strategic metrics.

4.1 Current Average Length of Stay

Average Length of Stay (ALOS) is a well-instantiated and widely -adopted metric used to measure how long the average patient stays in the hospital [19]. Since most hospital inpatient services are paid (reimbursed) by diagnosis and not cost or services rendered, there is a strong incentive for management to minimize days spent in the hospital. As a simplified example, an insurance company will pay roughly the same amount for patients with same diagnosis if the patient spends 2, 4, or 5 days in the hospital. Our concern with reporting ALOS was that the metric was always retrospective – the time in house was already complete once the metric was calculated. Simply knowing the prior month's ALOS did not help management anticipate or influence the metric in the future.

To address this problem, we introduced a derivative metric we called "Current Average Length of Stay" (CALOS). This metric reported a rolling day-to-day length of stay of all inpatients in house. This enabled senior management to anticipate where LOS would fall at the end of the month. To further introduce a predictive and proactive metric, each day we distributed a list of patients who had exceeded 6 days length of stay. In separate analysis we determined 6 days as an estimated financial break-even point for most chronic disease admissions. The hospital's case management team already reported internally within their office patients with more than 4 day LOS. Our rolling CALOS and Patients with LOS > 6 days reported this data widely across the hospital silos.

4.2 No PCP

Current efforts to reform the way health care is delivered emphasize greater utilization of out-patient services, less reliance on in-patient services, and greater coordination of care among an entire team of clinicians [1, 5, 6, 14]. A crucial network component of this shift is linking patients to out-patient clinics and primary care providers. As patients were registered for Emergency Department and inpatient services at the hospital we noticed that a field in the electronic registration system labeled "PrimaryCareProvider" was often blank or filled with a "null" character. Suspecting that this may be a data entry issue, we researched prior visits for patients recorded as not having a primary care provider (PCP). As we suspected, in several instances the database would show that a particular patient had a sustained relationship with a specific physician but in this instance the registration process omitted that data. The omission was problematic because nurses in the in-patient units would refer patients without a PCP to a clinic and often make a follow-up appointment for the patient after discharge. In these cases, the assumption that up-stream data entry was accurate or mindful proved precarious. Frustrated clinicians would report to us that they would spend considerable time linking a patient to a PCP only to find out that the patient already had a long relationship with a physician. In addition, if a PCP was not listed on admission, hospital clinicians would not call the patient's physician for advice, reporting, or care coordination.

Process improvement activities associated with clinical operations are highly critical of duplicative processes, work-arounds, and non value-added steps within a system [8]. While a clinician could simply ask patients if they had a PCP there were multiple individual data points within each patient's file and we agreed with the clinicians that data integrity meant that upstream data should come to the next step accurate. Nurses and physicians should be accountable for their own data integrity and clinical leadership and not be required to recognize and "do-over" data entry pieces already conducted at registration.

We developed the "Patients without PCP/Missed PCP" metric to measure daily the accuracy of registration clerks completing the PrimaryCareProvider field when registering a patient. For each patient listed as not having a PCP we conducted a backwards search for every prior visit to 2007 to see if they had a PCP registered to them on a prior visit. In cases where it was evident that a patient had a long-standing relationship with a PCP we documented that physician as the patient's PCP. Thus, in addition to the visual metric, we also included a list of patients registered that day without a PCP and the name of the PCP most recently associated with the patient (if any). This enabled us to measure accurate registrations, fix the PCP errors so the next level of clinical care could better coordinate services, and determine which patients were new (and percent of total patients new) to our hospital network (without a prior history).

5. Methods

To calculate both metrics, we used the hospital's electronic data base, a Meditech Data Repository [20]. We wrote Structured Query Language (SQL) programs for each metric. Each SQL program was run daily as part of a host of metrics we reported. Figure 1 documents the SQL code for the CALOS query for patients with LOS greater than 6 days. The CALOS metric was adopted into our regular reporting on December 1, 2010.

Figure 1. SQL Query for CALOS Metric

```
select
convert(varchar(10),ad.AdmitDateTime,23) as AdmitDate,
convert(varchar(10),nur.DateTime,23) as CensusDate,
(CASE
  WHEN datediff(dd, ad.AdmitDateTime, nur.DateTime) = 0
THEN 1
  ELSE datediff(dd, ad.AdmitDateTime, nur.DateTime)
END) CLOS,
DATEDIFF (yy, BirthDateTime, AdmitDateTime) Age,
AccountNumber,
DischargeAbsServiceID as ServiceID,
DischargeDateTime as DischargeDate,
LocationID,
FinancialClassID,
PtStatus,
ObservationPatient,
ReasonForVisit

from AbstractData ad join AdmNursingCensus nur on ad.VisitID
= nur.VisitID

where nur.DateTime = CONVERT(varchar(10),'yyyy-mm-
dd',23)
and LocationID in ('MSU2', 'MSU3', 'ICU')
and DischargeDateTime IS NULL
and datediff(dd, ad.AdmitDateTime, nur.DateTime) > '6'
```

Figure 2 documents the SQL code for the NoPCP query. The NoPCP metric was initially introduced in 2010 as a simple list of patients registered without a PCP. In January 2011 we experimented with looking up past history to see if a PCP could

be determined from previous visits. The combined metric (no PCP + Missed PCP) was formally adopted on March 1, 2011.

Figure 2. NoPCP SQL Query

```
Select ad.Name,
ad.AccountNumber,
ad.PtStatus,
ad.ObservationPatient,
CONVERT(Varchar(10),ad.AdmitDateTime,23)
AdmitDate,
CONVERT(varchar(10),ad.DischargeDateTime,23)
DischargeDate,
ad.ReasonForVisit,
ad.LocationID,
ad.FinancialClassName,
ap.AdmitProviderID AdmPhysician,
ap.ErProviderID ErPhysician,
isnull(ap.PrimaryCareProviderID, ap.FamilyProviderID) as
PrimaryCareProvider

from AbstractData ad join AbstractProviders ap on
ad.VisitID = ap.VisitID

where LocationID in ('MSU2','MSU3','ICU')
and (PtStatus = 'IN' or ObservationPatient = 'Y')
and CONVERT(varchar(10),AdmitDateTime,23) between
'2012-05-31' and '2012-05-31'

order by PrimaryCareProvider
```

The metrics were distributed among a list of 9 other metrics to hospital managers and senior leaders, including the CEO by email. Managers responsible for registration (NoPCP) and Case Management (Length of Stay) were included in the email distribution as well as their supervisors. We also met individually with those whose areas were measured by the metric to explain the metric, the importance of the measurement, and the larger up-and-down stream processes that were influenced by the specific activities measured by the metric.

Figure 3 displays the visual graph used to communicate the CALOS metric on March 17, 2011. The metric displays data from January, February, and March 1-17.

Figure 3. CALOS Visual Metric

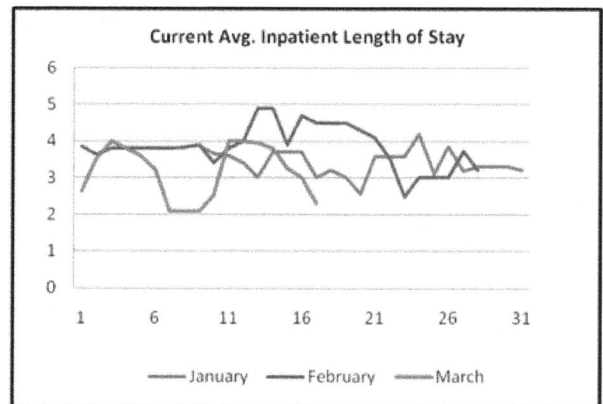

Figure 4 displays the visual graph used to communicate the NoPCP metric on March 18, 2011. We titled the graph "Every Patients a PCP" to identify the purpose of the measurement.

Figure 4. NoPCP Visual Metric

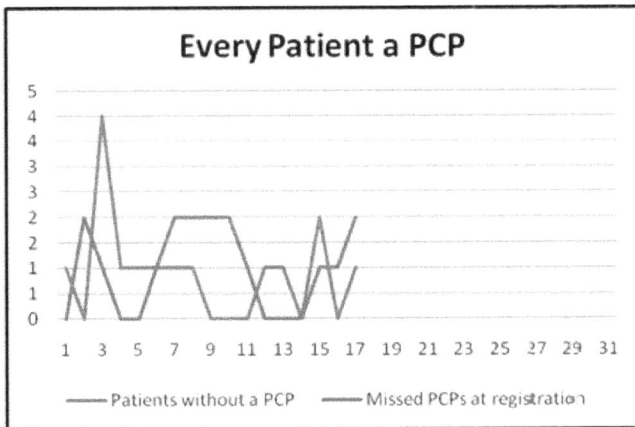

The graph displays patients without a PCP and patients who were mistakenly registered as not having a PCP. As noted above, accompanying the graph we included a list of the patients who were mistakenly registered without a PCP and the name of the PCP last attributed to that patient. After two months of distribution, we changed the visual to a bar graph which readers suggested was easier to understand.

6. Results

To determine the success of the CALOS metric, we calculated the average daily number of patients whose LOS exceeded 6 days and the average daily maximum LOS from November 1, 2010 (when we began recording pilot data) to November 30 2011 (lower numbers are better). We also recorded the average daily severity level of patients (mcmi) to ensure that LOS was not influenced by sicker patients.

To calculate the success of the NoPCP metric we retroactively looked at the percent of patients recorded without PCP versus those who actually did not have a PCP from January 2011 to May 2012.

In January 2012, the hospital implemented an upgrade to their Electronic Medical Record. A problem with the implementation took down the Data Repository and our ability to calculate (and report) any metrics from January 2012 to early March 2012. We have been able to reconstitute the NoPCP performance during this period but have not yet examined the CALOS. The downtime provided the unintentional benefit of a second metric test in which we could see if no reported metric influenced organizational performance. In addition, a new Vice President responsible for hospital quality was hired in mid-June 2012. Her portfolio included Case Management and by connection, patient LOS.

6.1 CALOS

As Figure 5 shows, the initial 4 months showed a decrease in the number of patients with a LOS greater than 6 days. Over the same time, the maximum length of stay for any one patient also decreased in 3 of the 4 months. One month (Feb) showed an increase in the maximum LOS due to one patient who had a 41-day LOS.

Despite initial success, over the next three months the measures increase exceeding the initial starting metric in June. June also included an outlier. However, even without the outlier the total number of patients with stays longer than 6 days increased between April and June. From June-October, the time after the new Vice President joined the organization, the measures decline before rising slightly in November.

6.2 NoPCP

Figure 6 displays the results of the NoPCP metric. The graph shows NoPCP documentation errors from January 2011 through May 2012. The top (solid) line records the total percent of patients who were registered without a PCP. The middle line (dashed) shows the error rate (percent of patient wrongly recorded without a PCP. The bottom line shows the actual number of patients without a PCP. The error rate declined from January 2011 to November 2011. It increased in December 2011 through March 2012.

Figure 5. CLOS Performance After Metric Introduction

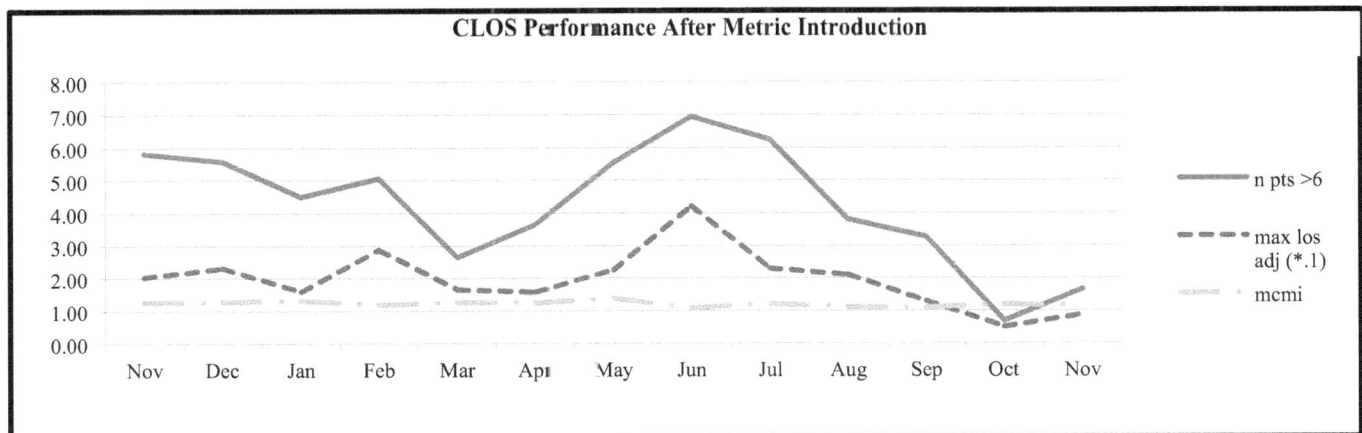

Figure 6. NoPCP Performance After Metric

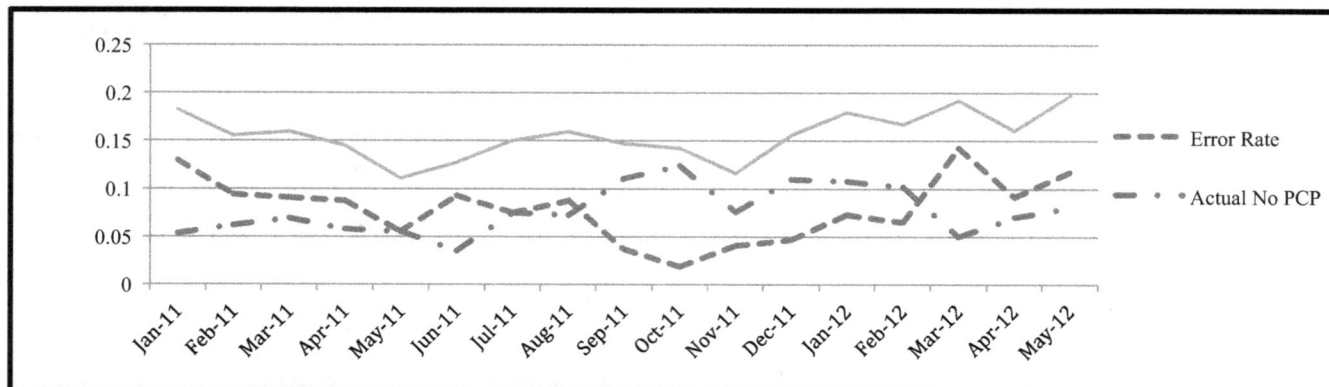

7. Discussion

The metrics appeared to have some initial influence on work performance. The NoPCP metric seems to have more sustained success. However, the improvements made during the reported period were given back over subsequent periods. These findings seem to indicate that the introduction of metric itself is not sufficient to sustain prolonged organizational change. We conclude that the metric requires some additional accountability provisions to ensure success.

In the case of the CALOS, simply reporting the metric seemed to have some influence but without accountability or other organizational activity attached to meeting the metric it should not be surprising to see the organization give back it gains. The instantiation of a new Vice President in June appears to have had considerable influence on performance. The severity of patients does not change, but the number of patients staying longer than 6 days drops rather dramatically to October. In this case, the additional supervisory function supports the metric. We should note that the new VP specifically requested that we continue to distribute (to her and widely) both the metric and the list of patients with LOS greater than 6 days.

The downtime NoPCP performance (January-March 2012) suggests some association between reporting the metric and work performance. The error rate drops in March and April once the metric resumed. However, the error rate increases again in May.

8. Conclusion

This study discussed the implementation of two new visual metrics on hospital administrative operations in order to introduce the topic and themes of visual analytics in healthcare to a technical communication audience. The project required designing a new way to communicate more effective patient management (CALOS) and more effective ways to coordinate patient care post-discharge (NoPCP). Both metrics were tied to granular hospital activities – preparing patients for discharge prior to the actual day of discharge and accurately reporting whether or not a patient has a PCP.

We entered the project (and the larger project of reporting hospital metrics generally) assuming that reporting performance data and making that data more transparent hospital-wide would inspire more effective performance. For example, we assumed that if staff registering patients knew that 12% of patients were incorrectly registered, clerks would become more careful when interviewing patients and entering patient data.

Similarly, we assumed that if clinical staff could see the number of patients with prolonged stays they would improve bed management. Unfortunately, these assumptions proved naïve over prolonged time. After some initial improvement it appears that more ingrained historical practices resumed over the longer term.

As a larger conclusion, our experience encourages researchers and practitioners to see nuanced value in visual forms for reporting operations data. The relationship between metrics, designing communication, and organizational performance is complicated and with significant issues beyond information and knowledge transfer. This may not be new information for many readers and we acknowledge numerous studies examining the political and social realities of organizational change [29]. At the same time, the growth of large data sets, availability of electronic data, and emergence of data mining, analytics, and metrics as renewed and promising fields offer the temptation to overlook the troubling social dynamics of organizations. As Pike et al. caution, "as visual analytics is concerned with the relationship between visual displays and human cognition, merely developing novel visual metaphors is rarely sufficient to trigger…insight (where insight may be a new discovery or confirmation or negation of prior belief)" [21, p.263]. While Pike et al. are more directly writing about interactive visuals for information processing we find this caution appropriate for more static, descriptive metrics as well.

For example, Fitzgerald and Dadich [13] in their implementation of visual analytics in a hospital emergency department integrated metrics of patient flow, room capacity, staff capacity, and equipment use into a visually-displayed virtual process model. As each individual metric was adjusted, clinicians could see the result on the larger operational arena of the emergency department. Further, adjusting metrics for ancillary departments (radiology, labs) could visualize the interrelatedness of processes between departments. This more global implementation (beyond single processes) seemed to help clinicians, managers, and supporting technologists visualize and thus better understand how their specific task (registering a patient's PCP for e.g.) fit within the hospital's larger performance.

Emerging as an interdisciplinary field, new studies of analytics integrate data mining, knowledge discovery, systems modeling, societal dynamics, and communication design. As such, the field represents an important meeting space for design, technology, and studies of humanity. As such, it is a field of practice and theory in natural alignment with rhetoric, information theory, and the design of communication.

9. ACKNOWLEDGMENTS

Our thanks to Community Hospital for allowing us to report our data from this project.

10. REFERENCES

[1] Andersen, R. and Davidson, P. 2007. "Improving access to care in America: Individual and contextual indicators" in *Changing the U.S. Health Care System: Key Issues in Health Services Policy and Management*, R. Andersen, T. Rice, and G. Kominski Eds. San Francisco: John Wiley & Sons, 3-32.

[2] Baker, S. 2008. *The Numerati*. Boston and New York: Mariner Books, Houghton Mifflin Harcourt.

[3] Berger, S. 2005. *The Power of Clinical and Financial Metrics*. ACHE Management Series, Health Administration Press. Chicago, IL.

[4] Blokzijl, W. and Andeweg, B. 2007. "The Effect of Text Slides Compared to Visualizations on Learning and Appreciation in Lectures," *Professional Communication Conference, 2007. IPCC 2007. IEEE International* pp.1-9, DOI: 10.1109/IPCC.2007.4464074 URL: http://ieeexplore.ieee.org/stamp/stamp.jsp?tp=&arnum ber=4464074&isnumber=4464038

[5] Breslow, L. and Fielding, J. 2007. "Public health and personal health services" in *Changing the U.S. Health Care System: Key Issues in Health Services Policy and Management*, R. Andersen, T. Rice, and G. Kominski Eds. San Francisco: John Wiley & Sons, 591-608.

[6] Brownlee, S. 2007. *Overtreated: Why too much medicine is making us sicker and poorer*. New York: Bloomsbury.

[7] Caldwell, J. 2009. "Safety icons and usability: A Peircean reanalysis," *Professional Communication Conference. IPCC IEEE International*, 1-8, doi: 10.1109/IPCC.2009.5208720 URL: http://ieeexplore.ieee.org/stamp/stamp.jsp?tp=&arnum ber=5208720&isnumber=5208666

[8] Chalice, R. 2007. *Improving Healthcare Using Toyota Lean Production Methods: 46 Steps for Improvement 2nd ed*. Milwaukee, WI: ASQ Quality Press.

[9] Corne, D., Dhaenens, C., and Jourdan, L. 2012. "Synergies between operations research and data mining: The emerging use of multi-objective approaches. *European J. of Operational Research* 221, 469-479. DOI= http://dx.doi.org/10.1016/j.ejor.2012.03.039

[10] Davenport, T. and Harris, J. 2007. *Competing on Analytics: The New Science of Winning*. Cambridge MA: Harvard Business Press.

[11] Davenport, T., Harris, J., and Morison, R. 2010. *Analytics at Work: Smarter Decisions Better Results*. Cambridge: Harvard Business Press.

[12] Dlugacz, y., Restifo, A., and Greenwood, A. 2004. *The Quality Handbook for Health Care Organizations*. Jossey-Bass, San Francisco, CA.

[13] Fitzgerald, J.A. and Dadich, A. 2009. "Using visual analytics to improve hospital scheduling and patient flow. *J. Theoretical and Applied Electronic Commercial Research* 4(2), 20-30. DOI: 10.4067/S0718-18762009000200003.

[14] Gawande, A. 2011. "The hot spotters". *New Yorker 24 January 2011*, 40-51.

[15] Heer, J., and Agrawala, M. 2008. "Design considerations for collaborative visual analytics." *Information Visualization* 7(49) 49-62. DOI=10.1057/palgrave.ivs.9500167.

[16] Ishizaki, S. 2001. "A model of aesthetic experience." *Professional Communication Conference (IPCC), 2011 IEEE International* 1-3. doi: 10.1109/IPCC.2011.6087208 URL: http://ieeexplore.ieee.org/stamp/stamp.jsp?tp=&arnum ber=6087208&isnumber=6087180.

[17] Kleim, D., Andrienko, G., Fekete, J-D., Gorg, C., Kohlhammer, J., & Melancon, G. 2008. "Visual analytics: Definition, process, and challenges." *Information Visualization, LNCS 4950*. Berlin & Heidelberg: Springer-Verlag, 154-175.

[18] Klein, P. and Cetin, N. "User-centered development of real-time dispatcher clients." *Professional Communication Conference (IPCC), IEEE International* 210-213. doi: 10.1109/IPCC.2010.5530011 URL: http://ieeexplore.ieee.org/stamp/stamp.jsp?tp=&arnum ber=5530011&isnumber=5529803

[19] Moseley, G. 2009. *Managing Health Care Business Strategy*. Sudbury, MA: Jones & Bartlett.

[20] Meditech Corporation http://meditech.com/productbriefs/pages/productpagedr.htm

[21] Pike, W., Stasko, J., Chang, R., O'Connell, T. 2009. "The science of interaction." *Information Visualization 8* (263), 263-274. DOI=10.1057/ivs.2009.22.

[22] Rodak. S. 2012. "Breaking down silos to improve patient flow, hospital efficiency. *Becker's Hospital Review*. DOI = http://beckershospitalreview.com/capacity-management/breaking-down-silos-to-improve-patient-flow-hospital-efficiency.html.

[23] Roy, D. 2008. "Using concept maps for information conceptualization and schematization in technical reading and writing courses: A case study for computer science majors in Japan," *Professional Communication Conference IPCC. IEEE International*, 1-12. URL: http://ieeexplore.ieee.org/stamp/stamp.jsp?tp=&arnum ber=4610238&isnumber=4610190

[24] Shannon, R. et al. 2006. Using real-time problem solving to eliminate central line infections. *Joint Commission J. on Quality and Patient Safety 32*(9) 479-487. DOI= http://macoalition.org/Initiatives/infections/general/feb4-2008/Using%20Real%20Time%20Problem%20Solving%20t o%20Eliminate%20Central%20Line%20Infections%20Articl e.pdf

[25] Spinuzzi, C. 2003. *Tracing Genres Through Organizations*. Cambridge, MA: MIT Press.

[26] Spinuzzi. C. 2008. *Network: Theorizing Knowledge Work in Telecommunications*. Cambridge UK: Cambridge UP.

[27] Swayne, L., Duncan, W., Ginter, P. 2006. *Strategic Management of Health Care Organizations 5th ed*. Malden, MA: Blackwell.

[28] Thomas, J., and Cook, K. 2005. *Illuminating the Path*. IEEE Society Press, Los Alamitos.

[29] Zachry, M. and Thralls, C. (eds). 2007. *Communicative Practices in Workplaces and the Professions: Culture Perspectives on the Regulation of Discourse and Organizations*. Amityville, NY: Baywood.

Investigating Usability and "Meaningful Use" of Electronic Medical Records

Christa B. Teston
University of Idaho
208 Brink Hall
Moscow, ID 83843
cteston@uidaho.edu

ABSTRACT

In this paper, I summarize research regarding known issues with Electronic Medical Record (EMR) software design and subsequent implementation. I consider the Centers for Medicare and Medicaid Services' cash incentive for EMR adoption, and the "meaningful use" criteria that mediate that incentive (Table 1). Based on this research and my own small-scale study of real time EMR use, I outline the ways that the same problems had by EMR usability researchers are also had by actual EMR users, themselves. Specifically, questions about how to account for both embodied and cognitive effects, how to discern noise from useful information, and how to make useful what is available are all concerns shared by both care providers using EMRs and those who study EMR usability. As a result, I propose that communication design researchers design usability studies that use Mol et al's [9] construct of "care" (as a practice) as the gold standard for "meaningful use." That is, meaningful use of EMR software ought to be articulated less in terms of task-oriented record-keeping practices and the time it takes to accomplish them, but in terms of Mol et al's three components of good care: embodied practices, attuned attentiveness, and adaptive tinkering.

Categories and Subject Descriptors

D.2.2 (Design Tools and Techniques/User Interfaces)

Keywords

Electronic medical records; meaningful use; design; care; usability

1. Introduction

George W. Bush claimed that electronic medical records (EMRs) would "help change medicine and save money and save lives" [1, 2]. But according to the U.S. Department of Health and Human Services, as of 2011, only 57% of office-based physicians used EMRs [3].

Advocates for the shift away from pen and paper medical records toward EMRs claimed that EMRs would reduce medical errors, eliminate the time consuming nature of handwritten clinical notes, increase consistency of medical record keeping practices, and create a storehouse of medical data that could be mined for

research [4]. While some have overstated the promise of the EMR as a way to "save money and save lives" [1], more recent research suggests that when EMRs are designed and deployed in certain ways, they change how care is provided in potentially useful ways.

Specifically, researchers deployed a robust natural-language querying strategy to mine text from annual foot examinations in diabetes patients' EMRs and were able to more accurately diagnose foot problems [5]. Additionally, scholars in medical decision-making have argued that EMRs can function like wikis in that they allow for the co-management of complex patient cases through asynchronous methods of communication [6]. Researchers have also used structured clinical data from EMRs to identify patients who were at risk for hospital-acquired acute kidney injury. They developed a model of patient risk for hospital-acquired acute kidney injury to predict which patients might benefit from intervention and/or increased monitoring [7]. And yet, clinicians are slow to adopt the use of EMR software in their practices.

Researchers who study Health Information Technology argue that one of, if not *the* main reasons healthcare practitioners in the US have been slow to adopt EMRs in their practices is because EMR software interfaces have poor usability. So while the adoption of EMRs in clinical practice was a response to a "demand for data transparency, reduced costs, and better health care" [8], those who are asked to deploy said software argue that it creates a greater cognitive and material workload, decreases efficiency, and does not afford the kind of multidisciplinary medical collaboration practitioners hope for [1, 2].

It no longer behooves us to compare the efficacy of electronic medical record keeping with pen and paper medical record keeping, or resist the so-called technologizing of care. Pen and paper are, after all, technologies; and technologies in healthcare have always existed (i.e., thermometers, stethoscopes, etc.). Mol et al. [9] argue that we ought not regard technology either as a mere functional tool or a usurper of care. Instead, they argue we should see machines as holding and performing various sometimes conflicting and sometimes harmonious concepts of good care. Mol et al define "good care" as "persistent tinkering in a world full of complex ambivalence and shifting tensions" (p. 14). Moreover, for the authors, technologies do not "work or fail in and of themselves." Instead, technologies depend on "people willing to adapt their tools to a specific situation while adapting the situation to the tools, on and on, endlessly tinkering" (p. 15). Mol et al, therefore, do not theorize care outside of already also theorizing technology. The authors discuss the ways that the hard work of *care* includes a complex of embodied practices, attuned attentiveness, and adaptive tinkering.

It is not within the scope of this paper to make definitive assertions about how EMR software ought to be redesigned, regulated, or standardized. Instead, in this paper, I heed Popham and Graham's [10] call for "more research in the areas of electronic organizational communication" (p. 149) in health fields. As such, in what follows, I

- summarize research on known issues with EMR design,

- describe some of the methodological problems associated with conducting usability studies with EMRs,

- deconstruct the government's criteria and measures for "meaningful use" of EMRs, and

- propose ways communication design researchers might reframe usability investigations of EMRs (and the EMR software systems, themselves) in order to account for Mol et al's construct of "care."

2. Issues with EMR Design

Researchers in medicine, ergonomics, health economics, cognitive science, and biomedical informatics have conducted several studies on the design of EMRs. Methods for these studies include modeling eye gaze patterns in clinical-patient interactions, conducting lag sequential analyses, surveys of care providers, and cost-benefit analyses [11, 12]. Findings from these studies suggest issues related to the design of EMRs and privacy, collaboration, memory, and efficiency (among others).

A small-scale study wherein I observed real time use of EMR software in the clinical moment, interviewed medical professionals who had adopted their use, and conducted an analysis of three EMR software system's interfaces (AllScripts, eClinical Works, and Centricity) reflected similar findings. Almost all EMRs contain a problem list, medication list, allergy list, notes, health maintenance information, and results retrieval (including blood work and imaging results). EMRs also contain computerized prescribing tools and the computerized ordering of scans and bloodwork. Each of the three EMR software systems I studied also provides varying degrees of space for the free forming of notes. The physician I studied deployed workarounds to the clunkiness of most EMR screens by developing a series of macros and shortcuts. So, in a few combinations of certain keystrokes, prefabricated text can be pasted over and over again across patients' records for the convenience of the healthcare provider. In what follows, however, I explicate issues users encounter with EMR software.

2.1.1 Privacy
With respect to concerns about EMR design and privacy issues, a wide-ranging survey of healthcare providers and patients resulted in negative attitudes from a rather substantial minority of participants about the secondary use of de-identified health information. Specifically, only 58% of patients responded that they believed that the benefits of sharing de-identified medical information outweighed the risk of privacy loss. This was especially true for participants who are already avid computer users [13].

2.1.2 Ergonomics of Collaborative Decision-Making
With regard to impacts the move from paper to computer has had on collaboration, scholars in medical informatics claim that, "the tangibility of paper to facilitate interaction is lost; the creation and display of information is different; the ergonomics are possibly a problem, and non-verbal interaction mechanisms require

consideration" [14, p. 97]. Morrison, et al. [14] provide several images of the ergonomic and embodied implications of paper versus electronic medical record-keeping for a group of interdisciplinary healthcare providers on rounds.

McGrath, Arar, and Pugh [15] conducted a study wherein six physicians were videotaped during consultations with 50 patients. Their analysis revealed that EMR use not only caused a loss of eye contact between the doctor and patient, but that doctors were "more physically oriented toward their computers than their patients" (p. 1). Researchers made suggestions about the importance of the "gaze" during the medical interview, and argue that physicians should deploy "breakpoints," or short periods of no computer use and sustained eye contact with patients in order to help reduce information loss (p. 3).

2.1.3 Memory
Cognitive scientists [16] have explored the ways moving from paper to computer impacts memory, or recall of significant patient information. Specifically, they explore the implication of the missing "narrative" from the patient record as a result from moving from paper to computer to store patient records. Other researchers argue that it is not necessarily the computer, itself, that creates issues surrounding physicians' recall of patient narrative detail. They argue that the design of the EMR software affords or constrains these activities [17].

2.1.4 Time and Cost
One of the chief complaints about EMRs is that their use does not save time and it costs too much [18, 26, 27, 30, 34]. Some clinicians find the design of the EMR software to be too generic. For instance, prevention-oriented physicians see the same interface as orthopedists [19], and so the options provided to them may not be relevant, and the options they use most may not be as easily accessible. Clinicians argue this decreases efficiency (wherein efficiency is measured by time to task and perceived cognitive workload). While some EMR software designers provide the overall architecture of the EMR interface and then allow physicians and other potential EMR users to contribute the medical terminology specific to that practice, patient body, or specialty, researchers who studied these users found that physicians resented the amount of additional time they were asked to contribute to the design of a product they feel they already paid too much money for in the first place [17].

2.1.5 Over Engineering
During a small-scale study in a general practitioner's office wherein I observed the use of EMRs in real time and interviewed its users, it was reported that the EMR software system this particular office used suffered from what Brown [20] calls over-engineering. Specifically, medical professionals were frustrated by the more than twenty point-and-clicks they had to get through just to pull up a single patient's record after logging in. Alerts in the form of pop-up boxes and interrupting text that appears on the screen often frustrated the physician I studied—something Connolly [21] calls "alert fatigue." Moreover, this particular EMR software did not allow the physician to be logged in to the system in more than one location. So, when the physician whose practices I studied would pull up a patient's laboratory results in his private office prior to meeting them in the examination room, he had to endure another lengthy login in the exam room. While this particular design feature was probably implemented as a way to maintain privacy, over engineering of the EMR interface leads

to feature fatigue and difficulty in discerning noise from information.

3. Methodological problems with studying EMR software

Many researchers who report on EMR use report some type of methodological complication associated with doing this research, itself. Specifically, there is some debate about the affordances of different kinds of usability methods for assessing the EMR [28, 29]. Among them include user testing, heuristic evaluation, cognitive walkthrough, and pluralistic usability walkthrough [31, 32]. Each approach yields different kinds and forms of data, but researchers seem to consistently report that they note complications with studying EMR usability because

- researchers have difficulty making generalizible recommendations for EMR redesign because not all medical specialties need or use the same portions of the EMR,

- researchers who are unfamiliar with medical terminology and other discipline-specific discourse experience difficulty when making recommendations about EMR content,

- researchers require permission from both practitioners and patients in order to study real time use of EMRs, so they often observe mock clinical moments with task-based objectives, and

- when researchers do observe real time, *in situ* EMR use, their observations are isolated events of clinical encounters and do not include tracing a single EMR over time and between collaborating care providers.

4. "Meaningful Use" of EMRs

At the time of this paper, there is not a standard for how EMR software should be designed. This creates its own list of adoption resistances—including fear that the EMR software system that hospitals or clinicians purchase and take the time to learn will soon become obsolete or incompatible with other hospitals' or clinicians' systems [22, 33].

While there is no standardization or governmental oversight on the design of EMR software, what counts as "meaningful use" of an EMR software system has been specified, and measures for assessment have been articulated. Specifically, the Obama Administration has tried to combat resistance to the adoption of EMR software with the Health Information Technology for Economic and Clinical Health Act (HITECH). The HITECH Act authorizes cash incentives through the Centers for Medicare and Medicaid Services to both clinicians and hospitals upon their adoption and meaningful use of EMRs. The list of mandatory steps medical practitioners must take in order to achieve meaningful use includes 15 objectives and corresponding measures by which the achievement of those measures are assessed (Table 1; note that here EMR is synonymous with Electronic Health Record, EHR).

Table 1. HITECH Act's "Meaningful Use" Objectives and Measures (Adapted from Blumenthal and Tavenner [23])

	Objective	Measure
1	Record patient demographics	>50% of patients' demographic data must be recorded
2	Record vital signs and chart changes	>50% of patients 2 years or older must have height, weight, and blood pressure recorded
3-5	Maintain up-to-date problem list of current and active diagnoses, medication lists, allergy lists	>80% of patients must have at least one entry recorded for each of the three lists
6	Record smoking status for patients 13 years of age or older	>50% of patients 13 years of age or older must have smoking status recorded
7	For individual professionals, provide patients with clinical summaries for each office visit; for hospitals, provide an electronic copy of hospital discharge instructions on request	>50% of patients must be provided with clinical summaries within 3 business days of an office visit; >50% of patients who are discharged from inpatient or emergency departments must be provided with an electronic copy of their discharge instructions if they request it
8	Provide patients with an electronic copy of their health information if they request it	>50% of requesting patients receive electronic copy within 3 business days
9	Generate and transmit permissible prescriptions electronically	>40% are transmitted electronically
10	Enter patients' medications using computer provider order entry	>30% of patients with at least 1 medication in their medication list have at least one medication ordered through CPOE
11	Implement drug-drug and drug-allergy interaction checks	Functionality is enabled for these checks for the entire reporting period
12	Implement capability to electronically exchange key clinical information among providers and patient-authorized entities	Perform at least one test of HER's capacity to electronically exchange information
13	Implement one clinical decision support rule and ability to track compliance with the rule	One clinical decision support rule implemented
14	Implement systems to protect privacy and security of patient data in the EHR	Conduct or review a security risk analysis, implement security updates as necessary, and correct identified security deficiencies
15	Report clinical quality measures to CMS or states	For 2012, electronically submit measures

In addition to these 15 objectives and measures, there is a list of 12 objectives and their corresponding measures from which health care practitioners, hospitals, and other eligible care professionals only have to choose five in order to be eligible for HITECH funds [23].

Discussions about what counts as meaningful use with respect to the adoption of EMR software in the clinical moment is an opportune moment for those of us committed to studying the design of communication to participate. Callon, Lascoumes, and Barthes [24] argue that socio-technical controversies (of which the adoption of government-mandated meaningful-use criteria may be considered) "reveal the multiplicity of stakes associated with one issue, but also...make the network of problems it raises both visible and debatable" (p. 31). They argue that these controversies also "allow the exploration of conceivable options by going beyond the list established by the official actors" (p. 31). As EMR software designers assess the usability of their product, they might consider ways that these meaningful use criteria might be modified to reflect EMR use as more than an attempt at record-keeping, but a complex human activity wherein human and nonhuman actors and verbal and nonverbal communication intersect.

For instance, how many of the 15 meaningful use criteria listed in Table 1 explain activity outside of activity? In other words, what makes each of those activities actually *meaningful*? Said another way, is there a way we might reconceive of meaningful use as more than a series of record-keeping related tasks, but as Witte and Haas [25] argue, a complex system of material, functional, and structural relations that hinge on considerations of design, construction and cost? Like Witte and Haas' speedbump as mediational means, the EMR directs and controls behavior and regulates activity. As such, in order to implement and subsequently assess meaningful use of EMR software, there ought to be a separation between the object of analysis and the analysis itself [25, p. 153].

Witte and Haas [25] argue that the essence of technology design is the "transferring [of] human competencies onto material objects through the process of either inscription or incorporation or both" (p. 148-149). If we think of the EMR as "infralinguistic" in that it "induces speech, talk, and the statement of propositions" [24, p. 53], how might measures of meaningful use be more aptly articulated? For Callon et al, "there is no world on one side and statements about the world on the other, but a thick and extensive layer of interwoven traces and statements linked and connected up to each other" [24, p. 54]. What are the interwoven traces and statements facilitated by EMR software design that allow physicians and patients to make the move from record-keeping to decision-making? How do we articulate, quantify, and assess those traces?

5. Designing Future EMR Usability Studies

While the audiences, means, and ends for EMR usability study results and the government's "meaningful use" criteria may be different, I propose that successful design of future EMR software systems might benefit from a co-articulation of the two assessments. Mehlenbacher [35, 36] argues that "design is wicked, messy, and inexact" [35, p. 90] and cites Schon's argument that "designers juggle variables, reconcile conflicting values, and maneuver around constraints—a process in which, although some design products may be superior to others, there are no unique right answers" (p. 42). My research suggests that users of EMR software systems and researchers who study the systems' usability struggle with similar design-related issues: privacy, efficiency, accounting for both cognition and embodiment, and discerning noise from data.

Software designers and policy-makers alike must leave enough designerly room to achieve a balance between what Spinuzzi [37] calls "inflexible and rule-bound" and "chaos" (p. 21). All parties involved in the providing of care—peripheral or otherwise—must

find a balance between absolute chaos and a set of sociotechnical lockins that discourage the agency of human and nonhuman actors. Algorithmic pathways and prescriptive criteria that do little in the way of actually describing the meaningfulness of use might be avoided if designers (of health and software) embrace Mol et al.'s [9] argument for care over control.

5.1 Considering Care

Specifically, Mol et al. [9] explain "care" as a complex of embodied practices, attuned attentiveness, and adaptive tinkering. They argue that "local solutions to specific problems need to be worked out" (p. 13). For them, "good care" is not something to "pass a judgement on, in general terms and from the outside," but, they argue, "something to *do*, in practice" (p. 13, emphasis in the original). Willems [38] challenges two dominant perspectives about the ways technology and good care are conceived. Specifically, he counters notions of technology that "crowd out real care" and the notion that "technical objects will not do anything we humans do not want them to do"—technology as a "means to an end" (p. 257). So what does this look like in practice? How can we articulate traces of meaningful use in ways that meet policy-makers' high expectations and the high stakes associated with human health?

Rather than proposing a set of propositions or heuristics for how meaningful use might be rearticulated to account for Mol et al.'s [9] construct of care, I will explain two snapshots from the same real life clinical care moment.

5.1.1 Snapshot One

A female patient presents at her doctor's office with a history of thyroid disease. Over the last three years she has gained, lost, and gained back 20-30 pounds, suffered fatigue, and reports major decreases in her ability to concentrate. A nodule on her thyroid appeared in an ultrasound two years before this particular doctor's visit. During this visit, the patient sat next to the physician's computing station, facing the doctor. The doctor immediately faced his computer, with a peripheral view of the patient. The doctor pulls up the images from the patient's latest ultrasound and said, "well, it all looks good," and moves on to discuss the adjustment of her medication to include cytomel alongside synthroid. The patient appears shocked and asks the doctor to explain the ultrasound results further. He reads verbatim from the ultrasound report. The patient then explains to her physician that during the ultrasound, the technician apologized for taking so long to image her neck because she was trying to "measure all the nodules." The doctor gives the patient a look of disbelief, stands up, pulls out his chair, and invites the patient to come around and sit down in his chair and see on the screen the actual images from her ultrasound. As she observes that there are no nodules on her thyroid according to the images on screen, he points and explains the unproblematic nature of variation of light and dark on the screen.

5.1.2 Snapshot Two

A female patient presents at her doctor's office for a follow-up appointment. Again, the patient sits next to the physician's computing station, facing the doctor. The doctor faces his computer, with a peripheral view of the patient. As the physician logs in to this patient's EMR, the patient apologizes to the physician that she did not get the bloodwork done that he asked of her in the previous visit. He asks, "what's your aversion to just getting your blood drawn?" She pulls up her sleeves to scars on both arms that extend from her wrist to approximately four inches up her arm. She explains that she's embarrassed to reveal the scars to a phlebotomist. During her explanation, the doctor maintains eye contact with the computer screen and appears to keep typing or scrolling through the patient's record. He replies to the patient, "so, tell me again…when did that happen?" She describes struggles with depression and how she's currently seeing both a psychologist and a psychiatrist.

5.2 Designing for Care

While the above two snapshots represent only a fraction of the clinical care moment—no longer than a total of two full minutes in either case—they are important moments in the providing of care. In these moments, doctor-patient trust is being negotiated through verbal and nonverbal means, and the EMR plays an interesting role in this negotiation. Specifically, in both snapshots, the EMR acts as more than a record-keeping device wherein symptoms of hypothyroid or suicide attempts are documented. Rather, the software and screen act as a kind of infralinguistic inscription or incorporation [25] wherein a patient's health is documented and doctor-patient trust is negotiated.

Continued research of EMR design and the space it inhabits will help communication design researchers make a case about meaningful use criteria and care. Embodied practices, attuned attentiveness, and adaptive tinkering are all a part of the act of good care. Long-range, mixed methods studies and meta-analyses of both EMR users and usability studies, themselves, will assist communication design researchers in not only creating heuristics for how to measure and assess these care practices, but then articulate them as meaningful to policy-makers.

6. REFERENCES

[1] Fletcher, M. 2005. President promotes switching to electronic records. *Washington Post*. January 28.

[2] Pagano. 2009. Converting to an Electronic Medical Record: Dialectics of Organizational Change. Conference Paper Presented at the National Communication Association. February 3, 2009.

[3] Hsiao, C., Hing, E., Socey, T., Cai, B. 2011. Electronic Health Record Systems and Intent to Apply for Meaningful Use Incentives Among Office-based Physician Practices: United States, 2001-2011. *NCHS Data Brief* 79. 1-8.

[4] Bates, D., Ebell, M., Gotlieb, E., Zapp, J., and Mullins, H.C., 2003. A Proposal for Electronic Medical Records in U.S. Primary Care. *Journal of the American Medical Informatics Association 10*. 1. 1-10. DOI 10.1197/jamia.M1097

[5] Pakhomov, S., Bjornsen, S., Hanson, P., and Smith, S. 2008. Quality Performance Measurement Using the Text of Electronic Medical Records. *Medical Decision Making* 28. 462-470. DOI 10.1177/0272989X08315253

[6] Naik, A., and Singh, H. 2010. Electronic Health Records to Coordinate Decision Making for Complex Patients: What Can We Learn from Wiki? *Medical Decision Making* 30. 722-731. DOI 10.1177/0272989X10385846

[7] Matheny, M., Miller, R., Ikisler, T.A., Waitman, L., Denny, J., Schildcrout, J., Dittus, R., Peterson, J. 2010. Development of Inpatient Risk Stratification Models of Acute Kidney Injury for Use in Electronic Health Records. *Medical Decision Making* 30. 639-650. DOI 10.1177/0272989X10364246

[8] Gunter, T.D. and Terry, N.P. 2005. The emergence of national electronic health record architectures in the United States and Australia: Models, costs, and questions. *Journal of Medical Internet Research, 7*(1):e3.

[9] Mol, A., Moser, I., and Pols, J. (eds.). 2010. *Care in Practice: On Tinkering in Clinics, Homes and Farms*. Verlag, Bielefeld, Transcript.

[10] Popham, S., and Graham, S. L. A Structural Analysis of Coherence in Electronic Charts in Juvenile Mental Health. *Technical Communication Quarterly 17*. 149-172. DOI: 10.10.1080/10572250801904622

[11] Miller, R., and Sim, D., 2004. Physicians' Use of Electronic Medical Records: Barriers and Solutions. *Project HOPE—The People to People Health Foundation*. 116-126. DOI 10.1377/hlthaff.23.2.116

[12] Montague, J.X., Chen, P., Asan, O., Barrett, B., and Chewning, B. 2011. Modeling Eye Gaze Patters in Clinician-Patient Interaction With Lag Sequential Analysis. *Human Factors: The Journal of the Human Factors and Ergonomics Society* 53. 502-518. DOI: 10.1177/0018720811405986

[13] Perera, G., Holbrook, A., Thabane, L, Foster, G., and Willison, D. 2011. Views on Health Information Sharing and Privacy From Primary Care Practices Using Electronic Medical Records. *International Journal of Medical Informatics* 80. 94-101. doi:10.1016/j.ijmedinf.2010.11.005

[14] Morrison, C., Fitzpatrick, G., and Blackwell, A. 2011. Multi-disciplinary Collaboration During Ward Rounds: Embodied Aspects of Electronic Medical Record Usage. *International Journal of Medical Informatics* 80. E96-e111. doi:10.1016/j.ijmedinf.2011.01.007

[15] McGrath, J.M., Arar, N.H., and Pugh, J.A. 2005. *Doctor-Patient Communication: The Influence of Electronic Medical Record Usage on Nonverbal Communication in the Medical Interview*. Veterans Evidence-based Research Dissemination Implementation Center, L. Murphy Memorial Veterans Hospital and University of Texas Health Science Center at San Antonio.

[16] Sharda, P., Das, A., Cohen, T., and Patel, V. 2006. Customizing Clinical Narratives for the Electronic Medical Record Interface Using Cognitive Methods. *International Journal of Medical Informatics* 75. 346-368. doi:10.1016/j.ijmedinf.2005.07.027

[17] Bleich, H., and Slack, W. 2010. Reflections on Electronic Medical Records: When Doctors Use Them and When They Will Not. *International Journal of Medical Informatics* 79. 1-4. doi:10.1016/j.ijmedinf.2009.10.002

[18] Tevaarwerk, G. Electronic Medical Records. *Canadian Medical Association Journal* 178, 10. 1323. DOI:10.1503/cmaj.1080032

[19] Smelcer, J., Miller-Jacobs, H., and Kantrovich, L. 2009. Usability of Electronic Medical Records. *Journal of Usability Studies* 4. 70-84.

[20] Brown, N. 2005. Driving EMR Adoption: Making EMRs a Sustainable, Profitable Investment. *Health Management Technology,* 25. 47-48.

[21] Connolly, C. 2005. Cedars-Sinai Doctors Cling to Pen and Paper. *The Washington Post*, p. A01.

[22] DesRoches, C., Campbell, E., Rao, S., Donelan, K., Ferris, T., Jha, A., Kaushal, R., Levy, D., Rosebaum, S., Shields, A., and Blumenthal, D. 2008. Electronic Health Records in Ambulatory Care—A National Survey of Physicians. *The New England Journal of Medicine* 359. 50-60.

[23] Blumenthal, D. and Tavenner, M. 2010. The "Meaningful Use" Regulation for Electronic Health Records. *The New England Journal of Medicine* 363. 501-504. DOI 10.1056/NEJMp1006114

[24] Callon, M., Lascoumes, P., and Barthe, Y. 2011. *Acting In an Uncertain World: An Essay on Technical Democracy.* Cambridge, MA, MIT Press.

[25] Witte, S. and Haas, C. 2005. Research in Activity: An Analysis of Speed Bumps as Mediational Means. *Written Communication* 22. 127-165. DOI: 10.1177/0741088305274781

[26] Alder-Milstein, J., and Bates, D., 2011. A Survey of Health Information Exchange Organizations in the United States: Implications for Meaningul Use. *Annals of Internal Medicine* 154. 666-671.

[27] Evans, D., Nichol, W.P., and Perlin, J. 2006. Effect of the Implementation of an Enterprise-Wide Electronic Health Record on Productivity in the Veterans Health Administration 1. 163-169. doi:10.1017/S1744133105001210

[28] Hoffman, S. and Podgurski, A., 2008. Finding a Cure: The Case for Regulation and Oversight of Electronic Health Record Systems. *Harvard Journal of Law & Technology* 22. 103-165.

[29] Healthcare Information and Management Systems Society HER Usability Task Force. June 2009. *Defining and Testing EMR Usability: Principles and Proposed Methods of EMR Usability Evaluation and Rating.*

[30] Hussain, A. 2011. Meaningful Use of Information Technology: A Local Perspective. *American College of Physicians,* 154. 690-692.

[31] Jaspers, M.W. 2009. A comparison of usability methods for testing interactive health technologies: methodological aspects and empirical evidence. *International Journal of Medical Informatics* 78(5):340-353.

[32] Hollingsed, T., and Novick, D. 2007. Usability Inspection Methods After 15 Years of Research and Practice. In Proceedings of the 26th ACM International Conference on Design of Communication (SIGDOC, El Paso, TX, USA).

[33] Ludwick, D.A., and Doucette, J. 2009. Adopting electronic medical records in primary care: Lessons learned from health information systems implementation experience in seven countries. *International Journal of Medical Informatics* 78. 22-31. doi:10.1016/j.ijmedinf.2008.06.005

[34] Wang, S., Middleton, B., Prosser, L., Bardon, C., Spurr, C., Carchidi, P., Kittler, A., Goldszer, R., Fairchild, D., Sussman, A., Kuperman, G., and Bates, D. 2003. A Cost-Benefit Analysis of Electronic Medical Records in Primary Care. *American Journal of Medicine* 114. 397-403. doi:10.1016/S0002-9343(03)00057-3

[35] Mehlenbacher, B. 2007. Multidisciplinarity and 21st Century Communication Design. *SIGDOC* 59-65.

[36] Mehlenbacher, B. 2009. Triangulating Communication Design: Emerging Models for Theory and Practice. *SIGDOC* 87-94.

[37] Spinuzzi, C. 2003. Tracing genres through organizations. Cambridge, MA: MIT Press.

[38] Willems, D. 2010. Varieties of goodness in high-tech home care. In Mol, et al. (Eds.) *Care and Practice.*

Uncovering Analogness and Digitalness in Interactive Media

Jeffrey Tzu Kwan Valino Koh

NGS, Keio-NUS CUTE Center
21 Heng Mui Keng Terrace
#02-01-01, Singapore, 119613
+65 6516 5951
jtkvkoh@gmail.com

Roshan Lalintha Peiris

NGS, Keio-NUS CUTE Center
21 Heng Mui Keng terrace
#02-01-01, Singapore, 119613
+65 6516 5951
roshan82@gmail.com

Kening Zhu

NGS, Keio-NUS CUTE Center
21 Heng Mui Keng terrace
#02-01-01, Singapore, 119613
+65 6516 5951
kenju850915@gmail.com

Doros Polydorou

ADM, Nanyang Technical University
81 Nanyang Drive, Level 3
Singapore, 637458
+65 6790 4828
dorosp@gmail.com

Ryohei Nakatsu

NGS, Keio-NUS CUTE Center
21 Heng Mui Keng terrace
#02-01-01, Singapore, 119613
+65 6516 5951
elenr@nus.edu.sg

ABSTRACT

In this paper we analyze the works of the Keio-NUS CUTE Center at the National University of Singapore in order to uncover the dispositions of "analogness" and "digitalness" in regards to the relationship between users and interfaces. By comparing concepts of embodiment from a philosophical perspective, paired with the computer science treatment of analog and digital data, we derive a contingent definition for analog-like and digital-like interaction. With case studies as reference, we outline a continuum to describe types of interfaces based on these dispositions, which could then be further analyzed using characteristics for designing analog-like, digital-like or hybrid-like interactive systems. Finally, we propose a new methodology for designing novel interactive systems that are analog in nature, called interactive analog media (IAM).

Categories and Subject Descriptors

H.5.2 [**Information Interfaces and Presentation**]: User Interfaces – *Benchmarking, Theory and methods, User-centered design.*

General Terms

Design, Human Factors, Measurement, Standardization, Theory.

Keywords

Analogness, continuous, digitalness, discrete, embodiment, interactive.

1. INTRODUCTION

Since the advent of the lever and button [7] we have seen an increasing amount of methods in which users interact with machines. Major breakthroughs in interface development such as tangible user interfaces (TUIs) [12], multitouch interfaces [25], and more recently, organic user interfaces (OUIs) [23] have afforded new ways for human-computer interaction (HCI) researchers the means to create innovative, interactive systems.

Likewise theories of the relationship between interactive systems and users has been explored though concepts of embodiment ever since Descartes published his Mediations on First Philosophy [8] right through to Merleau-Ponty and his theories regarding phenomenology [16], to Dourish's incorporation of phenomenology into HCI [9], and beyond. With the dawn of ubiquitous computing, Mark Weiser attempts to extend this notion of phenomenology with new digital computing technologies. By "weave(ing) themselves into the fabric of everyday life" Weiser tries to bring digital technologies into the analog world around us [24]. However, as we move into the 21st Century, a dichotomy between what is analog and what is digital has emerged [1]. This duality provides an opportunity to discuss and analyze interactive systems that have tendencies towards either analog-like or digital-like interaction characteristics, or even a hybrid of both. Here, the duality addresses the relationship between the user and the interactive interface in terms of the action by the user and the reaction of the system and vise versa.

Using case studies derived from the extensive body of published works developed and studied at the Keio-NUS CUTE Center at the National University of Singapore, we discuss in this paper the topic of embodiment within HCI as well as in the humanities. We then outline in this paper the characteristics of "analogness" and "digitalness" regarding the relationship between interactive systems and users. From this point we then define a taxonomy for types of interactive systems (analog-like, digital-like, hybrid-like), and propose a continuum for analog-like-to-digital-like interaction.

By creating the Analogness-Digitalness Continuum (ADC), we can then begin to define a new methodology for designing novel interactive systems based on their analog-like versus digital-like tendencies, and propose a new field of research to counterbalance interactive digital media (IDM) [19] based on interactive analog media (IAM).

The main motivation to create such a method of classification is two-fold. Firstly, the ADC in of itself can be used to study and classify all interactive systems.

Secondly, the ADC in conjunction with the proposed characteristics found in this manuscript can be used to direct development of such systems in order to achieve particular styles of interaction and user/system relationship.

In the next section we present a philosophical overview to the notion of embodiment and its contemporary representation in interactive media. Through this discussion we define "analogness" and "digitalness" for interactive systems. The following section presents a prototypical Example of an Interactive Analog-like Interface, which analyses some well-known works and concepts in interactive systems research, in terms of their analogness and digitalness. We then introduce our grounding characteristics to define the analogness or the digitalness of an interactive system. These characteristics are further expanded and explained in the next section titled characteristics for Defining Systems with Analog-like and/or Digital-like interactions. Next in the Case Studies section we analyze some works of the Keio-NUS CUTE Center, and then move to propose the Analogness-Digitalness Continuum, after which we conclude the paper by inviting researchers and practitioners of all interested fields to further define guidelines derived from the characteristics as outlined in this paper.

2. ON EMBODIMENT

There is no widespread acceptance regarding a universal definition on immersion and embodiment, therefore it is important before moving on to place them into context. As this paper concentrates on human-computer interactions with a special emphasis on their embodied potentialities, embodiment will be referring to a state where one has the ability to interact with a system through an interface, as well as receive and cause stimuli and experiences within a given space. This section will explore the notions of disembodiment as well as issues of phenomenology as proposed and discussed by Descartes, Merleau-Ponty and Mark Hansen. The phenomenological theories will then be applied in creating a distinction between the interactions of a user with a digital-like and an analog-like system.

The philosopher René Descartes suggested the idea of disembodiment in the 17th century. In his unfinished treatise *The Description of the Human Body*, Descartes describes the human body as a machine, where heat from the heart causes all the movement in the body. Veins, just like pipes, carry blood from all parts of the body towards the heart, where it serves as nourishment for the heat that is there. He believed that the most agitated and lively part of the blood would be taken to the brain where it would compose a subtle wind, called the animal spirit or the soul, that enabled the brain to experience, think and imagine [20]. The soul, according to Descartes, is in fact a separate nonmaterial entity that exists inside and controls the body. This idea had been proposed also by Plato centuries before who believed that the body is from the material world whereas the soul is from the world of ideas, united temporarily with the body and separated at death when it would return to the world of Forms. This dichotomy of the body and soul – commonly referred to as dualism or the Cartesian split – serves as the basis for modern ideas about disembodiment,

inhabitation of virtual avatars and transfer of consciousness from one body to another.

Jacquelyn Ford Morie, looking at immersion from a phenomenological point of view, argues in her paper Performing in *(Virtual) Spaces: Embodiment and Being in Virtual Environments* that "VEs engage the body as kinesthetic input via the specialized interface devices that not only permit but require bodily actions to be performed sensorially, kinesthetically and proprioceptively – within a full 3d spatial yet virtual construct" [17]. She goes on to mention that since the VR equipment mediates our perception, we must try and understand what constitutes a mediated environment.

The French phenomenological philosopher Maurice Merleau-Ponty on the other hand, views the phenomenal body as our primary access to our reality. Even though there are several approaches to phenomenology, Merleau-Ponty views the individual and the world not as part of a whole but rather as separate entities subjected to the phenomenon of the individual. Hansen, in his book *Bodies in Code* celebrates and expands this idea to the domain of new media art [11]. He argues that technologies can change or enhance our sensory experiences consequently affecting our view of embodiment. Wanting to move away from what he calls "the clichés of disembodied transcendence" Hansen envisions a world with a fluid interpenetration of the virtual and the physical realm [11]. Deriving his theories from Merleau-Ponty's notion of "reversibility" and the idea that the body has an ability of inverse sensorial duality (for example, it can see and can be seen), the main focus of Hansen's book is how vision needs to be combined with touch in order to shorten the gap between ocularcentrism and a body's inherent simultaneous multi-sensations.

Going a step further, Hansen argues "Motor activity" – not representationalist verisimilitude holds the key to fluid and functional crossing between virtual and physical realms [11]. According to Hansen the success of generating compelling virtual experiences comes not from representational aesthetics but rather by simulating tactile, proprioceptive and kinesthetic sense modalities. Expanding on a theme addressed in his previous book *New Philosophy for New Media*, Hansen couples the sense of reality with touch and the perception of spatial depth and argues that by including bodily movement the formula has enough elements to "synthesize" the other senses; therefore perception is transformed into experience [11]. He calls this notion Mixed Reality and defines it as "The eschewal of representationalism and embrace of a functional perspective rooted in perceptuo-motor activity" [11].

In HCI, the controls of an analog interface can be directly integrated or expanded into a perceptuo-motor activity, as there is no technological mediation between the interface and the system. Digital interfaces on the other hand are not a direct result of "the organism within" but rather on the representation of the action as mediated by the technology (what Merleau-Ponty refers to as the body image).

Hansen, in his first chapter in *Bodies in Code* defines Merleau-Ponty's body image and body schema as "...The body image characterizes and is generated from a primary visual apprehension of the body as an external object, the body schema emerges from what, with autopoietic theory, we have called the operational perspective of the embodied organism" [11]. Merleau-Ponty offers an account of the body schema as "a flexible, plastic, systemic form of distributed agency encompassing what takes place within the boundaries of the body proper (the skin) as well as the entirety of the spatiality of embodied motility". In other words the body image refers to how the body is represented whereas the body schema refers to the organism within, which is caused by movement and subsequently causes it [16]. As Hanson phrases it: "Because it is responsible for linking proto sensory bodily sense (proprioception) with perception and motility the body schema is a source of embodied potential" [11].

Discussing along the same lines, Brian Massumi in his book *Parables for the Virtual* argues that the digital realm has potentiality but what really produces the possibilities (which he calls inventions) is the analog. "Whatever inventiveness comes about, it is a result not of coding itself but of its detour into the analog. The processing may be digital – but the analog is the process. The virtuality involved, and any new possibility that may arise, is entirely bound up with the potentializing relay. It is not contained in the code" [15].

As this paper is mainly concerned with the user experience and the embodied interaction between a user and a system, a clear differentiation can be noted between a user interacting with the body schema and one that is not. When an action comes from "within one's organism", as a direct continuation of an embodiment in space, it becomes intuitive and analogous to the data it represents. When the interface is of a digital form, the action does not flow naturally but rather is broken down and rebuilt in a discrete manner dependent on the rules specified by the mediated technology, resulting into a dichotomy of the embodied potential and the intended result.

With this established, we now look to computer science and engineering for another dichotomistic definition in which the above discussed ruminations regarding embodiment can be synthesized with. By drawing comparison between a philosophical treatments of what is analog and digital and the computer science attitude towards analog and digital data (data being the embodiment of information with which a user can manipulate and interact with), we can attempt to define analogness and digitalness within the context of HCI.

3. DEFINING ANALOGNESS AND DIGITALNESS

In the past, philosophers such as David Lewis discussed the troublesomeness of distinguishing analog and digital classifications [14]. He mentions that even though it is relatively easy to make the distinction in practice, the analysis of such representations from a philosophical standpoint is difficult.

Yet from a computational standpoint, the distinction is much more defined. Dale and Lewis attempt to describe analog and digital data: "Analog data is a continuous representation (as represented in Figure 1), analogous to the actual information it represents. Digital data is a discrete representation (as represented in Figure 2), breaking the information up into separate elements." [6].

From Dale and Lewis' definition in comparison with concepts of embodiment discussed in the previous section of this paper, we can derive and adapt our own definition for analog-like and digital-like interaction:

Analog-like interfaces create a continuous experience for both the user and the system, analogous to the actual information it represents. Digital-like interfaces create a discrete experience, segregating the users' interaction with information and the system's interaction with the user into separate events.

Adopting this definition helps us outline the differences between interactive systems and highlight features that are disposed to analog-like versus digital-like tendencies when representing interactive content to users. The differences can then become identifiable characteristics that could help in the development of interactive systems, which are discussed in detail later on in this paper. Yet before continuing, an analysis of well-known HCI projects using the above-proposed definition should be made.

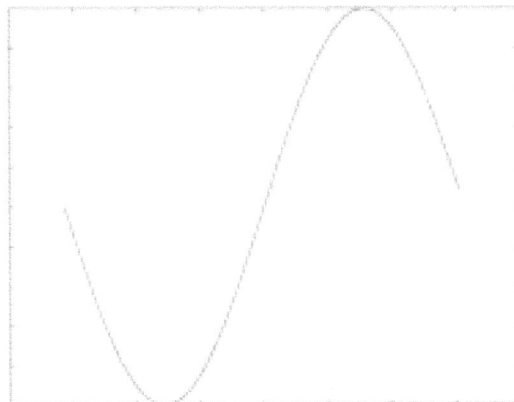

Figure 1. A continuous, analog signal.

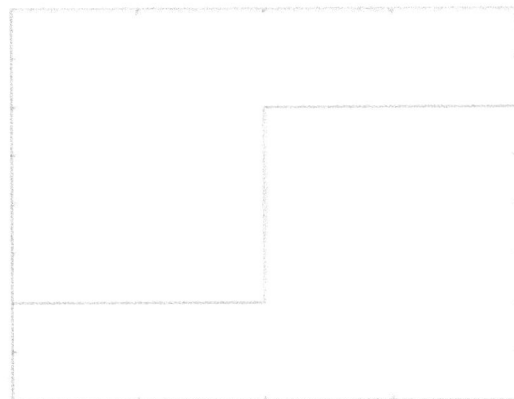

Figure 2. A discrete, digital signal.

4. A PROTOTYPICAL EXAMPLE OF AN INTERACTIVE ANALOG-LIKE INTERFACE

Adhering to this early classification of the digitalness and analogness of interactive systems, we investigate Ishii's work on Tangible Bits [12], in this context. We investigate the work presented in Tangible Bits due to its wide acceptance as the work that defines the notion of "tangible bits". Furthermore, to our understanding, this work contains both digital-like and analog-like affordances that would help us to define the true digitalness or analogness of interactive systems.

Tangible Bits represents a wave of new interface technologies that lets users grasp and manipulate digital information. Thus, the work here mainly focuses on the interface aspects of the interaction. In completing the equation, this paper introduces the user into the scenario and addresses her involvement with the interface, the interaction and the embodiment of these aspects with relation to the user.

The vision of tangible bits is introduced through the three main design projects of metaDESK, transBOARD and ambientROOM. These projects present various ways of representing digital information through tangible objects. Thus here, we analyze some of these interfaces and interactions in terms of their digitalness or analogness.

In the metaDESK, there are few tangible objects such as the "phicons", etc. which represents various interactions for the user. They are used on a tabletop setting to which the graphical user interface is projected on to the surface. The user interacts with this graphical user interface (GUI) using tangible objects. Here, the phicons are picked up, placed, rotated, etc. by the user on the tabletop. These various actions represent various reactions such as identification, rotation, zooming and so forth in the GUI. Thus, these intuitive actions that we would use on such a tangible object represent the interactions with the system. In addition, the interaction is continuous, as we would interact with a tangible object, without having to follow a discrete set of steps. Thus, the actions are embodied within the object or the interface. Hence, the phicons interface contains analog-like characteristics.

However, the output of the system here is a projection onto the tabletop. According to our earlier discussions this creates a dichotomy between the interface and the media, as it is not combined in a singular fashion. The interface (in this case, the table) does not have any particular representation of media or content. Thus simply changing the table to a wall would not have any effect on the media or the content, as it is a digital representation that is displayed as the output. This disconnection we see as a main characteristic of a digital-like system.

These key characteristics are seen in some of the early works of tangible user interfaces. In [12] again, similar to TUI's, physical pucks are used on a "sensetable" as the input devices. By relocating and rearranging these pucks the user can change various parameters of the system that is visualized through the output image projected onto the table. Here too, the use of physical pucks and their various orientations are intuitively engineered. This can be seen as an intuitiveness that leads to continuous interaction with this interface. In other words, the change in the orientation of the puck directly changes the parameters and causes a continuous interaction. However in contrast to this analogness of the input, in terms of the output of the system, once again, the projection creates a dichotomy between the projected content and the interface. The projection is not defined by the interface. Even if the interface was a scroll button of a mouse, or the output surface was a tabletop or a wall the projection is unhindered. As mentioned before this discontinuity or the discreteness between the output and the interface becomes a characteristic of a digital system.

This use of analog-like characteristics and digital-like characteristics presents a hybridized architecture for these technologies. This is one of the key characteristics of tangible user interfaces where the focus is mainly on the tangibility of the interface rather than its form or function. In addition, it only focuses on the interface and limits its involvement of the user and her role in the interface. Thus, the analog-like and digital-like characteristics are mixed more often in these technologies.

Thus moving ahead from tangible user interfaces, researchers of more recent fields like organic user interfaces started refining the characteristics of the interface itself [23]. Adhering to the three tenants of OUI's, input equals output, form equals functions and form follows flow [23], OUI's focused on the ergonomics of the interface to define its function and interaction. Thus, textiles, paper, and many other forms of flexible daily objects have become interfaces. Consideration of the ergonomics of the objects helps the interfaces to encompass more analog characteristics to its design. However, here too the lack of consideration of the user's involvement of the design of the interaction process has led to these systems to be more hybrid in nature as well.

For example, many of the recently developed fabric displays too fall under this category of organic user interfaces. However, there is a keen interest in combining media such as light emitting diodes (LEDs) and electroluminescence materials [4]. Thus, in the context of an embodied interface, such displays or interfaces fall short of using extended characteristics of the textile itself and rather superimpose a foreign object or material creating a vivid dichotomy between the material and the interface. Hence, the user's interaction is in fact with the LED or the EL wire, which represents the digital information and not the actual "fabric" itself as an interface. Therefore, the extension of the interface is to a foreign material making it more digital-like in nature.

Analyzing these concepts such as tangible user interfaces and organic user interfaces makes it clearer that most of these concepts focus their definitions towards the interfaces themselves. Thus, in determining the analogness or the digitalness of the interface and more importantly the interaction, we stress the importance in considering the user and the extension of user's notion of embodiment towards the user interface. Just as Mark Weiser depicted that "the most profound technologies are those that disappear" [23], the extension of the interface and more importantly the interaction as a single embodiment becomes important throughout the definition of the analogness and the digitalness of the interface and the interaction. Thus, in defining these characteristics and analyzing the previous concepts, we identify the following main points to define these characteristics:

- Analog-Like Interactive Systems: Content and Media are Singular in Embodiment

- Digital-Like Interactive Systems: Content and Media are Dichotomistic in Embodiment

- Analog-Like Interactive Systems: Interaction is Continuous

- Digital-Like Interactive Systems: Interaction is Discrete

- Analog-Like Interactive Systems: The Interface is Intuitive

- Digital-Like Interactive Systems: The Interface is Mediated

- Hybrid-Like Interactive Systems: Fulfills Some or All of the Afore Mentioned Rules

5. CHARACTERISTICS OF SYSTEMS WITH ANALOG-LIKE AND/OR DIGITAL-LIKE INTERACTION

Analog-Like Interactive Systems: Content and Media are Singular in Embodiment

Just as analog data in a computational system can be described as analogous to the actual data it represents, so do analog-like interactive systems represent data to users as a singular embodiment where content and system are one and the same.

Digital-Like Interactive Systems: Content and Media are Dichotomistic in Embodiment

In digital computational systems, data is represented discretely, breaking up information into separate elements. A digital-like interactive system therefore separates content and interface so that data delivered by the interactive system can be changed and replaced by different data. Content and media are therefore mutually exclusive and represent two separate embodiments.

Analog-Like Interactive Systems: Interaction is Continuous

Much as analog data is a continuous and infinite representation, so is the interaction method in analog interactive systems.

Digital-Like Interactive Systems: Interaction is Discrete

In digital computational systems, data is finite and compartmentalized into limited data sets. Therefore digital-like interactive systems are precise in their interactions, meaning that there is a limited selection of variables when interacting with the system.

Analog-Like Interactive Systems: The Interface is Intuitive

From a user standpoint, analog-like interactive systems feel natural to use. They are extensions of the body and when used, become part of the embodiment of the user.

Digital-Like Interactive Systems: The Interface is Mediated

Digital-like interfaces are always accessed through a discrete interface method or technology. Users must use a tool with a precise function and method of use in order to interact with the system.

Hybrid-Like Interactive Systems: Fulfills Some or All of the Afore Mentioned Rules

Hybrid-like interactive systems exhibit some or all of the characteristics of both analog-like and digital-like interactive systems.

The characteristics of systems with analog-like and/or digital-like interaction can be used as a lens to analyze the relationship between interactive systems and users. In the following section, we will attempt to differentiate projects by their analogness and digitalness by applying the characteristics to a series of case studies.

6. CASE STUDIES

In this section we will analyze six existing interactive systems from Keio-NUS CUTE Center [5], in the context of interactive analog and digital media. By apply the rules described in the last section, we divide these projects into three main categories: analog-like, digital-like, and hybrid.

6.1 Analog-like Relationship Between User and System

In this section we discuss projects with analog-like characteristics by looking at the Living Media and Huggy Pajama projects.

Living Media [3] is a new form of interactive ambient media using living organisms to communicate social, human or ecological information, such as the status of health, environmental pollution, and remote interactions between friends. As shown in Figure 3, in a Living Media system, information is semantically coupled into a living plant, in this case cabbage.

Situating Living Media with the proposed characteristics, it can be seen that Living Media communicates information through the intrinsic properties of living creatures, such as shape-changing and color-changing characteristics. Therefore the content and the media are naturally singular. In terms of the continuousness of user interaction, Living Media using cabbage to perform the output with the slow and gradual change of color under chemical solution with different pH values. Furthermore, the input information is from the natural environment, which is continuously changing; this also implies that there is no limited or specific set of input data for the living media, which means users can map any type and range of variable to ambient Living Media. In addition, the results of a user study for Living Media shows that it is visual and easy for user to understand information data through, and generate empathy for natural living creatures. Therefore, Living Media falls in the category of analog-like interface.

Figure 3. One of the Living Media projects, Babbage Cabbage was demonstrated at Laval Virtual 2009 in Laval, France.

Huggy Pajama [22] is a wearable system to allow parents and children to communicate over the Internet by physically hugging each other through a novel hugging interface. A demonstration and user study of the system is shown in Figure 4.

Figure 4. User study and demonstration of Huggy Pajama in Singapore, 2010.

In the Huggy Pajama system, the pajama with embedded actuators generates the remote physical hug. Without wearing the pajama, users cannot experience the remote hugging interaction, which means the hug sent through the Internet cannot be separated from the pajama. The input data for Huggy Pajama, such as touch and pressure, are continuously sensed in a wide range by the embedded Quantum Tunneling Composite (QTC) circuits. On the other side, the air pressure in the pajama changes slowly in a continuous way under a closed-loop controlling system. According to the user study, users showed interest to use Huggy Pajama to hug each other remotely, and it doesn't take effort to use the interface, as only touching input is required. With this analysis, we categorized Huggy Pajama as an analog-like interface.

6.2 Digital-like Relationship Between User and System

In this section we discuss projects with digital-like characteristics by looking at the Poetry Mix-up and Confucius Computer projects.

Poetry Mix-up [10] is an extension of the existing text-messaging paradigm to a new level of self-expression and cultural communication, combining visual art and poetry. Mixing and generating poetry based on users' input messages is the major element of this system, which transforms the users into experiencing the state of being a poet. An installation of Poetry Mix-up is shown in Figure 5.

Figure 5. Poetry Mix-up demonstrated at Art Center Nabi in Seoul, South Korea in 2011.

In the context of interactive analog media and digital media, in Poetry Mix-up the generated poems that are finally displayed to the public are stored in a database. Therefore, the stored poems are not bond to any specific media, such as workstations, displays and messaging devices. In addition, the poem is generated in a set of discrete steps using natural language processing, and mobile communication devices mediate the interaction. Therefore, we can argue that Poetry Mix-up is a digital-like media.

Confucius Computer [2] is a new form of illogical cultural computing based on the eastern philosophy of balance and harmony. The system enables users to have meaningful chatting with a virtual Confucius, as shown in Figure 6, to explore the Confucius philosophy, and even solve personal problems on occasion. Similar to Poetry Mix-up, it employs extensive advanced information retrieval and natural language processing techniques.

Therefore, Confucius Computer shares similar characteristics with Poetry Mix-up. It does not attach to any special hardware, and is available online. The virtual Confucius generates a related reply from analects in a series of discrete steps. As well as being mediated by the traditional computer interface, Confucius Computer can be also categorized into digital-like media.

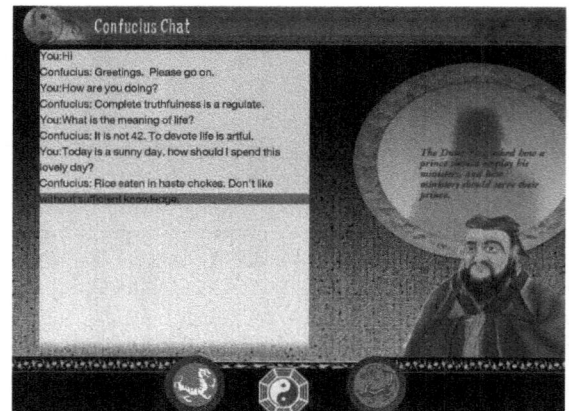

Figure 6. A screenshot of the Confucius Computer chat interface.

6.3 Hybrid-like Relationship Between User and System

In this section we discuss projects with hybrid-like characteristics by looking at the Metazoa Ludens and Age Invaders projects.

Metazoa Ludens is a revolutionary system that enables humans to play computer games with small animals in a mixed reality environment [21]. In this system as shown in Figure 7, the human user controls a movable robotic arm through a virtual reality game where the robotic arm is represented as a human avatar. The virtual-reality game is not bound to any special computer, and is mediated by the keyboard interface. On the other hand, for the pet user, within the large running environment, it chases freely and continuously after the robotic arm and the pet itself is the content and the media during the interaction, as its body is captured and recognized by the camera. In addition, based on the user study of the desire for pet to play this system, the pet hamster showed great interest in chasing the physical robotic arm. Therefore a mixture of both analog-like and digital-like media is shown, which makes Metazoa Ludens a hybrid-like interactive system.

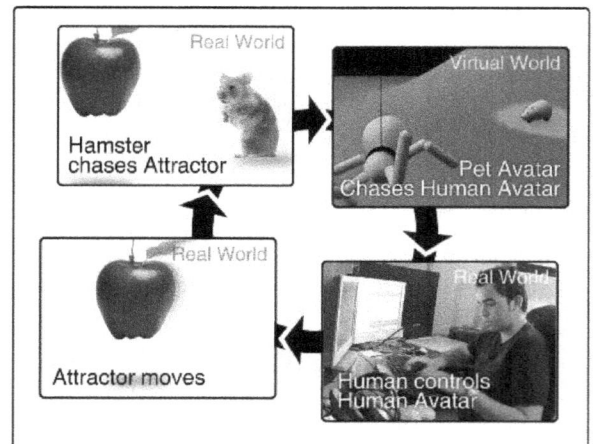

Figure 7. Hamster-Human interaction in Metazoa Ludens.

Age Invaders (Figure 8) is a novel interactive intergeneration physical game that allows the elderly to play harmoniously together with children in physical space, while parents can participate in the game play in real-time through the Internet [13].

Figure 8. Elderly users of the Age Invaders interactive, physical game system.

With the similar features of mixing physical reality and virtual reality as found in Metazoa Ludens, users can perform free and continuous play with their body using gestures and movement on the interactive floor, which senses the users' positions. Other users can also interact with players on the computer screen in virtual reality. Therefore, Age Invaders provide a hybrid relationship between users and media.

In summary, Living Media and Huggy Pajama fulfill all the features of analog-like media while Poetry Mix-up and Confucius Computer fall into the digital-like media category. Metazoa Ludens and Age Invaders provide a hybrid-like media experience for the user. Therefore, we can use the characteristics for analog-like and digital-like interaction to analyze and exam all interactive systems. This can also be used to develop digital only interaction (interactive digital media), or analog only interaction (interactive analog media). The analysis of case study projects is summarized in Table 1.

7. THE ANALOGNESS-DIGITALNESS CONTINUUM (ADC)

Similar to the Virtuality Continuum concept proposed by Paul Milgram [17], the Analog-Digital Continuum (or ADC) attempts to describe the continuous relationship of attributes in an interactive system, which could embody any combination of digital-like to analog-like qualities as described in the previous section, Characteristics of Systems with Analog-Like and/or Digital-Like Interaction. The ADC is meant to encompass not just the type of interaction an interactive system provides, but also the method of the embodied relationship between system and user. It therefore differs from other continuums in such that it not only represents the external world, as does the Virtuality Continuum describes, but also the intimate relationship of person and machine. The ADC can therefore be utilized with any HCI implementation when concepts of embodiment and human-factors are involved.

The main motivation to create such a method of classification is two-fold. Firstly, the ADC in of itself can be used to study and classify all interactive systems.

Secondly, the ADC in conjunction with the proposed characteristics found in this manuscript can be used to direct development of such systems in order to achieve particular styles of interaction and user/system relationship.

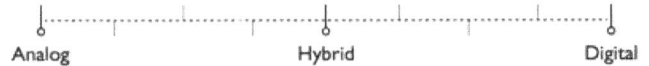

Figure 9. The Analogness-Digitalness Continuum (ADC).

As depicted in Figure 9, the ADC offers two polarizing dichotomies. On one end is the Analog descriptor. This represents systems with completely analog relationships with the interacting user. On the other extreme, completely digital-like interactive relationships between the system and user are represented. Varying scale points between both positions qualify a systems' interaction as hybrid. Depending on how analog-like versus digital-like a system interaction could be would govern its tendency to lean towards a particular polarity on the scale. Discerning the position is measured by scoring a system in relation to the proposed rules, as described by the characteristics of analog-like and/or digital-like interfaces, previously presented in the paper.

8. ON INTERACTIVE ANALOG MEDIA (IAM)

By clearly defining what it is for an interface to have notions of analogness and digitalness, a sub-field of interactive media has emerged. By taking the *Characteristics of Developing Systems with Analog-Like and/or Digital-Like Interaction* into account when developing interactive systems, interactivity of a purely analog-like nature can now be specifically designed. From this point the authors propose a new area of research; that of one that takes into account the analogness of interactive systems in order to develop truly continuous and intuitive interfaces that are wholly one with the user and the data it presents as a singular embodiment (Figure 9).

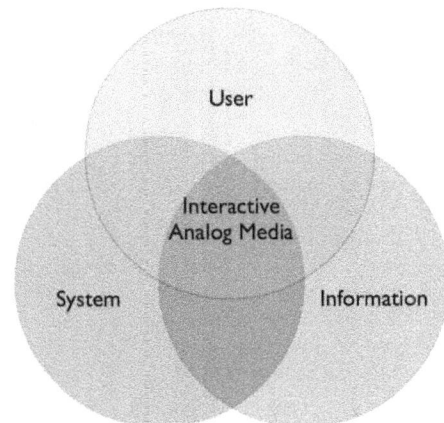

Figure 9. User, system and data as a singular embodiment.

In an era where media has increasingly become digital, the desire for analog-like interaction with the world around us becomes more desirable. The authors hope that the proposed field of IAM will elevate ubiquitous computing as a mainstay for human-computer interaction in our everyday lives.

Table 1. Summarization of project analysis in the contact of analog-like and/or digital-like interaction.

The Interface is Intuitive	Interaction is Continuous	Content and Media are Singular in Embodiment	System	Content and Media are Dichotomistic in Embodiment	Interaction is Discrete	The Interface is Mediated
X	X	X	Living Media			
X	X	X	Huggy Pajama			
			Poetry Mix-up	X	X	X
			Confucius Computer	X	X	X
X	X		Metazoa Ludens	X		X
X	X		Age Invaders	X	X	X

9. CONCLUSION

In this paper we presented characteristics in which interactive systems can be defined and developed, possessing aspects and characteristics of digitalness and analogness with specific regard to the relationship and embodiment of the user and system in mind. This was achieved by first discussing theories of embodiment from a humanities perspective, and how it could relate and be integrated with computer science and engineering by defining what it is for data to be digital or analog.

We then attempted to integrate both concepts into a new definition of analog-like and digital-like interactivity with the presentation of characteristics for interactive analog and digital media and through the analysis of a prototypical example of an interactive system.

We further supported these characteristics by analyzing published research projects from the Keio-NUS CUTE Center in the National University of Singapore as case studies, and categorized each project in relation to this.

We go on to present the Analog-Digital Continuum (ADC) in order to easily plot and classify interactive systems depending on their analogness or digitalness.

Lastly, we propose a new field of research that looks to develop the analogness of interactive systems called interactive analog media (IAM).

The presentation of this paper is by no means meant to be steadfast when describing interactive systems that possess digital-like and/or analog-like characteristics. On the contrary, the authors hope that the contents of this manuscript creates discussion and dialog between researchers, theorists and practitioners of all disciplines ranging from the sciences to the humanities, who are concerned with the analysis and application of interactivity and embodiment. We invite the wider community to challenge, refute, alter and augment our characteristics with the belief that they can be better defined for the benefit of all.

10. ACKNOWLEDGEMENTS

Development of this project would not have been possible without the invaluable assistance from the following people: Karin Aue, Hooman Samani, James Teh, Ingrid Hoofd, Newton Fernando, Lawrence Wong, C.C. Hang, Steven Miller and members of the National University of Singapore's Interactive Digital Media Institute, Keio-NUS CUTE Center and NUS Graduate School for Integrative Sciences and Engineering (NGS).

This research is carried out under CUTE Project No. WBS R-7050000-100-279 partially funded by a grant from the National Research Foundation (NRF) administered by the Media Development Authority (MDA) of Singapore.

11. REFERENCES

[1]. Analog/Digital Transaction. http://cultureandcommunication.org/deadmedia/index.php/Analog/Digital_Transition

[2]. Cheok, A. D., Khoo, E. T., Liu, W., Hu, X. M., Marini, P., and Zhang, X. Y. Confucius computer: transforming the future through ancient philosophy. In *ACM SIGGRAPH 2008 new tech demos* (SIGGRAPH '08). ACM, New York, NY, USA, , Article 10 , 2008, 1 pages.

[3]. Cheok, A. D., Tan, R. T. K.C., Fernando, O. N. N., Merritt, T., and Sen, J. Y. P. Empathetic living media. In *Proceedings of the 7th ACM conference on Designing interactive systems* (DIS '08). ACM, New York, NY, USA, 2008, 465-473.

[4]. Co, E. and Pashenkov, N. 2008. Emerging display technologies for organic user interfaces. *Commun. ACM* 51, 6, 2008, 45-47.

[5]. CUTE Center, http://cutecenter.nus.edu.sg/

[6]. Dale, N. B., and Lewis, J. *Computer Science Illuminated* (1st ed.). Jones and Bartlett Publishers, Inc., 2002, USA.

[7]. DeRouchey, B. (http://www.slideshare.net/billder/history-of-the-button-at-sxsw)

[8]. Descartes, R. *Mediations on First Philosophy,* 2005.

[9]. Dourish, P. Where the Action Is: The Foundations of Embodied Interaction, volume 54. The MIT Press, 2004.

[10]. Fernando, O. N. N., Cheok, A. D., Ranasinghe, N., Zhu, K., Edirisinghe, C. and Cao, Y. Y. Poetry mix-up: a poetry generating system for cultural communication. In *Proceedings of the International Conference on Advances in Computer Entertainment Technology* (ACE '09). ACM, New York, NY, USA, 2009, 396-399.

[11]. Hansen, M. *Bodies in Code. Interfaces with Digital Media.* New York: Rutledge, 2006.

[12]. Ishii, H. and Ullmer, B. Tangible bits: towards seamless interfaces between people, bits and atoms. In *Proceedings of*

the *SIGCHI conference on Human factors in computing systems* (CHI '97). ACM, New York, NY, USA, 1997, 234-241

[13]. Khoo, E. T., Lee, S. P., Cheok, A. D., Kodagoda, S., Zhou, Y. and Toh, G. S. Age invaders: social and physical inter-generational family entertainment. In *CHI '06 extended abstracts on Human factors in computing systems* (CHI EA '06). ACM, New York, NY, USA, 2006, 243-246.

[14]. Lewis, D. Analog and Digital. *Noûs* 5, no. 3, 1971, 321-327.

[15]. Massumi, B. *Parables of the Virtual: Movement, Affect, Sensation.* Durham: Duke University Press, 2002.

[16]. Merleau-Ponty, M. *Phenomenology of Perception.* London: Routledge, 2005.

[17]. Milgram, P., Takemura, H., Utsumi, A., and Kishino, F. "Augmented Reality: A class of displays on the reality-virtuality continuum". In *Proceedings of the SPIE Conference on Telemanipulator and Telepresence Technologies*, Vol. 2351, 1994, pp. 282-292.

[18]. Morie, J. F. "Performing in (virtual) spaces: Embodiment and being in virtual environments." *International Journal of Performance Arts and Digital Media*, 3:2 & 3, 2007, 123-38.

[19]. Pentland, A., Gips, J., Dong, W. and Stoltzman, W. Human computing for interactive digital media. In *Proceedings of the 14th annual ACM international conference on Multimedia* (MULTIMEDIA '06). ACM, New York, NY, USA, 2006, 865-870.

[20]. Ross, G. M. Descartes - *Description of the Human Body* (1975). Retrieved 10 12, 2011, from http://www.philosophy.leeds.ac.uk/GMR/hmp/texts/modern/descartes/body/body.html.

[21]. Tan, R. T. K. C. , Cheok, A. D., Peiris, R. L., Vodorovic, V., Loi, H. C., Loh, C. W., Nguyen, D. T. K., Sen, J. Y. P., Yio, E. Z. Y. and Derek, T. B. S. Metazoa ludens: Mixed reality interactions and play for small pets and humans. *Leonardo*, (3):308--309.

[22]. Teh, J. K. S., Cheok, A. D., Peiris, R. L., Choi, Y., Thuong, V. and Lai, S. Huggy Pajama: a mobile parent and child hugging communication system. In *Proceedings of the 7th international conference on Interaction design and children* (IDC '08). ACM, New York, NY, USA, 2008, 250-257.

[23]. Vertegaal, R. and Poupyrev, I. Introduction. *Commun. ACM* 51, 6 (June 2008), 2008, 26-30

[24]. Weiser, M. The computer for the 21st century. *Scientific American,* 1991

[25]. Wellner, P. The DigitalDesk calculator: tangible manipulation on a desktop display. In *Proceedings of the 4th annual ACM symposium on User interface software and technology* (UIST '91). ACM, New York, NY, USA, 1991, 27-33

Tracing The User Experience of Participation: What is It and Why Does it Matter?

Dave Jones
Old Dominion University
The Nerdery
Bloomington, MN, United States
dljone01@gmail.com

ABSTRACT

Digital applications and web-based user experiences increasingly incorporate social web technologies that enable the user to become a participant, or someone who actively co-constructs content, context, and meaning in digital ecosystems. This paper explores the *user experience of participation* by establishing a working definition of the concept and discussing why it is important to researching and designing digital communication tools. The case study presented in this paper explores the ways that user-generated content produced with the game *LittleBigPlanet* and the community that this content supports are intricately linked to local inventions embedded within cultural practices that improve support people's efforts to learn how to participate within the social web ecosystem. I demonstrate that participation relies on one's ability to coordinate with other participants via social web ecosystems in order to explore digital tools and perform knowledge work. Thus, the user experience of participation can be traced to these local inventions and the culturally situated practices of participants that leverage digital applications to develop, document, and share knowledge with each other. The conclusion to this paper offers preliminary concepts necessary to defining the user experience of participation and to theorizing participation as a critical component of researching and designing social web ecosystems.

Categories and Subject Descriptors

H.5.3 [**Information Interfaces and Presentation**]: Group and Organization Interfaces – *Asynchronous interaction, Collaborative computing, Computer-supported cooperative work, Evaluation/methodology, Organizational design, Synchronous interaction, Theory and models, Web-based interaction*

General Terms

Design, Human Factors

Keywords

User Experience, Participation, Social Web, Research Methodology

1. INTRODUCTION

The user-generated production and sharing of digital content across networked digital applications is now a ubiquitous form of engagement for those who use digital software and social web applications. In the research and design of social networking systems and social web tools, both scholars and industry practitioners have started pushing beyond the boundaries of single users interacting with single applications. Crumlish and Malone [5] state that it is crucial for designers to "take a step back" from the granular features and components of digital applications to consider the "underlying principles" that are critical to designing social web tools. In doing so, we need to critically examine how we theoretically situate the people that leverage social web tools in the production and sharing information.

This paper is a call to action that extends Potts' argument that networked applications and user-produced content must be better understood as elements of larger ecosystems [22, 23, 24]. These networks form cultural spaces in which people and technologies assemble to perform coordinated, collaborative knowledge work. Users are now crucial *participants* in the production of information and knowledge in the social web [22; 2; 11; 33]. I argue that communication researchers and designers need to theorize *participation* as a crucial element of the research and design of social web experiences. More specifically, I argue that by understanding how local, culturally bound creative and learning practices intersect with larger networks of systems, tools, and people, we can begin formulating an approach to the research and design of ecosystems that stretches beyond designing a single software or tool. We can then design ecosystems wherein people participate with systems, tools, and groups in more contextually-aware ways.

The following sections first explore how participation and user experience design are discussed in their respective fields, and then leveraging recent research of technical communication scholars to posit the possibilities of a bridge between these parallel lines of theory. Following that, I trace examples from collaborative and participatory activities surrounding the game *LittleBigPlanet* to illustrate how focusing on local contexts and explicit coordinative work can help researchers and designers better understand the user experience of participation.

2. CULTURAL STUDIES, USER EXPERIENCE, AND TECHNICAL COMMUNICATION AS MIXED METHODS

To better situate this discussion, this section provides a brief overview of recent published literature in various fields that touch on the concepts of *participation* and *user experience design* (commonly referred to as "UX"). The case study featured later in this paper is drawn from a larger, longitudinal research project that uses a mixed methods approach drawn from cultural studies, UX, and technical communication. Combining these fields of discourse provides a rich framework for producing an ethnographic narrative of online cultures and the ways in which technological design impacts their participatory practices and collaborative knowledge work.

Though *participation* and UX receive heavy critical attention in different fields, researchers have only recently started to trace an intersection between the two. Each line of research provides useful concepts for developing a more rigorous methodology that conceptualizes participation as a key element of the user experience of social web tools and user-produced content. By critically examining these parallel research lines, we can begin to conceptualize a more useful approach to researching and designing for culturally situated experiences rather than individuals interacting with a single software or device.

2.1 Cultural Studies and Digital Participation

Cultural studies research most often situates the concept of *participation* within a framework aimed at studying fan cultures, or communities in which people gather around common cultural texts for which they share a mutual affinity [6; 9; 10]. These communities then take on the task of constructing new meaning around these texts by injecting themselves into the production of the text itself. These fans produce and share various forms of content through a "cultural logic" in which they shift from passive consumers to becoming active participants in the construction of these texts [10, 11].

Jenkins argues that participation is a "collective process wherein coordinated and collaborative practices allow people to collaboratively generate culturally situated knowledge" [11]. This knowledge is derived from the content that they create. In the social web, this content can take many different forms, including blog posts, wiki updates, and forum discussions to name only a few. In the case study presented here, this content appears primarily in three different forms: player-generated game levels created and shared using the game *LittleBigPlanet 2*, digital images and videos capturing in-game content, and forum discussions wherein participants analyze this content in order to generate knowledge that is useful for their creative and participatory practices. These examples point to moments of "user-led innovation" wherein coordinated, collaborative work among participants produces new types of content and information that then support the growth of knowledge [1].

Thus, participation can be understood as a collective activity in which different people and groups collaboratively work to uncover data and synthesize it into information that supports the production of culturally situated knowledge. Social web services and applications are critical tools for facilitating participation when these cultures emerge online. Indeed, as services such as Facebook, Twitter, and Pinterest grow in popularity, they gain not only individual users in their services but also become integrated across many different spaces on the internet. Many company websites now feature links to social media pages they have constructed on Facebook and Twitter. And Facebook's Connect API (application programming interface) embeds interactive features for sharing content on Facebook in nearly every major news and information service on the web.

These are major steps towards the entire internet becoming more deeply integrated with people's online cultural practices. As a result participatory activity and collective knowledge work are ubiquitous.

2.2 User Experience and the Social Web

UX literature often presents the designer's challenge as a puzzle that complicates the relationship between a user's needs and the digital tools that they use. The designer's task is to design "well-orchestrated interfaces" [4] that accommodate those needs [7; 19; 20]. Methods for solving this puzzle take many different forms. User experience designers draw on ethnographic research and contextual inquiry that studies a user's everyday contexts of use [2; 14]. They may also leverage various forms of usability testing that range from quantitative statistical measures to qualitative one-on-one interviews [37]. Others discuss the need for well crafted conceptual and architectural organization of information within digital spaces [17; 18].

These books, articles, and other texts tend to situate the designer's task as one in which they are seeking to understand an individual's relationship with a single application. This has been critical to driving software design and development as a user-centered process rooted in understanding those who design software applications.

As the social web has become more and more ubiquitous as both a personal and professional tool, industry texts have indeed turned to discussions of user experience design for social applications. The most notable of these books is Crumlish and Malone's *Designing Social Interfaces*, which argues that designers should "leave things incomplete" in order to allow the people to take hold of the digital tools at their disposal and grow the space organically [5]. Still, the approach outlined in this book treats the space as one in which the individual person is leveraging a single application to connect with other people. There is no rigorous approach to understanding or considering what it means to be a digital participant or cultural practices within these spaces.

2.3 Technical Communication and Turning Towards the Local

Within academic research, the field of technical communication has expanded its interdisciplinary reach in recent years to include UX and its related subdomains (such as interaction design, experience design, and information architecture). In addition, this research has explicitly tackled the ways in which people leverage social web tools to share information and produce knowledge. Spinuzzi has discussed ways in which networks impact the "local innovations" of workers [30], as well as ways in which distributed participants must explicitly coordinate their efforts in order to sustain collaborative relationships [32]. Similar research from Potts [23] and Potts & Jones [25] illustrates ways in which social web tools can enable or constrain these efforts.

Additional research efforts often trace the rhetorical impact of communication via digital tools within distributed, collaborative ecosystems [28; 29; 30, 31, 32; 36]. Other researchers have examined backchannel communication via various social media services [15], the ways that social media are leveraged in workplaces [16; 34; 38], and the impact of social web tools on disaster communication [23; 26].

Within technical communication research, the emphasis has been on contextualizing individual creative practices against the backdrop of people's cultural and digital spaces. In other words, technical communicators have been tracing an intersection between information, user-production of content, and social practices of producing knowledge via networked spaces.

For this reason, we are uniquely situated to look at participation and UX in order to trace the parallel strands of research between them and highlight their intersections. By doing so, we can theorize participation as an element of user experience. Tracing these intersections allows us to extend our research of communities and communicative practice to the design not just of individual digital tools and systems, but of larger ecosystems of people, groups, tools, and practices, as well.

3. THE CASE STUDY

One area in which we can begin tracing the concept of participation is within participatory communities that emerge around games that support user-generated content. Such games provide unique examples of online cultures using digital tools for producing and sharing content through multiple software packages (including the game software). Participants collect and produce content through these games, and then re-purpose their creations by sharing them in different digital forms across multiple social media systems.

3.1 Data Collection

The data presented in this case study is from larger research project studying the intersection between cultural participation and the design of social web ecosystems used by online communities. The data set was collected over a period of two years, from June 2010 to July 2012. However, the data itself dates back to at least November 2008. Due to the ways that many internet discussion forums assign dates to online posts, precise origination dates can be difficult to determine. For example, many forums forgo specific dates using the day, month, and year in favor of a narrative style similar to "Posted 4 months ago." Such design choices can make tracking specific dates of origin for user-generated content difficult, if not impossible.

3.2 The *LittleBigPlanet* Game

This paper's case study traces interactions between a digital participant named NyghtHawk and his peers and their creative practices with the game *LittleBigPlanet*. These participants leverage well-known copyrighted characters as creative tools for not only producing and sharing content, but also for coordinating knowledge work that enables them to trace the capabilities of the digital tools at their disposal. These are critical practices to their online community, enabling them to better learn how to improve their participatory skills. Understanding this work allows researchers and designers to design not just for individuals, but for ecosystems of people and technologies situated within social cultures.

LittleBigPlanet is a game developed by Media Molecule in 2008. The company released its sequel, *LittleBigPlanet 2*, in 2011. These games are available only on Sony's Playstation 3 console and allow owners to use in-game assets and tools to produce playable game levels, characters, character costumes, and stories that they can then share online. To share this content, players must have an internet connection and access to Sony's proprietary online system, the Playstation Network (or PSN). Through this connectivity, players can upload the content they have produced in *LittleBigPlanet* to the PSN where others who have access to *the* game can play these levels or collect the costumes that participants produce.

In addition, Media Molecule and Sony provide a number of other digital tools to support participation, including discussion forums accessible through a standard web-browser. Forums such as LittleBigWorkshop.com are popular digital spaces in which participants discuss their creative practices and participatory activities. There is also LBP.me, which is a service connected to the player's PSN account information and allows him or her to share data about the content they've produced, including how many times levels have been played and favorite by other participants, as well as screencaptures of in-game assets.

Thus, *LittleBigPlanet* is an ecosystem of different tools in which participants' activities can stretch far beyond the game as they share their work via multiple services. In doing so, they forge digital linkages that support social and cultural linkages. Thus, a greater understanding of the social and cultural significance of these practices is crucial to effective design of tools that support participatory activity.

4. TRACING LOCAL INNOVATIONS WITHIN KNOWLEDGEWORK

In the *LittleBigPlanet* ecosystem, participants are active "creators" [27], producing and sharing content in several different ways. NyghtHawk [21] uses in-game assets to produce costumes that are based on popular film and comic book characters. Figure 1 shows an example of these costumes—in this case one based on the popular character The Joker from DC Comics and recent Hollywood films. *LittleBigPlanet* provides the participant with color palettes, texture palettes, and clothing items to dress the game's main avatar, the sackperson. Using a variety of different in-game tools, participants can apply these assets and customize them in order to produce distinct characters and game levels.

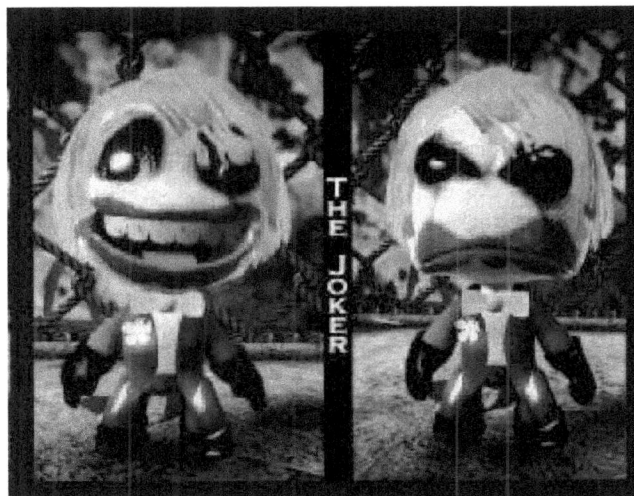

Figure 1. The Joker costume created by NyghtHawk in *LittleBigPlanet.*

Figure 1 also illustrates NyghtHawk's participation within the *LittleBigPlanet* ecosystem in several ways. Not only is he using the game to produce costumes and recreate popular characters from comics and movies, but he is sharing these costumes with others by taking screen captures of them and posting them to a forum discussion on the popular site LittleBigWorkshop.com.

Thus, NyghtHawk transforms his in-game creations to static images that he uploads to these forums.

His goal is to inspire others in the ecosystem to "try out their skills" for producing costumes with in-game assets [21]. NyghtHawk is leveraging the capability of digital content to move "fluidly" within a digital information space [13] in order to support learning amongst his peers. His creations can transform from one file type to another in order to move from one space to the next. He can capture an image of the in-game content and post it in a discussion group, asking for feedback and suggesting that he might be able to help others learn the ecosystem itself. Through this transformation of content and movement of it across digital spaces within the *LittleBigPlanet* ecosystem, NyghtHawk and his peers are taking advantage of digital content's ability to grow context through movement [12; 25].

In response, another participant identified as PhadedWun posts a response in the forum, asking NyghtHawk "how did you get the red along his mouth so small?" [21]. In this example, the participant is asking NyghtHawk a technical question to better understand how to use digital assets and tools within the game. NyghtHawk responds that the effect is achieved by using "2 of the same stickers flipped and overlapped" [21]. By leveraging a well-known character as an example for producing costumes within the game, NyghtHawk is also leveraging other participants' familiarity with the character in order to support feedback.

This is an example of a "local innovation" that supports the creative and social practices of these linked individual users [30]. By using these costumes, NyghtHawk and his peers reinforce their roles as participants. They not only produce content and share it, but leverage that content as a tool for exploring the capabilities and constraints of the creative tools available to them within the *LittleBigPlanet* ecosystem. They are further enriching their knowledge of what participation entails within the ecosystem and how they can improve their skills to maximize their participatory capabilities.

5. COORDINATING WORK ACROSS THE ECOSYSTEM

The example traced through Figure 1 also illustrates the need for participants to explicitly coordinate work across social web tools. As Potts & Jones describe, moving content is "a critical affordance" that supports the linkages that help to further contextualize information [25]. Meaning for participants emerges as information moves from one space to the next. This movement deeply embeds individual practice within larger cultural contexts.

Another example from the *LittleBigPlanet* ecosystem appears in the customer service forum, GetSatisfaction.com. The site is a discussion forum designed to promote conversations between customers and the companies that produce the products that these customers buy and use. Media Molecule maintains a forum within GetSatisfaction.com to encourage feedback about the games and players' experiences producing and sharing content. Within that forum, a poster named Harry Bellis suggests several changes to the ways that participants can moderate comments by others on their own levels [8]. One of his suggestion is to allow the comments sections to be turned off and on by the participant that owns the level. His suggestions stem from his perceptions that some participants within the community "like to abuse" the commenting tools "for their own amusement, bullying of others, etc." [8].

Similar to NyghtHawk's example, Harry Bellis has initiated a discussion within one section of the *LittleBigPlanet* ecosystem about events within another—in this case, GetSatisfaction.com is used as a tool for addressing problems within the in-game commenting systems. Five months after he posts his request, another forum participant named Shadowriver posts Figure 2.

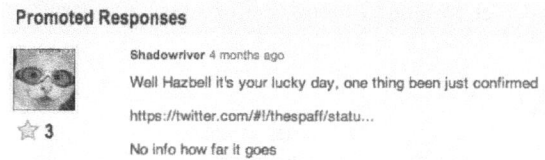

Figure 2. Shadowriver's response to Harry Bellis's request in GetSatisfaction.com.

Shadowriver's post indicates that "one thing [has] just been confirmed," and points to a tweet by linking it within the forum. In GetSatisfaction.com's case, the forum automatically turns posted URLs in to clickable links, enabling participants to quickly forge connections between the forum and other digital tools. Therefore, it can forge links between different people working within those spaces. Because movement is such a vital part of participating in the social web, participants must coordinate their creative and social activities across digital applications and social web tools in order "to hold together to form dense interconnections" [32]. These interconnections simultaneously support the movement of content while also being enriched by this movement. Broadly speaking, ecosystems of people, technologies, groups, and content both construct and are constructed by such linkages.

Figure 3 shows what Shadowriver is linking to. In this case, it is a Twitter post by a Media Molecule game designer, James Spafford. This tweet states that the development team for *LittleBigPlanet* is working on a comment moderation system similar to the one that Harry Bellis has requested.

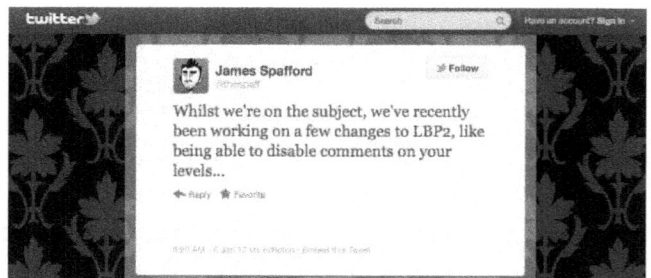

Figure 3. James Spafford's tweet discussing a user-controlled comment moderation system.

Just as importantly, Figure 4 suggests that Media Molecule has linked Harry Bellis's forum post in GetSatisfaction.com to company's decision to allow these types of actions by participants. His original request receives a special flag shown in Figure 4 in the upper right hand corner. This flag, stating "Under Consideration," can only be added by a company representative running the Media Molecule forum at GetSatisfaction.com. It is impossible to trace a full history of these events that shows step-by-step how one did or did not lead to another. However, the linkages have been created, and largely the participants within the ecosystem have created them.

Figure 4. Harry Bellis's post is marked with an "Under Consideration" flag in the upper right corner.

In this case, we see information moving from one space to another, enabled by the productive and social practices of the participants within these spaces. Shadowriver must track the discussion of this particular topic across multiple, disparate social web systems and produce a link between them. As Figure 3 shows, Shadowriver's post is also highlighted as a "Promoted Response." This means that other participants in this discussion have noticed the importance of his link and rated it positively. The effect is that his response is then automatically pushed by the forum software to the top of the list of responses under Harry Bellis's original post. Movement and coordination of information becomes key both across different tools within the ecosystem, and within one tool that is used to produce and support one specific digital space.

This linkage of information allows the participants in the forum to not only better understand the ways they can produce content within the *LittleBigPlanet* ecosystem, but to become what Spinuzzi would label as a "strong rhetor" in a space where networked participants "sorely need to learn how to make arguments" [32]. In Spinuzzi's analysis of networked communication among organizational workers, the dense interconnections among people, groups, and technologies also encourages the need to "build trust and stable alliances," as well as the need to "negotiate and bargain and horse trade across boundaries" [32]. This is also a fitting description of the work performed here by Harry Bellis, Shadowriver and others in the GetSatisfaction.com forums. They leverage their cultural knowledge of a problem and combine that with their ability to use social web tools in order to change how the commenting moderation system works.

The movement of people and information across the social web enables this participation, but also demands that these participants constantly seek to coordinate this information in a useful way. In this case, Shadowriver's linking of the Spafford's tweet happens approximately five months after Harry Bellis's original posted requests. In doing so, Shadowriver is demonstrating the importance of the topic. That is post is promoted by others illustrates the importance of his critical information to others participating within the discussion.

6. THE IMPORTANCE OF MOVEMENT

The movement of content and the ability of such movement to support local invention among community members becomes critical to these participants. It is now a cultural practice that supports the knowledge work necessary for participants to analyze and understand how they can better participate within the ecosystem. We see the "cultural logic" described by Jenkins at work [11], wherein participants learn by doing, encouraging them to participate further, forming more social and technological connections among people and tools available to them.

These ecosystems are digital environments in which participants prioritize what Johnson-Eilola describes as the "fluid movement of information and, just as important, the ability of users to move around within that information space" [13]. In such ecosystems, this movement allows for the combination, disordering, and then re-combination of information in order to seek out and test new ideas. In doing so, participatory communities collectively produce new knowledges through their collaborative practices. These new insights inform how they produce and share content, as well as why they do so and the culturally situated meaning that encourages their digital participation.

As the case study illustrates, these connections support movement in two ways. First, participants can move from one digital space to another within the ecosystem. Shadowriver, for example, moves back and forth between Twitter and the GetSatisfaction.com forums in order to collect relevant pieces of information. NyghtHawk's efforts are an example of the participant moving between the *LittleBigPlanet* game software, another unidentified digital tool for capturing the screen images of his costumes, and the online forum in which he posts his images to generate discussion.

Second, participants must be able to move information from one space to another. Sometimes, this means simply posting a link that is easily clickable and leads back to the original source for that information. At other times, this movement requires posting some form of inscription that potentially transforms and carries that information from one space to another. As NyghtHawk's example shows, he cannot transport the actual costumes that he produced within the *LittleBigPlanet* game software into a discussion forum. Thus, he had to capture static screenshots of them and post the images of those costumes as a point of discussion. Thus, other participants within the forums cannot grab the costumes as digital assets and recreate NyghtHawk's techniques so simply.

7. CONCLUSIONS

The user experience of participation is a critical element of researching and designing for the social web that must be rigorously explored by both scholars and industry practitioners moving forward. The examples traced through *LittleBigPlanet* and its surrounding ecosystem of people and digital tools illustrate the importance of three key concepts that technical communication scholars are already addressing.

1. **Local Innovations**—what people are doing to support their own needs as participants within their own online cultures

2. **Explicit Coordination of Information and Systems**—the ways in which participants trace and link information and digital tools across the ecosystems in which they work

3. **Movement of People and Content**—how systems support or constrain the ability of people and data to move from one space to the next in contextually-aware ways

The intersection of these three concepts forms a basis for understanding participation as a culturally situated user experience. At this intersection, researchers and designers can find tools for both exploring the importance of culturally relevant activities and for tracing explicitly participatory activities through social web tools.

7.1 Expanding the Call to Action

These three concepts are not an exhaustive exploration of the user experience of participation. User experience design, cultural studies, and technical communication are themselves all multidisciplinary fields that draw from multiple avenues of research in order to shed light on the concepts that are central to this paper. Thus, this paper serves only as a call for further rigorous research into participation as a critical element of the user experience. Scholars and designers should seek to expand upon the three key elements identified here, as well as problematize my application of them.

Through exploration grounded in rigorous methodologies, we can better theorize participation within the social web, empowering us as researchers and industry practitioners to design better digital tools for enabling contextually-aware communication.

8. REFERENCES

[1] Banks, J. and Deuze, M. 2009. Co-creative Labour. *International Journal of Cultural Studies*, 12.5, 419-431.

[2] Beyer, H., and Holtzblatt, K. 1998. *Contextual Design: Defining Customer-Centered Systems*. San Diego, CA: Academic Press.

[3] Bruns, A. 2009. *Blogs, Wikipedia, Second Life, and Beyond: From Production to Produsage*. New York: Peter Lang Publishing.

[4] Cooper, A., Reimann, R., and Cronin, D. 2007. *About Face 3: The Essentials of Interaction Design*. Indianapolis, IN: Wiley Publishing.

[5] Crumlish, C. and Malone, E. 2009. *Designing Social Interfaces*. Sebastopol, CA: O'Reilly Media.

[6] Deuze, M. 2007. *Media Work*. Malden, MA: Polity Press.

[7] Garrett, J. J. 2003. *The Elements of User Experience: User-Centered Design for the Web*. Indianapolis, IN: New Riders.

[8] Harry Bellis. 2011. Basic Moderation Tools for Authors on Their Levels. *GetSatisfaction.com*. Retrieved from https://getsatisfaction.com/littlebigplanet/topics/basic_moder ation_tools_for_authors_on_their_profile_levels.

[9] Jenkins, H. 1992. *Textual Poachers: Television Fans and Participatory Culture*. New York: Routledge.

[10] Jenkins, H. 2004. The Cultural Logic of Media Convergence. *International Journal of Cultural Studies*, 7.1, 33-43.

[11] Jenkins, H. 2006. *Convergence Culture: Where Old and New Media Collide*. New York: NYU Press.

[12] Jones, D. and Potts, L. 2010. *Best Practices for Designing Third-Party Applications for Contextually-Aware Tools*. In the Proceedings of the 28th ACM International Conference on Design of Communication. Sao Paolo, Brazil. 95-102.

[13] Johnson-Eilola, J. 2005. *Datacloud: Toward a New Theory of Online Work*. Cresskill, NJ: Hampton Press.

[14] Kuniavsky, M. 2003. *Observing the User Experience: A Practitioner's Guide to Use Research*. Morgan Kaufmann.

[15] McNely, B. 2009. *Backchannel Persistence and Collaborative Meaning-Making*. In the Proceedings of the 27th ACM International Conference on Design of Communication. Bloomington, IN. 297-303.

[16] McNely, B. 2010. *Exploring a Sustainable and Public Information Ecology*. In the Proceedings of the 28th ACM International Conference on Design of Communication. Sao Paolo, Brazil. 103-108.

[17] Morville, P. 2005. *Ambient Findability*. Sebastopol, CA: O'Reilly Media.

[18] Morville, P. and Rosenfeld, L. 2006. *Information Architecture for the World Wide Web: Designing Large-Scale Websites*. Sebastopol, CA: O'Reilly Media.

[19] Norman, D. 1988. *The Design of Everyday Things*. New York: Doubleday Press.

[20] Norman, D. 2004. *Emotional Design: Why We Love (or Hate) Everyday Things*. New York: Basic Books.

[21] NyghtHawk. 2008. Customer Character Creations. Forum Thread at *LittleBigWorkshop.com*. Retrieved from http://forums.littlebigplanet.com/t5/General-Discussion/Custom-Character-Creations/m-p/13244/highlight/true#M5624.

[22] Potts, L. 2008. *Designing with Actor Network Theory: A New Method for Modeling Holistic Experience*. In the Proceedings for the International Professional Communication Conference. Montreal, Canada. IEEE.

[23] Potts, L. 2009. Using Actor Network Theory to Trace and Improve Multimodal Communication Design. *Technical Communication Quarterly*, 18.3, 281-301.

[24] Potts, L. 2010. Consuming Digital Rights: Mapping the Artifacts of Entertainment. *Technical Communication*, 57.3, 300-318.

[25] Potts, L. and Jones, D. 2011. Contextualizing Experiences: Tracing the Relationships Between People and Technologies in the Social Web. *Journal of Business and Technical Communication*, 25.3, 338-358.

[26] Potts, L., Seitzinger, J., Jones, D., and Harrison, A. 2011. *Tweeting Disaster: Hashtag Constructions and Collisions*. In the Proceedings of the 29th ACM Conference on Design of Communication. Pisa, Italy.

[27] Robinson, M. 2008. *LittleBigPlanet* Interview. *IGN.com*. Retrieved from http://ps3.ign.com/articles/940/940711 p2.html.

[28] Sherlock, L. 2009. Genre, Activity, and Collaborative Work and Play in *World of Warcraft*: Places and Problems of Open Systems in Online Gaming. *Journal of Business and Technical Communication*, 23.3, 263-293.

[29] Slattery, S. 2007. Undistributing Work Through Writing: How Technical Writers Manage Texts in Complex Information Environments. *Technical Communication Quarterly*, 16.3, 311-325.

[30] Spinuzzi, C. 2003. *Tracing Genres Through Organizations: A Sociocultural Approach to Information Design.* Cambridge, MA: The MIT Press.

[31] Spinuzzi, C. 2007. Introduction to TCQ Special Issue: Technical Communication in the Age of Distributed Work. *Technical Communication Quarterly*, 16.3, 265-277.

[32] Spinuzzi, C. 2008. *Network: Theorizing Knowledge Work in Telecommunication.* New York: Cambridge University Press.

[33] Spinuzzi, C. 2009. Starter Ecologies: Introduction to the Special Issue on Social Software. *Journal of Business and Technical Communication*, 23.3, 251-262.

[34] Stolley, K. 2009. Integrating Social Media into Existing Work Environments. *Journal of Technical Communication*, 23.3, 350-371.

[35] Swarts, J. 2007. Mobility and Composition: The Architecture of Coherence in Non-places. *Technical Communication Quarterly*, 16.3, 279-309.

[36] Swarts, J. 2009. *The Collaborative Construction of "Fact" on Wikipedia.* In the Proceedings of the 27.h ACM International Conference on Design of Communication. Bloomington, IN. 281-288.

[37] Tullis, T. and Albert, W. 2008. *Measuring the User Experience: Collecting, Analyzing, and Presenting Usability Metrics.* Morgan Kaufmann.

[38] Zhao, D. and Rosson, M. B. 2009. *How and Why People Twitter: The Role that Micro-blogging Plays in Informal Communication at Work.* In the Proceedings of GROUP '04. Sanibel Island, FL. 243-252.

Left to Their Own Devices:
Ad Hoc Genres and the Design of Transmedia Narratives

Elmar Hashimov
Ball State University
Department of English
Robert Bell Building #297
Muncie, IN 47306
ehashimov@bsu.edu

Brian McNely
University of Kentucky
Writing, Rhetoric, and Digital Media
1315 Patterson Office Tower
Lexington, KY 40506
brian.mcnely@uky.edu

ABSTRACT

In this paper, we apply a writing, activity, and genre research (WAGR) framework to explore how research participants designed complex transmedia narratives during a two-semester experiential learning course that was conducted in concert with a major state museum. We focus here on two specific cases from our larger ethnographic study to illustrate participants' self-directed, adaptive development and use of situated genre ecologies to mediate their work. In doing so, we describe how participants navigate among genres and artifacts within a minimum of three overlapping genre assemblages to design transmedia narratives: (1) the course genre assemblage, (2) their discipline-specific assemblage, and (3) their individual genre ecology. We explore individual genre ecologies in detail, describing how participants frequently incorporated *ad hoc* genres into their workflow as a way of navigating the expectations and genre norms of broader, overlapping assemblages.

Categories and Subject Descriptors

H.5.3. [**Information Systems**]: Group and Organization interfaces—computer-supported cooperative work

General Terms

Human Factors, Theory

Keywords

Genre, transmedia, activity theory, WAGR, mediation

1. INTRODUCTION

In 1964, Marshall McLuhan argued in his germinal book, *Understanding Media: The Extensions of Man*, that "the personal and social consequences of any medium—that is, of any extension of ourselves—result from the new scale that is introduced into our affairs by each extension of ourselves, or by any new technology" [12, p. 7]. Often cited in rhetoric, media, culture, and communication studies, McLuhan's dictum has been largely

applied to media in its stricter modern sense—print news, television, radio, internet, etc. However, as this quote indicates, McLuhan used the term "medium" interchangeably with "technology." That is, every piece of technology—every tool, every artifact, and every genre that *mediates* our human experience—can be an "extension of ourselves." These tools, he argued, have personal and social consequences, and they change our experiences.

In this paper we explore such mediation and the ways in which "mediating artifacts qualitatively change the entire activity in which workers engage" [20, p. 38]. We apply a writing, activity, and genre research (WAGR) framework [16, 22] to investigate how participants in a project-based, experiential-learning course about transmedia storytelling at a large research university in the Midwestern United States navigate the complex assemblages of artifacts and genres that mediate their work. The tools that comprise these assemblages include "traditional" genres of writing and documentation (such as pen and paper, whiteboards, and text editors) as well as complex, discipline-specific digital genres (such as photo, video, audio, and web-editing applications). Viewing their work from the perspective of WAGR helps us understand how participants move between the complex assemblages of genres inherent in the emerging narrative form known as transmedia storytelling [6, 7, 8].

The first and largest genre assemblage we encountered, encompassing two other assemblages, is that of the entire course—including 30 students and two instructors who collaborated on a transmedia storytelling project over two semesters. Within this genre assemblage, the instructors set specific objectives for the course, including the creation of a transmedia story told across a variety of media platforms and through a variety of mediating tools and artifacts. To move toward this objective, participants from different disciplinary backgrounds and with different skill sets organized into smaller discipline-specific groups—writers, designers, and audio/video experts. Within these more localized genre assemblages, participants were given—and sometimes developed—specific components of the broader transmedia story, components that involved graphic design deliverables, infographics, written narratives, videos, or interactive websites, to name just a few. Participants negotiated and adapted the genres specific to these story components in often collective and decentralized ways, while instructors provided ongoing direction and scaffolding from within the course genre assemblage.

Finally, each discipline-specific group was comprised of individual participants who carried their own tools, artifacts, and norms into contact and negotiation with the two broader genre assemblages described above. At the individual level, these sets of tools and practices may best be understood as genre ecologies, following the work of Spinuzzi [20]. In this paper, we focus on these individual genre ecologies because a given participant's work at this level was largely self-directed, with little or no guidance or scaffolding from the instructors. To negotiate their way into the expert-group level of work (discipline-specific genre assemblage) and further into accomplishing the larger tasks of the class (course genre assemblage), every participant often had to adapt and develop their own genre ecologies "from scratch," incorporating *ad hoc* genres into their workflow to address everyday problems. This often involved learning and using new tools while navigating the expectations and norms of broader genre assemblages.

In the remainder of this paper, we examine the development of two representative participants' genre ecologies and consider the ways in which these ecologies are developed within the context of overlapping genre assemblages. First, we provide the broader context for our study and explain transmedia storytelling in more detail. Next, we describe our theoretical and analytic perspective before detailing our research methods. We then explore individual genre ecologies by describing in detail the work of two of our participants. Finally, we discuss the implications of our findings for the design of communication community.

2. CONTEXT
In August of 2011, two professors of journalism at a large research university in the Midwestern United States began a year-long team-teaching experiment that would bring the emerging practice of transmedia storytelling to an interdisciplinary group of students. This project-based, experiential learning course was carried out in partnership with the preeminent historical museum in the professors' state. Their work with students ultimately produced a complex series of publicly intertwined narratives that spooled out as fictional and nonfictional threads across a variety of artifacts and sites, and across a variety of genres and media delivery channels. This project was highly visible in both the professors' university and the state museum, and was relevant among a host of important community stakeholders. In this section, we provide some context about this unique research site, and we describe some of the key dimensions of transmedia storytelling—the primary object of study and practice among our participants.

Transmedia Storytelling (referred to hereafter as TMStory) was a course offered as a part of the university's immersive learning program. This program is in turn a part of a campus-wide initiative that has supported a number of project-based courses in which students from across disciplines collaborate with each other, their professors, and community partners to create various products that are used beyond the classroom, primarily in local contexts around the state where this study was conducted. As part of a strategy for developing invaluable professional experience, therefore, immersive learning students work directly with local community partners to make meaningful contributions to businesses and non-profits. TMStory was a three-credit, two-semester sequence offered through the Department of Journalism in both the Fall 2011 and Spring 2012 semesters. By the end of the project, 30 students collaborated to create a 45,000-word interactive, tablet-based narrative about state history that combined fiction and nonfiction components across several media platforms, including an ebook, a series of photos, videos, and podcasts, a series of feature-rich websites, and an in-person showcase at the state museum.

The TMStory study participants included 22 upperclassmen (primarily seniors) majoring in a broad range of disciplines—journalism, graphic design, digital media, rhetoric and writing, music technology, telecommunications, communication studies, anthropology, and creative writing. 9 of our participants were male and 13 were female, and their average age was 21; participants were largely demographically homogeneous and hailed from the Midwest. 10 of our participants were enrolled in the course for both semesters (Fall 2011 and Spring 2012); 7 were enrolled only in the fall, and 5 only in the spring.

As we mentioned above, to achieve the larger course objective of creating a complex transmedia narrative, several of the participants organized into discipline-specific groups that worked on the particular components of the larger story. For example, there was a group of self-identified fiction writers who quickly coalesced into a "writers' group." Similarly, individual journalism graphics majors—several of whom knew one another from previous classes—also coalesced into three smaller groups working on narrative components relevant to their expertise. One such group worked over both semesters on a complex non-fiction website that provided rich, multimedia content about the history of a particular town that was central to the overall narrative. Another group developed an interactive infographic about the state's natural history. And telecommunications and music technology students worked together in an audio/video group to produce a host of interrelated story assets, including a series of interconnected short films and podcasts. The work of participants in these discipline-specific teams, therefore, contributed artifacts that, when articulated together, formed the core of the overarching transmedia story.

In transmedia storytelling, these various artifacts and genres work together to tell different parts of a unified story, with each type of media making a distinct contribution to the overarching narrative. These different storytelling artifacts and genres thus provide different entry points into the story at different times, for different audiences, extending the storytelling experience over time and space [7]. In this way, a complex transmedia story is "dispersed systematically across multiple delivery channels for the purpose of creating a unified and coordinated entertainment experience" [9, p. 944]. Each TMStory participant, therefore, had to negotiate his or her work within the expectations and genre norms of at least three overlapping genre assemblages, which we detail below: (1) the TMStory genre assemblage, (2) a discipline-specific genre assemblage, and (3) his or her own individual genre ecology.

2.1 The TMStory Genre Assemblage
The larger TMStory genre assemblage was where the participants moved toward the major course objective—to create a complex transmedia story across a variety of narrative assets and media delivery channels, for a public audience. This genre assemblage, then, brought together the work produced by students in the other two genre assemblages. At the same time, however, this assemblage included a host of stabilizing genres such as the course syllabus, lectures, and a series of "producer meetings" coordinated by the course instructors. The TMStory genre assemblage also included genres and artifacts from overlapping activity systems—other groups of stakeholders beyond the course, chief among them those of the university and the state museum with whom they partnered on this project. As Russell and Yañez have demonstrated, "Activity systems are not hermetically sealed"

[17, p. 348]; our TMStory participants, much like the participants in Russell and Yañez's study, struggled with negotiating the inherent contradictions between multiple, overlapping activity systems and attendant genres.

In the course genre assemblage, then, each discipline-specific subgroup with their respective genre ecologies and broad range of disciplinary backgrounds engaged in complex interactions with each other to build the final product. In order to coordinate these complex interactions, participants engaged in a fair amount of inter-group communication. We repeatedly observed participants who moved between discipline-specific groups, and there were at least two participants who self-identified as members of two discipline-specific groups.

For example, Samantha (all personal names are pseudonyms to protect participant identities) worked with both the writers' group and one of the graphic design groups over both semesters. She often coordinated artifacts between these two genre assemblages. For one narrative asset in particular, she worked with the writers to identify a specific graphic symbol from the story that could be developed as a material and digital artifact. She then created the material version of the symbol herself (with a stencil and paint), and worked with her design-conscious collaborators to create and adapt subsequent digital versions. But these kinds of coordinating activities among discipline-specific groups within the larger genre assemblage evolved over time, partly in response to dealing with the complexity of the overlapping activity systems noted above, and the course genre assemblage that was designed to coordinate work within them.

2.2 Discipline-Specific Genre Assemblages
At the level of discipline-specific genre assemblages, participants worked in their areas of expertise and collaborated with each other in subgroups within their group-specific systems of genres and tools. The majority of the participants truly acted as experts on this level, as many of them were recruited for the project specifically for their disciplinary backgrounds and skill sets that they had already developed before the course began. As experts, participants worked toward understanding the broader TMStory genre assemblage and engaged in the broader activity system of the course by focusing their work in the genres with which they were most familiar.

For the majority of the time in TMStory, students worked within their discipline-specific genre assemblages: for instance, the writers' group worked collaboratively to compose both fiction and nonfiction content for the ebook, moving between the same tools (e. g., word processors, Google Docs), coordinating the same artifacts, and sharing discrete objectives within the discipline-specific level of activities. As we mentioned above, many participants moved between groups, gradually developing fluency in two or more discipline-specific genre assemblages.

2.3 Participant Genre Ecologies
Spinuzzi has drawn a distinction in his work between assemblages of genres and genre ecologies. He describes genre assemblages, for example, as "collectively oriented set[s] of solutions" [22, p. 367] to ongoing, situated needs. Drawing on Propen and Schuster (2010), he notes that "genres are rarely deployed alone: They interact in *genre assemblages* to collectively address complex cyclical activities," leading to a situation where "many genres shape the cyclical activity within which they are mobilized" [15, p. 367, emphasis in original]. As we have seen, the course and

discipline-specific genre assemblages collectively address the work of transmedia production. But what of genre and artifact use at the individual level of participants? How do individuals use genres to mediate their everyday practice?

For Spinuzzi, genres and artifacts at the individual level strongly *mediate* actions. In other words, mediating genres change individual actions as contingencies change (such as Samantha's need to develop a material symbol imagined by a writer). In this process, mediating genres related to individual actions overlap and interweave among members in discipline-specific groups and the broader community, changing the scope and tenor of the transmedia story itself. These genres do not merely communicate; they are involved in shaping individual practice, and in so doing, they help shape group practice. Focusing on individual genre ecologies, as we do below, highlights genres and artifacts that may be invisibilized (such as stencils and paint) when subsumed within broader assemblages (such as the digital representations of the discipline-specific graphic design group).

Most importantly, individuals use genres and artifacts in an ecology to jointly mediate their work [19]. In Figure 1 (see next page), we can see some of the material artifacts that comprise one small part of our participant Kayla's genre ecology. Her work here is jointly mediated by several tools at once—a sketchbook and pen (out of frame, to her right), two separate Photoshop layers, her MacBook Pro, an external hard drive, a mobile phone, and the verbal and phatic interactions of a collaborator (to the far left of the frame). As we describe below, of particular interest in our study is how participants bring *ad hoc* and often novel genres and artifacts into their ecology to mediate their work. In the next section, we describe our theoretical frame for exploring this kind of complex mediation.

3. THEORETICAL FRAMEWORK
Spinuzzi argues that "Genres have proven to be valuable particularly in studies of work and learning, since they help researchers to conceptualize and study how people produce and interpret artifacts" [21, p. 115]. More importantly, genre theory may be productively articulated with work in activity theory; indeed, Russell has recently argued that this fusion should be seen as writing, activity, and genre research (WAGR) [16], and Spinuzzi has worked on approaches for adapting WAGR to knowledge work environments [22]. In this section we detail our approach by first describing some of the major tenets of activity theory and its emphases on situatedness and mediation; we then articulate these ideas with our WAGR framework.

3.1 Activity Theory and Mediation
We began this manuscript with McLuhan because, writing in the 1960s, we believe he was onto something with the idea of tools as extensions of ourselves. Today especially, we cannot imagine our daily lives and activities without our cell phones, laptops, and other gadgets. We also surround ourselves with "low-tech" tools as well—pens, pencils, sticky notes, notebooks, etc. We communicate and create *meaning* through these tools. Activity theory provides a helpful descriptive framework that takes into consideration the entire activity (comprised of sometimes discrete and often overlapping actions and operations) and accounts for: the subject (the person or persons conducting the activity); the activity object or objective (what the motivated actions are aimed to achieve); the socio-cultural context; and the numerous tools used to jointly mediate individual actions.

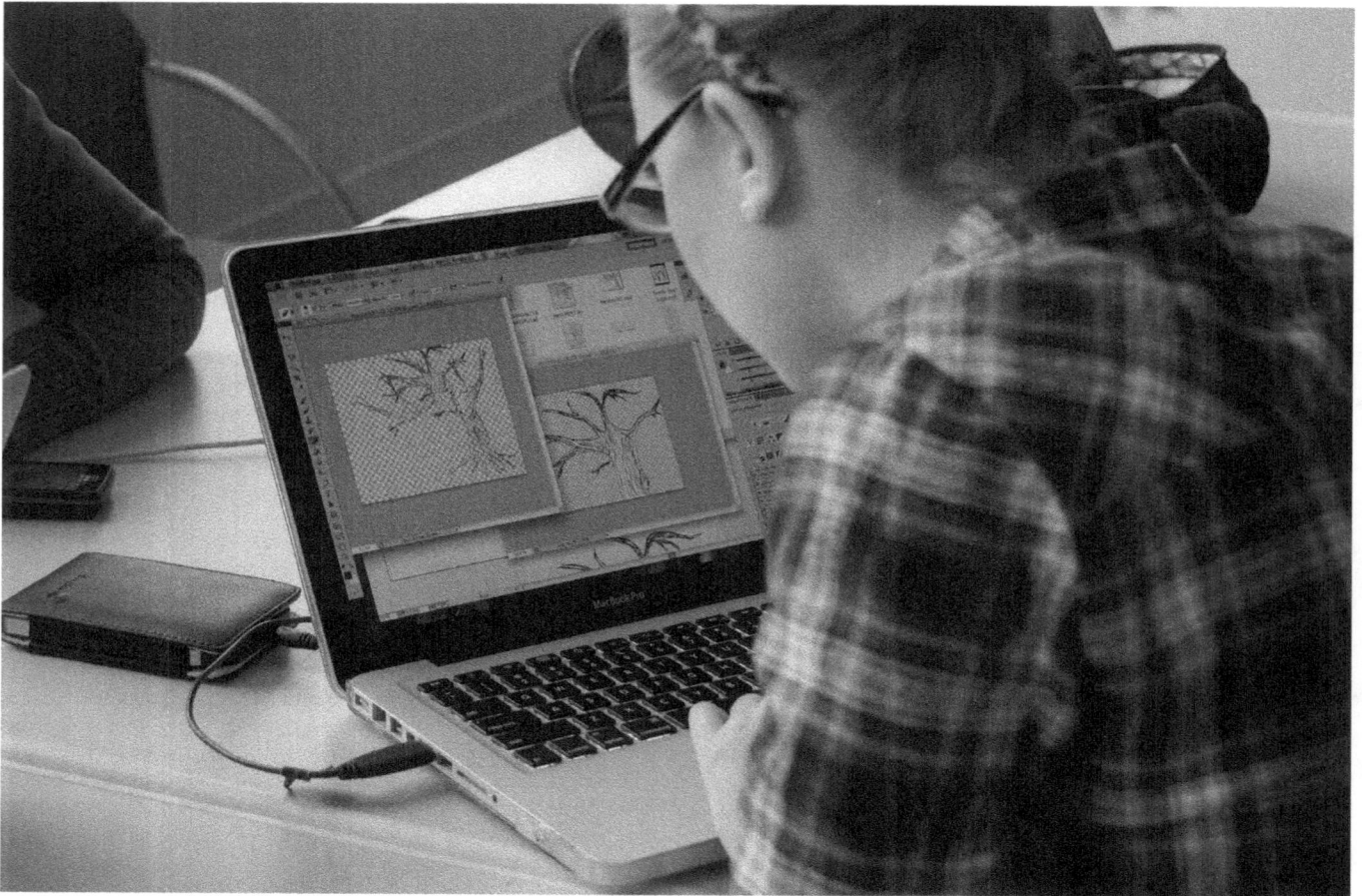

Figure 1: Kayla's Genre Ecology

"In activity theory," Kaptelinin and Nardi argue, *"people* act *with* technology; technologies are both designed and used in the context of people with intentions and desires" [10, p. 10]. More importantly, activity theory considers the "relationship between people and tools as one of *mediation*; tools mediate between people and the world" [10, p. 10]. Thus, "activity theory proposes a strong notion of mediation—all human experience is shaped by the tools and sign systems we use" [10, p. 10]. Our mediations consist in human interactions with tools, artifacts, and genres: "Mediators connect us organically and intimately to the world; they are not merely filters or channels through which experience is carried" [10, p. 10]. Finally, the unit of analysis in activity theory is an activity system: an object-oriented, socially situated, and culturally mediated human activity [2].

Activity theorists and empirical researchers who use activity theory emphasize the socio-cultural, socio-historical situatedness of every activity—its time and place in real life. Nardi (1996) argues, "Consciousness is located in everyday practice: you are what you do" [13, p. 7], while Lave and Wenger (1991) point out, "there is no activity that is not situated" [11, p. 33]. Nardi (1996) also contends that activity theory "focuses on practice [...] The object of activity theory is to understand the unity of consciousness and activity" [13, p. 7].

Situatedness also means that activity is *embodied*: in their research in workplace literacy, Haas and Witte explore the notion of writing as embodied practice [4, p. 416]. They note

that while "the *body* is a cultural, social, and linguistic construct, *embodiment* is a lived experience" [4, p. 417]. In other words, when analyzing an activity system, one should pay attention to the processes and mediation in which people and artifacts are engaging (not just the artifacts themselves) to reveal meaning in lived experience. Eskola, in his comparison of human activities to fish swimming in the ocean, argues that "the analysis must start not with water but with swimming" [3, p. 112]—that is, with embodied practices. This grounding in situated practice is what makes activity theory so useful: it reveals knowledge of everyday, situated activities; in addition, because activity theory provides a common conceptual framework, it allows us to talk about activity in a more generalizable way across disciplines.

3.2 WAGR and Genre Ecologies

For writing, activity, and genre research (WAGR), genre is a unit of *social action* [16]. Genres are typified responses to recurrent problems and challenges that are at once societally conditioned and socially grounded. In WAGR approaches, genre is potentially "a unit of analysis in its own right," and viewing genre from this perspective can help researchers understand systems of activity [15, p. 42]. Written genres are especially important, since writing is "arguably the most powerful mediational means for organizations and institutions" [16, p. 40]. Activity theoretical approaches, Russell argues, help researchers consider and reconcile, in "principled and systematic" ways, relationships between macrolevel social structures and microlevel actions [16, p. 43]. This is precisely where we locate our research in this study, and it is why WAGR is particularly suited to our exploration of individual genre ecologies within broader, overlapping genre assemblages.

Within these complex, shifting, overlapping activity systems and genre assemblages, therefore, subjects interact with numerous artifacts as part of their ongoing activity. That is, they use tools in overlapping sequences and systems—we write down grocery lists while talking on the phone; we look up directions to a concert venue online, coordinating with a friend through IM while writing directions on a slip of paper; we text one friend while talking to another face to face, and so on in endless combinations. We live, work, and play in situated *ecologies of genres*. Spinuzzi uses "the term *compound mediation* to refer to the ways that people habitually coordinate sets of artifacts to mediate or carry out their activities" [19, p. 98, emphasis in original]. He contends that "tools are connected in multiple, complex, and often nonsequential ways. ... The ecology itself—not its individual tools—is the mediator of the activity" [19, p. 100]. This concept of genre ecologies is especially congruent with WAGR approaches.

Genres and genre ecologies as social action, Russell notes, may be seen as "an array of strategies or tactics" marshaled by individuals in the service of goal-directed activity [16, p. 44]. "Studies of tools-in-use," Russell argues, "show actors consistently selecting, rejecting, and abandoning genres in the course of their work, individual and collective" [16, p. 44]. As we will see, participants in our study displayed similar characteristics; but more importantly, they incorporated into their ecologies genres that were often novel and *ad hoc*—that is, devised for a particular purpose at a particular time. This finding emerges from our focus on participants' motives, a focus specifically supported by a WAGR framework. In the remainder of this paper we describe our methods for conducting the broader ethnography of TMStory, while detailing the reduced dataset under consideration. We then explore the individual mediated actions within the genre ecologies of two of our participants.

4. METHODS
In this section, we delineate our methodology for the larger TMStory study and describe the process of data collection. We then detail our purposive reduction of the data to focus on two participants' individual genre ecologies.

4.1 Larger Study and Methodology
In our study of TM Story, we used an ethnographic research methodology to explore what participants "get out of" immersive-learning courses, how their experiences in these courses may be different from being in a more traditional class, and what their collaborative work and genre ecologies look like. Thus, the chief method of data collection for the larger project is based in intensive fieldwork in the classroom and small-group planning sessions, supplemented by semi-structured interviews, brief video observations, and the collection of textual and graphic artifacts produced by students and instructors (written documents, designs, videos, photos, audio files, notes, etc.).

We began our systematic collection of data in August 2011, continuing through the end of the Spring 2012 semester. In the Fall 2011 semester, we took turns observing every TMStory class, taking detailed fieldnotes, writing analytic memos,

conducting interviews, taking photos and videos, and collecting artifacts. In Spring 2012, as the class began to move into more intensive production work and we moved toward preliminary analysis of our data, we conducted 6 classroom and meeting observations while continuing semi-structured interviews and artifact collection.

We interviewed 22 participants, ten of whom participated in the class and the study both semesters. More than half of the participants did a follow-up interview toward the end of the second semester. By using semi-structured interviews, we have allowed for participants' own voices to be heard, following work in previous ethnographies of written communication [1, 5]. These unique participant-voices provide insights that would be impossible to acquire through observation alone.

Overall, we generated over 100 typed pages of fieldnotes (>60,000 words), and we collected 40 audio files (primarily participant interviews, averaging 20 minutes each), approximately 300 photos and screenshots, and 21 videos. These data provide rich insights into the classroom dynamics, the activities that took place in the class, the various actions that compose these larger activities, the overlapping genre assemblages and genre ecologies, and participants' perspectives on all of the above.

4.2 Purposive Data Reduction
To illustrate some of our observations of participant genre ecologies, we chose two participants—Jason and Kelly. Our purposive selection of these two participants is based on our observation of patterns during fieldwork, and while they do not necessarily represent the entire group of participants, they do provide tangible examples of how TMStory participants use tools in their genre ecologies, often moving into *ad-hoc* genres and using idiosyncratic ways of adapting to the changing expectations of the class.

Indeed, not all participants showed the same complex, self-directed interaction with genres: Amanda, for example, represents a divergent case. In her work, she exhibited a fairly simple and linear use of a limited number of tools and did not seem to move out of her expert "comfort zone." In her second interview, she indicated that she did all of her work in InDesign and Muse, and communicated with her collaborators through email, but did not venture beyond those tools. She explained: "I don't think I've used anything outside of that. I don't have a smartphone either, so I think that hinders it to a point. ... I saw a lot of people have little notebooks. I think that's 'in' right now or something, a little notebook, but I don't have one of those [laughs]." When asked if she used any other software, she simply replied, "No." However, we have observed that the majority of the participants did engage in complex genre ecologies, which we discuss in the following section.

5. CASE NARRATIVES
In this section, we provide detailed narratives of our two chosen cases. For clarity and ease of reading, we have lightly edited fieldnotes for typos, and spelling and punctuation errors; in addition, we have edited many phatic interactions out of interview transcript excerpts (utterances such as "uh," "um," "like," and "sort of"). Finally, we constructed brief narrative snapshots of Jason and Kelly. The short case narratives, following this section, are built on one specific class observation (from February 2, 2012), in which some of the most interesting

behavior was featured prominently, as well as 4 interviews—two with each participant. Thus, we base the following case narratives on the prominent themes drawn from the fieldnotes and relevant transcriptions of the four interviews.

5.1 Case 1: Jason

At the time of the study, Jason was a senior majoring in telecommunications and digital media. He was a part of TMStory since the beginning of the Fall 2011 semester, so at the end of Spring 2012, he was something of an expert among experts in the project. Jason and a few of his collaborators were responsible for the video, audio, and some online graphic strands of the transmedia story. Jason is an outgoing young man, often making jokes, laughing in class, and engaging in banter with one of the instructors. With his amiable personality, as well as his fascinating use of writing tools and navigation of complex genre ecologies, Jason represents a exemplary case. Based on our observations over the course of two semesters, he exemplified the typified shifts within the complex genre ecologies (habitual movements and uses of tools) described by Spinuzzi [19].

One idiosyncratic aspect of Jason's work in TMStory is that he always carried around a number of high-tech and low-tech tools with him to class. The following excerpt from our fieldnotes paints a fairly typical picture of how he worked on an individual task:

> [Jason] pulls out a protractor and a piece of drawing paper and draws a rectangle with a mechanical pencil. [Adam] asks him, surprised, "You carry around a protractor?" "Yes," answers [Jason], "In fact, I carry a whole drawing kit." He pulls out a (faux?) black-leather pencil holder and spills out its content—pencils, pens, a ruler. They laugh.

> [Jason] draws what appears to be a storyboard panel; he passes it to [Brandon], who sits two people away…

In this situation, Jason exhibits what, based on his interviews, turns out to be fairly typical behavior for him. He begins a task with "low-tech" tools—paper, pencil, a ruler, or, in this case, even a protractor. In his first interview, he states:

> I always start on paper and then move to a digital format. So, I'll write out just sort of a brainstorm of ideas, maybe do some sketches, and then from that I'll put it into either Celtx [screenwriting software] or just an email with actual script of it, and then from there I generally go back to paper to do storyboards, and then email that out either by taking a picture of it with my phone and send it that way, or just scan it in or something like that.

Jason explains that he does this often—going from paper to digital, then back to paper, and then to digital once again. This movement seems to be an important part of his workflow: he initially brainstorms ideas on paper, but he mentions in the same interview that he is "not very organized" with paper, so he prefers to have the ideas saved digitally, usually through email (which he checks regularly on his phone), as he notes several times in the interview. While the class uses Google Docs and Dropbox (collaborative online tools) extensively, Jason is more comfortable with using email for keeping track of his ideas. When it is time to be creative again with the ideas saved in an email—say to sketch storyboards—he goes back to paper and

pencil; but to make sure he does not lose his work, he digitizes it once again.

In our observations, we noticed other instances of Jason's tool-switching. Here is another excerpt from the same day of fieldnotes:

> [Jason] and [Brett] are now talking about photos of an open casket [taken for the project]. [Jason] twirls his pencil in his hand; he then checks something on his iPad. He pulls out a slim black wireless keyboard and begins typing. […] He taps-and-holds something on the iPad screen and selects a block of text. He continues typing.

At this point, Jason was working on a script, for which he uses Celtx. What we also noted was that even when he did use "high-tech" tools, like his iPad in this instance, he kept his paper and pencil nearby. In this example, he was twirling the pencil after he finished sketching the storyboards and before he began typing in Celtx on his iPad. While this action may seem simply mechanical, based on our observations, it links the two discrete actions into an ecology. Another linking tool, similarly not always used to perform a clearly identifiable task, is Jason's iPhone. It usually sits to the side of his other tools, as noted in the following excerpt from the same day of fieldnotes, less than an hour later:

> [Jason] is typing something in a text document. He also looks at what looks like a series of text messages on his iPhone, which sits to the left of the wireless keyboard (to the left of the phone sits the mechanical pencil). He drinks water from a blue Nalgene-type bottle.

These idiosyncratic uses of tools and artifacts—iPad, keyboard, Celtx, text editor, iPhone, texting app, paper, pencil, and even the blue water bottle—comprise part of Jason's unique genre ecology. He navigates between them in sequential and non-sequential ways, and some of these embodied movements function in perceivably small but nonetheless important ways—like the twirling pencil or the bottle from which Jason sips sporadically. In addition to these tools, in another interview, Jason discusses his habit of using sticky notes to keep track of his tasks as well. All of these artifacts are necessarily part of his genre ecologies. Through his typified interactions with them over time, through switching between them, and through habitual assigning of specific functions to them—pen and paper for more creative work, digital word-processing software and iPad for typing out more solidified ideas, and other seemingly minor tools to help him move between the two—Jason plans and subsequently achieves his tasks. In doing so, Jason embodies discrete actions, which create chains of actions aimed to achieve the objects of the activities—like a fictional conspiracy-theory video that Jason describes in his interviews.

Another interesting aspect of Jason's work (we noted this over and over again in his and other participants' work throughout the study) is that he often has to improvise and self-direct in the discrete tasks that build up to the activities within his discipline-specific genre assemblage, since the course instructors, whether by design or due to time constraints, provided less guidance and scaffolding than instructors in a traditional class would. Jason explains:

> I guess another thing I've learned was to see an end goal and realize the things that I need to go through

and learn to actually make that happen, even if I don't have any idea how I'm going to do it. ... Go figure out what you want to do and figure out how to do it, which is what I'm going to need in the real world.

This is an important move: Jason, like many other participants, often had to devise *ad hoc* genres in his individual genre ecology: for instance, figuring out what software to use for a specific video-production-related task, then finding a tutorial online, learning the software, and finally applying it to his task. By navigating these *ad hoc* genres, Jason would negotiate his individual work within the collective work of the expert group (discipline-specific genre assemblage) and further to contribute to the broader course work (TMStory genre assemblage).

5.2 Case 2: Kelly

Kelly was a creative-writing and French major. She was a part of the TMStory class only in the Spring 2012 semester, during which she was actively involved in creating and revising some of the fictional and nonfictional writing content for the project. Kelly is a quiet and reserved student, and she generally kept to herself in class. She also spent most of her time on her laptop, so our fieldnotes contain few details on her behavior during class. However, her interviews reveal fascinating details about her course-related activities.

Kelly, like Jason, surrounds herself with complex genre ecologies. In her first interview, she said that she used a number of tools in her workflow within TMStory: in addition to Google Docs and Dropbox used for course documents (which she, like Jason, also did not use for planning her individual tasks), she has a spiral-bound planner or "agenda," a sticky-note app on her laptop, and three dry-erase boards and multi-colored dry-erase markers—these constitute her main genre ecologies for planning work.

In her first interview, Kelly told us that when it comes to planning her work, she has a set *system*, but it is "a mess of a system," as she admits herself. She explains:

> If I get a new assignment, [...] I'll write in my agenda. If something is due in the next day or two, that I need to be working in the next day or two, then I have [digital] sticky notes up on my [computer] desktop that... I'll write down emergency things that I need to look at that night. And when there're things that might not be due for... Or they'll just tell me to start thinking about, but you don't have to do it yet, [...] on one of my dry-erase boards in my room at home. I'll write down, "While you're just sitting at your computer, start thinking about this. Maybe look something up," or something. So, when it's more abstract... that they might ask you any day, 'So what do you have on this so far? How do you think about it?" I can say, "Oh well, glad I reminded myself.." '

Similarly to Jason, when Kelly planned or wanted to remind herself of a more general, abstract task, she used a "low-tech" set of tools: her dry-erase boards and markers. She told us she had three dry-erase boards in her room—two above her desk, where she usually worked, and one to the side, on the wall. All three of them were about twice the size of a standard letter-size paper, she explained. The notes she wrote to herself on the dry-erase boards—"Things that I need to start thinking of"—were color-coded. Kelly used a different-colored marker for each

class. Transmedia is green (she explained, partly because the original blue marker that she used for the study was "dead").

Also noteworthy, Kelly would print off some of the Google Docs used in class (like draft scripts, for instance) and would take notes, highlight, and draw "arrows and circles ... all over the place" to help her make mental connections and help her plan her own work related to the draft. In those printouts, she wrote down *in pencil* what "needs to be done." But these are again, longer-term tasks. The more concrete plans went directly into her "agenda," in which she wrote with *a pen*. She pointed out that the "agenda" is for things that are "more concrete," like specific deadlines and events. She would check the agenda regularly throughout the week and adjust what is on her dry-erase boards and sticky notes accordingly.

So, for more urgent tasks, Kelly explained, if something was due "in the next day or two. I have sticky-notes on my desktop." She would remember "what's more pressing, based on where it is"—in the "agenda," on the dry-erase boards, or on her virtual sticky-notes. The sticky notes were for the most "pressing" tasks; and each task had its own sticky note. To help her coordinate her tasks, she color-coded the sticky notes the same way she color-coded notes on her dry-erase boards. So, the sticky notes for TMStory were also green.

Thus, Kelly would move between her own idiosyncratic tools and ecologies, often working with them simultaneously to organize her course-related activities, and did so in a very habitual way. Each tool was always assigned a very specific role, based on her traditional uses of them, and as a task approaches temporally, it also shifts spatially from one tool to another, almost always from a low-tech to a high-tech medium.

As a new student to TMStory in the spring semester, Kelly often felt that she had to "figure out" (in one interview, she used that phrase 9 times) what was required of her and how she was supposed to go about contributing to her discipline-specific group and the project at large. Like Jason, she often had to devise, "figure out" her genre ecology, often involving idiosyncratic uses of tools and artifacts, without any help from her collaborators or course instructors. Like Jason, Kelly found ways of accomplishing her individual tasks and negotiating her way into the discipline-specific genre assemblage, as well as further into the course genre assemblage.

6. IMPLICATIONS

Our two cases illustrate a number of interesting themes: TMStory participants inhabited and developed over time their own genre ecologies—that is to say, their own complex tool systems that mediate their actions and the habitual, typified, embodied *ways* in which they use these tools. From the WAGR point of view, the participants worked within complex, shifting, and overlapping genre assemblages and ecologies, many of which share activities and objectives (production of video, a script, or a web page). However, when it came to the individual-level work, being left to "figure things out" on their own, they often engaged in idiosyncratic ways of navigating genre ecologies and turning to *ad hoc* genre uses.

This intricate navigation within overlapping genre assemblages and ecologies, and movement between individual and overlapping or nesting collective activity systems, fits well with the activity theory framework, which bridges the gap between the individual subject and the social context. As Leont'ev argued, "the social does not dictate [the] individual… That is, the members of a group engaged in an activity will not think in precisely the same way or react identically to events" [14, p. 4]. Thus, Jason and Kelly's individual ecologies do not necessarily set them apart from the larger activity systems within TMStory; at the same time, it does allow them to engage in individually motivated, goal-directed actions—in this case in planning and organization—and to use tools to which they volitionally assigned various roles and functions in accordance with their individual genre ecologies.

More specifically, our findings indicate that some of the TMStory participants, like Jason and Kelly, assigned specific roles and functions to different types of tools: they tended to engage in more abstract, creative, and open-ended types of writing with the use of more "low-tech" tools—pencil and paper, dry-erase boards, etc. When their actions took a more specific direction, became more structured, more urgent, and more "concrete," as Kelly put it, they moved to digital platforms—email, Celtx, virtual sticky notes, etc. Often these tool-mediated actions were linked into chains, composing the larger activity, by various tools—pencil, marker, water bottle, etc. These integral parts of the participants' genre ecologies made their movements from one mediating artifact to another more fluid and more recursive. Furthermore, their *ad hoc* genre uses and individual negotiations of genres helped them self-direct into more complex genre assemblages, ultimately allowing them to contribute to the creation of the final public TMStory products.

A deeper understanding of scenarios involving *ad hoc* genre uses is important for teaching and learning communities: as educators, we can help our students become more self-aware of how they devise and adapt their genre ecologies and practices to a variety of contexts. The importance of understanding *ad hoc* genres, however, extends beyond formal education. Similar scenarios are at play in virtually all communities of practice—that is, in all groups of people who share a domain of interest and collectively engage in regular learning and interaction within that domain (see [23]). The importance of this understanding lies in what is at stake for participants in every community of practice, in what it portends for individuals reconciling their genre ecologies with broader genre assemblages, and the attendant norms and expectations embedded in their communities of practice.

7. CONCLUSION

To conclude, this discussion of themes that arose from the two cases within Transmedia Storytelling provides some important insights into the activity systems, genre assemblages, and genre ecologies of participants in experiential learning and transmedia storytelling courses. However, a deeper investigation of the full set of data collected for the larger ethnographic research study would be necessary to further develop the insights discussed here. Data drawn from the remaining 20 participants can provide a deeper, and richer understanding of TMStory participants' work in all three overlapping levels of genre assemblages. More generally, WAGR can provide useful approaches for revealing and understanding, genres, genre assemblages, and *ad hoc* genre uses in a broad variety of communities of practice, which would provide invaluable insights for the design of communication community.

8. REFERENCESS

[1] Black, L. 1998. *Between talk and teaching: Reconsidering the writing conference.* Logan: Utah State University Press.

[2] Engeström, Y. 1999. Activity theory and individual and social transformation. In Y. Engeström, R. Miettinen, & R. Punamäki (Eds.), *Perspectives on activity theory* (pp. 19–38). Cambridge: Cambridge University Press.

[3] Eskola, A. 1999. Laws, logics, and human activity. In Y. Engeström, R. Miettinen, & R. Punamaki (Eds.), *Perspectives on activity theory* (pp. 107–114). Cambridge: Cambridge University Press.

[4] Haas, C. & Witte, S. P. 2001. Writing as an embodied practice: The case of engineering standards. *Journal of Business and Technical Communication, 15*(4), 413–457.

[5] Herrington, A. J. & Curtis, M. 2000. *Persons in process: Four stories of writing and personal development in college.* National Council of Teachers of English. Berkeley: University of California University Press.

[6] Jenkins, H. 2003. Transmedia storytelling. *Technology Review.* Retrieved from http://www.technologyreview.com/biomedicine/13052/

[7] Jenkins, H. 2006. *Convergence culture.* New York: New York University Press.

[8] Jenkins, H. 2009, December 12. The revenge of the origami unicorn: Seven principles of transmedia storytelling. [Web log post]. Retrieved from http://henryjenkins.org/2009/12/the_revenge_of_the_origa mi_uni.html

[9] Jenkins, H. 2010. Transmedia storytelling and entertainment: An annotated syllabus. *Continuum: Journal of Media & Cultural Studies, 24* (6), 943–958.

[10] Kaptelinin, V. and Nardi, B. 2006. *Acting with technology: Activity theory and interaction design.* The MIT Press, Cambridge, MA.

[11] Lave, J. & Wenger, E. 1991. *Situated learning: Legitimate peripheral participation.* New York: Cambridge University Press.

[12] McLuhan, M. 1965. *Understanding media: The extensions of man.* New York: McGraw-Hill.

[13] Nardi, B. A. 1996. Activity theory and human-computer interaction. In Nardi, B.. A. (Ed.), *Context and consciousness: Activity theory and human-computer interaction* (pp. 7–16). Cambridge: MIT Press.

[14] Palmquist, M., Kiefer, K., & Salahub, J. 2009. Sustaining (and growing) a pedagogical writing environment: An activity theory analysis. In D. N. DeVoss, H. A. McKee, & S. Selfe (Eds.), *Technological ecologies and sustainability.* Logan: Utah State University Press. Retrieved from http://ccdigitalpress.org/tes/index2.html/

[15] Propen, A. D., & Schuster, M.L. 2010. Understanding genre through the lens of advocacy: The rhetorical work of the victim impact statement. *Written Communication 27*(1), 3–35.

[16] Russell, D. 2009. Uses of activity theory in written communication research. In A. Sannino, H. Daniels, & K. D. Gutiérrez (Eds.), *Learning and expanding with activity theory.* New York: Cambridge University Press.

[17] Russell, D., & Yañez, A. 2010. 'Big picture people rarely become historians': Genre systems and the contradictions of general education. In Bazerman, C. & Russell, D. R. (Eds.), *Writing selves/writing societies: Research from activity perspectives* (pp. 331–362). Fort Collins: The WAC Clearinghouse.

[18] Spinuzzi, C. 2002. Compound mediation in software development: Using Genre Ecologies to Study Textual Artifacts. In Bazerman, C. & Russell, D. R. (Eds.), *Writing selves/writing societies: Research from activity perspectives* (pp. 97–124). Fort Collins: The WAC Clearinghouse.

[19] Spinuzzi, C. 2003. *Tracing Genres through Organizations*. Cambridge, MA: MIT Press.

[20] Spinuzzi, C. 2004. Four ways to investigate assemblages of texts: Genre sets, systems, repertoires, and ecologies. In *SIGDOC '04: Proceedings of the 22nd annual conference on Design of communication*. ACM Press, New York.

[21] Spinuzzi, C. 2010. Secret sauce and snake oil: Writing monthly reports in a highly contingent environment. *Written Communication, 27*(4), 363–409.

[22] Spinuzzi, C. 2011. Losing by expanding: Corralling the runaway object. *Journal of Business and Technical Communication (25)*4, 449–486.

[23] Wenger, E. 1998. *Communities of practice: Learning, meaning, and identity*. New York: Cambridge University Press.

Interaction History Visualization

Benedikt Schmidt,
Sebastian Doeweling
SAP Research Darmstadt
62483 Darmstadt, Germany
firstname.lastname
@sap.com

Max Mühläuser
Telecooperation Group,
Technische Universität
Darmstadt
62489 Darmstadt, Germany
max@informatik.tu-
darmstadt.de

ABSTRACT

Interaction histories have been identified as a promising direction to support information workers in the execution of their work processes. However, to increase the workers' awareness about the structure of their work and to help them with the execution of their work processes, a suitable visualization is necessary. Up to now, interaction histories have typically been visualized with the classical Gantt, bar or line charts, neglecting the information contained in links between the individual items in an interaction history. Moreover, clear and empirically grounded guidance for the choice of the visualization is currently lacking. We present two graph-based visualizations for interaction histories and evaluate them against the classical visualizations in a controlled experiment. From the results, we derive a set of recommendations for the visualizations best suited for the different tasks within information workers' work processes.

Categories and Subject Descriptors

H.4.1 [**Information Systems Applications**]: Office Automation

General Terms

Human Factors

Keywords

human-computer interaction, task execution support, context, knowledge work support

1. INTRODUCTION

Information work is characterized by non-routine problem solving and a highly context-dependent execution of work processes. Moreover, frequent switches between work items are typical for this kind of work, making frequent adaptation and reevaluation of the work context necessary. As the work structure emerges ad-hoc, it is difficult for the information

worker to keep track of all ongoing activities. The non-standardized execution of work processes, however, prevents the use of common workflow management systems.

Interaction histories [21] have been proposed as a promising approach to increase information workers' awareness of their own work processes, and to support them with resources relevant to their current work context. They answer typical questions like "What was the last document i worked on and where can i find it?" or "How much time did i spent reading a report?" History features in web browsers, the journal in Outlook, Social Wakoopa [8] and Rescuetime [9] are examples for this. Yet, up to now, little work has been conducted on the optimal visualization for this type of data.

Current systems often rely on the obvious choices: Gantt –, bar- and line charts. However, these visualizations neglect the information contained in links between resources used for tasks in information work (e.g. documents opened at the same time, emails sent while reviewing a presentation, etc.). Questions like "Where is the document i read while i wrote a mail to colleague yesterday morning?" cannot be answered from these visualizations. This aspect is present in graph-based visualizations; conversely, typical graph-based visualizations do not display temporal relations.

Thus, in this paper, we propose two new hybrid visualizations: the *compound graph* and the *timeline graph*. Both embed a graph visualization into a temporal one – the former focuses on the transfer of process information, using a task-centric temporal structuring of work; the latter provides a task-independent, overall perspective on the work process.

Further on, we found that there is currently no systematic evaluation of the efficiency of different visualizations for interaction histories to guide the design of interaction history based software. To address this, we use a series of tasks generated by typical questions occurring during information work activities, and evaluate both task completion time and error rate for the proposed and the established interaction history visualizations.

The rest of this paper is structured as follows: we start with a definition of interaction histories and a short summary of work in their dominant application domains; we then identify the different types of tasks information workers have to complete with regard to their work structure and derive requirements for visualizations that support these tasks, drawing upon Gestalt theory and existing work on graph understanding. Subsequently, we review related work with regard to these requirements, and, addressing the limitations, propose two new visualizations for interaction histories. We then report on the results of a first evaluation of the different visualizations for the tasks identified before. We conclude with a set of recommendations for interaction history visualizations to inform the design of future support tools for information workers.

2. BACKGROUND

This section describes interaction histories and their relevance for information retrieval and work process awareness. The work on these aspects is fundamental to the assessment of interaction history visualization in this paper - the nature of interaction histories and the relevance for information retrieval and process awareness help to identify general tasks that need to be solved by an interaction history visualization in the next section.

2.1 Definition of interaction histories

Basically, interaction histories (see figure 1) are datasets that provide information about human activities. In the context of human-computer interaction, interaction histories refer to information about performed operations and accessed information objects.

An interaction history consists of interaction history elements. Each interaction history element stands for a logged user-system interaction, i.e. each interaction history element stands for an event that was logged when a user interacted with the system, and has temporal information about its occurrence. The granularity of the logged events depends on the used logging application. The minimum granularity focuses foreground events for information objects (e.g. when a user brings the webbrowser with the google page in the foreground, then google scholar and then Word with a document, results in the creation of three interaction history elements)[1] - typically some sort of filtering or aggregation is applied, before this information is presented to the user.


```
<event eventName="FOREGROUND_WINDOW_CHANGED" atTime="01.02.2011 16:19:26.484" eventCategory="Process"><eventattributes>
        <eventattribute name="processname" type="String" value="POWERPNT" />
        <eventattribute name="windowtitle" type="String" value="Microsoft PowerPoint - [Planning-Roundup_v3.pptx]" />
        <eventattribute name="associatedFile" type="String" value="\BaseNamedObjects\MSCTF.Shared.SFM.AFDB" />
        <eventattribute name="associatedFile" type="String" value="C:\Documents and Settings\evaluationuser3\Desktop\Work\Planning-
Roundup_v3.pptx" /></eventattributes></event>
<event eventName="FILESYSTEM_OBJECT_DELETED" atTime="01.02.2011 16:19:26.828" eventCategory="Filesystem"><eventattributes>
        <eventattribute name="name" type="String" value="C:\Documents and Settings\evaluationuser3\Desktop\Work\Planning-
Roundup_v3.pptx" />
        <eventattribute name="notifyfilter" type="String" value="FileName" /></eventattributes></event>
<event eventName="FILESYSTEM_OBJECT_CREATED" atTime="01.02.2011 16:19:26.828" eventCategory="Filesystem"><eventattributes>
        <eventattribute name="name" type="String" value="C:\Documents and Settings\evaluationuser3\Desktop\Work\Planning-
Roundup_v3.pptx" />
        <eventattribute name="notifyfilter" type="String" value="FileName" /></eventattributes></event>
<event eventName="MSPOWERPOINT_EVENT_THROWN" atTime="01.02.2011 16:19:26.968" eventCategory="Application"><eventattributes>
        <eventattribute name="title" type="String" value="Planning-Roundup_v3.pptx" />
        <eventattribute name="content" type="String" value=" Planning Demand and Master Planning Roundup Introduction Author: Andreas
Goeb&#xD;Date: 2011/02/01 Demand Planning Purpose&#xD;improve decisions affecting demand accuracy &#xD;calculation of buffer or
safety stocks &#xD;Results: &#xD;Demand Plan&#xD;Benefit:&#xD;Increased performance of each supply chain entity Master Planning
Purpose&#xD;synchronize the flow of materials along the supply chain&#xD;Range: Mid-term : At least one seasonal
cycle&#xD;Contents:&#xD;Production&#xD;Transport&#xD;supply capacities&#xD;Seasonal stock &#xD;balancing of supply and
```


Figure 1: Excerpt from an interaction history.

2.2 Applications of interaction histories

There are two main areas of application for interaction histories: information retrieval and work processes awareness.

2.2.1 Use in information retrieval

Interaction histories support different information retrieval tasks. For these tasks, the use of interaction histories is twofold:

Collection creation.

Interaction histories are used to create collections of information objects. These collections may be input to recommender systems or useful structures to support quick manual information object access. The interaction histories may support the manual creation of such collections or the automated creation based on given criteria.

Manual creation Interaction histories can support users, when they create collections of information that belongs together. This strategy has been implemented in the UMEA system [10] and Sphere Juggler [15].

Automatic creation In contrast to the manual collection creation, a system might identify information objects in the workprocess that are relevant and that can be grouped by a certain criterion. A simple criterion is access time. The visualization of access time based collections can be found in most modern applications, e.g. in the form of "recently used files"-lists, web-browsing histories or completion proposals for search fields.

Another frequently used criterion is the task: systems try to identify information objects that belong together as they belong to the same task. This is a complex operation, as it needs operationalize relevance and relatedness and measure it for resources in possibly multitasking work processes (e.g. do a Google Scholar site and an an email accessed while a browsing this site belong to the same collection?). Systems often use textual content of accessed resources and temporal information to create information object clusters. Examples for such systems are the CAAD system [20], Swish [16] and Transparency [22].

Recommendation.

Interaction histories are also used to create proactive recommendations: based on interaction histories, the system compares a current user work context with stored information about work contexts to identify information potentially supportive to the current activity.

Such information may be collections - possibly also created by interaction histories - that seem to fit to the users' work context. This identification is often implemented using supervised machine learning – the complexity of this task lies in the demand for measures of similarity in interaction histories and the need to identify task switches. Systems that address this are the Task Tracer System [23], the aposdle monitor [14] and UICO [19].

The examples show that information retrieval support based on interaction histories has been implemented both in the form of standalone applications and as an application feature.

2.2.2 Use for work process awareness

Interaction histories give a detailed insight into work processes, which is beneficial for weakly structured and weakly formalized work. Interaction data has already been used in the 80s to improve the understanding of such work processes, e.g when Bannon analyzed users' activity organization for command lines[1].

Recently the application of interaction histories to improve information workers' understanding of their own work processes gained attention [5, 8, 9]; this improved understanding is achieved by visualizing interaction histories for the user:

The Student Activity Monitor and the Contextualized Attention Metadata Dashboard are learning analytics tools [5]:

[1] An information object is a discrete entity that carries information following a defined encoding scheme and that typically is interpreted by an application.

interaction history elements are considered as traces of attention and visualized as charts to learner and teacher to improve learning processes. Other analytics applications are Social Wakoopa [8] or Rescuetime [9].

Social Wakoopa is a social network that visualizes application- and information object usage for an individual and his/her contacts, using lists, bar and line charts. Rescuetime displays executed work in the form of bar- and line charts, and provides features to support more focused work (e.g. the system denies access to certain resources during a specified period of time). The Outlook journal offers the feature of logging Microsoft Office specific information object access (emails, tasks, presentations, spreadsheets and documents). For the logged information objects open and close times are collected and visualized in a list or a Gantt chart.

The given examples illustrate that bar-, line- and Gantt charts are currently the preferred visualization types for interaction histories.

3. REQUIREMENTS

To maximize the benefit of interaction histories in the described application areas, easy consumption and simple integration of interaction history access into work processes is crucial. A visualization of interaction histories can be considered useful in this context if it allows users to easily solve interaction history related tasks.

This section identifies typical tasks information workers solve with an interaction history visualization and discusses the mental effort for decoding the respective visualization. From these tasks (and the task-specific decoding workload) requirements for useful interaction history visualizations are deduced, and criteria to check for the requirements are identified.

3.1 Task classes for interaction history visualization

Information retrieval and improved process awareness have been presented as domains that benefit from interaction data. In the following, we present four classes of tasks that are fundamental for the application of interaction data in the named domains. The task classes are result of a review of functionalities offered in the context of interaction history visualization, discussions with information workers and a review of usage scenarios of the respective features in commercial products.

3.1.1 Task classes for interaction history related information retrieval

To use interaction histories for information retrieval, we distinguish two different types of retrieval: retrieval by description and description by relatedness in the work process:

DC Tasks (retrieve by DesCription).
Keyword-based search for an information object included in the interaction history.

Answers to: "Where can I find the document *doc* that I accessed earlier?", "I am looking for the document that is described by keywords a,b, which I accessed earlier..."

Example: The user searches an information object "sales report.docx" based on descriptive keywords.

Referred to-as: DC tasks

RO Tasks (find by RelatiOn).
The RO task is an information object search, based on the usage context of an information object. A user remembers certain objects he interacted with or a timeframe and wants to identify the related resources. This especially addresses a context based memory.

Answers to: "I search an information object I accessed earlier, but I do not know enough to find to find it by description. But I know what else I did at the same time time."

Example: A user remembers that there was an interesting document, but does not know enough to enter a description; however, he/she remembers another document while he/she wrote the first document. He/she searches for the remembered document and identifies the related document.

Referred to-as: RO tasks

3.1.2 Task classes to improve work process awareness

To use interaction histories for improving work process awareness, we consider temporal information as relevant: usage times and durations with start and end times.

UD Tasks (identify Usage Duration).
The time spent with an activity is difficult to identify for users [2]. However, an improved temporal understanding of work is useful for planning future work as well as for time reporting (e.g. relevant for agile development methods).

Answers to: "How much time was spent with an information object?"

Example: A user worked on a contract proposal named "contract.docx" for a couple of days. To settle the proposal creation, he/she needs to identify the time that was required to create the contract. He/she uses the actual working time with the document as an important hint to the total time needed.

Referred to-as: UD task

UT Tasks (identify Usage Time).
This class involves tasks, in which users identify what was done at a certain point in time, which activities followed other activities, or a sanity check whether a certain activity was actually performed.

Due to the number of accessed information objects, and complex planning and replanning processes that are involved in information work, individuals forget aspects of their work process [3]. An improved structural understanding of work helps to avoid retrospective and prospective memory failures. Retrospective memory addresses remembering what was done. Prospective memory addresses remembering what was planned to be done. Especially in the context of interruptions both memory types are crucial, as failures of both types result in higher failure rates when work processes are intended to be resumed after interruptions [4].

Answers to: "What was done in the beginning of the process?" "What was continuously relevant?" "How did the work process proceed?"

Example: A user is asked to tell a colleague, how he/she created a document. He/she needs to remember what he/she initially did and reviewed, what he/she did after that and so on. Therefore, he/she needs to get on overview of the work process.

Referred to-as: UT tasks

In the following, we will focus on the RO, UT and UC tasks. The DC task will not be investigated further, as it is a classic information retrieval task, that is not focus of this work.

3.2 Characteristics of interaction history visualization

To solve tasks with an information visualization, the required information needs to be identified in and decoded from the visualization. Although, decoding is an individual process, it follows certain regularities. In the following, general rules of visualization comprehension are discussed. The gained insight is applied to the previously identified interaction history tasks, to derive requirements for interaction history visualization.

3.2.1 Human information visualization decoding

Interaction history visualization needs to consider how visualizations are encoded by humans. Reading of visualizations is different from the reading of text. Good information visualization uses this effect and helps to understand information quicker with less errors [24]. This benefit only holds if the visualization is perceived without high mental effort. Important aspects of graph understanding are summarized in the following. The summary follows a theory of graph understanding by Pinker that relates graph understanding and mental effort [18].

Graphs communicate n-tuples of values on organized scales. Scales and values are encoded as visual objects that apply visual features to display information (length, position, lightness, shape, etc.). Graph understanding requires 1) an encoding of the physical dimensions of graphical elements and 2) an understanding of the meaning of the scales, the elements and the objects they stand for. The interplay of both aspects is crucial. A complex visualization requires high mental effort to decode the image and to identify the scales and the relation of objects to the scales. Objects that represent scales may realize a coordinate system. Based on the coordinate system, other elements are perceived and compared.

An easily consumable visualization is understood almost effortless. To realize this, perception laws need to be applied to optimize the graph drawing with respect to the visualization goals. Important perception laws are formulated by Gestalt theory: proximity, similarity, common fate, good continuation, closure, figures, ground and connectedness [7]. The laws hint to those graphical formations that are decoded almost effortless by an individual.

Pinker [18] stresses that first the spatial organization of objects (following Gestalt theory), and then trained attributes are decoded following a decoding likelihood: the unconscious decoding of spatial organization reveals objects which are decomposed into scales and values. Values are directly decoded as being relative to the scales, and as being relative to all existing values. Only in a second step, conscious processes can enhance the understanding of the graph, requiring, however,

mental effort and time. Different limiting factors complicate graph understanding. Individual processing capacity is limited. Human beings can separate between four and nine elements at a time. The amount of elements is even fewer if processing resources are devoted to a concurrent task.

3.2.2 Requirements for useful interaction history visualizations

Pinkers work shows that visualizations can be optimized with respect to the mental effort required to solve a specific task.

To optimize interaction history visualization for the identified task classes, certain requirements must be met - the following list contains requirements that stem partly from the general principles for useful visualizations as discussed above, partly from several personal discussions about comprehension of activity data – on the on hand with experts in information visualization, on the other hand with users of existing tools that integrate interaction history visualizations. The term simple encoding refers to the application of Gestalt laws to simplify encoding for the specific information type:

RO-Tasks requirements:

(RQ1) Simple encoding of relations: Relations between interaction history elements should be easily identifiable, i.e. when the user has switched from one information object to another, this needs to be clearly visible.

(RQ2) Weighted relations: Relations should be weighted to display their relevance, i.e. when a user has switched frequently between two information objects, the frequency should be visible in the visualization.

(RQ3) Simple encoding of timeframes: Time should be decomposed into discrete time periods, so called timeframes, to structure interaction history data. Thus, a user can identify a certain time period like "yesterday morning" and see which activities were performed in that period.

UD-Tasks requirements:

(RQ3) also applies.

(RQ4) Simple comparability of time data: Temporal data should be associated to a scale that enables easy identification of timeframes, i.e. a user should be able to extract information like "happened before", "happened after" or "'happened while" easily.

(RQ5) Preservation of process information: Interaction history element presentation should show how the visualized work process was structured, so that a user can assess easily that information object A was accessed in the beginning, whereas information object B was accessed towards the end of the timeframe under consideration.

UT-Tasks Requirements:

(RQ6) Simple encoding of usage times: The overall time the user accessed an information object in a specific timeframe should be easily decodable. Thus, the user can easily see how much time information object A was accessed between e.g. 4PM and 5PM yesterday.

(RQ7) Simple comparability of usage times: Usage time should be associated to object scales (following Gestalt laws) to enable a simple identification of values and direct comparison of the respective values. This way, a user can easily compare different duration times to extract "longer than" or "shorter than" information.

General Requirements:

(RQ8) Limit amount of perceptual units: The visualizations needs to be understandable for large interaction histories. As human perception capability is limited, the visualization needs to find useful ways of structuring large data sets.

(RQ9) Easy to learn: The visualization should not require extensive learning effort.

4. RELATED WORK

Different interaction history visualizations are currently used both in commercial applications and in research prototypes to solve the discussed tasks. These tools use lists, line- and bar charts, Gantt charts, or grouped object sets (as proposed by Rattenbury[20]). In the following, we will focus the discussion of the visualization requirements on bar-, line- and Gantt charts.

We will not discuss lists and grouped object sets in more detail, as the former suffers from the large cognitive effort required to decode information as the list grows, and the latter focuses on DC tasks and does not encode time or relation information beyond grouping objects according to a shared context.

Bar- and line charts.

Bar- and line charts are the dominant visualizations for interaction history-based analytics. These charts use graphical elements that allow an easy identification of value information on a coordinate system (see figure 2). Based on the coordinate system, the elements are directly relatable among another. Bar charts are especially useful to compare values against each other. Line charts are useful to identify trends in data. The visualization is well known, thus usually requires little learning. For large data sets, however, bar- and line charts become complex to read.

Bar and line charts are capable of a simple encoding of timeframes and durations in the coordinate system. The displayed shapes can be compared among another. Relations are not visualized, and can only implicitly be deduced based on information objects included in a timeframe. Thus, for RO tasks, bar- and line charts are not suitable due to the lack of relation information. For UT tasks, they are only partly suitable, as the relation between the different visualized timeframes is not encoded, which complicates the understanding of the process (e.g. once a user wants to know if an information object was used in the beginning of the reviewed time only, he/she needs to check each timeframe). For UD tasks, however, the bar- and line charts are suitable, as usage times are encoded in a way that makes them easy to decode and compare.

Examples: Social wakoopa [8], rescue time [9], the CAM dashboard [5] and the student activity monitor [5].

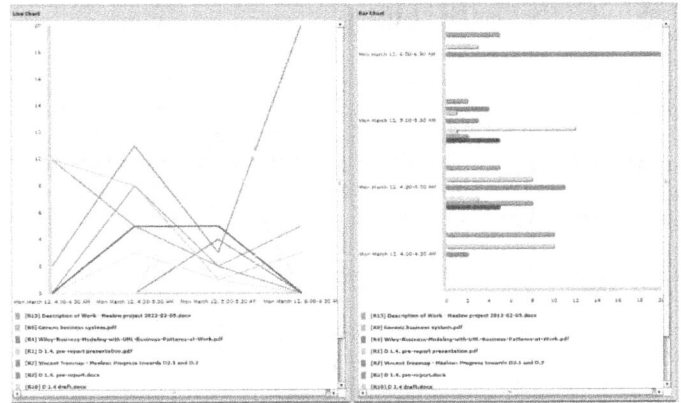

Figure 2: Bar and line chart visualization.

Gantt Charts.

When Gantt charts are used for visualization of interaction histories, this implies a (two-dimensional) coordinate system, with rows of text identifiers on the y-axis representing one or more interaction history elements, and a continuous timeline on the x-axis (see figure 3). Access durations are visualized as blocks with a start, an end and a duration that is expressed by the extent of the block. Relations among elements are visually represented by the proximity or the overlapping of blocks on the timeline. Gantt charts are well known, therefore require little learning. For huge data collections, they may, however, become overly complex.

For RO tasks, an encoding of relations is given, although it is not necessarily simple, in particular for elements with long duration. The weight of a relation is the number of similar information object successions, i.e. similar bar successions in the visualization that need to be manually counted. The identification of timeframes with gantt charts is simple, as they are simply encoded in the timeline.

The given aspects make Gantt charts a better choice for RO tasks than bar- or line charts, but they are still complex to read. For UT tasks, a simple encoding of timeframes is given. Comparison is complex, as the length of shapes at different y-positions needs to be compared. The process information is well preserved in gantt charts. One can assume that solving UT tasks with Gantt charts works well, but requires time for compare operations and search along the timeline. UD tasks are complex with Gantt charts, as the usage duration is spreaded across the timeline, or encoded in additional text, which makes the tasks solvable, but requires high metal effort.

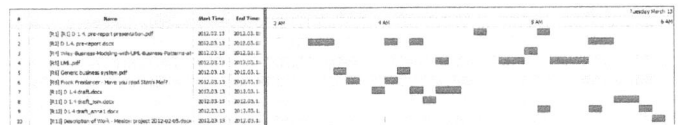

Figure 3: Gantt chart visualization.

Example: The Outlook journal provides a Gantt chart visualization of information object usage. Each information object has a dedicated row. In this row, a bar denotes the time the respective resource was open.

5. CONTRIBUTION

To our best knowledge, existing visualizations of interaction histories do not make use of graphs. This is surprising, as there is a need to display elements that have more than one predecessor and more than one successor (e.g. when interaction history elements for the same information object are aggregated). To visualize such a structure with numerous connections, graphs are useful, as they apply the law of uniform connectedness[2]. An important requirement for graphs is good readability, even when they contain many elements. [6] studies on nodes with 50 and more vertices show an increasing complexity of graph decoding and understanding.

Two specific types of graphs have gained increasing relevance [12] and are of specific importance for this paper: *dynamic graphs* address the visualization of time in graphs. Element evolution is displayed by the addition or deletion of edges and nodes, e.g. using animation. *Compound graphs* are static graphs organized based on semantic clustering, i.e. a second type of order, e.g. hierarchy or group is used to organize sets of nodes. Compound graphs are used e.g. in plate notation and UML diagrams.

In the following we shortly discuss a straight forward visualization of interaction histories with graphs, which reveals difficulties w.r.t. readability and temporal understanding of the visualized data, especially when the interaction history contains many elements. We then propose two new visualizations to address the readability and the visualization issue: the *timeline graph*, a new variant of dynamic graphs, and a *compound graph*, a variant of the compound graph applying a hierarchical structure.

5.1 Limitations of simple graphs for interaction history visualization

A straight forward graph visualization uses vertices to show interaction history elements and edges to show relations between the objects. Temporal information is added as label to nodes. This type of visualization has been integrated into a research prototype and was evaluated. 9 users used the research prototype for 2 weeks. This use was accompanied by a series of questionnaires that tracked trends in the perception of the named tool.

Most participants initially expected the graph representation of their work to be useful or very useful (6 of 9). After two weeks in which they used the tool in a normal work context, however, a number problems became apparent: the appreciation of the graph representation for the work decreased significantly (not useful (2 of 9), partly useful (2 of 9), moderately useful (2 of 9), useful (3 of 9)). 5 of 9 users considered reading the graph to be very complex. In a subsequent interview, all participants stated that they found the graph view interesting, but did not find a connection to their daily work tasks, and that it was time consuming to interact with the visualization, especially due to its size (after 8 hours of work a graph sometimes contained far more than 100 nodes, see figure 4). Also, the problem of decoding temporal information from the graph was mentioned informally by different participants.

---

[2]The law of uniform connectedness describes the effect that humans consider elements as related when they are connected by a visual element, e.g. a line. Palmer [17] argues that the law of uniform connectedness is the strongest of all gestalt laws.

The two visualizations presented below address in particular these concerns.

Figure 4: Interaction history visualization with a simple graph, data collected from 8 hours of work.

5.2 Timeline graph

The timeline graph addresses the central demands of RO tasks by combining temporal and relation visualization. The lower part of the visualization shows a timeline that displays the periods for which time interaction history data exists. A timeframe can be selected in the timeline to investigate in the selected period. For the selected period, the upper part displays a graph of interaction history elements. The graph encodes weighted relations by edges with different thicknesses; vertex size encodes the usage duration of the interaction history elements.

The period selected on the timeline can be moved to visualize the transformation of the visible graph by animations.

The combination of a timeline with a graph addresses the requirements for RO tasks; the encoding of a timeframe and comparability based on node size address those of UT and UD tasks. The disadvantage for UT tasks, however, is the way process information is coded in the graph: the user needs to actively change the visible timeframe to get an overview of the process. Also, UD tasks may be challenging, as the user needs to identify the timeframe that contains the information objects he/she is interested in, before they can be compared.

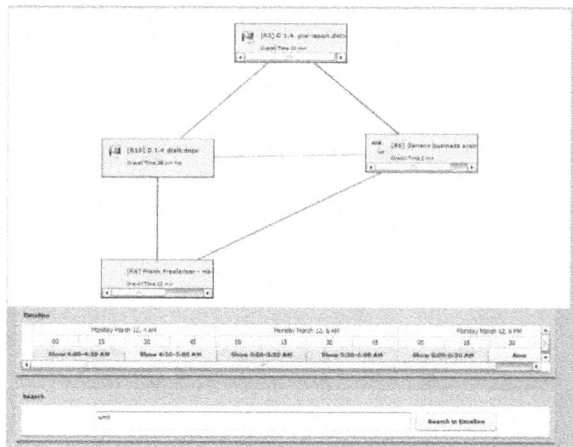

Figure 5: Timeline graph visualization.

5.3 Compound graph

The compound graph has been designed to address those requirements of UD tasks which have not been addressed completely by any of the previously discussed visualizations. In particular, the other visualizations failed to provide an easy means to transfer process knowledge. The compound graph organizes the displayed graph with respect to hierarchically ordered groups (see figure 6), i.e. elements are organized in several layers of interconnected boxes that are, in turn, embedded into a temporal coordinate system.

Each box stands for a period of time and contains a graph for interactions. An interaction history visualization is added to a box, only if all interaction history elements that is aggregated was only used during the timespan that is covered by the box and if it does not fit into the timeframe of a smaller box. The y-axis structures the duration time: the longer the box, the longer the duration. The x-axis is a timeline: the x start and end postion of the box hint to the length of the displayed period. The boxes are hierarchically ordered. The highest level contains one box with the width of the complete visualization. The level below the highest level is decomposed into two equally width boxes for two shorter periods. The lower level again, has twice the boxes, each with a width half the width of the boxes representing again shorter periods.

The hierarchical structure simplifies the process of identifying timespans of interest. The boxes restore a kind of "fuzzy process knowledge" in the visualization that structures interaction history data along questions like "What did i do in the beginning?" or "What was always relevant?". For example, in the lower left box are only those resources that were interesting only in the beginning. In the lower right box are those activities that were only performed at the end of the timeframe.

The graph fulfills all requirements for UT tasks: timeframes are encoded in a coordinate system that transfers process knowledge based on hierarchical structure. Representation of durations by vertex size enables comparability between elements. The requirements for RO tasks are also met: weighted relations are easy to decode and timeframes are clearly displayed. Only for long timeframes, the navigation of the compound graph is likely to be more complex than for the previosuly presented timeline graph. Finally, the requirements for UD tasks are met, although time comparation is presumably simpler using bar- or line charts.

6. COMPARATIVE STUDY

While the basic suitability of the respective visualizations for the identified tasks has already been analyzed, we set up a user study to substantiate the claims made.

6.1 Hypothesis and study design

We define suitability or usefulness of a visualization for a task by operation success (when a user solves a task with a visualization, the task can be solved correct, can be solved incorrect or can be considered as unsolvable with the specific visualization) and time investment. We posed three hypotheses for the suitability, focusing on the performance of the two proposed visualizations, the timeline graph and the compound graph, with respect to the other visualizations:

H1 The number of errors is lower for a) compound graph and b) timeline graph than for all other visualizations.

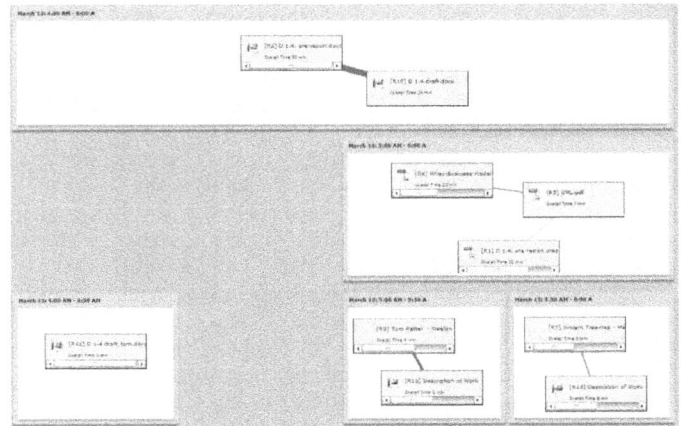

Figure 6: Compound graph visualization.

H2 Task completion time is lower for a) compound graphs and b) timeline graphs when compared to bar-, line and Gantt charts for most (at least 4) tasks.

H3 One of the graph-based visualizations outperforms the other in all tasks (in terms of task completion times and error rates).

To test these hypotheses, we created six tasks; each of them lies in one of the task classes discussed before, and each task class is represented by two different tasks (doc refers to any information object):

Task1 How much time was worked on *doc*? *(Task class: UD)*

Task2 When was *doc* used during the work process? (e.g. from 4.00-6.00 AM, from 5.00-5.30 AM, from 4.00-5.00 AM, ...)? *(Task class: UT)*

Task3 Which documents were connected to *doc* in the workprocess? *(Task class: RO)*

Task4 List the documents that were accessed only between 4.00 am and 4.30 am. *(Task class: UT)*

Task5 You have read an interesting book about patterns, when working on *doc*. Can you identify it? *(Task class: RO)*

Task6 Find 3 resources that were overall used for more than 18 min? *(Task class: UD)*

6.2 Study setup

To evaluate the performance of the visualizations on the six defined tasks, a prototypical interaction history visualization tool has been created. Initially, the tool shows a questionnaire. Then, the tool asks for the solution of the six presented tasks with the different visualizations. We have created interaction history data sets inspired by real interaction histories created during a normal working day as input for the tool.

The amount of resources has been restricted to allow an execution of the study with all 24 tests in 30 minutes. In this configuration, the visualizations display more than 7 discrete elements to assure that interaction history size is reflected in the dataset, although the scalability of the visualization with respect to very large datasets is thus not in the focus of our study. Each data set contains 13 resources, and shows 8 to 13 resources at a time. The data shows a timeframe for two hours for March 12, 4-6AM. Each task has to be executed with every visualization. To rule out learning effects, the tool randomizes among the tasks sequence, the visualization sequence and among four different data sets that are used. The different datasets share the same structure – only task completion times and information object names have been changed. The similarity among the datasets garuantees a similar complexity for the same task solved with different datasets.

To represent a realistic work process, the data sets tackle a focus topic, but also include information objects that belong to different tasks to mimic multi-tasking. The focus topic for the data sets are: 1) Software engineering/UML modeling, 2) Software engineering/Design patterns, 3) Lessing's "Hamburgische Dramaturgie", 4) Eccentric Pump Sales.

For each task, the solution provided by the user and the time spent (in ms) were logged. After the study, each participant was shortly asked to identify the visualization he/she liked the most/less.

Eleven participants were recruited for the study using convenience sampling - 10 were male, 1 female, their age was the between 25 and 60. All participants use computers heavily during their daily work processes.

6.3 Results

The initial questionnaire elaborated on interaction history use and process awareness. Ten participants stated that they use history features like timelines or history based auto-completion fields during their daily work. Four participants knew the outlook journal. With respect to memorization of work processes, 3 stated that they have problems remembering their work (2 not good, 1 okay), whereas 7 stated that they generally can remember their work processes (6 well, 1 good). Nevertheless, no one stated that he could remember all documents he worked on during the morning of the study day (study activities were all performed in the afternoon), 7 stated they remember most, 2 some of these documents – there was, however, no further inquiry to validate these reports. Only two participants stated that they spend little time with searching for documents they accessed earlier, the others spend a considerable amount of time with searching for this type of information (7 some time, 2 much time).

Number of errors.

Each participant completed 24 tasks. Each task could be solved with a correct solution, an incorrect solution, or a note that the task was not solvable with the visualization. The absolute number of errors and rejections for the tasks and visualization is visible in figure 7. It is important to note that a solution existed for each task and each visualization, although the complexity of finding it naturally differed among visualizations.

Line- and bar charts The charts show most errors (11) and most statements that a task is not solvable. Most errors and unsolvable statements occur for task 3 (9 unsolvable, 2 errors) and task 5 (3 unsolvable, 3 errors), which belong to the RO task class. This underlines the problem of visualizing relations in this chart type (they are only implicitly encoded in the timeframes). The UT and UD tasks show fewer errors,

without being considerably good results. The difficulties for UT and UD relate to the complexity of bar chart reading for many elements. The comparability features disappear due to the conscious limitations.

Gantt charts The Gantt chart showed 13 unsolvable statements and 11 errors. The participants had problems with RO tasks in particular. Although relations are encoded in Gantt charts, the identification of the relations among the different rows is error-ridden, and sometimes even discarded by users due to its complexity. Considering the three task classes, the Gantt chart performed best for UD tasks, as process information is visible based on the timeline. UT tasks showed difficulties, as the users had to identify all bars for each row to identify usage times.

Timeline graph The timeline graph showed good results for all tasks with no unsolvable consideration and only five errors. The errors mainly occurred for task 4, a UD task. As the timeline graph does not include a simple encoding of the process, the participant needs to identify the work process on the period successions in the timeline which is complex and error-ridden.

Compound graph Overall, the compound graph showed the best results. Only one error and one unsolvable statement occurred for task 4.

		Task1	Task2	Task3	Task4	Task5	Task6
Barchart	unsolv	1	2	9	4	3	3
	■ Error	4	1	2	0	3	1
	■ TRUE	6	8	0	7	5	7
Gantt Chart	unsolv	0	0	5	3	3	2
	■ Error	1	0	5	2	3	0
	■ TRUE	10	11	1	5	5	9
Compound Graph	unsolv	0	0	0	1	0	0
	■ Error	0	0	0	1	0	0
	■ TRUE	11	11	11	9	11	11
Timeline Graph	■ Error	0	0	1	4	0	0
	■ TRUE	11	11	10	7	11	11

Figure 7: Correct solutions, false solutions and "unsolvable" notes (per task)

Summing up, we can confirm H1a and H1b, as the timeline graph as well as the compound graph overall showed better results with regard to the number of errors than the other visualizations.

Usage time.

All tasks were executed between 7000 ms and 120000 ms (see the scatter chart in figure 8). To make statements about the time distribution among the different visualizations we need to show significance, using an ANOVA test. This requires a normal distribution and variance homogeneity.

To test for normal distribution, the Shapiro Wilk test is applicable for a data set of the given size. During the study execution some people started to execute tasks before they understood them and spent time to think about the task. This produced outliers which were eliminated following the three sigma rule (99.73% of the values lie within 3 standard deviations of the mean) and replaced by the mean value (c.f. [13]). Shapiro Wilk shows that a normal distribution for an alpha level of 0.05 can be assumed for all but two dataset (the data for the dynamic graph in task 3 and the data

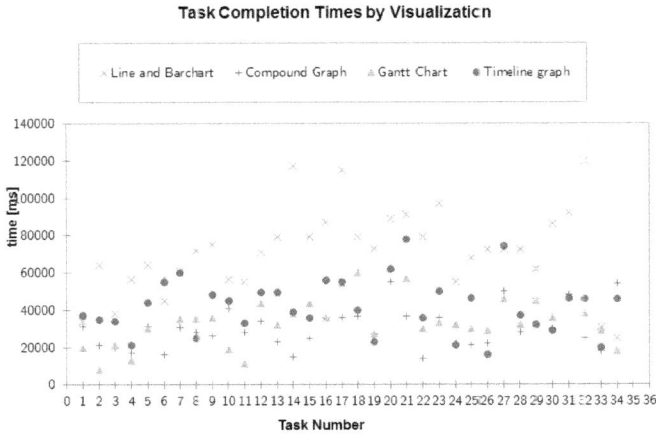

Figure 8: Task completion time (per task)

Task	Line and Barchart	Gannt Chart	Compound Graph
1	56446,27273	39735,53636	26446,27273
2	87247,92727	47628,09091	30801,65455
3	75305,77273	37942,14545	31446,28182
4	30008,27273	43099,16364	32181,81818
6	77801,64545	45619,82727	28454,54545

Table 1: Distribution of the average values forfor compound graph vs. classical charts in ms

Task	Line and Barchart	Gannt Chart	Dynamic Graph
1	56446,27273	39735,53636	25958,67273
2	87247,92727	47628,09091	44041,32727
3	75305,77273	37942,14545	36082,64545
4	30008,27273	43099,16364	36256,2
6	77801,64545	45619,82727	45504,12727

Table 2: Distribution of the average values for timeline graph vs. classical charts in ms

for the bar chart in task 4). We subsequently applied the Levene test for homogeneity, finding that the homogeneity is acceptable. For task 5 homogeneity assumption needs to be rejected.

As most data is normally distributed and variance homogeneity holds for all but one distributions we are allowed to apply an ANOVA test (c.f. [11]). Only task 5 was excluded, as homogeneity was rejected.

Compound graph vs. classical charts The compound graph, the bar/line chart and the gantt chart time series per task (rows) and visualizations (columns) have been used as input to a two factor ANOVA with replication. The result shows significance columns. The value for the columns is of interest as this describes the difference between the different graph types ($F(3,06) = 96,41$, $p < 0.001$).

Based on the average task completion times, one can investigate this further. In table 1 the average values of the task completion time per visualization and task are given. Based on this information, the strength and weaknesses of the different visualizations can be identified. It is striking that the compound graph outperforms the other visualizations (=lowest average value) for all tasks, except task 4. The identification of usage time and usage duration seems to be simple with the graph. The compound graph seems to fit the requirements for UT, UD and RO tasks very well. Only in some cases, like the UD timeframe identification of task 4, which is straight forward for the timeframe in question in that task, bar/line charts show their strength.

Summing up, we can confirm H2a.

Timeline graph vs. classical charts The timeline graph, the bar- and line chart and the gantt chart time series per task (rows) and visualizations (columns) have been used as input to a two factor ANOVA with replication. The result shows significance for columns that shows that there is significant difference between the used visualization ($F(3,94) = 13,41$, $p < 0.001$).

Again, we consider the average values of the time spent with each visualization for each task (see table 2): the

average values are better for all tasks, except task 4 and 6. These tasks ask to identify usage time and usage duration. The timeline graph performs especially good for RO tasks. Although the results for UD and UT tasks are worse, they are still convincing.

Summing up, we can confirm H2b.

Timeline graph vs. Compound graph To compare both graph visualization, the respective time series per task have been used as input to a two factor ANOVA with replication. The result shows significance for the columns. The effect of visualization types (columns) on task completion time gives: $F(3,94) = 13,41$, $p = 0.0004$. The null-hypothesis that the values are significantly different can be accepted. The average values of the compound graph are better than the results of the dynamic graph with timeline for all UT and UD tasks.

The graph-based visualizations show very good results with respect to task completion time and error rate for all three task classes. Still, the study does not allow a decision on one visualization which performs better for all tasks (no significant difference between the two graph-base visualizations with regard to task completion time). Therefore, H3 needs to be rejected.

Post-test interview.

After their trials, participants were asked for the visualization they appreciated the most/the least. All, except 2 considered the compound or the timeline graph as the most suitable visualization; bar- and line charts were the least appreciated visualization. This is very much in line with results given above: the graph visualizations are less prone to error, and have significantly smaller task completion times.

7. CONCLUSION

In this paper, we have discussed the challenges and requirements of interaction history visualization. Based on the application areas of interaction histories, we have identified four task classes that can be solved, using interaction histories: DC (retrieve by DesCription), RO (find by RelatiOn), UD (identify Usage Duration) and UT (identify Usage Time)). For these tasks, requirements for interaction history visualization have been specified. We have identified line charts, bar charts and Gantt charts as visualization types that are typically used to visualize interaction histories. These visualization types show weaknesses for UD and RO tasks. We have proposed two new graph-based visualizations: the timeline graph, specifically suitable for RO tasks, and the compound graph, specifically suitable for UT tasks. For all named visualization types, we have conducted a study to assess number of errors and task completion time for the execution of tasks belonging to the three classes.

Overall, the compound graph and the timeline graph have shown very good results for tasks of all three classes. Bar- and line charts and Gantt charts have shown weak results, in particular with respect to the number of errors. Bar- and line chart did, however, show good results for UT tasks, if the scale of the graph fits the searched time period. The Gantt chart showed good results for UD tasks, although the error rate was higher than for the compound graph. The best performance for RO tasks was shown by the timeline graph. The compound graph had the best overall performance, although it did not outperform the timeline graph in all task significantly.

Future work will focus on the scalability of the visualizations for very large collections of activity data. Additionally, we plan a new graph visualization which creates compounds for selected timelines. The combination of compound and timeline would combine the strengths of both graph visualizations.

8. REFERENCES

[1] L. Bannon, A. Cypher, S. Greenspan, and M. Monty. Evaluation and analysis of users' activity organization. In *Proceedings of the SIGCHI conference on Human Factors in Computing Systems*, number December, pages 54–57. ACM, 1983.

[2] V. Bellotti, B. Dalal, N. Good, P. Flynn, D. Bobrow, and N. Ducheneaut. What a to-do: studies of task management towards the design of a personal task list manager. In *Proceedings of the SIGCHI conference on Human factors in computing systems*, volume 6, pages 735–742. ACM, 2004.

[3] Benedikt Schmidt, Eicke Godehardt, and Björn Pantel. Visualizing the work processSituation awareness for the knowledge worker. In *3rd IUI Workshop on Semantic Models for Adaptive Interactive Systems (SEMAIS 2012)*, 2012.

[4] M. Czerwinski, E. Horvitz, and S. Wilhite. A diary study of task switching and interruptions. *Proceedings of the SIGCHI*, 2004.

[5] E. Duval. Attention Please ! Learning Analytics for Visualization and Recommendation. *Educational Technology*, 2011.

[6] M. Ghoniem, J.-d. Fekete, and P. Castagliola. On the readability of graphs using node-link and matrix-based representations : a controlled experiment and statistical analysis. (October 2004):114–135, 2005.

[7] S. Han and G. Humphreys. Uniform connectedness and classical Gestalt principles of perceptual grouping. *Attention, Perception, & Psychophysics*, 61(4):661–674, 1999.

[8] Http://social.wakoopa.com/. Social wakoopa.

[9] Http://www.rescuetime.com/. Rescue Time.

[10] V. Kaptelinin. UMEA: translating interaction histories into project contexts. In *Proceedings of the SIGCHI conference on Human factors in computing systems*, number 5, pages 353–360. ACM, 2003.

[11] S. Kuiper and J. Sklar. *Practicing Statistics: Guided Investigations for the Second Course*. 2012.

[12] T. V. Landesberger and A. Kuijper. Visual analysis of large graphs. *of Euro-Graphics:*, 2010.

[13] H. Liu, S. Shah, and W. Jiang. On-line outlier detection and data cleaning. *Computers & Chemical Engineering*, 28(9):1635–1647, Aug. 2004.

[14] R. Lokaiczyk and M. Goertz. Extending Low Level Context Events by Data Aggregation. *Proceedings of I-KNOW 08 and I-MEDIA '08*, pages 118–125, 2008.

[15] R. Morteo, V. Gonzalez, J. Favela, and G. Mark. Sphere juggler: fast context retrieval in support of working spheres. *Proceedings of the Fifth Mexican International Conference in Computer Science, 2004. ENC 2004.*, pages 361–367, 2004.

[16] N. Oliver, G. Smith, C. Thakkar, and A. Surendran. SWISH: semantic analysis of window titles and switching history. In *Proceedings of the 11th international conference on Intelligent user interfaces*, pages 201–209. ACM, 2006.

[17] S. Palmer and I. Rock. Rethinking perceptual organization: The role of uniform connectedness. *Psychonomic Bulletin & Review*, 1(1):29—-55, 1994.

[18] S. Pinker. A Theory of Graph Comprehension. In *Artificial intelligence and the future of testing*, pages 73–126. Lawrence Erlbaum Associates, 1990.

[19] A. S. Rath and S. N. Lindstaedt. UICO: An ontology-based user interaction context model for Automatic Task Detection on the Computer Desktop. (Ciao), 2009.

[20] T. Rattenbury and J. Canny. CAAD: an automatic task support system. In *Proceedings of the SIGCHI conference on Human factors in computing systems*, pages 696–706. ACM, 2007.

[21] B. Schmidt and E. Godehardt. Interaction Data Management. In *Knowlege-Based and Intelligent Information and Engineering Systems*. Springer, 2011.

[22] B. Schmidt, J. Kastl, T. Stoitsev, and M. Mühlhäuser. Hierarchical Task Instance Mining in Interaction Histories. In *Proceedings of the 29th annual international conference on Design of communication (SIGDOC)*. ACM, 2011.

[23] J. Shen, L. Li, and T. Dietterich. Real-time detection of task switches of desktop users. In *Proceedings of the International Joint Conferences on Artificial Intelligence*, volume 7, pages 2868–2873, 2007.

[24] C. Ware. *Information visualization: perception for design*. Morgan Kaufmann, 2004.

A Knowledge System for Promotion of Selecting, Sharing, and Circulation of Multilingual Technical Knowledge

Keita Minowa,Reiko Hishiyama
Graduate School of Creative Science and Engineering
Waseda University
{ keita-x@asagi., reiko@ }waseda.jp

ABSTRACT

A "knowledge system" is a system to allow users to select technical knowledge on a lexical basis from technical papers written in English and share that knowledge. It supports users to read technical paper written in English, understand technical knowledge in English, and complement knowledge with other users' knowledge. We experimented for accumulating English special knowledge, translating it to Japanese, and adding information how much people know the knowledge. And we evaluated the complementation and comprehensiveness of the technical knowledge between two different systems that we proposed and among the users. The experiment(s) showed that the number of Japanese-translated words tends to increase with increasing number of users and the environment facilitates acquiring technical knowledge in their mother language. Using this system, users can collect knowledge comprehensively. In addition, the system provides an effective way to create a high-quality environment for helping users to read English-written technical papers.

Categories and Subject Descriptors

H.5.3 [**Group and Organization Interfaces**]: Computer-supported cooperative work.

Keywords

Technical Knowledge and Words, Comprehension of Technical Knowledge and Words

1. INTRODUCTION

In the international community, with the development of new research areas, it has become very important for researchers and students to get knowledge about expert fields so they can learn about the latest advanced theories, cutting-edge technologies, and research results. To acquire such knowledge rapidly, a lot of information in documents written in English must be understood, and that is difficult for people whose mother language is not English. To avoid this problem, machine translation is one of the solution, but it does not translate words or terms which is used in research

area that require expertise to understand. Using parallel texts and multilingual dictionaries is still not enough to support non-English speakers because the cost for collecting examples and words for registration is high.

People in a technical community mainly exchange information about how much technical knowledge they have face-to-face or one-sidedly. Nevertheless, this way of information exchange is not efficient, and it does not make it easy for people who have just started to research new specialized areas to find out who to ask for support and what to investigate.

Considering the above-described issues, we propose to create a knowledge system that makes it possible to select expert knowledge on a lexical basis from technical papers published in English on-line and in Journals. And the system make people be able to share the knowledge so that they can read the English paper, gain technical knowledge in English, and complement knowledge each other in university laboratories, etc.

2. RELATED WORKS

2.1 Multilingual communication tool

Exchanging information in multilingual has been regarded as very important from long years ago, and the importance increases as one's level of expertise gets higher. In medical institutions, many dictionaries, such as the *Multilingual Dictionary of Disaster Medicine and International Relief* by S.W.A Gunn[1], have been published, and they support information exchange among medical personnel in a multi-language environment. Moreover, in recent years, many kinds of machine-translation systems have become available with the development of the Internet. Certain words and terms depending on a certain community can not be translated exactly because of lingual diversity and rapid development of research areas.

To solve the above-described problems, Tanaka[6] proposed to create an open-source multilingual community web site based on the Language Grid. This web site supports people who want to communicate with other people who speak another language, and it is created with some basic function, one of which is like a multilingual BBS with a translation system, and needed in multilingual communication. People who can translate a document side-by-side with the original text translate the original words or terms into the target language according to their expertise and register the translations on the website. The web site was made for the purpose of smoothing multilingual communication by the activity. However, this proposal did not consider personal characteristics and knowledge, but it only assessed functions of the site and sharing translation results.

2.2 Knowledge dictionary

The number of electronic articles stored on-line has tended to increase rapidly in recent years. It is, however, still very difficult to extract desired information from them and search for common tendencies. Unfortunately, as yet, there is no established way to solve this information-extraction problem.

Sakurai[2] proposed a tool for composing a knowledge dictionary for text mining. This tool supports knowledge engineers who do not have language-specialized knowledge. It consists of a function for creating a dictionary from a list of expressions. A lot of unknown words and incorrect words exist in daily business. In such a situation, the time taken searching for information and making requests increases.

2.3 Collaborative learning system

In certain areas or communities, knowledge (and the rules organizing it) exists in abundance, and, naturally, people in such a community can not comprehend all of it. Until recent years, the way to transmit information has been "passing on knowledge as communication;" in other words, it is one-way traffic. For example, teachers impart contents that they created to students, who, in turn, acquire the knowledge through listening or reading. From the viewpoint of a situation in which knowledge is mutually spread widely, this teaching/learning process does not create an optimum environment because it is possible that similar knowledge or contents overlap. Recently, research on human-computer interaction[7] focused on this problem in the case of collaborative work in some communities.

Parakh[5] proposed a collaborative learning platform for acquiring knowledge in a community. The platform enables users to not only learn the contents but also use them in a learning community. Not only do teachers impart their knowledge to their students but also students impart their knowledge to other students. Moreover, each student not only uses the contents they have but also uses other students' contents through the system and adds the contents that other students are interested in and learned from others' contents to their own system. As to optimization of leaning environment, Kim[4] also reported the importance of a personalized learning system.

2.4 Crowd-sourcing translations

Demand for translation of the document is increasing because of economic globalization. However, the number of professional translators is limited. Therefore, we need new translation process in which professional translators can work more efficiently.

For the problem, Crowd-Assisted Translation (CAT) is proposed. CAT is translation process using crowd-sourcing and post-editing. Crowd-sourcing is a type of employment for entrusting many people who is on the Internet to do tasks for the area. Post-editing is translation process by translator revises machine translation. CAT uses Crowd-sourcing in combination. CAT process is also used as a module operating on Language Grid Toolbox[3][8].

But collecting translations by crowd-sourcing the task to non-professional translators yields dis-fluent, low-quality results if no quality control is exercised.

2.5 Placement of this research

The above-described related works show the importance on the researches, multilingual communication, knowledge dictionary, Collaborative learning system, and Crowd-sourcing translations. However, little researches extended to other field has been reported.

For instance, the research about multilingual communication in on-line community did not consider personal characteristics and knowledge. It is unreliable because we do not understand how much knowledge the people have. On the other hand, multilingual environment is not established but only monolingual environment in the research of knowledge dictionary and knowledge circulation system which we brought up.

In the present study, we built a "knowledge-circulation system" that enables users (mainly college students and graduate school students majoring in engineering who have to read academic papers in English) to acquire technical knowledge, exchange knowledge with other students (so as to compensate for deficiencies in related works), and combine the acquired and exchanged knowledge.

3. KNOWLEDGE-CIRCULATION SYSTEM

3.1 Summary

The proposed knowledge-circulation system helps the users to understand words used in particular technical areas (hereafter called "technical words") and share them. This system creates an environment that allows users to extract information for acquiring knowledge about certain technical fields ("technical knowledge" hereafter) and more easily understand theories, technologies, and the forefront of research from English technical paper.

With the system, users read technical papers in English and acquire knowledge relevant to their research area. They can collect technical words through browsing technical knowledge that other users have accumulated on a language basis and add information about whether they already know or not ("add comprehension to technical words" hereafter). Through the activity with some users, technical knowledge is stored in the system. This system aims to encourage users to exchange technical knowledge with each other and share the knowledge.

3.2 System

Figure 1 shows a conceptual diagram for activity between the proposed knowledge-circulation system and users.

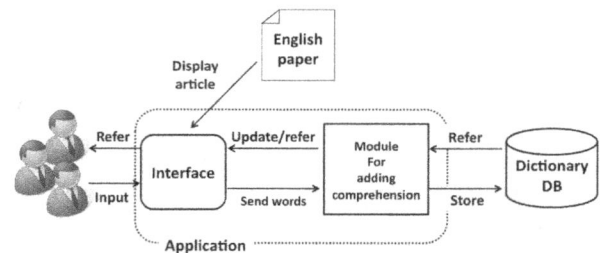

Figure 1: Activity between the system and users

This system is composed of an application interface, a dictionary database, and a module for adding comprehension information to technical words. While reading a technical paper in English (which they will read in their known range), a user collects technical words and registers them in the dictionary database through the system. At the same time, the user adds comprehension and Japanese translation to the technical words and if they know the Japanese translation. Through several users performing this procedure, a dictionary database is constructed with technical words, thereby creating an environment for knowledge circulation that can prompt users to share knowledge with each other. Each part of this system is explained in the following sections.

3.2.1 Application interface

Users operate the system via an application interface only. After preparing a technical paper in English which they read, they read the paper, collect the technical words, and add comprehension to them. The functions which users use in the activities are described in Section 3.3.

3.2.2 Module

The module for adding comprehension information judges how much users know about technical words and convert them to symbols according to its rules. The definitions of comprehension are explained in Section 3.4, and the converted symbols are described in Sections 4.1 and 4.2.

3.2.3 Dictionary database

The dictionary database stores the technical words sent from the application interface and the user's users' comprehension to the words. The information inside the database can only be updated through the interface.

3.3 Interface

The system has two interfaces. The first one, shown in Figure. 2, is for reading papers in English and collecting technical words, and the second one, shown in Figure. 3, is for confirming users' comprehension of technical knowledge. Each system is composed of the three functions described below.

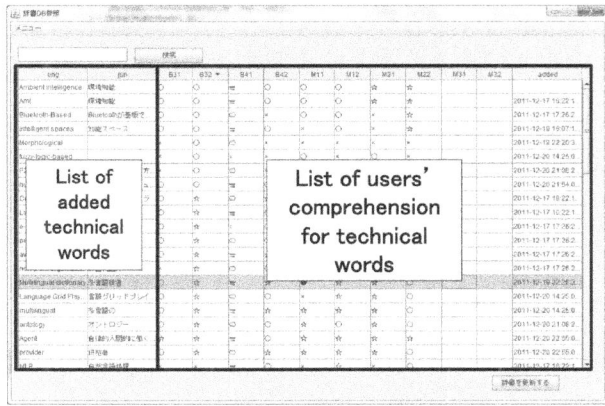

Figure 2: Interface for reading papers

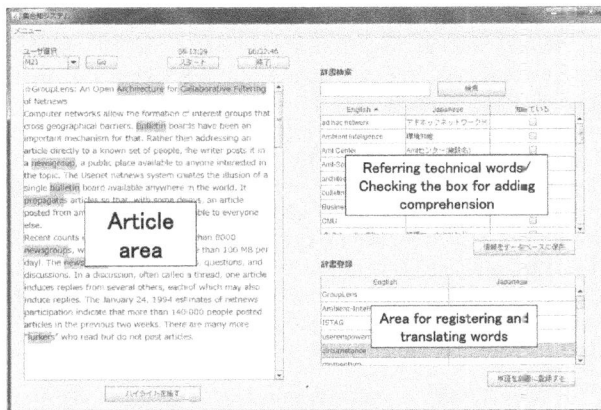

Figure 3: Interface for checking comprehension

3.3.1 Collecting technical words

Users register technical words that they collect from English papers in the article area and add the Japanese translation to the words when they read an article through the field shown in Figure 2. They can send the words and Japanese translation to the module for adding comprehension information by pushing the button on the bottom-right when they register them. Words already registered in the dictionary database are then highlighted so as not to register the same technical words twice. Users can browse all of them and their Japanese translations on the same interface if the translations exist. And they can register the words to the best of users' technical knowledge because the system does not have limitation for registration for flexibility.

3.3.2 Registration of understanding

Users can add the comprehension to technical words which are collected when users read technical paper or have been registered already. The check boxes next to the English and Japanese lists in Figures 2 and 3 can be used for adding comprehension information. The words that have been already added to the dictionary database are displayed in the list. After checking the box, the information is sent to the module with technical words. The information is sent by pushing the bottom at center right in Figure 2 and inputting the symbols of comprehension into the list shown in Figure 2.

3.3.3 Browsing users' comprehension

After users add comprehension to technical words, the module for adding comprehension information changes it to symbols. Users can browse how many words there are and how other people understand the technical words through the interface shown in Figure. 3. The user can then see what research areas other users are specialists in and how much they know about the words by seeing comprehension symbols

3.4 Definition of comprehension

The five situations in which the system can specify when users add comprehension are defined as follows.

(a) words that users already know and have already been added to the Japanese translation in the database

(b) words that users already know (and can add Japanese translation to) and have already been added (with no Japanese translation) to the database

(c) words that have not been added to the database and that users can add Japanese translation to

(d) words that have not been added to the database and that users can not add Japanese translation to

(e) words that users do not know

These situations can tell users "whether users know the words or not" but not "to what degree users know the words." Accordingly, the situation for "users already know" is divided into two classes for the words that users already know ((a) - (c)).

1. words that users have already acquired knowledge about, and they can explain

2. words that users have already seen or heard but do not know or can not explain very much

The former class is named "I know" and the later "I have heard", and words that they do not know the meaning of or the Japanese translation for are called "I don't know". In the experiment, two systems ere used: the previously described system for classifying users understanding for technical knowledge into the five situations, and a system for dividing the words that they already know into two classes.

4. EXPERIMENT

To verify the effectiveness of proposed system, testees who have technical knowledge and two experiments as follow on collecting technical words and adding comprehension information were conducted.

4.1 Experiment1

The testees were 10 Japanese university students, of which three were forth-year undergraduate students, four were graduate school student in first grade, and three were graduate school student in second grade.

We prepare the article (400 - 500 words / 1 excerpted article. It is comparatively easy to understand what the article is about.) of Ambient Intelligence (AmI), Web Service and Language Grid from some paper for testees reading, and testee read the 3 articles and collect and register the technical words with this system. After the activities, we analyzed how the technical words are gathered. Testees were allowed to use only electronic dictionary and judge the words whether they are technical words or not and register it. The each article differs from other article. Three different articles (400 to 500 words long) on AmI, Web Service, and Language Grid were prepared for the testees to read. Each testee read the three articles, collected technical words, and registered them with this system. After the tests, the manner in which the technical words were gathered was analyzed. Testees were allowed to use only electronic dictionary and judge the words whether they are technical words or not and register it.

The symbols of comprehension were changed by the module for adding comprehension information according to the rules below.

○ ⋯When the testee adds the information of "I know" to the words which have been already registered

◎ ⋯When the testee collects technical words and registers the words with Japanese translation

△ ⋯When the testee collects technical words and registers the words with no Japanese translation

□ ⋯When a testee adds a Japanese translation to the words that have already been registered

vacant ⋯When a testee adds no information to words or does not know the words.

Since the experiment targeted whether the testees could acquire technical knowledge or not, the word "vacant" was used for comprehension when a testee did not add comprehension or did not know technical words.

Table 1 lists the characteristic of the testees.

No.	Grade	Research area	English Skill
1	M1	Language Grid	Good
2	M2	Web Service	Good
3	M1	Web Service	Good
4	B4	Other area	Poor
5	B4	Ambient Intelligence	Good
6	M1	Language Grid	Good
7	B4	Web Service	Poor
8	M1	Ambient Intelligence	Good
9	M2	Other area	Poor
10	M2	Language Grid	Good

Table 1: Characteristics of testees in Experiment 1

4.2 Experiment 2

We made the system that is improved from the system of Experiment 1. Parameter exchange for comprehension is needed to see the difference between the two systems. In Experiment 2, we did a small preliminary experiment for determining the best weight when we change the symbols for comprehension. Then we determined the weight for "I have heard it" and made the weight for "I know it" 1.

The testees for the preliminary experiment were three students with the most knowledge in their respective research area. The testees for the main experiment were three third-year undergraduate students, three forth-year undergraduate students, and three second-grade graduate-school student.

Two systems were tested in the experiment: a system that can classify comprehension and used in Experiment 1 ("system 1" hereafter), and a system that can classify comprehension more accurately than system 1 ("system 2" hereafter). In the experiment, the testees do not read English articles which we prepared but add comprehension to the technical words collected in experiment 1 with both systems. After testees added comprehension, we classified the technical words into three categories (AmI, Web Service, and Language Grid) and made the rate of testees' comprehension in each research area numerically to make graph. The experiments therefore determined whether the systems can show the testees' personal comprehension for technical knowledge exactly or not. In the preliminary experiment, after testees add comprehension to the words with system 2, we determined the best weight that can show testees' comprehension exactly for "I have heard it".

The symbols of comprehension in system 1 were changed by the same rules in Experiment 1 and in system 2 were changed by module for adding comprehension information by the rules below.

☆ ⋯When the testee adds the information "I know" to the words that have already been registered.

★ ⋯When the testee adds the information "I know" to the words that have already been registered with a Japanese translation.

○ ⋯When the testee adds the information "I have heard it" to the words that have already been registered.

● ⋯When the testee adds the information "I know" to the words that have already been registered with a Japanese translation.

□ ⋯When the testee collects the words from articles, registers them with a Japanese translation, and adds the information "I know" to the words.

■ ⋯When the testee collects the words from articles, registers them with a Japanese translation, and adds the information "I have heard it" to the words.

△ ⋯When the testee collects the words from articles and registers them with no Japanese translation.

× ⋯When the testee adds the information "I don't know" to the words that have already been registered

vacant ⋯When the testee does not add the comprehension.

In experiment 2, testees do not use the function for collecting technical words so the situations for "□", "■", and "△" were not evaluated. For reflecting comprehension about technical words, we used "☆" and "★", "○" and "●" as the same weight of comprehension. Tables2 and 3 list the characteristic of the testees.

Table 2: Testees for preliminary experiment

No.	Grade	Research area	English Skill
1	M1	Ambient Intelligence	Good
2	M2	Web Service	Good
3	M1	Language Grid	Good

Table 3: Testees for main experiment

No.	Grade	Research area	English Skill
1	B4	Ambient Intelligence	Good
2	M1	Web Service	Good
3	B4	Web Service	Good
4	M1	Language Grid	Good
5	B3	Language Grid	Good
6	B3	Ambient Intelligence	Good
7	B3	Web Service	Good
8	M1	Ambient Intelligence	Good
9	B4	Web Service	Good

5. RESULTS AND DISCUSSION

5.1 Experiment 1

Figure 4 shows the results of experiment 1.

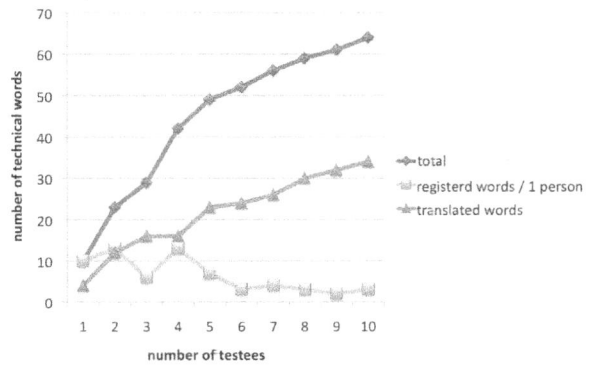

Figure 4: Shift of a number of technical words

Figure.4 shows the total number of technical words and how a number of the words increase. When a number of testees who resister the words are few, they can not refer to a database so that they tend to collect and register many words. But we can find that a number of the words which testee collect and register decrease by a number of testees increase. This result means that the keywords which are needed when users read a technical article are collected with users collecting and registering words, and the number of technical words that have to be registered decrease gradually. It also indicates that the environments where we can acquire technical knowledge are constructed gradually.

The number of words which are finally translated are half of all registered words, but tends to rise with increasing number of testees. This result indicates that technical words can be collected comprehensively with this knowledge-circulation system. And the translated words will be increase with increasing number of the system's users.

In regard to the result for the fourth testee, the number of translated words did not increase however the tester registered the 13 words. There are two main reasons to explain this result. First, the fourth testee had not studied in the field from which the extracted articles were prepared. Second, since he is not familiar with English technical words (because he does not often read English papers), his English ability affects the result.

Table 4 shows the part of the collected technical words and the comprehension. It shows which testees have knowledge about the words and how testees understand them. In addition, according to a number of the users' comprehension, it indicates that the technical words are basic words, limited words, or new words with new methods in research area.

5.2 Experiment 2

In experiment 1, it indicates possibility of acquiring technical knowledge. But we can not say that adding comprehension information is not done exactly from the result. For instance, when we see the table4 at "Ambient Intelligence", we can not understand how much testees know about the words but only can notice whether the testees know about the words or not. To avoid this problem and make the difference between "I know it" and "I have heard it", we decide the weight for "I have heard it" in preliminary experiment and use it for observing and evaluating in main experiment. And we observed the difference among students' grade. The reason to decide the weights is that it is hard to see the difference of comprehension among the systems from each lists of comprehension. We think that making a graphs for 2 systems are needed to see the difference easily.

English	Japanese	1	2	3	4	5	6	7	8	9	10
Ambient Intelligence	環境知能	◎	○	○	○	○	○		○	○	○
Collaborative Filtering	協調フィルタリング	◎		○						○	
QoS	サービスの質	△	□	○	○	○	○	○	○	○	
WSRec		△									
Language Grid	言語グリッド	◎	○	○		○	○	○	○		○
NLP	自然言語処理	△						□			
taxonomy of lexicon		△									
LMF (Lexical Markup Framework)		△									
ISO TC37/SC4		△									
LAICA	人にやさしい都市を目指した環境知能研究所	◎									
AmI	環境知能	◎		○	○	○	○		○	○	○
Bluetooth-Based	Bluetooth が基板である		△			□				○	

Table 4: Part of the list of technical knowledge and the comprehension

5.2.1 preliminary experiment

We use the equation for numeric conversion of comprehension of technical words.

$$x_{jk} = \frac{\sum_{i=1}^{n_j} \omega_{ijk}}{n_j}$$

<Description for variables>

x_{jk} level of comprehension for testee k of research area j. ($j=\{1,2,3 \mid$ AmI, Web Service, Language Grid$\}$)

n_j Number of technical words belonging to area j. ($n_1=25$, $n_2=25$, $n_3=22$)

ω_{ijk} the comprehension of the word i belonging to area j for testee k(in System1 $\omega_{ijk}=\{1$(if testees add comprehension for "I know it"), 0(if testees add comprehension for "I don't know it")}, in System2 $\omega_{ijk}=\{1$((if testees add comprehension for "I know it"), $0.05 \leq x \leq 0.95$((if testees add comprehension for "I have heard it"), 0(if testees add comprehension for "I don't know it")})

At ω_{ijk}, the weight for comprehension of technical words is changed from 0.05 to 0.95. Figures5, 6, 7 show the part of the shift to change the weight.

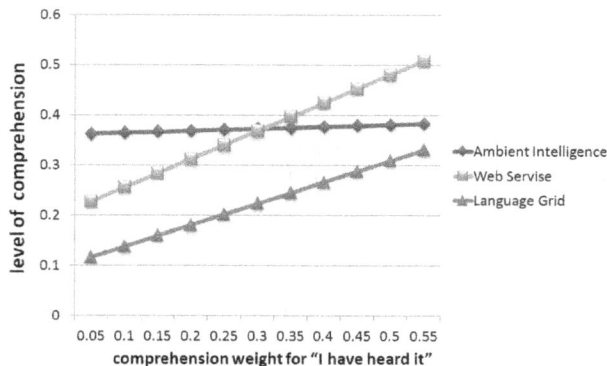

Figure 6: Changing the weight for the testee studying on Web Service

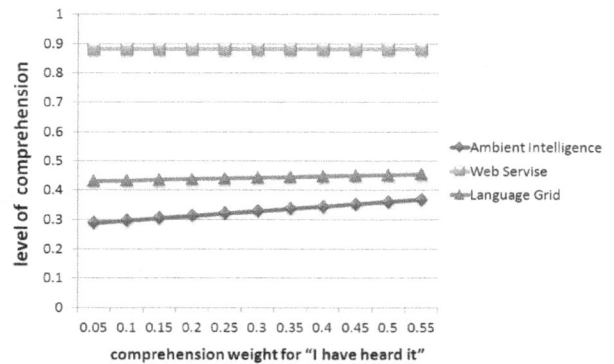

Figure 5: Changing the weight for the testee studying AmI

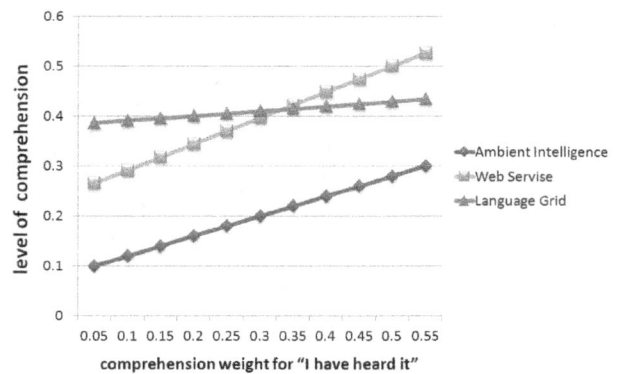

Figure 7: Changing the weight for the testee studying on Language Grid

The level of comprehension of the testee researching on Web Services does not change, even when the weight on "I have heard it" changes. It may be the reason that there were many comprehension scorings to every research area.

Referring to a testees' graph of AmI and Language Grid, the score for the research area that each testee is specialized in is highest from 0.30 and below. However, for the score of the testee researching on AmI, there is little gap at 0.30, so if we set the value 0.30, it is uncertain whether good effect appears or not after this experiment.

According to the preliminary experiment, we decide the weight for "I have heard it" was set to under 0.25. However, we consider it dubious that it is a suitable weight for a reflection of comprehension at nearby 0, so we set the weight as 0.25 in the main experiment.

5.2.2 Main experiment

In the main experiment, the system was improved; that is system 2 can add comprehension in more detail than system 1. Figure8 plots the average comprehension in each research area in order to compare systems 1 and 2.

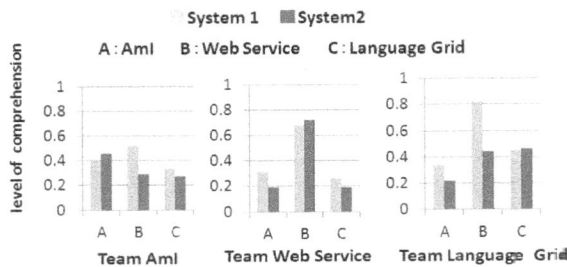

Figure 8: Comparison between system 1 and system 2

In the case of system 1, the every average score for "web service" are the highest because of vague additional information for "I know it" however highest score should be their research area's one. There are a lot of technical words which people have heard them in usual if they are technical. So there is a big gap in scoring between Web Service, Ambient Intelligence, and Language Grid. Because there are a lot of words that people have not heard in usual in research area of Ambient Intelligence and Language grid. That does not reflect testees' comprehension exactly to the graph for system1. On the other hand, system 2 reflects testees' comprehension exactly because it has a middle level of comprehension.

For analyzing the between value of comprehension and a grade, we observed what is the difference of value from third-year undergraduate student to first grade at graduate school student. The difference of value of comprehension is shown in Figure5.

a grade	No.1	No.2	No.3	average
M1	0.434	0.383	0.395	0.40365
B4	0.325	0.385	0.437	0.38228
B3	0.306	0.417	0.266	0.32937

Table 5: Average total comprehension for each academic year

The table indicates that the scores tend to increase with the number of years at university. For acquiring technical knowledge, researchers generally read papers and books, and they know technical words through some activities. The students who just joined the lab do not know technical words and it is hard to understand

some research area. Namely, for creating knowledge, it is proved as numerical so that they need to learn the base words.

For the above results, we can understand the proposed knowledge circulation system indicates which users have technical knowledge and how much of it they have. There is also possibility of the knowledge-circulation system to facilitate sharing technical knowledge.

6. CONCLUDING REMARKS

A multilingual knowledge-sharing-and-circulation system was proposed. Up till now, some correct translations have not been attached alongside technical words. This system can create an environment in which technical knowledge can be collected, shared, and circulated. It can also demonstrate the subsidiary of knowledge among users and reflect their comprehension by increasing the amount of technical words in a dictionary database.

However, we need to improve this knowledge system. Translated technical words increased with using this system. Even if some system's users' English skill are low, the users can easily read English technical paper with translated words. But the outcome is heavily dependent on users' effort and knowledge. Accordingly, there is a limit to collect English technical words with people whose English skill is not high. Moreover, some words which users can not translate easily might increase with spreading and complexation of study area, and it is hard for the users to translate many words. To solve this problem, the function which can collect technical words automatically from Web page is needed. And further studies are needed to extend the system to another language environment using Language Grid, put the system on-line, and collect more detailed information from papers written in English.

7. REFERENCES

[1] S.W.A Gunn,: Multilingual Dictionary of Disaster Medicine and International Relief Kluwer Academic Publishers, Dordrecht, Holland, pp. 23-24, 1990

[2] Shigeaki Sakurai, Yumi Ichimura, Akihiro Suyama, Ryohei Orihara: Inductive learning of a knowledge dictionary for a text mining system,*Engineering of Intelligent Systems 14th International Conference on Industrial and Engineering Applications of Artificial Intelligence and Expert Systems, IEA/AIE 2001 Budapest*, pp.247-252, 2001

[3] Toru Ishida: Language grid: an infrastructure for intercultural collaboration, *Applications and the Internet, 2006. SAINT 2006. International Symposium*, pp. 5 - 100, 2006

[4] Won Kim: Starting Directions for Personalized E-Learning, *Lecture Notes in Computer Science, Volume 4823*, pp.13-19, 2008

[5] Parakh, P., Venkiteswaran, B., Ramanathan, C.: SCORM for e-Learning: Towards implementing a collaborative learning platform,*Technology for Education (T4E), 2010 International Conference on*, pp. 236-237, 2010.

[6] Masahiro Tanaka, Yohei Murakami, Donghui Lin,Toru Ishida: Language Grid Toolbox: Open Source Multi-language Community Site, *4th International Universal Communication Symposium (IUCS 2010)*, pp. 104-110, 2010.

[7] Keith Andrews: Human-Computer Interaction, *Journal of digital imaging the official journal of the Society for Computer, Applications in Radiology Volume 24*, pp. 794-803, 2011

[8] Bayu Distiawan Trisedya, Ruli Manurung: A GrAF-compliant Indonesian Speech Recognition Web Service on the Language Grid for Transcription Crowdsourcing ,*The 6th Linguistic Annotation Workshop in conjunction with ACL-2012, Jeju, Republic of Korea*, pp 67-74, 2012

Activity Streams: Building Context to Coordinate Writing Activity in Collaborative Teams

William Hart-Davidson
Michigan State University
WIDE Research Center
7 Olds Hall
(517) 353-9184
hartdav2@msu.edu

Mark Zachry
Human Centered
Design & Engineering
University of Washington
(206) 616-7936
zachry@uw.edu

Clay Spinuzzi
University of Texas at Austin
208 W. 21st St., Stop B5500
Austin, TX 78712-1038
(512) 410-0247
clay.spinuzzi@utexas.edu

ABSTRACT

This paper evaluates the features and benefits of a new kind of writing tool – activity streams – for use by collaborative writing teams engaged in distributed work. Activity streams are continuously updated, shared records of project activity that include explicit references to project participants, shared objects, and actions performed over time. Drawing on case studies of distributed work in multiple settings conducted by the authors, the cases are discussed in relation to the affordances of activity streams in areas related to coordinating work.

Categories and Subject Descriptors

K.4.3 [**Organizational Impacts**]: Computers-Supported Cooperative Work

Keywords

Lifestreaming, Workstreaming, Activity Streams, Proposals, Collaboration

1. DISTRIBUTED WORK AND THE NEED FOR ACTIVITY STREAMS

Proposal writing and other kinds of knowledge work often involve groups of people collaborating with one another, creating documents, meeting with one another or with clients, etc. Traditional methods for supporting knowledge workers' needs to share digital files with one another in a shared repository or content management system (CMS) can leave critical pieces of context out of the overall picture: actions.

When someone involved in a project looks at a shared repository of digital objects, they may or may not be able to recover a detailed history of the project. Such objects are not, as Whittemore demonstrates, spaces that readily aid recall or help users tell stories about projects [28]. Often, all that is discernable in a CMS repository is a list of things – documents – and none of the context for how those objects were created. Project management (PM) software offers some help for this problem by linking project timelines and milestones to deliverables (objects). But PM software can create a misleading vision of a project based on a plan rather than on the day-to-day events that actually transpired.

One way to address the problem of missing context may be to allow workers to access a detailed project history for the purposes of coordination. Ideally an ongoing record of project activity, such histories have become more commonplace in the last several years in the context of specific software and services. The "news feed" in Facebook is one such example. In this paper, we will refer more generally to an "activity stream" as a continuously updated, shared record of some activity that includes explicit references to participants, shared objects, and actions performed over time. It may be helpful in the context of workplaces to think of an activity stream for specific projects, where projects are defined generically as collections of people (e.g., project team members), information objects (digital files), and actions. Certainly, a specific individual might have several project streams to monitor at one time.

Because activity streams are an emerging phenomenon and are not yet well-integrated into workplace practice, we see some value in revisiting previous work on distributed writing teams in order to understand how these new kinds of texts (and supporting technologies) might be productively leveraged in the near future. In the proceeding analysis, we pay particular attention to the "coordinative work" that distributed writing teams must do to ensure that they meet shared goals on a project and that they work efficiently and effectively across projects. We then draw on this analysis to offer recommendations for future systems to integrate activity streaming.

Our previous work on collaborative teams [12,13,29-32] has shown that members of collaborative writing teams have several areas of need that fall under the heading of *coordination* when performing distributed work. These are needs that, as the case studies that follow indicate, team members currently address with ad-hoc solutions rather than any one specific technology such as an activity stream.

Distributed writing teams:

- **Engage in multiple initiatives**. Many team members contribute to many activity streams, each corresponding to a project or shared initiative.
- **Distribute coordination**. Team members create, update, and monitor project status through mobile devices (and, thus, need to process multiple command, updating, and reporting protocols).

Permission to make digital or hard copies of all or part of this work for personal or classroom use is granted without fee provided that copies are not made or distributed for profit or commercial advantage and that copies bear this notice and the full citation on the first page. To copy otherwise, or republish, to post on servers or to redistribute to lists, requires prior specific permission and/or a fee.

SIGDOC'12, October 3–5, 2012, Seattle, Washington, USA.

Copyright 2012 ACM 978-1-4503-1497-8/12/10...$15.00.

- **Manage digital objects**. Teams must manage associations among digital objects and workstream updates to build context for these objects in a shared repository.
- **Narrate project histories**. Teams must be able to analyze and view project histories over time.
- **Map member contributions**. Team members must be able to view individuals☐ contributions across a variety of projects.

These aspects of writing activity are relatively unrelated to the production of texts, but are nonetheless critical to the success of specific writing teams such as the grant writers we studied. Moreover, writing tools that these teams use to create texts typically do not have all the tools they may need to engage in coordination of literate activity. As a result, we see a quite complex picture of technology use surrounding the coordination of distributed work. We believe that activity streaming technology holds some promise for the coordinative needs of distributed writing teams.

2. ACTIVITY STREAMING: BACKGROUND

Our interests in activity streaming have been influenced by various strands of research involving the coordination of literate activity: lifestreaming, workstreaming, distributed work, and activity streams. We offer the following review here as a background for others – researchers and designers – ahead of our discussion of collaborative, distributed work. At the end of this paper, we return with some implications for researchers and designers regarding applications for activity streaming for supporting collaborative work.

2.1 Lifestreaming

Lifestreaming—maintaining a comprehensive list of events in a chronological sequence—is a concept that has existed in the human-computer interaction literature since at least 1996. However, users have recently embraced the term and the concept in their use of diverse web services. We see this shift as significant in terms of online identity formation and ambient awareness of affiliated users, particularly collaborators.

Lifestreaming is a term that has been used in many ways, generally to indicate an interface that presents a comprehensive list of events in a chronological sequence. Although the term "lifestreaming" was first used in the Lifestreams project [8,10], the practice of recording and posting streams of events has recently gained substantial attention on the Web, where it is used for self-mediation and ambient awareness. When people post information to multiple services, such as social bookmarking services, blogs, and photo sharing services, these multiple posts can be aggregated in a lifestream and displayed in reverse chronological order. What emerges is a comprehensive picture of the public texts that the individual has produced, sometimes intermingled with others' texts.

Lifestreaming follows in the footsteps of accountability genres such as timesheets, running logs, weightlifting logs, and weight watching journals. But lifestreaming is based on general, recorded events (often recorded automatically), and cuts across activities. Early variations were meant for individual use, as a substitute for the desktop metaphor of personal computing. But contemporary variations are more directed toward ambient awareness among members of loosely defined groups. We speculate that these more recent variations respond to distributed work structures [24].

In the Lifestreams project [8,10], all documents were kept in a time-ordered stream that functioned as a diary of electronic life. Individual documents were not given names. In this early project, Lifestreams was desktop-oriented, not collaborative, and strictly functioned as an interface to documents rather than as a tool for sharing and monitoring document use per se. It represented timestamped systems events. However, authors suggested that Lifestreams could eventually be implemented "on the Net" [10] so that any device used by an individual would contribute to her lifestream. Similarly, any document sent to a person—starting with her electronic birth certificate—would be added to her lifestream.

Like Lifestreams, TimeScape [21] was a desktop environment. But unlike Lifestreams, this Java-based environment acknowledged the value of spatially organizing files. TimeScape worked by "combining a spatial arrangement of information with a chronological navigation mechanism" (p.46). This environment provided different visualizations, such as desktop, timeline, and calendar views, and it provided search results with time indexes. Like Freeman and Gelernter, Rekimoto argued that events should be shared among devices such as desktops, PDAs, and digital whiteboards. In addition, Rekimoto argues for linking events with physical contexts and time (p.51).

Later work along these lines was more restricted and less ambitious in implementation. The UMEA project [15], for instance, monitored an individual's Microsoft Office usage and updated project contexts on the basis of its monitoring. TaskTracer [6] was a system to help highly multitasking individuals to rapidly locate, discover, and reuse past processes that they had successfully used to complete tasks. TaskTracer assumed that knowledge workers organize work into tasks, with processes, information resources, and tools. TimeSpace [21] was a system for "activity-based temporal visualisation of personal information spaces" (p.46), using hierarchical, network, spatial, activity-based, and temporal models to achieve these visualizations.

2.2 Workstreaming

Loosely speaking, workstreaming is the application of lifestreaming to work. It can be used individually, but is often applied to facilitate collaborative work.

For instance, DISCIPLE was "a collaboration-enabling framework which allows multiple team members in disparate, geographically diverse locations to work together on a project" [2]. Bianco reported on DISCIPLE's EventStreams, "a series of tools which aid in the visualization and review of a collaborative project" (p.ii), including streams, substreams, timelines, persistent and transient views, session replays, and the "Squish" view pioneered in the Lifestreams project [10] (a summary document describing the contents of many similar documents) (p.33). Mehra later extended this work with Interaction Streams, which provided collaboration history [17].

At about the same time, Carriero and Gelernter [4] suggested that the original Lifestreams project had potential as "a powerful communication and collaborative system" (p.81), one that could be used for coordination.

More recently, TransientLife [23] gathered transient information from existing services (such as blogs and instant messaging) and allowed viewers to share that transient information with others. TransientLife had a client-side architecture consisting of a modular browser sidebar with a history calendar, IM names, today messages, blogs, and profiles. It dynamically maintained activity logs and to-do lists. Transient Life allowed broadcasting, but no collaborative orientation or visualization.

TransientLife's leveraging of existing services, however, points to the fact that lifestreaming has potential to spread as a practice among those who use such services. Facilitated by time-stamped formats for exchanging information, most prominently RSS, nonacademic lifestreaming systems have emerged "in the wild" (sometimes characterized as datastreaming, lifelogging, or workstreaming). Advocates argue that they are online so much, and logging so much of their existence via separate Web services, that they should be able to compile a timestamped record of their online existence. And since that existence intersects heavily with offline existence, they can provide a second memory of their activities.

In the workstreaming subgenre, lifestream-related efforts have approximated Carreiro and Gelertner's "powerful communication and collaborative system" [4]. Rather than "a sort of automatic cultural history of object development and use," lifestreams represent a sort of automatic cultural history of service development and activity.

2.3 Distributed work

As one of us has argued elsewhere, the shift to distributed knowledge work has meant that workers have been separated in time, space, and organization [24] (p.262). In the segments of the economy most characterized by this new work organization, workers are often not collocated at all—they do not share working space—and often they belong to entirely different organizations, coming together temporarily to work on projects before dispersing [29]. At the same time, work is often more collaborative due to the lower cost of electronic communication. Work is more mobile [25] and more distributed across geographical boundaries [20], and consequently it requires new strategies to be "undistributed," i.e., to be brought into structures coherent enough for work to take place [22]. Work is also more fragmented [5, 11]: workers tend to work on more projects at the same time, switching between them and incurring overhead as they switch tasks. To put it colloquially: in distributed work environments, workers cannot gather around the water cooler to catch up with each other, create a working community, or check informally on the status of each others' work.

It is in these segments of the economy that workstreaming applications appear to be most applicable: segments in which workers primarily work on their computers, in which interactions with applications are nearly continuous, in which sharing information about activities is easier through a computer interface than through face-to-face contact, and in which tasks are constantly switched, requiring a more complete record of work.

2.4 Activity Streams Open Standards

Since 2008, activity streams have been taken up in the social media development community as well, as both developers and users have noticed the potential for using them within and especially across various kinds of social media services [7, 19]. A group that includes Chris Messina, Jyri Engestrom (son of Yrjo

Engestrom, the activity theorist whose work is most strongly associated with Third Generation Activity Theory) and other notable social media developers launched the activitystrea.ms project to create specifications for social media services to implement shared protocols, allowing activity in one service to be aggregated, analyzed, and displayed in other services [18].

The work of developing standards has revealed that at their most straightforward, activity streams might be thought of in grammatical terms as lists of clauses that include an agent, one or more actions, and one or more direct or indirect objects. Nouns—agents, objects, and direct objects—correspond to digital objects and/or data structures in an online system or service. Verbs are actions and operations performed by users or by the system itself. Specific systems would support and provide reporting methods for specific verbs that correspond to actions performed in that particular system or service.

According to the activitystrea.ms wiki:

> "The activity in ActivityStreams is a description of an action that was performed (the verb) at some instant in time by someone or something (the actor) against some kind of person, place, or thing (the object). There may also be a target (like a photo album or wishlist) involved." [1]

3. APPLYING ACTIVITY STREAMS TO GRANT & PROPOSAL WRITING

Grant and proposal writing are complex collaborative activities that involve multiple people, texts, and contingencies [3,14,26]; for an overview see [30]. They involve a high degree of coordination and collaboration, both among authors and with granting agencies, clients, and more distant collaborators. As such, these are cases that seem well-suited to the apparent affordances of activity streams. To be clear, the people we considered did not use (nor did they have access to) activity streams as we see them emerging and/or in use in 2012. But they were working to assemble accounts of distributed activity described in section 2 using the means available to them. We can thus glean from each case some details about how best to integrate activity streams into the work environments of distributed writing teams.

3.1 Case 1: Pitching and coordinating projects in small businesses

The first example is very elementary and demonstrates how proposal writers are moving toward shared, coordinated literate activity without activity streams per se. (Author 3) studied how nonemployer firms pitched and coordinated projects.

Nonemployer firms (NEFs) are self-employed individuals or small partnerships whose firm has no paid employees, has business receipts over $1,000, and is subject to federal income taxes (United States Small Business Association Office of Advocacy 2011). NEFs typically take on a client, then enlist a temporary network of subcontractors to handle parts of the client's job. These subcontractors could be anywhere—in town or across the globe—and they may not have even met the NEF. Just as importantly, unlike traditional employees, these subcontractors work in multiple networks and have multiple income streams; they know that if they don't perform well, at worst, they may lose one of these many streams of income. Their fate is not necessarily bound up in their performance for any one contractor. Author 3 studied the following NEFs (Table 1): bound up in their

Table 1. Participants in two studies

Study 1

Pseudonym	Industry	Position	NEF Description (from website)
Sophie	Graphic design	Principal, GD1	"a web design and graphic design studio"
Bob and Tom	Graphic design	Co-Owners, GD2	"a creative agency"

Study 2

Pseudonym	Industry	Position	NEF Description (from website)
Albert	Internet	President	"a digital services agency"
Benny	Internet	President/Creative Director	"Drupal website design and Social Media services and events"
Cory	Graphic Design	Owner and Designer	A "graphic design & web design company"
Denise	Marketing and Advertising	Owner	A "technical copywriting company"
Ed	Internet	Web Developer, Consultant, and Strategist	"Experienced, reliable web consulting and development."

Crucially, NEFs must appear to be a larger firm in order to gain the client's confidence. In front of the client, they present themselves as "we"—whether they're meeting clients face to face or interacting with them electronically. But behind the scenes, they must coordinate extensively to lead their subcontractors in a team performance. How do they coordinate their subcontractors?

This question was critical, since poor coordination could badly disrupt the team's performance. As Cory lamented about one subcontractor, "It was supposed to be like four hours ... and it took him like two to three months." Ed similarly reported that one subcontractor "overcommitted himself because he wasn't just doing my work, he had other work he was doing. And he couldn't

get all the work done. So, he would let projects slide." One subcontractor could hold up an entire project. To avoid that problem, NEFs turned in part to coordinative texts—texts that represented a rudimentary form of activity streams.

As the face of the organization—and the one with the most to lose—the NEF had to coordinate the team's work. As Albert put it, "it's my job ... to send them out to the subcontractors, to hire the right people, to make sure that the graphic designer is aware of the schedule, of the timeline. Make sure that he knows that, hey, we are going to have a conference call on this date." The NEFs used a range of texts to coordinate their teams: project management software; spreadsheets, forms, and notes; and emails and instant messages.

Project management software. Many NEFs chose to use project management software. For instance, Albert, Bob and Tom used Basecamp, while Denise used Privia, which was specialized proposal management software. Bob and Tom also used OmniFocus for tracking tasks. (Although Ed had Project Management Professional certification, he did not mention using project management software.) As Albert explained, project management software served as a way to communicate the project's parameters without micromanaging the subcontractors—and it doubled as a communication medium. Similarly, Bob and Tom sometimes brought clients into their Basecamp project so that the clients could see GD2's progress.

Project management software covered many of the characteristics of activity streams (Table 2).

Spreadsheets, printed forms, and notes. Those NEFs who did not mention project management software tended to use other tools to coordinate tasks. For instance, Benny used a spreadsheet to coordinate the tasks that his team worked. Cory used sticky note software to track basic tasks that his contractors were completing. Finally, Sophie tracked tasks by filling out printed forms.

Spreadsheets, forms, and notes covered only two of the characteristics of activity streams (Table 2).

Emails and IM. Beyond communicating with subcontractors, Cory reported using his email inbox for tracking progress. Bob and Tom coordinated with their contractors over instant messaging.

In addition to texts, and often in concert with them, NEFs frequently conducted backstage meetings with their subcontractors. In these backstage meetings, NEFs coordinated work—often in informal ways—but also built relationships and trust that served to fine-tune the team's performance. These meetings sometimes happened over telecommunication devices and sometimes in person.

Emails and IM covered only one of the characteristics of activity streams (Table 2).

Skype and phone conversations. NEFs reported conducting direct phone calls (Albert, Benny, Cory, Sophie, Bob and Tom), conference calls (Benny, Denise), and Skype conversations (Benny) to coordinate subcontractors, especially when they were not local. Such conversations often focused on how to divide the labor and develop the timeline. For instance, Benny reported that at the beginning of a project, he would assemble his team on Skype, discuss the project, then record the tasks and time estimates on a spreadsheet. The finished document served to coordinate the project and set client expectations

Skype and phone conversations covered only two of the characteristics of activity streams (Table 2).

Meetings. For local subcontractors, NEFs sometimes conducted face-to-face meetings (Denise, Ed, Sophie, Bob and Tom). For instance, in Study 1, Sophie met with a subcontractor at her dining room table, where they went over and discussed client documents, then planned tasks and timeline. Sophie also used the meeting to coach her subcontractor extensively on how to present herself to the client—that is, she used the backstage meeting to coordinate the front stage performance.

Meetings covered only two of the characteristics of activity streams (Table 2).

3.1.1 Conclusion: Proto-activity streams.

The NEFs that Author 3 studied did not use activity streams per se. But, due to the inherently distributed nature of the work they performed, they drew on various coordinative genres to maintain situational awareness of the project across the entire ad hoc subcontractor network. These genres helped them to (a) determine the scope, timeline, cost, and division of labor for the project, and (b) monitor progress once the project was underway. Yet, as Table 2 shows, these genres covered only some of the characteristics of activity streams.

Table 2. Characteristics of activity streams in Case 1

Characteristic of Activity Stream	Managed through...
Multiple initiatives	Project management software; Skype and phone conversations, meetings
Distributed coordination	Project management software; emails and IM; Skype and phone conversations; meetings
Digital object management	(None)
Project histories	Project management software; spreadsheets, forms, and notes
Contribution mapping	Project management software; spreadsheets, forms, and notes

4. CASE 2: ASSEMBLING DISTRIBUTED TEAMS FOR PROPOSING WORK

Our second case concerns the development of a small core group of participants working out of an academic research center at a large public research university. We will focus here on their efforts to assemble a much larger team in the process of developing a $25M multi-institutional "center" grant for a U.S. federal agency. This was only one of several proposing projects that each member of the core group was working on, but it took up a substantial portion of their effort. There were just three members of the core group based at "HumanityNet," the center acting as the home base for the proposal effort (see Table 3, below). But in order for the proposal to be successful, Dave, the

Principle Investigator, reported that he would need to coordinate a team consisting of more than 20 faculty, graduate students, and staff members across multiple disciplines in the Social Sciences from three different universities.

Table 3. Participants in core group for Case 2

Pseudonym	Position	Scope of Routine Work
Dave	Professor	Center administration; teaching; research
Sara	Fiscal Officer	Project pre and post-award budget coordination and reporting
Candace	Academic Specialist	Grant coordination and writing; manage timeline and ensure all components come in as required

Dave and his team had been awarded a planning grant to support the phase of work that they logged during the study period. The primary goal of this work was to assemble the team and write the proposal for the final round of funding. The planning grant funded several face-to-face workshops meant to allow the team to meet, coordinate, and decide on the focus and trajectory of the next proposal. Much of the project activity Dave logged during the two-week period we observed was related to planning the first of these workshops. Dave completed a number of tasks that we might not typically associate with grant writing like sending invitations to the workshop via e-mail, soliciting and posting profiles of workshop participants on a website built specifically for the event, and creating workshop schedules and a "program" to prepare participants for the event.

Candace had the task of editing the profiles that participants sent in so that "nobody sounded inappropriately more important than anyone else," according to Dave. In all, the work of preparing the workshop was a major effort in creating working relationships among a highly accomplished (and therefore very busy) group of people.

4.1 Snapshot of an Activity: "Setting Up the Workshop"

The core team used several types of texts to do something all agreed to call "setting up the workshop."

E-mail to the participants and a website. Each participant in the workshop was being courted for the larger team, and so Dave wanted things to appear very well organized so that the participants would feel their time would be well spent. At the same time, Dave had to leave much of the substantive material related to the Center grant itself unspecified so that participants would feel that they had an opportunity to shape the intellectual trajectory of the project as it moved forward. Dave addressed the large group with e-mails sent via a listserv list. But members would reply back with questions and concerns to Dave individually.

This meant that, for Dave, setting up the workshop was a delicate process involving a lot of follow-up messages via e-mail between Dave and the participants. As new participants came on board, Dave would post profiles for the team to see. This was key, he explained, to getting others to commit because they would not want to be left out of what was shaping up to be an impressive group. As information came in, Dave would harvest it from e-mail messages and add it to the website by creating participant profiles, adding to the online program or the schedule. Parts of these tasks got offloaded to Candace, who was the primary contact for scheduling space, arranging catering, etc. She also did much of the final copyediting. But Dave was the only member of the team who knew how to post things to the website, so he ultimately posted all of the materials as they became ready to share.

Face-to-face meetings and phone calls. As participants' concerns over various details of the workshop surfaced, the core team had to respond which meant that Dave needed to coordinate with Candace on issues like meeting times, locations and menu choices and with Sara on all matters that influenced the budget. They would do much of this at a standing weekly grant coordination meeting on Monday mornings. They would also come to one another's offices or, less frequently, call one another on the phone. This was necessary because the offices HumanityNet used were spread across several physically separated sites on two different floors of a building. Dave and Sara worked close enough to call out to one another if both had their doors open. But Candace worked around a twisting corridor several hundred yards away from Dave.

Excel spreadsheet. At the weekly grant coordination meeting, the core team tried to account for tasks they had completed and tasks upcoming across all of the projects they were working on, including setting up the SLC grant workshop. They used an Excel workbook for this, kept by Sara. Reviewing and updating the spreadsheet was Sara's primary activity during the grant coordination meeting.

The activity "setting up the workshop" continued throughout the two week-period of the study. Some work days for Dave involved few or no actions on the activity, while other days nearly all of Dave's reported proposing work was devoted exclusively to this activity. Candace logged at least some "setting up the workshop activity" every day. Sara logged workshop-related activity least often, only listing the once-weekly grant coordination meeting and a few e-mail messages from Candace regarding billing for workshop catering. She anticipated that much more activity lay ahead for her, however, as she would have to plan travel for all the participants once the dates had been set.

Table 4. Characteristics of activity streams in case 2

Characteristic of Activity Stream	Managed through...
Multiple initiatives	Excel spreadsheet; grant coordination meeting; ad-hoc meetings
Distributed streaming	Emails, ad-hoc meetings, phone calls
Digital object management	Emails, website (Joomla CMS)
Project histories	Excel spreadsheet; grant coordination meeting
Contribution mapping	Spreadsheet

Not all of this activity was visible from Sara's spreadsheet. But when we combined the spreadsheet with the activity logs from our study, we started to reveal some of the details. Taken together

it could have formed something like an activity stream in which all core team members' activity was accounted for a given activity. But even the less detailed version of the teams' collective effort – Sara's spreadsheet—was mostly only visible to Sara and only updated weekly.

5. CASE 3: ACTING IN AN IMPROMPTU NETWORK TO PROPOSE ON A SHORT TIMELINE

Our third case is a self examination of the experiences of one of the authors, considering proposal writing in the context of an ad hoc team or co-workers coming together temporarily to develop a significant proposal to take advantage of a one-time opportunity. In this case, the temporary team produces a shared activity stream notable for its intensity, though limited to a discrete window of time.

In some workplace contexts funding opportunities arise that can be pursued only if a group of employees works together outside and beyond their routine institutional roles. In academic workplaces, for example, funding opportunities sometimes arise that can be competitively addressed in a proposal when an appropriate team of individuals agrees to cooperate on pursuing an idea that is not part of their normal workflow.

In this case, an announcement of a grant deadline was passed on to an academic department chair. Less than one week later, a temporarily formed team of 8 individuals had submitted a major proposal (~$875,000) for a grant with a government agency. After the intense sprint of activity that made this possible, the individuals involved (including one of the authors) all returned to their routine work (which was displaced by the effort) to await a decision scheduled for several months later.

What kind of effort is involved in such a disruptive, intense effort that draws resources away from routine work and that makes an ad hoc network of individuals productive? What we can learn by peering into the shared activity stream of such a team that might be valuable for learning about work in such contexts?

In order to respond to a one-time opportunity, this temporary project team needed to make available time and resources outside the scope of each individual's normal work routines. Development of a competitive proposal required significant and rapid idea development, with plans and commitments that articulated to resources not necessarily already allocated to the individual members of the team.

Because the opportunity available to the team in this case was a one-off event for all participants, and because the response time was notably short for an ad hoc team that was not routinely engaged in such a collective effort, the affordances of an activity stream became critical for coordinating work. In this case, a relatively short (~30 minute), impromptu kick-off meeting ended with the individual team members immediately beginning to enroll their relevant ideas and resources, which in turn were translated into a shared repository (the web-based service Dropbox).

Shared repository. The Dropbox repository provided a central location for maintaining shared access to the master set of files that would constitute the proposal submission, but its activity stream contributions were relatively small in terms of the coordination knowledge required by all team contributors. Dropbox itself provided system notifications when files were checked in, but it did not provide other utilities and notifications to make activity histories shared and explorable by team members. Some of these missing features are connected to the features of a version control system in which members of a collaborating team can monitor the owned and historical status of textual elements that are being (or have been) edited by team members.

Email messages. Given the limitations of Dropbox as a repository and the absence of project management software, email messages were used by the team to communicate status updates among members (who were working concurrently at an accelerated pace) and to coordinate version control so that files were developed successively rather than synchronously. A synchronous collaborative editing tool like Google Docs may have helped resolve some of these issues, but was not selected because the team needed to produce text files with format characteristics not supported by Google Docs.

Consequently, due to the rapid iteration of proposal elements among team members, email messages proliferated at the rate of dozens per hour during peak production windows as team members checked files in and out of Dropbox and provided meta comments and requests to others while developing the elements of the proposal.

Telephone conversations and meetings. Given the compressed schedule for proposal development in this case, rapid decision-making on matters that were complex or complicated by subtleties were most effectively handled in telephone conversations. A brief meeting at the beginning of the project was followed by a weekend of activity during which it was unfeasible (and unnecessary) for team members to meet. A brief meeting occurred after this initial weekend activity push to identify issues related to next steps of work, but this was only necessary to rapidly move into next phases of proposal development work. A final meeting just before submission of the proposal provided a verification check that tasks collectively agreed upon by the distributed team were orally confirmed as done (or to be done within the next hour) so that the submission would be made in time to meet the sponsor deadline.

The sporadic telephone conversations became traceable in the activity stream only as decisions were articulated in subsequent proposal development work and/or email exchanges.

Table 5. Characteristics of activity streams in Case 3

Characteristic of Activity Stream	Managed through ...
Multiple initiatives	Organizational systems associated with contributors' pre-existing roles; meetings; telephone conversations
Distributed streaming	Email messages; meetings; telephone conversations
Digital object management	Dropbox
Project histories	Email inbox; submission status in external sponsor's system
Contribution mapping	Email status updates

6. DISCUSSION & APPLICATIONS

In all of the cases, people need to communicate, coordinate, and collaborate. Currently the people in these cases must cobble together different solutions because (a) no one environment handles all of these well and (b) independent workers do not necessarily use the same tools.

But also in all cases, people needed to see the trail and traces of each other's work in order to be effective in their own tasks. They needed enough ambient awareness of work context that they could effectively communicate, coordinate, and collaborate. The taxonomy we have proposed here allows us to discuss what tools they recruited for these efforts. Table 6 indicates areas of coordinative work that happened, for the most part, outside of the technological environments writers used for document creation and editing.

Table 6. Areas of need for activity streams across cases

Characteristic of Activity Stream	Case 1	Case 2	Case 3
Multiple initiatives	√	√	√
Distributed coordination	√	√	√
Digital object management	?	?	√
Project histories	√	√	√
Contribution mapping	√	√	?

Given the trends we have noted, we expect workgroups to move, when they have the chance, toward environments that support more activity streams for work coordination. At the same time, we expect that work will continue to become more distributed, meaning that one-size-fits-all solutions may not adequately fit the needs of workers distributed across locations and organizations.

One reason is that the specific *verbs* any given system must support to enable activity streams that effectively mediate coordination will likely be specific to the genres of writing and even the subject-matter domains that writers are working within. All of our cases involve proposal writing, for instance, in which – we suspect—certain coordinative activities (e.g., meeting deadlines, ensuring that important requirements specified in RFPs are met) are more important than they might be for writers working primarily in reporting genres, for instance.

Activity streams will almost certainly become more important as collaboration occurs in distributed collaborations, but they will also continue to represent clusters of systems rather than single products. For instance, Google Plus could represent an integrated toolset for supporting the activity streams of distributed teams (with Docs, Hangouts, Sites, and other properties talking to each other). But even work teams who use Google Plus wholeheartedly will likely need to reach beyond it to leverage unintegrated tools for workflows in their specialized projects.

6.1 Applications of Activity Streaming to Collaborative Writing Environments: Implications from the Research

We offer the following implications as suggestions that may be taken up by designers, researchers, and users of social networking services and other stream-capable environments.

For teams writing together, verbs matter. Across all of our cases, teams felt the need to come together online or face-to-face to set goals, name and assign specific actions to fulfill those goals, and monitor progress toward goals on a regular basis. They were, in short, monitoring goal-oriented actions to try to maintain an updated picture of the overall activity. This, in turn, allowed individuals to map their contributions to the project and anticipate where others' contributions might have implications for their own work.

Project management (PM) software and spreadsheets provided adequate support for goal setting and task assignments in most situations, but staying updated on progress toward goals was a messier affair. Across all three cases, updating required meetings followed by someone entering status reports—usually informal ones—into PM software, spreadsheets, or their functional equivalent.

We see opportunities for designers of shared authoring services such as Google Docs and even for shared repository services like Dropbox or Google Drive (as we write this, Google has announced a merger of Docs and Drive) to incorporate a "verbs" toggle in displays of shared artifacts that would allow team members to see a list of artifacts as direct or indirect objects (grammatically speaking) in a narrative consisting of verbal phrases. Why not have a Dropbox with an activity stream?

Activity streams, coming to writing environments near you? At this point, we see more social networking services like Facebook and LinkedIn supporting verbs with features like Facebook's *timeline* and LinkedIn's *updates* view. But we do not yet see many services pitched at writers that offer activity streams for coordinating work among collaborative teams. One exception worth noting is a service called *Flowdock* offered by a Finnish startup company. Marketed as a "team inbox," *Flowdock* allows multiple team members to track shared "issues" and monitor an activity stream to see who is working on what and stay notified when progress toward shared goals has been made [10]. We think activity streams like the one in Flowdock will soon be part of most writing environments, allowing members to connect services like e-mail, PM software, spreadsheets, e-mail, SMS and microblogging to update a shared activity stream.

Activity Steam standards make sense for domain-specific verb support. It makes perfect sense that a service like LinkedIn tracks verbs related to making new professional relationships, making career changes, etc. Users receive notifications when the system records an action such as a first-order contact receiving a promotion (something LinkedIn knows about when that user updates her profile). LinkedIn can reliably limit the number of verbs it tracks in an activity stream to those associated with professional networking. But writing services have a much less well-defined set of potential verbs to support, as we noted above. So what is to be done?

A standards-based approach seems to make the most sense where teams could then be able to designate important verbs that an activity stream would display, actions in various systems that would trigger notifications, and of course display preferences (by user or user role) for receiving notifications.

The categories of coordinative action represented in Table 6 serve as a useful start. For each, several specific actions could be specified and tools identified that would be sources for reporting on actions. For instance, in the category of "contribution mapping" a team might specify "commits to a document versioning system" as a source of verbs related to document production. If the document versioning system supported an activity stream standard, it might then produce a stream update something like this:

> *"Danielle **revised** SpaceCo proposal (version 1.4), at sections 2.3 Literature Review" and 4.5 'Implications.'"*

We see real advantages for systems that can produce rich accounts of collaborative activity that, practically speaking, simply result from team members doing their work as they normally would.

7. ACKNOWLEDGMENTS

We would like to offer our thanks to the people in our cases for their time, including those who documented their work, adding an additional layer of coordination to an already complex work schedule. We also thank our anonymous reviewers for their helpful feedback.

8. REFERENCES

[1] Activitystrea.ms Wiki. http://wiki.activitystrea.ms/w/page/1359261/FrontPage

[2] Bianco, M. An Interface for the Visualization and Manipulation Of Asynchronous Collaborative Work within the DISCIPLE System. Unpublished master's thesis, Rutgers, New Brunswick, NJ. 2000.

[3] Broadhead, G. & Freed, R. Variables of composition: Process and product in a business setting. Carbondale, IL: SIUP & NCTE. 1986.

[4] Carriero, N. and Gelernter, D. A computational model of everything. *Communications of the ACM 44*, 11 (2001), 77-81.

[5] Czerwinski, M., Horvitz, E., and Wilhite, S. A diary study of task switching and interruptions. *CHI '04: Proceedings of the SIGCHI conference on Human factors in computing systems*, ACM Press (2004), 175-182.

[6] Dragunov, A.N., Dietterich, T.G., Johnsrude, K., McLaughlin, M., Li, L., and Herlocker, J.L. TaskTracer: a desktop environment to support multi-tasking knowledge workers. *IUI '05: Proceedings of the 10th international conference on Intelligent user interfaces*, ACM (2005), 75-82.

[7] Engestrom, Jyri. Why some social networking services work and others don't - Or: the case for object-centered sociality. Zengstrom. 2005. http://www.zengestrom.com/blog/2005/04/why-some-social-network-services-work-and-others-dont-or-the-case-for-object-centered-sociality.html. Retrieved 5/30/12.

[8] Fertig, S., Freeman, E., and Gelernter, D. Lifestreams: an alternative to the desktop metaphor. *CHI '96: Conference*

companion on *Human factors in computing systems*, ACM (1996), 410-411.

[9] FlowDock. About. https://www.flowdock.com/about.

[10] Freeman, E. and Gelernter, D. Lifestreams: A Storage Model for Personal Data. *SIGMOD Rec. 25*, 1 (1996), 80-86.

[11] Gonzalez, V.M. and Mark, G. "Constant, constant, multi-tasking craziness": Managing multiple working spheres. *CHI '04: Proceedings of the SIGCHI conference on Human factors in computing systems*, ACM Press (2004), 113-120.

[12] Hart-Davidson, W., Spinuzzi, C., and Zachry, M. Visualizing writing activity as knowledge work: Challenges & opportunities. *SIGDOC '06: Proceedings of the 24th annual international conference on Design of communication*. ACM Press (2006), 70-77.

[13] Hart-Davidson, W., Spinuzzi, C., and Zachry, M. Capturing & visualizing knowledge work: results & implications of a pilot study of proposal writing activity. *SIGDOC '07: Proceedings of the 25th annual ACM international conference on Design of communication*, ACM (2007), 113–119.

[14] Ding, H. The use of cognitive and social apprenticeship to teach a disciplinary genre: Initiation of graduate students into NIH grant writing. *Written Communication 25*.1. 2008.

[15] Kaptelinin, V. UMEA☐: Translating Interaction Histories. *New Horizons*, 5 (2003), 353-360.

[16] Krishnan, A. and Jones, S. TimeSpace: activity-based temporal visualisation of personal information spaces. *Personal Ubiquitous Comput. 9*, (2005), 46-65.

[17] Mehra, P. Interaction Streams: An Approach for Workspace Management in Collaborative Environments. *Evaluation*, 2003.

[18] Messina, C. Where we're going with activity streams. FactoryCity. http://factoryjoe.com/blog/2008/12/20/where-were-going-with-activity-streams. 2008.

[19] Messina, C. Adding richness to activity streams. FactoryCity. http://factoryjoe.com/blog/2008/06/11/adding-richness-to-activity-streams/. 2008.

[20] Paretti, M.C., McNair, L.D., and Holloway-Attaway, L. Teaching Technical Communication in an Era of Distributed Work: A Case Study of Collaboration Between U.S. and Swedish Students. *Technical Communication Quarterly 16*, 3 (2007), 327-352.

[21] Rekimoto, J. Time-machine computing: a time-centric approach for the information environment. *UIST '99: Proceedings of the 12th annual ACM symposium on User interface software and technology*, ACM Press (1999), 45-54.

[22] Slattery, S. Undistributing work through writing: How technical writers manage texts in complex information environments. *Technical Communication Quarterly 16*, 3 (2007), 311-326.

[23] Smale, S. and Greenberg, S. Transient life: collecting and sharing personal information. *OZCHI '06: Proceedings of the 20th conference of the computer-human interaction special interest group (CHISIG) of Australia on Computer-human interaction: design: activities, artefacts and environments*, ACM Press (2006), 31-38.

[24] Spinuzzi, C. Guest Editor's Introduction: Technical Communication in the Age of Distributed Work. *Technical Communication Quarterly 16*, 3 (2007), 265–277.

[25] Swarts, J. Mobility and composition: The architecture of coherence in non-places. *Technical Communication Quarterly 16*, 3 (2007), 279-309.

[26] Tardy, C.M. A genre system view of the funding of academic research. *Written Communication 20*.1. 2003.

[27] United States Small Business Association Office of Advocacy. Firm Data. 2011. http://archive.sba.gov/advo/research/data.html.

[28] Whittemore, S. Metadata and Memory: Lessons from the Canon of Memoria for the Design of Content Management Systems. *Technical Communication Quarterly 17*, 1 (2008), 88-109.

[29] Spinuzzi, C. Working Alone, Together: Coworking as Emergent Collaborative Activity. *Journal of Business And Technical Communication 26*, 4 (2012).

[30] Zachry, M., Spinuzzi, C., and Hart-Davidson, W. Researching proposal development: accounting for the complexity of designing persuasive texts. *SIGDOC '06: Proceedings of the 24th annual conference on Design of communication*, ACM Press (2006), 142–148.

[31] Zachry, M., Spinuzzi, C., and Hart-Davidson, W. Visual documentation of knowledge work: an examination of competing approaches. *SIGDOC '07: Proceedings of the 25th annual ACM international conference on Design of communication*, ACM (2007), 120–126.

[32] Zachry, M., Hart-Davidson, W., and Spinuzzi, C. Advances in understanding knowledge work: an experience report. *SIGDOC '08: Proceedings of the 26th annual ACM international conference on Design of communication*, (2008), 243–248.

A Process Documentation Model for DCMI

David W. Talley
University of Washington iSchool
Seattle, Washington
dtalley@preciserecall.com

ABSTRACT

The Dublin Core Metadata Initiative (DCMI) often must develop instructional materials associated with its mission to provide essential metadata vocabularies. DCMI undertook an effort to create a consistent framework for documentation that would streamline creation of instructional resources specific to internal tools, processes, and activities. Extensive documentation also describes applications of the Dublin Core metadata schema, but those materials require their own structure and content priorities.

DCMI's preferred meeting management tool, Open Conference System (OCS), was used as an exemplar to develop a comprehensive and flexible structure for documentation of internal tools, procedures, and activities. The model rests on a solid foundation of theory and experience accumulated by researchers. The resulting integrative review informed development of a theoretically justified and practically useful template for internal DCMI documentation.

Categories and Subject Descriptors

H.5.3 [Group and Organization Interfaces]: Computer-supported cooperative work; I.7.2 [Document Preparation]: Format and notation

General Terms

Documentation, Design, Human Factors, Standardization

Keywords

Dublin Core, DCMI, process documentation, minimalist documentation, streamlined step model

1. INTRODUCTION

The Dublin Core Metadata Initiative (DCMI) encounters frequent needs to develop instructional materials associated with its mission to provide essential metadata vocabularies that facilitate interoperable systems for discovery and management of information resources. Instruction becomes a priority in central DCMI efforts around linked data to enhance semantic interoperability and more generally around support for exchanges between separately maintained metadata resources built on mutually incompatible frameworks. DCMI organizes meetings among these and other constituencies, resulting in a second tier of instructional priorities for meeting management and applications of supporting technologies.

Recognizing this priority, DCMI undertook an effort to create a consistent framework for documentation to streamline creation of internal instructional resources of the second type discussed above. Much of its documentation describes applications of its metadata schema. Those materials require their own structure and content priorities and are not addressed by the framework presented here. The documentation model developed here applies specifically to internal DCMI processes and activities undertaken in support of its mission.

This effort to build a template for internal process documentation focused on DCMI's preferred meeting management tool, Open Conference System (OCS), as an exemplar. The result is a comprehensive and flexible structure for documentation of tools, procedures, and activities to be adapted for instructional needs in a range of areas. While the template is intended specifically to guide development of documentation for procedures involving OCS, it also should have general applicability to task and process documentation across DCMI's internal operations and activities.

Such a general-purpose documentation model must rest on a solid foundation of theory and experience accumulated by researchers investigating priorities for effective practice. That need motivated a literature review to inform development of a theoretically justified and practically useful template.

2. LITERATURE ON DOCUMENTATION EFFECTIVENESS

Considerable work was completed in the middle and late 1990s, with relatively settled results summarized and selectively extended by researchers working in the following decade. Eiriksdottir and Catrambone [1] provide a rather comprehensive summary of this literature. Another comprehensive review by van der Meij, Karreman, and Steehouder [2] addresses specifically printed documentation for novice users lacking background in a system or process. DCMI needs a review more closely targeted to its particular situation than these wide-ranging surveys, so discussion here will emphasize applicability of established findings within its specific operating environment.

At its most basic level, "procedural discourse is largely about telling someone who is in one set of circumstances how to transition to another set. In other words, . . . procedural discourse describes system states and actions that change system states"[3, p. 42]. The task of developing documentation breaks down to an effort to describe three system states and transitions between them [3, 4]. The prerequisite state defines a starting point that establishes essential supporting conditions, including collection of data inputs, that allow a process to begin. The interim state obtains when process activities are underway toward achievement of a desired state, which represents the preferred process outcome. A fourth unwanted state describes variation from the three-step sequence, resulting in corrective action to restore progress toward the desired state [4].

Documentation can engage this sequence at varying levels of detail, depending on the learner's situation and instructional needs. A three-tier high-level model has emerged [1, 4], beginning with tutorial documentation suited to pure beginners whose lack of experience with a process creates a need for comprehensive information. In particular, tutorial documentation provides extensive background detail about process context and objectives. Procedural documentation meets the needs of users already familiar with that context and focused on accomplishing particular tasks. Reference documentation supports quick access by relatively experienced users to specific facts essential for completion of otherwise well-understood tasks.

This usage from the instructional literature may create a possibility for confusion with applications of the term *reference* in library and information settings. Much of the instructional material produced by DCMI is properly reference documentation under the library meaning of the term – content accessed by discrete look-up to obtain specific information, as opposed to sequential reading of a complete resource for full understanding. Use of the term *reference* within this discussion of the DCMI process documentation model addresses the meaning specific to instructional documentation – information intended for experienced users needing quick access to particular facts that allow them to complete the documented process or procedure.

Considerable discussion has addressed the inclusion in task instruction of contextual information about the process and environment of which the task is part. A minimalist model of documentation describes system functions only as they directly help to complete user tasks [5, 6]. This task focus derives from analysis of user needs with the intention of transforming a mere inventory of all possible system actions into useful instruction that puts system resources to work for practical purposes [4]. Delanghe asserts, however, that "although dressed up as 'user tasks,' most manuals still simply describe features" [7, p. 201]. Farkas observes that some high-context instructional situations are best served by adoption of "rich-step" models, which embed background information into direct task instruction [4]. Even paragraph-formatted discussion, he says, can sometimes help to "emplot" the learner [8], or embed the learner in an unfolding story involving system functions, which promotes personal identification with a complex context.

Indeed, instructional goals are formulated within a situation broader than just the learning itself. According to Lentz and Pander Maat [9, p. 395], "instructive texts have as their main purpose to explain to people how to use a product, but they often also attain secondary persuasive purposes . . . for example, acceptance of a new technology." Those authors identify three essential sections of an instructional document, Background, Problem, and Solution, then they "introduce a fourth: the Motivation. This is a section that presents the motivation (or justification) for solving this problem" [9, p. 395]. DaSilva and Henderson agree that the purposes of an instructional document strictly defined do not include such "relational purposes" but those ancillary goals "clearly imply additional constraints on the design space" [10, p. 213].

Hovde [11] ties the practical success even of basic procedural documentation to a complex act of authorship that creates new meaning and knowledge rather than merely recounting system capabilities and listing actions to implement them. She describes a four-way interaction between understandings of users, organizational environment and constraints, system functions and features, and conventions of documentation genres, resulting in a sophisticated new process discourse especially suited to specific learner needs within a particular context. She describes the technical communicators she studied as having "accomplished tasks more complex than that of merely rewording the specifications. They created new procedural meaning—a task more challenging than merely repackaging existing declarative knowledge" [11, p. 167].

Research on the effectiveness of instructional documentation tends to narrow that broad context and focus instead on how learners develop strong mental models to support task completion. At a minimum, learners approach task-focused learning already in possession of tacit knowledge gained within their environment [4, 11]. The task environment also includes colleagues who "know the relevant subset of the relevant missing knowledge of a confused user" [12, p. 423], leading learners to consult experienced users before resorting to documentation. Dabbagh and Denisar describe a more individual process of mental modeling. In particular, they question assumptions that structured discourse must imply a rigidly hierarchical outline [13]. Instead, they make a case that heterarchical networks of information nodes support learning through "relational or network-like hypermedia representations of ill-structured problems or cases" [13, p. 20]. In particular, "the heterarchical case structure facilitated more exploratory-type tasks, which put students in control of problem solving, encouraging them to try out different strategies and hypotheses and observe their effects" [13, p. 20].

Learners often favor such exploration strategies, according to Eiriksdottir and Catrambone: "providing explicit invitations to explore helps to keep them motivated and relates the instructions to the tasks that they want to complete" [1, p. 760]. While exploration induces mental modeling by learners, who set new goals for themselves or adopt the goals embedded in the system as their own, they still need to acquire domain knowledge to guide practice in new skills. Directed problem-solving supports that modeling more effectively than does more general exploration [1].

Roy reports some benefits from early introduction of a procedure's focus through an "object-sentence first" structure that may "help readers to mentally animate the final goal, even before reading through the step-by-step process" [14, p. 161]. Steehouder observes that "steps were read faster when they were preceded by outcome information" [15, p. 2]. Users studied were able to increase both the amount of text read within a given time and understanding of the material when step outcome was stated first, followed by steps for achieving that outcome. Karreman and Steehouder report no improvement in initial task success when instruction text contains contextual information, but retesting learners after a delay reveals some improvement in longer-term error recognition and understanding of system logic [16].

So a need for mental modeling may provide some rationale for including explanation of context and principles in task-focused instructions [1], still practical task completion defines the milestones and nodes within the mental model. Manning describes a process where learners initially work from schemas, or mental models built on past experience, to structure new perceptions and create hypotheses, which they immediately test by acting on their provisional understanding [6]. In this process, Manning states, they ignore contradictory indications or evidence not directly and immediately relevant to accomplishing their intended tasks. Accomplishing goals in this way reinforces the original mental schemas [6]. Similarly, Carroll acknowledges that learners function in context but notes also that they come to understand their situations by observing the outcomes of their actions [5]. A user is ready to learn something new when a current understanding fails to accomplish goals [6], that is, when trial results in error.

Many researchers agree with Knapheide [12] that users tend to seek help from documentation only when they encounter problems, and they typically read only enough to resume progress toward task completion. Even where they seek help from colleagues, it is because those advisors' awareness of task context and history allows them to suggest quick fixes [12]. Karreman and Steehouder observe that "system information," or contextual explanation of a procedure, does not improve initial task success, and it reduces errors "only if the information describes the internal functioning of the product, not when it merely stresses motivational aspects or general principles" [16, p. 34]. In fact, these authors suggest that such system information could actually impede task learning by increasing cognitive load on learners while also increasing their perceptions of system complexity, which may reduce their feelings of self-efficacy.

Roy describes contextual information within task instruction as a potential source of learner frustration rather than assistance, because "instructional designers often create instructions involving the whole assembly context (global context), while readers often may have a smaller or limited context (local context) in mind" [14, p. 149]. This sort of disconnect is sometimes evident in style of presentation, as well, where learners mostly favor a "focused" style emphasizing practical coaching and concrete examples while technical writers tend toward a "dynamic" (exploratory) or exhaustively "rigorous" style [7].

To establish the right level of contextual information in relation to procedural detail, Farkas describes a minimalist model of system documentation centered on a decision-action sequence that "enables users to quickly decide (while reading the initial components) whether the particular procedure meets their needs, and if the procedure is appropriate, to move crisply from decision-making to carrying out actions" [4, p. 45] . Barber warns of increasing risk from omission of detail in situations where failure due to inexperience can lose or corrupt data [4]. To control this risk, task guidance can anticipate user error and provide topical warnings along with action-relevant recovery steps [4, p. 80]. Delanghe also suggests giving significant amounts of detail only with error recovery information and otherwise summarizing enough to support task completion [7]. Eiriksdottir and Catrambone conclude that "users who do read procedural instructions often scan large parts of the instructions and read carefully only when they need clarification" [1, p. 753].

Detail provided in system documentation must balance support for learners with "letting go" that frees them to engage the system and discover via self-directed learning both what actions to take and how they fit together [17, pp. 7-8]. Invitation to explore within an "On Your Own" section of an instructional document can cue the right sort of exploration to discover important context for current conceptual or procedural elements. Oberman emphasizes the value of promoting such self-regulation, even where gaps in minimalist documentation may leave learners momentarily confused. "Students who cannot successfully self-regulate encounter frustration which often results in failure. 'Constructive frustration' or better yet 'controlled frustration,' however, may stimulate self-regulation and, therefore, help students sharpen their reasoning abilities" [18, p. 25].

3. ELEMENTS OF A DOCUMENTATION MODEL

If DCMI is to adopt a rather minimalist documentation model, excluding most background and context discussion, then what elements should that model *include*? Prerequisites to start a procedure are stressed by van der Meij and Gallivej, potentially including specification of system states, user skills, and user knowledge [17, p. 7]. Explicit statement of a starting screen may be especially important. Steehouder [15] confirms the selection of elements from Farkas [4, pp. 46-48], which begins with a "nearly mandatory" title that helps the learner judge the relevance of the procedure to a task at hand. An optional conceptual element may help to confirm that judgment. A list of procedure steps, the only universally mandatory element according to Farkas, explicitly describes system responses to user actions, sometimes with a "facilitating modifier" such as the location of a required control in the user interface. Subheads may cluster related steps within a complex procedure, stated with an infinitive verb indicating the desired outcome (e.g., "To set up the first part, …"). Optional notes may be interspersed within steps to surface warnings and links to related procedures.

Farkas gives more detailed guidance for development of the essential core of procedure in a "streamlined step model" [4, p. 45]. Each step must incorporate:

1. A short action statement (or two) per step

2. Simple formatting

3. Phrasing based on an imperative verb

4. Little or no explanatory information (Some explanation may follow in notes.)

5. "Layering" via hyperlinks within online documentation to give access to contextual information at the learner's discretion

Other authors confirm the emphasis by Farkas on layering to control levels of detail confronting learners. This structure includes only basic instruction in a procedure step, but learners may click or hover on-page controls, where appropriate, to display additional detail at their option [4, pp. 67-68, 444-445; 6].

In contrast, repetition even of basic information may result when multiple procedures involve similar steps. In such a case, the technique of "fading" can gradually decrease detail in instruction for basic-skills tasks with recurring step sequences. Fading provides "successively less complete reminders . . . [which] change from predominantly procedural instructions toward conceptual information" [17, p. 7]. Eiriksdottir and Catrambone agree that learners respond well where procedures decrease detail and increase abstract information in second and later appearances of similar step sequences, or when they combine familiar steps [1, p. 766]. These authors note that fading works better when it drops the last step in a procedure than when it omits the first step.

The number of steps within a procedure is important to manage the scope of the learning presented. Multiple authors agree with van der Meij and Gallivej that an optimal sequence contains three to five steps, or five steps plus or minus two, especially where a user must memorize a sequence to complete a task [17]. Longer procedures can group steps within task-specific subheadings to avoid overly long sequences.

Farkas advocates use of imperative verbs in step content, creating relatively direct commands that promote clarity and learner engagement [4]. DaSilva and Henderson discuss a Rhetorical Structure Theory model for overall documentation planning that may also help to guide step content creation [10]. RST defines "segments" of an overall text, composed of "nuclei" which are essential to understanding and "satellites" that provide supporting information. A segment articulates a relationship between segment elements, usually one nucleus and one satellite (e.g., solution

DCMI/OCS Documentation Template

Roles: Conf. Information Mgr. - Conf. Program Mgr. - Reviewer - Designer

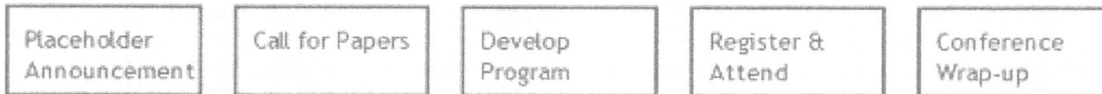

Placeholder Announcement	Call for Papers	Develop Program	Register & Attend	Conference Wrap-up

1.1 Procedure Title [1]

Brief text summary of procedure scope & objectives [2]

Responsible: Conf. Information Manager [3]

Required: State any prerequisistes to completing the procedure, including data and/or files to be collected for uploading, images, approvals, etc. Anything the user must have before proceeding to complete the steps. [4]

1. Process steps numbered, starting with definition of required preconditions - system states, prior procedures completed, user skills, user knowledge [5]
2. List includes 3-7 steps (5 +/- 2) [6]
3. Short, declarative statements of 1-2 actions per step [7]

> Warning! Notes interspersed in steps and called out with special formatting highlight warnings of probable errors and/or guide user in recovering from probable errors [8]

4. For users who need explanation about a step provide More detail . . . [9]
5. But AVOID Mr. Clipit-style intrusiveness - keep layered detail under user control!! [10]

Next Procedure: 1.2 Next Procedure Title [11]

Fig. 1: Screen image illustrating the documentation template.
Colors and other visual elements are intentionally exaggerated to emphasize that no attempt was made to finalize a stylesheet.

isSolutionFor problem). Some relationships can link multiple elements of equal importance (e.g., eventA precedes eventB precedes eventC). DaSilva and Henderson illustrate relationships as diagrams, providing visual indicators of formal content structure that may help to focus procedure steps on essential outcomes.

In addition to steps within instructional procedures, practical examples can emphasize task-based problem-solving. Judicious use of practical examples may combine benefits of specific steps and more general system information in context of one another to "help people instantiate abstract concepts and provide them with an instance of how a rule governing the task applies to a particular situation" [1, p. 756]. This strategy brings some risk of overly literal interpretation of examples rather than extrapolation from those instances to more general procedural actions.

Timely warnings interspersed with procedure steps provide important protection against error as well as guidance in recovery

from errors that occur [4]. To avoid errors, van der Meij and Gallivej emphasize a see-think-act sequence in procedure step construction [17]; in contrast, discussion of error recovery and problem-solving should emphasize a detect-diagnose-correct sequence, with emphasis on just-in-time detection of errors, because early intervention limits damage. Graphic illustrations of procedures, especially screen images, are most effectively used for error prevention and recovery. In particular, images help to emphasize goal states achieved by correct actions [4]. Graphics should illustrate interim states only to highlight warnings and prevent or recover from errors, in most cases [4, 15].

Roy [14] cites Tufte [19] in asserting that illustrations can effectively provide instructional text in procedural context by incorporating labels within graphic process depictions. This combination reduces the need for learners to switch between instructional elements. Indeed, "labels may contain the most important text in the document" [14, p. 150].

Farkas emphasizes use of illustrations, especially flowcharts, as support for learners' construction of mental models [4]. In particular, flowcharts can represent conditional procedures with less linear paths than streamlined steps describe. Steehouder tested task completion by learners working from text step lists, tables, flowcharts, and logical tree illustrations [15]. Flowcharts and logical tree charts were linked to the highest learner performance, and text step lists to the worst. However, learners sometimes preferred less effective but more familiar formats. Steehouder concluded that "any

1.1 Procedure Title [1]

Brief text summary of procedure scope & objectives [2]

Responsible: Conf. Information Manager [3]

Required: State any prerequisistes to completing the procedure, images, approvals, etc. Anything the user must have before proce

Fig. 2: Procedure heading elements.
Elements include a required task name numbered in sequence, the role responsible, and prerequisites for task completion. A brief summary of task objectives is optional.

292

graphical format is preferred to prose," at least for tasks involving conditional selection among alternatives [15, p. 2].

4. A PROCESS DOCUMENTATION MODEL FOR DCMI

DCMI relies heavily on volunteers engaging with narrow sets of tasks to complete much of its work, and this reality powerfully affects adaptation of the results reported so far to its need for instructional process documentation. Training materials must carefully position instruction within the tutorial-procedural-reference sequence with little expected benefit from learner familiarity. DCMI cannot expect learners to take time to work through extensive tutorial documentation, since most engage with its processes in roles ancillary to their primary responsibilities. These users can be expected to focus on near-term task completion within a limited scope, so the procedural level of documentation will have the greatest prominence for DCMI.

This is especially true of engagement with OCS, because the episodic nature of meeting planning tends to expose users to tasks within annual or longer cycles. Procedures repeated so infrequently may not be retained from one meeting cycle to the next, creating a need to refresh memory. Nevertheless, some users important to DCMI do work regularly with its systems, so its documentation may need to support reference lookup to retrieve limited information about specific functions.

DCMI can expect little opportunity for its learners to consult colleagues for task guidance, as described by Knapheice [12]. Its volunteers work mostly independently in a distributed network of individual contributors, so they will need to rely on document artifacts for their learning.

Such task-focused, directed problem-solving is especially important for documentation of OCS functions within DCMI activities, because users will be coming to role-based tasks out of context of their familiar daily activities. Individuals may also lack a mental model of the overall conference process, since much of it proceeds outside the boundaries of any one specific role. Even if context information can aid long-term system understanding, as some researchers report, DCMI's process needs are more episodic, with time intervals between tasks, responsibility for which is spread among multiple individuals. That dynamic may be expected to impede long-term retention, so a minimalist, task-focus model best suits DCMI's needs.

The streamlined step model of Farkas represents a good overall structure for DCMI documentation, with some amendments [4]. A combination of effective title and concise statement of a procedure's key objective will help both procedural and reference learners to scan for instruction relevant to their task. A clear statement of prerequisites for a procedure, such as data to be gathered and a

starting point, will help to orient unfamiliar learners. Concisely phrased steps based on imperative verbs should form the basis for any procedure, with layering controls that give access to additional context information at the learner's discretion. DCMI may consider defining categories for such layering information and tracking user access via web analytics to determine which sorts of context information users choose to access. Analysis of event logs could help to refine this step content and layering strategy.

Step documentation for OCS may be too simple to benefit from the complexity of Rhetorical Structure Theory, as described by DaSilva and Henderson [10]. However, RST diagrams bear a strong visual relationship to linked data triples, an area with significance for other DCMI activities. That resemblance may suggest a useful role for the technique within any DCMI instruction developed around linked data.

Screen captures and similar illustrations within step lists may provide useful context in OCS documentation, and in DCMI process documentation in general, as described by Barber and by van der Meij and Gellevij [3, 15]. A highly configurable environment like OCS presents a significant risk of overuse of screen illustrations, perhaps driven by an attempt to depict all possible settings. Screen captures should be included judiciously, in cases where they can help users to avoid likely confusion or error, similar to guidelines for warning notes. The principle of layering might be applied, as well, presenting a cropped or thumbnail-sized image and allowing a user to click or hover to display a more detailed image. As in 'more detail' text links, this tactic would control potentially overwhelming visual detail at first glance and for relatively experienced users while still making full information available for users who choose further exploration.

User interactions with OCS are strongly procedural, emphasizing a predictable linear event sequence more than a conditional if-then structure. Illustrations highlighting that sequence may support learners' mental modeling by arranging tasks along a timeline. Such a graphic device would have to accommodate variation in user roles over the duration of an event-management process. A timeline could accommodate the matrix of process sequence and user role by grouping tasks by the phase of their occurrence within an event's lifecycle, with color-coding or icons (or both) to highlight specific user roles associated with particular tasks. A tabular matrix could do the same job but at the risk of overwhelming individual learners with information not relevant to their immediate needs for task completion. A tabular display would also be less visually concise than a graphical timeline. Other processes within DCMI likely involve less linear sequences, so graphic modeling in those cases may have to accommodate more complexity.

DCMI would have to resolve questions about how to implement graphical or other access methods to guide users to parts of process documentation relevant to current tasks. Most such materials would be posted for online access, probably involving a content management platform. Most current CMS tools implement navigation as HTML lists, formatted for display by cascading stylesheets (CSS). Flexibility inherent in CSS would allow display either in traditional list format or as a linear model with relationships indicated by background images. Familiar techniques of collapse-

1. Process steps numbered, starting with definition of required preconditions - system st completed, user skills, user knowledge [5]

2. List includes 3-7 steps (5 +/- 2) [6]

3. Short, declarative statements of 1-2 actions per step [7]

- -

Warning! Notes interspersed in steps and called out with special formatting highlight warnings of probable errors and/or guide user in recovering from probable errors [8]

- -

4. For users who need explanation about a step provide More detail . . . [9]

5. But AVOID Mr. Clipit-style intrusiveness - keep layered detail under user control!! [10]

Fig. 3: Streamlined step elements.
Layering gives access to more information under user control.

expand and flyout menus could help to control the amount of procedural detail confronting learners, or fully expanded lists could display comprehensive detail. Multiple list formats might be combined in a single display, perhaps to present a graphic model of an overall process as a top-level menu with an expanded submenu listing detailed procedures that form part of a particular process step.

Outside OCS, such linear flows may be ill-suited to aid mental modeling of some instructional situations within DCMI.

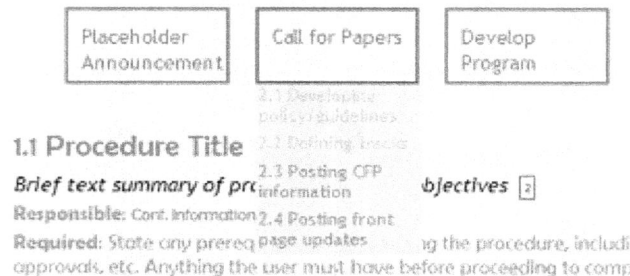

Fig. 4: Process navigation.
Tasks break down process sequence, with color coding and/or icons to indicate role responsibility. HTML list coding allows specification of look and feel by stylesheet rather than embedded graphics.

In some cases, navigation within a flexible heterarchical network structure, as described by Dabbagh and Denisar, may help learners to move from a current task to related tasks in a more ad hoc process [13]. Such a heterarchical structure may suit DCMI's involvement in the Learning Linked Data program, for example, and possibly other instructional situations.

The international reach of DCMI's volunteer base may also affect decisions about how to structure process documentation. McCool [20] describes a laborious process of identifying influences on success of process documentation by variations in learners' cultural values and expectations. Simple restatement in a different language was found to fall short, while evaluation of deeper cultural expectations helped to achieve effective adaptation and localization for specific user and learner communities. Even basic assumptions underlying minimalist documentation may require reevaluation, depending on the audience to be served: "Taskoriented procedures are not always the best method for presenting information to international audiences primarily because some cultures prefer narrative and thick description" [20, p. 70]. The timeline of event planning makes a linear organization appropriate for documentation of processes using OCS, but documentation may need adaptation for cultural considerations to effectively support learning in less constrained processes.

5. ACKNOWLEDGMENTS

The author is grateful for guidance and consultation though the project from Stuart Sutton, CEO of the Dublin Core Metadata Initiative. Additional thanks for careful review and thoughtful comments are due to DCMI Executive Committee members Diane Hillmann and Tom Baker.

6. REFERENCES

[1] Eiriksdottir, E., and R. Catrambone. 2011. Procedural instructions, principles, and examples. *Human Factors* (53)6: 749-770.

[2] van der Meij, H., j. Karreman, and M. Steehouder. 2009. Three decades of research and professional Practice on Printed software tutorials for novices. *Technical Communication* 56(3): 265-292.

[3] Farkas, D. 1999. The logical and rhetorical construction of procedural discourse. *Technical Communication* 46(1): 42-54.

[4] Barber, T. 2003. *Writing software documentation: A task-oriented approach,* 2nd ed. New York: Longman.

[5] Carroll, J. M. (1990). *The Nurnberg funnel: Designing minimalist instruction for practical computer skill.* Cambridge, Mass.: MIT Press.

[6] Manning, A. 1998. Minimalism beyond computer documentation. *IEEE Transactions on Professional Communication* 41(3): 200-204.

[7] Delanghe, S. 2000. Using learning styles in software documentation. *IEEE Transactions on Professional Communication* 43(2): 201-205.

[8] Goodwin, David. 1991. "Emplotting the reader." Journal of *Technical Writing and Communication* 21, no. 2:99–115.

[9] Lentz, L., and H. Pander Maat. 2004. Functional analysis for document design. *Technical Communication* 15(3): 387-398.

[10] DaSilva, N., and P. Henderson. 2007. Narrative-based writing for coherent technical documents. SIGDOC'07, October 22–24, 2007, El Paso, Texas, USA.

[11] Hovde, M. 2010. Creating procedural discourse and knowledge for software users: Beyond translation and transmission. *Journal of Business and Technical Communication* 24(2): 164-205.

[12] Knapheide, P. 2000. Synergy and subsidiarity: The systematic determination of software, user, and operating instructions. International *Journal of Human-Computer Interaction* 12(3-4): 415-430.

[13] Dabbagh, N., and K. Denisar. 2005. Assessing team-based instructional design problem solutions of hierarchical versus heterarchical web-based hypermedia cases. *Educational Technology Research & Development* 53(2): 5–23.

[14] Roy, D. 2007. Significance of configuration and sub-assemblies in sequential procedural instructions and role of text-graphical aid: An explorative study. *IEEE Transactions on Professional Communication* 50(2): 147-162.

[15] Steehouder, M. 2004. Acquiring procedural knowledge of a technology interface. *IEEE Transactions on Professional Communication* 47(1): 1-4.

[16] Karreman, J., and M. Steehouder. 2004. Some effects of system information in instructions for use. *IEEE Transactions on Professional Communication* (47)1: 34-43.

[17] van der Meij, H., and M. Gellevij. 2004. The four components of a procedure. *IEEE Transactions on Professional Communication* (47)1: 5-14.

[18] Oberman, C. 1983. Question analysis and the Learning Cycle. *Research Strategies* 1(1) (Winter): 22-30.

[19] Tufte, E. 1983. *The visual display of quantitative Information.* Cheshire, Conn.: Graphic Press.

[20] McCool, M. 2006. Information architecture: Intercultural human factors. *Technical Communication* 58(2): 167-183.

Development and Application of a Heuristic to Assess Trends in API Documentation

Robert Watson
University of Washington
Seattle, WA
1-206-543-2567

rbwatson@uw.edu

ABSTRACT

Computer technology has made amazing advances in the past few decades; however, the software documentation of today still looks strikingly similar to the software documentation used 30 years ago. If this continues into the 21st century, more and more software developers could be using 20th-century-style documentation to solve 21st-century problems with 21st-century technologies. Is 20th-century-style documentation up to the challenge? How can that be measured? This paper seeks to answer those questions by developing a heuristic to identify whether the documentation set for an application programming interface (API) contains the key elements of API reference documentation that help software developers learn an API. The resulting heuristic was tested on a collection of software documentation that was chosen to provide a diverse set of examples with which to validate the heuristic. In the course of testing the heuristic, interesting patterns in the API documentation were observed. For example, twenty-five percent of the documentation sets studied did not have any overview information, which, according to studies, is one of the most basic elements an API documentation set needs to help software developers learn to use the API. The heuristic produced by this research can be used to evaluate large sets of API documentation, track trends in API documentation, and facilitate additional research.

Categories and Subject Descriptors

D.2.2 [Software Engineering]: Design Tools and Techniques—*Software libraries*

H.5.2 [Information Systems]: User Interfaces—*Training, help, and documentation; Evaluation/methodology*

General Terms

Documentation; Human factors.

Keywords

Application programming interface, API, API reference documentation, Software documentation, Software libraries.

1. INTRODUCTION

Application programming interfaces (APIs) are the interfaces through which one computer program can access the features or services provided by another program or software library. The number of these libraries and APIs is growing rapidly. Microsoft's .NET Framework is just one API of the many that Microsoft pro-

duces and it grew from 35,470 members (individual interface elements of an API) in 2002 to over 109,000 in 2007 and continues to grow [1]. If you count the work of all the other commercial independent software vendors (ISVs) and include the independent, open-source developers who also produce software libraries and APIs, the number is larger still.

At the same time, the number of software developers who use these software libraries and APIs is also growing. Whereas in the past, it was more common to write your own function rather than use one from a software library [2], the tremendous time-to-market pressures and the wide variety of software libraries available today encourage software developers to use functions provided by existing software libraries wherever possible. At the same time, today's software developers face a dual challenge of keeping up with the APIs they are familiar with as those APIs evolve and learning new APIs as they appear in the market, so they can stay current with the state-of-the-art. These conditions make it important for documentation to be effective and easy-to-use.

Thirty years ago, the situation was different—software developers did not have as many software libraries or APIs to choose from compared to the selection they have today. During the 1980s and 1990s, the personal computer boom fueled an increase in software, software libraries, APIs, and also software developers. These were the times that shaped the software documentation format that is still common today. Yet, clearly much has changed since then. Today, many more software developers are using many more software libraries and APIs under very different circumstances than existed 30 years ago. We must question, therefore, whether this documentation format from the 1980s is up to the demands of 21st-century software development. If it is, how much longer will these 20th-century formats serve the software developers of the 21st-century? More to the point, how can we find out before it is too late?

Unfortunately, it might already be too late. What few studies have been done in this area indicate that our 1980s documentation technology might no longer be up to the task and might not have been for a while. In 2002, Nykaza, et al. [3] published a study listing items that API documentation should contain. In 2009, Robillard [4] described how API users of today and tomorrow need a better way to learn about APIs by concluding: "the way to foster more efficient API learning experiences is to include more sophisticated means for developers to identify the information and the resources they need." In in their 2010 study of what makes APIs difficult to learn, Robillard and DeLine identified "inadequate API documentation as the most severe obstacle facing developers learning a new API" [5]. This observation is disappointing given that software documentation has had over 30 years to "get it right." On the other hand, such an observation invites research to find out why and what can be done about it.

This paper reviews the existing research and published literature in order to identify criteria with which to study and evaluate API reference documentation from a user-centered perspective. The resulting criteria are then used to evaluate a spectrum of API documentation from the past and present so as to test the criteria and identify challenges or gaps in their application. A method for evaluating API reference documentation at a high level in a consistent manner is the result that will enable researchers to study API reference documentation over time and ultimately improve it to meet the needs of future software developers.

2. BACKGROUND

The first methodological choice for studying a content set might seem to be content analysis. While content analysis would identify and measure elements of a documentation set and be able to track changes to those elements over time, it would not necessarily measure the suitability of a documentation set to a specific task or audience—that is, measure its "fit." While content analysis will be more valuable when the documentation is examined in more detail, for a high-level study, a structural analysis of user-centered requirements is more appropriate for determining the fit between the user and a product. That is, structural analysis helps one assess whether a documentation set has the basic structure required to meet the user's needs as identified in the literature.

The literature reviewed for this paper is divided into the following categories: API design and usability, online documentation design, software developers' use of documentation, and the application of heuristic evaluation.

2.1 API Design and Usability

References discussed here describe the fundamentals of API design and the factors used to characterize the APIs described in API reference documentation. API design refers to the design of the interface, which is related to, but separate from, the design principles of the software that actually performs a task. Consequently, these references do not necessarily describe how to implement a function with software, just how the interface a software developer uses should look and behave. While this paper focuses on API documentation, the API itself is often the first, and usually the preferred and most trusted, form of documentation [6]. As such, these design principles form the foundation of the documentation principles for APIs and they provide a means by which the design elements can be identified, measured, and compared.

Cwalina and Abrams [6] and Tulach [7] discuss the elements of an API that comprise sound design practices in object-oriented programming. Cwalina and Abrams describe design principles that are intended to provide "consistent functionality that is appropriate for a broad range of developers." They encourage a user-centered, scenario-driven approach to designing frameworks or software libraries. While Cwalina and Abrams describe their principles in the context of Microsoft's .NET Framework, many of their recommendations also apply or can be adapted to other programming environments. Tulach offers a similar design guide for software developers who create software libraries and APIs in Java, and, like Cwalina and Abrams, Tulach encourages user-centered, scenario-driven design methods.

Bloch [8] and Henning [2] discuss specifically why usability is important to consider in API design and they describe the consequences of what happens when APIs have usability problems. Bloch lists several characteristics of a good API including "Easy to learn" and "Easy to use, even without documentation" and advocates a user-centered, scenario-driven approach [8]. Henning [2] cites examples of APIs that are difficult to use successfully and easy to use in a way that reduces the program's performance and reliability. The APIs that Henning describes are designed in a way that is contrary to what Rico Mariani described as making it easy to use the API correctly and to "make it hard to do things the wrong way" [6].

Arnold [9] and Clarke [10] encourage a user-centered approach to API design by looking at the API design problem from the perspectives of human factors and usability. Arnold describes some examples of applying the user-centered design principles of understanding the audience and using progressive disclosure and Clarke describes how to characterize an API and its users along 12 different cognitive dimensions.

2.2 Software Developer's Documentation Use

One of the key tenets of technical writing is to know your audience and to write for them [11, 12]; however, this is complicated when the audience has diverse information-seeking goals and methods. Clarke [10] describes three groups of software developers, each with a different approach to software development and a different learning style. The three groups are opportunistic, pragmatic, and systematic [13].

Nykaza et al. [3] studied a software installation and observed how developers felt about the documentation. They listed eight ways to reduce the learning curve of an API and seven things to include in the content of a software development kit (SDK, usually a collection of software libraries, documentation, and tools necessary to include the features of third-party software into a program), and six ways to present the content. Their study, however, is now over ten years old, so some of their suggestions are now less popular, such as providing printed documentation. At the same time, studies that are more recent still arrive at many of the same conclusions.

Robillard [4] surveyed 80 software developers at Microsoft to identify the challenges they experienced learning new APIs. Robillard and DeLine [5] followed this with a more in-depth analysis to identify five dimensions of obstacles to learning an API: intent documentation, code examples, matching APIs with scenarios, penetrability, and documentation format. From their research, they derive seven implications of what software developers need in their documentation.

Rouet's TRACE model of document processing [14] is a task-oriented model of document search and information retrieval that is well suited to examining the just-in-time type of information retrieval that is frequently used by consumers of API documentation [13]. Rouet's model is a more detailed version of Wright's document interaction model [15, 16] as referenced by Nielsen: searching, understanding, and applying [17].

2.3 Online Documentation Design

Web content design in general has received a lot of attention; however, it is challenging to find a succinct resource that addresses the design patterns necessary to support a software developer's information-seeking needs. Redish [12] describes online document design for the user who "skims and scans." She goes on to describe some of the key design elements for this type of audience such as home pages, pathway pages, and how much content to include on a content page, elements that agree with Robillard and DeLine's [5] findings about API documentation.

Video is becoming more popular as a medium for online instruction and studies have shown that video tutorials can help users learn technical topics [18, 19, 20]. However, it is unclear how video and other new media formats can help software developers learn about an API.

2.4 Heuristic Evaluation of Web content

Nielsen [17] describes using heuristic evaluation as "a systematic inspection of a user interface design for usability" and a "discount usability engineering" method. The application of the heuristic studied in this paper is consistent with Nielsen's description of heuristic evaluation.

3. METHOD

A user-centered heuristic was derived from the published literature to study the structure of a documentation set at a high level. The resulting heuristic was tested by two coders who used it to evaluate a variety of API documentation sets.

The primary task context of the heuristic consists of the searching and understanding [17] stages of online documentation use while using API reference documentation to learn a new API. API reference documentation might have many other uses that could benefit from different heuristics, if not completely different methodologies, but they are outside the scope of this paper.

In the context of searching and understanding, readers can be divided into two groups: new readers who have not seen the site before and returning readers who have. The heuristic assumes a new reader of the documentation for several reasons. First, new readers are the more demanding of the two groups. Second, because software developers are unlikely to return to the same section of API reference documentation frequently, many characteristics of new readers apply to returning readers in this context. While it is true that returning readers might be familiar with the nature of the API when they return to the documentation, they are likely to reacquaint themselves with the site's organization if it has been a while since their last visit. In that case, the returning readers will need to search and find the information like new readers.

Additionally, the heuristic focuses only on learning to use a new API. It assumes that readers come to the documentation with a sufficient understanding of how to write a program in the context of their task and need only to learn about the features of the software library being studied.

One complication of a user-centered heuristic in this scenario is characterizing the user sufficiently. Software developers span a wide range of learning and programming styles and the software they use spans an equally diverse range of intended software development styles. The supporting literature [3, 4, 5, 12, 14], however, studied a wide range of audiences and learning styles, so the elements of the heuristic that results from this literature should also apply to a similarly diverse set of audiences.

3.1 Heuristic Used

The heuristic used to examine an API's documentation is based on Rouet's TRACE mode of information seeking [14], Redish's characterization of web document usage [12], and Robillard and DeLine's lists of what software developers need in API documentation [5]. Figure 1 lists the elements of the heuristic.

The heuristic has three categories: the *initial impression*, the *experience* of using the documentation, and *additional data*. Together, these categories correspond to the select document, process content, and document relevance steps in the TRACE mode and "information foraging" described by Redish [12]. The factors of the initial impression describe the elements a reader would use to evaluate the nature of the site to determine if it warrants further investigation. The experience factors evaluate the elements of the documentation that affect the reader's experience after he or she

decides to explore the site, and the additional data are used to collect information about the site and its evaluation.

3.1.1 Initial impression

The initial impression of the documentation was evaluated by observing the following elements: the entry page content and the presence of overview information.

Initial impression

- Entry page content
- Overview information

Experience

- Top-level navigation type
- Reference topic format
- Code examples
  - Code snippets
  - Tutorials
  - Sample apps

Additional data

- Advanced pages
- Video tutorials
- Comments

Figure 1. Summary of heuristic elements

The <u>entry page</u> is the page seen at the top of the documentation content hierarchy. Typically, this is the page that the reader sees when he or she clicks a "documentation" link on the product's home page or it is one of the first links returned in a search for the API's documentation. This page acts as a home page for the API or the API documentation in the context of Redish [12], but it is called an *entry page* in this context to avoid confusion with the cases where it is different from the site's overall home page. The content of the entry page is a key element that a reader uses to determine the relevance of the page to his or her search and whether the site is worth exploring further. In this paper, the information elements found on the entry page were described by the coders and reviewed after all the sites had been studied.

<u>Overview information</u> explains the purpose or application of the API at a high level in a single page. The overview information helps characterize the *intent documentation* [5] that software developers need to orient themselves in the API. Ideally, the documentation contains an overview topic, which provides information about the scenarios for which the API was designed [3, 5]. In some cases, the entry page contains this content, while in others, this information was found on another page. In the cases where the overview information was not in the entry page, the coders used the navigational affordances of the entry page to find the overview information. If overview or intent information could not be found, this element was coded as not present.

3.1.2 Experience

The experience of using the documentation was evaluated by identifying the following design elements: top-level navigation type, reference topic format, and the availability and type of code examples. The navigation style and reference-topic design elements directly characterize the documentation set's hyperlinking structure and how a reader navigates the content, which relates to how a reader maintains his or her orientation in the content [5].

The <u>top-level navigation type</u> used by the site describes the navigation affordances the site offers to the reader for navigating among the topics in the documentation. The sites studied used one of two different navigation styles and were coded as either hub-and-spoke or menu-content.

In the *hub-and-spoke* model, one central table-of-contents linked all other documentation. In the cases where there was no specific table of contents, this attribute was assigned if the interaction resembled such a structure, as would be the case in a breadcrumb-only navigation style, for example.

In the *menu-content* model, the pages were divided into a menu portion and a content portion—usually with the menu displayed in a narrow column the left side of the page—and the content that corresponds to the reader's menu selection displayed in a larger area to the right of the menu.

With regard to maintaining orientation in the document set, the hub-and-spoke model provides a view of the content that is limited to the current node and its sub nodes in the documentation's hierarchy, while the menu-content model generally offers a context that includes more levels of the hierarchy. For simple topics and small APIs, the view of the content offered by the hub-and-spoke model can be sufficient. In larger and more complex APIs, however, the menu-content model provides an organizational framework for the reader.

The reference topic format describes how the documentation of individual API elements is presented on the page. The API reference content could be presented as individual topics in the single-element-per-page format or as a group of elements that relate to a single object or other high-level concept in the multiple-element-per-page format.

API reference documentation usually contains a description of an element (where an element is an individual programming component provided by the software library, such as an object, class, interface, method, function, or data structure) and its parameters. These descriptions can vary in detail from simply showing the prototype or definition of the element to presenting extensively detailed descriptions of the element, including boundary cases, error returns, and other information that could be useful to the software developer. The detail an API element description requires depends on the element and its intended audience. Studying the contents of an API element description requires a more detailed examination and so they are not included in this analysis.

Code examples are an important aspect of API reference documentation [3, 5]. Robillard and DeLine [5] categorize code examples by size and complexity as code snippets, tutorials, sample applications, and production code. The first three categories can be found in published API documentation, while the fourth is usually available only to software developers who have access to the software library's source code. This looks only for code snippets, tutorials, and sample apps. For production code, the user of an open-source software library is presumed to have access to the source code behind the API, while the users of commercial software libraries are presumed not to have access to the software library's source code.

Code snippets were measured by reviewing the API reference topics to see if they included short samples of code that illustrated how that element was used. If code snippets were easily or frequently found in the documentation's topics, this value was coded as "present." If they were infrequent or could not be found in the reference topics, the value was coded as "not-present."

Tutorials, while not specifically part of API reference documentation, are important tools that help software developers understand how to use an API element or group of elements in a programming context. Software developers also use tutorials as a source

from which to copy program code that they include into their own program's [5]. If tutorials could be found easily from the entry page or overview information, this value was coded as "present." If tutorials could not be found easily, the value was coded as "not present." The quality of the tutorials, such as their detail or breadth of coverage was not evaluated.

Software developers also use sample apps to understand how to use the elements of an API in context and as another source from which to copy program code [5]. Where a tutorial typically will focus on a single feature or a set of related features, a sample app is a complete application that includes examples of the API as well as the other functions that comprise a complete program, such as display, data input/output, and error handling.

3.1.3 Additional data

In addition to the initial impression and experience data, the coders recorded the presence of these additional documentation elements to help characterize their experience with the documentation: advanced pages, video tutorials, and coder comments. These elements were selected to record the use of new media and technologies in API reference documentation.

Advanced pages are reference topics that allow user interaction. In contrast, a basic page uses only HTML and CSS to display content that consists of images, text, or HTML samples. Animation examples were considered basic pages unless the reader could interact with them. Advanced pages would be pages that contained elements that were more interactive or dynamic than basic pages. As an example, the *HTML5 <audio> Tag* page on the W3Schools.com site [21] would be considered an advanced page because it allows the reader to interact with the code example. Only API reference pages were considered when coding this field. Interactive tutorials or demonstration programs were not considered when coding this field.

Video tutorials were scored as "present" if video explanations about how to use the API were easily found from the entry page, overview topic, or a reference page. A video would only count if it was a narrated video clip that explained or demonstrated some aspect of the API.

The coders also recorded any Comments about the site as they reviewed the documentation.

3.2 API Documentation Studied

The goal was to develop a heuristic that can used to evaluate API documentation. To test the resulting heuristic, a collection of API documentation was selected for its variety in terms of API size, API source, the size of the entity that produced the API, the technology for which the API was developed, and the intended use of the API. The goal of testing the heuristic on a diverse collection of API documentation was to increase the likelihood of finding any problems with the heuristic or its application. If the heuristic proves to be valid, it could provide interesting and useful information about the sites used to test it. The intentional diversity of the APIs selected for this test also provides some insight into the current state of API documentation, even if the sample is not a statistically valid random sample that could be generalized to a larger population.

Table 1 lists the 43 software libraries that were identified to provide the desired diversity. Eight of these libraries (as indicated by an asterisk in Table 1) could not be studied for various reasons such as an inability to locate the documentation or the library did not have a conventional API. In one case, for example, a library provided a template interface and was documented more like a programming language than an API that was documented in the context of a programming language. The 35 software libraries that were studied with this heuristic supported technologies and languages such as C/C++, Java, JavaScript, PHP, Ruby, Ruby on Rails, and VAX/VMS. Of the software libraries, 29 were for a web technology, while 6 were intended for native or client software. Open-source software libraries made up 28 of the software libraries studied and 7 software libraries came from commercial independent software vendors (ISVs). The 1:4 ratio of commercial to open-source software libraries could be misleading, however. Some of the commercial libraries studied are individual libraries from commercial vendors who offer hundreds of similarly organized and authored libraries with a cumulative total of many thousands of API objects and elements. Therefore, the commercial libraries studied represent a much larger volume of API documentation topics than their numbers might otherwise indicate.

Table 1. APIs selected to test the heuristic

Amazon SES	express*	knockout.js	Rails
ARM 4.0	fixtext*	lettering.js*	Raphaël
Backbone	Google MAPS	minitest	require.js
batik	guard*	Mocha	rspec
boost	Hadoop	mustache.js*	sinon.js
Cake PHP	handlebars.js*	node.js	Underscore
CodeIgniter	Infovis	OpenVMS RTL	Microsoft Windows Documents & Printing
d3.js	Jasmine	paper.js	wire.js
Devise	Java 2 Platform Ent. Ed. V 1.4	phantom.js	WordPress
Drupal	JQuery	Processing*	YUI
ember.js*	JQueryUI	protovis	

* These APIs could not be studied.

The libraries sizes were measured by estimating the number of high-level objects they provided in the API. These could be objects or classes, in the case of object-oriented APIs, or functions, in the case of procedural APIs. Table 2 shows the size of the libraries used to test this heuristic.

Table 2. Software library size

Size	API Objects	Total Count of Libraries Studied	Open Source Libraries
Huge	>1000	4	1
Large	100-999	10	8
Med	10-99	15	14
Small	<10	6	5

3.3 Documentation Aspects Not Studied

The heuristic is intended to identify elements of an API documentation set along several key dimensions of utility to software developers as identified in the literature. It is designed to identify those API documentation sets that might make the APIs they document harder to learn, but this heuristic does not examine API documentation content at a detailed level. While a detailed heuristic would be a valuable tool, it is outside the scope of this paper. This heuristic identifies whether an API documentation set contains some of the aspects of API documentation that Robillard and DeLine [5], Nykaza, et al. [3], and others list as helpful to software developers learning an API, specifically, intent documentation and penetrability; however, it does not evaluate the quality of those elements.

While the usability of an API affects how a software developer learns it and what sort of documentation is required [4], this heuristic does not measure the usability or suitability of the API documentation to any particular learning style or application. The purpose of this heuristic is to study the presence or absence of documentation elements to answer the question, "does the API documentation contain the elements that help a software developer learn an API?"

3.4 Coding

Two experienced, professional software developers applied the heuristic to the 35 APIs that could be studied. At least one of the software developers studied each API and 15% of the results were selected at random to review for coding errors. A total of 11 coding errors were found out of 286 values coded, for an error rate of 4%. The coding errors were corrected and recoded before the data were analyzed.

4. FINDINGS

This section reports the observations of using the heuristic tool and of the data collected by using the heuristic.

4.1 Using the Heuristic

The heuristic was applied to a wide range of software libraries and API documentation styles with few coding errors. Most of the coding errors reported above resulted from having insufficiently precise operational definitions of some of the categories. For example, the "Video tutorial" category was intended to identify videos of people explaining or demonstrating a topic to the viewer. The original definition of this category, however, was worded such that it could be interpreted as any tutorial that included some video content. The documentation for a graphics library, however, included in its tutorials animated elements that demonstrated animation functions of the library. These elements were originally coded as video tutorials. However, because they did not have any presenter, they were subsequently recoded and the definition was made more specific.

Because this heuristic looks only for specific elements of a documentation set, evaluating an API documentation set is relatively quick. Coders reported spending about 10 minutes to evaluate each documentation set. The variety of documentation styles, however, provided examples that did not cleanly fit the categories described by the heuristic. For example, wiki-based documentation offered a variety of navigation styles. Some examples retained a menu, while others relied on a breadcrumb trail to show the reader where they were in the documentation. Having a breadcrumb trail alone made it difficult to maintain orientation, which is one of the problems of hypertext documentation identified by Robillard and DeLine [5].

Except for the criteria definitions that needed refinement, the heuristic seemed easy to use and apply consistently.

4.2 Data Collected by the Heuristic

In the course of applying the heuristic across the different sets of API documentation, an interesting view of the API documentation landscape emerged.

4.2.1 Document elements

Figure 2 shows the presence of the elements that help software developers learn an API. Overview information was found in 27 of the API documentation sets evaluated and code snippets were included in the reference topics of 22 of the 35 API documentation sets evaluated. Tutorials and sample apps were less common in this collection of documentation and most sites studied used basic pages for their reference topics with only six documentation sets using advanced pages. Even fewer documentation sets used video tutorials.

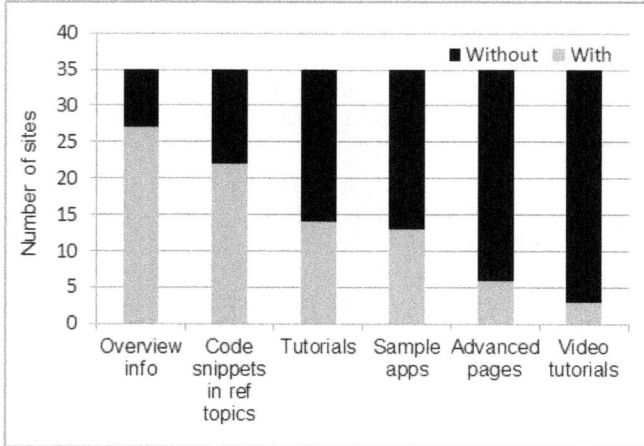

Figure 2. Document elements found in the API documentation studied

Figure 3 shows the elements found in the entry pages of the API documentation sites studied. The entry pages studied included such content as value propositions, which could serve as intent documentation, getting started topics, links to tutorials and the API reference, tables of contents, and in the case of a small API, the entire documentation set. Of the 35 sites studied, 12 had value propositions on their entry pages, 14 had a table-of-contents to their documentation, and 9 had getting started topics or links to getting started topics.

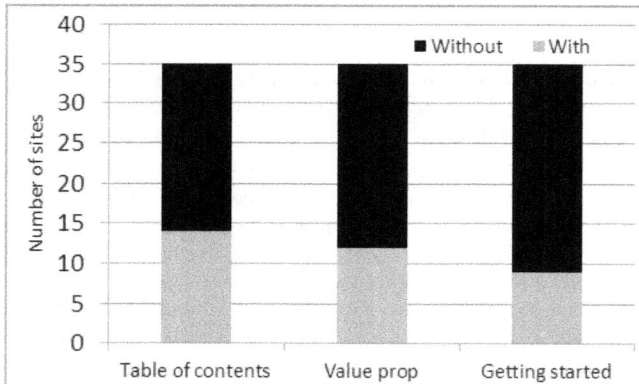

Figure 3. Entry page contents

4.2.2 Navigation elements

The navigation model and the reference-topic page format describe the site's affordances for document navigation. Figure 4 shows that the multiple-element-per-page format was the most common format seen in the documentation studied, by a factor of about 3 to 1. The multiple-element-per-page topic model includes on a single page all the content that relates to a high-level object such as a class, interface, or object.

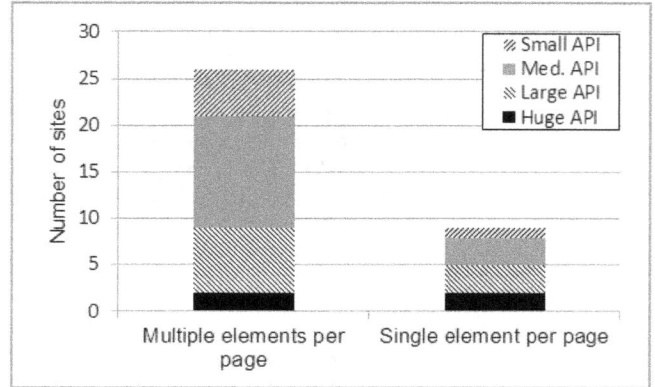

Figure 4. Reference topic format by API size

However, Figure 5 shows that the preference for reference-topic page format within documentation studied varies with API size. The larger APIs favored the simpler, single-topic-per-element page format, where each topic page described only one single element of an API, for example, a method, function, or structure. Smaller APIs, on the other hand were more likely to have pages in the multiple-element-per-page format, where the related elements are all on a single page.

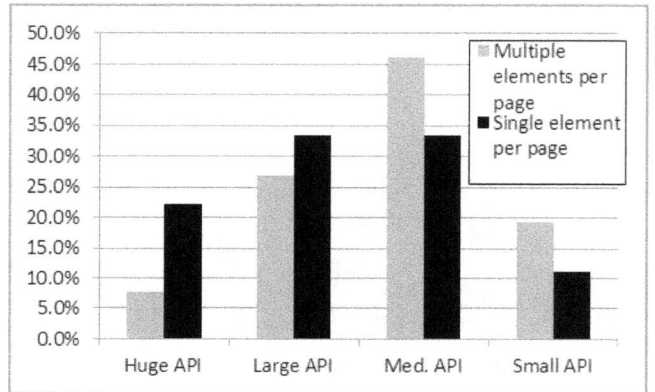

Figure 5. Reference topic format distribution by API size

Figure 6 shows that the menu-content style of navigation was twice as popular as the hub-and-spoke style in this collection. However, Figure 7 shows that unlike the reference topic format, the navigation model preference did not change significantly with the size of the API.

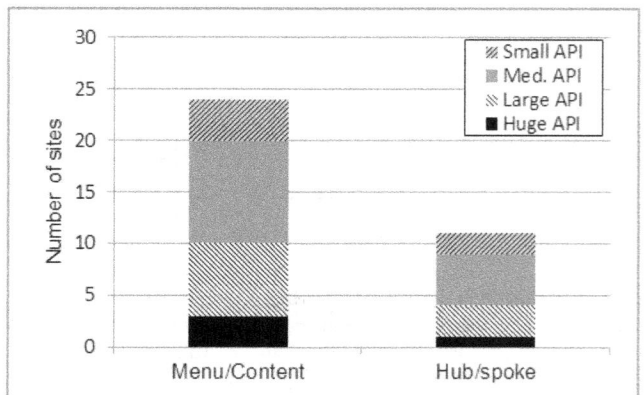

Figure 6. Navigation model by API size

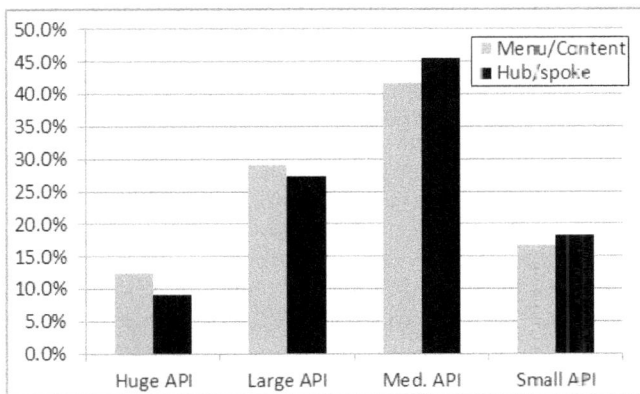

Figure 7. Navigation model distribution by API size

5. DISCUSSION

The goal of this project was to develop and test a heuristic for evaluating API documentation. The heuristic developed seemed easy to apply and accurately describes a documentation set in terms of having the high-level documentation elements that software developers need to learn an API. Because the heuristic tests for only the high-level elements of a documentation set, it is more useful to characterize a collection of API documentation than a single documentation set. Using this heuristic to survey a collection of APIs, such as those described in this paper, provides a high-level view of how that collection of documentation addresses the documentation needs commonly expressed by software developers [5].

Studying this collection of API documentation provides some interesting insights in API documentation that might warrant further investigation. For example, while video tutorials are useful and effective in teaching technical topics, very few of the API documentation sets studied included them. Somewhat more common than videos, but still found in less than half of the sites studied are the elements most desired by developers in Robillard and DeLine's [5] study: tutorials and sample apps.

Code snippets and overview information were the most common documentation elements found in the sites studied; however, eight, almost 25% of the sites studied, did not have any overview information. This is surprising considering that overview information is some of the easiest content to write and offers the much needed orientation and intent information for the API. In one example without an overview, the documentation appeared to assume the reader understood the overview and intent by going right into applications and examples. In another, it appeared that the overview was divided into sub-overviews that did not seem to relate directly to the API documentation reviewed. This particular API was huge so it is possible that the overview was elsewhere in the documentation. However, even if that was the case, it still seems risky to assume the reader will always know how to find the overview content without an affordance in the reference content.

Additional aspects of API documentation were also encountered while testing the heuristic. For example, some API documentation could not be found by online searches due to name collisions. One API had a name that was descriptive to a fault. Its name described its function by using a term that matched a common industry term. As a result, the search results contained mostly references to the term in its industry context, not the API's. As a result, the documentation was not found and so it could not be included in the

APIs studied. Another aspect that was not coded by this heuristic was the usability of the site from the perspective of the coder. In the comments, some sites were noted as being easy to navigate while others were extremely difficult. These observations might be worthy to model and note in a future revision of this heuristic, but they were not modeled in this heuristic.

6. CONCLUSIONS AND FUTURE WORK

Good API documentation begins with the API and extends into the online documentation [6, 8]. Heuristics have been applied to measure the usability of an API [10] but not to the API's documentation. This heuristic is a step towards being able to measure the usability and suitability of API documentation sets for software developers and their tasks. It can also be used to study large collections of APIs over time to track trends.

Some of the directions that future research could take include going broader and deeper. Going broader, the heuristic could be applied to larger or targeted sets of APIs to generalize the nature of those APIs. Going deeper, new heuristics could be developed to study the documentation elements in detail to evaluate their usability and effectiveness. Other measures to evaluate include how easy the site is to find through search, how easy the site is to navigate, and the user's satisfaction with the site.

While the literature reviewed describes what software developers would like to see in API documentation, it is unclear that having those elements actually improves a software developer's learning experience, satisfaction, or ability to complete a programming task. Starting with the elements identified by this heuristic, experiments could be designed to test an API's effectiveness in specific scenarios. For example, two types of reference topic formats are described in this paper: multiple-element per page and a single-element per page. While the multiple-element per page format was more common, it is unclear whether what format makes it easier for a software developer to learn an API. With specific elements and scenarios defined, experiments could be designed to test the performance of the different elements in those scenarios.

7. ACKNOWLEDGEMENTS

I would like to thank Dr. Jan Spyridakis and her Internet-Based User-Experience Lab in the University of Washington's Department of Human Centered Design & Engineering for their help in collect and coding this data.

8. REFERENCES

[1] Abrams, B. 2008. *Number of Types in the .NET Framework*. 17 March 2008. [Online]. Available: http://blogs.msdn.com/b/brada/archive/2008/03/17/number-of-types-in-the-net-framework.aspx. [Accessed 23 January 2010].

[2] Henning, M. 2007. API design matters. *ACM Queue*. pp. 24-36, May/June 2007.

[3] Nykaza, J., Messinger, R., Boehme, F., Norman, C., Mace, M. and Gordon, M. 2002. What programmers really want: Results of a needs assessment for SDK documentation. In *Proceedings of the 20th Annual International Conference on Computer Documentation* (Toronto, Ontario, Canada, 2002).

[4] Robillard, M. P. 2009. What makes APIs hard to learn? Answers from developers. *Software, IEEE*. vol. 26, no. 6, pp. 27-34 (November/December 2009).

[5] Robillard, M. P. and DeLine, R. 2011. A field study of API learning obstacles. *Empirical Software Engineering*. pp. 703-732 (2011).

[6] Cwalina K. and Abrams, B. 2009. *Framework Design Guidelines: Conventions, Idioms, and Patterns for Reusable .NET Libraries.* Indianapolis, IN: Addison Wesley.

[7] Tulach, J. 2008. *How to Design a (Module) API.* [Online]. Available: http://openide.netbeans.org/tutorial/apidesign.html. [Accessed 26 April 2008].

[8] Bloch, J. 2005. *How to Design a Good API and why it Matters.* 19 October 2005. Available: http://lcsd05.cs.tamu.edu/slides/keynote.pdf [Accessed 27 January 2010].

[9] Arnold, K. 2005. Programmers are people, too. *ACM Queue,* pp. 55-59 (June 2005).

[10] Clarke, S. 2004. Measuring API usability. *Dr. Dobbs Journal Special Windows/.NET Supplement.* pp. S6-S9 (May 2004).

[11] Markel, M. 2007. *Technical Communication,* 8th ed., Boston, MA. Bedford/St. Martin's.

[12] Redish, J. 2007. *Letting Go of the Words: Writing Web Content that Works.* San Francisco, CA: Morgan Kaufmann Publishers.

[13] Clarke, S. 2003. *Using the Cognitive Dimensions, Continued - Learning Style 24 Nov 2003.* Available: http://blogs.msdn.com/stevencl/archive/2003/11/24/57079.aspx. [Accessed 2 February 2010].

[14] Rouet, J. F. 2006. *The Skills of Document Use: From Text Comprehension to Web-Based Learning,* Mahweh, NJ: Lawrence Erlbaum Associates.

[15] Wright, P. 1983. Manual dexterity: A user-oriented approach to creating computer documentation. In *Proc. ACM CHI '83 Conf.* (Boston, MA, 1983).

[16] Wright, P. 1991. Designing and evaluating documentation for I.T. users. In *Human Factors for Informatics Usability.* Shackel, B. and Richardson S., Eds., Cambridge, Cambridge University Press, pp. 343-358.

[17] Nielsen, J. 1993. *Usability Engineering,* Boston, MA: Academic Press.

[18] Bowles, T. M., Hensley M. K. and Hinchliffe, L. J. 2010. Best practices for online video tutorials: A study of student preferences and understanding. *Communications in Information Literacy.* vol. 4, no. 1, pp. 17-28 (2010).

[19] DeVaney, T. A. 2009. *Impact of Video Tutorials in an Online Educational Statistics Courses,* Dec. 2009. [Online]. Available: http://jolt.merlot.org/vol5no4/devaney_1209.htm. [Accessed 30 May 2012].

[20] Bridge, P. D., Jackson, M. and Robinson, L. 2009. The effectiveness of streaming video on medical student learning: A case study. *Wayne State University School of Medicine.* 19 August 2009. [Online]. Available: http://www.ncbi.nlm.nih.gov/pmc/articles/PMC2779626/pdf/MEO-14-RES00311.pdf. [Accessed 30 May 2012].

[21] W3Schools. 2012. *HTML5 <audio> Tag.* [Online]. Available: http://www.w3schools.com/html5/tag_audio.asp. [Accessed 30 May 2012].

9. ABOUT THE AUTHOR

Robert Watson developed software professionally for 17 years. After writing software for many products and designing many APIs, he stopped writing software and started writing about software as a programming writer at Microsoft. As a programming writer, he has been writing about software for software developers for almost 10 years. He holds a Master of Science degree in Human Centered Design and Engineering from the University of Washington with a focus on user-centered design and is currently studying for a PhD in Human Centered Design & Engineering and Global Technical & Communication Management.

Development Framework Components as Commonplaces

Tom Lindsley
Iowa State University
206 Ross Hall
Ames, IA 50011
1(515) 294-2180
lindsley@iastate.edu

ABSTRACT

This paper examines the practice of using front-end web development frameworks and associated plug-ins to develop web application interfaces and suggests returning to a rhetorical foundation for determining the propriety of code use and vetting of an open-source community's plug-ins. Additionally, this paper asks developers and those teaching developers to further problematize development framework usability and its implications for designer judgment and agency.

Categories and Subject Descriptors

D.2.2 [**Software Engineering**] Design Tools and Techniques – *user interfaces*. D.2.13 Reusable Software – *reusable libraries*. H.5.2 [**Information Interfaces and Presentation**]: User interfaces – *user-centered design*.

General Terms

Your general terms must be any of the following 16 designated terms: Documentation, Performance, Design, Human Factors, Standardization, Theory.

Keywords

Front-End Development, Development Frameworks, Code Libraries, Rhetoric, Topoi, Commonplaces, Design, User-Interfaces, Extreme Usability.

1. INTRODUCTION

Within the last ten years, an increasing number of scholars in the digital humanities and UX-associated disciplines have been sounding a collective call for information designers to not only design user experiences, but to build those user experiences as well [18, 3, 14, 4, 5]. Fortunately for those new to programming and markup, many open-source communities have created development frameworks, code libraries, and a wealth of custom plug-ins that aid programmers in the rapid development of software, websites, and apps for desktop and mobile devices. Many of these frameworks rely on APIs (Application Programming Interface) that simplify multiline functions into single word calls from the script line. Essentially, a combination of an API-accessed code library and open-source community plug-ins creates a coding experience that allows a developer to rely heavily on the existing functions and plug-ins within a framework, while avoiding the burdensome task of rewriting simple animations, data queries, and output loops.

While this practice is in the interest of ease and efficiency, novice programmers run the risk of relying too heavily on the prefabricated work of others, ceding agency, and context-based decision making to the community or developer responsible for the reused code, a user experience focused more on ease than skill, what Bradley Dilger [3] terms "extreme usability." Additionally, such a practice allows a novice to be unaware of larger cultural or functional contexts that may have called for simpler customized solutions. Rhetorical theory, specifically with its concepts of the topoi and commonplaces, provides a heuristic for understanding the communicative dangers of relying too heavily on context-absent code.

This paper examines the practice of using front-end web development frameworks and associated plug-ins to develop web application interfaces and suggests returning to a rhetorical foundation for determining the propriety of code use and vetting of an open-source community's plug-ins. Additionally, this paper asks developers and those teaching developers to further problematize development framework usability and its implications for designer judgment and agency.

2. DEVELOPMENT FRAMEWORKS

2.1 Frameworks

Broadly defined, development frameworks are "a set of tools, libraries, conventions, and best practices that attempt to abstract routine tasks into generic modules that can be reused" in the process of application development (*this paper considers web frameworks specifically, though there are many development frameworks for software as well) [2]. Some frameworks such as jQuery and MooTools are specifically front-end or client-side frameworks whose sole purpose is to abstract routine "presentation" code into modular chunks of information that allow for quicker building and greater replication. Other web development frameworks such as Zend, Rails, and CodeIgniter provide libraries and abstracted routines for server-side programming, or the functional part of the web application that processes, stores, and outputs data. Partially a result of the web-standards movement, and partially a result of a need for efficient and expedited coding, both front-end and back-end development frameworks are providing powerful standardization of common web writing practices. An example of a framework's power can be explained in terms of quantity of work: while it might take a developer twenty lines of code to program, from scratch, a common function for data retrieval, a framework could provide a set of short codes or an API that serves as mechanism of communication between the application and the framework's library, allowing the developer to call the same function in no more than two lines.

Additionally, most frameworks offer a collection of "plug-ins" or collections of functions that perform specific tasks such as calendars, online shopping carts, and mail systems. In other words, while a framework might make a "slide" animation faster to code, a plug-in provides something such as a full-fledged image-gallery, pre-built and ready for use in any application compatible with the framework language. In terms of the web, these prefabricated functions and plug-ins combine together with mark-up and styling to create an interface between the user and the web application.

The field of rhetoric and professional communication has been increasingly interested in how interfaces mediate our retrieval and use of information [6,13], situate users within the power relations of technology use [16], and shape arguments about our own identities [1]. At the base of these many inquiries is the understanding that an interface is an argument made up of visual claims, functional affordances, and appeals to a user's values and sense of universal truths. And if we are to continue to situate interface design and technical communication in the rhetorical tradition, we will benefit from drawing on all ancient practices of argument construction and invention. In terms of web development frameworks that draw on abstracted or pre-built collections of code, this paper will argue for resurrecting the concepts of the topoi and commonplaces to move toward a rhetorically-based heuristic that allows developers, specifically novice developers, to gauge the propriety and value of the arguments available on the web and within the development frameworks themselves, thus being better able to make context-specific arguments without overusing common rhetorical appeals within the interface.

2.2 Commonplace Arguments

If we are to consider the interface as a collection of visual and functional arguments, it seems appropriate that rhetorical theory could have many analogues or "cognates" [7] to ancient concepts of argumentation, style, and delivery. Two concepts, the topoi and the commonplace, share a similar purpose with the function of development frameworks and code libraries.

For Aristotle, Quintilian, and Cicero, the topoi (or topics), were the functional building blocks used in the invention of an argument. In other words, they were heuristics that provided an argument with clarifying frames such as who, why, to what degree, by what definition, etc. For Cicero, specifically, the topics did not function as full arguments, but merely as means to an end. As Michael Leff has written, Cicero believed the topics "offer material - timbers or planks ... that may prove useful in constructing an argument and which, when combined with other resources, contribute to appropriate management of a case" [9:447]. In many arguments, these "other resources" were "commonplace arguments."

The commonplaces were stock epithets, figures of speech, proverbs, quotations, praises or censures of people and things, and brief treatises on virtues and vices, all well known or respected turns of phrase or position statements that were commonly understood to find universal acceptance with audiences. Practiced during early schooling, the commonplaces served as a bank of prefabricated arguments that could be called upon to add "amplification" to an argument. Of course, this amplification was entirely dependent on the context of use and the skill in which the rhetor was able to deploy the commonplace within the arrangement of the spoken composition. As Leff explains, arguments discovered and constructed by use of the topoi and commonplaces "must arise through knowledge of the case at hand, and a decision about whether and how they are used cannot be specified by topical method, per se, but must depend upon situated judgment" [9:448].

Quintilian stresses the importance of situated deployment of the commonplaces, suggesting that they are much like "weapons which we should always have stored in our armoury ready for immediate use as the occasion demands" [13:II.i.12]. It is a practice of poor argumentation to memorize a commonplace and insert it carelessly into the argument without paying any attention to the context of the argument or the audience at hand. Quintilian argues that while the commonplace, however beautiful, can be called upon and deployed at any moment, it should be "ready," not "wanted," for careless use is almost always "superfluous and sometimes even noxious" [13:II.iv.32]. Essentially, the use of common arguments must be reserved and shaped for specific rhetorical situations as to avoid diluted power and cliché.

Much like ancient rhetoricians, contemporary writers, web developers, and programmers have similar banks of arguments available for deployment. However, instead of building these commonplaces into verbal arguments, development frameworks allow developers to build plug-ins and widgets into interfaces, sometimes quite easily. And for novice developers, it is this ease of usability that can limit the developer's ability to exercise agency and sound judgment in the development of an interface.

2.3 Usability and Judgment

As usability studies have transitioned from user-friendly design, to user-centered design, to user experience design, the streamlined "ease" of product use and interface use has been a central concern [12, 10, 8]. This ceding of problem solving abilities and judgment to our interfaces is the subject of Bradley Dilger's [3] critique of consumerist values of "ease" and simplicity driving current work in usability studies, a trend he calls "extreme usability."

Dilger argues that while usability evangelists such as Jakob Nielsen and Don Norman promote multi-faceted definitions of usability, much of their message focuses on the ease of products and their ability to make consumers' lives easier and avoid the extraneous work of figuring technology out for themselves. Steve Krug [8] has gone so far as to make this consumerist demand central to his best selling usability manifesto, which he titled *Don't Make Me Think*. Dilger suggests that this version of usability, in extending the ideological framework of "ease" and consumerist values of speed and convenience, encourages an "out-of-pocket rejection of difficulty and complexity," and that it "displaces agency and control to external experts, and represses critique and critical use of technology in the name of productivity and efficiency" [3:52]. The result for the novice user, is that the "frictionless and transparent nature of extreme usability becomes self-perpetuating; because novice users develop only instrumental knowledge of a system...their need for extreme usability - and their need for the system to know their "needs" - can be perpetual" [3:56]. By perpetuating the novice/expert binary and relying on products and systems which disconnect the novice from the cultural and historical contexts of their technologies, "extreme usability" essentially black boxes the expertise and the reasons for why technologies were invented, built, and deployed.

While Dilger's critique of extreme usability might be more focused on physical products and GUI interfaces, his arguments regarding user agency and a general deskilling of novice users are salient to the discussion of development framework usability as well. For as Jakob Nielsen reminds us, even an alpha-numeric command line is a kind of interface, also [11].

2.4 Usability and Developers

All developers, regardless of expertise, reuse code. A central tenet of programming states that "no problem should ever be solved twice" [19]. Reuse of common functions and structures is a survival skill one must learn in order to meet the demand for efficiency and expedited work, which is a primary reason for the creation of development frameworks. However, when novice developers scour the web for framework plug-ins to enhance the aesthetics of a page, they may be trying to answer problems different from those of the developer who originally built the plug-in. The open source communities that share these plug-ins attempt to show transparency in their work by providing a wealth of tutorials that demonstrate the plug-ins and also display and explain the code. Unfortunately, a tendency exists within the novice community to grab code, paste it into applications, and ignore the implications of plug-ins built for specific purposes.

In the example of jQuery, the popular JavaScript framework and library, many techie forums and programmer blogs have castigated "noobs" or novice users for perpetuating the use of the JavaScript language through jQuery without necessarily knowing how to use it, without knowing how to use it well (writing bad code), and without knowing the specific developer culture that it's grown from. And though many of these posts or forum titles may hint at an elitism of programmer culture, these concerns are hinting at the existence of a growing population of web writers who are changing the notion of expert in web development communities. This change provides impetus for a focus on rhetorical foundations to framework reliance, code-reuse, and analysis of plugin propriety for specific contexts of use

3. TWITTER BOOTSTRAP: A CASE

To elucidate the concerns central to the use and misuse of front-end development frameworks, this section will examine one of the most popular front-end frameworks in use at present, Twitter Bootstrap.

Originally developed by Mark Otto and Jacob Thornton as a collection of libraries to aid the development of user interfaces for internal data management applications at Twitter, Twitter Bootstrap was released as open-source in 2011 and is at the time of this writing the most watched project on GitHub, the collaborative versioning and revision control network for software and web development projects. Bootstrap provides a powerful HTML, CSS, and jQuery-based framework for the rapid development of "cross-everything" compatible web pages/applications that retain their integrity on desktop monitors, tablets, and mobile devices [cite the Bootstrap site]. The framework provides a simple CSS class-based initialization for many of the plugins, such as dialog boxes, carousels, and dropdown menus, allowing developers to introduce components to their web pages with single word class declarations in their HTML. Additionally, since Bootstrap 2.0, the framework defaults to a responsive layout, allowing the display of the page to render differently depending upon the device being used.

While such features are a boon for developers building cross-compatible applications that rely heavily on common JavaScript functions, Twitter Bootstrap has attracted criticism from the expert developer community for its often replicated stock layouts available with a default loading of the framework. Others have raised concern about Bootstrap's bloated javascript collection, which, novice developers may leave "unpared," sometimes causing unintended conflicts with external scripts. In his recent article, "Great, Another Bootstrap Website," Paul Scrivens, web

designer and social media expert at North Social, describes a worrisome trend in the design of web-based information where using development tools are becoming synonymous with programming knowhow. Describing both Bootstrap and the popular Ruby framework Ruby on Rails, Scrivens writes, "This is the danger behind frameworks. Ruby on Rails is great for a lot of people, but there are some who learn how to program from it and in the end don't really learn how to program at all. If you are a designer and you are using Bootstrap as your learning tool then you might be in for a rude awakening when you finally have to venture out on your own and create a custom design" [17]. Scrivens cites Bootstrap's showcase gallery of sites using Bootstrap, and laments the glaring similarities between them, arguing that front-end frameworks should exclusively be used as a code base for developers, not an aesthetic silver bullet. However, developers such as Reuven M. Lerner, see that for a programmer "who is design-challenged, the introduction of design frameworks has made it possible… to make a Web application that doesn't cause people to go screaming into the night" [10]. Both Scrivens and Lerner bring their disciplinary biases to their arguments, the designer tired of visual clichés, and the developer relying on those clichés for "good design." While this dichotomy represents the common concerns about Bootstrap between designers and developers, we should be complicating this question further if we are to vet and use front-end frameworks responsibly. Does Twitter Bootstrap, or similar front-end development frameworks represent what our fields describe as effective communication? Does an unquestioning allegiance to a framework's default code set, structure, and aesthetic ever achieve this goal? The answer to these questions should be a resounding "Maybe" if we are to understand our work as a rhetorical and context-based enterprise. However, in order to have full control over our communication, we must help novice developers master the tools, their languages, and their topical and aesthetic landscapes in which they exist in order for their communication to be products of "situated judgment."

4. COMMONPLACES, USABILITY, AND RESPONSIBLE CODING

As our UX-related fields continue arguing for information designers to shape interface design and write code, we must include in these discussions questions of agency, expertise, and argumentative best practice. Borrowing from Cicero and Quintilian's discussions of the topoi and the commonplaces and problematizing the usability of frameworks through the lens of extreme usability, we might find rules of thumb and assertions to follow as we design and build.

Primarily, we must reiterate that what we build are interfaces and that interfaces mediate information dispersal and communicate arguments. The building blocks of those arguments will only be as effective as the skill with which a developer deploys programmed functions and prefabricated plug-ins and the level of awareness she has for the micro and macro contexts where the interface will be used. If, as Quintilian suggests, our commonplace arguments - in this case framework plug-ins - exist as weapons available for use at the appropriate time, we must be aware of user needs and user goals before we deploy plug-ins for interactivity's sake. Overuse of common tropes or figures will dilute our arguments and run the risk of cliché, and eventually diminished use of our applications and websites.

Additionally, we must acknowledge the imbalance of power we accept if we are to build with highly usable frameworks and also question the intentions of communities that provide frameworks that function at such a high level of abstraction that manipulating at the source is reserved only for expert builders. At a pragmatic level, relying on the expertise of framework developers limits our options as designers and developers to whatever currently exists. Such an approach to design cripples the invention process and, continuing Quintilian's battle metaphor, forces us to work with the army we have, rather than the one we need.

Finally, if we are going to take building seriously, we need to be thinking about source code as an interface as well. Some in the Digital Humanities and Critical Code Studies communities are doing just this. However, as information designers, we have an immense amount of experience with audience analysis, text design, and document usability to inform the interrogation and development of best practices for web designers.

Ease will surely remain an illegitimate rhetorical justification for how to compose and design situated communication for as long as our associated disciplines exist. As such, ease is also rarely justifiable in user-centered development, because ease in the development process is enjoyed solely by the developer — as well as the institution, organization, or corporation black-boxing and controlling the overall design of that communication.

Developing new practices that move away from usable code experiences may be uncomfortable for developers. Though, if we can avoid the seamless user experiences made possible by development frameworks and APIs, we can break the novice/expert binary, reclaiming agency and building applications better fit to user needs and specific contexts of use.

5. REFERENCES

[1]   Arola, K. (2010). The design of web 2.0: The rise of the template, the fall of design. Computers and Composition, 27, 4-14.

[2]   Croft, J. (2007). Frameworks for designers. Alistapart, 239. Retreived from http://www.alistapart.com/articles/frameworksfordesigners/

[3]   Dilger, B. & Rice, R. (2010). From a to <a>: The keywords of markup. Minneapolis: University of Minnesota Press.

[4]   Ghajar, L.A. (2012). I code, you code, we code…why code? The notebook. Retrieved from http://www.leeannghajar.com/i-code-you-code-we-code-why-code/

[5]   Hart-Davidson, W. (2001). On writing, technical communication, and information technology: The core competencies of technical communication. Technical Communication, 48(2), 145-155.

[6]   Johnson-Eilola. J. (2003). Datacloud. New York: Hampton Press.

[7]   Kostelnick, C. H., & Robert, D. (1999). Desiging visual language: Strategies for technical communicators. New York: Longman.

[8]   Krug, S. (2005). Don't make me think. Berkeley: New Riders Press.

[9]   Leff, M. (1996). Commonplaces and argumentation in cicero and quintilian. Argumentation, 10, 445-452.

[10] Lerner, R. (2012). At the forge: Twitter bootstrap, Linux Journal. 218(6).

[11] Nielsen. J. (1993). Usability Engineering. Burlington: Morgan Kauffman.

[12] Norman, D. (1990). The design of everyday things. New York: Basic Books.

[13] Quintilian. (2006). Institutes of oratory. L. Honeycutt, Ed., (J.S. Watson, Trans.). Retrieved May 1, 2012 , from http://rhetoric.eserver.org/quintilian/ (Original work published 1856).

[14] Ramsay, S. (2011). On building. Stephen Ramsay. Retrieved from http://lenz.unl.edu/papers/2011/01/11/on-building.html.

[15] Rosinski, P., & Squire, P. (2009). Strange bedfellows: Human computer interaction, interface design, and composition pedagogy. Computers and Composition, 26, 149-163.

[16] Selfe, C.L., & Selfe, R.J. (1994). Politics of the interface: Power and its exercise in electronic contact zones. College Composition and Communication, 45(4), 480-504.

[17] Scrivens, P. (2012). Great, another bootstrap site. Retrieved from http://drawar.com/d/great-another-bootstrap-site/

[18] Stolley, K. (2009). The lo-fi manifesto. Kairos. 12(3). Retrieved from http://kairos.technorhetoric.net/12.3/topoi/stolley/

[19] Widner, M. (2012). Learn code, learn code culture. HASTAC. Retrieved from http://hastac.org/blogs/michael-widner/2012/02/16/learn-code-learn-code-culture

Designing for Selective Reading with QuikScan Views

David K. Farkas
Department of Human Centered
Design & Engineering
University of Washington
Seattle, WA 98155
farkas@uw.edu

ABSTRACT

Many people—especially knowledge workers—experience information overload, lack sufficient time to read, and therefore choose to read selectively within texts. QuikScan Views is a new Web-based reading environment that provides extensive support for selective reading. It is an enhancement of QuikScan, an empirically validated document format that employs a multiple summary approach to facilitate selective reading, enable quick access to specific ideas in the body of the document, and improve text recall. QuikScan Views provides a hyperlinked table of contents for global navigation, displays QuikScan summaries in a scrolling window (as well as within the body of the document), and adds an extra level of summarization by means of a hyperlinked structured abstract. A QuikScan Views document gives the reader choices of pathways through the document corresponding to the time the reader wishes to invest and the reader's desire to increase their recall of the document.

Categories and Subject Descriptors

H.5.4 **[Information Interfaces and Presentation]**: Hypertext/Hypermedia—*Navigation*; I.7.2 **[Document and Text Processing]**: Document Preparation—*Format and notation*

General Terms

Design, Human Factors

Keywords

Literacy, Reading, Summarization, Selective Reading

1. INTRODUCTION

Many people—especially knowledge workers—experience information overload [21, 5] and don't think they have enough time to read all the texts they think necessary to keep up with their job duties and areas of expertise [12, 11]. For these individuals reading selectively within a document is a professional survival skill [14, 11]. There are also arguments, backed by some empirical research and many anecdotal reports, that various societal changes associated with the digital age are reducing peoples' attention spans and willingness to read extended texts [3, 4, 16, 2, 15]. In other words, there may be increasing numbers of well-educated people who will read many Facebook posts and tweets but—at least under certain

circumstances—resist reading extended texts even if they are not pressed for time.

For centuries our medium-to-long documents have often included affordances that support selective reading, that make it easier for overworked or resistant readers to bypass certain portions of a document and focus instead on portions of greater interest. These affordances include the abstract, the table of contents, headings, appendices, and within-document hyperlinks. But now seems like a good time to devise and adopt new designs that are more effective in supporting selective reading.

QuikScan is a recently developed document format that effectively supports selective reading within documents by means of multiple within-document summaries [22, 23, see also http://www.quikscan.org/]. Here I introduce a new multiple summary design: the QuikScan Views reading environment. QuikScan Views is a variant of the QuikScan format optimized for the Web. While classic QuikScan texts can be published as HTML and PDF as well as print, QuikScan Views is Web-specific because it relies heavily on hyperlinking and windowing. The value of QuikScan Views is that it gives the readers more well-supported reading pathways than does QuikScan.

Below I briefly describe QuikScan, pointing out the strong experimental evidence demonstrating its value. Then I briefly describe one other design, SwitchBack, because it sheds light on the "loss of context" problem that pertains to QuikScan, QuikScan Views, and indeed all multiple summary designs. Then I turn to QuikScan Views explaining what it does, the various ways in which it benefits readers, and how it is implemented. (For an advance look at QuikScan Views, look ahead to Figure 3.)

2. QUIKSCAN

QuikScan employs numerous summaries placed strategically within a document, very often directly following a heading. As shown in Figure 1, these summaries are formatted as numbered list items that correspond to target numbers placed within the body of the document. Busy or impatient readers can read just the summaries, choose between summaries or sections of the full text depending on their level of interest, or (by using the numbers) scan quickly from an idea in a summary to the specific location in the body of the document where the idea is fully discussed. More committed readers can read the summaries as previews while they read the full text.

Empirical studies demonstrate that reading QuikScan summaries as previews impressively improves text recall, [22, 18, 19, 20], that QuikScan enables better navigation within the document [24], and is well accepted by readers [22, 18]. Furthermore, because QuikScan promotes more efficient reading, readers who read the summaries and the full text require no more reading time than readers who just read the full text [18, 19].

Procedure

14} Three redcedar trees were harvested. Two were limbed and their trunks were chipped. The third was chipped with branches and foliage.

15} The two limbed trees were used as the raw material for round wood particleboard furnish while the third tree was used for whole tree furnish. See figure 1.

16} We made 18 single-layer particleboard panels from the round wood furnish and 18 single-layer panels from the whole tree furnish.

17} Test samples were prepared based on ASTM D-1037 specifications.

{ 14 Three eastern redcedar trees with an average of 10.3-inch diameter at breast height (DBH) were harvested in Goldsby, Oklahoma. Two of the trees were limbed and only their trunks were chipped. The third tree, after being bucked into smaller segments, was chipped with branches and foliage using a commercial chipper. The chips were reduced into particles using a laboratory-type hammer mill without screening. Later, the furnish was dried to 5 percent moisture content in a 30-ft.^{3} capacity dryer.

{ 15 The two limbed trees were the raw material for round wood particleboard furnish. The other tree was used for whole tree furnish. Both kinds of furnish are shown in Figure 1.

Figure 1. Whole tree and round wood furnish.

{ 16 Thirty-six single-layer mats with dimensions of 20 x 22 x 0.5 inches were manually formed in a frame prior to being pressed into particleboard panels. Eighteen mats were composed of round wood furnish and 18 were composed of whole tree furnish. Urea-formaldehyde resin with a solids content of 65.8 percent was used as binder for the panels. The furnish for each panel was mixed with 7 percent resin in a rotating-drum mixer for 5 minutes. No wax was used in this process.

{ 17 Test samples were prepared based on ASTM D-1037 specifications and conditioned at a temperature of 70 degrees Fahrenheit and 55 percent relative humidity before any tests were carried out. Modulus of elasticity (MOE) and modulus of rupture (MOR) were determined on a Titus Universal system and a Comten tensile tester was employed for internal bond strength (IB) tests.

Results and Discussion

18} Modulus of elasticity (MOE) values, modulus of rupture values (MOR), and internal bond strength (IB) were ascertained (Table 2). The round wood particleboard exceeded ASTD specifications. The

Figure 1. A portion of a QuikScanned document showing a QuikScan summary (gray box) and corresponding target numbers in the body of the text.

QuikScan was designed to accommodate the wide variations in formatting we regularly see in the many genres of expository texts. For example, there are four different kinds of QuikScan summaries and three different numbering systems for the list items and target numbers. Because QuikScan is a complete and flexible document specification, you can QuikScan a document with one or multiple columns, figures and tables, few or no headings, multiple levels of closely spaced headings, bulleted lists, etc. You can write a document with QuikScanning in mind or you can QuikScan an existing document. QuikScan has drawbacks, the main one being the extra work entailed in writing and formatting the summaries and adding the target numbers to the body of the document. Summaries, however, can be formatted efficiently using various shortcut techniques available in full-featured word processing applications. Also, a recent addition to the QuikScan specification makes QuikScan easier to format than it was originally (see "Simpler QuikScan" in http://www.quikscan.org/). Even so, because of the extra effort, QuikScan will most often be used for relatively high-value documents, such as documents that will be broadly distributed or will be the basis of important decisions.

3. SWITCHBACK AND THE LOSS OF CONTEXT PROBLEM

Selective-reading designs employing the multiple summary approach are not rare. For example, many book-length documents provide a summary before each chapter. The influential STOP format [17, 6] consists of two-page modules, each with a summary ("thesis statement"). Still another example is a BBC Website, *India-Pakistan Troubled Relations* [1]. This Website features nine pages each describing a phase in the conflict between the two nations. Each page begins with a brief abstract so that the reader can choose between the abstract and the full discussion.

While multiple summary designs give readers the choice between reading the summary or the corresponding section of the full text, they are also subject to what can be termed the "loss of context problem": When a reader opts for a summary instead of the full text, the resulting information deficit may cause problems for that reader later on in the document.

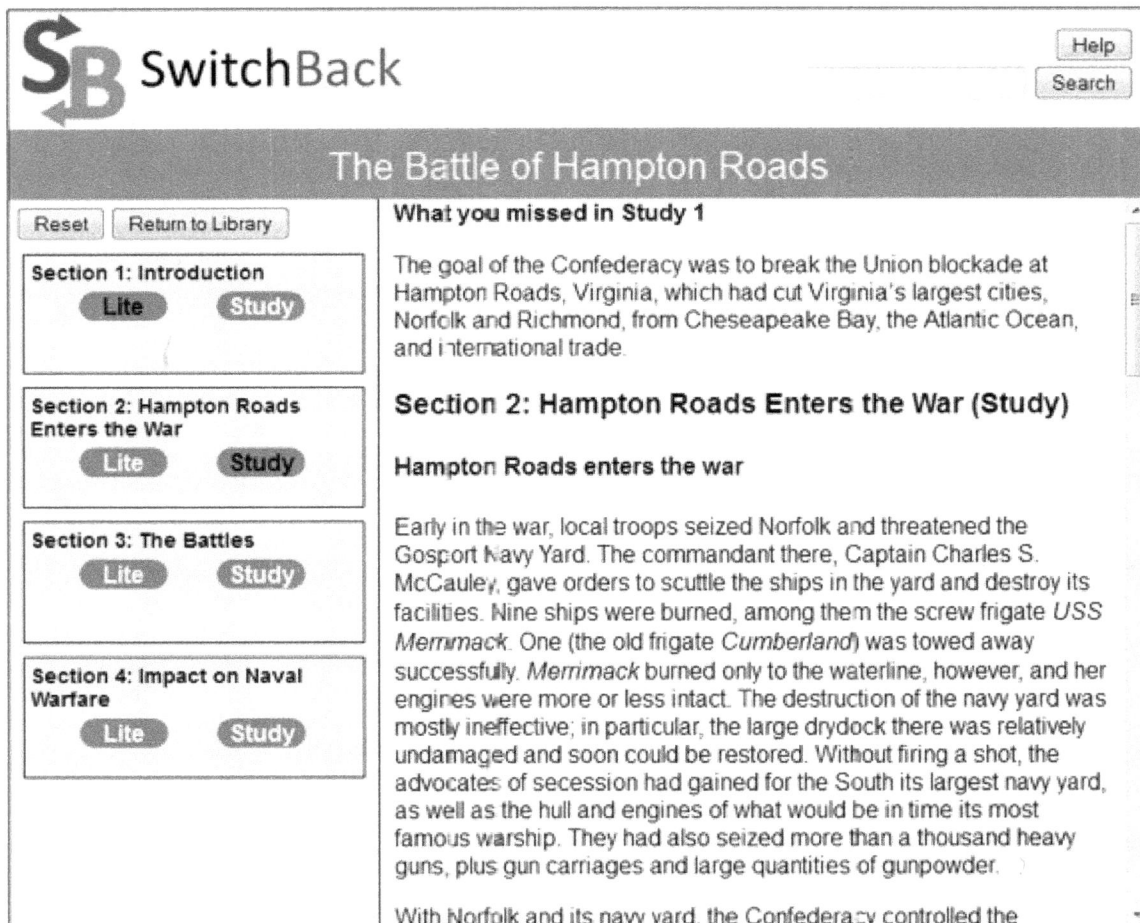

Figure 2. A sample SwitchBack document showing the reading paths available to the reader and the text SwitchBack displays in response to the reader's choices.

SwitchBack, developed by Farkas, Raleigh, and the SwitchBack Research Group at the University of Washington, is a working prototype designed to address and to explore this loss of context problem [7, see also http://faculty.washington.edu/farkas/ SwitchBack.html]. A SwitchBack document is shown in Figure 2.

SwitchBack addresses the loss of context problem by tracking the reader's path through the document and interposing any information the author deems necessary to prevent the problem. In the figure, we can see that the reader chose to read the Lite (summarized) version of Section 1 and then switched to the Study (complete) version of Section 2. SwitchBack has interposed the prerequisite information (the goal of the Confederacy) that the reader missed by not reading the Study version of Section 1). The reader, therefore, is not hindered by the lack of prerequisite information as she reads the Study 2 component. We refer to this interposed prerequisite information as a "bridge component." If the reader had read Lite 1, Lite 2, and Study 3, SwitchBack would have interposed Bridge Components 1 and 2 (rather than just Bridge Component 1). We usually display bridge components to readers under the heading "What you missed in Study X." The essence of SwitchBack is simply this: Whenever the reader makes a switch from Lite to Study content, any prerequisite information is interposed as a bridge component. Authoring a SwitchBack document is significantly more arduous than QuikScanning. The author must (1) keep track of all the pathways a reader can follow when choosing between lite and study components, (2) write the appropriate bridge components (.txt files), and (3) upload numerous SwitchBack files to the appropriate SwitchBack folders on the server. To limit the complexity of this task, the practical limit to the number of sections in a SwitchBack document is five.

Working with both QuikScan and SwitchBack yielded insights regarding the loss of context problem in multiple summary designs. First, the likelihood and severity of the problem increase with the reader's lack of familiarity with the subject matter, the reader's discomfort with incomplete information [10], and (unless bridge components are interposed) how many times the reader chooses a summary before switching to the full text. The problem also increases when summaries are relatively short in proportion to the sections of text being summarized. Shorter summaries (say 10% or less of the length of the summarized section) enable busy readers to save more time than do longer summaries, but cause larger information deficits. We also recognized that SwitchBack is worth doing only if summaries will be short. With longer summaries (say 25% of the length of the summarized section), there are fewer instances of the loss of context problem to protect the reader from and less reason to go to the extra trouble of authoring a SwitchBack document. In the case of QuikScan, which does not interpose prerequisite information, longer summaries are advisable, and the QuikScanner should strive to write informationally rich summaries that will minimize the loss of context problem. A final insight is that while a SwitchBack or QuikScan author can do a reasonably good job in anticipating the information needs of the mainstream reader, readers with special interests (idiosyncratic information needs) will not find the information they are seeking in the summaries and bridge components and should read the full text. These insights significantly influenced the design of some interim prototypes (not discussed here) and then QuikScan Views.

4. QUIKSCAN VIEWS: MORE CHOICES FOR READERS

QuikScan Views, the culmination of this paper, is a Web-based version of QuikScan with significant enhancements. First, I explain the QuikScan Views user interface and its features. Then I explain how users benefit from the extra pathways. Then I proceed to implementation and conclude with future plans. A QuikScan Views document is shown in Figure 3. Examples are available at http://www.quikscan.org/QuikScanViews.html.

4.1 More Choices for Readers

A standard QuikScan document does not allow the reader to navigate instantly among the sections of the document. Instead, you turn pages or scroll linearly through the document. However, QuikScan Views' persistent table of contents (TOC), shown at the upper right in Figure 3, provides immediate access to each section of the document (global navigation).

Below the TOC is the (scrolling) QuikScan summary window. This window displays all the QuikScan summaries (along with hyperlinked headings of the document) but none of the intervening body text—very convenient if you opt to read just the summaries. Finally, there is a structured abstract [9, 13], partly visible in the upper left. Structured abstracts, like conventional abstracts, enable a reader to preview the document, but are divided into sections with headings that map to the headings of the document. The headings of QuikScan structured abstracts are hyperlinked to the headings of the document. Also, because the sections of these structured abstracts are usually just one or two sentences, the structured abstract provides an additional, more abbreviated level of summarization than do the regular QuikScan summaries.

A QuikScan Views document can be displayed without horizontal scrolling on any desktop and almost any laptop computer (even down to a net book (880 pixel requirement). If the browser window is reduced in width for display on a tablet, the QuikScan summary window will overlap the QuikScanned document—an awkward situation. To avoid this problem, the tablet user can hide (and then restore) the summaries using the link in the TOC. In addition, the summaries can be displayed in a new browser tab. Finally, a link at the top (not visible in the figure) displays a PDF version of the QuikScanned document.

4.2 The Loss of Context Problem

QuikScan Views addresses the loss of context problem in a simpler way than SwitchBack. Just as with QuikScan, the relatively long summaries minimize the problem. Also, the reader can use the browser's Find feature to search the full document for prerequisite information he or she didn't find in a summary.

Readers who only read one or more sections of the structured abstract and then jump into the body of the full document are quite likely to experience a loss of context problem because these very short sections provide relatively little prerequisite information. But these readers stand a good chance of finding the prerequisite information they need by scrolling through the QuikScan summary window. Unfortunately, the very busy or impatient readers who opt for the structured abstract are exactly those who will be tempted to accept confusion on a point rather than taking time to find the prerequisite information. But the convenience of the summary window may be the tipping point [8] that motivates them to resolve their confusion.

4.3 Traditional and Modified Structured Abstracts

Standard structured abstracts map only the first-level headings of the document they summarize. Because structured abstracts are especially prevalent in scientific and technical journal articles, we usually see headings such as these in structured abstracts: Background, Procedure, Results, Discussion, and Conclusion. But what if the document does not divide neatly into a limited number of first-level headings? What do we do, for example, if the document contains a large and important section introduced by a second-level heading? The QuikScan Views specification allows for one or more second-level structured abstract headings (indicated with indentation) and—as necessary—other variations from the standard structured abstract. The QuikScan Views document "War of the Poppies" (http://www.quikscan.org/Poppies/) is an instance in which the QuikScanner supplied headings in the body of the document (marked with brackets to show them as the QuikScanner's additions) that were then used to write the structured abstract. If structured abstracts are going to be adopted in disciplines outside the sciences and in a wider range of genres, the general model for structured abstracts should probably be relaxed to allow for the inclusion, when appropriate, of a document's second-level headings.

4.4 Implementation

In most cases, it's best to create a QuikScan Views document by first creating a QuikScan version in MS Word (or another full-featured word processing application). You can export a (filtered) HTML file from Word into any HTML editor or use Dreamweaver's Import feature. An alternative is to build the QuikScan version directly in HTML, especially if you use Simpler QuikScan formatting (http://www.QuikScan.org/SimplerQuikScan.html).

Once the QuikScanned document is in HTML format, just a few hours of intermediate-level Web-building work is required—especially because QuikScan.org provides detailed instructions, fully commented sample documents, and a template which includes the simple JavaScript that hides the summary window. The only extra writing is the structured abstract, which in any case is a desirable addition to most documents. Because QuikScan, SwitchBack, and QuikScan Views are in the public domain, they can be used and modified freely.

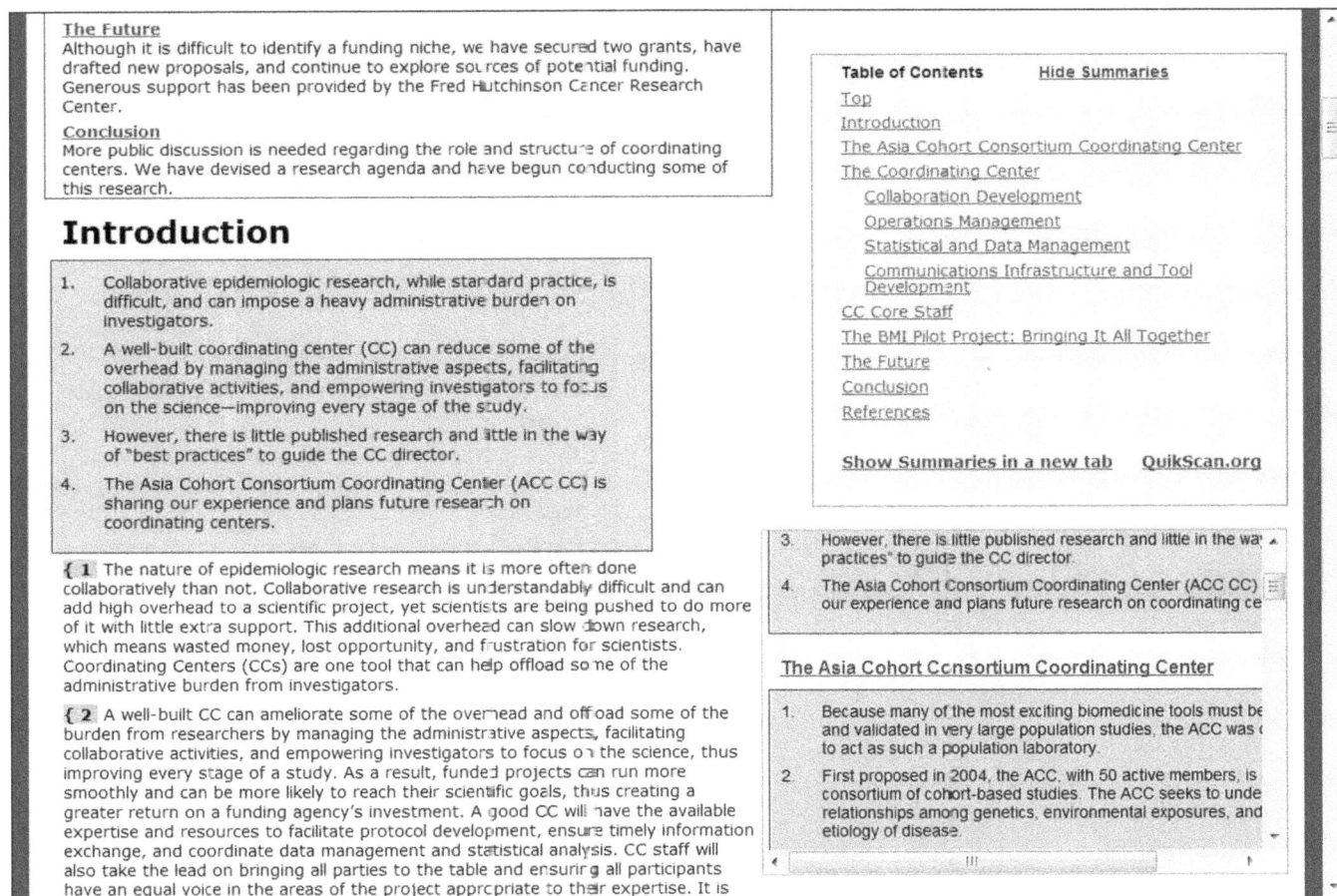

The Future
Although it is difficult to identify a funding niche, we have secured two grants, have drafted new proposals, and continue to explore sources of potential funding. Generous support has been provided by the Fred Hutchinson Cancer Research Center.

Conclusion
More public discussion is needed regarding the role and structure of coordinating centers. We have devised a research agenda and have begun conducting some of this research.

Introduction

1. Collaborative epidemiologic research, while standard practice, is difficult, and can impose a heavy administrative burden on investigators.
2. A well-built coordinating center (CC) can reduce some of the overhead by managing the administrative aspects, facilitating collaborative activities, and empowering investigators to focus on the science—improving every stage of the study.
3. However, there is little published research and little in the way of "best practices" to guide the CC director.
4. The Asia Cohort Consortium Coordinating Center (ACC CC) is sharing our experience and plans future research on coordinating centers.

{ 1 } The nature of epidemiologic research means it is more often done collaboratively than not. Collaborative research is understandably difficult and can add high overhead to a scientific project, yet scientists are being pushed to do more of it with little extra support. This additional overhead can slow down research, which means wasted money, lost opportunity, and frustration for scientists. Coordinating Centers (CCs) are one tool that can help offload some of the administrative burden from investigators.

{ 2 } A well-built CC can ameliorate some of the overhead and offload some of the burden from researchers by managing the administrative aspects, facilitating collaborative activities, and empowering investigators to focus on the science, thus improving every stage of a study. As a result, funded projects can run more smoothly and can be more likely to reach their scientific goals, thus creating a greater return on a funding agency's investment. A good CC will have the available expertise and resources to facilitate protocol development, ensure timely information exchange, and coordinate data management and statistical analysis. CC staff will also take the lead on bringing all parties to the table and ensuring all participants have an equal voice in the areas of the project appropriate to their expertise. It is

Table of Contents   Hide Summaries
Top
Introduction
The Asia Cohort Consortium Coordinating Center
The Coordinating Center
    Collaboration Development
    Operations Management
    Statistical and Data Management
    Communications Infrastructure and Tool Development
CC Core Staff
The BMI Pilot Project: Bringing It All Together
The Future
Conclusion
References

Show Summaries in a new tab   QuikScan.org

3. However, there is little published research and little in the way practices" to guide the CC director.
4. The Asia Cohort Consortium Coordinating Center (ACC CC) our experience and plans future research on coordinating ce

The Asia Cohort Consortium Coordinating Center

1. Because many of the most exciting biomedicine tools must be and validated in very large population studies, the ACC was to act as such a population laboratory.
2. First proposed in 2004, the ACC, with 50 active members, is consortium of cohort-based studies. The ACC seeks to unde relationships among genetics, environmental exposures, and etiology of disease.

Figure 3. A QuikScan Views document as it appears on a desktop or laptop computer.

5. CONCLUSION

Because classic QuikScan documents are embedded without change within QuikScan Views, it is highly plausible that the well-demonstrated benefits of QuikScan apply as well to QuikScan Views. Direct experimental testing of QuikScan Views, however, presents significant challenges because the essence of QuikScan Views is to give readers multiple choices (pathways through the document), choices that reflect the complex pressures, motivations, and trade-offs that arise in actual use, but are hard to simulate realistically in a controlled study. A better plan is an extended observational study conducted with a group of readers who have used one or more QuikScan Views documents to achieve authentic reading goals.

With so many busy and impatient readers, it seems desirable to support selective reading through good design. Multiple summary designs are an excellent design approach, even though the loss of context problem must be addressed in some way. QuikScan, SwitchBack, and QuikScan Views each offers its own features and benefits. The special strength of QuikScan Views is that it empowers the reader by providing many more pathways through the document.

6. REFERENCES

[1] BBC. 2005. *India-Pakistan: Troubled Relations.* http://news.bbc.co.uk/hi/english/static/in_depth/south_asia/2002/india_pakistan/timeline/default.stm.

[2] Bosman, J. and Richtel, M. 2012. Finding your book interrupted ... By the tablet you read it on. *New York Times* March 4. http://www.nytimes.com/2012/03/05/business/media/e-books-on-tablets-fight-digital-distractions.html?pagewanted=all

[3] Carr, N. 2010. *The Shallows: What the Internet Is Doing To Our Brains.* WW Norton & Company.

[4] Connolly, R. 2010. *What's Wrong with Online Reading?* http://randyconnolly.com/blog/?p=210.

[5] Eppler, M. J. and Mengis, J. M. 2004. The concept of information overload: A review of literature from organization science, accounting, marketing, MIS, and related disciplines. *The Information Society* 20, 325-344.

[6] Farkas, D. K. 2005. The explicit structure of print and on-screen documents. *Technical Communication Quarterly* 14(1), 9-30.

[7] Farkas, D. K. and Raleigh, C. 2012. Designing documents for selective reading. *Information Design Journal* 20(1&2), (forthcoming).

[8] Gladwell, M. 2000. The Tipping Point: How Little Things Can Make a Big Difference. New York: Little, Brown, & Co.

[9] Hartley, J. 2004. Current findings from research on structured abstracts. *Journal of the Medical Library Association* 92(3), 368-371.

[10] Lee, M. J. 2005. Expanding hypertext: Does it address disorientation? Depends on individuals' adventurousness. *Journal of Computer-Mediated Communication* 10(3), article 6. http://jcmc.indiana.edu/vol10/issue3/lee.html.

[11] Liu, Z. 2005. Reading behavior in the digital environment: Changes in reading behavior over the past ten years. *Journal of Documentation* 61, 700-712.

[12] Menzies, H. and Newson, J. 2007. No time to think: Academics' life in the globally wired university. *Time and Society* 16, 83-98.

[13] Nakayama T, Hirai N, Yamazaki S, and Naito, M. 2005. Adoption of structured abstracts by general medical journals and format for a structured abstract. *Journal of the Medical Library Association* 93(2), 237-42.

[14] Nicholas, D., Huntington, P., Jamali, H. R., Rowlands, I., Dobrowolski, T., and Tenopir, C. 2008. Viewing and reading behaviour in a virtual environment: The full-text download and what can be read into it. *Aslib (Association for Information Management) Proceedings* 60, 185-198.

[15] Nielsen, J. 2008. How little do users read? *Alertbox* May 6. http://www.useit.com/alertbox/percent-text-read.html.

[16] Rich, M. 2009. Curling up with hybrid books, videos included. *New York Times*, September 30. http://www.nytimes.com/2009/10/01/books/01book.html.

[17] Tracey, J. R., Rugh, D. E., and Starkey, W. S. 1965. *Sequential Thematic Organization of Publications (STOP)*, Internal report for the Hughes Aircraft Company. Reprinted in the *Journal of Computer Documentation*, 23(3), August 1999. Available from the ACM Digital Library at ACM.org.

[18] van der Meij, H. and van der Meij, J. 2011. Improving text recall with multiple summaries. *British Journal of Educational Psychology* 81(4), 1–13. DOI: 10.1111/j.2044-8279.2011.02024.x

[19] van der Meij, H., van der Meij, J., and Farkas, D. K. Forthcoming. QuikScan formatting as a means to improve text recall. *Journal of Documentation*.

[20] Weiss, L. A. 2012. *Improving Texts with Multiple Summaries by Aiding Readers To Build a Text Model*, Master's Thesis, University of Twente, The Netherlands.

[21] Wurman, R. S. 1989. *Information Anxiety*. New York: Doubleday.

[22] Zhou, Q. 2008. *QuikScan: Facilitating Document Use Through Innovative Formatting*. Dissertation, University of Washington, USA.

[23] Zhou, Q. and Farkas, D. K. 2010. QuikScan: Formatting documents for better comprehension and navigation. *Technical Communication* 57(2), 197-209.

[24] Zhou, Q. and Farkas, D. K. 2009. QuikScan: Facilitating reading and information navigation through innovative document formatting. In *Proceedings of the IEEE International Professional Communication Conference (IPCC)*.

Designing Graphical User Interfaces Integrating Gestures

François Beuvens
Université catholique de Louvain
Place des Doyens, 1
B-1348 Louvain-la-Neuve, Belgium
+3210478179
francois.beuvens@uclouvain.be

Jean Vanderdonckt
Université catholique de Louvain
Place des Doyens, 1
B-1348 Louvain-laNeuve, Belgium
+3210478525
jean.vanderdonckt@uclouvain.be

ABSTRACT

The world of today and its new technologies like smartphones, tablets, or any flat interaction surface has increasing the need for graphical user interfaces integrating gestural interaction in which 2D pen-based gestures are properly used. Integrating this interaction modality in streamlined software development represents a significant challenge for designers or developers: it requires important knowledge in gestures management, in deciding which gesture recognition algorithm should be used or refined for which types of gestures, or which usability knowledge should be used for supporting the development. These skills usually belong to experts for gesture interaction and not actors usually involved in user interface design process. In this paper, we present a structured method for facilitating the integration of gestures in graphical user interfaces by describing the roles of the gesture specialist and other stakeholders involved in the development life cycle, and the process of cooperation leading to the creation of a gesture-based user interface. The method consists of three pillars: a conceptual model for describing gestures on top of graphical user interfaces and its associated language, a step-wise approach for defining gestures depending on the end user's task, and a software that supports this approach. This method is exemplified with a running example in the area of document navigation.

Categories and Subject Descriptors

D.2.2 [**Software Engineering**]: Design Tools and Techniques – User interfaces. H.5.2 [**Information Interfaces and Presentation**]: User Interfaces – Graphical user interfaces. I.3.6 [**Computer Graphics**]: Methodology and Techniques – Interaction techniques.

Keywords

Method engineering, model-driven architecture, user interface, pen-based gesture, sketch.

1. INTRODUCTION

Gesture-based user interfaces are getting more popular last years with the emergence smartphones, tablets, and any other flat interaction surface that could accommodate pen-based gestures. These new platforms usually require gesture-based interaction with – often but not always – finger or pen as inputs. Despite their recent increased popularity, such user interfaces are considered for a long time and several tools have been realized in order to bring support during their creation.

Pen-based gesture recognition [2,4,14] typically consists in interpreting hand-made marks, called *strokes* [1,7], made with a pointing device (e.g., a mouse, a stylus, a light pen) on a flat constrained vertical or horizontal surface (e.g., a table, a wall or a graphic tablet). Pen-based gestures are applicable to a large area of tasks (e.g., music editing, drawing, sketching, spreadsheets, web navigation, equation editing) in many different domains of activity (e.g., office automation [32], ambient intelligence [10], multimodal systems [30]) and a growing set of devices, ranging from smartphones to tabletop interaction. Pen-based gestures can even be considered across several platforms: starting on a smartphone and finishing on a tabletop [10]. When the locus of input is different from the locus of output (e.g., with a graphic tablet), gestures are drawn outside the main display, thus posing a visual discontinuity problem. When locus of input and output match, a risk of occlusion occurs since the gesture is drawn on top of the main display. The surface used for pen-based gestures is however used as a way to constrain the gesture, thus helping its recognition.

Pen-based gestures have received considerable attention in both research and development, namely for addressing the scientific problem of modeling, analyzing, learning, interpreting, and recognizing gestures in a large spectrum of setups. The large inclusion of pen-based gestures in widely-available interactive applications has however not reached its full potential due to at least the following reasons: designers and developers do not know which recognition algorithm to select from such as large offer, how to tune the selected algorithm depending on their context of use, and how to incorporate the selected algorithm into streamlined User Interface (UI) development in an effective and efficient way. Incorporating pen-based gestures may also involve using Application Programming Interfaces (APIs), libraries, toolkits or algorithm code that could be considered hard to use [31]. Consequently, in this paper, we do not address the scientific problem for modeling, analyzing, interpreting, and recognizing gestures. Rather, we are interested in integrating the results provided by this body of research [3,9,21,22,23,25] into streamlined UI development with device independence, extensibility, and flexibility

2. RELATED WORK

2.1 Motivations for pen-based gestures

Pen-based gestures are appreciated by end users for several reasons: they are straightforward to operate [5], they offer a better precision than finger touch [8], which make them particularly adequate for fine-grained tasks like drawing, sketching. Most people found gestures quick to learn and to reproduce once learned, depending on properties [15,32]:

Iconicity («memorable because the shape of the gesture corresponds with this operation» [17]). When humans are communicating, they are using gestures to increase the understanding of the listener and obviously, the gesture usually means what the speaker is saying. Iconicity principle is based on this. It means that gestures that are designed are close to the interpretation of this reality. For example, Fig. 1(a) depicts the "Delete" action by a pair of scissors, which denotes the activity of cutting something.

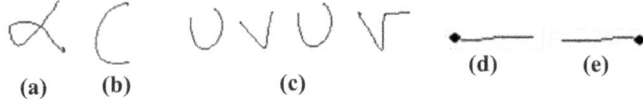

(a)   (b)   (c)   (d)   (e)

Figure 1. Some pen-based gestures for "delete" (a), "copy" (b), "u" and "v" letters (c), move forward (d), move back (e).

Learnability. Users sometimes forget gestures because they are numerous or because they are complex or not iconic. 90% and more participants held that pen-based gestures with visual meaningful related to commands are easy to be remembered and learned [5]. Another option suggested in [8] to increase the rememberability of the users was to represent a gesture as the first character of the command name. For instance, Fig. 1(b) depicts the "Copy" action because «C» stands for Copy, which is an alternative provided that shortcuts are available. If users spend their time for checking which pen-based gesture is convenient for executing which command in the manual, they will get bored soon.

Recognizability. Naive designers often create pen-based gestures that the computer viewed as similar and thus were difficult to recognize [15]. There is a trade-off between improving the gesture recognizability for the gesture recognizer and optimizing the recognizability for the end user. For instance, Fig. 1(c) compares two alternate designs for writing the "u" and "v" letters. The right one improves the system recognition rate of the system, but deteriorates the end user recognition (since the gesture looks like a square root), while the left one is the opposite: natural for the end user, hard for the system to differentiate.

Compatibility and coherence. Gestures [8] are also better learned and used when they are compatible and coherent. Gestures are best perceived when they are introduced in a uniformed and stable way. For instance, the gesture of Fig. 1(d) depicts "moving forward or right" since the gesture indicated the direction, which is natural to understand for the user, while Fig. 1(e) means the opposite direction.

2.2 Motivations for integration in UI development
In this subsection, some significant related work is reviewed by referring to some of their shortcomings.

Accessibility. Pen-based gesture recognition algorithms are usually made accessible as APIs, libraries, toolkits, platforms or procedural code. A recognition algorithm may become available either in one or many of these heterogeneous forms, thus making their integration in application development a permanent challenge. When a same algorithm is found in different sources, the source choice is even more challenging. Some platforms, like iGesture [26] and InkKit [21,25] offer several algorithms though, but they are more intended for recognition benchmarking.

Hard Algorithm Selection. Certain platforms help the designer to create a gesture set or to benchmark recognition algorithms in a general way. But, to our knowledge, none of them is able to drive the designer through the different steps of selecting a recognition algorithm that is appropriate for a particular gesture set, of fine-tuning its parameters in order to optimize its performance, and for integrating this fine-tuning in UI development.

Satin [3] is a toolkit created for making effective pen-based UIs easier. The two important facets are the integration of pen input with interpreters and the libraries for manipulating ink strokes. Built on top of Satin, *Denim* [6] consists in web site design tool

aimed at the early stages of information, navigation, and interaction design. It may be used by designers to quickly sketch web pages, create links among them and interact with them at runtime. *Silk* [4] is an interactive tool that allows designers quickly prototyping a UI by sketching it with a stylus. GART [8] is a UI toolkit designed to enable the development of gesture-based applications. It provides an abstraction to machine learning algorithms suitable for modeling and recognizing different types of gestures. The toolkit also proposes support for the data collection and the training process. GT2k [19] provides a publicly available toolkit for developing gesture-based recognition components to be integrated in large systems. It provides capabilities for training models and allows for both real-time and off-line recognition.

Many gesture recognition algorithms exist and few comparative studies for comparison are published. *DataManager* [13] is a toolkit providing automatic evaluation of gesture recognition algorithms. *iGesture* [14] also helps developers selecting a suitable algorithm for specific needs, and additionally supports them to add new gesture recognition functionality to their application. *InkKit* [11] may be used to perform recognition benchmarking too. *Quill* [7] assists developers in the task of creating well-designed gesture sets, both in terms of computer recognizability and likelihood of confusion among gestures by people.

All these tools provide help during a specific step of the process leading to the creation of a gesture-based user interface. To our knowledge though, none of them is able to fully support all the steps of this process. Following section first outlines the different actors it involves, gives some insights of a system fostering their collaboration, and finally defines a method describing the different steps to be followed by the actors of the user interface creation with the help the system. The two next sections respectively present a model describing the system and give an implementation of this system.

Pen-based gesture recognition may have several finalities. Among them, many tools support the field of document manipulation in different ways. An example is PapierCraft [15], which is pen-gesture-based command system combining graphical and gestural modalities for paper-based interfaces. Fifth section shows through a concrete example how such a system could be easily created through the defined method, with the help of the system. Last section finally concludes and presents future work.

Lack of extensibility and flexibility. It is usually very hard to extend the current implement with another recognition algorithm or another variant of an existing algorithm. Some platforms, like iGesture [26] and InkKit [25], already hold several recognition algorithms with room for extension, but this task is more intended for highly-experienced developers. In addition, they do not help in selecting which algorithm or interpretation of an algorithm is most appropriate for a certain task.

Incorporation in UI development. Most of the time, the incorporation of pen-based gestures should be achieved in a programmatic way, by hand, with little or no support [14]. This is probably one of the most challenging shortcomings. There is no continuity between the design phase of pen-based gestures and the development phase of incorporating the algorithms in the final interactive application. Wilhelm *et al.* describe a trajectory-based approach that is applied to support device independent dynamic hand gesture recognition from pen devices. Feature extraction and recognition are performed on data recorded from the different devices and transformed them to a common basis (2D-space).

This paper is believed to be original in that it provides a method (and a software support) for integrating 2D pen-based gesture interaction in software development of Graphical User Interfaces straightforwardly, with device independence, extensibility, and flexibility.

3. METHOD

Creating a user interface is a complex task requiring many skills. In the perfect case, all these skills would belong to a single developer that would then be able to conduct the whole process of creating the user interface alone. In practice, it is rarely the case since it is difficult for a single developer to acquire all the needed knowledge for each sub-process involved in the user interface creation.

The usual process of creating a user interface can be divided in two distinct parts: during the *conception* phase, the engineer/architect analyzes the user preferences, environment parameters, and miscellaneous requirements, and elaborates the specifications of the interface with the help of the designer. Based on these specifications, the programmer actually codes the user interface during the *implementation phase*.

We are here interested by the specification of user interfaces including gesture or sketch (in the rest of the paper, we will refer to gesture or sketch as equivalent) manipulation. Taking such a feature into account would impact the two phases of the user interface creation. A gesture specialist helps the engineer/architect and the designer during the conception phase. The programmer codes the gesture mechanism based on the specifications during the implementation phase, or is helped by a second programmer specialist in this domain.

We thereby define two phases and four roles characterizing the creation of gesture-based user interfaces:

1. *Conception phase*: outputs a UI description.

    - The **engineer/architect** analyzes the different requirements elicited by the user, the environment, or any other input and identifies the different parts to be included in the user interface (widgets) as well as the behavior enabling interaction with the user and between the widgets. He is taking care of the ergonomics of the system.

    - The **designer** is in charge of the aesthetics of the user interface. His role is to choose the right layout parameters (size, color, font, etc.) for each part of the user interface, and follow aesthetics rules based on metrics such as density [18] or balance [9]. He helps the engineer/architect ensuring good ergonomics.

    - The **gesture specialist** is devoted to the recognition mechanism specification with its different parameters.

2. *Implementation phase*: based on the UI description elaborated in conception phase, outputs the final code of the UI.

    - The **programmer(s)** are the builders of the user interface. Based on the specifications of the conception phase, they actually code it. This includes the recognition mechanism, i.e. the algorithms and the gesture datasets.

The roles defined in the conception phase are well delimited, but in practice, they are more interfering and lead to a real cooperation. Additionally, if the conception and implementation phases remain independent, they will rarely be performed one time each.

After the conception and the implementation, the generated user interface is tested, often leading to a conception refinement. The different phases are then repeated until convergence on a satisfying user interface. Our goal is to provide a system supporting the conception and implementation phases, enacting the interaction between the different actors.

At this point, we have considered providing a system that can be **used** by engineers/architects, designers, gesture specialists and programmers to create a gesture-based user interface. But how to tune such a system? What widgets, behavior, algorithms, elements of design, etc. should be proposed? We are not specialists and we do not have competences to make any assumptions on what is important or not. Furthermore, technologies are constantly evolving, how to update the system in order to reflect them?

The system should be flexible and extensible to be able to easily acquire new knowledge from skilled people. These people are engineers/architects, designers and gesture specialists, helped by programmers. Instead of being users of the system, they become **feeders**.

At this level, the role of the programmer(s) is slightly different since it consists in programming the engines allowing the automatic generation of the user interface specification (i.e. every element of knowledge determined by engineers/architects, designers and gesture specialists) in final code, rather than directly programming the user interface by transforming the specifications "manually" (thanks to the direct mapping between the XML specifications and Java code provided by WindowBuilder, presented in Section 5). In this view, the role of the programmer(s) as user(s) of the system is not useful anymore and may then be suppressed for this level.

Around these different descriptions, we are now able to formalize a method enacting the creation of gesture-based user interfaces. For this purpose, we define three different roles acting at three different levels of interaction:

- The **Interface Users (IU)**: end users of the interface.

- The **System Users (SU)**: first group of engineer(s)/architect(s), designer(s) and gesture specialist(s) using the system in order to produce the user interface for the Interface Users.

- The **System Feeders (SF)**: second group of engineer(s)/architect(s), designer(s), gesture specialist(s) and programmer(s) feeding the system with knowledge allowing SU creating user interfaces.

The roles are not exclusive. People acting as System Feeders may be System Users (e.g., a gesture specialists that create an algorithm and then tune and include it in the user interface) or Systems Users may be Interface Users (e.g., engineer(s)/architect (s), designer (s) and gesture specialist(s) wanting to use the interface they have created with the system), etc.

The method is then defined in seven steps:

1. Interface Users define user interface requirements.
2. Based on the UI requirements, System Users define system requirements.
3. If system requirements not met: based on the system requirements, System Feeders feed the system.
4. Based on UI requirements, System Users use the system to produce the user interface.
5. If UI requirements not met: System Users refine system requirements, then go back to step 3.

6. Interface Users use the produced user interface.
7. If Interface Users not satisfied: Interface Users refine UI requirements, then go back to step 4.

When the interface users are satisfied, the method stops iterating. The whole process is illustrated in Figure 2.

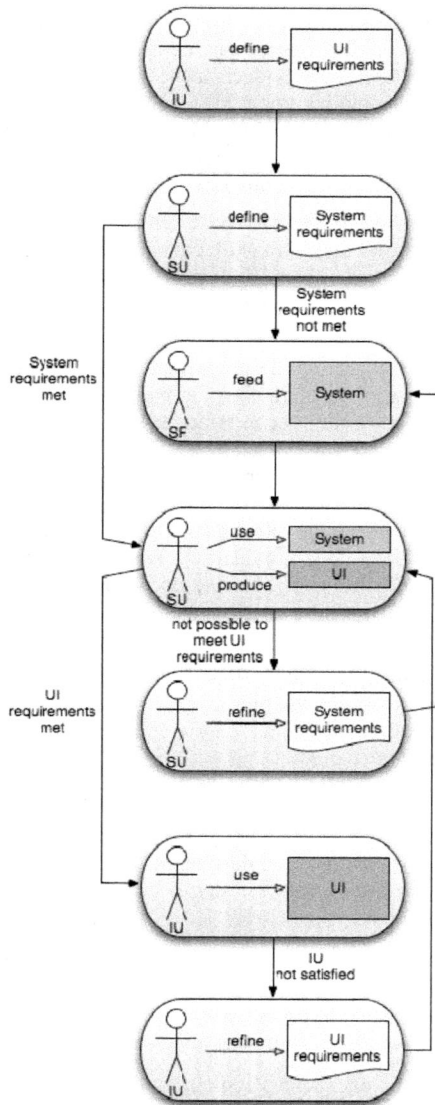

Figure 2. Method.

The main advantage of such a system is its ability to evolve through the different user interfaces creations. It may be viewed as a structured repository of gesture-based user interfaces knowledge. The more user interfaces are produced, the more the system is fed with knowledge, allowing any system users taking profit of all the experience acquired during previous work.

Next section presents the choices we made to model the system on which the method is relying.

4. MODEL

The Cameleon Reference Framework [1] defines the description of a user interface at different levels of abstraction: Tasks & Concepts, Abstract User Interface (AUI), Concrete User Interface (CUI) and Final User Interface (FUI). Each level is formalized by a User Interface Description Language (UIDL) representing the user interface for the specific level. Different mechanisms of forward and reverse engineering allow translating one level into another one.

The user interface description elaborated during the conception phase of the method proposed in previous section actually corresponds to the CUI UIDL. CUI is then transformed in FUI in the implementation phase. This is the modeling approach chosen to support the method.

The CUI UIDL we decided to adopt is Eclipse XML Window Toolkit (XWT) [22]. This language allows specifying user interfaces with XML representation by relying on Standard Widget Toolkit (SWT) [16], which is an open-source widget toolkit for Java. XWT provides a very interesting piece of work, including the description of an important set of SWT widgets as well as a tool supporting the XWT and graphical edition of user interface (see next section). The chosen FUI language is naturally Java since it is directly supported by XWT.

Although XWT constitutes a very useful basis, it is not sufficient to achieve the targeted method. SWT proposes many widgets with design and behavior features. As aforementioned, XWT provides an XML description of an important part of them, but this description only concerns the widgets themselves with their elements of design. The behavior part is not fully described by XWT: although it is possible to specify listening to events, launching an action provided some condition is not possible with XML syntax. Furthermore, no mechanism is devoted to gesture interaction. We then chose XWT as our core model, extended to meet our requirements.

Figure 3 depicts the model including the XWT package, with the behavior extension part (bottom block) and the sketch extension part (top-left block). The three next subsections respectively detail XWT, behavior and gesture parts.

4.1 XWT Package

Only a subset of the XWT model is represented since the whole model is too big and contains useless information at this level. The attributes are not shown for the same reasons.

The main principle of this model is that most entities are derived from the concept of *Widget*, which defines a set of methods and attributes. *Control* and *Scrollable* both add other methods and attributes to *Widget* to increase the available functionalities. These three classes are sub-classed by many concrete classes as *Button, Label,* etc. Among them, three important widgets will be the starting points for the behavior and gesture extensions:

- *Composite*: container of widgets.

- *Canvas*: special container defining a paintable zone.

- *Shell*: root container representing the user interface.

Additionally, *Color* entity is represented since it will be useful for the gesture block.

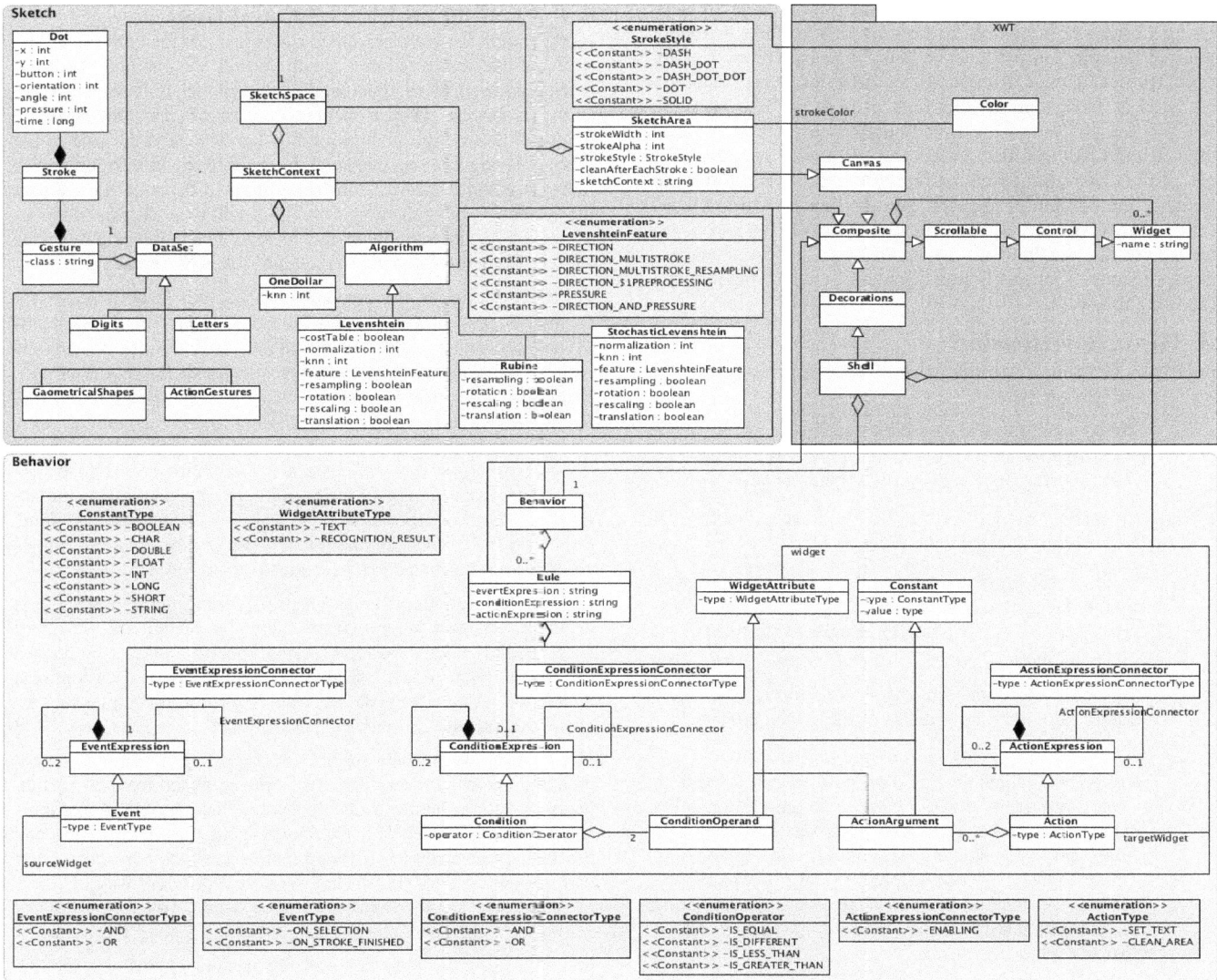

Figure 3. Conceptual model for defining graphical user interfaces and the integration of behavior and gestures.

4.2 Behavior Extension

The extension proposed for the behavior is articulated around two main entities:

- *Behavior*: main behavior entity enclosing all the needed information in a set of *Rule*. It is unique for a user interface and belongs directly to the *Shell*.

- *Rule*: represents an Event-Condition-Action rule (ECA rule). "eventExpression", "conditionExpression" and "actionExpression" attributes are the string representations of the rules elements described in the followings.

An ECA rule in its basic form allows specifying an action to be launched when an event occur, under a certain condition. In order to add more expressivity, we considered event expressions, condition expressions and action expressions instead of events, conditions and actions. The corresponding entities in the model are *EventExpression, ConditionExpression* and *ActionExpression*.

An event expression is a set of events interconnected by connectors. Additionally, subsets of events may be interconnected with other subsets of events, or simple events. *EventExpression* is ei-

ther a simple event, or a group of two *EventExpression* interconnected with an *EventExpressionConnector*, which allows modeling the described event expression. The simple event is modeled with *Event* entity, which has a source widget and an event type. There is no explicit constraint between the source widget and the type of event, but the programmer must take care of associating the possible combinations during the implementation phase.

The condition expressions and the action expressions follow, with different types of connectors, the pattern adopted for the event expressions. However, conditions and actions are different from events. A condition is represented by *Condition* entity, which is a couple of two operands linked through an operator. These operands may be either a constant (integer, string, etc.) or a widget attribute (represented by *WidgetAttribute* entity). An action is modeled with *Action* entity, which has a target widget on which the action applies, an action type and a list of arguments to be taken by the action type. There is no explicit constraint between the target widget, type of action and the arguments, but the programmer must take care of associating the possible combinations during the implementation phase.

317

Let's finally notice that both *Behavior* and *Rule* entities are sub-classing *Composite* entity. With this way of modeling –strongly suggested by common practices in XWT and partly imposed by the tool (presented in next section) – the behavior and the rules are considered as being entirely part of the interface. It is usual in XWT, since it allows reusing already defined entities with useful attributes and functionalities. In this case, *Behavior* and *Rule* take profit of the *Composite* functionalities, but have a visibility set to false since they do not need graphical representation in the interface. We only chose these two elements to be explicitly part of the interface because we think specifying the event, condition and action expressions as strings is less constraining, more flexible and more straightforward.

4.3 Gesture Extension

Similarly to behavior extension, gesture extension relies on entities sub-classing *Composite*:

- *SketchSpace*: main sketch entity enclosing all the needed information in a set of *SketchContext*. It is unique for a user interface and belongs directly to the *Shell*.

- *SketchContext*: defines a sketch context gathering different algorithms and datasets.

- *DataSet*: collection of gestures, themselves composed of strokes, themselves composed of dots. Dots gather different information of position, time, and stylus state (if can be applied).

- *Algorithm*: represents the engine able to classify a new gesture, provided the datasets of the sketch context parent.

- *SketchArea*: paintable area linked to sketch context in order to provide recognition feature to the gesture being drawn on it. "sketchContext" attribute is the widget name of the sketch context it is linked to. "strokeWidth", "strokeAlpha" and "strokeStyle" provide control on the stroke aspect, and "cleanAfterEachStroke" indicates if the area must be cleaned each time a stroke is drawn.

As *Behavior* and *Rule*, *SketchSpace*, *SketchContext*, *DataSet*, and *Algorithm* are not intended to be visible in the FUI, while *SketchArea* is a visible component. The other entities are not part of the core description of the gesture extension and will be explained in the next subsection.

4.4 Feeding and Using the System

At this point, we have presented the entities of the core model describing the system aimed at supporting the method. In other words, without more specification this model is "naked", it describes a system ready to acquire any knowledge, but currently empty of knowledge. Increasing this knowledge is the role of the System Feeders. At model level, it corresponds in refining and/or increasing some specific entities in order to describe the features the system supports. The System Users will then use this model as a kind of documentation of the system. The way we expect the System Feeders to extend the model is different for each part.

We think the behavior extension allows an advanced expressivity for many rules or composition of rules. However, the types of events, conditions, actions and widgets attributes are missing, as well as the connector types between expressions. For this part, *EventType*, *ConditionOperator*, *ActionType*, *WidgetAttributeType*, *EventExpressionConnectorType*, *ConditionExpressionConnectorType*, and *ActionExpressionConnectorType* are the enumerations to be increased in order to specify the possible events, conditions and actions, and the way they are connected. We already provide some possibilities for each enumeration. They are given as examples and must not be considered as mandatory attributes.

For the gesture extension, the way of adding new knowledge is different. The sketch contexts must actually contain sub-classes of *DataSet* and *Algorithm*, representing specific datasets composed of several *Gesture*, and specific algorithms with their options. Again, we provide some datasets and algorithms examples that we elaborated during a previous experiment [1].

The datasets we provide (digits, letters, action gestures and geometrical shapes) are built from gestures collected from 30 participants through a platform developed for this purpose. Algorithms we provide (Rubine [12], OneDollar [21], Levenshtein [5] and Stochastic Levenshtein [10]) and their extensions constitutes a set of well-known algorithms. They all have a different way of working and cover together many situations with different needs. They are not described here since it is beyond the scope of this paper.

In addition to the behavior and the gesture extensions, System Feeders may add other new functionalities. The XWT widgets may be extended in order to add any new component with a specific purpose. This new component may then be linked to the behavior extension or even the gesture extension if needed.

Next section shows the tool we developed in order to implement the system. It is described by the model presented in this section and supports the method.

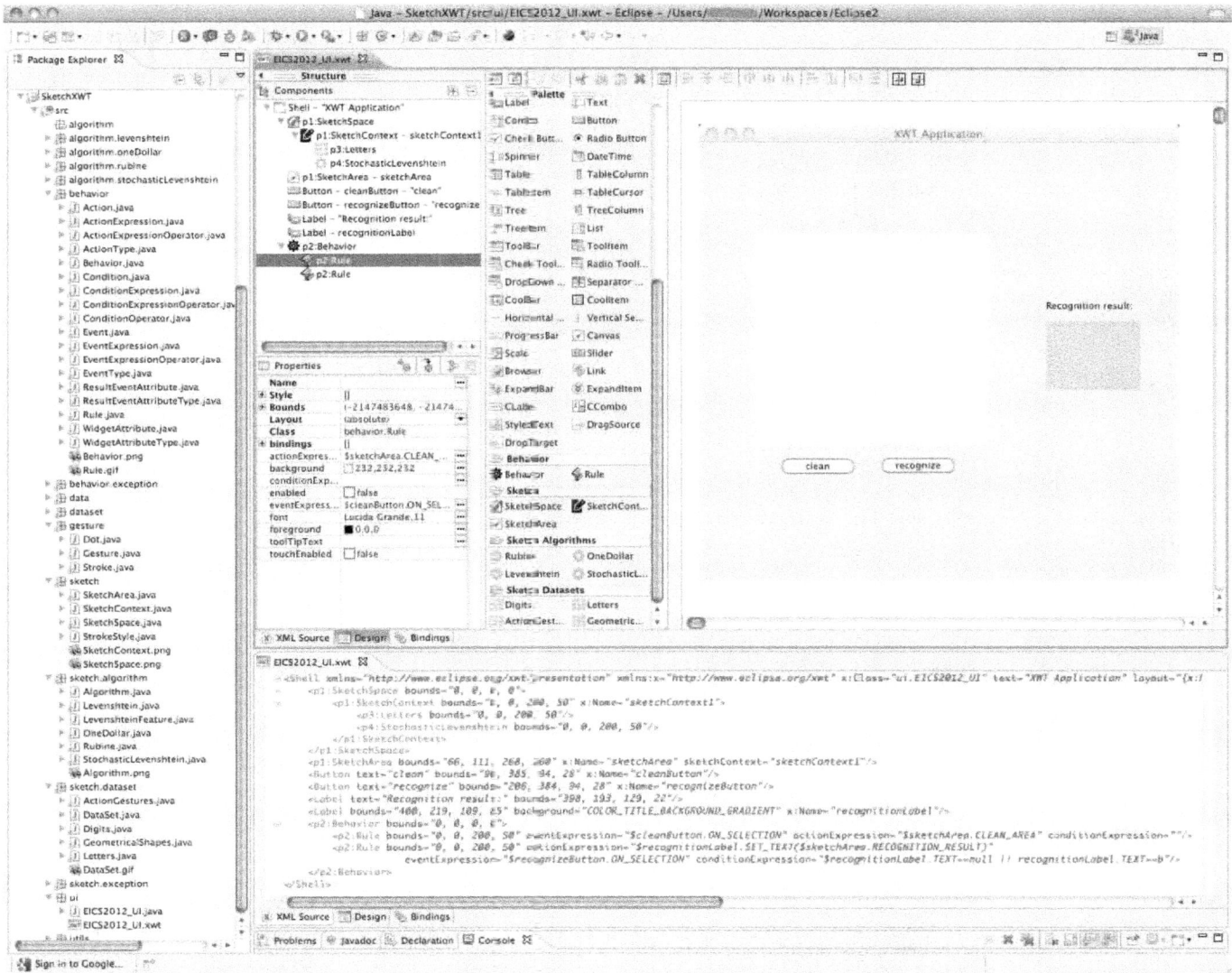

Figure 4. The software environment for integrating gestures.

5. TOOL

WindowBuilder [20] is a powerful and easy to use bi-directional Java GUI designer built as an Eclipse plug-in. It supports different toolkits, including SWT and its XML representation XWT. It may be viewed as a visual CUI editor outputting XWT user interface specifications. Moreover, it provides a Java rendering engine for the XWT package described in the previous section. We decided to choose this tool since it fits our requirements by providing a CUI editor and a Java rendering engine to produce the FUI from the CUI. Nevertheless, it must be improved in order to support the behavior and gesture extensions.

5.1 Using the Tool

Figure 4 shows a screenshot of the extended WindowBuilder environment (it may also be seen in action at the following address: http://dai.ly/GJduWS) The top-right part is the visual CUI editor allowing, through the widget palette, manipulating standard SWT widgets as well as behavior and gesture widgets, in order to build the description of a gesture-based user interface. A tree representing the interface is available along with a properties panel useful to specify any option or attribute of a widget. The bottom part of the tool shows the XWT sources of the specification of the interface.

For editing the user interface specifications, System Users have three choices: through the visual CUI editor, by editing the tree representation, or directly by updating the XWT description. In the three cases, the changes are reflected in the other representations.

To build an interface, System Users place widget elements in the visual editor, in the tree, or directly write them in the XWT specification. They define the behavior with one and only one *Behavior* widget in the *Shell* and add a set of *Rule* to it. Each *Rule* may be specified with event, condition and action expressions as String attributes, as described in the model.

The tool adds an interesting feature on the behavior by providing validation. It is used to throw an exception when the System Users specify a malformed or invalid event, condition or action expression. The validation may be turned off via an attribute in the *Behavior* widget in order to let the possibility of describing a different syntax than the one expected by the system. In this case, the running interface provided by WindowBuilder may not work, but in some cases it may be useful to create a specification based on a custom syntax. Concerning the gesture part, System Users are expected to place one and only one *SketchSpace* widget in the *Shell* and add a set of *SketchContext* to it. These *SketchContext* gather one or many *Algorithm* and *DataSet* that can be tuned with the different options described in the model. The *SketchArea* is the sketch element with a visible representation in the interface, allowing the user drawing on it and performing recognition on the gesture drawn. The *SketchArea* has many options, and must be linked to a *SketchContext* through one of them.

The specifications of the user interface are described in the *.xwt* file generated when a new XWT application is created. In order to actually produce the user interface, the System Users have to run the *.java* associated file, which will parse the CUI specifications and render the FUI in Java.

5.2 Feeding the Tool

The left column of the tool provides a view on the sources of the system implementation. Each entity described in the model has a class corresponding to its implementation.

System Feeders may add enumeration constants to *EventType*, *ConditionOperator*, *ActionType*, *WidgetAttributeType*, *EventExpressionConnectorType*, *ConditionExpressionConnectorType*, and *ActionExpressionConnectorType* classes in order to increase the behavior possibilities. The four first ones allow increasing respectively the set of events, conditions, actions and widget attributes, while System Feeders may add new connectors respectively between the events, the conditions and the actions through the three last ones.

The schema of the aforementioned validation feature is set in *EventType*, *ConditionOperator*, *ActionType* and *WidgetAttributeType* classes. Indeed, each constant of these enumerations can optionally take one or several arguments in its constructor, indicating the schema of validation:

- *EventType*: takes a table of *Class* objects as source specification in order to specify the allowed widget types from which the event may be issued.
- *ConditionOperator*: takes a first *Class* object as left operand specification and a second *Class* object as right operand specification to specify the allowed types than may be compared.
- *ActionType*: takes a *Class* object as target specification in order to specify the allowed widget type on which the action may be applied, and a table of *Class* objects as argument specification in order to specify the allowed types for each action argument.
- *WidgetAttributeType*: takes a table of *Class* objects as specification in order to specify the allowed widget types from which the widget attribute may be called.

For the constants of the four enumerations, no schema specification means no restriction. Validation exceptions are thrown if the System Users do not respect these specifications, use a malformed syntax, or try to use inexistent widgets, events, actions, etc.

Feeding the gesture recognition mechanism is done by providing new algorithms or datasets. A new algorithm is added by subclassing the *Algorithm* class and providing it all the wanted options with getters and setters. It is the way WindowBuilder works to show an attribute in the visual editor. New datasets are added by sub-classing *DataSet* class and providing option attributes with getters and setters. The new algorithms and datasets must then be added to the widget palette of the tool (simply by adding a new

component to the palette through the contextual menu, and then selecting the newly created class).

At this point, no recompilation of the tool or any further action is required from the System Feeders: the System Users are able to use the new elements of behavior or gesture mechanism in the user interface specification. However, new elements are not implemented for working during the runtime yet. The rendering engines have still to be updated in consequence by the programmer(s) to reflect the new types of events, conditions, actions and widget attributes, the new types of connectors or the new algorithms and datasets. For the behavior part, the programmer(s) must edit the *EventExpression*, *ConditionExpression*, *ActionExpression*, *Event*, *Condition*, *Action* and *WidgetAttribute* classes. Each new feature (new types of event, condition, action, or new types of connections between them) must be handled in one specific method of one of these classes.

For the gesture part, the programmer(s) must modify each new sub-class of *Algorithm* and of *DataSet*. For each algorithm subclass, *train* and *recognize* methods must be implemented in order to train the algorithm and return the string class of the gesture to recognize. For each dataset sub-class, *dataset* method must be implemented in order to return set of *Gesture*. For the implementation we provide, all the logic allowing fulfilling the methods are contained in *algorithm* and *dataset* packages. All the used gestures are provided as text files and located in the *records* folder.

This section has given a description of the few pieces of code to update in order to increase the tool possibilities, the rest of the platform is expected to remain unchanged. It globally shows how the platform is articulated, but does not constitute an exhaustive documentation, which is present in the code.

Next section presents an example showing how the method, model and tool are used to build a pen gesture-based user interface.

6. EXAMPLE

The user interface chosen for the example target document manipulation, and more specifically document navigation. The goal is to show how the method, the model and the tool can be used in order to create a system such as PapierCraft [15], which allows using gesture as commands for manipulating a paper-based interface.

Additionally, at the beginning we assume that the system is empty of any knowledge, i.e. without sub-class of *DataSet* and *Algorithm*, and with empty enumerations in the behavior part. We will start from user interface requirements produced by Interface Users and show how the System Users with the help of the System Feeders will build the user interface by iterating through the different steps of the method.

The user interface for the example has been imagined sufficiently simple to avoid useless information but sufficiently expressive to highlight all the steps defined in the method (Figure 2).

- *Step 1 – IU define UI requirements*

The user interface is a viewer for a document containing several pages. The viewer must have the capability of changing the current page to previous or next page by using gestures.

- *Step 2 – SU define system requirements*

The system must propose a component on which it is possible to specify a background corresponding to the current page of the document, and triggering the recognition of left and right action gestures as the actions for going to previous and next pages. The system requirements are not met then go to step 3.

- *Step 3 – SF feed the system*

Engineer(s)/architect(s), designer(s) and gesture specialist(s) update the CUI UIDL by creating a *ActionGestures* dataset and a *Stochastic Levenshtein* algorithm with options. They create a new *PageViewer* component on top of a sketch area allowing specifying different pages. They additionally update *EventType*, *ActionType*, and *WidgetAttributeType* by providing them respectively ON_STROKE_FINISHED (for monitoring the end of an action gesture on the document viewer); PREVIOUS_PAGE and NEXT_PAGE (for modifying the current page on document viewer); RECOGNITION_RESULT (for getting recognition result on the document viewer). They add also a *IS_EQUAL ConditionOperator*. The programmer(s) then fulfill the *dataset* method of *ActionGestures*, the *train* and *recognize* methods of *Stochastic Levenshtein*, the *perform* method of *Action* and the *getWidgetAttribute* of *WidgetAttribute* in order to implement the rendering engines reflecting the knowledge introduced in the CUI UIDL.

Figure 5. Example, first version.

- *Step 4 – SU use the system to produce the UI*

SU put the document viewer component in the UI and specify the different pages. For the behavior, they add a first rule triggered for the event expression "$documentViewer.ON_STROKE_ FINISHED" and, if the condition "$documentViewer. RECOGNITION_RESULT == LEFT", launching action expression "$documentViewer.PREVIOUS_PAGE". This rule express the the action for going back to the previous page. Similarly, they add a second rule for handling the possibility for going to next page. This second rule is triggered by event expression "$documentViewer.ON_STROKE_FINISHED" and, if the condition "$documentViewer.RECOGNITION_RESULT == RIGHT", launching action expression "$documentViewer.PREVIOUS_PAGE". The produced user interface is depicted in Figure 5 (the red line represents a right action gesture).

For the SU, the UI requirements are met then go to step 6.

- *Step 6 – IU use the UI*

IU are not satisfied with produced UI then go to step 7.

- *Step 7 – IU refine the UI requirements*

For the IU, even if the recognition is good, it is too slow and should be fastened. They also would like receiving a feedback indicating the current page they are watching.

- *Step 4 – SU use the system to produce the UI*

With the current system, SU are unable to create the user interface respecting the new UI requirements.

- *Step 5 – SU refine the system requirements*

The system needs to propose a faster algorithm. Additionally, a label is required with the possibility to specify a text, corresponding the page currently visualized.

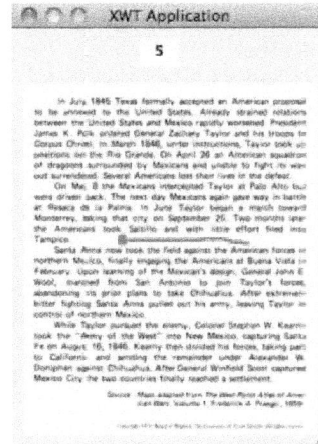

Figure 6. Example, second version.

- *Step 3 – SF feed the system*

SF will add a label component to the CUI UIDL and implement the original *Levenshtein* algorithm (less good performances but less time consuming), and a *SET_TEXT ActionType* on the label component.

- *Step 4 – SU use the system to produce the UI*

SU are now able to add a label on top of the document viewer in order to indicate the current page. The behavior possibilities have been increased in order to allow linking the page viewer with the label. The generated UI is depicted in Figure 6.

For the SU, the UI requirements are met then go to step 6.

- *Step 6 – IU use the UI*

IU are not satisfied with produced UI then go to step 7.

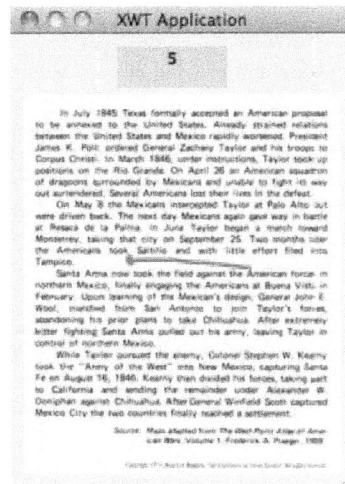

Figure 7. Example, final version.

- *Step 7 – IU refine the UI requirements*

IU finally want the label in blue and bigger because they think it is more beautiful.

- *Step 4 – SU use the system to produce the UI*

System already allows addressing this new UI requirement. The color of the label is then changed and the produced user interface is proposed to the IU, which are finally satisfied. This user interface specification may be viewed in the tool screenshot (Figure 4), with the corresponding XWT. The final generated user interface is depicted in Figure 7.

7. CONCLUSION AND FUTURE WORK

In this paper, we proposed a method enacting the creation of gesture-based user interfaces. This method (Figure 2) defines seven steps through which, with the help of the system, different categories of actors will cooperate on the creation of the gesture-based user interface targeted by end users. The system is described by an extension of the XWT model (Figure 3) allowing supporting behavior and gesture missing features. For implementing the system, we relied on a extended version of WindowBuilder (Figure 4). Through a concrete example applied to document manipulation, previous section showed the process of cooperation between the different actors leading to the creation of a gesture-based interface. If the considered user interface is simple, it is sufficient to highlight the different steps and the way achieving them. The same principles may be applied for more elaborated interfaces. Furthermore, although the method has been developed for handling the specific gesture feature, it may be generalized to take other features into account.

The big advantage of the described system is its ability to acquire and structure new knowledge. It may be viewed as a customizable gesture-based user interface factory: it is expected to evolve through the different creations of gesture-based user interfaces and be refined by System Feeders accordingly to the evolution of new technologies and needs. With time and experience, needs for updating the system will decrease, since it will contain the information needed for most user interfaces. This will lead to an improvement of the process of creating the gesture-based user interfaces. Indeed, the steps for feeding the system will be skipped, letting all the efforts focused on the direct conception of the user interfaces. When this level is reached, only the System Users and the Interface Users are needed to collaborate for producing the interface.

As a next step, we aim at improving the system in such a way that the Interface Users alone would be able to create the user interface. The idea is to rely on recommendation principles. An extension to the system would be developed in order to capture a series of rules defined by conception actors such as engineers/architects, designers and gesture specialists. It would add "intelligence" to the system, being then able to drive the final users in the creation of their user interfaces, even without any knowledge in ergonomics, UI architecture, design or gesture mechanism.

Although the current implementation of the system only targets Java language and more specifically SWT toolkit, it underlies how the method can be concretized in a general way. Thanks to the separation of concerns between the conception and the implementation phases, the whole part of the system devoted to the conception can be kept whatever the platform targeted. However, in order to implement other languages and hence support other platforms, we aim at adding a translation engine from XWT to UsiXML [17] language. UsiXML is an XML-based UIDL sup-

porting the different levels of abstraction of Cameleon Reference Framework. It defines rendering engines from its CUI to many FUI such as HTML5, Java, etc., and would allow our system outputting final user interfaces in different languages. Relying on UsiXML brings the advantage of reusing many already defined rendering engines, but these rendering engines are sometimes not sufficient to translate the XWT syntax increased by System Feeders engineers/architects, designers and gesture specialists. As UsiXML is extensible, the role of the System Feeders programmers would then become improving UsiXML rendering engines to support new features or languages fitting the increased XWT syntax. With this future integration, we hope even more increasing the System Users experience by avoiding them additional efforts when specifying a user interface for a new language since one specification would be automatically transformable in many languages.

8. REFERENCES

[1] Beuvens, F. and Vanderdonckt, J.: UsiGesture: an Environment for Integrating Pen-Based Interaction in User Interfaces. In Proc. of RCIS'12 , 339-350.

[2] Calvary, G. et al.: A Unifying Reference Framework for Multi-Target User Interfaces. Interacting with Computer 15, 3 (2003), 289-308.

[3] Hong, J. and Landay, J., Satin: a Toolkit for Informal Ink-based Applications. In UIST'00. ACM, 63–72.

[4] Landay, J. A.: SILK: Sketching Interfaces Like Krazy. In: CHI'96, ACM, NY (1996), 389-399.

[5] Levenshtein, V. I.: Binary codes capable of correcting deletions, insertions, and reversals. Soviet Physics Doklady 10, 8 (1966), 707–710.

[6] Lin, J., Newman, M., Hong, J., Landay, J.: DENIM: Finding a Tighter Fit Between Tools and Practice for Web Site Design. In: CHI'2000, 2 (1), 510-517.

[7] Long, A.C.J. quill: A Gesture Design Tool for Pen-based User Interfaces. PhD Thesis, Univ. of California at Berkeley, 2001.

[8] Lyons, K., Brashear, H., Westeyn, T., Kim, J.S., Starner, T.: GART: The Gesture and Activity Recognition Toolkit. In Proc. of HCI'07, LNCS, 4552, 718–727.

[9] Ngo, D. C. L., Byrne, J. G.: Another Look at a Model for Evaluating Interface Aesthetics, AMCS 11, 2 (2001), 515-535.

[10] Oncina, J., Sebban, M.: Learning stochastic edit distance: Application in handwritten character recognition. Pattern recognition 39 (2006), 1575–1587.

[11] Plimmer, B., Freeman, I.: A Toolkit Approach to Sketched Diagram Recognition. HCI, Lancaster, UK (2007), 205-213.

[12] Rubine, D.: Specifying gestures by example. SIGGRAPH Computer Graphics (1991).

[13] Schmieder, P., Plimmer, B., and Blagojevic, R. Automatic Evaluation of Sketch Recognizers. In: SBIM'09 ACM Press (2009), pp. 85–92.

[14] Signer, B., Kurmann, U., and Norrie, M. C. iGesture: A General Gesture Recognition Framework. ICDAR'2007, Los Alamitos (2007), 954-958.

[15] Liao, C., Guimbretière, F., and Hinckley, K.: PapierCraft: a command system for interactive paper.

[16] SWT: http://eclipse.org/swt/.

[17] UsiXML: http://www.usixml.org.

[18] Vanderdonckt, J.: Visual Design Methods In Interactive Applications. Mahwah : Lawrence Erlbaum Associates (2003), 187-203.

[19] Westeyn, T., Brashear, H., Atrash, A., Starner, T.: Georgia Tech Gesture Toolkit: Supporting Experiments in Gesture Recognition. Proc. of ICMI'03 (2003), 85-92.

[20] WindowBuilder: http://eclipse.org/windowbuilder/.

[21] Wobbrock, J. O., Wilson, A. D., Li Y.: Gestures without libraries, toolkits or training: a $1 recognizer for user interface prototypes. In Proc. of UIST'07, 159– 168.

[22] XWT: http://wiki.eclipse.org/E4/XWT.

Understanding Conceptualizations of Anatomy: Designing a Browser for the Foundational Model of Anatomy

Melissa Clarkson
University of Washington
Seattle, WA 98195
mclarkso@uw.edu

ABSTRACT

The Foundational Model of Anatomy (FMA) ontology is a reference ontology for the domain of human anatomy. Although the FMA has been developed as a computer-parsable resource that is intended to enable computers to reason about human anatomy, it is also important to present the FMA in a manner that can be more easily understood by humans. Current interfaces for accessing the FMA do not adequately reveal the structure of the FMA to the user, nor do they support intuitive navigation through the ontology. As the first step toward designing a new interface, this paper describes an extensive inquiry into conceptualizations of both anatomy and the FMA. This user-centered process led to a design that will serve as a basis for the implementation of a web-based browser.

Categories and Subject Descriptors

H.5.2 **[Information Interfaces and Presentation]**: User interfaces – *graphical user interfaces, screen design, prototyping, user-centered design*

Keywords

Network visualization, ontology, medicine

1. INTRODUCTION

Biomedical research is becoming both more data- and knowledge-intensive and more interdisciplinary—drawing researchers and practitioners from medicine, life sciences, and computational fields. Great progress has been made in developing computer systems to store, organize, and access this biomedical data and knowledge, but less effort has been invested in understanding how to present this information to the users.

The contribution of this paper is to demonstrate how research to understand conceptualizations of a particular knowledge network (the Foundational Model of Anatomy ontology) and the domain of the knowledge it represents (anatomy) guided the design of the interface for accessing the network. The work described here focuses solely on supporting browsing of the network.

1.1 Knowledge and data

Biomedical researchers make use of repositories of both *knowledge* and *data*. Knowledge bases are maintained by curators

who strive to represent the current state of understanding of a domain for the purpose of creating a community resource. Databases are collections of observations gathered for the purpose of analysis.

This distinction has implications for the design of tools to present the contents of these repositories to users. The work described in this paper is based on the premise that because a knowledge base presents a structured view of a domain, the design of the interface should facilitate communication of that view. This need may be less critical for the interface of a database, where the emphasis is on querying and analysis.

1.2 Biomedical networks

Much biomedical knowledge and data can be conceptualized as networks: entities and the relationships between pairs of those entities. Examples of these networks include biochemical pathways [1], protein binding networks [2], biological neural networks [3], and cell lineages [4].

In order for biomedical networks to be useful, three types of research contributions are required: (a) discovering and documenting the components of networks, (b) modeling networks as computer-parsable symbolic representations, and (c) designing presentations of the network that are accessible to users. The work described in this paper is a visualization design study, which places it in the final category.

Because the goal of this work is to develop an interface that reflects a specific domain of knowledge, this project did not use as a starting point existing methods and tools for network visualization [reviewed in 5, 6]. Instead, the design is a reflection of the structure of the network and users' conceptualizations of the domain of knowledge it represents.

1.3 The Foundational Model of Anatomy

Ontologies are a type of knowledge network. They consist of terms—formally specified as classes—and relationships between those classes. Ontologies provide a semantic framework that supports logic-based models for describing a domain of knowledge in a way that is both computer-parsable and human-readable.

This paper reports on work to design a web-based interface for a biomedical ontology called the Foundational Model of Anatomy (FMA) [7,8]. The FMA is a reference ontology for the domain of human anatomy and one of the largest biomedical ontologies in existence. It is considered to be a *reference* ontology because it is not intended for any specific use or user group. It can be used for any application requiring anatomical knowledge and can be extended to any specialized domain of anatomy. The FMA currently has over 90,000 classes, 175 types of relationships, 2.5

million relationships between classes, and remains under active development [José L. V. Mejino, personal communication].

The fundamental purpose of the FMA is to allow computers to reason about human anatomy, but a user-friendly interface for viewing the FMA is also necessary. There are two general use cases for this interface. The first is to allow people to develop an understanding of the structure and content of the FMA. This is important for researchers who will be using the FMA in their projects, biomedical informatics students learning about ontologies, and software engineers who will build tools to computationally access the FMA. The second use case is to assist users in locating specific classes within the FMA. The FMA serves as a standardized terminology for annotating data, and therefore researchers need to locate specific classes during annotation[1]. For example, a researcher who has a collection of data pertaining to different regions of the liver will need to locate the corresponding classes within the FMA.

2. CURRENT INTERFACES

The FMA has been developed in the Protégé frame-based authoring environment [10] and is available for download as a Protégé file, allowing researchers to create their own FMA database and view it within the Protégé system [11]. But because the vast majority of users have no need to maintain their own database, alternative methods for accessing the FMA are available.

2.1 The Foundational Model Explorer (FME)

The Foundational Model Explorer (FME) was developed for the purpose of accessing the FMA over the web [12, 13]. The interface of the FME includes a hierarchical tree displayed as an indented list on the left (see Figure 1). This allows the user to navigate through class and part relationships. (See Figure 2 for an explanation of these relationships.) Details about a selected class are displayed on the right. A text search function is also provided.

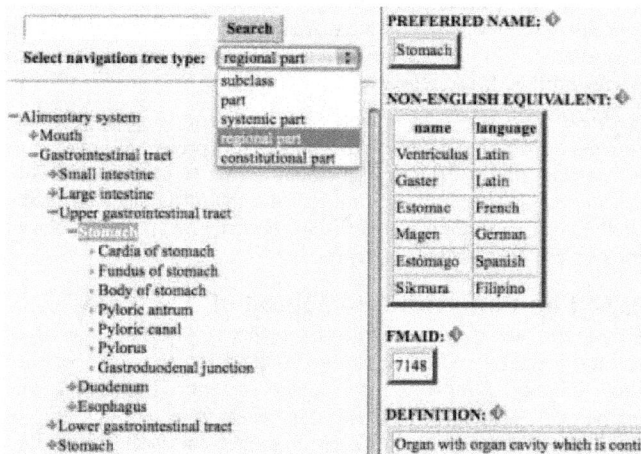

Figure 1. Interface of the FME

The FME has provided access to a weekly-updated version of the FMA for over a decade, but it has a significant number of usability issues. One participant in this study described it as

---

[1] There has been research to develop tools to assist with the task of data annotation by presenting small, relevant subsets of the FMA to annotators (for example, see [9]). However these tools will not completely replace the need for researchers to view and browse the entire FMA.

"totally non-intuitive". Another said that it "needs to more transparently distinguish regional and constitutional part hierarchies by which one entity can be represented in two different ways." This comment reflects the way these hierarchies are selected and displayed in the FME. The drop-down menu provides four options for display: regional part, constitutional part, systemic part,[2] and simply "part". This last option combines components of the regional part and constitutional part hierarchies without distinguishing them.

2.2 Node-and-link representations

The FME was constructed specifically for the FMA, but a number of more general tools for browsing ontologies also exist. One of these is the Ontology Viewer, which was created using the FMA as a demonstration ontology (Figure 3, top) [14]. Another is the FlexViz tool deployed within BioPortal, a repository of biomedical ontologies (Figure 3, bottom) [15, 16].

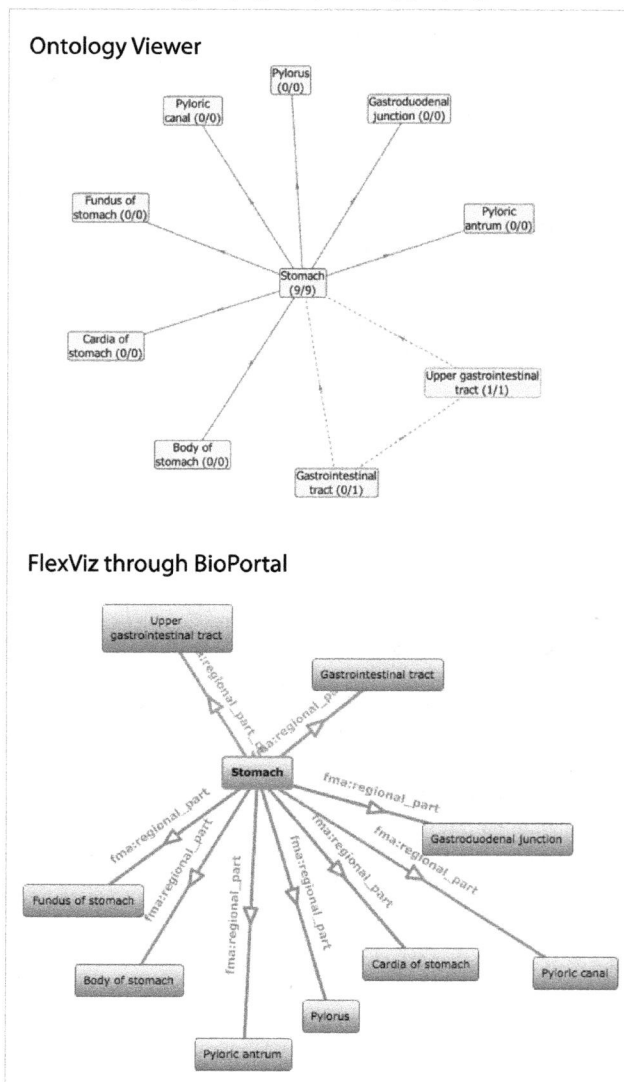

Figure 3. Node-and-link representations

---

[2] The systemic part relationship was an effort to represent functional relationships early in the development of the FMA, but has now been abandoned.

The class relationship

Each anatomical entity is a class, and these classes are arranged in a hierarchy

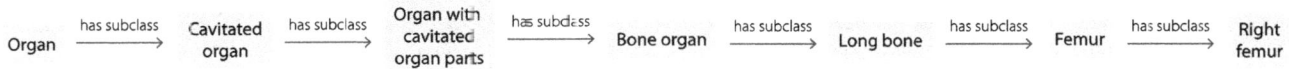

Organ → has subclass → Cavitated organ → has subclass → Organ with cavitated organ parts → has subclass → Bone organ → has subclass → Long bone → has subclass → Femur → has subclass → Right femur

The regional part relationship

Spatial subdivisions of the body

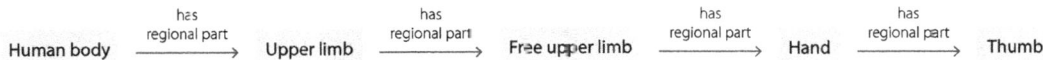

Human body → has regional part → Upper limb → has regional part → Free upper limb → has regional part → Hand → has regional part → Thumb

The constitutional part relationship

Divisions based on composition (as a structure is divided into constitutional parts, the parts become simpler in composition)

Stomach → has constitutional part → Wall of stomach → has constitutional part → Mucosa of stomach → has constitutional part → Epithelium of stomach

Figure 2. The major relationships that structure of the FMA, demonstrated by traversing different hierarchies leading to the classes Right femur, Thumb, and Epithelium of stomach

Both of these tools use node-and-link representations. They allow the FMA to be viewed as a network of different types of relationships, instead of a strictly hierarchical tree. However, because they are general-purpose tools intended for viewing any ontology, they do not reflect the domain of anatomy nor do they help to reveal the fundamental structure of the FMA. In addition, like all node-and-link representations, they become increasingly difficult to interpret as the number of visible nodes increases.

3. THE DESIGN PROCESS

The design process proceeded in two phases: an exploratory phase followed by a design phase.

3.1 Exploratory phase

The purposes of the exploratory phase were to understand the structure of the FMA, to identify the users for the browser and the types of tasks they want to perform, and to generate ideas for the design of the browser.

Two types of activities were conducted:

- Three biomedical researchers who have expert knowledge of the FMA were interviewed individually. During the interview the participant was asked to sketch a map of how they conceptualize the FMA. They were asked how they divide the FMA into "chunks", their entry point(s) when thinking about the FMA, and any important paths through the FMA. The interviews were between 45 and 60 minutes in length. Interviews were recorded, transcribed and then analyzed for themes and methods of visual representation.

- An hour-long focus group was conducted with five biomedical researchers who either have expert knowledge of the FMA or have used the FMA in their own research. In order to generate ideas for different styles of visual representation, participants were asked to sketch ideas for visualizing the FMA that were inspired by the wayfinding strategies described by David

Gibson (the Landmarks model, Streets model, Connector model, and Districts model) [17]. Architects and graphic designers use these types of strategies when constructing systems to help people navigate through physical spaces.

3.1.1 Finding 1: Anatomy and ontologies occupy separate conceptual spaces and have distinct representations

Participants drew two types of visual representations: outlines of bodies or organs (sometimes divided into regions) and node-and-link diagrams that corresponded to classes and relationships within the FMA. One participant referred to these as the "spatial" and "symbolic" representations (Figure 4), and commented, "I think it is very important for me to keep the two sides separate."

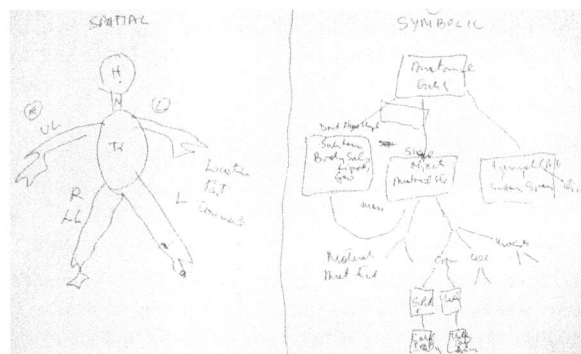

Figure 4. Example of a participant's sketch demonstrating different representations for anatomy and an ontology

These two styles of representations are products of two different conceptual spaces. The spatial representation reflects an understanding of anatomy as three-dimensional structures and their locations within the body. The symbolic representation is a collection of statements about anatomy, represented by the classes and relationships within the ontology. These two spaces can be described as "What is my understanding of anatomy itself?" and "What is my understanding of how anatomy has been modeled in the FMA?" Participants moved between these two conceptual spaces based on the topic or task of the moment.

Design implication: Provide separate entry points into the FMA to accommodate these different conceptual spaces.

3.1.2 Finding 2: The FMA has multiple entry points, and these reflect different purposes and tasks

The FME uses the class Human body as the entry point. When the FMA is displayed in general tools such as the Ontology Viewer or FlexViz, the entry point will be the class Anatomical entity at the top of the class hierarchy. But these may not be the most helpful entry points. When participants were asked where they mentally entered the FMA, they responded with several strategies. One strategy was to begin with the class Human body and move through the regional parts. Another was to begin with the organ most relevant to the class they wanted. A final strategy was to first decide which subclass of Anatomical structure (such as Organ system, Organ, or Portion of tissue) was appropriate.

Design implication: Provide several entry points into the FMA.

3.1.3 Finding 3: Three relationships are used for global navigation of the FMA

During both the interviews and the focus, group participants were asked to describe types of paths they would like to navigate through the FMA. Participants described two types of navigation: global and local. Global navigation relied on class, regional part, and constitutional part relationships to reach a class of interest. Local navigation took place around that class of interest, and could incorporate relationships such as "continuous with" for navigating through arteries or "articulates with" for bones.

Design implication: It is most critical to support navigation through the class, regional part, and constitutional part hierarchies in a browser that is primarily for finding classes of interest and understanding the structure of the FMA.

3.2 Design phase

The purposes of the design phase were to identify common sources of confusion about the structure or content of the FMA, to develop methods to represent the content of the FMA and to browse the FMA, and to validate that the emerging design made sense to researchers who are unfamiliar with the FMA.

Four types of activities took place:

- Extensive conversations were conducted with José Mejino, who has been working on the development of the FMA for over fifteen years and is currently the sole author and curator.

- An informal survey of methods for graphical representation of anatomy was undertaken. This included examining stylized representations of anatomy within collections of clip art on stock image websites and illustrations of organ systems in medical textbooks and on websites.

- Graphics and screen layouts for the interface were sketched and refined. These were shown to a total of six biomedical researchers who had some familiarity with the FMA. A

feedback session had between one and three participants and lasted between 30 and 60 minutes. These feedback sessions were also repeated at a later stage of the design process. Participants were asked to interpret the graphics I had drawn to represent FMA classes, to describe what information they would like to see on each screen, and to suggest any alternative designs for the navigation or graphics. Photos from these sessions are shown in Figure 5.

- The nearly-completed prototypes were shown to two biomedical researchers unfamiliar with the FMA. They were asked for their interpretation and feedback. These sessions lasted between 30 and 45 minutes.

Figure 5. Feedback sessions during the iterative design process, showing participants discussing graphics and sketching their ideas

3.2.1 Finding 1: A number of mismatches exist between common conceptual units and FMA classes

During the survey of methods for graphically representing anatomy a number of "common conceptual units" of anatomy were identified. These are concepts such as "heart", "kidney", or "hand" that are widely recognized by a common name and have a fairly standard graphic representation. One of my focus group participants described a similar phenomena as "salient concepts", explaining that these are "names people recognize as visible structures, and they use these to locate smaller [parts]."

After compiling a set of approximately two dozen common conceptual units, two types of mismatches between some of these common conceptual units and the corresponding class in the FMA were identified (Figure 6).

The first type of mismatch exists when the standard graphic representation conflicts with the FMA class. For example, the standard graphic of a kidney will include not just the kidney, but also sections of the ureter, renal artery, and renal vein. A graphic of a stomach will show sections of the esophagus and small intestine. This type of mismatch could lead to two difficulties. The first is that a user could assume that a class contains a part that it does not. For example, someone could navigate to the class Heart with the expectation of finding the class Aortic arch as a part of it. The second difficulty arises when designing graphics to accurately represent these classes. Figure 7 shows explorations to represent the class Stomach. Two approaches are: (a) to add context to the graphic by showing the position within the body or adding dotted lines to show the "missing" parts, and (b) to place the class within

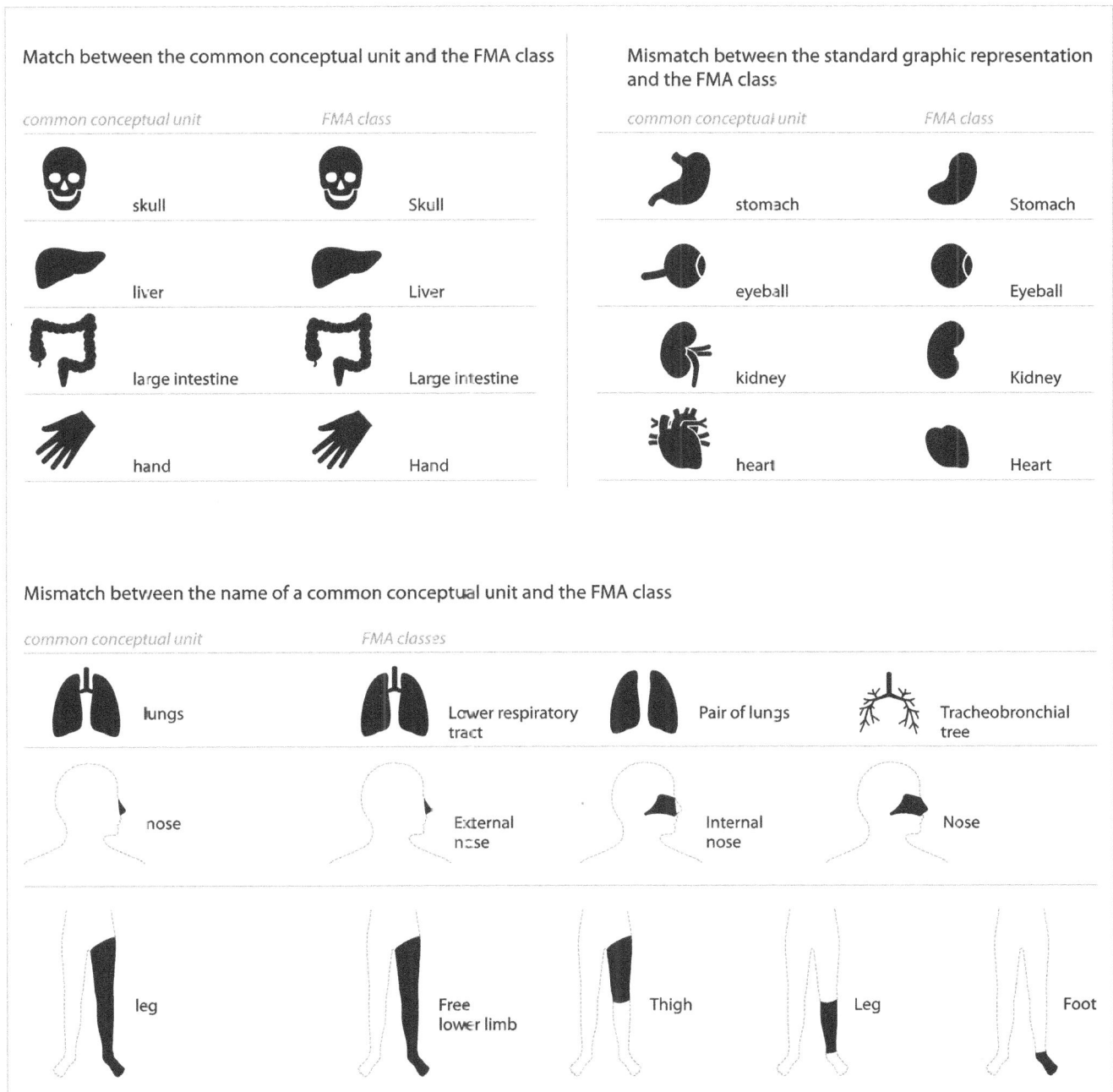

Match between the common conceptual unit and the FMA class

common conceptual unit		FMA class	
(skull)	skull	(Skull)	Skull
(liver)	liver	(Liver)	Liver
(large intestine)	large intestine	(Large intestine)	Large intestine
(hand)	hand	(Hand)	Hand

Mismatch between the standard graphic representation and the FMA class

common conceptual unit		FMA class	
(stomach)	stomach	(Stomach)	Stomach
(eyeball)	eyeball	(Eyeball)	Eyeball
(kidney)	kidney	(Kidney)	Kidney
(heart)	heart	(Heart)	Heart

Mismatch between the name of a common conceptual unit and the FMA class

common conceptual unit		FMA classes					
(lungs)	lungs	(lungs)	Lower respiratory tract	(pair of lungs)	Pair of lungs	(tracheobronchial tree)	Tracheobronchial tree
(nose)	nose	(external nose)	External nose	(internal nose)	Internal nose	(nose)	Nose
(leg)	leg	(free lower limb)	Free lower limb	(thigh)	Thigh	(leg)	Leg	(foot)	Foot

Figure 6. Comparisons of common conceptual units and the corresponding FMA class

a larger, more recognizable class, such as using a graphic for the class Gastrointestinal tract instead of Stomach.

The second type of mismatch exists when the name of a common conceptual unit does not match the corresponding FMA class, but instead refers to a different class. For example, the common conceptual unit of "leg" corresponds to the class Free lower limb. The class Leg is the regional part of the class Free lower limb between the thigh and foot.

Design implications: (a) There should be a strict correspondence between a graphic and the FMA class it represents, but this can lead to challenges in creating recognizable graphics. (b) Graphics

can help people to locate classes within the FMA even if the name of the class is unexpected.

3.2.2 Finding 2: The organ systems provide an intuitive way of entering the FMA, and these can be represented graphically

Anatomy can be taught by two methods: (a) a regional approach in which students learn about all structures within a region of a body (such as the head) before moving to the next region, or (b) a systems approach in which the organ systems (such as the cardiovascular system) are studied one at a time, regardless of

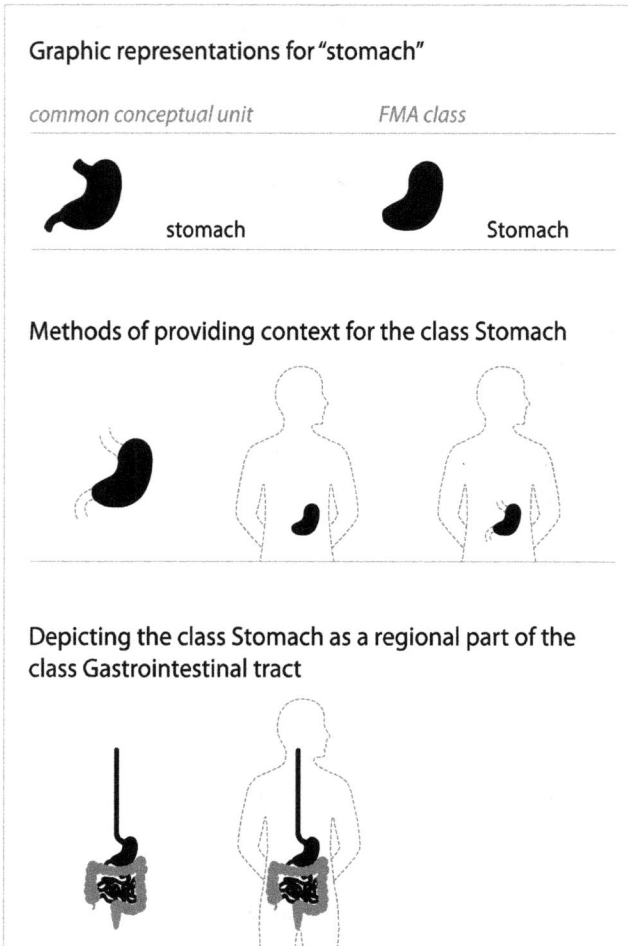

Figure 7. Graphical representations of the class Stomach

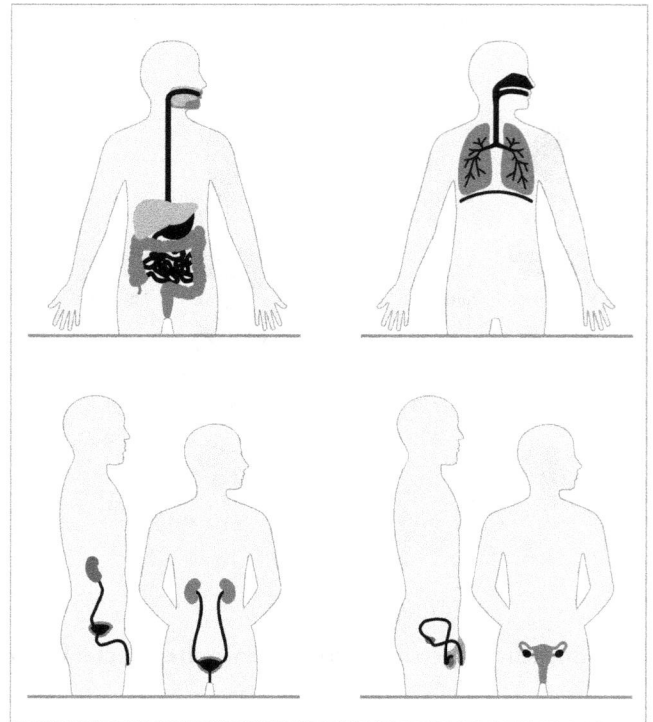

Figure 8. Examples of graphics developed for the subclasses of Organ system (Alimentary system, Respiratory system, Male and Female urinary system, Male and Female genital system

their locations within the body. This systems approach has strongly influenced how people conceptualize anatomy. In order to help align the design of the browser with people's existing understanding of anatomy, a series of graphics were designed to represent the organ systems of the FMA (see examples in Figure 8). Participants in the feedback sections were generally able to recognize the organ systems represented by the graphics, and small changes were made in response to feedback.

The FMA represents some organ systems separately for males and females. For example, the class Urinary system has subclasses Male urinary system and Female urinary system. It is important for the graphics to indicate if the organ system is represented separately for males and females, and this was successfully conveyed by using graphics that show either a single body or side-by-side male and female bodies (Figure 8).

Design implication: Graphics representing the subclasses of Organ system provide a good entry point to the FMA, and can be used to convey that some organ systems are modeled separately for males and females.

3.2.3 Finding 3: Several levels of the regional parts hierarchy can be successfully navigated using graphics if the graphics maintain context

Many participants wanted an option to select regional parts using a graphic of a human body. Therefore, several methods were explored to allow users to graphically navigate the first few levels of the regional part hierarchy. The final scheme is shown in Figure 9. Each selection reveals an additional graphic presenting the regional parts of the previous. This allows the user to return to the previous graphic and make a new selection, and it also helps to give context to the new graphic. If a series of graphics would require more screen space than is available, showing only the last two graphics (with an option to scroll to earlier graphics) was acceptable to participants.

With the exception of the initial graphic, the entire body is not shown. Each new graphic is an enlargement of the region of interest in order to prevent regions from becoming too small to display and select.

Design implication: Several levels of the regional part hierarchy can be successfully navigated using graphics.

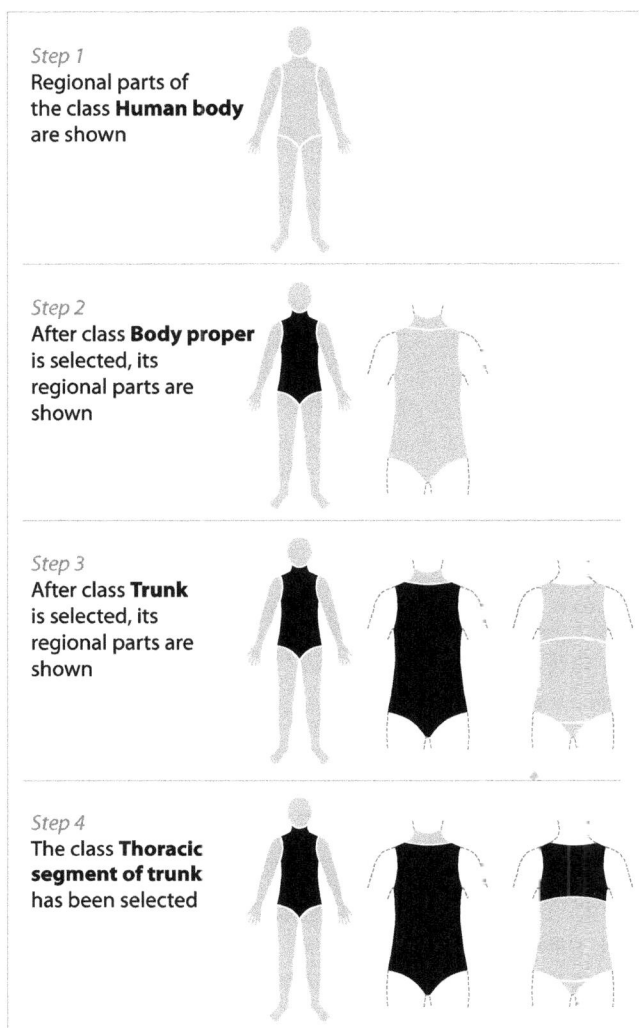

Figure 9. A scheme for selecting regional parts of the class Human Body

Step 1
Regional parts of the class **Human body** are shown

Step 2
After class **Body proper** is selected, its regional parts are shown

Step 3
After class **Trunk** is selected, its regional parts are shown

Step 4
The class **Thoracic segment of trunk** has been selected

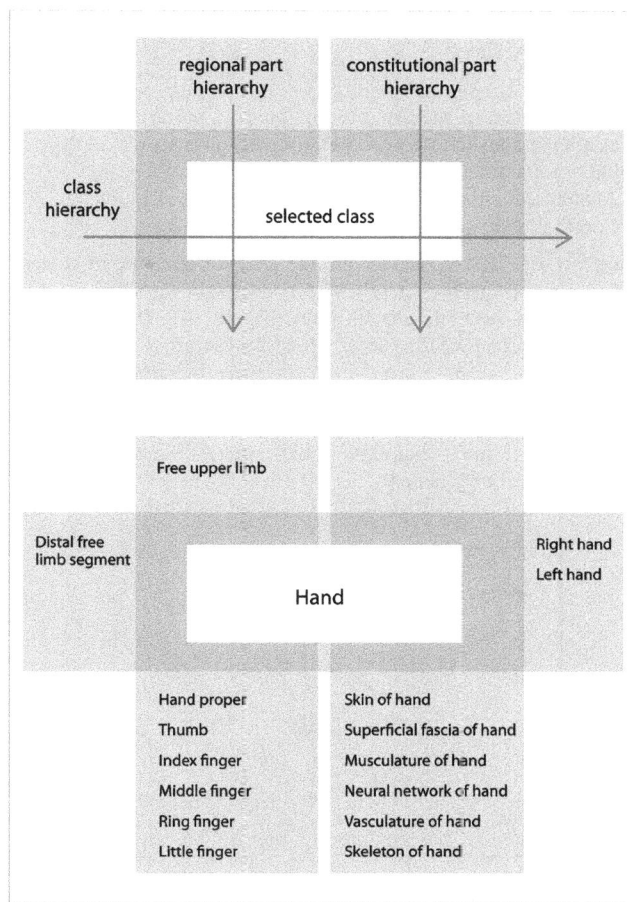

Figure 10. General layout of the hierarchy browser (top) and an example with the class Hand selected (bottom)

3.2.4 Finding 4: By centering on a single class, a browser can simultaneously display the position of that class within the three hierarchies of class, regional part, and constitutional part relationships in a way that is intuitive to users

To address the task of global navigation, participants were shown a sketch of a hierarchy browser similar to Figure 10. Participants responded favorably to this design. For participants unfamiliar with the FMA, this layout not only clarified how a single class can exist within these three hierarchies, but also helped them to understand the differences between the three hierarchies.

Design implication: The layout shown in Figure 10 will support navigation through the class, regional part, and constitutional part hierarchies and help users to understand the structure of the FMA.

4. THE DESIGN PRODUCT

The design for the FMA browser is summarized in Figure 11. The initial screen will present the user with four entry points:

- *A collection of selected classes (including Heart, Liver, Eyeball).* These classes are intended to reflect common conceptual units, particularly the major organs. Selecting a graphic will reveal the regional and constitutional parts of that class, and may also provide an explanation of that class and short list of related classes. This entry point is provided so that users can quickly compare their understanding of common conceptual units to the way they are modeled in the FMA.

- *The organ systems.* The FMA defines nine classes as subclasses of Organ system (including the Alimentary system, Respiratory system, and Musculoskeletal system). Selecting one of these graphics will reveal the names of the regional and constitutional parts of that class. For those systems modeled separately for males and females, the user must select either the male or female class for that organ system before viewing regional and constitutional parts. The Musculoskeletal system will include a graphical selector for regional parts, allowing users to navigate to classes for muscles, bones, and joints.

- *Regional parts of class Human body.* A graphic of the human body divided into regional parts will be presented. The user will navigate two to four levels into the regional part hierarchy by selecting a sequence of regions (such as Upper limb, Free upper limb, Hand).

- *The upper classes of the ontology.* For users entering from an ontology conceptual space, an option to view the upper classes as a node-and-link tree will be provided. This view will display the top five levels of the class hierarchy (from the class Anatomical entity through classes at the level of Body, Cardinal body part, Organ system, and Organ).

Once the user has navigated through a set of entry point screens with graphical displays, navigation deeper into the FMA will be done through the hierarchy browser (Figure 10). The name of a class will be displayed in the center of the hierarchy browser, and the placement of that class within the three hierarchies of class, regional part, and constitutional part relationships will be shown (Figure 10). Selecting the name of a class within one of those hierarchies will move that class to the center of the screen and the hierarchies will be updated.

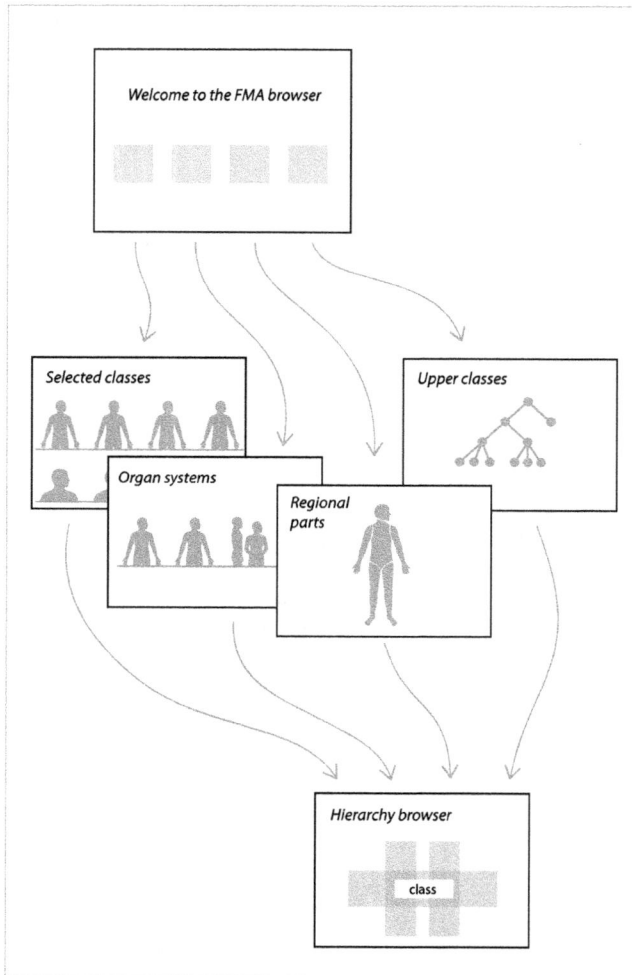

Figure 11. Summary of the design for the FMA browser

5. DISCUSSION

This project has highlighted a number of issues in the use of graphics and in navigating through hierarchies.

5.1 Using graphics at entry points, then losing the graphics

This design relies heavily on graphics to support navigation through the entry points. But navigation through the rest of the FMA is done within the hierarchy browser. There are three reasons for this design decision:

- It is labor-intensive to produce graphics, and therefore not feasible to produce graphics for all 88,000 classes. (Although it may be possible to design a system that dynamically constructs some graphics from a library of smaller parts.)

- Because the FMA continues to grow, new classes will be added and their relationships may be modified over time. The classes and hierarchical structures at the chosen entry points are not expected to change. (Although the number of classes available in the "selected classes" entry point could be expanded.) In contrast, the hierarchy browser can accommodate any new classes and modifications to relationships because the information displayed for each class will be directly retrieved from the knowledge base.

- Not all classes can be represented graphically. Most of the classes for which graphics were designed correspond to common conceptual units or their regional parts. It is much more difficult to create graphics for classes that are constitutional parts. (For example, is it possible to create a graphic for the class Mucosa of stomach that is more easily recognized than the text label itself?) Classes near to the top of the class hierarchy are also difficult to create graphics for. (How would you represent the class Solid organ, except by providing a number of examples?)

5.2 The uses of graphics: to recall knowledge or to form new knowledge

The graphics that have been created for this project are intended to act as navigation aids and should represent anatomical concepts already familiar to the user. They are not intended to provide new knowledge about anatomy. For this reason, the graphics are very stylized, with a minimal amount of detail.

This contrasts with the purpose of graphics in textbooks and anatomy atlases, where the graphics themselves are intended to support the learning of anatomy. (See [18] for a discussion of this topic.)

5.3 Visualizing multiple hierarchies

A number of other tools have been created to visualize one or more nodes that exist simultaneously within multiple hierarchies. (Reviewed in [19].) The design of the hierarchy browser that resulted from this work is distinct from these previous tools. The task that this browser will supported is very limited—viewing the neighbors of a single node within three separate hierarchies. The tasks supported by other tools are more extensive (for example, mapping the positions of multiple nodes between several hierarchies). Therefore, the tools designed by other authors tend to display larger regions of the hierarchies and they take on a variety of forms of representation (including tree maps and matrices) because they are intended to support a greater number of tasks or to visualize multiple shared nodes.

6. CONCLUSION

The work has provided insight about how people conceptualize anatomy, investigated how people want to interact with the FMA, and identified a number of non-intuitive aspects of the FMA. All of these findings had implications for the design of the interface for browsing the FMA.

The design provides multiple entry points into the FMA, relies on graphics to convey meaning for many of the classes near these entry points, and supports navigation through the class, regional part, and constitutional part hierarchies.

This design will provide a solid foundation for moving forward with implementation of the web-based browser. In addition, the design of the hierarchy browser should be applicable to browsers for other ontologies that contain both class and part relationships.

7. ACKNOWLEDGMENTS

I wish to thank my dissertation adviser Jim Brinkley, as well as José (Onard) L. V. Mejino for helpful discussions. I also thank the researchers who participated in my interviews and focus group, and two anonymous reviewers for their helpful comments.

This work was supported by a pre-doctoral training fellowship from the National Library of Medicine, T15 LM007442-10

8. REFERENCES

[1] Deville, Y., Gilbert, D., van Helden, J., and Wodak, S. J. 2003. An overview of data models for the analysis of biochemical pathways. *Briefings in Bioinformatics* 4, 3 (Sept. 2003), 246–259. DOI= http://dx.doi.org/10.1093/bib/4.3.246.

[2] Uetz, P., et al. 2000. A comprehensive analysis of protein-protein interactions in *Saccharomyces cerevisiae*. *Nature* 403: 623–627. DOI= http://dx.doi.org/10.1038/35001009.

[3] White, J. G., Southgate, E., Thomson, J. N. and Brenner, S. 1986. The structure of the nervous system of the nematode *Caenorhabditis elegans*. *Philosophical Transactions of the Royal Society of London, Series B* (Nov 1986) 314, 1165 1–340. DOI=http://dx.doi.org/ 10.1098/rstb.1986.0056.

[4] Sulston, J.E., Schierenberg, E., White, J.G., and Thomas, J.N. 1983. The embryonic cell lineage of the nematode *Caenorhabditis elegans*. *Developmental Biology* 100, 1 64–119. DOI=http://dx.doi.org/10.1016/0012-1606(83)90201-4.

[5] Pavlopoulos, G. A., Wegener, A.L., and Schneider, R. 2008. A survey of visualization tools for biological network analysis. *BioData Mining* 1, 12. DOI=http://dx.doi.org/10.1186/1756-0381-1-12.

[6] Suderman, M. and Hallett, M. 2007. Tools for visually exploring biological networks. *Bioinformatics* 23, 20 2651–2659. DOI=http://dx.doi.org/10.1093/bioinformatics/btm401.

[7] Rosse, C. and Mejino Jr., L. V. 2003. A reference ontology for biomedical informatics: the Foundational Model of Anatomy. *Journal of Biomedical Informatics* 36, 478–500. DOI=http://dx.doi.org/10.1016/j.jbi.2003.11.007.

[8] Rosse, C. and Mejino Jr., J. L. V. The Foundational Model of Anatomy Ontology, in Burger, A., Davidson, D., and Baldock, R, eds., *Anatomy Ontologies for Bioinformatics: Principles and Practice*, Springer, NewYork, 2008, 59–118.

[9] Franklin, J. D., Mejino Jr., J. L. V., Detwiler, L. T, Rubin, D. L., and Brinkley, J. F. 2008. Web service access to semantic web ontologies for data annotation. *AMIA 2008 Symposium Proceedings,* 946.

[10] Noy, N. F. Musen, M. A, Mejino Jr., J. L V., and Rosse, C. 2004. Pushing the envelope: Challenges in frame-based representation of human anatomy. Data and Knowledge Engineering 48, 3 (March 2004) 335–359. DOI = http://dx.doi.org/10.1016/j.datak.2003.06.002.

[11] Protégé ontology editor and knowledge acquisition system, developed by the Stanford Center for Biomedical Informatics Research, http://protege.stanford.edu.

[12] Detwiler, L. T., Mejino Jr, J. L. V., Rosse, C., and Brinkley, J. F. 2003. Efficient web-based navigation of the Foundational Model of Anatomy. *AMIA 2003 Symposium Proceedings*, 829.

[13] Foundational Model Explorer, developed by the Structural Informatics Group at the University of Washington, http://fme.biostr.washington.edu/FME/index.html.

[14] Yngve, G. 2008. *Visualization for biological models, simulation, and ontologies*. Doctoral dissertation. University of Washington, Seattle.

[15] Falconer, S. M., Callendar, C., and Story, M. A. 2010. A visualization service for the semantic web. *Lecture Notes in Computer Science* 6317, 554–564. DOI= http://dx.doi.org/10.1007/978-3-642-16438-5_45.

[16] BioPortal, developed by the National Center for Biomedical Ontology, http://bioportal.bioontology.org.

[17] Gibson, D. 2009. *The Wayfinding Handbook: Information Design for Public Places*. Princeton Architectural Press.

[18] Rosse, C. 1999. Anatomy Atlases. *Clinical Anatomy* 12, 293–299. DOI=http://dx.doi.org/ 10.1002/(SICI)1098-2353(1999)12:4<293::AID-CA13>3.0.CO;2-4.

[19] Graham, M. and Kennedy, J. 2009. A survey of multiple tree visualization. *Information Visualization* 9, 4 (winter 2010) 1–18. DOI=http://dx.doi.org/10.1057/ivs.2009.29.

Participatory Design in the Development of a Web-based Technology for Visualizing Writing Activity as Knowledge Work

Sarah Read
Writing, Rhetoric & Discourse
DePaul University
sread@depaul.edu

Anna DelaMerced
Human Centered
Design & Engineering
University of Washington
avmd@uw.edu

Mark Zachry
Human Centered
Design & Engineering
University of Washington
zachry@uw.edu

ABSTRACT

This study raises the question of how to make an analytical tool developed for and by researchers for visualizing writing activity as knowledge work into a useful tool for a broader community, and in particular students. The development of GEMviz, a web-based technology for creating Genre Ecology Models in research and instructional contexts, provides the context for this study. Our study examines the process of using participatory design techniques to develop GEMviz with students and researchers working in different institutions. The study illustrates a 4-stage participatory design process in which contributors voluntarily participate in varied events that contributed to the design effort, refining the technology that is meant to provide insight into the communicative practices of knowledge workers. This paper reports on this design process in light of six design and functional requirements for visualizations of writing activity and knowledge work more broadly. The paper concludes with proposing an additional design and functional requirement for visualizing writing activity and future directions for the technology.

Categories and Subject Descriptors

K.3.1 [**Computer Uses in Education**]: Computer-assisted instruction (CAI)

General Terms

Human Factors, Design, Theory

Keywords

Knowledge work, participatory design, web-based learning technologies, genre ecologies, visualizations

1. DEVELOPING TOOLS FOR VISUALIZING WRITING ACTIVITY AS KNOWLEDGE WORK

New analytical techniques for studying and understanding writing activity in knowledge work are actively being explored [2, 6, 7, 9, 10, 11, 14, 16, 21]. Since writing activity is increasingly distributed geographically, temporally and technologically, the ability to visualize this activity is essential to making it comprehensible to stakeholders, as well as for understanding how to improve and refine workflows.

An expressed aim of much of the recent research in this area is to find ways to visualize writing activity as knowledge work in order to "support writers' reasoning about their work" [11]. Studies in this vein have developed tools in different contexts and for different user groups, including workplaces [e.g., 12, 16], classroom contexts [e.g., 14] and community-based projects [e.g., 2, 7]. The development process reported on in this paper shares similarities with both classroom-based and the community-based projects. However, the design process reported on in this paper differs in that the work is guided by the overall aim of developing a useful web-based tool for a broad user group by beginning with a theoretical analytical tool developed for and by researchers.

Past efforts [11] to develop visualization tools for knowledge workers have resulted in a set of design considerations for the types of visualizations such a technology should produce. In summary, the visualizations should be 1. Data driven to depict practice in a detailed and accurate way; 2. Represented by explicit, but flexible, categories so that representations are stable enough to be shared and read by multiple people; 3. Interactive so that users can update, sort, expand, extend and refresh them during the course of a reasoning process; 4. Portable to follow around the site of work; 5. Timely in the sense of being available on demand; and 6. Able to answer key questions relevant to a given individual's needs as well as the domain or context of work.

The design of the visualization tool that is the focus of this study, GEMviz, has revealed that satisfying some of these basic functional requirements is easier than others. As this paper will develop, when implementing a theory-motivated analytical tool as a web-based technological tool, tensions arise between maintaining the theoretical validity of the tool and user-based and domain-specific functional needs. In other words, it is a challenge to develop a tool that can represent a wide range of contextually relevant data for users without losing focus on the analytical concept core to the visualization.

1.1 Genre Ecology Models

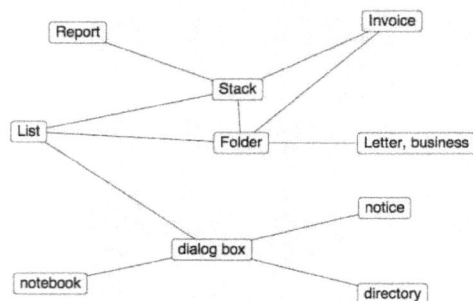

Figure 1: An informal genre ecology with sample genres [13].

The design study reported in this paper focuses exclusively on the development of GEMviz, a visualization tool that supports the creation of Genre Ecology Models (GEMs), such as in Figure 1. Genre ecologies were first introduced as a framework for conceptualizing and analyzing open systems of computer documentation [20] and subsequently refined [12, 17] as an analytical tool for visualizing knowledge work more broadly. The ecology metaphor is able to account for the dynamism and interconnectedness of multiple genres in a system, qualities that can be examined in the three interrelated dimensions of *contingency*, *decentralization* (or distribution) and *stability*.

The unit of analysis for a genre ecology is a socio-technical activity that is mediated by multiple, socially recognizable means, or genres. These multiple genres are interrelated in meditational relationships through which they co-mediate workers' activities in analyzable ways. In Figure 1, a set of generalized genres used to accomplish a hypothetical activity are represented as nodes and connected in order to represent the meditational relationships among genres. The spatial arrangement of the genres gives some indication as to the importance of the genres located in the center of the diagram to the particular work activity.

An example of a more complex, empirical example from research [17] is a GEM for the work activity of credit and collections workers at a telecommunications company. One aspect of their work is to contact customers with past due accounts and manage the documentation of deactivating and activating phone numbers. A genre ecology of these workers' activities situates the data-entry screen for the information system that tracked customer accounts at the center of the diagram, with the additional supporting meditational genres arrayed around it. A genre ecology can make visible how the data entry screens were the nexus of rippling relationships between genres in this ecology. These relationships make visible how meaning is transferred within the complex ecology of genres, making it possible for workers and managers to identify points of disruption to the work flow.

The features of the analytical tool of the genre ecology are relatively stable, although less stable features have been introduced. Stable features are illustrated in Fig. 1: the names of genres (rather than media) in otherwise blank "bubbles," or nodes, the 2-D arrangement of these bubbles, often, but not always, around a central controlling genre, and simple connector lines showing the existence of a meditational relationship between these genres. Less stable features [17] include arrows on connector lines between genre bubbles indicating directionality in the meditational relationship, and line thickness and numbers

hovering near a connector line to indicate the frequency of a meditational relationship between genres in the data.

Given that the features of a genre ecology are not rigidly defined, one of the core questions shaping the participatory design process of GEMviz, a genre ecology modeling tool, was what features should a web-based tool include? In other words, what qualities of a genre ecology visualization tool seem desirable for providing meditational support to a broad community of writers and researchers? This question drove the participatory design process for developing GEMviz.

The rest of this paper reports on the unique participatory design process of developing a visualization tool for a broad set of users, in particular students, from a theory-motivated analytical tool that was originally created for and by researchers.

2. PARTICIPATORY DESIGN WITH USERS IN MULTIPLE CONTEXTS

Since its inception, the development of GEMviz has followed a process in line with participatory design. Its development has involved both students and researchers in all phases of work, from ideation and initial design to development and contextual design studies. This development process is in line with recent calls to expand participation in design [5]. Unlike commercial design processes, this work has relied on the voluntary contributions of interested parties over time. Development work, consequently, has occurred in spurts, roughly corresponding to cycle times associated with academic calendars. At the same time, the project has benefitted from the motivated contributions of individuals who represent the envisioned end-users of the tool. Designing with a community of users is always a challenging process, but one that can yield better systems for the community who will benefit from the system under development [15].

In addition to following a design process that values the participation of individuals from multiple contexts, the process has also notably followed an open source paradigm in which the code base and related project resources have been available to interested parties.

3. THE DESIGN PROCESS
3.1 User Interviews

A key user group consulted in the development process was researchers who have addressed genre formations in papers published in the proceedings of ACM's Special Interest Group on the Design of Communication (SIGDOC) over the preceding 10 years. Interviewees were asked about the tools that they use to visualize writing activity in both their teaching and research practices. The purpose of these interviews was to understand how researchers knowledgeable about the theory of genre formations—including genre ecologies—used this knowledge in their research and instructional practices and to discern their values for a tool that could support this work.

The interviews with seven individuals, conducted during the spring of 2011, focused on current teaching practices and desired resources for supporting future teaching practices. When asked more specifically about teaching with genre ecology models, the interviewees provided details about how these models fit into the kinds of learning experiences they desire for their students. One interviewee describes his motivation for teaching with GEMs:

"I think the main reason for doing this kind of research or teaching is to help folks better understand the complexity of mediation, that things aren't simple or seamless, that there are ad-hoc genres that populate the real world and if those things aren't maps, then you can't truly understand how work is mediated in a given environment they are studying."

Teaching the logic of GEMS, however, is not a simple task because it represents a way of thinking about the mediation of knowledge in society that is not familiar to many undergraduates. One of our interviewees describes the challenge, "Students always have trouble getting their heads around this idea of genre ecologies. Like I said, they mix it up with medium, text, and sometimes even with actions, so they're looking for a really simple anchor and it's hard to kind of break them out of that."

Another interviewee offers some insight into how she works around this challenge:

"Whenever I start thinking about those maps, I always have some kind of narrative to go along with it, like a story…The thing that's usually missing from all of that is a story, and people usually don't have a shared narrative or some sort of common ground on what's happening…So we used the maps as a way to guide us through the story to talk about what's going on and how its going on."

In these interviews, we asked general questions about experiences with creating genre ecology models. The challenges described by individuals suggest that a tool for doing this kind of analytical work would be valued. As one interviewee describes her process,

"I typically read through a bunch of data and try to figure stuff out and I'll just start sketching on paper and I use different tools—whatever tool that happens to be on my desktop. I then hand that off to a colleague and ask them if it makes sense—like "Are the stencils I have created representative, does it look like what it should look like, can you understand what I'm trying to explain here?" The downside is that it doesn't automatically happen. You kind of just get lost in making sure the shape looks perfect and everything is aligned perfectly, and you've lost a day you will never get back, but your diagram is perfect. Something that will make that "automagic" would be awesome."

These challenges for the interviewees (all of whom create such models for their own research in addition to teaching them) translate into instructional issues in the classroom. One interviewee draws the connection between the effort required to create such models and students' willingness to iterate on their model designs:

"It takes a lot of work to make them look nice when they're using drawing tools. So its harder to get them to revise them too because they put so much effort into it they don't want to take it apart. If an ecology is alive, it's literally changing, so any one picture is just a snapshot away."

The challenges expressed by these interviewees strongly influenced our thinking about the design of the visualizer as it was being developed. The interview data made it obvious to us that there would be significant issues to be addressed in the design of a tool that would complement the needs of these researchers-educators, but that there would also be real value in a system that addressed those needs. As another of our interviewees expressed, "If I could send students somewhere and say "Okay, I've got this ecology that I've got to map" and they start to play around with the tool you guys are creating, then that would be really useful—that would cut down my time spent talking about how to do this exponentially."

These interviews informed design thinking during a development process that was guided by repeated interactions with people who were the likely users of such a system. As described below, this process included the creation of interaction prototypes that were tested with potential users, the development of high-fidelity wireframes that represented the ideas and needs of potential users, and deployment studies to understand the value of the tools when it was embedded in the learning activities of students. In addition, the development process also included the creation of an auxiliary tool to foster social interaction among individuals engaged in the work of creating GEMs.

Throughout this development process, that cast of individuals involved changed. Because the tool itself is being designed for researchers who have no official ties to one another and who work in varied institutional contexts and because the design work itself involves students who are engaged in the process to learn, a varied and dynamic group of people have participated in the design. While this fact added complications to the project, it also significantly broadened the range of users who had input into the development of the tool.

3.2 Representative User Prototype Feedback

Early in the development process, graduate students involved in the project treated themselves as representatives of the potential user population. In 2010, these students associated with the project talked with other project students to create initial design ideas. In this initial phase of developing GEMviz, the students engaged in task-focused, design artifact-based interviews with other students. These interviews were designed to discover basic design considerations in how students (as representative users) would likely use a ecology model building tool, including their thought processes and assumptions about a tool interface and functionality.

These interviews used a scenario to motivate interaction with sketches of design ideas. Students asked about the designs were asked to indicate how they would use features represented in the sketched design to do such things as create nodes in a diagram, associate one node with another via a connecting edge, and label nodes in the diagram. Through this process, the team discovered how potential users of the system reasoned about performing tasks with potential system interfaces for GEMviz. The team also learned about how new users would likely interpret interface elements upon first exposure to them.

After considering the responses of participants in this phase of the development process, the team developed higher fidelity wireframe representations of the system for additional research with students.

3.3 Potential User Opinions about High-fidelity Wireframes

To further explore the value of the emerging design for the visualization tool, the team created high fidelity wireframe prototypes of the planned system (See Figure 3 for an example).

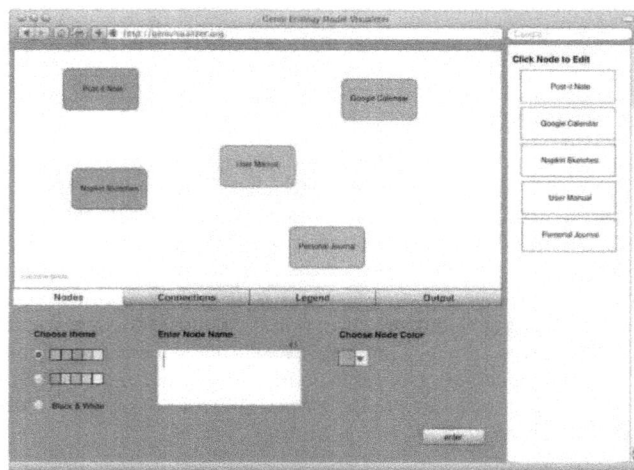

Figure 3. High-fidelity wireframe used to solicit responses to the design.

Those who saw these high-fidelity wireframes were free to give their opinions about them, such as

- perceived affordances of GEMviz based on the wireframe images
- interpretations of interface elements
- descriptions of anticipated actions with the system to achieve supportable goals
- desired features not included in the design

3.4 Working Prototype Development

Based on opinions gathered from students as potential users of a new system, a working version of GEMviz was developed in 2011 [1]. This initial version of the tool included the most fundamental functionality of the tool, but realized a fully working prototype deployed on the Web. In this version of GEMviz, which is further described in the classroom deployment studies below, allowed users to create basic GEMs with annotatable nodes and connector lines. The nodes and their related connector lines can be repositioned, causing the overall GEM to change shape and character based on the user's desires. Additional editing functionality, such as the ability to color code nodes or to provide a legend, were not included in this initial prototype. Later in this paper, we identify next steps in the design process for GEMviz based on deployment studies in which we gathered feedback on the design of this system from students.

Concurrent with the build of this working prototype version of the visualizer, an additional tool that allowed for sharing of GEMs was developed (Fig. 4). This tool, a social gallery for sharing and commenting on the work of other GEM researchers, was designed to support conversations among the dispersed individuals who were employing this technique and/or teaching it to students.

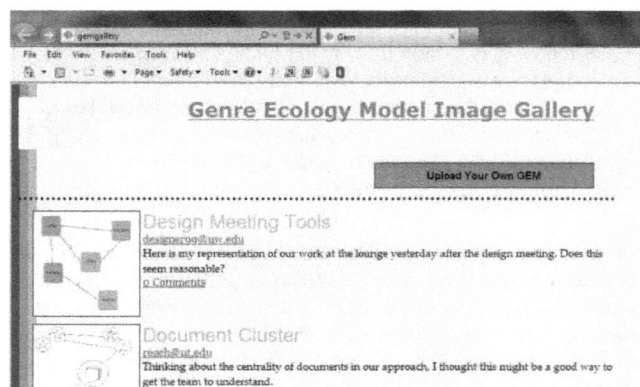

Figure 4. Working prototype of the GEM Gallery tool, designed to support social exchanges of ideas around working using this technique.

Adding this social dimension to GEMviz responded to a perceived user need discovered inadvertently during interactions with participants during earlier phases of the research. It became clear during the interviews that there was very little awareness of work being done in this area by researchers and students at other institutions. The fact that this technique was typically being used in relative isolation, we determined, limited the potential value of an online tool that would similarly only be used in discrete instances. Desiring to make the tool more relevant to a broader user base, and hoping to have that wider population participate in the future design of GEMviz, the visualization tool was bundled with a gallery (Fig. 4) in which people could have open exchanges about the GEMs.

4. FIELD DEPLOYMENT IN THE CLASSROOM

To better understand the value of GEMviz as a tool for training students to be more rhetorically aware knowledge workers, one of the authors used a working prototype version of the tool within the context of a class on writing in workplace contexts. Her goal was to use the tool both to teach the underlying theoretical concept of the genre ecology as well as have students use the tool to generate representations of data from their research sites.

4.1 Course Context

GEMs have been used as teaching tools in a variety of classroom contexts at the graduate and the undergraduate levels. The course was a 300-level undergraduate course called "Writing in Workplace Contexts" populated by Writing, Rhetoric & Discourse majors, minors and non-majors. The course was framed as a Writing Studies course that introduces students to the study of writing in workplace settings, while at the same time exposing students to conventional styles and genres of professional writing. Students assumed the role of writing researchers and chose a field site at which to research writing. Over a 10-week quarter, students learned fieldwork methods and analytical tools, including the genre ecology model (GEM). In this pedagogical context, GEMs were introduced as tools for researching the activity of workplace writing.

The GEM was introduced during the unit on genre as a tool for making visible the "ecology" of genres that mediated work activity at the students' field site. Introducing the concept and the practice of making GEMs, supported two course objectives. That students would be able to 1. Identify and analyze the genres of writing that constitute a workplace, profession or industry; and 2. Explain how these genres are (inter)related. In short, a GEM functioned as a researcher's tool for making visible the multiple genres that mediate work activity at the student's field site and for mapping how they are interrelated.

4.2 Affordances and Limitations of GEMviz for Novice Users

In this course the concept of a GEM was taught independently of the GEMviz tool. This meant that students were introduced to the concept of visualizing assemblages of genres [18], and GEMs in particular, and then offered the prototype version of GEMviz as one tool for generating their representation of workplace writing activity at their field sites. In addition, students were introduced to GEMs within the context of other theory-motivated tools from writing studies, such as intertextuality and genre sets [3] and internal and external sources of meaning in organizational communication [4]. Students spent time in class "playing around" with the GEMviz tool as a first attempt to visualize how multiple genres at their field sites are interrelated. Given the course context and content, the GEMviz tool presented both affordances and limitations for meeting the objectives of the course. Working through these affordances and limitations in a classroom setting produced additional findings on the desirable features for a gene ecology visualization tool that resonate with the basic functional requirements for such a tool [11] and the user comments in Section 3.1.

4.2.1 Affordances

Ethos: Students were intrigued by working with a web-based app that is in "beta" development by real researchers. Since the course already framed students as researchers, participating in tool development, however indirectly, reinforced their positioning within this ethos. In addition, students were given insight into the development process of tools for research, and a taste of the rhetorical and dynamic nature of analytical tools.

Limited functionality: The version of GEMviz accessible to students in the class had a limited functionality to create and name genre "bubbles," or nodes, to position these bubbles in a 2D space and to link the bubbles with a connector tool. The limited functionality of the prototype GEMviz tool had the advantage of limiting students' attention to the multiple genres and their mediational relationships for any given workplace activity. In a course where students were introduced to, and encouraged to synthesize multiple analytical tools, the limited functionality of the prototype GEMviz tool was effective for reinforcing a focus on the concept of mediation, a difficult concept for undergraduates to take up quickly. Such a limited functionality resisted hybrid maps that blend, and often confuse, theoretical concepts, such as mediation, intertextuality and internal and external sources of meaning. Figure 5 is an example of a GEM produced by a student in class using GEMviz of a fencing company's operations.

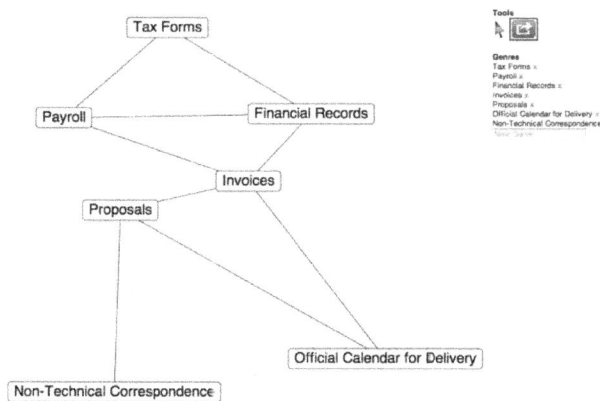

Figure 5: A student GEM of a fencing company's operations, including the GEMviz user interface.

Accessibility: As a web-based tool, GEMviz use was not limited to the classroom space or dependent upon the specifications of a personal or campus lab computer. Thus far in development, however, the prototype tool had accessibility problems, which will be addressed below.

4.2.2 Limitations

Limited Functionality: Although the limited functionality of the tool forced the exclusion of visualizing elements that deviated from the most stable form of a GEM [19], the tool does not have the functionality to distinguish between different types of mediatory relationships among genres [8, 17]. When the tool was introduced to students after a discussion of the various types of mediatory relationships between genres, students were quick to ask whether they are restricted to using the GEMviz tool, or whether they could use a tool with more functionality to represent a variety of mediatory relationships.

The tool also resisted the representation of other empirical data that students gathered from their field sites. In particular, the tool resisted the representation of contextual boundaries (such as internal and external organizational boundaries) or the sequentiality of genres. Using other visualization tools, students used boxes, connector lines with arrows and "flow chart" arrows to represent this data. In other words, the tool resists the creation hybrid maps that are inclusive of less stable features of genre ecologies, but that are heuristically more intuitive for students. This limitation points to the advantages of using more flexible tools for creating visualizations, such as MS PowerPoint and Visio.

Figure 6 is an example of a student GEM built in MS PowerPoint. The activity that the map represents is named by the genre at the center of the diagram, "Grant," and refers to collaborative grant-writing at an educational institution. The various boxes and connectors arrayed around this genre are components (not necessarily all genres) of the activity of grant writing at this organization. The boxes are color-coded based on their unique relationship to the central genre. These relationships are explained in the key adjacent to the map.

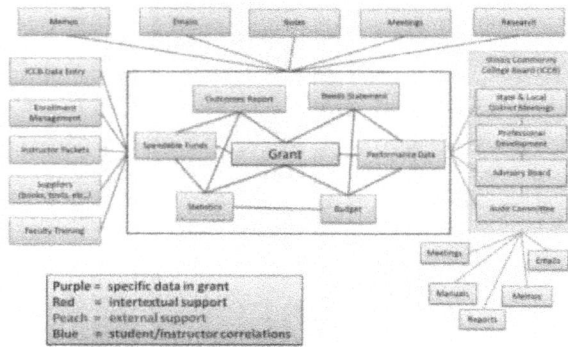

Figure 6: A hybrid GEM developed using MS PowerPoint.

While this map would not be in direct conversation with other more orthodox GEMs, it does present a richer and more contextually specific visualization of the elements that constitute the activity of grant writing at this organization. As a heuristic tool for students developing conclusions about writing activity in a particular workplace context, hybrid maps enabled a more complex synthesis of data that included more fluid understandings of genres and the types of relationships among elements. Finally, and in keeping with the research frame of the course, by building more flexible visualizations students also became theory and tool producers as they critiqued and adapted the analytical tools of scholars to the conditions of their own field research.

Scope: The application of activity theory-based analysis to any set of empirical data raises the problem of scope. A tool that limited users to the representation of finely grained data, such as the names of genres and the relationships among particular genres mediating a discrete activity, limited the scope of representation to a local activity in which contextual representation (such as internal and external organizational boundaries) had no bearing. For the representation of activity at an organizational or even industry level, however, such boundaries were important. Figure 7 shows a GEM built with the GEMviz tool that demonstrates the potential for an overlay of contextual information with a simple boxing tool. This GEM was generated by taking a screen shot of the original GEMviz representation and using another application to overlay the contextual information.

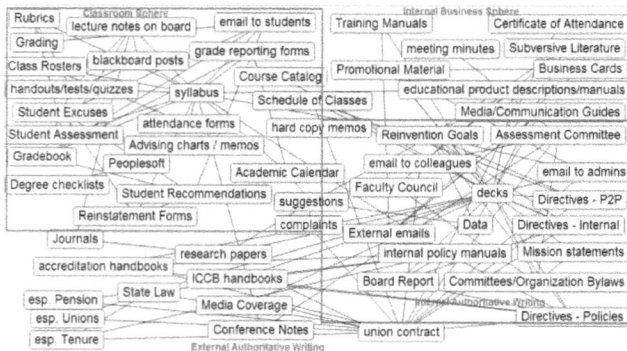

Figure 7: Analysis of the GEM created for this research site revealed four distinct, but related, writing environments within the organization (marked by the red boxes and labels).

Accessibility: Students had trouble getting the tool to work reliably, and in particular on PCs. This unreliability was a serious limitation for students who expected to be able to do their classwork at any time and from anywhere. When this prototype version of GEMviz failed to meet this expectation, they quickly found alternative tools for mapping their field data.

4.3 Design Recommendations from Deployment Observations

Based on these experiences using GEMviz with students in 3 classes during the 2011-2012 academic year, we have identified new features for development, including the functionality to:

1. Delete genre bubbles (nodes) and connectors
2. Duplicate GEMs easily
3. Draw lines, boxes and other overlaying design objects to annotate GEMs with contextual boundaries and other similar data
4. Create color fills for genre bubbles (nodes), and differently colored connectors to visualize different types of mediatory relationships
5. Indicate directionality for connectors (arrows)
6. Insert text boxes that are differentiated from genre bubbles (nodes) in order to caption the GEM
7. Support collaborative design and other social activities.

5. ADAPTING AN ANALYTICAL TOOL FOR RESEARCHERS FOR A BROADER COMMUNITY OF USERS

The participatory design process for developing GEMviz has produced interesting outcomes for the six design and functional requirements [11] laid out in the introduction. This section will review those six requirements and propose a seventh requirement that is suggested by this study.

5.1 How Does GEMviz Stack Up?

Data driven to depict practice in a detailed and accurate way: The tool satisfies this requirement in its fundamental design. Genres identified in the field as mediating a work activity are directly transposed into the genre nodes produced by the tool. The number of nodes increases linearly with the number of genre identified. This regular feature of the tool enables the emergence of visible patterns in the data either across multiple GEMs or within one.

Represented by explicit, but flexible categories so that representations are stable enough to be shared and read by multiple people: This requirement is linked to the first one, in the sense that the tool interface enforces a standardized representation of genres and the links among them ensuring consistency among diagrams. On the other hand students in the field deployment often found that the tool was too rigid, or limited, in its options for representing genres and how they are linked. Often, students turned to another tool that enabled "hybrid" maps to more fully represent the complexity of their data from their field sites. These rigidities can be addressed in the next development cycle of the tool.

Interactive so that users can update, sort, expand, extend and refresh during the course of a reasoning process. The functional interactivity of the tool was addressed during the working prototype development phase with the design of the social gallery. These features are not yet built into the working prototype, but are slated for the next development cycle.

Portable to follow around the site of work and available on demand. By design, GEMviz is a Web 2.0 tool, which by definition accommodate these two design and functional requirements.

Able to answer key questions relevant to the individual's needs as well as the domain or context of work. This is the most complex requirement in terms of developing a tool for a broad user community that is based on a theory-motivated tool developed for and by researchers. As the interviews with the researchers and the classroom deployment revealed, the theoretical concept behind genre ecologies—mediation—is difficult for novice users to grasp. However, understanding this concept is essential to a meaningful and collaborative use of the tool. Short of this understanding, users will turn to tools that are more accommodating to their intuitive understanding of their field data.

The willingness of users to choose alternative, more flexible tools reveals both an affordance and a limitation of GEMviz: On the one hand, the tool enforces a narrow implementation of genres and mediation; on the other hand, the tool does not include support for users to expand their understanding of mediation or to accommodate how mediatory relationships between genres are represented to be context-sensitive. The question remains whether it is important for users to use the tool heuristically for any pay-off or learning about their data, or whether it is important that users are limited to a reasoning process about mediation. This stand-off points to a seventh design and functional requirement for a visualization tool designed for a broad community to best support research and reasoning about knowledge work.

5.2 A Proposed Seventh Design and Functional Requirement

This study points to a proposed seventh design and functional requirement for visualizations that support writing activity, or knowledge work more generally: *Intuitive and/or includes instructional support for the conceptual foundation behind the tool.*

This requirement suggests an additional cycle of participatory design in order to implement design and content elements that would support users' understanding of the theoretical concepts behind the tool. In the case of GEMviz, these elements would support the concepts of genre, genre formations and mediation.

In addition to providing conceptual support to users, these additional elements would also serve to intervene in the persuasive process of getting users to follow-through on their reasoning using this tool, as the supporting elements would educate users about the reasoning process at the same time that they learned how to operate the features of the tool. The GEM Gallery Tool (Figure 4) is designed to address these social needs for interacting around models, but it has not yet been studied in conjunction with GEMviz.

6. FUTURE OPPORTUNITIES

As described in this study, GEMviz has been developed following a participatory design process with the intention of creating a web-based tool to render meditational aspects of communicative interactivity visible for a broad community. Its participatory

design process is unique in that it has implemented the transformation of an analytical tool developed by researchers into a tool that meets the design and functional requirements necessary to serve the needs of users in multiple contexts. As articulated in this study, the development of this tool is not finished and new design goals have already been articulated.

The code base for GEMviz is now available on GITHub, where interested parties could follow the development directions identified here or pursue their own development agendas. Such work is likely to be pursued by the authors within their institutional contexts based on student interest and motivation to engage in the work to be done.

7. REFERENCES

[1] Abrahamsen, P., DelaMerced, A., Divine. D., Nguyen, C., and Zachry, M. 2011. Designing a system to create a community: the GEMviz project. In *Proceedings of the 29th ACM international conference on Design of communication (SIGDOC '11)*. ACM, New York, NY, USA, 289-290.

[2] Diehl, A., Grabill, J.T., Hart-Davidson, W., Iyer, V. 2008. Grassroots: Supporting the knowledge work of everyday life. *Technical Communication Quarterly*, 17(4), 413-434.

[3] Devitt, A. J. 1991. Intertextuality in tax accounting. In C. Bazerman & J. Paradis (Eds.), *Textual Dynamics of the Professions* (pp. 336-357). Madison: The University of Wisconsin Press.

[4] Driskill, L. 1989. Understanding the writing context in organizations. In M. Kogen (Ed.), *Writing in the Business Professions* (pp. 125-145): NCTE.

[5] Fischer, G. 2011. Beyond interaction: meta-design and cultures of participation. In *Proceedings of the 23rd Australian Computer-Human Interaction Conference (OzCHI '11)*. ACM, New York, NY, USA, 112-121.

[6] Geisler, S., Slattery, S. 2007. Capturing the activity of digital writing. In *Digital Writing Research: Technologies, Methodologies, and Ethical Issues*. Hampton Press. 185-200.

[7] Grabill, J.T. 2010. On being useful: Rhetoric and the work of engagement. In J. Ackerman & D. Coogan (Eds.), *The Public Work of Rhetoric: Citizen-scholars and Civic Engagement*. Columbia: University of South Carolina Press, 193-208.

[8] Gygi, K., & Zachry, M. (2010). Productive tensions and the regulatory work of genres in the development of an engineering communication workshop in a transnational corporation. *Journal of Business and Technical Communication*, 24, 358-381.

[9] Hart-Davidson, W. Modeling document-mediated interaction. *Proceedings of the 20th Annual ACM International Conference on Design of Communication (SIGDOC'02)*, Toronto, Ontario, Canada, 60-71.

[10] Hart-Davidson, W. Seeing the project: Mapping patterns of intra-team communication events. *Proceedings of the 21st Annual ACM International Conference on Design of Communication (SIGDOC'03)*, San Francisco, CA, 28-34.

[11] Hart-Davidson, W., Spinuzzi, C., & Zachry, M. 2006. Visualizing writing activity as knowledge work: Challenges and opportunities. *Proceedings of the 24th Annual ACM International Conference on Design of Communication*

(SIGDOC'06), Myrtle Beach, South Carolina. ACM, New York, NY, USA, 70-77.

[12] Hart-Davidson, W., Spinuzzi, C., & Zachry, M. 2007. Capturing and visualizing knowledge work: Results and implications of a pilot study of proposal writing activity. In *Proceedings of the 25th Annual ACM International Conference on Design of Communication (SIGDOC'07)*. ACM, New York, NY, USA, 113-119.

[13] Hart-Davidson, W., Spinuzzi, C., & Zachry, M. 2009. Visualizing patterns of group communication. In *Digital Writing* (workshop packet). Penn State University: RSA 2009 Workshop.

[14] Kaufer, D., Ishizaki, S., Collins, J., Vlachos, P. 2004. Teaching language awareness in rhetorical choice: Using IText and visualization in classroom genre assignments. *Journal of Business and Technical Communication*. 18(3), 361-402.

[15] Merkel, C. B., Xiao, L., Farooq, U., Ganoe, C. H., Lee, R., Carroll, J. M., & Rosson, M. B. 2004. Participatory design in community computing contexts: tales from the field. In *Proceedings of the eighth conference on Participatory design: Artful integration: interweaving media, materials and practices - Volume 1 (PDC 04)*, Vol. 1. ACM, New York, NY, USA, 1-10.

[16] Slattery, S. Research methods for revealing patterns of mediation. *Proceedings of the 21st Annual ACM International Conference on Design of Communication (SIGDOC'03)*, San Francisco, CA, 35-38.

[17] Spinuzzi, C. 2002. Modeling genre ecologies. In *Proceedings of the 20th Annual ACM International Conference on Design of Communication*, Toronto, Canada. ACM, New York, NY, USA, 200-207.

[18] Spinuzzi, C. 2004. Four ways to investigate assemblages of texts: Genre sets, systems, repertoires, and ecologies. In *SIGDOC' 04: Proceedings of the 22th Annual International Conference on Design of Communication*, Memphis, TN.

[19] Spinuzzi, C., Hart-Davidson, W., & Zachry, M. 2006. Chains and ecologies: methodological notes toward a communicative-mediational model of technologically mediated writing. In *Proceedings of the 24th ACM international conference on Design of communication (SIGDOC '06)*. ACM, New York, NY, USA, 43-50.

[20] Spinuzzi, C., & Zachry, M. 2000. Genre ecologies: An open-system approach to understanding and constructing documentation. In ACM *Journal of Computer Documentation*. Vol. 24, No. 3.

[21] Wilson, G., & Herndl, C. G. 2007. Boundary objects as rhetorical exigence: Knowledge mapping and interdisciplinary cooperation at Los Alamos National Laboratory. *Journal of Business and Technical Communication*. 21(2), 129-154.

[22] Zachry, M., Hart-Davidson, W. & Spinuzzi, C. 2008. Advances in understanding knowledge work: An experience report. In *Proceedings of the 26th ACM International Conference on Design of Communication (SIGDOC '08)*. ACM, New York, NY, USA, 243-248.

A Qualitative Metasynthesis of Activity Theory in SIGDOC Proceedings 2001–2011

Jennifer Stewart[1]
jlstewart2@bsu.edu

Nicki Litherland Baker[1]
nlbaker2@bsu.edu

Sarah Chaney[1]
sechaney@bsu.edu

Elmar Hashimov[1]
ehashimov@bsu.edu

Elizabeth Imafuji[1]
elfager@bsu.edu

Brian McNely[2]
brian.mcnely@gmail.com

Laura Romano[1]
ljromano@bsu.edu

Ball State University[1]
Department of English
Muncie, IN 47306

University of Kentucky[2]
Writing, Rhetoric, and Digital Media
Lexington, KY 40506

ABSTRACT

Activity theory has become an increasingly important theoretical framework for practitioners and researchers in a wide variety of fields. Offering a set of tools for exploring and theorizing everyday practice, activity theory has proven to be a useful lens for exploring how various artifacts and genres mediate social practices. This article systematically analyzes the use of activity theory by researchers publishing work in the ACM SIGDOC proceedings between 2001 and 2011. By paying attention to the cultural-historical situatedness of a given author, his or her terminology, and the ostensible function of activity theory within each piece, a more comprehensive understanding of the adaptive nature of activity theoretical approaches to design of communication emerges. And as activity theory continues to be used within disciplines relevant to design of communication, a framework for understanding both the previous and potential roles of activity theory in the scholarly literature is needed and is provided, in part, by our analysis.

Categories and Subject Descriptors

A.1 [**General**]: Introduction and Survey H.1.1.[**Models and Principles**]:Systems and Information Theory—*General systems theory, Information theory, Value of information*

General Terms

Theory

Keywords

activity theory, information ecologies, genre, lineage, terminology, function, writing

1. INTRODUCTION

Researchers in professional and technical communication have called on activity theory in their work for well over a decade. As this theoretical frame has been used to help understand everyday practices in a variety of communication design contexts, reflecting on how the frame itself is used within the discipline can provide useful direction to researchers and practitioners interested in continuing and expanding such approaches. Our research team, therefore, has systematically reviewed activity theoretical approaches to design of communication by analyzing ten years of SIGDOC articles that invoke activity theory.

Because activity theory is used within several disciplines, this review offers researchers and practitioners an understanding of the disciplinary norms of activity theory as an analytic frame. In the remainder of this paper, we will present a review of activity theory and detail the methods and methodology of our qualitative metasynthesis. We will then analyze the cultural-historical orientation of this purposeful sample of SIGDOC authors, considering in particular the ways in which they attend to activity theoretical terminology in their work. Finally, we will examine three of the key ways that activity theory functions within the sample articles: 1. as a primary theoretical frame; 2. as positioned alongside other theories; or 3. as a site for theoretical revision and expansion.

2. OVERVIEW OF ACTIVITY THEORY

For more than eight decades, the influence of activity theory has spread across a wide range of disciplines, such as behavioral psychology, education, technical and professional communication, human-computer interaction, and writing studies, to name just a few. Activity theory accounts for a number of notions that have proven helpful in several fields studying human activities: human subjects engage in intentional, complex, technology- and sign-mediated activity systems and work to achieve various objectives while being situated historically and culturally in the world [10, p. 10]. Moreover, technology and sign systems do not simply inform human activities, but rather shape them and intertwine with them organically in the world [16, p. 10].

As of 2012, activity theory is a commonly accepted approach across several disciplines. Spinuzzi contends that the popularity of using activity theory as a theoretical and methodological frame among technical and professional communication researchers stems from its ability to offer a "sociocultural case-study framework for writing studies" [29, p. 450]. Indeed, having a common framework allows researchers in the field to speak about mediated activities in a meaningful way and/or to theorize by using a common language [cf. 17]. For this analysis, however, it is important to establish, as best as possible, what exactly "activity theory" means for those within the design of communication community who use it. Engeström provides a helpful way to demarcate the development of activity theory: he suggests that

> the evolution of activity theory may be seen in terms of three generations, each building on its own version of the unit of analysis... The first generation built on Vygotsky's notion of mediated action. The second generation built on Leont'ev's notion of activity system. The third generation, emerging in the past 15 years or so, built on the idea of multiple interacting activity systems focused on a partially shared object. [4, p. 306–307]

Activity theory has therefore developed over time, and as we will discuss, aspects of both second and third generation activity theory were present in our sample, with preferred activity theory terminology changing slightly over the decade of research we investigated.

With our analysis, we argue that establishing patterns of the use of activity theory within work published in the last decade of SIGDOC Proceedings serves several important purposes. First, doing so develops an understanding of activity theoretical approaches that can be used broadly by researchers studying design of communication. Second, exploring activity theoretical articles in the field and the different ways that those scholars have applied an activity theoretical lens may provide useful insights into analytic norms in design of communication. Finally, the knowledge of previous uses of activity theory opens doors to other communication design researchers seeking to use this approach in their work, giving them the opportunity to ground their research with a theoretical lens that is more clearly defined and understood within the existing literature. Therefore, as scholars move forward with activity theoretical approaches to design of communication, they can understand the conventions of using this theoretical frame within their own work and can position how they use activity theory relative to previous scholarship.

3. METHODS

To our knowledge, a systematic examination of the use of activity theory within the communication design community has not been previously undertaken. Our approach, sometimes described as a systematic review of literature, may be better understood as qualitative metasynthesis, which Au defines as "part of a tradition of metaresearch that involves synthesizing the results of qualitative studies to gain a better understanding of the general nature of a given phenomenon" [1, p. 259]. Thus, our metasynthesis of activity theoretical SIGDOC proceedings articles was undertaken so as to provide a grounded, improved understanding of the specific ways in which our field has invoked, adapted, and extended activity theory.

Drawing on Au, Brereton, and Wiles et al, we first describe our sampling procedure and then detail our inductive systematic analysis of the articles in our sample [1, 2, 32]. Our dataset consists of 15 articles from the ACM Special Interest Group on the Design of Communication (SIGDOC) Proceedings for the years 2001–2011. To arrive at this sample, the full set of SIGDOC papers in the ACM Digital Library was initially searched using the following Boolean key word strings: "activity theory" in any field; "activ*" in the keywords field; and "activity + Vygotsky," "activity + Engeström," and "activity + Leont'ev" in any field. This first pass resulted in more than 50 articles. We excluded workshop abstracts and articles that did not use activity theory at all. We also excluded articles that only tangentially invoked or discussed activity theory, such as those not citing major work in activity theory and/or not explicitly claiming to employ activity theory for theoretical discussion or data analysis. The resulting 15 articles comprise our dataset; though we discuss these articles in more detail below, they are also identified by an asterisk in our References section.

While these 15 articles do not represent the total possible sample, as some researchers in the SIGDOC community may be influenced by activity theory and may even obliquely invoke activity theoretical approaches, the selected articles draw direct connections between design of communication concerns and activity theory. Considering the wide range of theoretical frames employed by design of communication researchers, the permanency of activity theory as a useable theoretical frame—a theory that has no specific origin or direct connection to this discipline—across this 10 year span is compelling and warrants further examination.

In order to explore this diverse set of articles, we focused on how sample authors invoked and deployed activity theory. This allowed us to take an inductive approach to a specific and easily identifiable phenomenon in the research literature: how authors marshaled activity theory. Therefore, two coders from our research team collaboratively coded the 15 SIGDOC articles from our sample using an inductive approach. In this way, the articles were systematically analyzed following emergent coding practices [cf. 20]. First-pass codes generally highlighted references to activity theory or the use of its terminology within the article. During coding, we identified potential themes that might emerge from a closer analysis of our codes. Consequently, we discussed and explored three potential themes after our first pass of coding:

1. Lineage—what theorists do the writers use to position themselves within the cultural and historical framework of activity theoretical scholarship?

2. Terminology—which terms do the writers use when discussing activity theory? To which theorists may these terms be linked? Do the authors use first-, second-, or third-generation activity theory terminology, or some combination thereof?

3. Function—how does activity theory function in articles as an analytic frame?

In our second pass at coding, we grouped new and extant codes and categories according to these emergent potential themes. Terminology was categorized according to the theorist who used the terms, and we found obvious congruence between *lineage* and *terminology* within the sample. Most importantly, through closer analysis during our second pass at coding, through constant comparison of codes generated by two researchers, and through

Table 1: Illustrated development of sample codes and emergent categories and themes

First-pass codes	Second-pass Categories	Theme
Vygotsky		Lineage
Leont'ev		
Orlikwski and Yates		
Nardi		
Kapetelinin		
Spinuzzi		
Engeström		
Mediation	Used by all	Terminology
Tool	Leont'ev's terms	
Rules		
Community	Engeström's terms	
Division of labor		
Knots		
Artifact	Spinuzzi's terms	
Genre ecology		
Primary method of analysis	Primary theoretical frame to analyze activity	Function
Activity triangle to show work flow		
Positioned alongside other theories (genre theory). Also seeks to expand the way AT is understood and used.	Positioned alongside or complicated by other theoretical approaches	
Positioned within other theories (Situated Action Theory) for analysis.		
Positioned alongside ANT		
Comparing AT to other frameworks, assess AT's effectiveness	Propose to assess, revise, or expand AT	
Add value to AT		
Complicates AT		
Analyzes AT's strengths and weaknesses, and proposes using it to solve a theory/practice debate		

analytic memos, the first-pass theme of *function* was understood as consisting of three important theoretical moves across authors in the sample:

1. Activity theory used as a primary theoretical frame to analyze activity

2. Activity theory positioned alongside or complicated by other theories

3. Proposals to revise or expand activity theory

Table 1 details representative codes, categories, and themes that emerged from our analysis of selected articles, arranged and shaded according to the themes that developed. Through two rounds of coding the 15 papers in our sample, we were able to determine some general patterns of activity theoretical research. Because some terms were used by multiple authors in activity theoretical lineage, the connection between terminology and lineage, while clearly supported by the data, was less direct than we originally hypothesized, as we describe in section 4.2. How

authors adopted or pushed the function of activity theory was especially important in our analysis, as we describe in section 4.3.

4. FINDINGS

In this section, we detail the key patterns we identified across our sample of activity theoretical approaches to design of communication research in the SIGDOC proceedings from 2001–2011. We found that how a given researcher positions his or her work relative to an activity theoretical lineage will understandably impact the terminology and function of their approach. However, because some SIGDOC researchers invoke activity theorists from across the spectrum, determining lineage is not always readily transparent and thus warrants deeper analysis. Moreover, we found that researchers sometimes mix and match terminology, even when their lineage seems apparent. But our key finding for future design of communication researchers involves the ways in which previous SIGDOC papers view the *function* of activity theory. Indeed, we found that most of the researchers in our sample called for critiques and expansions of activity theory for the design of communication community, a finding which supports Spinuzzi's assertion that the use of activity theory is becoming more "interconnected and multidimensional" [29, p. 470].

4.1 Lineage

How the authors oriented themselves among activity theory's existing body of literature varied considerably. The authors of the sample cited a total of 485 sources, 91 of which were citations that either explicitly referenced activity theory or were stated by the authors as being significant to the activity theoretical approaches. These figures produced a mean of 6.733 activity theory sources and a median of 6 activity theory sources per article within our sample.

Table 2. Distribution and Citation of Activity Theory-related Articles

Year	Number of SIGDOC articles	Number of AT sources cited
2002	2	9
2004	2	13
2006	1	29
2007	3	15
2008	1	2
2009	3	19
2010	2	13
2011	1	1

Table 2 represents how the articles from the sample were distributed from 2001-2011. With the exception of 2001, 2003,

and 2005, most years are represented by at least one proceedings paper that invokes activity theory in a meaningful way. However, a great variety exists within the number of activity theory sources from year to year. This variance can be attributed to the function activity theory plays in the article itself, which will be discussed in more detail in section 4.3.

When viewed in the broader context of sample authors' sources, those that involved activity theory took a prominent position in some reviews of literature. For example, Spinuzzi contained the highest percentage of activity theory sources (57.8 percent of his total references) [26], and Spinuzzi, Hart Davidson, and Zachry used the largest number of activity theory sources: 29 (54.7 percent) [29]. However, other authors' use of activity theory within their reviews of literature was understated. Mehlenbacher, for example, had the lowest percentage of activity theory sources (3.3 percent) [14], while Schmidt et. al used the smallest number of activity theory sources: 1 (4 percent) [20].

Figure 1 is a spatial and temporal representation of how the various authors situated themselves within the activity theory scholarship; authors are positioned according to the publication date(s) of their works. Authors who have multiple articles which were referenced by the sample authors are indicated by a parenthetical indicating the number of sources referenced. Darkened arrows indicate references to multiple articles from a single author; standard arrows indicate references to a single article from a single author.

Figure 1 illustrates the interconnected network of scholars within the SIGDOC community who invoke activity theory, and it also foregrounds their respective lineages: most authors use their review of literature to ground their work in activity theory's rich history. Because of their foundational theoretical work, Vygotsky, Engeström, and Spinuzzi are the most frequently cited authors. Vygotsky is cited six times, all from a singular work; Engeström

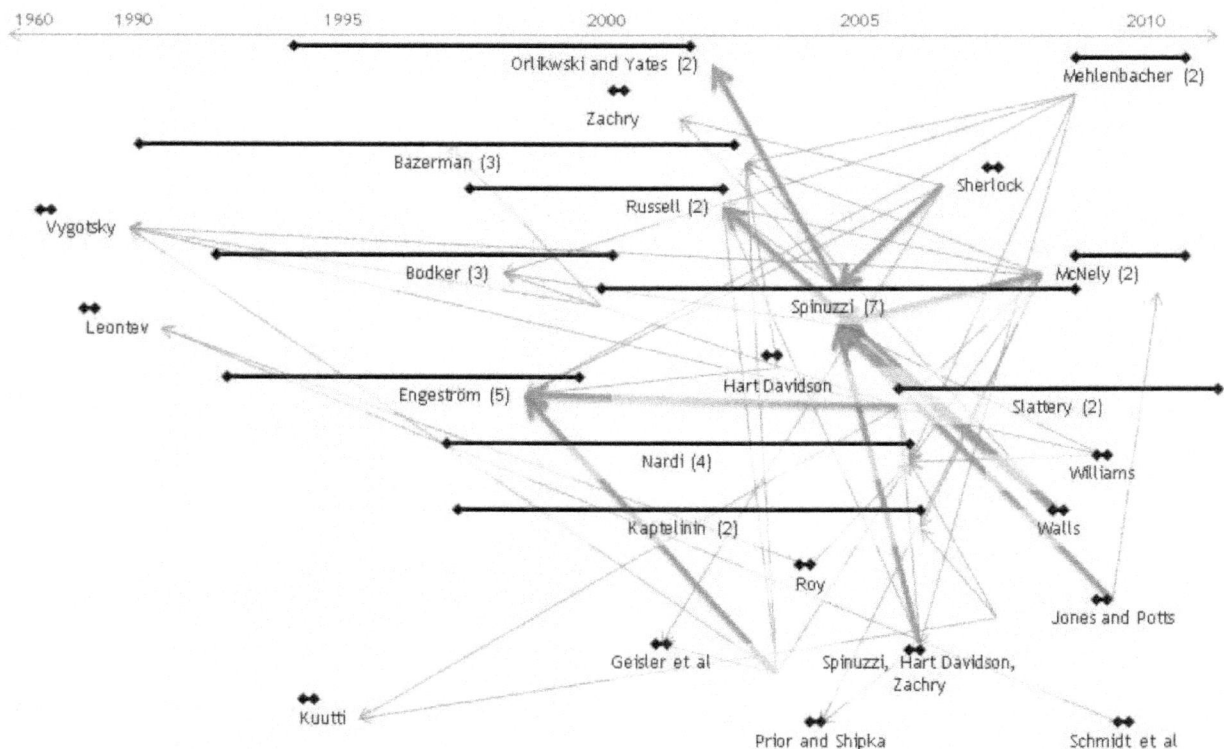

Figure 1. A referential and temporal model of activity theory authors' lineage

is cited nine times, from five of his works; and Spinuzzi is cited 17 times, from seven of his works.

4.2 Terminology

An author's activity theoretical lineage should shape the terminology they use. Toward that end, Nardi has argued that within activity theory there exists "a common vocabulary for describing activity that all HCI researchers would share. Activity theory has a simple but powerful hierarchy for describing activity that could be common coin for all HCI researchers [and, presumably, design of communication]" [16, p. 10]. With Nardi's assertion in mind, we identified instances of activity theory terminology as it was used in the selected SIGDOC papers. In all instances, the authors from our sample used this terminology to frame their analysis of activity or to position their work among the rest of the activity theory scholarship.

Figure 2 shows the interrelatedness of activity theory terminology and lineage as used by the authors from our sample. While the diagram does not truly represent the fluidity with which the authors in our sample used the terminology of the various generations of activity theory, it provides a useful method of examining the terms most frequently used in conjunction with the lineage of the term. From the figure, we see that *artifact* and *community* were the most frequently used activity theory terms among sample authors; this finding is unsurprising, as Engeström and Spinuzzi—both of whom use these terms—were most frequently cited.

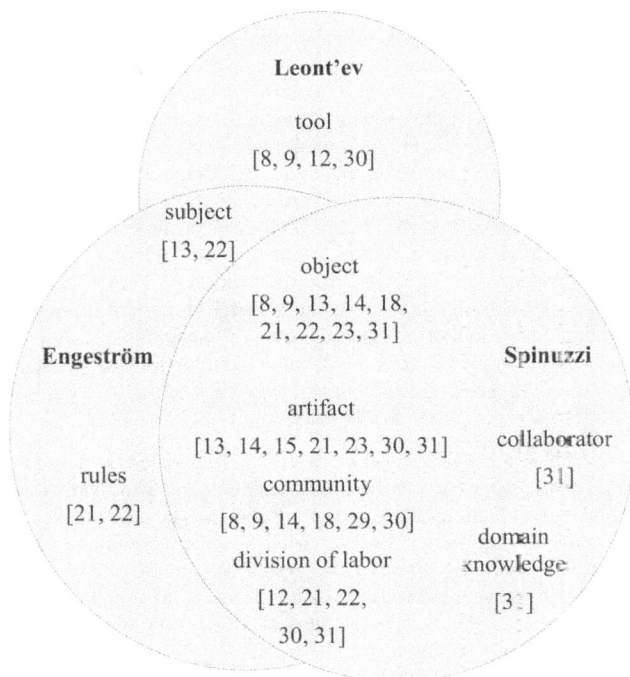

Figure 2. Activity theory-related terminology use and its lexical lineage among the selected SIGDOC articles

All authors in our sample use some aspect of Leont'ev's *subject/tool/object* terminology—per Engeström, second-generation activity theory—the most common being *object* [11]. Similarly, all authors embraced the third generation socio-cultural expansion of Engeström, using one or more of his terms (*community, division of labor*, and *rules*) [4]. However, none of the authors used the term *instrument* rather than *tool*.

Spinuzzi modified Engeström's language, replacing *tool* with *artifact*. He cited Bødker's (1996) concept of a "'web of artifacts' that jointly mediate activity" [24, p. 100]. After 2003, seven authors from our SIGDOC sample [13, 14, 15, 21, 23, 29, 30] adopted Spinuzzi's term *artifact*, while only four used *tool* [8, 9, 12, 29]. As authors chose to use Leont'ev's *tool* vs. Spinuzzi's *artifact* or to include Engeström's *rules/community/division of labor*, they situated themselves within the historical-theoretical framework and lineage of activity theory.

The interconnected nature of activity theory research's lineage and terminology exemplified in Figures 1 and 2 illustrates the rich socio-cultural history that researchers may adapt for the permutations of communication design. Our findings support Nardi's assertion that activity theory provides human computer interaction researchers with "a well-articulated conceptual apparatus and a core set of concepts that are useful for empirical analyses," and that "[b]asic concepts of activity theory can provide a solid framework with which to approach the analysis of data" [17, p. 245]. This analytic frame, we agree, also allows communication design researchers to investigate how communication works in various social and professional settings; to that end, our findings show that the researchers in our sample are not only grounding their work in activity theory, but they are also working to expand and complicate it.

4.3 Function

Knowing what researchers are doing with activity theory can tell us not only the particular strengths of activity theory in the area of communication design, but can also suggest activity theory's current evolutionary stage. The following account of the extensive theoretical discussion, compared to the few studies that put the theory to use, suggests that activity theory serves its fundamental purpose of providing researchers in communication design a theoretical means with which to analyze activities. It may also mean that theorists continue to adapt the potential possibilities of activity theory to meet their needs in technical and professional communication design; often they will call on the help of other theories to perform functions outside of activity theory's object-oriented boundaries [23].

As shown in Table 1, our second pass at coding and deeper thematic analysis of patterns within our sample revealed three categories of codes within the theme *function*:

1. Activity theory used as a primary theoretical frame to analyze activity
2. Activity theory positioned alongside or complicated by other theories
3. Proposals to revise or expand activity theory

In the following subsections we explore each category in more detail as we describe *function* as the most significant theme to emerge from our analysis.

4.3.1 Primary Theoretical Frame

Of the 15 articles reviewed, only Hart-Davidson, Slattery, and McNely use activity theory as their primary theoretical frame [8,

12, 23]. As the first to use only activity theory in the selected ten-year time span, Hart-Davidson is only "guided in part by work in activity theory" and looks at what is already happening with modeling literate activity that could help deconstruct "specific task situations" [8, p. 60]. Hart-Davidson uses activity theory as a guide for focusing on the utility of a document instead of simple content. He advises developers to improve their technical writing tool designs so that writers have better ways to regard their audiences' needs, and he suggests the same considerations for text and design assessment.

In a later study, Slattery analyzes Wikipedia's mediating-artifact role as well as plots its "technological functionality and the social conventions of its participants" to determine how these elements contribute to "networked fact-building" [23, p. 289]. The following year, McNely uses activity theory as a solitary framework for his methods and as a means to understanding specific information ecologies. He explores the use of blogs, microblogging, and online videos surrounding an international conference. More specifically, his activity theory methods lead him to the conclusion that *tummeling* (the creation of engaged conversation or connection) and phatic gestures in social networks, usually perceived as superficial, are important components in sustaining public information ecologies. It is interesting to find that only two out of 15 articles in our sample use activity theory as the primary theoretical framework; as we describe below, activity theory was more commonly used alongside other theories or critiqued and expanded.

4.3.2 Positioned Alongside Other Theories
Four papers within our sample position activity theory within or alongside additional theories or analysis techniques: Roy, Sherlock, McNely, and Jones and Potts [9, 13, 18, 22]. A year after Hart-Davidson employs activity theory alone, Roy follows by using both situated action theory and activity theory to offer "the groundwork for discussing the importance of a conversational design as part of a self-paced patient education module" [18, p. 29]. In studying the gaming community of World of Warcraft, Sherlock too needs more than activity theory to "identify the systems of texts and interactions that players use in their social gaming lives" [22, p. 19]. Activity theory coupled with genre theory helps ground Sherlock's analysis. McNely chooses to deploy actor network theory alongside activity theory in his analysis of digital backchannel persistence because, he argues, studying such environments "requires the simultaneous consideration of multiple theoretical frames" [13, p. 299]. Finally, Jones and Potts use both Morville's notion of findability and activity theory to study Twitter and "the design of [Twitter's] applications and the experiences suggested by those designs" [9, p. 96].

Rather than distort activity theory beyond its scope, as Spinuzzi, Hart Davidson, and Zachry caution us to avoid, these researchers are wise to recruit the different focal capabilities of situated action theory, genre theory, actor network theory, and information architecture [30]. Given the massive global capacity for participants in a given communication design study, researchers need to understand the potential benefits of only using activity theory and when to seek and enlist additional theoretical approaches. Such coupling has been widespread enough to name the combinations. Combining work in activity and genre theory, for instance, has come to be known as writing, activity, and genre research (WAGR), an approach in its own right [19, 27].

4.3.3 Revision and Expansion of Activity Theory
The majority of the articles included in this qualitative metasynthesis do not call on activity theory as a framework for research, but instead critique activity theory itself. These eight articles seek to revise activity theory, proposing expansions or adaptations [14, 15, 20, 23, 24, 30, 31, 32]. Although Spinuzzi does use his genre ecologies model to guide one of his studies, his research illustrates how genre ecologies, which are grounded in activity theory, can function as a formal modeling tool rather than as a mere heuristic [24]. In his next article, Spinuzzi returns to the genre ecology framework and discusses its functions, distinguishing it from three other genre frameworks. Spinuzzi explains how the genre ecology framework focuses on the mediation of an activity rather than focusing on the people performing the actions or on genres as simply communicative [24].

In 2006, Spinuzzi co-authors with Hart-Davidson and Zachry, drawing upon both activity theory and genre theory and proposing a "unified framework that describes both chains and ecologies" [30, p. 44]. Such arguments for incorporations of theories return persistently. Mehlenbacher, for example, puts forward a unique union, Gay and Hembrooke's mediational triangle that accounts for space and time with Engeström's mediational triangle, to address the theory-versus-practice debate [15]. Walls, who seeks "to expand activity theory to account for and make explicit how agent values assemble an activity system" [30, p. 258], accomplishes this task with activity theory and distributed usability in order to establish a Distributed Value System Matrix.

Likewise, Mehlenbacher continues to call for a merger of several theories. He argues that social theories alone—activity theory among them—or cognitive theories alone fail to provide a rich understanding of human learning for use by communication-design researchers. Therefore, it is necessary to "draw on research describing both cognitive and social perspectives" [14, p. 144]. Finally, Williams follows Mehlenbacher's call for integration by examining three common methods used to design web applications: one of those methods is activity-centered design, which is derived from activity theory [32]. Williams draws a similar conclusion as Spinuzzi [24], that designers should be investigating both the activities and their users. Schmidt, Stoitsev, and Mühläuser, though, close the ten-year span of our literature review by breaking away from the integration pattern to suggest another expansion of activity theory—the semantic hierarchical task model—which breaks down knowledge actions and desktop operations to get a more in-depth view of work processes. The authors test their model and find it methodologically sound.

One-fifth of the articles in this review, then, pursue an integration of theories, all proposing different combinations. Thus, only three articles found activity theory to be sufficient as a primary research framework. The other twelve articles either combined other theories to conduct research, suggested integrating theories and methods to create new research tools, or sought to expand activity theory to better suit the special demands of working with technical and professional communication design.

More recently, Spinuzzi has argued that the expansion of the understanding of object among 3rd generation activity theorists complicates analysis in activity theory. He argues that while the object is the "sense-maker," the "linchpin" of analysis, "the notion of object has expanded methodologically and theoretically over time, making it difficult to reliably bound an empirical case" [28,

p. 449]. When dealing with more global and/or less concrete phenomena, the object alone loses its usefulness as the unit of analysis. He concludes that researchers must contract the object and anchor it in more bounded cases. Spinuzzi identifies a series of countermovements that can help researchers do so, and given our review of the *function*, *terminology*, and *lineage* of activity theory in the recent design of communication literature, we see Spinuzzi's recent suggestions as particularly salient to our community.

4. CONCLUSIONS

Through our systematic analysis of these SIGDOC articles, we conclude that sample authors tend to draw on a similar corpus of works in activity theory, and that activity theory can provide a common terminology across multiple studies. Specifically, we identify Spinuzzi, Zachry, Hart Davidson, and Yates and Orlikowski—all of whom are writing studies/technical communication/communication researchers publishing in this community—as researchers comprising an emergent lineage, traceable over the ten-year period discussed here, which includes productive fusions of activity theory and genre.

Thus, our findings indicate that activity theory is not revealed to be a stable or monolithic theory for those within the design of communication community who invoke it; rather, it continues to be flexible and adaptable, as it has been throughout the decades of its development. The majority of the articles in this study addressed activity theory in order to revise or expand it, while one-third of the articles used activity theory alongside other theories.

Spinuzzi argues that activity theory holds promise in for communication studies if the crisis of the expanding object can be addressed. He asserts that "for the object to produce the multiple outcomes identified by different participants, it must become more definite: it must contract [29, p. 474]. He suggests that a linchpin of analysis, a sense-maker is needed in order to bound a case that that may include a large set of associations.

Ascertaining the *function* of activity theory within our sample articles is our most compelling finding. If the object as a unit of analysis is becoming less stable [29], then researchers in the design of communication will adapt theoretically as well; our findings show this to be the case. Thus, design of communication scholars and practitioners would do well to continue expanding activity theory and its use in new situations and in conjunction with other theories.

5. REFERENCES

[1] Au, W. 2007. High-Stakes testing and curricular control: A qualitative metasynthesis Educational Researcher 36 (5), 258-267.

[2] Brereton, P. 2011. A study of computing undergraduates Undertaking a systematic literature review. IEEE Transactions on Education 54 (4), 558-563.

[3] Engeström, Y. 1999. Activity theory and individual and social transformation. In Perspectives on activity theory, Y. Engeström, R. Miettinen, & R. Punamäki, Eds. (pp. 19–38). Cambridge University Press, New York.

[4] Engeström, Y. 2009. The future of activity theory: A rough draft. In Learning and expanding with activity theory, A. Sannino, H. Daniels, & K. D. Gutiérrez, Eds. (pp. 303–328). Cambridge University Press, New York.

[5] Engeström, Y. and Miettinen, R. 1999. Introduction. In Perspectives on activity theory, Y. Engeström, R. Miettinen, & R. Punamäki, Eds. (pp. 19–38). Cambridge University Press, New York.

[6] Eskola, A. 1999. Laws, logics, and human activity. In Perspectives on activity theory, Y. Engeström, R. Miettinen, & R. Punamaki, Eds. (pp. 107–114). Cambridge University Press, New York.

[7] Glaser, B. & Strauss, A. 1967. The discovery of grounded theory: strategies for qualitative research. Aldine Transaction, London.

[8] Hart-Davidson, W. 2002. Modeling document-mediated interaction. In SIGDOC '02: Proceedings of the 20th annual conference on design of communication. ACM Press, New York.*

[9] Jones, D. and Potts, L. 2010. Best practices for designing third party applications for contextually-aware tools. In SIGDOC '10: Proceedings of the 28th annual conference on design of communication. ACM Press, New York.*

[10] Kaptelinin, V. and Nardi, B. 2006. Acting with technology: Activity theory and interaction design. The MIT Press, Cambridge, MA.

[11] Leont'ev, A. N. 1978. Activity, consciousness, and personality. Prentice-Hall Press, Englewood Cliffs.

[12] McNely, B. 2009. Backchannel persistence and collaborative meaning-making. In SIGDOC '09: Proceedings of the 27th annual conference on Design of communication.ACM Press, New York.*

[13] McNely, B. 2010. Exploring a sustainable and public information ecology. In SIGDOC '10: Proceedings of the 28th annual conference on Design of communication. ACM Press, New York.*

[14] Mehlenbacher, B. 2008. Communication design and theories of learning. In SIGDOC '08: Proceedings of the 26th annual conference on Design of communication. ACM Press, New York.*

[15] Mehlenbacher, B. 2007. Triangulating communication design: emerging models for theory and practice. In SIGDOC'07: Proceedings of the 25th annual conference on Design of communication. ACM Press, New York.*

[16] Nardi, B. A. 1996. Activity theory and human-computer interaction. In Context and consciousness: Activity theory and human-computer interaction, B.A. Nardi., Ed. (pp. 7–16). The MIT Press, Cambridge, MA.

[17] Nardi, B. A. 1996. Some reflections on the application of activity theory. In Context and consciousness: Activity theory and human-computer interaction, B. A. Nardi, Ed. (pp. 235–246). The MIT Press, Cambridge, MA.

[18] Roy, D. 2004. A self-paced approach to hypermedia design for patient education. In SIGDOC '04: Proceedings of the 22nd annual conference on Design of communication. ACM Press, New York.*

[19] Russell, D. R. 2009. Uses of activity theory in written communication research. In Learning and expanding with activity theory, A. Sannino, H. Daniels, & K. D. Gutierrez, Eds., (pp. 40-52). Cambridge University Press, New York.

[20] Saldaña, J. 2009. The coding manual for qualitative researchers. Thousand Oaks, CA: Sage.

[21] Schmidt, B., Kastl, J., Stoitsev, T., & Mulhauser, M. 2011. Hierarchical task instance mining in interaction histories. In SIGDOC '11: Proceedings of the 29th annual conference on Design of communication. ACM Press, New York.*

[22] Sherlock, L. M. 2007. When social networking meets online games: the activity system of grouping in world of warcraft. In SIGDOC '07: Proceedings of the 25th annual conference on Design of communication. ACM Press, New York.*

[23] Slattery, S. P. 2009. "edit this page": The sociotechnological infrastructure of a wikipedia article. In SIGDOC '09: Proceedings of the 27th annual conference on Design of communication. ACM Press, New York.*

[24] Spinuzzi, C. 2002. Modeling genre ecologies. In SIGDOC 02: Proceedings of the 20th annual conference on Design of communication. ACM Press, New York.*

[25] Spinuzzi, C. 2003. Compound mediation in software development: Using genre ecologies to study textual artifacts. In Writing selves/writing societies: Research from activity perspectives, C. Bazerman, & D. R. Russell, Eds., (pp. 97–124). The WAC Clearinghouse, Fort Collins, CO.

[26] Spinuzzi, C. 2003. Tracing genres through organizations: A sociocultural approach to information design. MIT Press, Cambridge.

[27] Spinuzzi, C. 2004. Four ways to investigate assemblages of texts: Genre sets, systems, repertoires, and ecologies. In SIGDOC '04: Proceedings of the 22nd annual conference on Design of communication. ACM Press, New York.*

[28] Spinuzzi, C. 2010. Secret sauce and snake oil: Writing monthly reports in a highly contingent environment. Written Communication 27(4), 363-409.

[29] Spinuzzi, C. 2011. Losing by expanding: Corralling the runaway object. Journal of Business and Technical Communication (25)4, 449–486.

[30] Spinuzzi, C., Hart-Davidson, W., and Zachry, M. 2006. Chains and ecologies: Methodological notes toward a communicative-mediational model of technologically mediated writing. In SIGDOC '06: Proceedings of the 24th annual conference on Design of communication. ACM Press, New York.*

[31] Walls, D. 2007. Distributed value system matrix: a new use for distributed usability testing. In SIGDOC '07: Proceedings of the 25th annual conference on Design of communication. ACM Press, New York.*

[32] Wiles, R., Crow, G., and Pain, H. 2011. Innovation in qualitative research methods: a narrative review. Qualitative Research, 11(5), 587-604.

[33] Williams, A. 2009. User-centered design, activity-centered design, and goal-directed design: A review of three methods for designing web applications. In SIGDOC '09: Proceedings of the 27th annual conference on Design of communication. ACM Press, New York.*

Hosting an ACM SIGDOC Unconference

Sarah Egan Warren
ACM SIGDOC Faculty Advisor and
Student Relations Officer
NC State University
English Department Box 8105
Raleigh, NC 27695
+1 919 515 4121
seegan@ncsu.edu

Jennifer Riehle
ACM SIGDOC Webmaster and
Student Chapter Past President
NC State University
Outreach, Communications & Consulting Box 7109
Raleigh, NC 27695
+1 919 513 7924
jen_riehle@ncsu.edu

ABSTRACT

In this paper, we describe our experience hosting an "unconference" as a student chapter of ACM SIGDOC. This paper can serve as a starting point for other groups wanting to try this non-traditional approach to sharing information in a participant-driven event or meeting. We explain the unconference idea, our planning stages, technology we used implementation and delivery, lessons learned, and plans for the future. A checklist at the end of the paper details the steps to running a successful unconference.

Categories and Subject Descriptors

A.0. [**General**]: Conference Proceedings. K.3. [**Computers and Education**] K.4.0 [**Computing Milieux**]: Computers and Society, Computer supported collaborative-work.

General Terms

Management, Theory

Keywords

Unconference, event, planning, participant-driven, conference, community, training, technical, keynote, organization, NCSU, Raleigh, NC, student chapter

1. INTRODUCTION

The NC State University student chapter of SIGDOC teamed up with the Carolina Chapter of STC (Society for Technical Communication) to present SpeedCon 2011: An Unconference on Communication. Our SIGDOC student chapter had been discussing the idea of hosting a mini-conference when STC approached our group about hosting a joint conference. We have a history of partnering with the local professional chapter of STC and the timing was right for this collaborative effort.

The STC Chapter had sufficient financial resources, sponsorship connections, and door prizes to make it possible to host the event. The SIGDOC student chapter managed the location, scheduling, organization, and overall event details.

2. WHAT IS AN UNCONFERENCE?

An "unconference" is not a brand new concept; in fact, it has been around in various forms since the 1980s. However it is only in the last five to ten years that the concept has gained popularity [1]. An unconference is essentially a "participant-driven" meeting. It's often used as a format for conferences; however, sometimes it can be a smaller subset of a larger conference [2].

An unconference may be implemented in several ways, but it generally involves the conference participants "pitching" ideas for conference sessions on or shortly before the date of the event. This removes the lead time required for program submissions, ensuring the presentations are timely and much more targeted to the event audience.

3. WHY AN UNCONFERENCE?

There were several reasons why the "unconference" format was appealing to us. First, this conference was intended to bring together a professional STC chapter made up almost exclusively of full-time technical communicators and a SIGDOC chapter of graduate students: potentially very diverse audiences. We weren't sure how to begin soliciting session topics, let alone how to pick them. The idea of making the conference more flexible in scope and topic appealed to everyone.

Secondly, this was the first time that our SIGDOC student chapter had decided to try an event like this. We weren't sure how much participation there would be from STC or the rest of the Technical Communication community. We felt that an unconference format would allow us to work best with whatever turnout we got. The unconference would also let us be flexible with respect to start and end time of the event, and the number and length of sessions. Finally, with the event scheduled for a weekend day in the middle of fall there was concern about scheduling conflicts. The unconference format made it a more flexible and relaxed event, allowing users to come and go as needed.

Despite the reasons described above, the decision to go with an unconference was not an easy one and was not without its detractors. There were concerns that the conference would be too flexible. Several of the planners made the point that without a schedule, there's little to draw an audience; there were fears that people might not come if they didn't know what to expect. Complicating that was the unconference idea itself. Most of the SIGDOC planners were not familiar with the idea of an unconference and there was a great deal of concern that conference attendees wouldn't "get it" and therefore they wouldn't be interested and wouldn't come prepared to present. An unconference cannot exist without participation—it requires active interaction from its participants.

In order to help relieve these concerns we took several steps in the weeks leading up to the conference. First, we set up a website to provide a landing point for all the details of the conference. The first thing to go on that website was an explanation of what an unconference is and how it would work in this instance. Secondly, we decided early on that relying on sessions pitched on the day of the event would not be feasible. We agreed to seed the event with some topics so that participants would have an idea of what to expect.

Finally, we wanted to encourage others to think about and share their topics in advance if they desired. In order to make advanced topic submission easy, and to help potential attendees interact with that information, we used a website called UserVoice (http://www.uservoice.com/). UserVoice has a quick Talk Submission tool which allows participants to share their idea for a talk in advance. It also has a simple feedback mechanism: guests to the site can "vote" on the presentations they most want to see. This feedback helped immeasurably. Participants could now get a sense of what to expect, and beyond that they could see what types of presentations were most popular and use that information when pitching their own session. It was also extremely valuable for us when deciding how to schedule the sessions the day of the event. More popular sessions were given larger spaces and 30-minute time slots while sessions with fewer votes were given 15-minute "lightning talks" in smaller rooms. See Table 1 for topics and votes.

Table 1. Early Submissions and Vote Totals

Submitted Topic	Totals
21st Century Challenges to Technical Communication	11
Strategies for Simplicity	9
Creating an ebook... for free	8
Non-Traditional Resumes	8
The Genius of WordPress	8
Writing to Your Strengths: Writing and Personality Type	8
Documentation in an Agile World	7
Control from the Crypt: End-of-Life Documentation	6
Communication Metrics	5
Designing an infrastructure to support the publishing lifecycle	5
Welcome to Tiki Wiki CMS	5
Why Learning DITA Can Keep You Viable	4
Blogging Your Passion	3
Getting to Know Your Users Better	2

4. PLANNING OUR UNCONFERENCE: SPEEDCON 2011

SIGDOC and STC officers held one joint planning meeting and then finished planning by email. We dubbed our event: SpeedCon2011: an Unconference on Communication. Although an unconference does not require all the same management and organization that a full-fledged conference demands, certain logistical details must be considered. We scheduled SpeedCon on a Saturday from 9am-3pm in the NC State University student center. Because we held the event on a weekend, the student center was not crowded and participants had access to ample free parking. We used one main gathering room, three breakout rooms, and one planning room. Each room had a projector for laptops and white boards. Because the rooms were relatively small, we did not need to use microphones for the speakers.

In addition to the information on the website(s) described above we also used social media to inform and engage potential participants (and by extension, potential presenters). We posted to the NCSU Technical Communication Facebook page, website and listserv and also shared the information with related graduate programs. STC also shared the conference information through their channels and used EventBrite (http://www.eventbrite.com/) to manage the event registration.

5. DELIVERING OUR UNCONFERENCE

Our day-long unconference gave participants the opportunity to learn about communication from each other. Participants were students (full- and part-time graduate students—most also work full- or part-time jobs), faculty, alumni, and local professionals.

Like a traditional conference, on the morning of the event, SIGDOC officers arrived early at the student center and put up signs to direct participants to the main gathering room. As people arrived, we asked them to put on a nametag and enjoy a light breakfast (STC provided the light breakfast, a coffee break, and lunch for participants). Like a traditional conference, SpeedCon started with a welcome and opening remarks by the SIGDOC faculty advisor and the STC president. Then, SpeedCon became something very different from a traditional conference.

Although some speakers had submitted ideas to the UserVoice space, all participants who wanted to speak were asked to stand up and give a short (20-30 second) explanation of their topic. As the speaker explained their topic, one SIGDOC officer recorded the title and any constraints for the proposed session (technology needs, time of presentation, conflicting topics) on individual sheets of paper. After all the pitches were completed, a small group of officers moved to another room to construct the schedule while the keynote speaker presented.

Creating the schedule on the fly with a strict time limit (the keynote speaker was scheduled to talk for 25 minutes) was the most challenging aspect of the event. The SIGDOC officers grouped all the pitches into similar categories and then divided them up across the three rooms and five time slots.

Figure 1. SIGDOC Officers planning the schedule

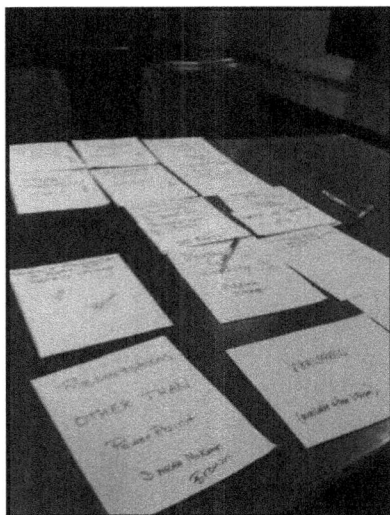

Figure 2. Schedule

After the schedule was established, we dropped the information into a pre-made schedule layout and uploaded it to the conference website [3]. We included a QR Code so that participants could scan the schedule and have it on their phone. In addition, we went low-tech and used large Post-It Notes on each door to indicate the topics and times for each room.

Topics included strategies for simplicity, communication metrics, DITA, ePUB eBook, writing and personality types, presentation tools, WordPress, blogging, and the future of technical communication (delivered by SIGDOC former chair, Brad Mehlenbacher). Some presenters had full-fledged presentations prepared; others had a general topic and invited conversations around a particular idea or aspect. Some presenters did brief technology demonstrations while others spoke without any visual aids.

After a day of sharing ideas, generating questions and conversation, and learning new tools, we closed SpeedCon by drawing tickets for door prizes and thanking participants.

6. LESSONS LEARNED

There were plenty of takeaways from the first SpeedCon. We did gather feedback from the attendees; eleven of the fifty attendees responded to our survey and many of their responses mirrored our own thoughts.

First, it was unanimous from our attendees that the unconference was a success and they would happily attend another event. They loved the unconference format and the flexible nature of the event. One user response: "Despite the informality of the overall experience, you folks were very well organized. Just enough structure... plenty of flexibility." Another survey respondent commented specifically on the structure of the day with respect to its weekend timeslot: "I enjoyed the informality and brevity of it. I get bored easily. Professional development on a Saturday should be fast-paced like SpeedCon."

Secondly, several of the attendees suggested a closing event that would tie everything together or allow some final opportunities for networking. Several respondents suggested having one or two of the most popular session from the day re-present to the entire group to finish off the event.

Third, from the feedback it was clear that we needed to find better ways to publicize the event: the majority of the respondents heard about the event from a friend. While we were happy with the turnout we feel like there would be major gains if we could improve our marketing

Several things impacted our efforts to reach the largest audience possible. First, the short turnaround of the event meant there was little time to spend on marketing or to efficiently spread the word. Secondly, multiple websites (SpeedCon, UserVoice, EventBrite, STC pages) meant that the user had to visit several sites to gather information and occasionally that information got out-of-date on one or more pages. Finally, our short turnaround also meant that we didn't have time to solicit vendor support, or endorsements with other communications-related professional groups in the area, either of which would have been an excellent way to reach a larger audience of potential attendees.

There were several other lessons learned in the planning of SpeedCon. Many of the challenges we had planning the event came from the fact that there were too many people planning the event. We had SIGDOC members working on logistics, but STC also had several people who contributed to various parts of the planning. There were times when efforts were duplicated or contributions conflicted and this resulted in a slower and less efficient process. For example, the SIGDOC group created the main website and the UserVoice site for submitting talks. However, STC also created several webpages: one for registration (through EventBrite) and another on their own STC site. Managing the information across four sites was largely unsuccessful and frustrating both for planners but also attendees.

One of the other big misses to the conference was the lack of vendor support. Because we planned and executed the unconference very quickly, we did not have a great deal of time to solicit vendors. We missed out on some of the bigger "perks" of most conferences such as more swag, an evening event, and more door prizes.

7. LOOKING TO THE FUTURE

We absolutely plan to have a second SpeedCon; we hope it will in fall 2012. In light of our successes and challenges with the 2011 event we expect to adjust our goals slightly, but stay on the same path.

We do plan to use the unconference format again and expect that we will once again seed the event and allow early feedback on the topics.

Table 2. Checklist

Phase	Decision/Action Item
Initial Planning	Identify unconference team
Initial Planning	Select date/time
Initial Planning	Select location
Initial Planning	Solicit sponsorship
Initial Planning	Arrange refreshments
Technology	Create unconference website & sign up
Technology	Advertise event
Technology	Explain unconference concept to participants
Technology	Solicit speakers
Technology	Encourage voting on early submissions
Technology	Send reminder email to participants
Logistics	Purchase name tags, markers, paper
Logistics	Verify participant numbers; place food orders
Logistics	Confirm rooms, AV equipment, tech support
Day of Event	Unconference team arrive early
Day of Event	Put up directional signs
Day of Event	Set up tables for name tags and check in
Day of Event	Welcome participants and explain process
Day of Event	Create schedule

We hope to consolidate the number of websites and try to manage the information both on those sites and in our larger social media marketing more efficiently. We would like to start planning much earlier and use vendor support to increase our reach, offset some costs, and improve the value for participants. Finally, we would like to modify the event to add more networking opportunities for attendees and to finish with a larger session either with repeats of popular talks, or perhaps offering a more interactive conversation on some of the more interesting and timely topics of the day.

8. CHECKLIST
Below, we share our checklist of required decisions and action items needed for hosting an unconference.

9. ACKNOWLEDGMENTS
Our thanks to the Carolina Chapter of STC for providing financial support; and to all the speakers and participants of SpeedCon 2011 for contributing to the success of the event.

10. REFERENCES
[1] Johnson, Laurie. (May 17, 2012). *Alternatives to Face-to-Face Technical Communications Conferences.* Retrieved from http://techwhirl.com/business/trends/alternatives-to-face-to-face-technical-communication-conferences/

[2] Unconference. (n.d.). In *Wikipedia.* Retrived from http://en.wikipedia.org/wiki/Unconference

[3] ncsumarit. (2011, October 29). Schedule [Web log post]. Retrieved from http://speedcon.wordpress.com/2011/10/29/schedule/

Structured Authoring Meets Technical Comics in TechCommix

Carlos Evia
Virginia Tech
Blacksburg, VA
carlos.evia@vt.edu

Michael Stewart
Virginia Tech
Blacksburg, VA
michael_stewart@vt.edu

Tim Lockridge
Saint Joseph's University
Philadelphia, PA
tlockrid@sju.edu

Siroberto Scerbo
Virginia Tech
Blacksburg, VA
scerbo@vt.edu

Manuel Perez-Quiñones
Virginia Tech
Blacksburg, VA
mperezqu@vt.edu

ABSTRACT

TechCommix is an XML grammar and GUI that allows technical communicators to build comics based on the principles of structured authoring. *TechCommix* XML uses elements of two markup languages—ComicsML and DITA—the combination of which offers a means of tagging elements connected to a comics narrative (such as speech, action, narration) and to structured technical documentation (such as context, step, example). The resulting language allows a technical writer to differentiate between instructional and entertainment content, facilitating content analysis and reuse. Additionally, the *TechCommix* GUI provides assisted means of building web comics from DITA input. In this online environment, a technical writer can transform an XML file into an HTML deliverable with multiple presentation options—extending usability and accessibility beyond the current standard of image-based web comics. Future work will examine the efficacy of these comics in communicating procedural information.

Categories and Subject Descriptors

H.5.2 [**User Interfaces**]: Training, help, and documentation; I.7.2 [**Document Preparation**]: Markup languages

Keywords

comics, structured authoring, XML, DITA.

1. INTRODUCTION

Inspired mainly by the impact of the online comic created by Scott McCloud to introduce Google Chrome, technical communicators are looking at comic books and comic strips as a genre for conveying technical information to audiences who would not read traditional documentation [1, 4, 9, 5, 3].

Using comics for technical purposes, however, represents unique challenges that begin with achieving the proper balance of entertainment and information content: it is often too easy to create a "funny" comic book that keeps important content hidden among jokes and character development. Additionally, a graphic genre like comics requires writing practices that might not be compatible with technical communication trends of structured authoring ("a publishing workflow that defines and enforces consistent organization of information"[6]) and content reuse,

potentially missing on benefits that "include clear, consistent information for customers and business efficiencies"[7].

This poster presentation reports on work in progress to develop *TechCommix*: an Extensible Markup Language (XML) grammar and online comic computing[8] environment that allows technical communicators to incorporate principles of structured authoring to balance out elements of content and humor. *TechCommix* is based on ComicsML[1] (a markup language for archiving comic books) and the Darwin Information Typing Architecture (DITA, an international standard for structuring technical documentation). Benefits from this treatment include enhanced accessibility of technical comics, as users who cannot follow images are able to listen to the content; opportunities for reusing, archiving, and searching content inside comics; and improved Return on Investment (ROI) metrics, allowing authors to justify the use of a comic by comparing its procedural content to that of traditional text-based documentation.

2. CREATING TECHCOMMIX

2.1 Marking up existing comics

The first stage of developing *TechCommix* involved extending ComicsML's Document Type Definition (DTD) to incorporate DITA tags and allow structured transcription of existing technical comics. Following DITA's three types of content (procedures, background or conceptual information, and quick reference information[2]), all speech and narration elements had to be tagged with a type attribute, starting with the generic plot and humor, and then specializing with *introduction, example, question, answer, explanation,* and *demonstration* (for conceptual and reference comics), and *context, prereq, step, choice, info, example, postreq, hazardstatement,* and *result* (for procedural comics).

Through a series of automated transformations based on Extensible Stylesheet Language (XSL), the structured transcriptions generated a Hypertext Markup Language (HTML) deliverable with options for viewing the content as a) comic only, b) comic and transcription, or c) transcription only. All transcriptions were automatically annotated to identify and label speech and narration types (step, example, prereq, postreq, etc.). Thus, a comic became a document with measurable and reusable content elements.

---

[1] http://jmac.org/projects/comics_ml

Preliminary evaluation of phase 1 asked students in an *Introduction to Professional Writing* course to adapt existing text-based instructions on topics of computer safety into comics created with the online comic generator Bitstrips[2]. Then, students had to use a text editor to code *TechCommix* transcripts of their comics. The following code displays a sample panel transcription of a student-produced comic:

```
<panel id="p03">
<img>img/3.jpg</img>
<panel-desc>
<action>Eddie sits. Ralph stands
up.</action>
<speech characterid="2" type="step">The
first thing you should do is run
MalWareBytes</speech>
<speech characterid="1" type="plot">But I
don't have MalWareBytes.</speech>
<speech characterid="2" type="humor">Stop
 interrupting; I'm getting to that.</speech>
</panel-desc>
</panel>
```

The students, who had basic knowledge of HTML but had not been previously exposed to XML or DITA, did not report problems working directly with code. However, they unanimously supported the idea of a graphical user interface (GUI) to simplify the process of building and transcribing technical comics. The main problem reported in this evaluation stage was the lack of a system for generating task-oriented panels. Conceptual and reference panels were relatively easy to build, with characters paraphrasing problems and solutions, but procedural panels demanded a faithful representation of all steps included in the original text-based task.

2.2 Facilitating task-to-comic translation

The next stage in developing *TechCommix* addresses the need for a comic computing GUI and facilitates proper adaptation of steps from a text-based task to a technical comic.

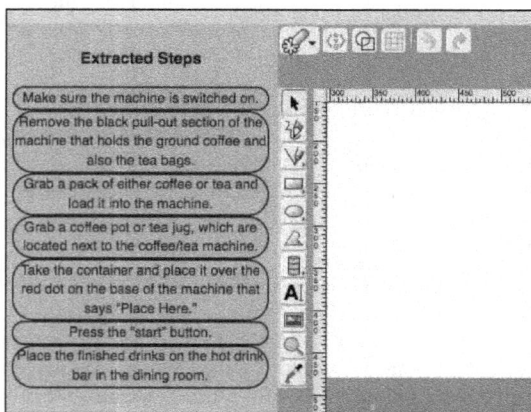

Figure 1: Steps extracted from a task

The authoring environment evolved to an online interface with four columns: 1) an area to drag and drop or open an existing DITA task for input, 2) an accordion-like list of automatically extracted elements from the DITA input, 3) an image editor based on SVG-edit[3], and 4) a *TechCommix* XML output. The user drops or opens a DITA task in column 1, then column 2 is automatically populated with the source file's structured content. The user can then open a stock comic panel (the project is using the open source DesignComics[4] panels) in column 3's editor and drag and drop step, prereq, example, etc. tags from column 2, which can be moved around the canvas and modified to become speech bubbles. Lastly, column 4 automatically generates the panel's XML transcription. **Figure 1** shows an example of columns 2 and 3, with extracted steps from a DITA task ready to be dropped into the editor. In its current version, the interface only works with DITA task topics, as phase 1 showed that concept and reference topics were easier to adapt into comics.

3. CONCLUSIONS

TechCommix facilitates the process of translating DITA tasks into comics and producing semantically representative XML for the resulting comic. The next phase will evaluate the efficacy of these comics in communicating the steps and other elements in the task. Additionally, it will include evaluating the usability of the comic computing environment and its resulting comics in contrast to comics produced using other tools, and in contrast to the effectiveness of source text-based tasks.

4. REFERENCES

[1] R. Bailie. Comics for consumer communication: Reaching users with word and image. http://www.boxesandarrows.com/view/comics- for-consumer, 2008.

[2] L. Bellamy, M. Carey, and J. Schlotfeldt. *DITA Best Practices: A Roadmap for Writing, Editing, and Architecting in DITA*. IBM Press, 2012.

[3] E. Noll Webb, G. Balasubramanian, U. OBroin, and J. Webb. Wham! pow! comics as user assistance. *Journal of Usability Studies*, 7(3):105–117, May 2012.

[4] M. Opsteegh. What technical communicators can learn from comics. *TechniScribe: Orange County STC Newsletter*, 47(9), 2008.

[5] A. Porter. Writing technical comics. *Intercom*, February 2010.

[6] A. S. Pringle and S. S. O'Keefe. *Technical Writing 101: A Real-World Guide to Planning and Writing Technical Content*. Scriptorium Publishing Services, Incorporated, 3rd edition, 2009.

[7] C. Robidoux. Rhetorically structured content: Developing a collaborative single-sourcing curriculum. *Technical Communication Quarterly*, 17(1):110–135, 2007.

[8] Tobita, R. Comic computing: creation and communication with comic. *In Proceedings of the 29th ACM international conference on Design of communication (SIGDOC '11)*. ACM, New York, NY, USA, 91-98. 2011

[9] E. Yuh. Trendspotting: The comic as a technical communication tool. *Coast Lines: Newsletter blog of the Society of Technical Communicators Canada West Coast chapter*, December 2008.

---

[2] http://www.bitstrips.com

---

[3] https://code.google.com/p/svg-edit/

[4] http://designcomics.org

Improving Rehabilitation Process After Total Knee Replacement Surgery Through Visual Feedback and Enhanced Communication in a Serious Game

Bernhard Maurer
Salzburg University of Applied Sciences
Urstein Sued 1
Puch/Salzburg, Austria
bmaurer.mmt-m2011@fh-salzburg.ac.at

Fabian Bergner
Salzburg University of Applied Sciences
Urstein Sued 1
Puch/Salzburg, Austria
fbergner.mmt-m2011@fh-salzburg.ac.at

Peter Kober
Salzburg University of Applied Sciences
Urstein Sued 1
Puch/Salzburg, Austria
pkober.mmt-m2011@fh-salzburg.ac.at

Rene Baumgartner
Salzburg University of Applied Sciences
Urstein Sued 1
Puch/Salzburg, Austria
rbaumgartner.mmt-m2011@fh-salzburg.ac.at

ABSTRACT

A common problem during rehabilitation after total knee replacement surgery is a lack of intrinsic motivation to do the necessary exercises at home. Doing the exercises at home without the supervision of a physical therapist raises the risk that patients do not execute the activities in a safe and effective manner

To address this problem, we developed a serious exergame to improve engagement and the efficiency of the rehabilitation process. A team of game developers, physiotherapists and a researcher collaborated to contribute to the design and prototype development. This led to a prototype using Microsoft Kinect as an input device to engage users combined with an individualized setup that provides visual rewarding and corrective feedback to the patient and a communication channel to the therapist to enable performance monitoring.

This interdisciplinary process we were engaged in has implications for the development of engaging exergames that communicate clinically relevant performance information to elderly patients through a visual feedback tool.

Categories and Subject Descriptors

H.5.2 [**Information Interfaces and Presentation**]: User Interfaces—*Prototyping, User-centered Design*; J.3 [**Life and Medical Sciences**]: [Health, Medical information systems]; K.8.0 [**Personal Computing**]: Games

Keywords

Serious games, interdisciplinary process, visual feedback, communication design, surgery rehabilitation

1. INTRODUCTION

Current problems in knee rehabilitation are mainly based around communication problems between the therapist and patient, resulting in wrong executed or overdone exercises and a lack of motivation of the patient to actually do the exercises. We developed a prototype exergame that acts as a controlled training environment to be used at the patient's home. Working together with physiotherapists we developed an interface that deals with the needs of patients as well as therapists: It enables the therapist to easily setup a training cycle for the patient (based on the individual patient's progress during rehab). It gives the patient an opportunity to do their exercises in a virtual and controlled training environment. Based on the therapist's suggestions we found out that knee bends are the most common exercise during the process. Therefore we decided that the prototype will focus on this particular exercise. Using Microsoft Kinect we are able to provide an easy approach for an individualized setup process, depending on the individual patient needs and the different progress of each patient.

Our prototype addresses current rehabilitation problems with current rehabilitation problems as follows:

- controlled movement via Kinect body tracking
- motivation through gameplay
- adjustability of exercises to the specific patient needs
- providing a feedback/reporting channel from patient to therapist

2. SETUP PROCESS

Doing the knee bend exercise in the right way depends on several *values* (maximum distance between the knees during the exercise, minimum/maximum bending distance) that have to be set up and communicated by the therapist. During an early therapy session these values are tracked by the Kinect and stored via a single button-press by the therapist. The stored values act as limiters for the knee-bend exercises done by the patient later at home.

As the patient's condition gets better (increased range of motion) the initial values for the exercises can be easily adapted to the current progress of the rehab process.

3. FEEDBACK PROCESS

The feedback given by the prototype is based on the values stored by the therapist during the therapy sessions. Providing a feedback is crucial for signaling to the patient when a certain movement is *overdone* or badly executed.

Our approach can be divided into two different phases in which the actual feedback takes place:

- Visual feedback given by the prototype application itself during the exercises in real-time

- Spoken feedback given by the therapist based on exercise statistics saved on a USB-drive during the therapy sessions

The virtually given feedback prevents the patient from executing the exercises in a wrong way and therefore replaces partially a present therapist at home.

3.1 Visual Feedback

If an exercise is done wrong the game will represent the feedback in an appropriate way. Overdoing an exercise results in a flashing indicator bar (representing the allowed maximum distance between the knees during the exercise) telling the patient exactly what was done wrong. On the other side positive feedback will be given to the patient if an exercise was completed in a good way, therefore increasing motivation by giving rewards.

3.2 Statistics and Reporting

Besides the visual feedback the prototype gives a detailed reporting to the therapist. Statistics over the progress of each patients training cycles are stored and saved to a USB-drive handed out to the patient. The USB-drive stores all the relevant values for both the training at home as well as the statistics of the training sessions. It gives the patients a physical device that they relate their rehabilitation progress with.

Back at the therapy sessions the data stored on the USB-drive tells the therapist exactly how how well the patient performed at home. The drive therefore acts as a missing link between home and therapy and fills this gap with a definite reporting tool. This enables the therapist to actually keep track of patients training behaviour at home and therefore give a more precise feedback based on this information. The statistics provide a base for upcoming therapy sessions and further adjustments of exercise values.

4. TEAM COMMUNICATION

The development of the prototype took place in an interdisciplinary process between developers, physiotherapists and researchers. For a better understanding of what physiotherapy after a total knee replacement actually means, training sessions with therapists and developers where planned. The therapists showed several exercises typical for the time period after a total knee replacement. These sessions were crucial to better understand the movement limitations a patient has after the surgery. Based on the experiences the team took from the training sessions the actual game idea and the understanding of what features and values we could base the game around came along.

5. CONCLUSION

To improve the communication during the rehabilitation process it is crucial to address both the needs of the therapist and the patient. The proposed prototype with its feedback channel and communication enhancements can increase the overall communication in the rehabilitation process.

The controlled training environment our prototype exergame provides, can contribute to a more efficient and accurate rehabilitation process.

Our prototype acts as a tool for improving communication between patient and therapist by addressing the needs of both sides during the rehabilitation process. It fills the gap between the different therapy sessions and makes the time where patients exercise from at home more efficient and save.

How Do Experts Read Application Letters?
A Multi-Modal Study

Joyce Locke Carter
Texas Tech University
Box 43091
Lubbock, TX 79409-3091
+1 (806) 742-2501 #237
Joyce.Carter@ttu.edu

ABSTRACT

Fourteen faculty participants each read two letters of application to a graduate program, and the data about how they read was collected using eye-tracking and think-aloud protocol. The eyetracking data show that expert readers not only "slow down" when they encounter grammatical and other errors, but also when they see words and phrases that match their program's mission or their own research interests. The think-aloud protocol data was used to verify eye-tracking results and also to allow for readers to expand on their impressions of the persuasiveness of a given letter. The project is not finished, but early impressions are that something akin to Kenneth Burke's concept of identification is a powerfully persuasive move in such letters—readers' eyes fixate on these identification moves and the participants identify those moves as positive and persuasive.

Categories and Subject Descriptors

H.1.2 [**Human Factors**]: Human information processing

J.5 [**Arts and Humanities**]: Linguistics, Literature

Keywords

eye-tracking, argumentation, persuasion, fixations

1. INTRODUCTION

When we look at the documents we write, whether they are informative, persuasive, argumentative, demonstrative, or task-oriented; whether they employ high or low style—our field has developed an impressive array of analytical tools we can use to both analyze and evaluate them.

However, we have less experience once we get to analyzing the reader, although we have borrowed from reader-response literary criticism and other audience-oriented approaches. A productive turn in past 10 years has been to employ user-centered design concepts and research techniques to understand readers as "users" of communication artifacts. Some have bristled at employing the verb "use" and its noun "user" to apply to the reader or the recipient of the communication message, but for the purposes of understanding rhetorical effectiveness, it seems like a perfectly suitable concept.

One of the biggest, most voluminous, and important rhetorical usage events is the evaluation of applications to a doctoral program. Each application is composed of many artifacts, from the purely factual (GRE, GPA, transcripts) to the overtly argumentative (letters of recommendation, statement of intent).

A strong statement of intent often reveals its rhetorical power fairly easily, and that its overall effectiveness is apparent quickly. This is also true of weak statements of intent. In both cases, my impression is that my reading time, my evaluation time, and my judgment time is not terribly lengthy, certainly not in comparison to the statements that are plausible, but not immediately overwhelming, arguments for admission.

It is apparent to me that this process involves two steps, the individual impression of materials and then the group norming and deliberation that happen when we bring those individual assessments into the committee room. And the literature confirms that while we know a lot about how we teach argumentation, we know virtually nothing about how we read argumentation and what we look for when we make decisions based on that argumentation.

The proposed poster details two research techniques the author is using in a study designed to learn how readers engage persuasive letters that call for the reader's decision. If the analysis is complete by the conference, then the results will be shared on the poster, as well.

2. RESEARCH QUESTION

How do experts read arguments that call for a decision? What words to they look for, how do they scan the sentences, what do they think as we encounter the transition from one sentence to the next?

3. RESEARCH DESIGN AND METHODS

3.1 Participants

I enlisted the help and expertise from 14 faculty members who were experienced in reading graduate application letters and making decisions.

3.2 Artifacts

Two letters of application were selected randomly from a vast pool of such letters received in previous semesters. They were scrubbed of all identifying characteristics and were formatted in two different ways. The first remained exactly as the letter was received (same layout, typeface, and so on). The second format broke the letter into a "one-paragraph-per-page" format, full-justified, with extra leading and a larger typeface. This second format was used during eye-tracking to facilitate the overlay of multiple participants, who would inevitably read a formatted letter in different ways, scrolling, moving, and so on.

3.3 The Study
Each participant read both letters in two different ways, first while wearing an EyeGuide eye-tracker in order to establish what the participants looked at, and second employing a think-aloud protocol, captured in audio and video with Morae. The order of the letters was randomized so that approximately half the participants began with Letter #1 and the other half with Letter #2.

4. ANALYSIS
4.1 Eye-Tracking
Nine of the 14 participants generated usable eye-tracks for all 11 paragraphs, and 11 participants generated usable data for at least half the paragraphs. I employed EyeGuide's analytical software to look for aggregate patterns, creating a heatmap (aggregated data from all valid recordings), as well as a bee-swarm and areas of interest.

4.2 Think-Aloud Protocol (TAP)
The second technique involved think-aloud protocol, a technique whereby research participants say what they're thinking in a kind of realtime braindump during the performance of a task. In conventional usability testing of a product or a service, during which the participant attempts to perform a task, think-aloud data is extremely useful in helping the analyst interpret task actions (including failure, frustration, success, and so on). In this case, though, the TAP was used to interpret the specific task action of arriving at a decision (yes/no).

The think-aloud protocol videos were marked up with a bottom-up category system (i.e. the categories I used to tag observations came from the participant pool themselves).

Typical markers generated by the participants included observations about mechanics, style, organization, genre, interest, scholarship, teaching, questions about meaning, anticipating the admissibility of the writer, imagining the suitability of the student for the graduate program, among others.

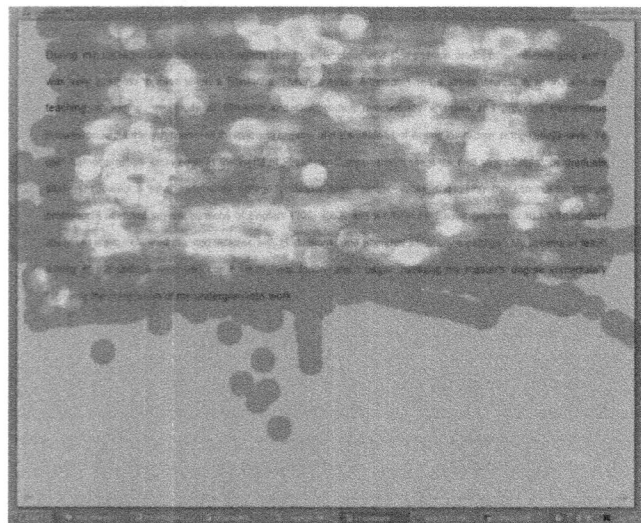

Figure 1: Typical Heatmap of Aggregate Results for One Paragraph

This category system was checked for reliability with another coder working independently, yielding an interrater reliability score of 86%.

5. RESULTS
Analysis is still ongoing, but there are early observations and results that this poster will discuss.

Preliminary results suggest that while some experts look for errors in these application letters, the places where the eye fixates and where the TAP also reveals that readers pause over often involve matches of interests between the writer and the reader. A fruitful scheme to describe this match may involve Kenneth Burke's concept of identification [1].

Another preliminary result involves where the eye pauses in higher-order thinking. I am defining this sort of pause as something different than what the eye-tracking literature [2] calls "fixations."

As the eye moves across a field, it pauses to gather information, then moves swiftly to another location. The mechanical pauses are called fixations, and this is where perception happens. The swift movements from one fixation to another are called saccades and current research demonstrates that no perception happens during these movements.

One expected outcome of the eyetracking portion of the study was that participants would pause over interesting words, confusing statements, errors, and so on. The literature on reading comprehension [3] demonstrates this phenomenon, and it also matches our common sense about how we read.

And the early analysis of the eyetracking data is that there are pauses over strategic places that are not errors, but rather areas of overlapping interest, or suitability for graduate study.

6. CONCLUSION
Eye tracking literature has focused on mechanical fixations and error-based fixations, but the field has yet to discuss what I am tentatively calling rhetorical fixations, or areas of interest in prose that most probably mirror areas of interest in the visual realm. Participants in my study appear to dwell on such areas as part of their personal decision-making process. If this conclusion is ultimately borne out in the completed study via TAP triangulation, then the fields of rhetoric (generally) and argumentation (more specifically) will have one of its first empirical studies into how readers engage with argumentative discourse and how their eyes see the prose in a critical reading. Not only will such an empirical model of argumentation be possible, but the field may be able to develop prescriptive models for writers of argumentation that take into account such empirical findings of readers.

7. REFERENCES
[1] Burke, Kenneth. 1950. *A Rhetoric of Motives*. U of California P.

[2] Just, Marcel Adam, and Carpenter, Patricia A. 1980. A theory of reading: From eye fixations to comprehension. *Psychological Review* 87, 4 (July 1980), 329-354.

[3] Rayner, Keith. 1998. Eye movements in reading and information processing: 20 years of research. *Psychological Bulletin* 124, 3, 372-422.

Tracing Digital Thyroid Culture: Building Communities of Support

Elizabeth Keller
Michigan State University
3D Olds Hall, East Lansing, Michigan 48824
kellere6@msu.edu

ABSTRACT

In this poster presentation, the author traces health communication in online spaces, especially conversations about hypothyroidism on Twitter. Specifically, the author looks at how participants on Twitter use the hashtag #hypothyroidism for patient agency and advocacy. The strength of ties between #hypothyroidism (the Twitter hashtag) and the actors necessary for its existence is also discussed. This poster presentation argues that Twitter can strengthen patient agency and advocacy in both online and offline relationships between hypothyroidism patients and healthcare professionals. Patient agency and advocacy is accomplished because Twitter helps to build communities of support between and among patients and professionals through the immediacy and accessibility of information.

Categories and Subject Descriptors

H.5.3 [**Information Interfaces and Presentation**] Group and Organization Interfaces—*Computer-supported cooperative work.*

Keywords

Social Web, Social Media, Twitter, Information Design, Hashtags, Health Communication, Hypothyroidism

1. INTRODUCTION

The social media tool Twitter is used as a communication platform for participants who suffer from the condition hypothyroidism. Twitter affords participants with hypothyroidism to immediately converse with one another in brief, 140-characters tweets about the symptoms of hypothyroidism, and how best to live with the condition daily. Moreover, Twitter acts as a space for hypothyroidism participants to collect and share information with one another, thereby distributing and transforming knowledge of hypothyroidism around the world.

Participants with hypothyroidism share stories and experiences about the condition across Twitter. These stories include coping with symptoms of hypothyroidism (fatigue, hair loss, weight gain, etc.), accessing current healthcare resources (health professionals, books/articles, online/offline support groups), and even managing the condition on a daily basis (synthetic and herbal medications, and diet changes).

As such, participants use keywords and hashtags to accomplish a myriad of tasks, including communicating with other participants in the Twitter stream, locating information about hypothyroidism within the stream, and organizing content about the condition. In this poster presentation, the author looks at how participants on Twitter use the hashtag #hypothyroidism for patient agency and advocacy. The strength of ties between #hypothyroidism (the Twitter hashtag) and the actors necessary for its existence is also discussed. This poster presentation argues that Twitter can strengthen patient agency and advocacy in both online and offline

relationships between hypothyroidism patients and healthcare professionals. Patient agency and advocacy is accomplished because Twitter helps to build communities of support between and among patients and professionals through the immediacy and accessibility of information.

1. WHAT IS HYPOTHYROIDISM?

Hypothyroidism is a condition in which the thyroid gland produces little or no thyroid-stimulating hormone [1]. Major contributors to hypothyroidism are autoimmune disorders, thyroiditis, too much or too little iodine, stress (both environmental and homeostatic stress), and removal of the thyroid gland itself [1]. An under-active thyroid can be associated with a variety of symptoms, including but not limited to anxiety and depression, fatigue, hair loss, weight gain, and cold intolerance. Other, more serious, symptoms can be goiter, infertility, and impaired memory or 'brain fog.' It is estimated that more than 12 million Americans have a thyroid condition of some sort [2]. While hypothyroidism cannot be cured, in many instances it can be controlled with medications, diet and exercise. Moreover, living with hypothyroidism can be easier on the individual if they keep others (family, friends, and health professionals) informed of their symptoms and over all health [1].

2. TWITTER: A SPACE FOR COMMUNITY BUILDING

Twitter is a "real-time information network that connects [people] to the latest stories, ideas, opinions and news" [8]. Through short, 140-characters tweets, participants can follow the tweets from other participants, provided that the participant has an unprotected account [8]. The '#' symbol, called a hashtag, is used to indicate keywords or topics in a tweet. Originally inscribed by users, the hashtag allows participants to search for and organize information that is important to them [9]. Clicking on a hashtagged word like #hypothyroidism, for instance, shows other tweets marked with the hashtag #hypothyroidism [6, 9]. Hashtagged words can be organized into an aggregation or stream using a social media dashboard (like Hootsuite or Tweetdeck) [6]. What's of most interest to this poster presentation is that Twitter publicly states that it "lends itself to cause and action" [8]. Further, Twitter, as an organization is "inspired by stories of people using Twitter to help make the world a better place in unexpected ways" [8]. This presentation shows examples of how hypothyroidism participants use hashtags on Twitter in order to share stories and generate knowledge about hypothyroidism.

3. HYPOTHYROIDISM CULTURE ON TWITTER: HOW COMMUNITY FORMS

Actor-network theory (ANT) [4], articulation theory [3], and activity theory [7] were used as methods in diagramming the figures for this poster. Both human and non-human actors were mapped as essential for the hashtag #hypothyroidism to exist on Twitter. The figures in this poster presentation examine the people, events, things, and activities necessary for the #hypothyroidism hashtag to exist. To this end, data (tweets) were collected for eight weeks during the summer of 2012, as part of a pilot study on tracing digital culture. Tweets having the hashtag #hypothyroidism were organized into a Twitter stream using a social media dashboard, which allowed the author to more easily observe and participate in the conversations about hypothyroidism. Participant tweets were screen captured using the application Grab, so that the author could reference them at a later time.

3.1 About the Maps

The first ANT map describes the actors involved in relation to the Twitter hashtag #hypothyroidism (see Figure 1). The symbols attached to this map represent the larger groupings of the people, events, and things associated with the hashtag. Adding visual representations to each actor is helpful for researchers as well as patients, participants, and doctors or other health professionals in making visible the structures needed for the hashtag to exist. The butterfly symbol (a symbol associated with the thyroid) acts as a visual connection to the thyroid community. Mapping the relevant people, events, and things in relation to the hashtag made evident the ways in which participants actively contribute to the thyroid community.

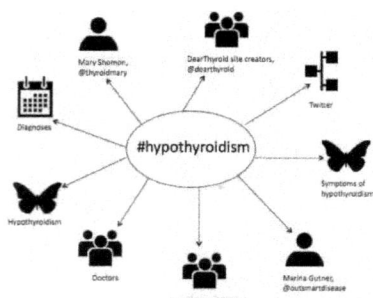

Figure 1. ANT Map of the actors involved in relation to the Twitter hashtag #hypothyroidism (with relevant shapes).

The second ANT map shows the strength of ties of the actors involved in relation to the Twitter hashtag #hypothyroidism (see Figure 2). This map shows the articulations that link structures to the hashtag, and data to information and knowledge. While all actors are necessary for the existence of the hashtag, the bolder arrows indicate that a particular tie is stronger than another. Figure 2 shows that one of the strongest actors in the hashtag network are participants on Twitter with hypothyroidism (as opposed to doctors and diagnosis, who have the weakest ties to the hashtag).

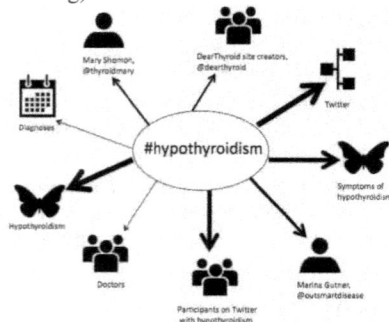

Figure 2. ANT Map showing the strength of ties of the actors involved in relation to the Twitter hashtag #hypothyroidism

The third and final map in this poster presentation uses second generation activity theory to "look at activity at a collective level" (see Figure 3) [7]. The eight questions proposed by Mwanza & Engeström in 2003 are explicated in Figure 3 [7]. A single tweet,

for example, is transformed through a series of other actions (replying, retweeting), which help to generate knowledge, resources and support for other participants with hypothyroidism. By using activity theory, the author more closely examined the tensions surrounding the existence of the hashtag #hypothyroidism.

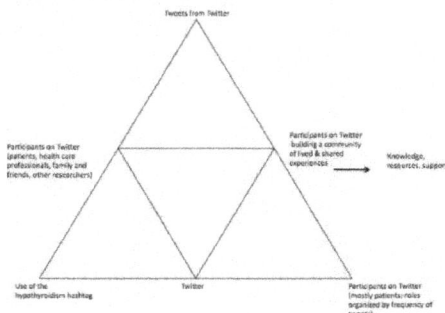

Figure 3. Activity Theory Map of the tensions within the hashtag #hypothyroidism as a single system.

4. IMPLICATIONS: PATIENT AGENCY AND ADVOCACY

Stories about hypothyroidism are plentiful on Twitter. And these stories primarily come from patients who suffer from the condition. Participants use the hashtag #hypothyroidism and interact with others in the Twitter stream by sharing information and knowledge [5]. Participants distribute knowledge to others in the network, and build an online community of support. This distributed knowledge reinforces patient agency and advocacy. The immediacy and accessibility of information on Twitter can provide hypothyroidism participants with a public space to make better their quality of life.

5. REFERENCES

[1] American Thyroid Association. 2012. *Hypothyroidism*. Available from http://www.thyroid.org/patients/patient_brochures/hypothyroidism.html.

[2] Garber, Jeffery R. 2012. *Thyroid Disease: Understanding hypothyroidism and hyperthyroidism*. Health Report. Harvard University.

[3] Kuan-Hsing C., and Morley, D. 1996. *Stuart Hall: Critical Dialogues in Cultural Studies*. New York, NY., Routledge.

[4] Latour, B. 2007. *Reassembling the Social: An Introduction to Actor-Network Theory*. New York, NY., Oxford University Press.

[5] Morville, P. 2005. *Ambient Findability*. Sebastopol, CA., O'Reilly.

[6] Potts, L., Seitzinger, J., Jones, D., and Harrison, A. Tweeting Disaster: Hashtag Constructions and Collisions. In *Proceedings of the 29th ACM International Conference on Design of Communication* (Pisa, Italy). SIGDOC '11. ACM, New York, NY, 235-240.

[7] Robertson, I. 2008. Sustainable e-learning, activity theory and professional development. In *Proceedings ascilite Melbourne 2008* (Melbourne, Australia). 819-826.

[8] Twitter. 2012. *About Twitter*. Available from https://twitter.com/about.

[9] Twitter. 2012. *What are hashtags ("#" Symbols)?* Available from http://support.twitter.com/groups/31-twitter-basics/topics/109-tweets-messages/articles/49309-what-are-hashtags-symbols#.

"I See You're Talking #HPV":
Communication Patterns in the #HPV Stream on Twitter

Angela Harrison
Old Dominion University
Norfolk, VA U.S.A
aharrisr@gmail.com

ABSTRACT

This poster reports data from a pilot study of the communication practices in the #hpv stream on Twitter. The pilot study found that, unlike other studies conducted on Twitter streams, the #hpv stream broadcasts information as opposed to interacting and conversing. The researcher plans to build upon this study by expanding the pilot dataset as a means to explore if preliminary findings in the initial study stand. The goal is to create a set of communication practices that happen within this ontology so that the space can be defined accordingly and compared with other streams of information on Twitter.

Categories and Subject Descriptors

E.4 [**Data**]: Coding and Information Theory

General Terms

Human Factors

Keywords

Social Web, Social Media, Twitter, Health Communication

1. INTRODUCTION

Twitter is a microblogging service in which people communicate using status updates in 140 characters or less. Recent scholarship by Scanfeld, Scanfeld and Larson [7] and Chew and Eysenbach [2] have examined the communication practices on Twitter in the wake of the H1N1 outbreak. However, there is not a large amount of scholarship that examines communication practices outside this particular topic. Based on the researcher's interest concerning information on Human Papillomavirus (HPV), this pilot study investigated the communication practices in a sample of fifty tweets from Twitter's #hpv stream in order to determine the ways that participants in the stream interact with one another and share information.

2. DEFINITIONS

The definitions the researcher used in this study are provided in order to clarify what contexts were used for the data coding process.

Table 1. Terms and Definitions for Data Coding

Term	Definition
Question	Asks a Question
Response	Response to a question or tweet
Command/Plea	Tells or asks others in the stream to do something
Informative	Contains information about HPV or a topic related to HPV
Other	Not relevant to the sexually transmitted disease HPV or unable to be determined

Other definitions that will be used include Twitter-specific terms such as Retweet [5], Hashtag [5], and @ [5].

2. METHODS

The researcher used content analysis as the method for determining what patterns were found in the dataset. The researcher used emergent coding [4] in order to ascertain what characteristics would be coded. The characteristics that emerged were: link usage, uses of the @ symbol as attribution or addressing another participant, what tweets were retweeted, what hashtags were present other than #hpv, and what specific kinds of tweets were present.

3. RESULTS

The following section is the results of the pilot study.

3.1 General Information

The tweets contained in this data sample are mostly in English and contain links. Of the fifty tweets, only one was not English and 2 did not contain links. The tweet that was not in English was in Portuguese.

3.2 Uses of the @ Symbol

Uses of the @ symbol included attributions, addressing, or a combination of the two. Of the fifty tweets, thirty-four were attributions to another participant, usually in the context of retweeting. Four of the tweets are addressing another participant, usually in the context of responding to a tweet or asking a question. Three of the tweets both address another participant and attribute at least a part of the tweet to another participant. Nine tweets did not contain the @ symbol.

3.3 Retweets
Most of the tweets contained in this sample were retweets of another tweet. However, within the sample, only four of the retweets were actually retweeted. All four of these tweets were retweeted a minimal amount; the most number of retweets of a particular tweet is three, and the others were only retweeted once.

3.4 Hashtags
The majority of the tweets in this dataset contained hashtags other than #hpv. Forty-four tweets contained other hashtags and six did not. #Cancer was the most prominent hashtag, used a total of thirty-three times. The second most prominent was #Gardasil, which was used five times. The third most prominent was #vaccination, followed by #pathogenposse, which was twice. #mRNA was used twice, and the rest of the hashtags were used only once.

3.5 Kinds of Tweets
The categories that were determined for the kinds of tweets include: Question, Response, Command/Plea, Informative, and Other. Forty-two of the tweets are informative. One was a Question, one was a Response, one was a Command/Plea, and one was classified as Other because it was in Portuguese. Three tweets were a combination of a Response and Informative, and one was a combination of Response and a Question.

4. CONCLUSIONS
In this sample, the vast majority of the tweets are in English, which was expected. Though only a tweet in one other language was present in this sample, it can be assumed that tweets in other languages will be present in a larger data set. The majority of tweets also contained links, which points to a trend of using references in order to supplement the content contained in the tweet.

The uses of the @ symbol have been examined by Honeycutt and Herring; in their study, 91% of @ signs were used to specifically tweet another person, and the second most common use was to refer to another person [2]. Based on their findings, Honeycutt and Herring concluded that conversation and collaboration were largely present in their sample [2]. In the #hpv stream, the findings were the opposite. The majority of the tweets were attributions and very few were used to address another person. This trend suggests that the #hpv stream is used primarily for the spread of information as opposed to conversations about the disease.

A previous study of boyd, Golder, and Lotan examined the practices of retweeting; they found that the reasons that people retweet are varied [1]. In the data sample, most of the tweets in the stream are actually retweets as opposed to original tweets. For the pilot study, the researcher chose to concentrate on tweets that were retweeted within the sample data set. Only four tweets were retweeted, and none of them were used in cases of commentary. All of them are simply the reproduction of original tweets verbatim. The exact reason is unknown, but possibilities that boyd, Golder, and Lotan that could be applied include spreading tweets to larger audiences and/or validation. A larger dataset will be needed in order to be conclusive. There is evidence present of some retweets being used to comment on the content of the original tweet.

In the case of the hashtags, it is probable that the presence of the hashtags are in conjunction with the concerns related to HPV. The most prominent alternative hashtag is #cancer, which suggests that the information related to HPV and cancer is the information of the most interest to the participants. The second and third most prominent hashtags suggest an interest in information that is related to Gardasil.

In conjunction with the lack of retweets and the use of the @ symbol to address another participant, Informative tweets were the most prominent kind. There are very little Questions, Responses, and Command/Pleas. Based on this dataset, the researcher concluded that the #hpv stream was used to broadcast information with very little conversation going on.

5. FURTHER WORK
The researcher plans to expand this dataset more and continue the process of content analysis in order to determine the patterns of communication in this space. The researcher also plans to define this space according to the patterns that are recorded and trace the information contained in the tweets that are the most prominent in the stream. The goal is to use this work in both technical and health communication.

7. REFERENCES
[1] boyd, d., Golder, S., and Lotan, G. 2010. Tweet, tweet, retweet: conversational aspects of retweeting on twitter. In *Proceedings of the 42nd HICSS* (Kauai, Hawaii, January 05-08 2010). IEEE Press, 1-10. DOI=10.1109/HICSS.2010.412

[2] Chew, C. and Eysenbach, G. 2010. Pandemics in the age of twitter: Content analysis of tweets during the 2009 H1N1 outbreak. *PLoS ONE (5)*11. E14118. DOI:10.1371/journal.pone.0014118

[3] Honeycutt, C. and S. Herring. 2009. Beyond Microblogging: Conversation and Collaboration in Twitter. In *Proceedings of the 42nd HICSS* (Kauai, Hawaii, January 05-08 2010). IEEE Press, 1-10. DOI=10.1109/HICSS.2009.89

[4] Neundorf, K. 2002. *The content analysis guidebook.* Thousand Oaks, Sage.

[5] O'Reilly, T. and Milstein, S. 2009. *The twitter book.* Sebastopol, CA.

[6] Scanfeld, D., Scanfeld, V. and Larson, E. 2010. Dissemination of health information through social networks: Twitter and antibiotics. *American Journal of Infection Control.* 38, 3. (2010). 182-188.

Developing Human-Centered Design Approaches: Preparing Professionals to Address Complex Problems

Monica E. Cardella
Purdue University
701 West Stadium Avenue
West Lafayette, IN 47907-2045
+1-765-496-1206
cardella@purdue.edu

Carla B. Zoltowski
Purdue University
701 West Stadium Avenue
West Lafayette, IN 47907-2045
+1-765-494-3559
cbz@purdue.edu

William C. Oakes
Purdue University
701 West Stadium Avenue
West Lafayette, IN 47907-2045
+1-765-494-3892
oakes@purdue.edu

ABSTRACT
In this poster, we describe the types of problems that the SIGDOC community addresses as complex, socially-situated and wicked. As we consider the future professionals who will address these problems, it is important to understand *how* we can prepare students and early career professionals to continue this work. To this end, we draw on research that describes different stages people might go through in developing design skills to meet human needs, and then suggest educational experiences that would help students and early-career professionals develop competencies in these areas.

Categories and Subject Descriptors
H.5.2. [**User Interfaces**]: User-centered design

General Terms
Design

Keywords
Human-centered design; design education

1. INTRODUCTION
Members of the SIGDOC community ("official" members as well as others participating in SIGDOC conferences or other scholarly exchanges) address a variety of complex, socially-situated "wicked" problems in contexts such as industry, recreation, education, science, and social exchanges. In 2011, the community discussed issues of social media [e.g 1], accessibility in relation to user interface [e.g. 2], serious games [e.g. 3], other aspects of learning [e.g. 4], formation of community (e.g. 5) and cross-cultural competence [e.g. 6]. These problems are *complex* in that they require approaches and knowledge from many disciplines (e.g. educational psychology, software design and human development); they are *socially-situated* as the researchers and practitioners working on these topics are addressing real human needs, and are cognizant of the need to include the people for whom they are designing throughout the design and research processes; and they are *"wicked"* [7] because these topics are very difficult to fully address, as they are ill-defined, involve many stakeholders with competing perspectives and needs, and change as technology and people's needs change over time.

Despite the challenge associated with tackling complex, socially-situated "wicked" problems, practitioners and researchers continue to address these problems. Reasons for doing so include the desire to work on socially-relevant problems/ meet real human needs and sheer enjoyment in working on something that is challenging and difficult, as well as motivations stemming from personal life experiences (e.g. living with a family member who is blind might motivate work on an interface for the blind). Alternatively, one might work on these problems simply because they are part of one's job assignment. Regardless of motivation, it is important to consider how future generations of usability experience professionals develop the skills that are necessary to address these problems. The goal of this poster, then, is to draw on research findings to consider the different types of experiences (both in school and out-of-school settings) that might prepare students and early-career professionals to be able to effectively address complex, socially-situated "wicked" problems. We describe the specific skills that we believe are necessary for future (and current) user experience professionals as *human-centered design* skills.

2. HUMAN-CENTERED DESIGN
Our educational approach is informed by design principles informed by human-centered design (HCD) literature and empirical research studies. From the literature, HCD is a design process in which there is a purposeful focus on the end users, clients and stakeholders throughout the design process. Key principles of HCD are: the active involvement of users, a clear understanding of the user and task requirements, and iteration of design solutions [8]. IDEO describes HCD as a process that begins by, "examining the needs, dreams, and behaviors of the people we want to affect with our solutions" [9].

Design researchers' efforts have identified novice-expert differences, which have informed educational practices [10-12]. In a recent empirical study we focused on different levels of understanding of HCD and learned that there are seven qualitatively different ways in which students experience and understand HCD:

1) As a technology-centered process

2) As service

3) As a process of gathering user information that is inputted into a linear process

4) As a process of keeping users' needs in mind

5) As design in context

6) As commitment to users' and stakeholders' needs

7) As empathic design [13]

These categories (or ways of experiencing/understanding HCD) differ in terms of students' understanding of their users as well as the level of their design skills and ability to integrate the knowledge [13]. The third through seventh categories are nested hierarchically, where moving from the third category to the seventh represents a more comprehensive understanding of HCD or designing for others [13]. Two categories that were distinct and not included in the main nested hierarchy of categories: those whose experiences lacked design processes (service) and those who did not appreciate the knowledge, experiences and perspectives of the users or the value of involving the users in the design (technology-centered).

3. EDUCATIONAL IMPLICATIONS

3.1 Understanding of Users and of Design

The results of the study suggest that students' understanding of the user and their ability to integrate that into their design are related in the development of more comprehensive ways of experiencing human-centered design. As the student designers understand users and the context better, they are then confronted with the need to take more factors/aspects into consideration into the design. Therefore, their awareness of the complexity of design increases. Similarly, as design and disciplinary skills increase and are brought to bear on the design, the student designers are more capable of incorporating more complex information about the stakeholders, as well as aspects related to feasibility and viability, that are not realized without those skills.

3.2 Experience with Real Clients and Users

The results suggest that critical or immersive experiences involving real clients and users were important in allowing the students to experience human-centered design in more comprehensive ways. For example, student designers whose experiences comprised the "Commitment" category all described critical experiences that challenged their assumptions. Situations that were described included problems associated with delivering a project or prototype to the client. This would suggest that it would be beneficial for undergraduate and graduate students to have experiences working on projects like acoustic interfaces for the blind [2] or creating a simulation game to train pre-service teachers in classroom management [4] with a requirement that students are able to work with real potential users.

3.3 Reflection

The interview process itself appeared to be a great learning opportunity for student participants. This is not surprising as the interviews guided them through a reflective experience. This is consistent with the literature on reflection and other metacognitive approaches to learning [14-15]. The study suggests that utilizing an interview or reflective activity in which the students explore their experiences designing for others could be an effective educational tool to help students as well as early career professionals understand what it means to use a human-centered design approach. Simply having an experience working with a real client or user may not be sufficient for the experience to become a "critical experience" without the opportunity for students and early career professionals to process the experience and deepen their learning related to human-centered design.

4. CONCLUSIONS

We believe that developing students' and early career professionals' human-centered design skills is crucial for the future of the many fields represented by SIGDOC. In the interactive poster, we plan to present an overview of our previous research which provides a framework for understanding stages a learner might go through in developing these skills as well as a variety of recommendations for approaches for promoting the development of these skills. This will, include the implications presented in this summary as well as additional approaches (e.g. service-learning approaches; our recent "alien-centered design" project). We further aim to promote interactivity by eliciting other participants' approaches.

5. ACKNOWLEDGMENTS

This work was made possible by a grant from the National Science Foundation (EEC 0935077). Any opinions, findings, and conclusions or recommendations expressed in this material are those of the authors and do not necessarily reflect the views of the National Science Foundation.

6. REFERENCES

[1] Kelly, A. and Kittle-Autrey, M. 2011. A Humanistic Approach to the Study of Social Media: Combining Social Network Analysis & Case Study Research. SIGDOC 2011.

[2] Ferati, M., Mannheimer, S. and Bolchini D. 2011. Usability Evaluation of Acoustic Interfaces for the Blind. SIGDOC 2011.

[3] Protopsaltis, A., Laurent, L., Dunwell, I., De Freitas, S. Petridis, P., Arnab, S., Scarle, S. and Hendrix, M. 2011. Scenario-based Serious Game Repurposing. SIGDOC 2011.

[4] Bouki,V, Metzelopoulos, M. and Protopsaltis, A. 2011. Simultation Game for Training New Teachers in Class Management. SIGDOC 2011.

[5] Abrahamsen, P., Delamerced, A., Nguyen, C. and Zachry, M. 2011. Designing a System to Create a Community. SIGDOC 2011.

[6] da Silva, R.L.P, Anacleto, J.C. and Balbino, F.C. 2011.Applying Cultural Knowledge to Multimedia Resources to Enrich Contextualized Applications. SIGDOC 2011.

[7] Rittel, H. and Webber, M. 1973. Dilemmas in a General Theory of Planning. *Policy Sciences* 4, 155-159.

[8] Maguire, M. 2001. Methods to support human-centered design. *Int. J. of Hum-Comput St*, 55, 3, 587-634.

[9] IDEO, "Human centered design toolkit," http://www.ideo.com/work/featured/human-centered-design-toolkit, accessed February 2010.

[10] Bailey,R. and Szabo, Z. 2006. "Assessing engineering design process knowledge," *Int. J. Eng. Educ.*, 22, 3, pp 508-518.

[11] Atman, C.J., Adams, R.S., Cardella, M.E., Turns, J., Mosborg, S. and Saleem, J. 2007. Engineering Design Processes: A Comparison of Students and Expert Practitioners. *J. Eng. Educ.,* 96, 4, 359-379

[12] Adams, R., Turns, J. and Atman, C. 2003. Educating effective engineering designers: the role of reflective practice. *Des. Stud.*, 24, 3, 275-294.

[13] Author. 2010. "Students' was of experiencing human-centered design," Doctorial dissertation, ProQuest Dissertations & Theses (PQDT).

[14] Bransford, J. D., Brown, A. L., & Cocking, R. R. (Eds.) 2000. *How People Learn*. Washington D.C.: National Academy Press.

[15] Bringle, R. G., & Hatcher, J. A. 1996. Implementing service learning in higher education. *J. High Educ.*, *67*, 221-239.

Promoting Behavior Change Through Community-Generated Digital Video

Jarman Hauser[1], Robert Racadio[1], William Wynn[2],
Beth Kolko[1], Richard Anderson[3], Ruth Anderson[3]

[1]Dept. of Human Centered
Design & Engineering
University of Washington
Seattle, WA USA 98195
{jarmanh, racadio, bkolko}
@uw.edu

[2]Evans School of Public Affairs
University of Washington
Seattle, WA USA 98195

wtwynn@uw.edu

[3]Dept. of Computer Science
& Engineering
University of Washington
Seattle, WA USA 98195
{anderson, rea}
@cs.washington.edu

ABSTRACT
The Health Videos for Global to Local project aims to impact health outcomes in South King County through digital video mediated behavior change. The project gives community members a platform to showcase positive health behaviors amongst peers, thus impacting communities from within. Through interviews, observation, meetings and workshops our evolving research is looking to identify effective strategies for creating health videos for socio-economically diverse communities.

Categories and Subject Descriptors
H.5.m [Miscellaneous]

General Terms
Design, Human Factors

Keywords
global health, public health, health, videos, behavior change, localization, community empowerment

1. OVERVIEW
South King County encompasses several cities in Washington State, including Tukwila, Sea-Tac and Federal Way. Its residents experience some of the worst health outcomes in the country. Diabetes prevalence in South King County is more than twice the rate of King County, while rates of obesity and heart disease are also disproportionately high. The incredibly diverse ethnic and linguistic makeup of the area also leads to residents' reduced access to healthcare facilities and services. [5].

A local organization, Global to Local [3], was established to help reduce these disparities by adapting and applying global health strategies in the local community. Currently, Global to Local has three community health promoters (CHPs) who serve the Somali, Eritrean / Ethiopian, and Latino communities of South King County. One model they have turned to is that of Digital Green, an India-based NGO, producing community-centered sustainable agriculture videos [2]. Digital Green's model of community involvement in video production and dissemination has proven to be successful at influencing agricultural behavior change. What makes Digital Green's model unique is the involvement of local community members to produce and star in the videos. Our project's goal is to adapt Digital Green's model of video creation

and dissemination to address health issues locally in South King County communities. By training Global to Local's community health promoters (CHPs), the project works to both build capacity within Global to Local for creating videos, while demonstrating healthy living and encouraging behavior changes within the communities.

2. PROJECT GOALS
The project began with a focus on creating a software tool to help produce and show digital health videos. The team interviewed the CHPs in order to gauge their comfort and familiarity with digital video and assess how such a tool might augment their existing knowledge, skills, and work context. However, it became clear that their technical and video expertise varied greatly. More concerning, all of the CHPs displayed some degree of anxiety regarding the process of video production, especially how the ideas for content would be formed and structured. Developing a new video tool to facilitate a not-yet-defined process would be premature, and we instead shifted our focus to create a process that allowed the CHPs to create and direct health videos using low cost or existing tools (such as cheap Flip-style camcorders and Windows Movie Maker). Our research currently focuses on how to design and facilitate a video creation process; later work will evaluate how this process can be improved.

3. CURRENT WORK
3.1 Adaptation of the Digital Green Process
During the initial stages of the project, much of the planning work was dedicated to learning from Digital Green's standard operating procedures (SOP). Their SOP includes detailed instructions on the process, from selecting partner agencies to the production and dissemination of videos. From this model, we extracted elements that were most relevant to the health workers, community and time constraints to develop our own SOP as a framework for the project. Additionally, we fleshed out some additional portions of the process that lacked clear guidance in the Digital Green SOP. One of these areas was with storyboarding, which included only a text instruction outline of what a storyboard might contain. Another area lacking clear guidance in the SOP was in shooting itself, such as understanding the different types of shots and angles that could go into creating a compelling video. After assessing the needs and constraints of the health promoters, including time constraints and language barriers, we realized that simply providing detailed documentation and equipment wouldn't be effective. Instead, we developed and presented a workshop and presentation that streamlined some of the general parts of Digital Green's process while providing structured guidance on

more complex aspects such as concept creation and storyboarding by creating activities and providing worksheets.

3.2 Workshop

We piloted our workshop with Global 2 Local's three health promoters and members of the Community Schools Collaborative (CSC), another South King County agency that works in adolescent peer health. During the workshop, we walked participants through the video conceptualization and filming process, asking them to develop and work through ideas of their own. At the end of the workshop, participants left with an understanding of the Digital Green model and how we want to use the model to promote healthy behavior change, as well as a storyboard and plans to get started shooting their own videos.

3.3 Shooting & Editing Videos

At present, we have recorded three videos, and we are currently working on editing and post-production.

The first video was conceptualized by Global to Local's Eritrean CHP and it demonstrates healthy Eritrean cooking. The video showcases a local Eritrean chef who specializes in creating healthy versions of traditional foods. A high school student member of the Eritrean community filmed the video and another is editing it.

The second video was conceptualized by the Latina CHP, and she demonstrates the plate method [1] for composing healthy meals. This video also features a testimonial from a local Latina woman who has adopted the plate method for herself and her family, which has improved their health as a result.

The third video was conceptualized and filmed by staff from CSC. It aims to get more high school students involved in peer health programs.

4. LESSONS LEARNED

Though we are still early in the process, we have learned many lessons on how to improve this process. Two of the most significant lessons follow.

4.1 Tradeoff between Flexibility & Structure

One of the first things we noted about the Digital Green SOP was that content generation and production is a very structured and top-down approach. Our efforts would differ from Digital Green's work in that we are working in a different context with diverse types of communities, where a more flexible approach may be more beneficial. Looking at the expertise of our community partners to create content that would be valuable to their community, we wanted to avoid strictly defining the idea creating process in a way that might lead to producing culturally inappropriate videos.

4.2 Evolving Goals

As we move from the planning to implementation, it has become apparent that the framework we have created needs to be expanded to address the sustainability and evolving goals of the project. The original intent, which focused on promoting self-efficacy with community members through peer generated content, shifted to include building capacity within Global to Local's infrastructure through incorporating aspects of technical skills building. Designing tools that guide and train participants through the whole process from idea → concept → storyboard → script → shooting → editing creates a more sustainable model that empowers the CHP's and community members involved to become self-sufficient in replicating the process to make additional videos on their own.

5. NEXT STEPS

The next steps for this work are to finish producing the videos and share them with the community. Once these videos have been produced and shared, we would like to reflect again on the process so that it can be improved and sustained. We also want to understand how training in video production impacts community member's self-efficacy. Additionally, we want to more deeply investigate the role that these types of community-created videos play in promoting behavior change by evaluating this work through the lens of various health behavior change theories such as the transtheoretical model of behavior change [4]. From this, we hope to draw out implications that can drive the design of tools that make videos like these more effective for promoting behavior change.

6. ACKNOWLEDGMENTS

Our thanks to our Praveen Shekhar for his work on planning and creating videos, and to our colleagues at Global to Local and the Community Schools Collaborative for their participation. We also thank the community members who kindly volunteered their time to be involved. This research was supported in part by National Science Foundation Grant IIS-1111433.

7. REFERENCES

[1] Create Your Plate: *http://www.diabetes.org/food-and-fitness/food/planning-meals/create-your-plate/*.

[2] Gandhi, R. 2007. Digital green: Participatory video for agricultural extension. *ICTD 2007*. (2007).

[3] Global to Local: *http://www.globaltolocal.org*.

[4] Prochaska, J.O. and Velicer, W.F. 1997. The transtheoretical model of health behavior change. *American Journal of Health*. (1997).

[5] Seattle's global health powerhouses turn their attention to south King County: 2012. *http://crosscut.com/2012/03/07/health-medicine/22017/Seattles-global-health-powerhouses-turn-their-atte/*.

The Case of Facebook Japan:
Cross-Cultural Design in Postcolonial Conditions

Huatong Sun
Interdisciplinary Arts & Sciences
University of Washington Tacoma
USA
huatongs@gmail.com

ABSTRACT
Centering on the unfolding development of Facebook Japan case, this work-in-progress research poster seeks to engage the audience in a conversation on critical sensibility the cross-cultural design community should develop in postcolonial conditions.

Categories and Subject Descriptors
H.5.m [**Information interfaces and presentation (e.g., HCI)**]: Miscellaneous.

General Terms
Design, Human Factors, Languages, Theory

Keywords
Facebook, SNS, cross-cultural design, culturally localized user experience, postcolonial computing, HCI4D

1. INTRODUCTION
One common problem in cross-cultural design is that static meanings out of context are transferred through design, influenced by a transmission model of communication [13]. As a result, the designed technology is usable, but local users don't relate to it. This is what happened to the Facebook Japan website as it required Japanese users to follow the American online social networking protocols when it was launched in Japan.

While this case could be interpreted as one of many examples of an instrumental design approach, driven by the mainstream engineering mindset in the HCI field, it should be investigated on a deeper level. In the lens of British cultural studies, cultural phenomenon is "neither aesthetic nor humanist in emphasis but instead political" [4]. As described in the proposal for "postcolonial computing": "Colonial relationships may have dissolved, and yet the history of global dynamics of power, wealth, economic strength, and political influence shape contemporary cultural encounters…. Colonial tropes characterizing certain people as in need of enlightenment, civilization, and development still persist today" [7]. The tension between power and discourse that defines online cultural phenomenon is never settled. As a matter of fact, postcolonial computing happens not just in developing countries when designers are engaged in HCI4D (HCI for developing countries), it is happening everywhere, including an affluent country with well-developed, unique and independent Internet culture as Japan.

By tracing the unfolding development of the Facebook Japan case with charts and data, this poster seeks to engage the audience in a conversation on the critical sensibility a cross-cultural designer should foster in postcolonial conditions.

2. THE CASE OF FACEBOOK JAPAN
Founded in 2004, the U.S.-based Facebook is the world's largest social networking website. According to its own data as July 2012, it connected "901 million monthly active uses at the end of March 2012. Approximately 80% of our monthly active users are outside of the U.S. and Canada." As Facebook has rapidly risen as the top SNS website in the world aiming for a billion users [2], many local SNS websites were kicked out of the game [3].

Though Facebook succeeds in many places of the world, it has had a difficult battle to win the Japanese SNS market. Why? Facebook asks its users to use real names and photos for profiles. This distinctive feature, which made Facebook a huge success in American culture where it originated, conflicts with Japanese Internet culture, where users like to use pseudonyms to interact with each other. Over 75% of Japanese social media users chose to do it this way around the time of 2009, which is supported by the top Japanese SNS website Mixi [12]. Consequently Facebook's penetration rate had been stagnating at 3% for a long time until fall 2011, even after a Facebook office was opened in Tokyo in September 2010. In stark contrast, its reach rate in its home country was 62% at that time [13].

To conquer this strategically important front of digital culture, Facebook has developed a number of bold initiatives to reach Japanese users such as designing a customized mobile interface, allowing users to syndicate Facebook posts on Mixi, and introducing a job search application for college students. Their efforts slowly paid off. By March 2012, Facebook announced that its users in Japan have surpassed 10 million and the number of users has doubled over the past six months, with a penetration rate of 10% [5]. The June 2012 Nielsen Report states 29.1 percent of Japanese Internet users now visit Facebook [1]. Apparently 2012 is a critical year for Facebook Japan, which will determine whether it could take over the Japanese SNS market and beat the indigenous SNS site Mixi. Indeed it might not be a surprise if Facebook wins this brutal competition in the end. As one of the richest IT companies at present, it has the capital to conquer every corner of the world as long as it has market access, not to mention altering and shaping Japanese way of online social networking.

The unfolding development of Facebook Japan offers much food for thoughts for the cross-cultural design community. While this case is one of the many examples that static meanings out of context are often transferred through cross-cultural design, neglecting local cultural preferences and use habits [13], the static meaning here is complicated with the ideology in postcolonial conditions. Even though we UX researchers and practitioners already began to celebrate the agency of local users in this increasingly globalized world and describe this stage as "glocalization"—a new stage after "cultural imperialism" and "globalization," which recognizes the tension between the global and the local and thus theoretically captures "receding center-periphery international arrangements and emerging decentralized, fragmented, and multifaceted patterns" [8] —cultural imperialism is still pervasive, even for an affluent country with self-sufficient Internet culture as Japan.

3. CROSS-CULTURAL DESIGN IN POSTCOLONIAL CONDITIONS

This Facebook Japan case dramatizes a dilemma cross-cultural designers have been facing: What design sensibility should we have when creating culturally sensitive design for local users at this later stage of globalization? In term of the Facebook case, are we more connected when only one online social networking mode is honored in this global village?

The disconnect of action and meaning [13] in this case suggests that the issues of power, identity, value, hegemony need a closer examination in cross-cultural design, and designers should foster a critical design sensibility to understand the postcolonial conditions where we are living through so that we could come up with culturally sensitive designs that are not driven by market revenues but by mindful listening, ethical standards, social responsibility, and the conscience of "design for social good."

Unfortunately postcolonial scholarship had been absent in technology and computing design discourse until lately [11], and this partially explains why culture is often interpreted narrowly and statically, and structure is mostly ignored in cross-cultural design practices. To address these issues, a postcolonial perspective will help interweave structure and culture in design practices and research by regarding a local site as "a heterogeneous space, one with uneven development, always under construction, and never complete," therefore, it will "open up critical space for new narratives of becoming and emancipation" [10].

My goal in this work-in-progress poster is to enrich and complicate the cross-cultural design philosophy of Culturally Localized User Experience (CLUE) [13] with a postcolonial rhetoric and extend the design implications of British cultural studies, one of the three key strands in the CLUE framework, which is closely connected with postcolonial scholarship. I will incorporate postcolonial work from global media studies [9, 10] and HCI4D [6, 7, 11], contextualize it in cross-cultural design, and link it to a dialogic model of communication on which the CLUE framework is built [13] as a way of further developing that model. For example, modes of glocalization and hybridization will be unpacked and compared to illustrate the asymmetrical diffusion of technological culture in current postcolonial conditions. My ultimate goal is to promote a critical design sensibility that is guided by the dialogic model of communication. To facilitate the conversation with the audience, a conceptual map will be included in the poster.

4. CONCLUSION

From the perspective of the articulation model, the Facebook Japan case is about the articulation between technological culture and power. Applying postcolonial scholarship from the fields of communication and HCI, I argue that participatory cross-cultural designers should foster a critical design sensibility that is founded on a dialogical model of communication for transformation and emancipation in postcolonial conditions.

5. REFERENCES

[1] Alabaster, J. (June 27, 2012). Facebook visitors from Japan have more than doubled in last year, says study. http://www.pcworld.com/businesscenter/article/258385/facebook_visitors_from_japan_have_more_than_doubled_in_last_year_says_study.html

[2] Chilana, P., Holsberry, C., Oliveira, F., Ko, A. Designing for a billion users: A case study of Facebook. In Proc CHI 2012, ACM Press (2012), 419-431.

[3] Cosenza, V. (June 2012). World map of social networks. http://vincos.it/world-map-of-social-networks/

[4] Fiske, J. 1987. British Cultural Studies and Television. Channels of Discourse, Reassembled: Television and contemporary criticism. R. Allen. Chapel Hill, NC, University of North Carolina Press: 284-326.

[5] Fujimura, N. (March 29, 2012). Facebook's Zuckerberg Says Japan Users Doubled in Six Months. http://www.businessweek.com/news/2012-03-29/facebook-s-zuckerberg-says-japan-users-doubled-in-six-months

[6] Irani, L. Dourish, P. Postcolonial interculturality. In Proc. IWIC 2009, ACM Press (2009), 249-252.

[7] Irani, L., Vertesi, J. Dourish, P., Philip, K., Grinter, R. Postcolonial Computing: A Lens on Design and Development. Proceedings of Conference on Human Factors in Computing Systems (CHI 2010). ACM, New York, 1311-1320.

[8] Kraidy, M. 2001. From Imperialism to Glocalization: A theoretical framework for the Information Age. Cyberimperialism? Global relations in the new electronic frontier. B. L. Ebo. Greenwood Publishing, Westport, CT, 27-42.

[9] Kraidy, M. 2005. Hybridity or the Cultural Logic of Globalization. Temple University Press, Philadelphia.

[10] McMillin, D. 2007.International media studies. Blackwell, Malden, MA.

[11] Merritt, S., Bardzell, S. Postcolonial language and culture theory for HCI4D. In Proc CHI 2011, ACM Press (2011), 1675-1680.

[12] Orita, A. and H. Hada, 2009. Is that really you?: an approach to assure identity without revealing real-name online. Proceedings of the 5th ACM workshop on Digital identity management. ACM, New York, 17-20.

[13] Sun, H. 2012. *Cross-cultural technology design: Creating culture-sensitive technology for local users.* Oxford University Press, New York.

Tracing and Responding to Foodborne Illness

Rebecca Tegtmeyer
Michigan State University
Kresge Art Ctr
600 Auditorium Road Room 26C
(517)432-1613
tegtmey2@msu.edu

Liza Potts
Michigan State University
WIDE Research
235 Bessey Hall
(517) 355-2400
lpotts@msu.edu

William Hart-Davidson
Michigan State University
WIDE Research
7 Olds Hall
(517) 353-9184
hartdav2@msu.edu

ABSTRACT

In this poster, we describe a how we use social web tools to track, trace, and respond to foodborne illness. Using a combination of data streams, analytical tools, bots, and dashboards, we propose solutions to the current challenges facing government officials, NGOs, and everyday people.

Categories and Subject Descriptors

H.5.2 [Information Interfaces and Presentation]: User Interfaces – *Natural language, Screen design, User-centered design.*

General Terms

Design, Experimentation, Human Factors

Keywords

Dashboards, Twitter, data mining, foodborne illness, disaster

1. INTRODUCTION

Foodborne disease outbreaks are particularly difficult to detect due to the highly complex and distributed nature of our food supply chain. In the short term, digital disease detection techniques that have been successfully used to detect flu and other infectious diseases could decrease the time it takes to detect outbreaks of foodborne illness. In the long term, digital disease detection data could be combined with sensor data collected throughout the food chain to form a "smart grid" for a more comprehensive system of rapid detection, warning and traceback.

2. ABOUT BIOSURVEILLANCE

2.1 The Problem

Each year 48 million Americans get sick, 128,000 are hospitalized and 3,000 die from foodborne illness. The current system for identifying outbreaks is highly labor-, and more importantly, time-intensive [1]. The CDC estimates that it takes on average 5-28 days to identify a case as part of an outbreak. Furthermore, for every case of salmonellosis reported, 28 cases go undiagnosed. This 28-fold attenuation in signal strength severely impairs the ability of the system to rapidly identify clusters of cases that public health officials rely upon to home in on the source of contamination [1].

2.2 The Opportunity

It has been demonstrated that digital disease detection can match or surpass traditional techniques for detecting infectious disease outbreaks such as flu and dengue [1, 2]. Early examples used data search queries (e.g. looking at how people searched for information on flu), but have progressed to include new streams of data, such as Twitter[2, 3]. In addition to passively looking at new data streams, there have been examples of users actively organizing themselves on Facebook for successful disease outbreak investigation. These techniques could be particularly useful for detecting outbreaks of foodborne illness where the vast majority of victims do not seek medical attention and, therefore, would not be detected under the current system, yet many of these individuals are likely to self-report via social networks [3].

2.3 Challenges

First, it will be necessary to demonstrate proof of concept using existing and emerging **data streams** (search queries, Twitter, Facebook, etc.) and **analytical tools** (intelligent search engines or robots that can detect an increase in volume and/or clusters in space and time). This will require developing a specific **ontology**: verbs and nouns, their misspellings and associations that act as indicators of foodborne illness. Historic data from a recent outbreak will be procured for an initial test of sensitivity, and then the model can be improved to proactively "listen" for new outbreaks.

3. TRACING EVENTS

Tracing foodborne illness through for the sake of mitigating a disaster involves issues concerning time and space. By this we mean that analytical tools must be able to locate the appropriate data stream for a given culture, location, and timeline for a specific event. In this section, we define these concepts further.

3.1 Across Time

Foodborne illnesess are bound by fairly standard lengths of time when the first outbreak occurs and the last person falls ill. Bound by time, being able to track specific issues across specific blocks of time is essentially for early detection. Using timestamps found in social web tools is one way to locate foodborne illnesses online. For example, Twitter tweets and Facebook status updates have timestamps, as do Yelp, Foursquare, and Facebook check-ins.

3.2 Across Space

Foodborne illnesses are also typically located in clusters in space. Using location-aware information from Twitter, Facebook, Yelp, and Foursquare would greatly aid in this detection. Of course, there are outliers – such as conferences, conventions, and tourism.

However, the data sets are typically large enough to show clusters.

4. RESPONDING
In order to respond to people during these outbreaks, we are using a three-pronged approach. Focusing on tracing, responding, and mitigating, we are working to deploy Twitter response robots, dashboards for organizers and officials, and linking to content-rich web sites and tools.

4.1 Deploying Robots
Responding to specific Twitter status updates, these robots (known as "bots") will reply to whoever initiates the tweet. The tweet response will notify the user about recent issues and encourage the participant to engage further on one of the partner websites. Engagement can be simply learning more about foodborne illness or participating in surveys about a current emerging outbreak. Future work will include building response bots for Foursquare, Facebook, and other social web tools.

4.2 Launching Dashboards
The major focus of our work is on this dashboard system. The system will allow for different levels of participation from users, a curious browser, affected reported, and active reviewer.

The basic components of the dashboard include a social media stream, tag cloud, location map, timeframe graph, and a form to submit reports. The social media stream pulls keywords and clusters related to foodborne illness preset by the system. It also displays invalid, valid, and pending reports. A user can locate the posts on the map and choose to login as an active reviewer to submit the post for further validation.

The tag cloud is animated and displays keywords and clusters from the social stream. The scale of words indicates the amount of usage in posts. A curious browser can add words of relevance to the tag cloud.

The map displays possible outbreaks by showing confirmed and unconfirmed reports. A curious user can search various locations within the U.S. The active reviewer can track, find, share, and save multiple outbreaks based on location.

The timeframe graph displays confirmed and un-confirmed reports correlated with time and the location. All users can interact with the timeframe graph to display data from the past, going back 14 days.

The report submission form is for affected reporters, they can chose to submit as a guest or create a reviewer profile. In the report submission form the affected reporter provides detailed information about their case and publishes it to the system.

4.3 Linking Websites
In order to close the feedback loop, both the robots and the dashboards will provide links to more robust content. In particular, we are exploring ways in which timely information from the Centers for Disease Control (CDC) and other organizations would benefit these response mechanisms.

5. Future Work
Early detection of foodborne illness outbreaks will substantially reduce casualties and their associated costs due to medical expenses, lost productivity, and damage to the food industry from loss of consumer confidence. The emergence and global adoption of social networks holds promise as a tool for early signal detection, but its usefulness will be realized only if it is widely accepted by public health agencies responsible for food safety. By their nature, regulatory agencies are slow to adopt new technologies and this will likely be the case for a social media-based system with its attendant data quality shortcomings. It is important, therefore, to develop a well-organized adoption strategy as an integral component of a web-based food safety biosurveillance project.

6. REFERENCES
[1] Brownstein, J.S., Freifeld, C.C.,& Madoff, L.C., M.D. (2009). Digital disease detection: Harnessing the web for public health surveillance. *N Engl J Med* 360. 2153-2157

[2] Hesse, B.W., & Shneiderman, B. (2007). eHealth research from the user's perspective," *Am. J. Preventive Medicine* 32.5S. S97-S103.

[3] Eysenbach, G. (2009). Infodemiology and infoveillance: Framework for an emerging set of public health informatics methods to analyze search, communication and publication behavior on the internet. *J. Medical Internet Research*11.1 e11.

[4] Jones, D. and Potts, L. 2010. Best practices for designing third party applications for contextually-aware tools. In *Proceedings of the 28th ACM International Conference on Design of Communication* (Sao Paolo, Brazil). SIGDOC '10. ACM, New York, NY, 95-102.

[5] Potts, L. 2009. Designing for disaster: Social software use in times of crisis. *International Journal of Sociotechnology and Knowledge Development* 1, 2, 33-46.

[6] Potts, L. 2009. Peering into disaster: Social software use from the Indian Ocean earthquake to the Mumbai bombings. In *Proceedings of the International Professional Communication Conference.* Hawaii: IEEE.

[7] Potts, L. and Jones, D. 2011. Contextualing experiences: Tracing the relationships between people and technologies in the social web. *Journal of Business and Technical Communication* 25, 3, 338-358.

[8] Potts, Seitzinger, Jones, and Harrison. 2012. Tweeting Disaster: Hashtag Constructions and Collisions. *Proceedings of the 29th ACM International Conference on Design of Communication* (Pisa, Italy). SIGDOC '11. ACM, New York, NY.

[9] Vander Wal, T. 2007. Folksonomy. *Vanderwal.net.* Available from http://vanderwal.net/folksonomy.html.

Technical Communication and Project Management

Kathie Gossett
Iowa State University
Department of English
203 Ross Hall, Ames, IA
kgossett@iastate.edu

ABSTRACT

This poster argues that recent theories in project management put technical communicators in a powerful position to move into project management—not just as managers of documentation and documentation projects but as managers of projects across industries.

Categories and Subject Descriptors

K.6.1 [**Project and People Management**], I.7.1 [**Document and Text Editing**]: Document Management.

General Terms

Management, Documentation, Design, Theory.

Keywords

Project management, technical communication

1. INTRODUCTION

The field of technical communication has embraced the expansion of the field beyond written communication into related fields such as user experience, usability, application design, etc. As emerging theories of project management favor people-centered methods and practices, which are traditional strengths of technical communication, it is time to consider project management as a potential field of practice for the technical communicator.

2. HISTORY OF PROJECT MANAGEMENT

The field of project management is "a relatively young field of study as an academic discipline" [4]. What began as a set of tools to optimize engineering and construction projects, which focused primarily on quantitative measures (money and time), has grown into a "transfunctional discipline" [4] that views project management as a set of methods, techniques, and tools that interact with other fields (e.g., general management, marketing, and business) to create a universal way of dealing with projects across multiple sectors (e.g., construction, engineering, information technology, etc.) [4]. That is, modern theories of project management combine quantitative and qualitative means to measure project success or failure.

A more comprehensive look at the historical development of the field of project management can be done by mapping out the relationship between theory and practice within the field. In creating a such a typological model Lalond, Bourgault, and Findeli [12] identified four distinct types of project management that are roughly chronological; that is, each type builds on the types that preceded it, as well as "implying a specific interpretation of the theory-practice link" [12].

2.1 Four types of project management

2.1.1 Type 1: Intuitive theories of project management

The first type of theory-practice relationship was one of the earliest types of project management (and somewhat counter-intuitively can still be found in some industries today). This type defines project management as an art: an activity, or group of activities, that is based on experience and intuition rather than any scientific theory. The belief that project management cannot be taught in the classroom but requires hands-on-experience is primary.

2.1.2 Type 2: Prescriptive theories of project management

Gradually efforts were made to organize and systematize the field by both professional organizations (e.g., the Project Management Institute) and management science researchers. These efforts can be directly attributed to the shortcomings found in the first type of project management [12]. During this period many of the mainstays of project management documentation/ methodologies such as the Gantt chart, the PERT (program evaluation review technique) process/chart, and critical path methods (CPM) were developed [3].

2.1.3 Type 3: Sociological theories of project management

One of the main premises of the third type was that rather than identifying the field as project management, it should be identified as the management of projects. It is during this project management type that the field expanded to become a truly interdisciplinary field. As a result, there are simply too many theoretical frameworks from too many disciplines at play to be able to identify a core theory and/or practice for this type of project management. (It must be noted, however, that this is the first type of project management that takes communicational aspects into consideration as a measure of the success of a project.)

2.1.4 Type 4: Pragmatist theories of project management

The fourth type of project management has emerged recently and seeks to incorporate "both rigorous scientific and practice-relevant research" [12]. This type has developed as the professionalization model has become a focus of some academic disciplines (e.g., business schools). This type of project management has as one of its goals to "to improve the welfare of workers, employees, organizational actors, customers, project managers, CEOs, and, broadly speaking, social communities" [12]. Thus, this fourth type focuses on how the theory and practice of project management impacts people: users, developers, investors, etc

3. PROJECT MANAGEMENT AND TECHNICAL COMMUNICATION

A brief review of the leading journals in the field of technical communication and the Technical Communication eServer reveals that the most dominant discussions of project management within the field of technical communication are: 1) how to work with a project manager [2, 7]; 2) how to maintain project management documents (AKA knowledge management) [6, 1]; 3) how to manage a documentation project (both as a group manager and as an individual consultant) [14, 5]; and, most recently, 4) how to manage content in a content management system [9, 13]. While these continue to be important topics of research and discussion, this poster argues that there is a fifth discussion that needs to be happening in the field: technical communicators as project managers.

A recent study of technical communication graduates and managers by Whiteside showed that one of the new roles technical communicators are increasingly being asked to do is project management [15]. The technical communication managers surveyed responded that the majority of their recent hires had solid foundations in written communication and the associated tools, but sixty percent of those managers indicated that "newly graduated technical communicators lacked project management experience" [15]. A review of the curriculum of technical communication programs in Whiteside's study supported this lack of training. While all ten of the schools she surveyed offered a large selection of writing, rhetoric, and tool-based courses, only two offered a course in project management.

While it may have been challenging to make the move into project management historically (under the first three types), the emerging emphasis on people rather than skills in current project management theories places technical communicators in a unique position. In addition to designing and managing many of the documents associated with project management, the work of analyzing and connecting people and tools to accomplish team and project goals has long been a core competency of the technical communicator [8]. Thus, project management is moving even more strongly into technical communication's purview.

4. CONCLUSION

Technical communicators are increasingly moving into project management roles across industry. As this trend continues, it will be vital to prepare our students to do this work. Kampf and Isohella have repeatedly argued for the inclusion of project management courses in technical communication and English studies program curricula [10, 11], but currently there are only a few programs that include such courses (and the majority of these programs are currently in Europe [11]). We need to continue to work to define ourselves as a field beyond written communication and prepare our students to continue this work. As we do this we will begin to fulfill Hart-Davidson's call for us to become the makers of systems rather than the writers of them [8].

5. REFERENCES

[1] Aikat, S. 1996. Using PERT to plan and schedule your documentation projects. *STC Proceedings*. Available from: http://www.stc.org/confproceed/1996/PDFs/PG7174.PDF

[2] Amidon, S., & Blythe, S. 2008. Wrestling with Proteus: Tales of communication managers in a changing economy. *Journal of Business and Technical Writing*, (January 208), 5-37.

[3] Cicmil, S., & Hodgson, D. 2006. Making projects critical: An introduction. In D. Hodgson & S. Cicmil (Eds.), *Making projects critical*. New York, Palgrave.

[4] Bredillet, C. 2010. Blowing hot and cold on project management. *Project Management Journal* (June 2010), 4-20.

[5] Dhanagopal, K. 2011. Managing Documentation Projects. *TC World*, India. Available from: http://www.slideshare.net/akashjd/kumar-project-management

[6] Dick, D. 2008. Documents that no project cannot be without. *Carolina Communique (STC)*, (January 2008). Available from: http://stc-carolina.org/newsletter/tiki-index.php?page=Documents+That+No+Project+Cannot+Be+Without

[7] Glick-Smith, J., & Steele, K. 1993. Managing your documentation monster: Project management for the 90's. *STC Proceedings*. Available from: http://www.stc.org/ConfProceed/1993/PDFs/Pg514.pdf

[8] Hart-Davidson, W. 2001. On writing, technical communication, and information technology: The core competencies of technical communication. *Technical Communication* (May 2001), 145-155.

[9] Hart-Davidson, W., Bernhardt, G. McLeod, M., Rife, M., & Grabill, J. 2007. Coming to content management: Inventing infrastructure for organizational knowledge work. *Technical Communication Quarterly* (December 2007), 10-34

[10] Kampf, C. 2006. The future of project management in technical communication: Incorporating a communications approach. *IEEE International Professional Communication Conference*.

[11] Kampf, C. & Isohella, S. 2009. A place for project management in English studies and communication studies curricula. *Nordic Journal of English Studies* (January 2009), 61-79.

[12] Lalonde, P., Bourgault, M., & Findeli, A. 2010. Building pragmatist theories of PM practice: Theorizing the act of project management. *Project Management Journal* (December 2010), 21-36.

[13] McCarthy, J., Grabill, J., Hart-Davidson, W., & McLeod, M. 2011. Content management in the workplace: Community, context, and a new way to organize writing. *Journal of Business and Technical Writing* (October 2011), 367-395.

[14] Slatterty, S. 2007. Undistributing work through writing: How technical writers manage texts in complex information environments. *Technical Communication Quarterly* (June 2007), 311-325.

[15] Whiteside, A. 2003. The skills that technical communicators need: An investigation of technical communication graduates, managers, and curricula. Journal of Technical Writing and Communication (December 2003), 303-318.

Author Index

www.ingramcontent.com/pod-product-compliance
Lightning Source LLC
Chambersburg PA
CBHW080708220326
41598CB00033B/5348

* 9 7 8 1 4 5 0 3 1 4 9 7 8 *